Children of the Revolution

ROBERT GILDEA

Children of the Revolution

The French, 1799–1914

Harvard University Press
Cambridge, Massachusetts
2008

Library of Congress Cataloguing-in-Publication Data

Gildea, Robert
Children of the Revolution : The French, 1799–1914 / Robert Gildea
p. cm.
Includes bibliographical references and index.
ISBN-13: 978-0-674-03209-5 (alk. paper)

1. France–History–1789–1900. 2. France–Politics and government–1789–1900.
3. France–History–Revolution, 1789–1799–Influence. I. Title.
DC251.G54 2008
944.06–DC22

2008019219

to Rachel, Georgia, William and Adam

Contents

List of Illustrations

Photographic acknowledgements are given in parentheses.

1. Fête de la Fédération, Champ de Mars, Paris on 14 July 1790. Engraving by Lecoeur based on contemporary drawing by Jacques Swebach-Desfontaines (akg-images)

2. Robespierre guillotining the executioner, having guillotined all French people, 1793 (The Art Archive)

3. Madame de Staël, by François Gérard, c. 1810, Château de Coppet, Switzerland (akg-images/Erich Lessing)

4. François-René de Chateaubriand, engraving by Aubry-Lecomte after Girodet-Trioson, 1823, Bibliothèque Nationale, Paris (Roger-Viollet/Topfoto)

5. Charles Maurice de Talleyrand, portrait by Ary Scheffer, c. 1830, Musée Condé, Chantilly (akg-images/Erich Lessing)

6. Marie-Joseph-Paul-Yves-Roch Gilbert du Motier, Marquis de Lafayette, portrait by Matthew Harris Jouett, c. 1825, National Portrait Gallery, Smithsonian Institution (Scala/Art Resource)

7. A street in old Paris by Gustave Doré, engraving, c. 1860 (Mary Evans Picture Library)

8. Building the avenue de l'Opéra, Paris, during Haussmann's civil engineering project, c. 1870, photograph by Marville, private collection (The Art Archive/Marc Charmet)

9. Louis-Adolphe Thiers, undated engraving by Bosselman (Mary Evans Picture Library)

10. Eugène Delacroix, self-portrait, 1838, Musée du Louvre, Paris (akg-images/Erich Lessing)

11. Félicité de Lammenais, undated portrait by Paulin Guérin, Châteaux de Versailles et de Trianon, Versailles (Roger-Viollet/Topfoto)

12. Victor Hugo, photograph by Charles Hugo, c. 1853–5 (adoc-photos)

Acknowledgments

First and foremost I would like to thank Ruth Harris, my fellow traveller in nineteenth-century French history, for her close reading of much of this book and her insightful advice. Belinda Jack encouraged me to write a history that would be of use to modern linguists as well as to historians. Julian Wright kindly invited Colin Jones, author of *The Great Nation*, and myself to discuss our approaches at an event on 'The New Cobbans' that he organized at the University of Durham in 2006. I would like to acknowledge the debt I owe to Theodore Zeldin, who supervised my thesis over thirty years ago, and whose revolutionary approach to French history stimulated some of my thinking about this book. My thanks go to Simon Winder, my editor at Penguin, for his guidance which was both firm and good-humoured, and to my agent Catherine Clarke for her sharp judgement and unfailing enthusiasm. Cecilia Mackay presented me with a vast range of rich images, only a sample of which are used as illustrations here. I am grateful to the editorial team at Penguin, notably to Peter James for his skilful copy-editing and to the editorial manager, Richard Duguid. I would like to thank Lucy-Jean for her support and affection, as ever. This book is dedicated to my children in the hope that they will learn a little more about the country they love.

Maps

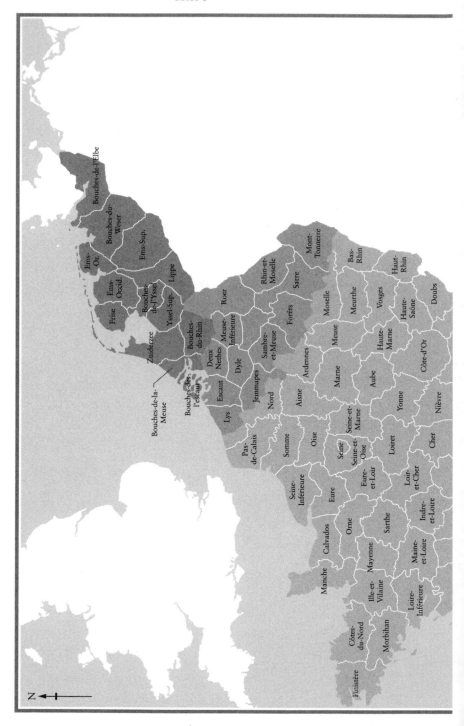

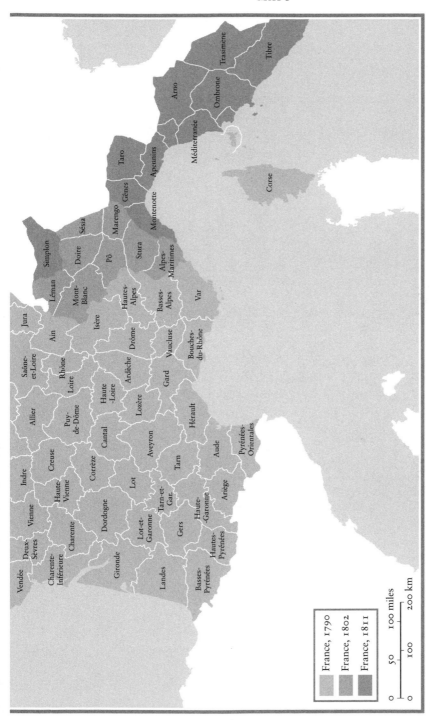

France, 1790–1811

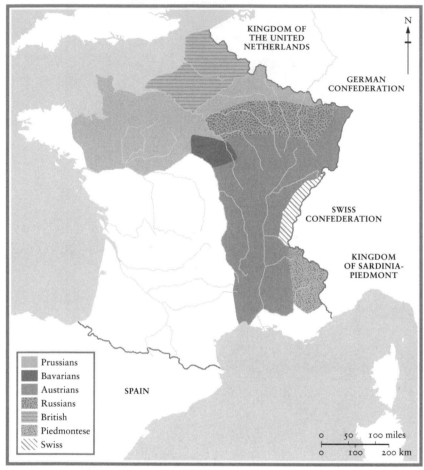

Occupation of France by the Allies, 1815

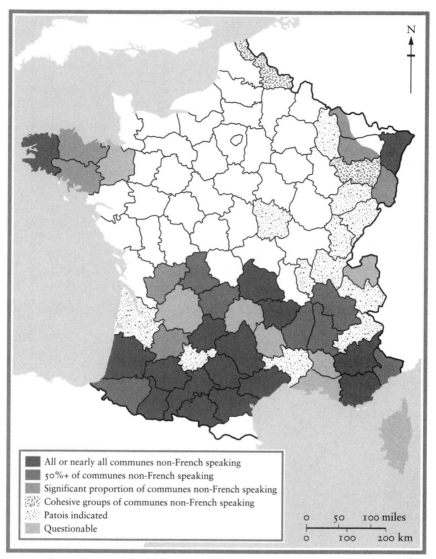

French and minority language/patois-speaking
departments, 1863

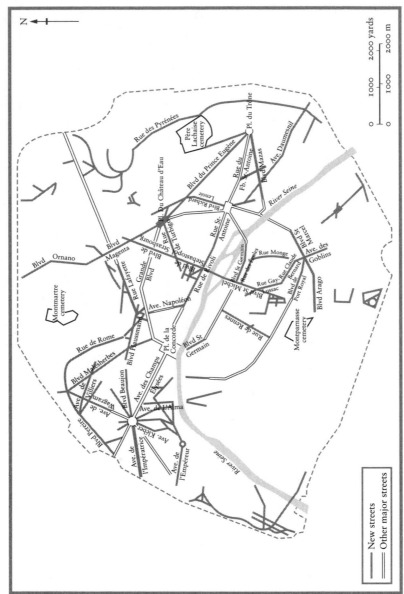

Principal new streets in Paris built between 1850 and 1870

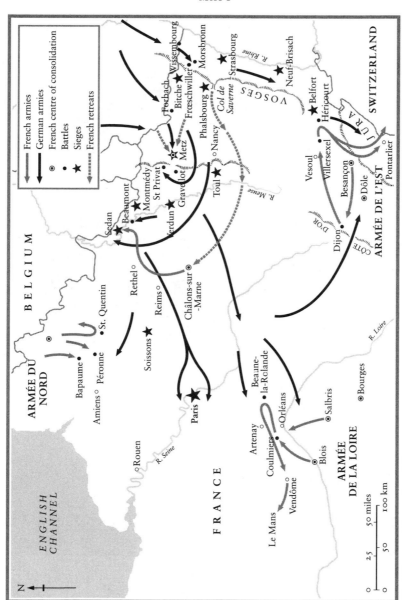

The Franco-Prussian War, 1870–71

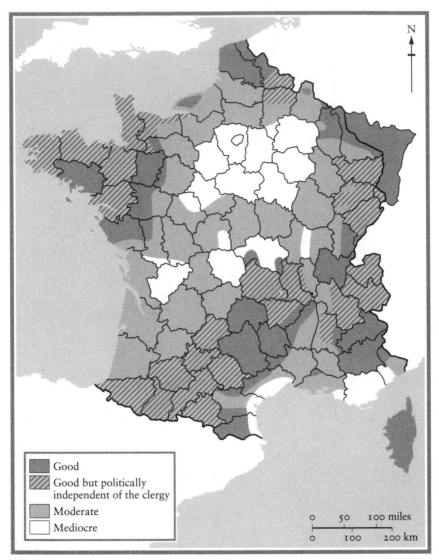

Religious practice in France, *c.* 1880

Introduction: The Children
of the Revolution

On every generation to which it gave birth the French Revolution left its mark. A mark of hope for a new dawn, a new order of the world, but also a mark of tragedy, of a project that came to grief in anarchy, bloodletting and despotism. It proclaimed the power of man's reason to achieve progress and happiness in the world, the rights of man to liberty and equality which every government should protect, the sovereignty of the people, the virtues of self-government, and the duty of French citizens to spread liberty among oppressed peoples abroad. And yet the Revolution spawned new tyrannies, the tyranny of the masses who insulted and abused their elected representatives, a revolutionary dictatorship that terrorized its enemies and the plebiscitary dictatorship of Napoleon Bonaparte who appealed to the disgruntled masses over the heads of the politicians. Liberty was sacrificed to equality, and difference was eliminated in the name of the public interest. The fanaticism attributed to religion was replaced by a revolutionary fanaticism that persecuted its enemies and then consumed its own in a fratricidal struggle. Revolutionaries spawned new armies that set fire to Europe for a generation in the first manifestation of total war.

The Revolution divided the French into two irreconcilable camps. Each had its own defined sense of what France should be, claimed total legitimacy for itself and demonized its opponents. One camp dreamed of bringing back the Ancien Régime, monarchy by divine right, a social hierarchy dominated by a noble caste, and the supremacy of the Catholic Church which sanctified the monarchy and was protected by it. It abhorred the Revolution, forgetting that for three years monarchy, Church and Revolution had coexisted, denouncing the violence it had unleashed from the taking of the Bastille on 14 July 1789, when the head of its governor was paraded on a pikestaff by the mob. Attempts to reform the Catholic Church quickly gave way to its destruction, the closure of churches, the massacre of priests and nuns, the silencing of bells. The monarchy was overthrown by a republic, and the Republic executed the king. A reign of Terror was orchestrated against the enemies of the Revolution, using the guillotine, grapeshot and drownings, and putting rebel provinces to fire and sword. For the counter-revolutionaries no compromise was possible with the Revolution: it would be terminated and those who had promoted it, beginning with the regicides who had voted for the king's death, would themselves be put to death. Neither could there be any deal with the regime of Napoleon to which the Revolution gave rise: he was regarded as a despot, a usurper and a warmonger.

The other camp, with the same passion, believed that the Revolution had been necessary to overthrow an Ancien Régime that had refused to reform itself and had violated the right of every man to liberty and self-government. The forces of the Ancien Régime had not given way but had brought in foreign armies and fomented civil war in the provinces. The Revolution had had to defend itself against its enemies, deposing a tyrant, crushing nobles and clergy who stirred up counter-revolution. The Republic was considered the perfect political order, enshrining liberty, equality and fraternity. It educated its citizens in patriotism or civic virtue – the sacrifice of their selfish interests to the common good – by a combination of republican schooling, participation in public festivals celebrating the Republic, and military service. Enrolled in revolutionary armies, citizens drove out the armies of kings and aristocrats who tried to destroy them and brought liberty and fraternity to peoples who were still oppressed. If the Republic came to an end in 1804 and the Revolution seemed to be over in 1814–15 with the restoration of the monarchy, this was because the education of citizens had not been thorough enough or because opposition had not been suppressed decisively enough. The Revolution and the Republic were unfinished business for revolutionaries, who returned to them repeatedly in the nineteenth century, in

1815, 1830, 1848 and 1871, in order to achieve them completely, permanently, better than before.

Each generation through the nineteenth century wrestled with these problems in their own way. Generations were not so much biological, born at the same time, as historical, shaped by the same events. These events might be the revolutions of 1789, 1830, 1848 and 1871. They might be the Hundred Days of 1815, when Napoleon returned briefly from exile to power until his overthrow at Waterloo, or defeat in the Franco-Prussian war of 1870, or the challenge to French power of British aggression in 1898 or German aggression in 1905 or 1911. These events gave shape to successive generations which differed because of the different events they experienced in their formative years, or later in life. The birth dates of a generation would gravitate around a key year, although individuals defined by the same event might actually be born ten years before or after, so long as they reacted in the same way, most as peers, others as masters or disciples. Not all members of the same generation responded to the same events in the same way. Some, for example, would be swept up in the revolutionary fervour, while others would be turned against it by persecution, the loss of loved ones or enforced exile. The great challenge of the nineteenth century was whether rival or even enemy units of the same generation could find common ground on which to build a political consensus and lay to rest the painful conflicts inherited from the Revolution.[1]

Five key generations were responsible for the making of France during and after the Revolution, and in turn were made by successive revolutions and wars. The Revolution of 1789 was propelled by a generation born around 1760, although the revolutionary decade 1789–99 drew in a range of age-cohorts born between 1750 and 1770. Initially it seemed as if the French people, subjects of absolute monarchy and divided into the two privileged legal orders of clergy and nobility and the unprivileged third estate, would be reconciled in a new nation of free and equal citizens. In his 1789 pamphlet *What is the Third Estate?* the Abbé Sieyès invented a new civic concept of the nation as 'a body of associates living under the same law and represented in the same legislature'. Elected a

3

member of the Estates General called by the king to resolve the government's financial crisis, he proposed a motion on 17 May 1789 that the three chambers for clergy, nobles and third estate become a National Assembly in which they all came together to make a constitution for the new France. The apotheosis of national consensus was the Fête de la Fédération of 14 July 1790, when 350,000 national guards formed from the citizen body assembled on the Champ de Mars in Paris to swear oaths to the nation, the law and the king. The masters of the ceremony were two members of the privileged orders who had thrown in their lot with the nation: Talleyrand, bishop of Autun, who said mass, and the Marquis de Lafayette, who had led French armies in the American War of Independence and as head of the Paris National Guard did his best to persuade the king to accept the Revolution.

The new order inaugurated by the revolutionaries reached into all parts of French life. They replaced the division of France into provinces and a multitude of other jurisdictions by division into eighty-three more or less equal departments, run by elected local administrations. The Catholic Church was reconciled with the Revolution by a Civil Constitution of the Clergy which permitted the election of priests and bishops by the citizen body, while the monopoly of the Catholic faith was ended by toleration accorded to Protestants and Jews. The abolition of privilege opened careers to talent, the abolition of primogeniture established the equal right of all children to family property, and the sale of church lands to solve the government's financial crisis spread property-ownership in French society. Women were emancipated through the legalization of divorce and the dissolution of religious congregations in which many of them traditionally spent their lives and they entered the political arena as agitators if not as citizens. Finally, freedom of the press and theatre unleashed political debate on an unprecedented scale.

The Revolution, however, was soon under threat from its enemies at home and abroad and a new unit of the revolutionary generation overturned the monarchy, proclaimed the Republic, tried and executed the king, and acceded to popular demands for a Terror aimed at all those suspected of frustrating the revolutionary project.

For a year between July 1793 and July 1794 the Republic was ruled by a Jacobin dictatorship of twelve men of the Committee of Public Safety of the Convention parliament elected in 1792 which was dominated by Robespierre. A ruthless centralization was imposed on a country that civil war threatened to split into rival provinces, departments and cities. Church reform was abandoned and a campaign of dechristianization tried to eliminate organized religion, now seen as a threat to revolution. The former privileged orders of nobles and clergy were persecuted, driven underground or into exile, as were the new rich who were seen to benefit from their monopoly of goods in short supply. Women were excluded from the political sphere and political dissent in the arts subjected to censorship. The Jacobin dictatorship and Terror divided France into two, driving into implacable opposition young nobles such as François-René de Chateaubriand, who lost his mother and sister in the Terror and fought briefly in the counter-revolutionary armies before going into exile.

In 1794 the revolutionary brotherhood consumed itself in fratricidal struggle, those who survived turning against Robespierre in July 1794 (*thermidor* Year II in the revolutionary calendar) and seeking to rebuild the Republic on a lasting basis. A younger generation of revolutionaries born after 1760 now became involved. Madame de Staël, daughter of Louis XVI's finance minister, Necker, confined to working behind the political scenes, and Benjamin Constant, a young Swiss intellectual and her sometime lover, endeavoured with many others to found a republic based on liberty instead of dictatorship, on the parliamentary rule of the propertied and educated instead of the rule of the mob and its demagogues. When this liberty collapsed into anarchy, the obvious solution was recourse to dictatorship by a general thrown up by the revolutionary armies who were establishing France as a Grande Nation in Belgium and the Netherlands, the Rhineland, Switzerland and Italy. There was more than one candidate among the revolutionary generals born in the 1760s, but it was General Bonaparte, conqueror of Italy after 1796 and Egypt and Syria in 1798, who emerged as dictator. Revolution as violence was ended and the principles of the Revolution were amalgamated with the need for order and unity. France was placed under extreme administrative centralization with prefects and mayors appointed by the central government. A new nobility was invented, made up of the regime's military and civil elite. The Catholic Church was restored under the Concordat, but more as a department of state than as an independent corporation. The freedom of women was subordinated to the priorities of the family and divorce by mutual consent abolished. The arts were restricted by censorship or harnessed to state propaganda, with the revolutionary artist Jean-Louis David and his pupils recruited to paint the Emperor and his glorious deeds.

A second generation, born around 1800, did not witness the Revolution at first hand, but were the offspring of those who had made and secured it, either in government or on the battlefield. The distinctiveness of this generation, who grew up under the Napoleonic Empire and reached maturity around 1820, has been remarked on by historians, in one case defined as the cohort born between 1792 and 1803.[2] They were also intensely self-aware, raised in a period of excitement and greatness, which was abruptly terminated by the final defeat of the Empire at Waterloo following Napoleon's Hundred Days return in 1815. Edgar Quinet, the son of a military bureaucrat, was taken as a child by his mother to visit his father at Wesel in the Rhineland. 'We lived in the palace of the prince of Prussia,' he recalled, 'and saw nothing but soldiers dragging sabres. They were cavalrymen who had returned from Austerlitz, who had a high opinion of me, and no one could separate me from them.' He was twelve when the Emperor returned from Elba and at that moment 'I began to be fascinated by him, not just by French armies.' After Waterloo and Napoleon's final exile to St Helena his parents sent him away to college. 'If I pitied my hero for the captivity he was to endure in the midst of the ocean, I found my own no less intolerable.'[3] Similarly Alfred de Musset, the son of a writer who also served as a military bureaucrat, observed in his *Confessions of a Child of the Century* that his generation were 'conceived between two battles and brought up in colleges to the roll of drums'. 'For fifteen years they dreamed of the snows of Moscow and the sun of the Pyramids,' but these vast horizons shrivelled after 1815. After that, 'When the children spoke of glory, they were told, "Become priests"; when they spoke of ambition, "Become priests"; of hope, love, strength, life: "Become priests".'[4]

This generation hated the attacks on the Revolution by the restored monarchy, the exile of the regicides, and the pernicious alliance of throne and altar. They wished to rediscover the Revolution as the bringer of liberty, equality and fraternity and to rerun the experiment, this time without the errors of violence, Terror or dictatorship that had discredited the project. One unit of the generation was composed of young liberal journalists who were active in Paris after the Restoration such as Adolphe Thiers, François Mignet and Charles de Rémusat. Thiers and Mignet wrote histories of the Revolution in the 1820s that presented it as a triumph of liberty and order against despotism and popular violence, and realized their dreams in the Revolution of July 1830 which installed a constitutional monarchy and rule of the propertied and educated elite. This outcome was attacked as a hijacking of democratic revolution that could be delivered only by the republic proclaimed by a rival group of this generation. Their fathers had been deputies of the Convention parliament of 1792–5 which had voted the death of the king and elected the Committee of Public Safety, or alternatively had been revolutionary or Napoleonic generals or officials. Among the first were Godefroy Cavaignac, whose father had been exiled to Brussels as a regicide and died there in 1829, and Auguste Blanqui, whose father had been elected to the Convention in 1793 when his home city of Nice was annexed by France. They joined forces with François Raspail, a former seminarist and schoolmaster from Carpentras whose family was in no sense revolutionary but who himself became a public figure whipping up local opinion in favour of revolution during the Hundred Days. These young men modelled themselves on Jacobins such as Robespierre, Saint-Just and Marat, calling their secret society of 30 July 1830 the Society of Friends of the People, after Marat's revolutionary newspaper, and then, after it was dissolved the following year, the Society of the Rights of Man. Godefroy Cavaignac died in 1845, but his friends were orchestrators of the Revolution of 1848, which proclaimed the liberty of the sovereign people to make their own constitution through an elected constituent assembly, equality through universal manhood suffrage, and the avoidance of violence by fraternal union. In the event these revolutionaries were unable to avoid both violence and dictatorship. The working people of eastern Paris rose in revolt in June 1848, demanding social as well as political equality. Ironically, Cavaignac's younger brother Eugène, a professional soldier, was entrusted with dictatorial powers to suppress it. Then in 1851 the president elected by universal suffrage, Louis-Napoleon Bonaparte, nephew of Napoleon Bonaparte, mounted a coup d'état against the constitution and set up a dictatorship. The following year he was proclaimed emperor. The generation of 1800, whether the revolutionaries of 1830 or those of 1848, thus suffered a double blow, and many of them went into exile or abandoned politics.

The generation of 1800 fought a long battle over the Church. One group were shocked by the recurrence of revolution in the Hundred Days of 1815 and became ardent defenders of the Catholic Church and monarchy. This included the curé d'Ars and Félicité de Lamennais, both of whom were born well before 1800 but were fired by the Hundred Days to be ordained in 1815 and begin the work of reconverting the French. Because of their commitment to the monarchy of 1815, which grew increasingly absolutist, the liberal unit of this generation became fiercely anticlerical, intent on destroying the alliance of altar and throne, which it achieved in 1830. At the same moment Lamennais concluded that religion was best secured not by alliance with absolute monarchy but by alliance with liberty and led a number of peers and disciples born around 1800 towards the promised land of religion and freedom, a path that was soon closed by the Pope. In 1848 Frédéric Ozanam, born at the tail end of this generation, attempted to reconcile religion with democracy. In the cultural sphere, which was political by another name, the generation of 1800 was the Romantic generation. Victor Hugo and Alexandre Dumas were both sons of revolutionary–imperial generals, while the painter Eugène Delacroix was rumoured to be the illegitimate son of Talleyrand. Their work explored themes of love, liberty and violence, tested new techniques and appealed to new audiences. Children of the barracks and mess also included a number of prominent women such as Delphine Gay, the daughter

8

of a Napoleonic officer for whom her mother had divorced under the revolutionary law of 1792, and George Sand, whose father, aide-de-camp to General Murat, was killed when she was four. These women were among the feminists antagonized by the prohibition of divorce in 1816 and sought a wider public role for women through journalism and fiction. Gay, now Delphine de Girardin, supported the Revolution of 1830, while George Sand committed herself to the Republic of 1848. As far as France's international standing was concerned, they were appalled by the defeats of 1814–15 and the inability of governments to restore the greatness to which revolutionary and Napoleonic France had laid claim. Spokesmen such as Jules Michelet and Edgar Quinet dreamed of restoring French greatness and of France once again bringing liberty and civilization to the world.

A third generation, born around 1830, scarcely had the time to form any illusions before they were lost, destroyed first by the violent insurrection of June 1848 and its brutal suppression, then by the coup d'état and dictatorship of Louis-Napoleon. Whereas the generation of 1800 were wedded either to the constitutional monarchy or to the Republic, that of 1830 were less ideological, more pragmatic and less committed to one particular form of government or another. It was a generation of builders rather than dreamers. Since 1848 equality in the form of universal manhood suffrage was a given; it was not abolished but restored by Louis-Napoleon in 1851. What was at stake was liberty, or rather liberty with order, for there was a fear that liberty as a sole end would tip into violence. Some of this generation such as Émile Ollivier worked within the Second Empire, trying to make it more liberal, and enjoyed some success with the constitution of 1870, endorsed just before the defeat. Others profited from the defeat of the Empire in 1870, becoming the founding fathers of the Third Republic, constructing a parliamentary regime which would avoid both the authoritarian Empire and the excesses of the Paris Commune of 1871. This group was spearheaded by Léon Gambetta, Juliet Adam – who presided over the salon that launched Gambetta's career – Jules Ferry and Auguste Scheurer-Kestner. Of course, not all of this generation were pragmatic and middle-of-the-road. A rival unit of this generation drew different conclusions from the events of 1848 and 1851. For them the brutal stifling of the cry for bread and freedom in the June Days and the coup d'état of 1851 expressed the violence which the bourgeoisie was prepared to adopt in order to safeguard its interests. They committed themselves to anarchism, following Pierre-Joseph Proudhon who was born late in the Romantic generation but was not fully politicized until the June Days. Alternatively they espoused the Jacobin revolutionism of Blanqui, who dispensed his philosophy from the prisons of the Second Empire, or Marxist socialism, which was becoming known through the meetings of the First Socialist International in the later 1860s. This unit included the likes of Jules Vallès, Henri Rochefort and Louise Michel, who avenged the June Days of 1848 with the Paris Commune of 1871.

The generation of 1830 made their views felt in other areas. They were decentralizers, happy with the centralization of political decision-making in Paris, but keen to see administration devolved to the departmental assemblies which advised prefects and to municipal councils, whose mayors should be elected. They had some influence under the Empire but realized concrete changes under the Third Republic. Since the Second Republic after the June Days and the Second Empire until 1860 restored the political influence of the Church, this generation aimed to reduce that political influence, especially by pruning back the ascendancy the Church had in education. Its anticlericalism was scientific rather than simply iconoclastic, as that of the generation of 1800 had been, for it developed a secular morality that would replace religious education in state schools, replacing fear of hell by fear of social disorder. Ernest Renan wrote a *Life of Jesus* based on scholarship, purged of mystery and placed in historical context. Jules Ferry, as education minister in the 1880s, excluded religious congregations and religious education from state schools. Since the education of women in particular was under the control of the Church, the generation of 1830 developed the state education of women, while the feminist wing of the generation, led by Maria Desraismes, campaigned in favour of the civil rights of women and obtained the legalization of divorce again in 1884. In

the arts the generation of 1830 was less Romantic than Realist.
Witnessing the defeat of dreams by naked political and military
power in 1848 and 1851, writers such as the Goncourt brothers,
Gustave Flaubert, Alexandre Dumas *fils* and Alphonse Daudet were
persuaded to look reality in the face. In the art world the Realist
Courbet was followed by Impressionists around Édouard Manet who
painted modern life rather than legends or histories. Internationally,
the defeat of France by Prussia on its road to a united Germany was
felt with particular pain. It was the formative event of the adult
years of this generation that sent many of them into deep reflection
about the identity of the French nation, which had suffered a massive
blow to its confidence. Ernest Renan, Fustel de Coulanges and Ernest
Lavisse all contributed, in the wake of defeat, to redefining French
national identity and to restoring the country's national consciousness and confidence.[5]

A fourth generation, born around 1860 and thus still children during
the Franco-Prussian war and Paris Commune in 1870–71, were less
marked by these traumatic events than were their parents. They
reached maturity during the early years of the Third Republic, when
the regime was well secured against the threats of royalist or Bonapartist restoration or of popular revolution. By the 1890s many
royalists and Bonapartists had 'rallied' to the Republic and even
Marxist socialists were committed to the democratic process. The
event which shaped it was the Dreyfus Affair of 1897–9 which
reopened old conflicts between republicans and anti-republicans,
anticlericals and Catholics, and sparked new conflicts between philo-
Semites and anti-Semites, revolutionary patriots and reactionary
nationalists. The main lesson learned by the generation of 1860 was
that such conflicts were aberrant and needed to be defused by a
process of what became known as *apaisement* or pacification. A
republic of the centre had to be constructed which incorporated as
many people as possible under its shade. The leaders of this generation, who assumed the reins of government after the Dreyfus Affair,
in the so-called Belle Époque down to 1914, were drawn from both
the centre-right and centre-left of the political spectrum. From the
centre-right came Raymond Poincaré, Louis Barthou and Joseph

Caillaux. From the centre-left were drawn former socialists who had flirted with anarchism, such as Aristide Briand, or socialists who had never really espoused Marxism, such as Alexandre Millerand and René Viviani. A serious Marxist such as Jean Jaurès did not hold power but steered the socialist party away from the rhetoric of revolutionary class war towards democratic socialism.

This generation were committed to rejuvenating the Republic in many ways. They challenged the system of administrative centralization that, with a few reforms by the 1830 generation, still held France in the iron grip of 1800. The Lorrainer Maurice Barrès, the Provençal Charles Maurras and the Languedocien Jean Charles-Brun were all serious campaigners for a more decentralized republic. On the religious front, they were committed to end the war of religion that was stirred up again by the Dreyfus Affair. Aristide Briand was a key negotiator in the Separation of Church and state which abrogated the Concordat under which the Catholic Church had received state funding but had to submit to state control. The Church now floated free as an institution, and it became once again possible to be fully Catholic and fully republican. This generation included a new generation of feminists, led by Marguerite Durand, editor of *La Fronde*, and qualified lawyers and doctors such as Jeanne Schmal who demanded that married women should have control of their earnings and Madeleine Pelletier, who campaigned for birth control and the right to abortion. In the cultural sphere the generation of 1860 was that of the Symbolists, who retreated from the modern world embraced by their fathers and sought a spiritual ideal that might be expressed in myth or legend or primitive art. They included poets such as Rimbaud and followers of Mallarmé like André Gide and Paul Valéry, Marcel Proust, disciples of Pissarro such as Seurat and Signac, and of Gauguin such as Édouard Vuillard and Maurice Denis, and musicians such as Debussy.

Unlike the generation of 1830, which was shocked by defeat in 1870, the generation of 1860 tended to antimilitarism and a lack of interest in national greatness. It sported a number of antimilitarist agitators such as Lucien Descaves and Georges Darien. However, the Dreyfus Affair and the Fashoda incident of 1898 exposed the weakness of France internally and internationally. Some members of this generation, such as Maurice Barrès and Charles Maurras, converted overnight to the cause of nationalism. At the higher end of the generational spectrum, old enough to have witnessed the impact of 1870, powerful political advocates of France's colonial empire, such as Eugène Étienne, were vindicated. Étienne had influence with soldiers who built the French Empire in Indo-China and Africa during the Third Republic, such as Galliéni and his deputy Lyautey. These were now joined by colonial soldiers born after 1860, notably Jean-Baptiste Marchand, who led the expedition to Fashoda, and Charles Mangin. International crisis prompted the political generation of 1860, headed by Poincaré and Barthou, to focus on the question of national greatness. Among socialists Alexandre Millerand who had previously questioned the use of soldiers to crush strikers now emerged as a strong defender of the French army and nation.

The last generation, born around 1890, was marked less by the political and religious struggles around the Dreyfus Affair than by the regime that emerged from it. Rather than seeing the pacification of old conflicts in a positive light, it took the view that the politicians of 1860 who held office in the Belle Époque had traded principle for power and ideological commitment for political compromise. They regarded the Republic of the centre as the product of horse-trading by political parties, notably the Radicals, and the sacrifice of the national interest by politicians who were too often Jewish, Protestant or freemasons. They adopted a position on the political extremes, either on the extreme left or on the extreme right. Many of them were inspired by antidreyfusards such as Maurice Barrès or Charles Maurras, and joined the latter's Action Française organization, which was committed to replacing the corrupt Republic by an energetic, popular monarchy. Others were disciples of Charles Péguy, a former dreyfusard who was disillusioned by the sell-out of former allies on the left and moved in the direction of patriotism and Catholicism.

The identity of this generation was publicized by a survey in 1913 entitled *Les Jeunes Gens d'aujourdhui*.[6] Statistically, its base was rather narrow and it concentrated on the intellectual elite of the universities, *grandes écoles* and best lycées, and in this sense it was no more than a version of studies of the student population of 1820. The generation born around 1890, it asserted, were completely different from that of 1860 that had become the decadent youth of the 1880s, before the Dreyfus Affair. The new generation, it announced, were characterized not by ennui or listlessness but by 'a taste for action', enthusiasm for team sports such as football and admiration for those new acrobats of the sky, the aviators. Whereas their fathers had been anticlericals, materialists and freethinkers who fought to diminish the influence of the Church in state and society, they themselves celebrated the beauty of religion and the grace of God and were the agents of a 'Catholic renaissance'. Many of them were members of the Christian-democratic youth movement founded by Marc Sangnier, the Sillon or Furrow, and were dedicated to rechristianizing the Republic after the Separation of Church and state. Although some of this generation were antimilitaristic, opposed to France's participation in the arms race that led up to 1914, their dominant view, according to the survey, was patriotic. They were shocked by manifestations of German aggression in 1905, when Kaiser William landed in Tangier to challenge France's bid for Morocco, or in 1911 when Germany sent a gunboat to Agadir for the same purpose. This was a generation that believed in French colonial expansion, which at this point focussed on Morocco, and responded to Barrès' campaign to put the recovery of Alsace-Lorraine at the front of France's national agenda.

The iconic representative of this generation was Ernest Psichari, the grandson of Ernest Renan, author of the humanistic *Life of Jesus* but also thinker about French national identity. Psichari graduated from the Sorbonne, a bastion of anticlerical thought, but converted to active Catholicism and rather than follow an academic career joined the colonial army, fought in Africa, and wrote novels on the subject of patriotism, greatness and the nobility of the sword. He was a model for the French officers who led France into battle in 1914 and was one of the first to be killed on the battlefield, in Belgium on 22 August. He was followed two weeks later by one of his mentors, Charles Péguy, killed on the Marne. These were

the leaders of the generation of 1890 which was the generation of
Verdun and the Chemin des Dames. It left a million and a half
of its number dead in the field, demonstrating the strength of the
French in national unity and finally burying the divisions inherited
from the Revolution.

PART ONE

France, 1799–1870

I

Revolution or Consensus?
French Politics, 1799–1870

SAVING THE REPUBLIC

On 9 October 1799 a thirty-year-old general landed at Fréjus on the south coast of France, having set sail from Egypt six weeks before. The most successful general to have been thrown up by the French revolutionary armies, he had in fact abandoned his army after a campaign that had been anything but a success, to seize the initiative from his political masters before they could act against him.

Bonaparte, a minor Corsican noble and graduate of the Paris École Militaire, combined military genius with both a political ability uncommon among soldiers and unbridled ambition. His first military exploit as an artillery commander in December 1793 had been to dislodge royalist rebels from the Mediterranean port of Toulon and to drive out the British fleet that was supporting them. Less than two years later, on 5 October 1795, he used his military command for political purposes, scattering with a 'whiff of grapeshot' a royalist insurrection against the Convention parliament which, having presided over the Terror, refused to dissolve itself fully and allow free and fair elections which royalists stood a good chance of winning. He was acting on behalf of his political master Paul Barras, a regicide of the Convention who had led the military forces which toppled Robespierre on 27 July 1794, and had become the uncrowned king of the five-man Directory which then ran the Republic.

In 1796 Bonaparte, a novice in love, married Joséphine de Beauharnais, a creole who was doubly a victim of the Revolution in that she had lost her first fortune in the West Indies as the result of war and her first husband on the scaffold after he surrendered Mainz to the Prussians. While writing to her daily, Bonaparte combined military and diplomatic skills commanding the French armies that invaded Italy in the spring of 1796 to take control of it from the Austrians. After the battle of Lodi in May he occupied Milan, after the victory of Rivoli in January he entered Mantua. On behalf of the Directory he forced the Austrians to sign the Treaty of Campo Formio (17 October 1797) under which France secured recognition of its control of Belgium, the left bank of the Rhine and the Cisalpine and Ligurian Republics based respectively on Milan and Genoa. Having set up one satellite republic in Holland in 1795 (the Batavian), in 1798–9 France set up others in Switzerland, Rome and Naples, after ejecting the pope and the Bourbon families. French power had never been so great, but Bonaparte's ambitions were even greater. He secured the approval of Talleyrand, now foreign minister, for an offensive by an Army of the Orient to Egypt, which belonged formally to the Ottoman Empire but was ruled by a military caste of Mamelukes. Domination of Egypt would allow France to control the whole of the Mediterranean and to disrupt Great Britain's lucrative trade with and growing Empire in India. On 19 May 1798 a French armada therefore set sail from Toulon under his command. En route it seized Malta from the Knights of St John, a blow to British sea-power in the Mediterranean. Landing in Egypt Bonaparte defeated the Mameluke army at the battle of the Pyramids on 21 July and entered Cairo in triumph on 25 July. Unfortunately, Nelson sank Bonaparte's fleet at the battle of Aboukir Bay on 1 August 1798, so that there was no easy return for his army. Bonaparte decided to fight his way out by marching north to Syria and confronting the Ottoman armies, but his attempt to take Acre by siege failed and he fell back on Egypt. On 25 July 1799 he won his own battle of Aboukir against the Ottomans, but having given his army this respite he decided that his next battle was to be waged on metropolitan soil, for the control of France.

By the summer of 1799 the French Republic was under siege. Having dominated half of Europe in 1798, it was now in retreat on all fronts. The mobilization of huge armies was increasingly resented by the population, and the country was awash with deserters and draft-dodgers who often made common cause with counter-revolutionary guerrillas. Failure to settle the religious question by any other means than persecuting the clergy and the faithful who looked to them achieved nothing other than to make counter-revolution popular. The state itself was also in crisis, besieged on the one hand by royalists campaigning for the restoration of the Bourbon monarchy, and on the other by Jacobins or radical republicans wanting to return to the virtuous, democratic Republic of 1793.

All these issues were connected. Bonaparte's invasion of Egypt unleashed the so-called War of the Second Coalition, declared against an overambitious France by the Ottoman Empire, Great Britain, Austria and Russia. In the spring of 1799 Bonaparte took on the Ottomans in Syria and Egypt, while Generals Jourdan and Bernadotte were sent across the Rhine into Germany. Just as Bonaparte failed in Syria, Jourdan was defeated by the Austrian emperor's brother, the Archduke Charles, at the battle of Stockach (25 March 1799) and both he and Bernadotte returned to France. In Switzerland General Masséna was forced to abandon Zurich to the Austrians on 6 June. General Macdonald abandoned Naples as power in the south fell into the hands of Catholic irregulars bent on destroying the short-lived French Republic at Naples: a Christian Army organized in Calabria by a buccaneering cardinal, Fabrizio Ruffo, and known as the Sanfedists, supported in the Naples area by a peasant leader who went under the name of Fra Diavolo. More seriously, the Austrian emperor had hired to command his forces in Italy the Russian General Suvarov, scourge of the Ottoman Turks in two wars and of the Poles after their insurrection in 1794. He defeated General Moreau at the battle of Cassano (27 April), entered Milan and Turin, and then defeated Macdonald at the battle of the Trebbia river on 21 June 1799.

The revolutionary armies demanded an unprecedented mobilization of men and resources. The French army reached a maximum of 750,000 in 1794 but declined to 270,000 in 1798. To meet the Second Coalition a law of 5 September 1798 sponsored by General Jourdan made all young men aged twenty to twenty-five liable for conscription and wasted no time calling them to the colours. Unfortunately the growing needs of the Republic were matched by its decreasing ability to enforce the law. In the Paris region and along the eastern frontier, where there was a tradition of soldiering, men answered the call, but many communities tried to prevent the departure of their young men. Those who were recruited often deserted and, now outlaws, took refuge with bands of brigands that roamed the countryside, looting and practising highway robbery. The Beauce south of Chartres was tyrannized by a gang known as the *bande d'Orgères* led by 'le beau François' which was finally rounded up and put on trial in March 1799; twenty-two of the band were executed in July 1800.[1] In the west and south-east of France brigandage often merged with counter-revolution, as bands targeted mail coaches, purchasers of church property, factories working to supply the army and republican officials, hacking down trees of liberty into the bargain. In Belgium, which had no tradition of conscription under the Austrians, the Loi Jourdan on top of religious persecution triggered a so-called peasant war, with rebel bands destroying conscription registers, taking Austrian colours and shouting 'Long live the Emperor!'[2] On the left bank of the Rhine French authority was challenged by the brigand leader Johannes Bückler, alias Schinderhannes, who won notoriety as the violent defender of local communities against French officials and Jewish middlemen until his arrest in 1802 and execution with nineteen accomplices outside Mainz in 1803.[3]

Most of these areas, from Brittany to Belgium and the Rhineland, were deeply Catholic, and resistance was provoked by conscription but sustained by the fierce opposition of communities to republican campaigns of dechristianization. The problem went back a long way. The National Assembly started in 1790 by trying to reform the Church, but split the clergy and their parishes between those who accepted the democratic principle of the Civil Constitution of the Clergy that parish priests and bishops should be elected, and those from the pope downwards who argued that this violated the doctrines of divine calling and apostolic succession. Only the minority of clergy who took the oath to the Civil Constitution were allowed to continue; the non-jurors who refused were ejected from their parishes and subjected to growing persecution. As France sank into civil war in 1793 the Catholic religion was imagined by revolutionaries, with some reason, to be fuelling counter-revolution, and a campaign of

22

dechristianization was launched. Churches were closed, sold off as granaries, warehouses or stables, or given over to temples of Reason. Sundays were replaced by *décadi* which came round only once every ten days, church bells melted down for cannon, shrines and calvaries vandalized, priests defrocked and married by force to nuns in bizarre ceremonies. At Nevers the Convention's representative on mission Joseph Fouché, himself a former Oratorian priest, had an atheistic message placarded on cemeteries, 'Death is eternal sleep.' At Nantes in December 1793 hundreds of priests were bound and herded on to barges that were then sunk in the Loire estuary.

After Thermidor there was a move to tolerate religious worship (21 February 1795), but on the condition that it was done without processions and vestments in public; bells were to be rung only on the *décadi* and national festivals. Gradually the practice of religion began to revive in local communities. Churches were recovered by the faithful, and services were held again on a Sunday. Pilgrimages to local shrines to ask for succour or pardon were revived. Clergy were in short supply since non-juring priests were still persecuted and constitutional ones were disliked, so sometimes masses had to be celebrated by the laity themselves. The republican authorities, however, remained to be convinced that the royalist sting had been pulled out of religion, and reverted to persecution at the slightest provocation. The way to separate religion from counter-revolutionary politics had yet to be found.

The constitution of 1795 attempted to secure the Republic on the basis of property and education, which were represented in the two assemblies of the Five Hundred and the Elders, while absolute rule was prevented by splitting the executive between five Directors. Since the Terror, however, property and education looked for peace and order and a restoration of the monarchy. The Directors, most of whom were regicides, responded to the threat of royalists winning elections by invalidating results and purging those elected, if necessary by military force. The Directors were also opposed by Jacobins or radical republicans who detested their corrupt and oligarchical regime and demanded a return to the democratic constitution of 1793, which they hoped would usher in a regime more accountable to the people, more virtuous and more patriotic. The Directors themselves, meanwhile, were prepared to slide one way or another, taking advantage of political crises to eliminate rival Directors.

Elections in 1797 confirmed the revenge of the royalists. Dominating the Council of Five Hundred they elected as president or speaker General Pichegru, who had conquered Holland for the revolutionary armies but now had contacts with Louis XVIII's court. This was an intolerable threat to the Republic for the Directors under Barras, who now turned to the army. On 4 September 1797 the threat of force supported a purge of about fifty royalist deputies from Pichegru down, and the dismissal of two Directors, including Lazare Carnot, formerly the 'organizer of victory' on the Committee of Public Safety now also suspected of making overtures towards royalists. Royalists who had emigrated from France but had since returned were now driven out again on pain of death. Military commissions sentenced forty-seven officers of counter-revolutionary armies and forty-eight refractory priests accused of fomenting sedition to be shot. Fourteen hundred priests were deported, of whom 187 died within two years.[4] This has sometimes been called the 'Directorial Terror', which was sharply focussed on the regime's enemies, backed by considerable force, and met with little resistance.

This shift to the left opened a way back for Jacobins. This faction supported revolutionary measures against seditious priests and nobles, but also wanted to dispose of the republican oligarchy. They were well organized in the Society of Friends of Liberty and Equality that in Paris met in the Manège near the Tuileries gardens and around radical newspapers such as the *Journal des Hommes Libres*. Their darlings and patrons were Generals Jourdan and Bernadotte. They did well in the elections of April 1798 but the regime was determined to keep them out of the political process. The Directors passed a law of 11 May 1798 which prevented 127 deputies from even taking their seats, 86 of them Jacobins. The following year, in March 1799, Jacobins exploited electoral apathy and made up a party of ninety-nine deputies as the Directors struggled to survive.[5]

The Directory's control over the assemblies which could less and less be described as elected might have been effective if the news from abroad had been good. In the spring and early summer of

1799, however, the news from Italy, Switzerland, Germany and Syria was uniformly bad. Public opinion grew angry and restless. 'This state of alarm and discontent comes from our armies' lack of success,' reported the Paris police authorities on 16 June 1799.[6] The Jacobin minority in the Council of Five Hundred bayed for heads to roll and for a more decisive and aggressive republic. At their head, General Jourdan, returning from Germany, denounced the incompetence and corruption of the Directors, war ministers and army contractors. For the first time it was the Councils that purged the Directors, not the other way around. The Abbé Sieyès, who had just been elected a director in May, could not be blamed but saw the opportunity to find new allies. Barras took the part of orchestrator of the coup of 18 June 1799, forcing the resignation of three of his rival Directors, replaced by three reliable nonentities. The failure of his foreign policy forced Talleyrand out as foreign minister, Joseph Fouché was appointed minister of police, General Bernadotte became war minister and the regime went into patriotic overdrive to remove the menace of counter-revolution from home and beyond the frontiers. All eligible conscripts were called up, a forced loan was levied to cover the deficit, and a law of hostages allowed the authorities to seize members of noble or émigré families in areas which had fallen prey to brigandage.

This mobilization was designed to support a new and decisive offensive, but things did not work out that way. The young General Joubert, who was the favourite of Talleyrand and Fouché and was viewed as a future dictator should one be needed, took command of the army in Italy, only to be mortally wounded at the head of his troops at the battle of Novi on 14 August, which was lost. Shortly afterwards the British landed a force in Holland, which was then the Batavian Republic, a satellite of the French Republic, and seized the Dutch fleet. Foreign defeat stimulated a fresh wave of counter-revolution aimed at displacing republican authorities from the towns and cities they controlled. In the Alpes-Maritimes local counter-revolutionaries known as Barbets were fortified by the addition of soldiers deserting from Italy. A royalist insurrection possibly 12,000 strong, consisting of peasants, artisans, draft-dodgers and deserters led by returned émigrés and non-juring priests, tried to seize control of the Jacobin city of Toulouse on 6 August; in the fighting a hundred republicans and a thousand rebels were killed.[7] The leaders of the Catholic and royal armies of the west of France, in close contact with the Bourbon court and the British, organized a series of attacks on republican towns in that area in October 1799. The Vendean leader Comte Ghaisne de Bourmont captured Le Mans on 14 October with 2,000 *chouans*. Georges Cadoudal, a burly peasant and *chouan* leader in the Morbihan, launched an assault on Vannes, while on 25 October Louis de Frotté, leader of the counter-revolution in Normandy, returned from exile in England to order a series of attacks on Norman towns. 'In the space of two months', reported police minister Fouché on 4 October, 'the activity of our enemies has redoubled, and they have exploited the momentary setbacks of our armies to reopen wounds that had healed only imperfectly in the west and Midi. The scourge of a war that already has devastated too much is not enough for them; they also want the horrors of a civil war.'[8]

The Republic was now in serious trouble. It was under threat from counter-revolutionaries backed by the allies of the Second Coalition. It was threatened by Jacobins who wanted to bring back some version of the revolutionary government of 1793 in order to seize control from the Directory. On 13 September, indeed, General Jourdan proposed a motion of *la patrie en danger* in the Council of Five Hundred. 'Our strongholds abroad have been surrendered by treachery,' he declared, 'and within our borders a vast royalist conspiracy holds the whole Republic in its web.'[9] To declare the country in danger was to declare a state of emergency. The last time this had happened was in July 1792 when the country was invaded by Austria and Prussia and it prefigured the fall of the monarchy and the Terror. Jourdan's motion was thus opposed by moderate republicans in the Five Hundred, led now by its president or speaker, Lucien Bonaparte, who wanted to avoid a return to revolutionary government. Accused of planning dictatorship he riposted, 'There is none among us who would not be ready to stab the first person who dared set himself up as a dictator in France.' Jourdan's motion was defeated 245–171, the war minister Bernadotte promoted by the Jacobins was forced to resign and the Jacobin threat was temporarily shelved. Perhaps Lucien Bonaparte knew that his brother was on a ship somewhere between Egypt and the south of France.

Napoleon Bonaparte landed with a number of his generals at Fréjus on 9 October 1799 and arrived in Paris on 16 October. Joséphine's house on the rue de la Victoire, where he stayed, was besieged by crowds and some sort of dénouement was keenly anticipated. The seizure of power when it came on 9–10 November (18–19 *brumaire* in the revolutionary calendar) was very much like previous coups since 1795: the 'black legend' of Napoleon's *brumaire* coup was not elaborated until his nephew took power by a similar coup against the National Assembly in 1851. It was, in the first place, a conspiracy orchestrated by Bonaparte and Sieyès, who used the crisis finally to get rid of leading Director Barras and bring in a stronger constitution in order to contain the royalist and Jacobin opposition. 'You want the power and Sieyès wants a new constitution,' said Talleyrand, who was also part of the conspiracy. 'Therefore join forces.'[10] Sieyès had influence in the Council of Elders, who voted early on 9 November to move the assemblies away from the revolutionary-infested capital to the nearby palace of Saint-Cloud and to appoint Bonaparte commander of the troops of the Paris region. When the Council of Five Hundred opened its proceedings at Saint-Cloud, surrounded by troops, on 10 November, each deputy renewed his oath to the constitution of 1795. News arrived of the resignation of Barras and they started to debate the election of his successor. Bonaparte left his guard at the door and entered the Council, but was greeted by shouts of 'Outlaw the dictator!' and 'Long live the Republic and the constitution of Year III!' Bonaparte hurried out in a panic and Lucien, who had promised to resist would-be dictators but made an exception for his brother, was prevented from leaving too by deputies who held him down in his speaker's chair. Napoleon's grenadiers now intervened, removing Lucien from the chamber. In the courtyard Lucien was able to steel the nerve of his brother and the assembled troops by claiming that Jacobin deputies were armed with daggers, ready to assassinate Napoleon and relaunch the Terror. The grenadiers were ordered to drive the deputies out of the chamber at bayonet point and that night a commission of three, headed by Sièyes and Bonaparte, was set up to draft a new constitution.[11]

Threats were followed by double-crossing and corruption. Sieyès envisaged himself in the role of a grand elector, receiving ambassadors, signing treaties and appointing one consul for internal and one for external affairs. Bonaparte would have none of this 'do-nothing king' and bullied Sieyès into accepting a team of three consuls, the first of whom would have the power to appoint the Council of State (which drafted legislation) and government ministers. At the last meeting of the commission on 13 December, Bonaparte called Sieyès' bluff by inviting him to propose the names of the three consuls. Reluctant to suggest himself, Sieyès proposed Bonaparte as first consul together with a former justice minister Cambacérès and Lebrun, former secretary of Louis XV's reforming chancellor Maupeou. Sieyès found himself fobbed off as president of the Senate. Bonaparte now appointed his brother Lucien, to whom he was in debt for *brumaire*, as minister of the interior, and it was Lucien who organized the plebiscite held on 7 February 1800 to endorse the new constitution. Given massive royalist hostility in Belgium, the west and the Midi, the only possible verdict on the outcome of the vote – 3,011,007 for and 1,562 against – was that it was a fiddle.[12]

The strategy of Napoleon was to bring over the republican political class which had nurtured him while removing the threat from the Jacobin revolutionaries when the moment presented itself. Republican politicians dominated the three assemblies provided for under the new constitution: an appointed Senate which would choose the members of a Tribunate that could debate laws but not vote them and a Legislative Body that could vote them but not debate them, drawn from a national list of 6,000 notables. After 1802 electoral colleges were set up in each department, composed of the 600 notables who paid the most land tax. Of the original sixty senators, then, thirty-eight had sat in a revolutionary assembly before *brumaire*, as had sixty-nine of the one hundred tribunes and 240 out of 300 deputies of the Legislative Body. Sieyès, as a veteran republican politician, hoped to use his influence in the assemblies to counterbalance that of Bonaparte, but having double-crossed him once Bonaparte did it again by offering him a large estate outside Versailles, which he accepted at the cost of his credibility.[13]

Dealing with the revolutionary threat was more difficult, for

Bonaparte's own legitimacy flowed from the Revolution and he was aware of leaders who had been carried away by trying to stop the revolutionary tide too soon. By the same token it was no longer seen as politic to guillotine revolutionaries; the preferred punishment was the 'dry guillotine' of deportation to some inhospitable colony. While he would have liked to deport sixty neo-Jacobins who were alleged to be carrying daggers in the chamber on 19 *brumaire*, including General Jourdan, along with seventy other former terrorists, immediately after the coup, public opinion was too strongly against it. The fact that Fouché himself, carried over as minister of police, was a former architect of the Terror, also made things difficult. Bonaparte had to wait for an opportunity to blacken his enemies. This came with a bomb attempt on his life as he went to the opera on Christmas Eve 1800, which he blamed on 'terrorists', and had 130 of his revolutionary opponents deported without trial to Guiana, the Seychelles, or the islands of Oléron and Ré off La Rochelle.[14]

In fact the Christmas Eve assassination attempt was the work of royalists, who had hoped that Bonaparte was going to pave the way for the restoration of the monarchy, but were disappointed when he told the Comte de Provence (the future Louis XVIII), 'You must give up all hope of returning to France: you would have to pass over a hundred thousand dead bodies.'[15] That he blamed the attack on revolutionaries says much about Bonaparte's strategy. He was keen to end the French civil war and to attract the support of royalists, so long as they gave up hope of a Bourbon restoration. Émigrés were allowed to return and recover their estates if they were prepared to accept the new regime. A truce was negotiated with the Vendean rebels on 18 January 1800. Talks were begun to restore the Roman Catholic religion in France, albeit under strict state control, and the Concordat between the regime and the Papacy was signed on 16 July 1801 and publicized on Easter Day, 18 April 1802. The anniversary of the death of Louis XVI, 21 February, was no longer celebrated.

Some royalists were indeed won over. François-René de Chateaubriand had fought in the émigré army of the Prince de Condé in 1792, had lost his brother, mother and sister as a result of the Terror and had been in exile in London and America. He returned in the spring of 1800 and, through the good offices of foreign minister Talleyrand, was appointed in 1803 first secretary at the embassy in Rome, re-established after the Concordat.[16] The Duc de Richelieu, great-great-great-nephew of the cardinal, on the other hand, who had served in the army of Catherine the Great after 1792, returned to France early in 1802 in order to recover his estates, but was unwilling to serve the new regime and went back to serve Tsar Alexander in 1803 as governor of Odessa.[17] The fate of royalist rebels who refused to lay down their arms against the Republic was more violent. Louis de Frotté, the leader of the Norman rebels, was captured, court-martialled and shot on 18 February 1800.[18] Georges Cadoudal, the *chouan* leader, obtained an interview with Bonaparte in March 1800, but they did not agree terms and he now flitted between France and England, organizing conspiracies, with the police snapping at his heels.[19]

The profile of those who supported Napoleon and those who opposed him changed as he sought to perpetuate his power. The Senate ruled that he could serve as consul for life in 1802, and this was ratified by popular plebiscite, with 3.2 million in favour, and only 7,200 against.[20] Republicans of a liberal persuasion saw this move as a threat first to liberty, then to the Republic. Benjamin Constant, who enjoyed the patronage of Sieyès and the favours of Madame de Staël, declared in his maiden speech to the Tribunate in January 1800 that 'a constitution is in itself an act of defiance, as it sets limits to authority'. Such defiance led to his removal from the Tribunate in 1802, and Madame de Staël, accused of using her salon and her writings to rally liberal opposition, in September 1803 was ordered to reside 40 leagues from Paris. In fact she went to Weimar and Berlin and began to write the famous work that Napoleon took to be an indirect criticism of his regime, *On Germany*. Meanwhile the salon of her friend and rival Madame Récamier became a meeting point of Bonaparte's brothers in arms, Generals Moreau and Bernadotte, equally successful generals in the republican army who were envious of the way in which Bonaparte was setting himself above them. Bernadotte remained cautious, but Moreau became entangled in a plot to kidnap Bonaparte planned by General Pichegru, his former commander. Pichegru had been deported to Cayenne as a royalist plotter after the 1797 coup but escaped and linked up with the tireless Georges Cadoudal and other prominent royalists. In the event Moreau was not won over by the royalists, as he would not compromise the Republic, although he was arrested with the other conspirators early in 1804 and sent for trial with them. Pichegru died in prison – whether strangled or committing suicide was unclear. Moreau used the trial in May 1804 to preach the virtues of a republican soldier without ambition and to observe, 'many were republicans then who are now no longer'; he was given a two-year sentence which he was able to swap for exile in the United States.[21] Cadoudal was executed with eleven other *chouans*, while death sentences against Armand and Jules Polignac, sons of Marie-Antoinette's former confidante and close to the Comte d'Artois (the future Charles X), were commuted to prison terms.

During the trial an even more dramatic event occurred. The Duc d'Enghien, thirty-one-year-old son of the Prince de Condé and a likely Bourbon pretender, was seized in Germany on Napoleon's orders and brought to the fort of Vincennes outside Paris, where he was summarily tried by a nocturnal court martial and shot. Fouché remarked that this was worse than a crime: it was a mistake. Chateaubriand recalled that this event 'changed my life, as it changed that of Napoleon'.[22] Seeing the blood of a regicide on Napoleon's hands he resigned his diplomatic post and broke with the regime. Napoleon, however, took the view that the Bourbon threat was so serious that only becoming an emperor or republican king himself would ensure the security of his position. To become hereditary emperor shut the door on Bourbon restoration, but also alienated many of the republican brotherhood. Lazare Carnot, who had served as war minister in 1800, declared in the Tribunate that while a temporary dictatorship had been necessary to save the Republic, a hereditary empire was a threat both to liberty and to equality, for it would usher in a new nobility.[23] In spite of this the Senate offered Napoleon a hereditary imperial title on 18 May 1804, a constitutional change that was endorsed by plebiscite, with 2.5 millions voting in favour and a mere 1,400 against.

CHARLEMAGNE'S EMPIRE

Napoleon was consecrated emperor in the cathedral of Notre-Dame on 2 December 1804. He received the crown, sword and sceptre said to have belonged to Charlemagne and brought from his capital of Aix-la-Chapelle, but in fact mocked up for the occasion by local Paris jewellers. Napoleon intended to recreate the western Empire of Charlemagne and needed the sanction of the pope. Pius VII was persuaded to cross the Alps for the occasion. He said mass and blessed the regalia but was not permitted to crown Napoleon for fear of reopening the conflict between Papacy and Empire that had dogged the Middle Ages; Napoleon placed the crown on his own head and also crowned his wife Joséphine. Napoleon then swore an oath to maintain the territory of the Republic, to safeguard the Concordat with the Church, and to uphold equal rights and civil and political liberty, to the massed acclaim of 'Vive l'Empereur!'[24]

The coronation of the first emperor of the fourth French dynasty after the Merovingians, Carolingians and Capetians required a royal family, a household and a military establishment. Napoleon and his brothers Joseph and Louis were pronounced princes of the blood; Lucien had been relieved of the Ministry of the Interior in 1800 and retired in high dudgeon to Rome. Napoleon's uncle, Cardinal Fesch, archbishop of Lyon, became grand almoner, Cambacérès arch-chancellor of the Empire and Talleyrand grand chamberlain. The coronation regalia were carried by some of the nineteen military chiefs who had been promoted marshal in May 1804. They included Joachim Murat, who had married Napoleon's sister Caroline and was now part of the family, Kellermann and Lefebvre, veterans of the republican armies of 1792–4, the victors of Valmy, Jemappes and Fleurus, and the brilliant generals of the Army of Italy of 1796 – Berthier, Masséna, Auguereau, Lannes. The Army of the Rhine, led by Moreau, a stronghold of opposition to Bonaparte's rise, was less favoured, although generals like Ney, who had served under Moreau at Hohenlinden in 1800, but did not follow him down the route of opposition, were promoted also.

The Empire of Charlemagne now had to be created in reality. Napoleon crowned himself king of Italy with the ancient crown of the Lombards in the Duomo of Milan on 26 May 1805. This was a kingdom of northern Italy that left the Papal States for the moment to the pope, but in March 1806 Napoleon ousted the Bourbon dynasty from Naples and entrusted this kingdom to his brother Joseph. At the other end of Europe he made his brother Louis, who had married Joséphine's daughter Hortense, king of Holland. Meanwhile with the defeat at Trafalgar on 21 October 1805 Napoleon lost control of the seas and gave up hope of invading Britain from the huge camp established at Boulogne. His Grande Armée of 200,000 men was moved swiftly via Strasbourg to Bavaria first to take on an Austrian army at Ulm and then to defeat a combined Austrian–Russian force in perhaps his most brilliant victory at Austerlitz on 2 December 1805, the anniversary of his coronation. Bavaria and Württemberg were raised to the status of kingdoms but became French client states, the heart of the Confederation of the Rhine, set up in July 1806, through which Napoleon looked to rule a Germany from which Austria and Prussia were squeezed out. On 6 August 1806 Emperor Francis of Austria dissolved the Holy Roman Empire that had lasted for a thousand years, becoming nothing but a Danubian prince himself and recognizing that Napoleon was now the Emperor of the West. The Confederation of the Rhine was enlarged at its northern end by the creation out of Prussian territories of the Grand Duchy of Berg, which was given to Murat. This provoked war with Prussia, but the redoubtable Prussian army was destroyed by Napoleon at the battles of Jena and Auerstädt on 14 October 1806. Napoleon occupied Berlin and removed the sword of Frederick the Great from its tomb, sending it back to the Invalides in Paris. The Russians were the next challenge and, after an indecisive bloodbath at Eylau on 7–8 February 1807, Napoleon defeated them at the battle of Friedland on 14 June 1807. Napoleon met Tsar Alexander in great pomp on a barge on the River Nieman on 7 July and concluded the Treaty of Tilsit. France and Russia joined in alliance, acknowledged their respective gains in Europe, and unceremoniously disposed of Prussia as a great power. Prussia was reduced to a shell with the invention of a kingdom of Westphalia in the west, of which Bonaparte's brother Jérôme became king, and in the east by the Grand Duchy of Warsaw, a client state that was given to the King of Saxony, both of which were incorporated into the Confederation of the Rhine.

The European Empire of Napoleon was a vast machine that provided soldiers and supplies for his armies and a cascade of kingdoms, principalities and fiefs in Italy, Germany and Poland to satisfy the greed and vanity of his brothers, dignitaries and marshals. Three of his brothers became kings, while his stepson Eugène Beauharnais became viceroy of Italy. Foreign minister Talleyrand became prince of Benevento, police minister Fouché duke of Otranto. Marshals were titled according to their fiefs or military victories. Berthier became prince of Neuchâtel and prince of Wagram, Bernadotte prince of Ponte-Corvo, Davout duke of Auerstädt, Lannes duke of Montebello, Masséna duke of Rivoli, Macdonald duke of Tarento, Soult duke of Dalmatia, Ney duke of Elchingen and Lefebvre duke of Danzig. These honours entitled the holder less to land than to a large income drawn from the occupied territories, the flow of which depended on the continued occupation of the territory. The generals and marshals were the elite of Napoleon's loyalists, but the rank and file of *grognards* or grousers had an even deeper affection. These were eligible for the Legion of Honour, instituted in 1802, numbering 38,000 by the end of his reign, and overwhelmingly used to reward soldiers. One of them, Jean-Roche Coignet, beaten by his stepmother and fleeing the family farm in Burgundy, found a surrogate family in Napoleon's army. Conscripted in August 1799, he was one of the troops commanded by Bonaparte at Saint-Cloud on 19 *brumaire*, was recruited to the Imperial Guard and awarded the Legion of Honour at the Invalides in June 1804. He was at the camp of Boulogne and then on the forced march to Strasbourg and Ulm, grumbling that 'our emperor makes war not with our arms but with our legs'. Such endeavours were compensated by the leadership of the emperor who visited his troops by torchlight the night before Austerlitz and was greeted by the massed cries of 'Vive l'Empereur!' For Coignet the emperor was in the midst of his troops at Jena and entered Berlin at the head of 20,000 grenadiers with a 'small hat and one-sou cockade . . . the worst-dressed man of such a splendid army'. Promoted corporal in 1807 after the battle of Eylau, still unable to read and write, sergeant after the capture of Vienna in 1809, and captain after the battle of Lützen in 1813, Coignet had a healthy disdain for 'all the men who [Napoleon] had raised to prominent positions' and had ultimately let him down.[25]

In the hope of consolidating his Empire Napoleon created an imperial nobility in 1808. By 1815 this nobility numbered 3,364, a hierarchy of thirty-four princes and dukes, 459 counts, 1,552 barons and 1,319 knights. Nearly 60 per cent of the new nobles were military men, 22 per cent high civil servants and 17 per cent notables such as senators and mayors. The title of prince was reserved for marshals and grand dignitaries of the Empire, that of count for generals, ministers, senators and presidents of the Legislative Body, that of baron for colonels, top magistrates, mayors of large towns and the presidents of electoral colleges.[26] One of the purposes of creating a nobility was to win over the old nobility from its loyalty to the Bourbons in pursuit of what Napoleon called a strategy of 'amalgamation' or 'fusion' of the Ancien Régime elite with that forged by the Revolution. 'I offered them ranks in my army, but they did not want them,' he said, 'offices in my administration, but they refused them. But I opened the antechambers of my household, and they rushed in.'[27] This witty analysis was not quite exact. Napoleon's armies did include figures such as the Alsatian noble Kellermann, the Burgundian nobles Davout and Berthier, whose father was ennobled by Louis XV, together with the Polish noble Poniatowski, who was made a marshal in 1813. The rapid turnover on the battlefield nevertheless meant that among generals the proportion of nobles fell from 33 per cent in the period 1792-1812 to 22 per cent under the Empire, although it still stood at 25 per cent in 1814.[28]

In the civil service, Napoleon used the post of *auditeur* in the Conseil d'État to win over young men of old noble families to the higher echelons of state service. The fathers of Mathieu-Louis Molé and Victor de Broglie had both been guillotined during the Terror, but Molé was appointed *auditeur* of the Conseil d'État at the age of twenty-five in 1806, and went on to become prefect of the Côte d'Or in 1807, director-general of the Ponts-et-Chaussées in 1809, count of the Empire, and minister of justice in 1813. De Broglie was appointed *auditeur* aged twenty-four in 1809, and was attached to the French armies in Austria in 1809 and Spain in 1811, then to the French embassy in Warsaw in 1812.[29] Stendhal, from a non-noble magistrate's family of Grenoble and serving in the Ministry of War, became an *auditeur* in 1800 and took part in the Russian campaign, but did not forge a brilliant administrative career such as his noble contemporaries Molé or de Broglie achieved.[30] Forty-two *auditeurs* went on to become prefects and the prefectoral body in fact became more dominated by nobles as the Empire reached its apogee, the percentage of noble prefects rising from 23 per cent in 1800 to 43 per cent in 1814.[31]

The court lent itself much more readily to the recruitment of the old nobility. Claire de Rémusat, great-niece of Louis XV's foreign minister Vergennes, became Joséphine Bonaparte's lady-in-waiting; her husband, Augustin de Rémusat, whose office at the Cour des Comptes of Provence had been abolished at the Revolution and was looking for 'office, of any kind', became prefect of the palace.[32] On the other hand, while the Duc de Luynes accepted nomination to the Senate in 1808 his wife, a former lady-in-waiting of Marie-Antoinette, dressed in the Ancien Régime fashion and never went near the Tuileries. Their daughter, the Duchesse de Chevreuse, was persuaded against her will to be a lady-in-waiting to the empress, but when she was required to attend the deposed Queen of Spain, in 1808, she refused, saying, 'I have been a victim, but I shall never be a gaoler.' For her sins Napoleon exiled her 50 leagues from Paris and she sickened and died, aged twenty-eight, in 1813.[33] Only 22 per cent of the imperial nobility were composed of old nobles, and 80 per cent of old nobles refused to rally to a regime which they regarded as illegitimate, tyrannical and warlike, and preferred to await the return of the Bourbon dynasty. This majority frequented each other's salons on the Faubourg Saint-Germain or hunted on the country estates they had recovered after returning from exile, waiting upon the return of the monarchy. Two very different nobles who remained on their estates were the Marquis de Lafayette and the Comte de Villèle. Lafayette refused a seat in the Senate and an embassy in America and remained on his estate in the Seine-et-Marne. Villèle, of an old noble family of Toulouse, joined the navy in 1788, spent most of the Revolution in the Indies, and bought property and married in Réunion in the Indian Ocean. He returned to France in

1807 where he recovered the family estate, became mayor of his village in the Haute-Garonne and president of the *conseil général*, but abstained from politics until 1814.

The survival of Napoleon's regime was entirely dependent on his ability to dominate Europe, and this became much more difficult after 1808. In order to contain British power he persuaded the Bourbons of Spain to partition Portugal with him in 1807. French forces under Murat occupied Madrid, and a revolt against them on 2 May 1808 was put down with extreme brutality. Napoleon now persuaded the Spanish king, Charles IV, and his son Ferdinand to renounce their claims to the throne, and he moved Joseph from the Kingdom of Naples, which he gave to Murat, to that of Spain. Unfortunately, French rule in Spain was opposed by Catholic royalist and liberal revolutionary opposition, supported by the British, and never established itself with any effectiveness. Meanwhile the Austrians now challenged French rule in southern Germany and Italy. Napoleon responded by annexing the Papal States and taking the pope prisoner, then by defeating the Austrians at the battle of Wagram on 5 July 1809 and annexing Trieste, Slovenia and much of Croatia, forging what he called the Illyrian Provinces on the Adriatic. Napoleon was now obsessed by the succession to his rule, for Joséphine who was now forty-five had not borne him an heir. The tsar refused him his fourteen-year-old sister Anna, so he fastened on Marie-Louise, the eighteen-year-old daughter of the Habsburg emperor. He divorced Joséphine in January 1810, and married Marie-Louise by proxy. The new imperial couple arrived in Paris on 1 April, parading through the unfinished Arc de Triomphe. Although half the French cardinals refused to accept the divorce and boycotted the ceremony, much to Napoleon's fury, his marriage into one of the European royal houses eased relations with the old French nobility and an heir, titled the King of Rome, was born in 1811.

Napoleon's invasion of Russia with a multinational army of 600,000 in June 1812 was supposed to complete his domination of a European empire of eighty million people. Despite the victory of Borodino in September 1812 and brief occupation of Moscow, however, he was forced to retreat and lost most of his army to attacks by Russian troops and partisans aided by the freezing winter. The absence of Napoleon provided an opportunity for a coup d'état by disgruntled republican generals Malet, who had resigned from the army after the coronation of Napoleon, and Lahorie, who was one of Moreau's men and the lover of Victor Hugo's mother. On 23 October they announced that Napoleon had died in Russia and attempted to seize power in Paris, but they were arrested, tried and shot.[34] Other military leaders who had resented Napoleon's rise to power now also entered the fray again. Marshal Bernadotte, who had invaded Sweden and was elected its crown prince in 1810, met up with General Moreau who returned to Europe from the United States in 1812. Bernadotte became commander-in-chief of a coalition of Russian, Prussian and Swedish forces which drove Napoleon's armies back after the retreat from Moscow. Madame de Staël, expelled from France again after the manuscript of *On Germany* had been seized, and fleeing to Britain by way of Russia and Sweden, corresponded frantically with Bernadotte and Moreau, whom she saw as the best options for liberal government in France and a guarantee against it falling under the sway of the royalists and Cossacks.[35] Unfortunately for Madame de Staël's hopes, Moreau died in September 1813, mortally wounded at the battle of Dresden, and Bernadotte refused to lead his army across the Rhine.

As Napoleon's military power collapsed, with Paris surrendering to the Allies on 30 March 1814, so the political class also deserted him. The key role was played by the once servile Senate, which sought to manage its transition to the new regime. In this it was guided by Talleyrand, who had resigned as Napoleon's foreign minister in 1807 and had been described by him in 1809 as 'a shit in silk stockings'.[36] On 31 March Talleyrand hosted a meeting with Tsar Alexander and the Prussian King Frederick William III in his Paris house and persuaded them to issue a proclamation that they would not treat with Napoleon. Then, on 2 April, he convened the Senate and persuaded it to depose the emperor, appoint a provisional government dominated by himself, and approve a draft constitution which preserved the main gains of the Revolution and, as an inducement, converted the Senate from an appointed to a hereditary body in which they would all keep their jobs. Marshal Ney, who had covered himself with glory during the retreat from

Moscow and had been promoted prince of the Moscowa, finally convinced the emperor that he must abdicate unconditionally, went off to join Louis XVIII at Compiègne, and rode behind the royal carriage as it entered Paris on 4 May 1814. The *girouette* or weather-vane, changing loyalty with every puff of wind, became a commonplace of political satire.[37]

This attempt to bind the hands of Louis XVIII was only partially successful. Louis was forced to concede a greater degree of representative government than the despotic Napoleon had allowed, but did not wish to receive a constitution from an assembly. He therefore rejected the Senate's draft constitution and issued his own Charter to the assembled Chambers on 4 June, replacing the hereditary Senate by a Chamber of Peers. However, he too had to attempt some degree of fusion of the political class between the Napoleonic elite and the returning émigrés, hungry for power. In the new Chamber of Peers, therefore, eighty imperial senators, including Talleyrand, were carried over, fifty-three new peers were created from the ranks of returning royalists, and fifty-seven of Napoleon's senators were excluded as politically unacceptable, including twelve regicides of the Convention.[38] Old noble families which had rallied to the Empire were cold-shouldered. Augustin de Rémusat, who had become superintendent of theatres under Napoleon, was not offered a post at the Restoration because, as his son Charles recalled, his family were 'sufficiently marked by the stigmata of the imperial regime to have only negative claims on the new regime'.[39] More fortunate were aspiring bourgeois like François Guizot. Though he later claimed that 'I entered public life only in 1814; I had served neither the Revolution nor the Empire,' he was in fact appointed professor of modern history at the Sorbonne, aged twenty-five, in 1812.[40] Despite this debut as an imperial functionary he made an easy transition to the restored monarchy, appointed secretary-general of the Ministry of the Interior, and drafting a law on the press.[41]

Building a consensus around the regime was if anything more difficult for the restored monarchy than for the Empire. Returning royalists wanted to recover office from the revolutionary–Napoleonic political class and had no particular love for the constitutional Charter. Under pressure from them, Madame de Staël observed, ministers defended it in public but mocked it in private. Benjamin Constant objected to the new press law drafted by Guizot, which reimposed press censorship, and argued for a British-style monarchy in which the king was above politics while his ministers were responsible to parliament.[42] As the political elite was reconfigured it became clear that the old rifts between revolutionaries and counter-revolutionaries were opening up. Lazare Carnot, who had criticized Napoleon's bid for a hereditary empire in 1804, attacked the restored monarchy in July 1814. His *Mémoire au roi* argued that while the return of the king had been universally acclaimed, even by ex-republicans, as ushering in a new consensus, the regime had marginalized what he called 'patriots' as 'suspects' and 'révoltés', whereas 'if you have the fortune to be a *chouan*, a Vendean, an émigré, a Cossack or an Englishman, then your loyalty is praised to the rooftops, and you are showered with tender thanks and decorations by the whole royal family.'[43] Meanwhile almost half of the imperial army was disbanded to save money and please the Allies and 12,000 officers were put on half-pay.[44] The Imperial Guard was replaced by a King's Household staffed by returning émigrés, and the officer corps filled up, Marshal Macdonald recalled, with 'a lot of beardless boys dressed in uniforms resplendent with gold lace, nearly all decorated with ribands, and with the epaulettes of senior officers'.[45] Finally, although Louis reassured those who had bought church properties during the Revolution that their titles were safe, country people feared that the returning nobles and clergy would soon restore the feudal dues and tithes that had gone with the Ancien Régime.

THE RETURN OF CIVIL WAR

The consensus built around the restored monarchy was therefore fragile when, on March 1815, Napoleon, escaping from his prison island of Elba, landed once again in the south of France and marched on Paris. By all accounts he should have been repulsed, but as he moved from Cannes to Grenoble and from Lyon to Paris he was greeted by the rural populations and old soldiers, many of them of peasant stock, like Captain Coignet, who rejoined the emperor at Auxerre. Napoleon later claimed, with only a little exaggeration, that 'I am not only, as has been said, the emperor of the soldiers; I am that of the peasants, the lower ranks in France . . . the popular fibre responds to mine.' The ruling class was paralysed and Napoleon boasted, 'I have but to make a sign, or rather to turn away my eyes, and the nobility will be massacred in all departments . . . But I will not be the king of a Jacquerie,' of a peasant revolt.[46] Popular support was crucial, but even more so was the attitude of the army. Before he set out to check Napoleon's progress Marshal Ney kissed Louis XVIII's hand and said that Napoleon was a madman who should be sent to Charenton madhouse or brought home in an iron cage. At Lons-le-Saunier in the Jura, however, he received a handwritten note from the emperor, then at Lyon, asking the marshal to join him: 'I shall greet you as on the morning of the Moskowa' (Borodino). The next morning, 14 June 1815, Ney drew up his troops and told them, 'The cause of the Bourbons is lost for ever . . . Vive l'Empereur!'[47] The defection of Ney toppled the monarchy and Louis and his court were obliged to abandon Paris and make for Ghent. Guizot, who went with them, deplored the way in which the return of Napoleon rekindled:

the old quarrel that the Empire had stifled and the Charter sought to extinguish, the quarrel between old France and new France, between the *émigration* and the revolution. In 1815 the struggle of 1789 began again, not only between political parties, but between rival classes . . . In the twinkling of an eye the Hundred Days destroyed the work of social pacification that had been pursued in France for sixteen years.[48]

Napoleon refused to preside over another popular revolution or Terror, but in order to avoid this he had to win sufficient support among the political class, and most of the political class was no longer willing to serve him. Comte Molé, for example, was offered the Ministry of Foreign Affairs or of the Interior, but declined such a high-profile post. He nominally resumed his old job as director of the Ponts-et-Chaussées, but soon disappeared to Plombières ostensibly to take the waters, returning to Paris only after Waterloo.[49] Napoleon was forced back on regicides as ministers, Carnot as minister of the interior and Fouché as minister of police. Of huge importance then was the decision of Benjamin Constant, who as late as 19 March had denounced Napoleon as worse than Genghis Khan or Attila, to rally to the new regime in an attempt to steer it towards liberal government. Since Louis XVIII had granted a Charter, he argued, Napoleon must match it in order to win over propertied classes now used to liberty. Constant met Napoleon at the Tuileries on 14 April, was made a member of the Council of State and drafted an Additional Act to the Constitutions of the Empire, soon nicknamed 'la Benjamine', which was designed to turn Napoleon into a constitutional monarch like William of Orange.[50] The new constitution was put to a plebiscite at the end of April but mustered only 1.5 million votes in support against 5,700 against out of an electorate of 7.5 million.[51] The truth was that the regime had control of very little of the country, with the west and south in particular in the hands of counter-revolutionaries. After the flight of Louis XVIII in March 1815 his nephew, son of his brother the Comte d'Artois, Louis-Antoine, Duc d'Angoulême, gathered a volunteer militia of 100,000 counter-revolutionaries to sustain what was effectively a separate kingdom in the south. He was forced to surrender on 8 April and go into exile in Spain. However, after the collapse of Napoleon's armies at Waterloo on 18 June counter-revolutionary militias took over a vast area from Toulouse to Toulon, under the Duc d'Angoulême's quasi-official authority, wreaking vengeance against those who had actively supported the Revolution and Napoleonic regime in what became known as the White Terror.

RESTORING THE ANCIEN RÉGIME?

Just as in 1814 Talleyrand had tried to manage the transition from empire to monarchy, in order to safeguard the interests of the political class, so in 1815 it was Fouché the regicide who tried to salvage what he could from the republican and imperial period as Louis XVIII and his court headed back to Paris. He persuaded the Duke of Wellington, who was very much arbiter of the situation, that he alone could control a Chamber of Deputies elected under the Additional Act that preferred a regency in the name of Napoleon's son to the restoration of monarchy, and likewise that he had control over the 25,000 *fédérés* or revolutionary volunteers in Paris who had sworn to prevent another restoration.[52] Wellington thus insisted that Fouché serve as minister of police in a government headed by Talleyrand who, just back from Vienna where he had signed a peace treaty with the Allies, must also be foreign minister.

This incongruous duo at the head of French affairs did not, however, long outlast the elections to the new Chamber of Deputies in August 1815. On the crest of the White Terror 350 ultra-royalists were returned to the so-called Chambre Introuvable or Matchless Chamber, a decisive verdict of an electorate of 75,000 propertied voters who had opposed the Revolution, endured Napoleon, but felt abandoned by the recycling of the political elite, tarnished by the Revolution or the Empire, whenever the monarchy was restored. One of their leaders was the Comte de Villèle, appointed mayor of Toulouse in July 1815 by the Duc d'Angoulême. He claimed to be against the worst excesses of the White Terror, but challenged the authority of Augustin de Rémusat, now prefect at Toulouse, and was unable to stop the brutal murder of General Ramel, commander of the National Guard in Toulouse, on 17 August. The final fall of Napoleon, according to Villèle, had to be used to 'deliver a mortal blow to the ideas of the Revolution which he represented'.[53]

The triumph of the ultra-royalists in the Chamber indeed brought about a settling of accounts with the old political class. The Talleyrand–Fouché ministry was driven unceremoniously from office, and replaced on 24 September by a ministry headed by the Duc de Richelieu. Richelieu was a high-profile émigré who had not only left the country but had served under Russian emperors he judged to be more legitimate than revolutionary assemblies or Napoleon, and finished up as governor-general of New Russia (the Ukraine). He was dismissed by Talleyrand as 'the Frenchman who knows the Crimea best', but in fact did what he could to maintain a moderate royalist line while constantly harassed by the reactionary court faction of the Comte d'Artois.[54]

The triumph of the ultras settled the fate of Marshal Ney, whose defection in March that year had forced the court to flee precipitately to Belgium. Tried by the Chamber of Peers in November 1815 he was found guilty of treason by 157 of the 161 peers, with just three finding extenuating circumstances and only one voting against. This was the thirty-year-old Victor de Broglie, whose best friend was Madame de Staël's son and who would marry her daughter in 1816; he refused to call into question Ney's fundamental patriotism.[55] De Broglie managed to rally seventeen peers in favour of deportation, but 139 voted for the death penalty, including weathercocks such as Marshal Marmont, who had deserted Napoleon in April 1814, and careerists who had rallied to Napoleon in the Hundred Days and were trying to refashion a royalist virginity, like Comte Molé.[56]

The triumph of the ultras provoked a purge of revolutionaries who were finally called to answer for their crimes. The instrument of proscription, used so effectively by the revolutionaries against their enemies, was now turned against the revolutionaries themselves. The most vindictive proposal of the Chambre Introuvable would have condemned 850 people to death or deportation. The law passed on 12 January 1816 singled out the regicides in particular for exile, their departure for Brussels or Geneva echoing the flight of royalists to Coblenz or Turin a generation earlier. Talleyrand, who was not a regicide, wriggled out again but justice finally caught up with Fouché who, hurried off to be ambassador in Dresden after he fell from power, was added to the list of exiles in 1816 and died in Trieste in 1820. Carnot, also exiled, died in Magdeburg in 1823.

In order to survive, however, the restored monarchy needed to be more than a tool of the ultras. Like any regime it needed to build bridges to a wider constituency. The role model for the Duc de Richelieu was Sully, the judicious first minister of Henri IV, who had ended the French Wars of Religion and whose statue on the Pont-Neuf, destroyed in the Revolution, was returned to its plinth with great ceremony in 1818.[57] His most influential minister was Élie Decazes, a bourgeois of Libourne in the Gironde, who under the Empire became a magistrate in Paris and secretary to Napoleon's mother, Madame Mère, and then to Napoleon's brother, Louis, King of Holland, managing his affairs in France. Too close to the imperial family to enjoy favour with the Bourbons in 1814, he steered clear of the emperor during the Hundred Days and after Waterloo used his role on the Paris National Guard to counter the threat of the *fédérés* and ensure the safe return to the capital of the royal family. Made Paris prefect of police by Talleyrand and minister of police under Richelieu, he also won the confidence of the childless Louis XVIII, who began to treat him as his own adoptive son, writing to him as 'mon cher enfant' and 'mon bon fils'.[58] The maxim of Decazes was 'to nationalize the royalty and to royalize France'.[59] He saw that at some point the ministry would need to break free of the grip of the Chambre Introuvable and obtained the ordinance of 5 September 1816 from the king to dissolve it. This was regarded as nothing less than a coup d'état by the ultras, and Chateaubriand, already smarting from not having been offered a portfolio in the government, unleashed a biting attack on the ministers whose policy since the Restoration, he alleged, had been to 'govern France in the revolutionary interest'.[60]

Decazes now emerged as the king's leading minister, first as minister of the interior in December 1818, then in November 1819 as president of the council. Among his advisers were the so-called Doctrinaires around Royer-Collard, the somewhat austere patron of the likes of Guizot. Their doctrine was that while the Revolution had committed many crimes – including the execution of his own father, of which Guizot never spoke – it had embedded certain institutional gains, such as constitutional rule, representative government, a free press and equality before the law, which must not be called into question by any regime. They were intellectuals reluctant to take office lest it compromise them, preferring to exercise influence through the Council of State, where they could draft laws, and in the Chamber of Deputies and the press, where they could influence opinion. They took credit for the electoral law of February 1817 which enfranchised a middle class that paid 300 francs in tax per year and a slightly more liberal press law of May 1819. They saw it as their task to keep the government maintained in this direction, to prevent it being swept off course by winds pushing too far to the right, or to the left.[61]

After the Chambre Introuvable had been disbanded, however, the next issue was how far the ministry should seek agreement with the liberal opposition, which had flourished briefly in the troubled year 1814–15 and now again became active. Benjamin Constant, *persona non grata* after his role in the Hundred Days, fled to England in 1815 but returned to France in 1816 to found two new liberal papers, the *Mercure* in 1817, and the *Minerve Française* in 1818, with a circulation of 10,000.[62] Madame de Staël died in 1817 but her message was delivered from the grave in her posthumous *Considerations on the French Revolution* (1818), which while condemning Terror and tyranny praised the moderate revolution aimed at by friends of liberty such as Lafayette. Financial backing for the liberals was provided by Jacques Laffitte, a rich banker whose father had been a carpenter in Bayonne and who, despite being governor of the Banque de France, felt snubbed by the aristocratic society of the Restoration. After the ultra landslide of 1815 the electoral system of 1817 went back to the Directorial method of renewing a fifth of the Chamber every year, but while the threat under the Directory had been from royalists, now it was from liberals. The liberal financiers Laffitte and Casimir Périer were elected in 1817, Lafayette and soldier-turned-lawyer Manuel in 1818, Constant himself and the Abbé Grégoire, former bishop in the Constitutional Church who had approved the execution of the king, in 1819. What stood between the liberal opposition and the ministry, however, was the question of amnesty for the regicides exiled in 1816. The verdict of the ministry, given by justice minister De Selves, a Doctrinaire who had unusually accepted office under Decazes, was 'Never!'[63]

The ministry's balancing act between ultras and liberals was ended on 13 February 1820 when the Duc de Berry, the son of the Comte d'Artois and heir to the throne, was stabbed at the opera. As Decazes rushed to the scene he announced, 'We are all assassinated!'[64] Chateaubriand, on behalf of the ultras, remarked that Decazes' own foot had 'slipped on the blood'.[65] Public opinion turned against the liberals, whose leaders were ejected from the Chamber in 1820 and 1821. Artois and the Duc and Duchesse d'Angoulême were able to prevail upon the king to dismiss Decazes, and Chateaubriand, trumpeting from his *Conservative* newspaper, claimed credit for promoting Villèle first to a post in the government and then to chief minister, in December 1821. The ambition of Villèle, proclaiming 'the union of the government with the royalists', was as far as possible to restore the Ancien Régime.[66] When a liberal ministry came to power in Spain in 1823 the Duc d'Angoulême led a French army flying the white Bourbon flag to remove it on behalf of the reactionary monarch, Ferdinand VII. Louis XVIII died in 1824 and was succeeded by Artois, darling of the émigrés and ultras since 1789. His coronation as Charles X in Reims cathedral was an occasion of absolutist pomp the like of which had not been seen since that of his ill-fated brother in 1775.

RE-RUNNING THE REVOLUTION

The attempt by the monarchy and its reactionary ministers to put back the clock to before 1789 triggered a re-run of the French Revolution. The main difference was that the contending parties were sharply aware of what had gone before and of the lessons that needed to be learned. The argument of the reactionaries was that constitutional limitations on absolute power handed the monarchy bound and gagged into the hands of liberals who were unable to check the tide of revolution rising behind them. The argument of liberals was that constitutional monarchy was the only guarantee of both liberty and order and this time they would be careful to stop the course of revolution once this limited gain had been achieved. Republic and empire were anathema and must never be allowed to recur.

As in 1789 the 1820s experienced a good deal of popular discontent. This time, however, it was defined by a generation of revolutionary and patriotic activity and looked back to both republican heroes and Napoleon. Former *fédérés* who had volunteered to defend Paris and other cities against the return of the Bourbons in 1815, *demi-soldes* or disbanded officers of Napoleon's armies on half-pay, former *grognards* who returned to their towns and villages with scarce a pension but dreams of military grandeur, middle-class professionals who had served the Napoleonic regime in one capacity or another and students born at the turn of the century whose ambitions were crushed by the Restoration were all elements of a

constituency that were not prepared to accept a return to the Ancien
Régime.[67] The reinvention of Napoleon as a popular leader during
the Hundred Days and his death in 1821 meant that there was a
powerful convergence between republican and Bonapartist opinion.[68]
Political activity was closely circumscribed and press censorship
tightened so that opposition was often covert or conspiratorial.
Goguettes or drinking clubs were favourite meeting-places for those
who wished to sing the political songs of Béranger or Debraux
exalting the banned tricolour flag or Napoleon's column in the place
Vendôme, pulled down in 1814, or exchange political prints such as
the *Grenadier of Waterloo* (1818) of former *fédéré* Charlet.[69] Secret
societies of Carbonari sprang up in which civilian activists linked up
with conspirators within the army and there was a spate of attempts
to provoke mutiny and insurrection in garrisons: Paris in 1820,
Saumur and Belfort in 1821, Strasbourg and La Rochelle in 1822.
The execution of the four sergeants who had mutinied at La Rochelle
was witnessed by Auguste Blanqui, a schoolboy in Paris, who hence-
forth saw politics as 'a ferocious battle to which one must commit
one's liberty and one's life'.[70]

Liberal politicians and journalists were in two minds about
conspiracy and revolt. Some, such as Lafayette and Manuel, were
nominally members of conspiratorial organizations and offered their
patronage without wanting to risk greater involvement. Others, like
Guizot, feared that revolt would bring back 1793; Guizot told Manuel
in 1822 that it was necessary for France to 'expel the revolutionary
spirit that still torments her'.[71] After his lectures at the Sorbonne and
École Normale were closed down by the Villèle government in 1822
he gave himself over to journalism, founding the liberal but severe,
legalistic and antipopular *Globe* in 1824. A new generation of young
liberals, born around 1800, were recruited to the cause. Guizot
brought to the *Globe* the twenty-seven-year-old Charles de Rémusat,
whose father Augustin had been dismissed from the prefectoral corps
by Villèle in 1822 and died the following year.[72] A young journalist
the same age as Rémusat, Adolphe Thiers, came to Paris from Aix-
en-Provence crowned by literary prizes and enjoyed the patronage of
Jacques Laffitte, who employed him on a rival paper, the *Constitutional*, which was more enthusiastic about revolutionary spirit.[73] What

Guizot and Thiers had in common, however, was a commitment to rewrite the French Revolution not as a spectre of Terror to be waved by reactionaries but as the source of legitimacy for those who wanted to contest attempts to restore the Ancien Régime. Guizot achieved this in his lectures on French and European civilization which he was allowed to give again after 1828, in which he argued that the Revolution was the fruit of an alliance against feudalism of the monarchy and Third Estate or bourgeoisie that had been developing since the rise of the medieval town.[74] In a hugely ambitious history of the Revolution that appeared between 1823 and 1827 Thiers demonstrated that it was an inevitable result of the awakening of the desire for freedom from the top to the bottom of the social scale, but while liberals such as Lafayette and the Girondins had rightly tried to reconcile liberty and order it had been thrown off course by the 'excesses of the multitude' and 'the vile populace' which relished dipping handkerchiefs in the blood of the beheaded Louis XVI.[75]

The contest was not only between partisans of the Ancien Régime and champions of the Revolution, but also between those who wanted a revolution to bring back the Republic or install the nineteen-year-old King of Rome as Napoleon II and those who wanted a constitutional monarchy to secure the legal gains of the Revolution of 1789 but to avoid revolution-as-violence at all costs. The liberals made a breakthrough in the elections of 1827 and Villèle resigned. His successor, Martignac, from a family of Bordeaux *noblesse de robe* or nobles of the judiciary, had taken part in the invasion of liberal Spain in 1823 but in 1828 made an attempt to build bridges to French liberals.[76] However, there was no room for a 'Decazes of Charles X' and he was summarily replaced in August 1829 by Jules de Polignac, son of Marie-Antoinette's favourite, a former soldier in Condé's army, imprisoned for conspiracy in 1804, and confidant of the Comte d'Artois, now Charles X. Together they were careless of public opinion, had no sense that a ministry should be responsible to the parliamentary majority and were prepared to violate the Charter in order to restore absolute monarchy.[77] In January 1830 Thiers founded a new paper, the *National*, in which he campaigned for what he saw as the British system after 1688, namely an inviolable monarch and hereditary peerage but ministers responsible to the majority in the Chamber of Deputies. The king's address to parliament on 2 March 1830 was uncompromising, and 221 opposition deputies signed an address to remind him that 'France wants anarchy no more than you want despotism.'[78] The king dissolved the Chamber, but new elections only increased the liberal opposition against him. In response Charles mounted a coup d'état with four ordinances issued from his palace of Saint-Cloud on 25 July which dissolved the Chamber that had not yet met, reduced the size of the electorate, called new elections in September and ended press freedom.

This provoked popular revolt in Paris on 27 July, involving among others printworkers whose livelihoods were threatened. Gunshops were raided, barricades thrown up, and insurgents – workers, students and veterans of the Napoleonic wars – clashed with the troops of Marshal Marmont, military governor of Paris, who lost control of the situation when his own forces fraternized with the rebels. On 29 July Paris was in the hands of the insurgents, and cries went up to bring back the Republic or Napoleon II. At this point the liberal journalists and deputies tried to regain the initiative and impose a sensible solution. Meeting at Laffitte's house they put Lafayette, based at the Hôtel de Ville or Paris Town Hall, in charge of the Paris National Guard, to defend against both royal troops and insurgents. He confirmed that 'my conduct will be, at 73 years old, what it was at 32', when he had fulfilled the same role.[79] On 30 July Thiers led a delegation to the Neuilly residence of Louis-Philippe, Duc d'Orléans, head of a younger branch of the Bourbon family, to offer him the post of lieutenant-general of the kingdom.[80] A rump of deputies under the chairmanship of Laffitte endorsed his acceptance on 31 July and Louis-Philippe came to the Hôtel de Ville where he was embraced by Lafayette; a lame Benjamin Constant was brought to the scene in a sedan chair.[81] The main concern of the liberals was to prevent what Thiers called the 'generous folly' of a republic, and on 9 August the deputies and peers who remained on the scene invested Louis-Philippe, who swore to defend the Charter that Charles X had violated, as king of the French.[82] Guizot in turn breathed a sigh of relief: 'in a week the revolution was ended and the government established.'[83]

The new leadership of France was composed of liberals who had been on the side of moderate reform since the last days of the Empire or early Restoration. Jacques Laffitte formed a ministry in November 1830 and saw through legislation in March and April 1831 lowering the parliamentary franchise to men paying 200 francs in tax instead of 300 francs, doubling the electorate to about 200,000, and making two million men eligible to vote in local elections. In March 1831 he was replaced by the more conservative liberal Casimir Périer, who dealt harshly with the revolt of the silkworkers of Lyon in November 1831 and disturbances in his native Grenoble, but died of cholera in May 1832.[84] In October 1832 Napoleon's former Marshal Soult fronted a powerful ministry which included Thiers at the Interior, Guizot at Education, and de Broglie at the Foreign Ministry and embedded the conservative liberalism of the July Monarchy.

The new regime had to see off the threat of counter-revolution, but wanted to avoid the extreme measures of 1793. Charles X was taken by an American steamer from Cherbourg to England, but there was great pressure to try his ministers, especially Polignac, arrested on 15 August. During the trial of the ministers by the peers that December, crowds gathered shouting 'Death to the ministers!' and were angry when, found guilty of treason, they were merely deported to England.[85] Showing more guts than the male members of her family the Duchesse de Berry, whose husband had been assassinated in 1820, landed near Marseille in April 1832 and tried to raise the Vendée in support of the claim of the heir she had borne her husband after his death, but to no avail. She was arrested in November 1832 on the orders of interior minister Thiers. Chateaubriand, who had attacked the 'bastard monarchy' stitched up by a parliamentary rump, which had banished the Bourbons and confiscated their estates, was arrested for complicity in the uprising but was defended by Pierre-Antoine Berryer, whose father had defended Ney in 1815, and was acquitted.[86]

More serious for the July Monarchy was the threat from republicans who shared the view that the new monarchy was bereft of legitimacy, and claimed that revolutionary legitimacy required the restoration of the Republic. An amnesty was granted to the eighty regicide members of the Convention, exiled in 1816, who were still alive, but with the king's blood on their hands they were seen as an embarrassment. 'No one shook their hand. They reappeared as strangers in their own house: their shadow alone would have made more noise,' noted the young republican Edgar Quinet.[87] The republican torch was taken up by a new generation of law and medical students, who were the same age as liberals such as Thiers or Rémusat, but more radical in their commitment, sometimes for family reasons. Godefroy Cavaignac's father had been exiled to Brussels as a regicide and died there in 1829. Blanqui's father had been elected to the Convention in 1793 when his home city of Nice was annexed by France, although he was not a regicide. The father of François Raspail was no friend of the Revolution, which ruined his business, but François was influenced by a radical priest at his seminary and by the White Terror at Carpentras, where he was teaching philosophy. Slightly younger, born in 1809, were Armand Barbès, the son of a military surgeon who had served in Egypt and the West Indies, and Charles Delescluze, son of a republican soldier and Napoleonic police commissioner.[88] These set up the Society of Friends of the People on 30 July 1830, saw themselves as heirs of Jacobins such as Robespierre, Saint-Just and Marat, demonstrated in favour of the death penalty for Charles X's ministers and used the funeral of Napoleon's Marshal Lamarque on 5 June 1832 to launch an insurrection in favour of the Republic. Dissolved, they reconstituted as the Society of the Rights of Man in 1833, and launched another insurrection in April 1834 in Paris and in conjunction with the silkworkers of Lyon.

These risings were brutally suppressed on the orders of Thiers, including the so-called massacre of the rue Transnonain in Paris, when twelve residents thought to be hiding rebels were put to the sword.[89] Some of the leaders of the insurrection, like Cavaignac, escaped, but 121 rebels of the Paris and Lyon movements were sent for trial for treason before the Chamber of Peers in April 1835. Armand Carrel, who had worked with Thiers on the *National* but had broken with him because he favoured the Republic, evoked the spectre of Marshal Ney, whom they had 'assassinated' in 1815, to call into question the peers' legitimacy.[90] Jules Favre, a Lyon barrister also born in 1809, attacked the government for provoking the rebels and made his name as one of the new generation of republican leaders.[91] That said, the sentences effectively destroyed the republican leadership, with dozens deported or sent to prison. Republicans were reduced to counter-productive violence, such as the assassination attempt on Louis-Philippe on 28 July 1838 using a home-made multi-barrelled gun by a disgruntled former Napoleonic soldier from Corsica, Joseph Fieschi. The king survived but eighteen people watching the review of the Paris National Guard were killed. Fieschi and two other conspirators were executed and stringent laws against the press and carrying arms were enacted in September 1836. Former members of the Society of the Rights of Man, now reborn as the Society of Seasons, tried to seize control of the Palais de Justice and Hôtel de Ville on 12 May 1839. Armand Barbès who was wounded and Auguste Blanqui who fled were sentenced to death but had their sentence commuted to perpetual detention after a campaign against the death penalty led by Victor Hugo and were imprisoned in the medieval fortress of Mont Saint-Michel.[92]

RE-RUNNING THE REPUBLIC

By 1840 the July Monarchy had reached an enviable level of stability. There was no fighting in the streets of Paris between 1839 and 1848. Politics remained in the hands of a coherent body of notables, an electorate of 250,000 electing a body of deputies two-thirds of whom paid 1,000 francs in taxes in 1840. A single ministry led by Guizot remained in power from 1840 to 1848, supported by a government majority two-thirds of whom were civil servants, a majority strengthened by the elections of 1846. To those who protested at their exclusion from the political process because they were not propertied enough to pay sufficient taxes, Guizot simply replied, 'Get rich.' His social life revolved around the salon of the Princesse Lieven, whose international connections satisfied Guizot's 'puerile ambition', in the opinion of Charles de Rémusat, 'to be incorporated into the Metternich clique of every country'.[93] Only electoral reform and in particular the introduction of universal suffrage would shift the government, but the Chamber of Deputies set its face against such reform in March 1847. Given the restrictions on public meetings the campaign for reform was confined to 'banquets' and Chartist-like petitions. At a banquet in Lille on 7 November 1847 the lawyer and republican deputy for Le Mans, Ledru-Rollin, called for universal suffrage. When the government banned another due in Paris it took place illegally on 22 February 1848 and violence broke out.

Guizot was finally dismissed on 23 February and Thiers formed a government which included another opposition leader Odilon Barrot and Charles de Rémusat. When, however, regular troops fired on demonstrators, provoking insurrection, and the National Guard sided with the demonstrators, Louis-Philippe abdicated. His son, the Duc d'Orléans, had died in a carriage accident in 1842, and the attempt on 24 February by his widow, supported by Barrot, to have the Chamber endorse a regency in favour of her nine-year-old son, the Comte de Paris, came to nothing as crowds invaded the Chamber. Meanwhile decision-making had shifted to the Hôtel de Ville. Ledru-Rollin and Alphonse de Lamartine, a poet and Legitimist politician who moved sharply to the left in 1842, went from the Chamber to the Hôtel de Ville where a provisional government was set up ahead of elections to a constituent assembly. They hesitated to declare a republic, and François Raspail, determined that the mistake of 1830 should be avoided, marched at the head of a column of building workers to the Hôtel de Ville on 25 February, and proclaimed the Republic to the crowd.[94]

Those who refounded the Republic on 24-25 February were clear that to succeed it must exorcize the demons of that of 1792, and not descend into another Terror. Raspail had emphasized as early as 1835 that 'the republic we desire is not what you describe as that of 1793'. Universal suffrage would provide liberty for all and fraternity would replace persecution and civil war.[95] Lamartine, having moved to the left, resurrected the Girondins, the moderate revolutionaries who in 1793 had been purged by Robespierre's 'Montagne' (so called because they sat on the Assembly's highest benches), as model republicans. 'They adored liberty. They founded the Republic,' he wrote. 'They died for refusing to allow liberty to be soiled.'[96] On 27 February, on behalf of the provisional government, he duly announced the abolition of the death penalty for political crimes, and there were no trials of Louis-Philippe's ministers. Victor Hugo, who wrote an ode to the coronation of Charles X at twenty-three, was converted to the cult of Napoleon two years later and became a peer in 1845, stood as a candidate in the 8th *arrondissement* of Paris. He told his electors that the Republic should not 'restart those two fatal machines . . . the *assignat* printing press and the pivot of the guillotine' but should be 'the holy communion of all French people . . . under the democratic principle'.[97]

The Second Republic certainly did not usher in the Terror, but its dream of fraternity did not prevent civil war and it did not, unlike that of 1792, take measures tough enough to prevent the enemies of the Republic using against it the liberty it proclaimed. The *commissaires* of the Republic sent out by Ledru-Rollin, the new interior minister, in place of the prefects, were former colleagues of the late Godefroy Cavaignac – Félix Pyat, sent to the Allier, Charles Delescluze, sent to Lille – or sons of former colleagues in the case of the twenty-two-year-old lawyer Émile Ollivier, sent to Marseille, but were far from being as effective as the Convention's representatives on mission during the Terror.[98] Elections to the Constituent Assembly were scheduled for 9 April, which did not give enough time, argued Auguste Blanqui and his supporters, for citizens just given the vote to be educated in republican ways by the popular press and political clubs which sprang up as they had in 1789. They obtained a postponement till Easter day, 23 April, when, as they feared, the republican message was not sufficiently disseminated and old social hierarchies ensured the return of many of the old politicians as effectively under universal suffrage as under a limited franchise. The Comte de Falloux, a Legitimist from Anjou, urged his supporters to use the opportunities provided by 'the government of all for all' and was elected as in 1846, while the Orleanist Charles de Rémusat, meeting his Legitimist friend Berryer after they had been re-elected, recalled that 'we could not stop ourselves laughing', so little had been changed by the Revolution.[99]

Ironically there were only a minority of confirmed republican deputies in the Constituent Assembly which opened on 4 May, much to the chagrin of the republican movement that was bubbling in the political clubs and popular press of Paris as it had in 1789, and confrontation was not long in coming. On 15 May the Assembly was invaded by Paris republicans led by Blanqui, Barbès and Raspail, who then attempted to set up a revolutionary government in the Hôtel de Ville. Overpowered by the National Guard, the leaders were arrested, tried and given long prison sentences. On 21 June unemployed workers who had been found work on building projects were suddenly thrown out of work when these 'national workshops' were closed down, the workers drafted into the army or sent back to their province of origin. Feared as hotbeds of socialist discontent, they were transformed into the base of a popular revolution which took control of the poorer, eastern half of the capital between 23 and 26 June, the so-called June Days. The Assembly handed over dictatorial power to the minister of war, Eugène Cavaignac, younger brother of the revolutionary Godefroy, who had made a career in the army conquering Algeria and now saw himself as a French Washington. The insurrection was brutally suppressed, with 500 deaths on the barricades, 3,000 summary executions and 12,000 men arrested and crammed into improvised prisons before 4,000 were deported to Algeria.[100] This repression was a formative influence on a whole generation who would become socialists and anarchists, for whom the bourgeois state was exposed in all its brutality. Pierre-Joseph Proudhon, who had just been elected in a by-election, said that 'the memory of the June Days will always weigh like a terrible remorse on my heart.' He was 'elected by the plebs, journalist of the proletariat', but was unable to lead the 100,000 rebels – a 'disastrous apprenticeship' which he urgently had to put right.[101] Jules Vallès, who came to Paris in 1848 to resit his *baccalauréat*, was appalled by the chain-gangs of rebels being led away to deportation. He resolved to write a book on the June Days but so awful were the memories he was never able to do so.

The constitution of the Republic was voted by the Assembly on 4 November 1848 and the election of a president for four years by universal suffrage took place on 10 December. Cavaignac was the favourite as a man of order who had saved the Republic, but his reputation among the populace was as a butcher, while he was too much a republican for the combined Orleanist and Legitimist leaders of what was now known as the 'party of order' such as Thiers,

Molé, Barrot, Berryer and Falloux who were looking for a way back into power. 'Not for a single day had the infant republic ceased being attacked by republicans,' said Falloux; it had to be entrusted to royalists who knew how to govern.[102] The dark horse was Louis-Napoleon Bonaparte, son of the emperor's brother Louis and Joséphine's daughter Hortense Beauharnais, who had been brought up in enforced exile in Switzerland and Italy, had fled to England after the failure of a military rising at Strasbourg in 1836, and had been captured and imprisoned, only to escape after a madcap landing at Boulogne in 1840. He had spent time thinking about how to reinvent his uncle's legacy for modern times and published *Napoleonic Ideas* in 1839. Napoleon, he argued, 'rooted the principal benefits of the great crisis of 1789 in France and introduced them all over Europe . . . he accelerated the reign of liberty by saving the moral influence of the Revolution and calming the fears it inspired.' If liberty had been restricted under Napoleon it was because of ongoing war and counter-revolution; dictatorship was temporary, and, he quoted Napoleon, 'a constitution is the work of time'. Napoleon had deferred to the people, said that his own fibre responded to theirs, and instituted a republican monarchy, legitimated by a popular vote. He had overcome the war of parties by bringing together those who had favoured the Revolution and those who had opposed it. 'To govern through a party is to become dependent on it sooner or later,' he had told the Conseil d'État. 'No one will get the better of me that way: I am national.' Louis-Napoleon paid homage to Napoleon I, but did not intend simply to copy him. 'March at the head of the ideas of your century, and those ideas will follow you and support you,' he said. 'March beside them, and they will drag you along. March against them, and they will overthrow you.'[103]

Elected to the Assembly in a by-election in Burgundy at the same time as Proudhon, on 4 June, and returning to France, he was an unknown quantity and thought mediocre by many who met him. 'With his long face and heavy features, a sickly colouring, his large parrot's nose, and awful mouth,' said Charles de Rémusat, he looked not like a Bonaparte but like a Beauharnais. Some people said, 'The man is an idiot,' but Rémusat became aware that he 'believed in the star of his dynasty' and represented a 'popular Bonapartism'.[104] This was echoed by a Burgundy newspaper which argued that the rural populations who voted for him 'focussed on the memory of the Emperor, whose name is still worshipped in our cottages'. This popular support was not an expression of peasant atavism, but a folk memory of the Napoleon of the Hundred Days who in 1815 had thrown out the Bourbons and their noble and clerical allies.[105] On the day, Louis-Napoleon was elected president with a massive 5.4 million votes, as against 1.4 million for Cavaignac, 400,000 for Ledru-Rollin and 37,000 for Raspail.

Despite this popular mandate the leaders of the party of order were persuaded, in Thiers' words, that Louis-Napoleon was 'a cretin we will manage'.[106] His first ministry was headed by Odilon Barrot, who had been the last chief minister of Louis-Philippe. The Comte de Falloux replaced Hippolyte Carnot, son of the regicide Lazare Carnot, as education minister, 'proof of an agreement', said Charles de Rémusat, 'between Bonapartism and the clergy, or rather the Catholic party'.[107] Another Legitimist, Alexis de Tocqueville, was appointed foreign minister. Elections to the Legislative Assembly on 13 May 1849 gave a majority of 500 to the royalist party of order, seeing off a hard-fought campaign by the Montagne under Ledru-Rollin which wanted to install a democratic and socialist republic but won only 200 seats. On 13 June the Montagnards took to the streets in an attempted insurrection which was crushed, and Ledru-Rollin fled to London. Louis-Napoleon now reshuffled his government to include the hard men of the party of order, not those such as Thiers tarnished by association with previous regimes but men of the same vintage who were less politically compromised. These included Achille Fould, a banker of Jewish origin and deputy for Paris who had financed Louis-Napoleon's presidential campaign and became minister of finance; Jules Baroche, a barrister from La Rochelle and protégé of Odilon Barrot, who as procurator-general tried the leaders of the 15 May and 13 June disturbances and became interior minister; and Eugène Rouher, a barrister from Riom and deputy for the Auvergne who became minister of justice.[108] These new ministers took the opportunity to wrap up the democratic experiment, clamping down on the press and public meetings, and restricting universal suffrage by a law of 31 May 1850 which disfranchised a third of the electorate, characterized by Thiers as the 'vile multitude'.

In this way France might have established a consensus as a conservative, Catholic republic, with the 'Montagne' destroyed in 1849 as it had been in 1794, the mass of the people deprived of a political voice and the royalists taking over the Republic as they had not been permitted to do by repeated coups against them under the Directory. Thiers told the Assembly in 1850 that the Republic was 'of all governments, that which divides us least'.[109] Although conservatives might not like it instinctively, it suspended the quarrelling between Legitimists, Orleanists and Bonapartists that broke up the unity of the party of order. Unfortunately, dynastic differences could not so easily be papered over. The death of Louis-Philippe in 1850 opened the possibility of 'fusion' whereby the Legitimist Comte de Chambord, son of the Duc de Berry, succeeded first, and if he had no issue would be succeeded by an Orleanist prince, but terms could not be agreed and the royalist branches again fell apart. Meanwhile Louis-Napoleon wished to revise the constitution of the Republic in order to permit him to run for a second term in 1852. This was blocked by the Assembly, in which a two-thirds majority was required. Victor Hugo, one of the deputies, argued that an attack on the Republic was an attack on the Revolution and sneered, 'Just because we had Napoléon le Grand, do we have to have Napoléon le Petit?'[110] Louis-Napoleon had the last laugh on 2 December when he mobilized his supporters in the army to dissolve the Assembly, issued a new constitution which restored the authoritarian regime of 1799 and the universal suffrage foolishly abrogated by the Assembly, and had it acclaimed by a plebiscite on 20 December 1851 by 7.5 million votes to 640,000 with 1.5 million abstentions.

RE-RUNNING THE EMPIRE

The coup d'état of 2 December ushered in a project to establish a different kind of consensus in France. Louis-Napoleon now demonstrated his ambition to become 'national'. Initially this meant dealing harshly with the royalist and republican oppositions. Royalist deputies and former ministers such as Berryer, Falloux, Tocqueville, Barrot, Rémusat and Thiers were sent briefly to Mazas prison to cool their heels, and Rémusat and Thiers spent a few months in exile in Brussels. The republican opposition to the coup, which included an attempt by representative Jean-Baptiste Baudin to raise the people of eastern Paris, with Baudin himself dying on a barricade, and a series of uprisings in south-east France, was more harshly dealt with. Some conspirators were sent to Cayenne, while representatives such as Victor Hugo and Edgar Quinet went into exile.

How to form a governing class without recourse to the political class that had run France since 1830, if not 1815, was no easy matter. The core of Napoleon's support came from his family. His half-brother, the Duc de Morny, son of Hortense Beauharnais after her separation from Louis, was the grey eminence of the coup d'état and became interior minister, while Comte Alexander Walewski, an illegitimate son of Napoleon I, was for a long time foreign minister.[111] His uncle Jérôme, former King of Westphalia, was briefly president of the Senate, a body of appointed marshals, admirals and cardinals, and including his son, Prince Jérôme-Napoléon, although both were jealous of Louis-Napoleon's imperial ambitions.[112] Victor Persigny, the son of a soldier in Napoleon's armies who was killed at Salamanca in 1812, was himself dismissed from the hussars in 1830 for republican conspiracy, offered his services to Louis-Napoleon in 1836 and shared his fortunes in London after the Strasbourg fiasco and prison after the Boulogne incident, remaining there till 1848. He was in the inner circle that planned the coup of 2 December and was rewarded with the Ministry of the Interior.[113] Whereas senior generals close to the Orleanist circles of power were unhappy about the coup, Saint-Arnaud, who had learned his trade during the pacification of Algeria, was a key player in the coup and was rewarded with the Ministry of War.[114]

A second circle was formed by the men of the party of order who had been his ministers in 1849–50. Achille Fould was again appointed minister of finance, Rouher returned to the Ministry of Justice and was a leading drafter of the 1852 constitution, while Baroche became president of the Conseil d'État, the administrative and legislative hub of the regime. Fould and Rouher together with Morny had vestigial

Orleanist sympathies and resigned in January 1852 when Napoleon ordered the confiscation of the property of the Orleans family, but Fould was promoted to the Senate where he formally proposed the re-establishment of the Empire in November 1852, Rouher became minister of public works, presiding over the rebuilding of Paris as an imperial capital, and Morny became president (speaker) of the Legislative Body in 1854. The restoration of the Empire was endorsed by 7.8 million votes in a plebiscite of 21 November 1852, with 250,000 against and two million abstentions. Louis-Napoleon, now Napoleon III, refused a coronation on the model of his uncle in 1804, his wedding to the Spanish noblewoman Eugénie de Montijo in Notre-Dame in 1853 serving a similar ceremonial function.[115] In addition, the feast of St Napoleon, the birthday of Napoleon I, which coincided with the Catholic Feast of the Assumption on 15 August, became a public holiday with much speech-making and merry-making.[116]

The regime combined the personal power of the emperor with a concentration of power in the army and bureaucracy, together with democratic legitimacy provided not only by the plebiscite when the constitution was changed, as in 1799–1815, but by elections to the Legislative Body or lower house. Elections were not left to chance, but there was no such thing as a Bonapartist party. Instead, prefects endorsed 'official candidates', who had standing as notables in the community and supported the government line, and put the power and money of the state behind their election. Typical of the prefectoral corps was Georges Haussmann, whose administrative career made only slow progress under the July Monarchy, as he vegetated in a series of subprefectures, and under the Republic, when he was offered the Var and the Yonne, but Louis-Napoleon appointed him prefect of the Gironde at Bordeaux in 1851 and prefect of the Seine in Paris in 1853.[117] As for the candidates they were to select, interior minister Morny advised them in January 1852, 'When a man has made his fortune by work, industry, agriculture, and if he has made himself popular through the noble use of his wealth, he is preferable to those who might have reputations as politicians, because he will bring a practical sense to the preparation of laws and support the government in the work of pacification and reconstruction.'[118] Thus, of the deputies elected in 1852, only 26 per cent came from the liberal professions, 15 per cent were high officials, generals or magistrates, while 59 per cent were landowners, bankers, merchants or industrialists, and this profile changed little in the elections of 1857, 1863 and 1869. Among the industrialists favoured by the regime were the cotton magnate Augustin Pouyer-Quertier in Normandy, the iron magnate Charles de Wendel in Lorraine, and in Burgundy the steel magnate Eugène Schneider, who was vice-president of the Legislative Body in 1852–67 and became its president in 1867.[119]

All holders of public office, including elective office, were required to take an oath of loyalty to the emperor. Even if they broke through the defences erected by the official candidate system, royalists and republicans would not be able to take their seats without forswearing their political allegiance. Among the Legitimists Tocqueville denounced the 'rule of the sabre' and 'bureaucratic and military despotism'.[120] He retired to write *The Ancien Régime and the Revolution* (1856) which can be read as a polemic against Bonapartism and a defence of liberty. The Comte de Falloux was unable to secure election in the Vendée although Berryer was elected at Marseille in 1863, virtually the only Legitimist mouthpiece in the Chamber. Orleanists hated the Empire which was the reverse of the parliamentary regime of the July Monarchy, at once too personal and too popular. The Duc de Broglie, whose salon was the meeting place of the Orleanist opposition, compared the arbitrary confiscation of the Orleans family property to the murder of the Duc d'Enghien.[121] Republicans also detested the Empire, but a gap opened up between the veterans of 1848 such as Cavaignac and Carnot, who could never be reconciled to the Empire and remained 'exiles of the interior', and republicans of a new generation who were less wedded to forms of government and thought that the Empire might be modified from within to become more liberal. Émile Ollivier, whose father Démosthène narrowly avoided deportation to Cayenne after the coup, was won over by Morny, elected to the Chamber in 1857 and was one of five republicans to take the oath, seeing himself as a 'disinterested moderator of the Revolution'.[122] Ollivier now married Blandine, the daughter of Liszt, and the salon of Marie d'Agoult, Liszt's former lover, became the preferred meeting place of 'little Olliviers' such as Jules Favre, another republican deputy who took the oath, along with Jules Ferry and Charles Floquet.[123]

'A constitution is the work of time,' Napoleon quoted his uncle, and not all times were propitious. The elections of 1857 were a setback for the government, and concerns increased about opposition in the press. The government attempted to close down newspapers like the *Revue de Paris* by trying Flaubert's *Madame Bovary*, which it had serialized at the end of 1856, for obscenity.[124] Then, on 14 January 1858, an attempt was made to assassinate Napoleon III on his way to the opera: eight people were killed, 148 wounded. The bomb was planted by an Italian patriot, Orsini, who believed that Italy would be liberated only by a European revolution. A general was appointed minister of the interior and France hovered on the brink of military dictatorship. Orsini was executed, and, fearing an imminent republican uprising, the government rushed through a law of general security, under which 430 suspects were rounded up, 380 of whom were deported in chains to Algeria. One of these was Benjamin Clemenceau, who had already been arrested in 1851 after the coup d'état. He was released at Marseille but the effect on his son Georges was decisive. Georges was himself arrested and imprisoned in February 1863 for stirring up a demonstration in honour of the Revolution of 1848. Georges was inducted into the republican university of Sainte-Pélagie prison, where he met the likes of Auguste Blanqui and the Alsatian deputy Auguste Scheurer-Kestner.[125]

The crisis was resolved by Napoleon III's alliance with Piedmont and war against the Austrians in 1859 to liberate northern Italy. The Empire's popularity soared, and Napoleon III took the opportunity to negotiate a more liberal regime that would win over much of the political class as well as the people in a time of relative peace and prosperity. 'You can put down a riot with soldiers and secure an election with peasants,' Guizot had said in 1851, 'but soldiers and peasants are not enough to govern; you need the support of the higher classes, who are the naturally governing classes.'[126] Reforms of 1860 gave the Legislative Body greater powers to amend the budget and debate the speech from the throne at the beginning of the session, parliamentary debates could be published in the press, though without comment, and ministers without portfolio, notably Rouher, were authorized to sit in the Legislative Body to engage with the opposition and put the government's point of view. Napoleon's 'reign as an absolute monarch is over', Thiers told an English observer in 1862. 'The next step will be to take his ministers from the chambers, and that is parliamentary government.'[127]

For the elections of 1863 a Liberal Union was formed which included the 'little Olliviers' and Orleanists who were now prepared to work for greater liberty within the Empire. Although Rémusat and de Broglie made no headway against official candidates, Adolphe Thiers was elected in Paris with the help of republican votes and re-entered national politics in January 1864 with a speech in the Chamber on the 'necessary liberties' to placate liberal opinion, including the end of official candidatures, freedom from arbitrary arrest, and a free press.[128]

The government responded with another instalment of reforms in 1868, when the press was given greater freedom and public meetings were allowed. Political activity returned to the cities for the first time since 1851, but as republicans used the act of political commemoration to make their point, so the government attempted to retain a whip hand to uphold the regime. Charles Delescluze launched a campaign to restore the dilapidated grave of Baudin, a deputy who had died resisting the coup d'état of 2 December. He was sent for trial in November 1868 for disturbing public order and inciting hatred of the government. His defence counsel, Léon Gambetta, used the trial to attack the government for the coup, and though the case was lost one of his political allies announced, 'The Republic is founded. Gambetta is the lion of Paris today.'[129] The name of Gambetta was made and he was duly elected to the Legislative Body in May 1869. These elections were fought in lively political meetings and in over a hundred new newspapers which were hostile to the government, such as Henri Rochefort's *La Lanterne*. Republicans won 31 per cent of the vote and were massively elected in the towns and cities.

The regime was now on a knife-edge between the authoritarian rule of Rouher and republicans on the march. Émile Ollivier grasped the opportunity by rallying 116 deputies on 6 July 1869 to demand greater association of the country in the direction of public affairs, above all a ministry responsible to parliament as well as to the emperor. Napoleon accepted the propositions and Rouher fell from power. In his speech to parliament on 29 November Napoleon announced, 'It is not easy to establish the regular and peaceful practice of liberty in France . . . I can provide order. Help me, messieurs, to save liberty.'[130] On 2 January 1870 Napoleon III invited Ollivier to form a government, and for the first time deputies were given ministerial office. Ollivier and the emperor collaborated on a more liberal constitution. It was imperfect, in that the emperor retained the right to appeal to the people over the head of parliament, and the right to chair the council of ministers, with Ollivier nothing more than minister of justice.[131] In spite of these shortcomings, the new liberal constitution of the Empire was approved by plebiscite on 8 May 1870 by 7.3 million votes to 1.5 million. Gambetta was forced to admit, 'The Empire is stronger than ever.'[132] Unfortunately, the lack of grip that Ollivier had on his ministry, notably his foreign minister Gramont, and the lack of a majority enjoyed by the ministry in the Legislative Body, meant that the combination of an irresponsible foreign minister and a Legislative Body smarting at German provocation led to an outcome that was fatal to the Empire: war.

2

Discovering France

On the evening of Tuesday 5 August 1834 Victor Hugo boarded a mail-coach in Paris and set off in the direction of Brittany. His goal was not literary but to catch up with his mistress, Juliette Drouet, with whom he had had a row and who had fled to her sister's near Brest. Hugo took the fastest form of transport then available, for the mail-coach travelled through the night, and he was in Brest at dawn on Friday 8 August. 'Three nights of whiplashes, as fast as the horses could go, without drinking, eating, scarcely breathing, with four diabolical wheels that simply ate up the leagues,' he wrote to his wife, as if she would sympathize. He was reconciled with Juliette but not impressed by Brittany, which seemed a backward and foreign country. 'Stupid country! stupid people! stupid government!' he exclaimed. Hugo nevertheless returned to Brittany two years later. By the time he got to Saint-Malo he had only one obsession, and wrote to a friend:

Poor Brittany! It has preserved everything, its monuments and its inhabitants, its poetry and its mire, its old colour and its old dirt on top of it. Wash the buildings, they are superb, but I defy you to wash the Bretons. Often, in one of those beautiful heather landscapes . . . under great oaks bearing their leaves down almost to your reach, you will see a charming cottage with smoke rising above its ivy and roses. You admire it, you enter. Alas, my poor Louis, this golden cottage is a horrible Breton shack where people and pigs sleep in the same room. You have to admit that the pigs get pretty dirty.[1]

This ride to Brittany points up an interesting paradox. On the one hand travel was becoming increasingly rapid, along good roads

built to move armies and officials at speed, and using high-perform-
ance horse-drawn vehicles. In 1785 a coach took three days just
to get to Rennes, 150 miles short of Brest.[2] On the other hand the
encounter with Brittany pointed up its strangeness to the Parisian
traveller, a sense of its backwardness compared to the civilization
of modern France. This contradiction was observed by writers such
as Victor Hugo, but also by those sent to administer such far-flung
provinces.

PREFECTS DISCOVER FRANCE

When Bonaparte seized power in 1799 France was on the verge of
collapse. Outlying areas of the country, notably the Vendée, Brittany
and the Midi, were in the hands of counter-revolutionaries, organized
into small armies under the leadership of nobles in communication
with the Allies, or into guerrilla bands which emerged at night, such
as the Breton *chouans*. Even larger areas of France fell victim to
bands of brigands, formed by draft-dodgers and deserters from the
revolutionary armies that were being conscripted to fight the war of
the Second Coalition. Both counter-revolutionary forces and brigands,
which might merge into one another, targeted mail-coaches that
carried money to pay for the regular army and attacked republican
officials who had demonstrated their greed and loyalty to the new
regime by purchasing church land. To deal with these threats Bonaparte as first consul resorted both to military measures and to
negotiation, but in the long term bringing order to the country relied
on the establishment of a centralized system of administration, the
prefect system.

France, run before the Revolution through a network of overlapping jurisdictions – military, fiscal, administrative, judicial and
ecclesiastical – was divided in 1790 into eighty-three more or less
equal departments, which provided the basic unit for all those
jurisdictions. Regimes had struggled in the 1790s to find an administrative system that worked, since the Revolution favoured
administration by elected bodies and officials who lacked clout, while
the representatives on mission sent out by the Convention parliament

in 1793–4 had discredited themselves as agents of the Terror. Bonaparte's solution under the law of 17 February 1800 was a centralized and hierarchical system by which each department would be run by a prefect, appointed by the head of state and directly responsible to him. The representation of opinions and interests was minimal, for elections to representative bodies had for ten years brought little but anarchy. A *conseil général* of a score or so notables, appointed for fifteen years after 1802 by the consul for life from names submitted by the department's electoral college, composed of the highest taxpayers, met for no more than two weeks every year, mainly to share out the tax bill. Each *arrondissement*, of which from four to six normally formed a department, would be run by a subprefect, also appointed by the head of state. Each of the 36,000 communes of France, cities, towns and villages, were to be run by a mayor, who would be appointed by the head of state where the population was over 3,000 and by the prefect where it was fewer. Below each mayor was a municipal council to which appointments for twenty years were made by the prefect from names submitted by the canton assemblies of the highest taxpayers. The exception to this was Paris, which was allowed no mayor, in case the capital become a power-base independent of the central government. Instead, it was divided into twelve *arrondissements*, each with its own mayor, but real power remained in the hands of two prefects, the prefect of the Seine and the prefect of police.[3]

The advantages of this top-down system in terms of uniformity and efficiency were plain to see. What was less clear was how much prefects appointed by the central government would know about the parts of the country they now had to run. Some prefects at least were acquainted with the region. In Brittany Jean-Pierre Bouillé was born at Auray (in what became the Morbihan after 1790) and later was a lawyer at Pontivy (in what became the Côtes-du-Nord). During the Revolution he became an administrator of the Morbihan and then became prefect of the Côtes-du-Nord. The prefect of the Finistère in 1800, however, was François-Joseph Rudler, a native of Alsace, who complained that of the 288 mayors 'about thirty do not read, write or speak French'.[4] Since knowledge was power, in 1801 minister of the interior Chaptal, doctor, scientist, chemical industrialist, administrator of the department of the Hérault, director of the national agency of gunpowder manufacture in 1793, ordered a statistical survey of France. Prefects were to collect information about population, local resources and the local economy, religion and customs, taking into account the legacy of the Ancien Régime and ten years of Revolution, in order to make possible their own governance.[5]

The collection of these data obliged prefects to make contact with local agricultural societies, learned societies, doctors, clergy, members of *conseils généraux* and the like, who could provide them with the information they needed. Not consulted for any political reason, they made the most of this 'scientific' survey to establish their credentials as members of the educated, urbane, national society that subscribed to science and reason. Called upon to interpret local customs for the purposes of the national survey, they did so by distancing themselves from 'the people' who, in their eyes, were still trapped in ignorance, rustic manners, localism, routine and superstition. Thus when a young secretary of the prefecture of Hautes-Pyrénées wrote of the region that 'local festivals are still essentially drunken orgies,' two local notables corrected the draft to read, 'local festivals attract only the lower classes.'[6]

Alongside this rather Enlightenment view of local and provincial life, however, ran another, Romantic notion that rural populations, even in places as backward as Brittany, were not as uncouth as might first be assumed. On the contrary, the manners and customs of local people were seen as vestiges of some bygone civilization that was somehow more authentic than the artificial and polished civilization of the French national elite. Jacques Cambry, the son of a naval engineer in Lorient and much travelled in his youth, was part of the revolutionary administration of Finistère during the Revolution and published an early version of the departmental survey, a *Voyage in Finistère, or State of the Department in 1794 and 1795*, in 1799. He reflected on the one hand on the province's intense localism since, with the exception of the few military roads built in the eighteenth century, travel along the sunken tracks in the *bocage* (where small fields were divided by tall hedgerows) was extremely difficult. The inhabitants of each *pays*, which corresponded more or less to the *arrondissement*, were characterized by a distinct natural, historic, religious and even linguistic identity. Cambry noted that:

the Breton dialect of the Léonais is purer, more sonorous and elegant than those of the other cantons. It is to these parts what Saxon is to the German language. In the Léon the dialect of Cornouaille and Tréguier is understood, but they can make no sense of that of Vannes . . . The peoples of Léon and Tréguier hate the inhabitants of Cornouaille as brutal and uncouth, with their strange habit of striking themselves on the head.[7]

On the other hand, Cambry developed the view that under the uncouthness of the Breton lay an ancient civilization and that beyond the localism was a proud imperial tradition. 'The Breton is externally a savage if you compare him to a French person civilized by imitation,' he wrote, 'but the natural French person is inferior to the Breton.' The fact that Bretons had preserved their distinct language, argued Cambry, had inoculated them against the pernicious ideas of modern philosophy and saved them from the worst of the French Revolution: 'there, people slept under Robespierre.' Again, Bretons might be considered superstitious, but under the Catholic practices that they had adopted and which had been attacked by the Revolution they had preserved a far more resilient Druidic religion. As they had resisted the French Revolution, so 2,000 years before they had resisted Caesar. Indeed they were the hub of a vast Celtic empire that had covered not only the British Isles and Ireland but Spain, Italy, Greece, France, Germany and Asia Minor. 'The language of the Scythians, who populated a good part of the world, was Celtic in times gone by.'[8]

When in 1802 Cambry became prefect of the Oise at Beauvais, north of Paris, he threw himself into the research required for Chaptal's statistical survey. He admitted that it was 'pictureque and anecdotal' rather than systematic. In fact he was looking for evidence for his theory that Celts had left signs of their passage everywhere in Europe. For example in the Oise he observed the popularity of a Celtic ball game called *soule* or *choulle*. The Oise, formerly the Beauvaisis, belonged to the Bellovacques, whom Caesar had called 'the bravest of the Belgians, as the Belgians were the bravest of the Gauls'.[9] In 1805 Cambry founded the Académie Celtique, and addressed its opening meeting in 1805. The Academy devoted itself to propagating the idea that France, rather than England, which had set up a Celtic Academy under Charles II, was the cradle of the Celtic people, and that the empire of the Celts stretched all over Europe and half of Asia. This was the territory that Napoleon's Empire was destined to recover. When he reached Moscow in 1812 Napoleon is alleged to have said, 'The civilisation of St Petersburg deceived us; these are still Scythians.'[10]

COUNTER-REVOLUTION AND PROVINCIALISM

Although prefects were supposed to be the all-powerful executors of the government's will, they were only as powerful as the support they obtained from the central government. Two invasions, three changes of regime and a civil war that broke out after Napoleon's second defeat at Waterloo not only undermined the prefectoral system, but also demonstrated the fragility of the system of centralized administration when stress was applied. Some counter-revolutionary elements, who had famously 'learned nothing and forgotten nothing' since 1789, wanted to go back to the provinces of the Ancien Régime, some of which, such as Brittany, Franche-Comté and Languedoc, had elected provincial estates dominated by the nobility and clergy. In fact, provinces had not stood out as the dominant administrative unit of the Ancien Régime and it was not until the departments were invented that nostalgia for the provinces developed. Perhaps because of this, the restored monarchy of 1814–15 saw no advantage in reverting to this system and, once it had recovered its grip, stuck with the institution, if not the personnel, of the Napoleonic prefectoral administration.

Franche-Comté, on the Swiss border, was formerly a province of the Habsburg monarchy, conquered by Louis XIV in 1678. Its vigorous military nobility, who had revived the provincial estates in 1787, had emigrated to join the counter-revolutionary armies of the Bourbon princes. One of them, Comte Pierre-Georges de Scey-Montbéliard, offered his services to the Austrian commander

Schwarzenberg in December 1813, asking him to revive the Franche-Comté under Habsburg protection. After the Austrians took Besançon, Scey-Montbéliard became unofficial governor of Franche-Comté. However, when the Bourbons returned in the spring of 1814, they refused to countenance such a plan; the most they did for Scey-Montbéliard was to make him prefect of the Doubs, one of the three departments into which the province had been divided in 1790. Moreover, though Scey led opposition to Napoleon during the Hundred Days from the Swiss frontier, he was not offered his prefectoral post back after Waterloo. The Bourbon regime favoured moderate royalists who collaborated with the centralized administration it was pleased to inherit from its arch-enemy Napoleon.[11]

Brittany, despite Cambry, had not slept under Robespierre, but had rather provided an adjunct to the Vendean uprising in the form of the less organized guerrilla warfare of *chouannerie*. Though the region had been pacified by Napoleon after 1800, his return in the Hundred Days was greeted by another rebellion. The towns generally remained loyal to him and he entrusted the Loire army to General Lamarque, who said of the uprising, 'the heart is in the Vendée: we must strike there.' One of the Vendean leaders, Louis de La Rochejacquelein, was killed on 4 June 1815, and Lamarque was able to force peace on the Vendean leaders at Cholet on 26 June. They were persuaded by Lamarque not to exploit Napoleon's defeat at Waterloo, since Prussian troops were moving into the area.[12] From this moment the Vendée became a part of Catholic and royalist historic memory rather than a military threat. The Marquise de La Rochejacquelein, widow of Louis, and widowed by another Vendean leader, the Marquis de Lescure, 'the saint of Poitou', published her *Memoirs* in 1815. In this she painted the Vendée as an ideal community, the polar opposite of a system in which citizens equal under the law were subjected to the authority of the state. Here, though feudalism had been abolished by the Revolution, she argued, 'a sort of union unknown elsewhere' reigned between peasants and their noble lords.[13] As they had hunted together and danced in the château courtyard, so they fought together against the intrusive power of the revolutionary state. The key chapter about Vendée society had in fact been ghostwritten by Prosper de Barante, who had met and worked with the Marquise de La Rochejacquelein when he was prefect of the Vendée in 1809–13. George Sand, who was at convent schools with the marquise's daughter, remembered her in practice as haughty and obsessed by caste. Despite this, the myth of the Vendée as an idealized microcosm of the Ancien Régime enjoyed enduring currency.[14]

Much more dangerous in terms of the collapse of the Napoleonic administration were events in the Midi. After Waterloo a broad crescent of the south from Toulouse to Toulon became a virtually autonomous kingdom under Louis-Antoine, Duc d'Angoulême, son of the Comte d'Artois and nephew of Louis XVIII. In the White Terror, volunteer militias 100,000 strong wreaked vengeance on those who had supported the revolutionary and Napoleonic regimes in the Midi. One flashpoint was the Gard department around Nîmes, the Ulster of France, where Catholic royalist bands known as *miquelets* took their revenge against the Protestants who had enjoyed political ascendancy since 1789. On 1–2 August 1815 a veritable St Bartholomew's massacre of Protestants took place in Nîmes.[15] Meanwhile, with the help of a British blockade of the coast, royalist bands took control of Marseille and Toulon. Napoleon's commander in Toulon, Marshal Brune, was given a safe conduct to Paris by the authorities, but on 9 August in Avignon, former apanage of the popes annexed by France in 1791 and hotbed of counter-revolutionaries, he was recognized by the crowd, lynched, and his body tossed into the Rhône. In a similar incident at Toulouse, the authority of the Bourbon prefect, Augustin de Rémusat, another royalist who had rallied to Napoleon and was now recruited by the restored monarchy, was not sufficient to prevent an attack by counter-revolutionary bands of *verdets* on Napoleon's General Ramel, who died of his wounds on 17 August.[16] The murders of Brune and Ramel were long held up as evidence of the ungovernability and cruelty of the populations of the Midi.

One of the outcomes of the loss of prefectoral authority after Waterloo was a failure of the administration adequately to influence the elections of 19–20 August 1815, and the consequent return of the ultra-royalist Chambre Introuvable. The tension between Chamber and government continued until chief minister Decazes dissolved the Chamber and called new elections, this time managed by prefects of his choosing. In the Gard things took a little longer but in 1817 a reliable prefect was appointed who sacked the two subprefects in the department, forty mayors and twenty judicial officials, in order to eliminate counter-revolutionary clientage and ensure a victory for government candidates in the elections of 1818. That said, none of the leaders of the White Terror was ever brought to justice.[17]

After the collapse of the Bourbon monarchy in July 1830, Charles X gave instructions from exile in England that there should be no insurrection. The only disobedience came from his daughter-in-law, the Duchesse de Berry, widow of the Duc de Berry assassinated in 1820. Unfortunately for her, a large number of servants of Napoleon had rallied to the July Monarchy, including Marshal Soult, now minister of war, who had strengthened the army in the south-east. Moreover, despite the myths of class harmony peddled in the work of the Marquise de La Rochejacquelein, the peasantry of Brittany and the Vendée did not rise in support of the Legitimist cause.[18]

After 1832 Legitimism no longer posed a political threat to the Orleanist regime. Elections limited to a small propertied electorate were managed by the government through a combination of corruption and pressure. In his *Deputy of Arcis* Balzac explored the 'making' of an election in 1839 by an alliance of the minister, the Comte de Rastignac, the subprefect of Arcis and the most influential of the local electors, dubbed the grand elector, the Comte de Gondreville, 'king of the Aube department'. An oath of loyalty to the regime was required of all officials and representatives, and Legitimist nobles who refused to take the oath retired to their town houses in the Faubourg Saint-Germain or to their country estates. Removed as prefects and mayors, they could exercise authority only indirectly. At Boismé (Deux-Sèvres), in the area broadly constituted by the Vendée, the mayor was a farmer and political straw man of the Marquise de La Rochejacquelein. The authorities disqualified him from standing in elections and therefore no elections took place in 1834 and 1837, because the other farmers of the marquise refused to vote for anyone else.[19] At Chanzeaux (Maine-et-Loire), in the part of the Vendée area known as the Mauges, the local landowner was Comte Théodore de Quatrebarbes, who was imprisoned after taking part in the Duchesse de Berry's conspiracy. Though neither mayor nor deputy, he and his wife exerted influence by means of the traditional hierarchy in the countryside, supplying grain, paying for work on roads and distributing charity in the hard winters of the 1840s.[20]

In face of the grip of prefects and grand electors on politics and administration, Legitimist nobles excluded from power could find some compensation by reconstituting in a virtual sense provinces that had existed before 1790 but had been destroyed by the Revolution and Napoleon. The Association Bretonne was founded in 1843 by Jules Rieffel, founder of an agricultural college at Grand-Jouan (Loire-Inférieure), who wanted to revive the agricultural society set up by the Breton estates in the eighteenth century. Also part of the Association, however, was the archaeological section, which concerned itself with the preservation of Breton monuments, musical instruments, costume, language and poetry.[21] A key figure here was Théodore Hersant de La Villemarqué, who published a collection of popular Breton songs, *Barzaz-Breiz*, in 1839, arguing in the German Romantic tradition that they were echoes of the Breton soul.[22] Against those who argued that Bretons would never be civilized until they learned to speak French, La Villemarqué argued that Breton had preserved Brittany from Calvinism, 'philosophical impiety and Voltaireanism', and that 'amid the storms of the Revolution the preservation of faith and social virtues among the Breton people was due essentially to their language.'[23]

WRITERS DISCOVER FRANCE

In 1837 the poet, novelist and artist Théophile Gautier noted that the vogue for young writers to tour the French provinces and to record their impressions was 'the veritable Don Quichottisme of our time'.[24] By 1830 the outlying parts of France had been brought under the heel of the central administration, and the collaboration of prefects and local notables in the management of elections ensured that the country was politically integrated as well. Communications with the provinces were better and faster. After the last burst of *chouannerie* in 1832 the July Monarchy invested heavily in strategic roads under a law of 27 June 1833, while local roads were also developed under a law of 21 May 1836. Public transport on the main arteries was provided by the imperial (later royal) stage-coach company (*messageries impériales/royales*), and the general stage-coach company (*messageries générales*) founded in 1828 and largely funded by Laffitte. These went only as far as Lyon, Toulouse and Bordeaux, after which other companies ran complementary services. The most rapid form of road transport, however, was provided by the mail-post, which alone was allowed to gallop and to stop only to change horses. Thus under Louis XVIII it took forty-eight hours to reach Bordeaux by stage-coach, but thirty-six hours by mail-post. That said, by the 1830s and 1840s transport was entering the steam age. Steamboats plied the major rivers, and the first railway, providing a short link between Lyon and Saint-Étienne, mainly for the transport of coal, opened in 1832, and another between Paris and Saint-Germain in 1837. It was a law of 11 June 1842, dividing responsibility between public authorities, which would take care of the infrastructure, namely the cost of expropriation, and railway companies, which would provide the superstructure of rails, rolling-stock and maintenance that launched the railway mania of the 1840s. A star of lines radiated out from Paris, reaching Lyon in 1845, and in 1848 it was possible to travel by railway from Paris to Marseille in less than twenty hours.[25]

Despite the growing speed of travel, Paris-based writers who were attracted to the provinces encountered them almost as foreign lands. Naturally, not all parts of France were equally strange. The central part of France around Paris seemed familiar, while the greatest differences were experienced in the west, especially Brittany, and the Midi. Balzac, who was brought up in Tours on the Loire until the age of fifteen in 1814, when his family moved to Paris, saw a clear difference between the Loire valley, where the most perfect French was said to be spoken, and Brittany. In the summer of 1827 he took a coach to Fougères, at the entrance to French-speaking Upper Brittany rather than Breton-speaking Lower Brittany in the west, but foreign enough to serve as the base for his historical novel, *The Chouans* (1829). He pictured a column of republican soldiers in 1799 isolated in hostile country controlled by *chouan* rebels who 'heated the feet' of informers in front of roaring fires, beheaded traitors and nailed their heads to the door of their cottages, and plundered the bodies of soldiers before sinking them into a lake. The double mission of the republican soldiers, explained the young officer Gérard, was to 'defend the territory of France' and to 'preserve the country's soul, the generous principles of liberty and independence, the human reason revealed by our Assemblies and which, I hope, will win people over. France is like a traveller carrying a light in one hand and a weapon in the other.' Yet Balzac hesitated between showing the goatskin-clad, forest-dwelling Bretons, isolated from modern civilization, as benighted assassins or as noble savages. They were 'as stunted intellectually as the Mohicans and Redskins of North America, but as great, as cunning and as tough as they'.[26]

The historian Michelet visited Brittany in the summer of 1831 and reported that the wearing of goatskins began at Laval, even before Brittany was reached, as the forests became denser. He argued that the true, Breton-speaking Brittany was 'a country quite different from ours, because it has remained faithful to our primitive state; scarcely French, so much it is Gallic', but that it was controlled by four essentially French towns – Nantes, Rennes, Brest and Saint-Malo – so that Breton 'resistance' to things French was gradually being eroded. In terms of difference he was just as much struck by the Midi, which he characterized as 'a country of ruins', Roman monuments, Roman law, Roman religion. Avignon in particular was 'the theatre of this decrepitude', combining ancient Roman architecture and the Roman Catholic religion. Along with its antiquity went a 'murderous violence' exploding in wars of religion against Albigensians and Protestants, and the demagogic rhetoric of the likes of Mirabeau.[27]

Michelet's analysis fed into his *History of France* in which he exalted 'that beautiful centralization by which France becomes France'. He imagined centralization not in administrative terms but in intellectual ones, 'a general, universal spirit' that was gradually conquering local differences shaped by material considerations such as soil, climate or race. 'England is an empire, Germany is a country, a race, France is a person.'[28] He drove home the same theory in his lectures at the Collège de France in 1838. Paris, he said, was not only the French capital but a European capital, a world capital. 'Every state today is seeking to imitate France by way of centralization.

Local sentiments are gradually dissolving in favour of a unifying spirit which animates all the parts.'[29] The work of national unification, begun by the monarchy, was completed by the Revolution and Republic, but on a higher intellectual plane. Into this context Michelet fitted his attack on the Vendée. 'Just as the world turned towards France and gave itself to her, becoming French at heart, one country made an exception,' he explained in the third volume of his *History of the French Revolution*, published in 1850. 'There was a people that was so strangely blind and so curiously misled that it took arms against the Revolution, its mother, against the public safety, against itself. And by a miracle of the devil that country was in France . . . that strange people came from the Vendée.'[30]

For many writers the south of France was even more barbaric and violent than the west. Prosper Mérimée, who toured France in his capacity as inspector-general of historic monuments, remarked that when he got off the steamboat that had carried him from Lyon to Avignon in September 1834, 'it seemed to me that I was leaving France . . . I thought myself in the middle of a Spanish town.'[31] Stendhal, who came across Mérimée during his tour of France, was impressed by the speed of the steamboat that took him on the same route from Lyon to Avignon in 1837, a distance of over 60 leagues in ten hours. When he reached Avignon, however, he was keen to confirm it as a violent city, and visited the room in the Hôtel du Palais-Royal where Marshal Brune had been killed in 1815. He reflected that it was incredible that Brune had decided to go to Paris via Avignon; 'it would have been so simple to go by Gap and Grenoble, where no one ever got murdered.' For Stendhal, a native of Grenoble, the Dauphiné was a 'country of fine minds and enlightened patriotism', quite different from Provence. Three weeks after Waterloo, he boasted, Grenoble was still trying to defend France against invading Piedmontese troops. The 'civilized part of France', he argued, was north of a line between Nantes and Dijon; south of that line there was only Bordeaux and Grenoble.[32] In his memoirs, *The Life of Henri Brulard*, he was even more explicit about where civilization stopped, describing 'the fatal triangle that stretches from Bordeaux, Bayonne and Valence. There they believe in witches, can't read and don't speak French.'[33]

Not all writers had such a negative view of the Midi. Flaubert, brought up among the green fields of Normandy, and promised a trip to the south with a medical colleague of his father's if he passed his *baccalauréat*, which he did in 1840, was fascinated by the classic beauty of the girls of Arles and Marseille, where he felt 'something Oriental' in the bright mixture of complexions, costumes and tongues. His fear of violence was projected on to the island of Corsica, where he was told by the prefect that at a formal dinner to which he was invited no member of the *conseil général* would be without a concealed dagger, while bandits roamed the maquis, women were treated like beasts of burden and murders were routinely committed by vengeance groups of extended families.[34] His trip to Brittany seven years later with his friend Maxime du Camp was altogether less challenging. They left Paris by train, going as far as Blois before deciding to continue on foot. The main distinction they drew, however, was between the Breton countryside, whose peasantry, attached to their families and village priests, spent as little time as possible in town on market day, and the towns where no one but maids wore the regional costume, and those working in government offices spoke French and read the newspapers. Gradually, Flaubert remarked, the town-dweller was 'becoming less Breton and more separate from the peasant, whom he increasingly despises and who distances himself all the more, as they each understand each other less'.[35]

CONQUERING PARIS

The educated, middle-class elite who began to discover France in the 1830s originated from Paris, but that did not mean that they were familiar with Paris life as a whole. The differences between the educated class and 'the people' that obtained in the provinces also obtained in Paris, perhaps even more so. However, just as the provinces were being explored by writers, so Paris was being explored first by officials responsible for public order and the public health and secondly, too, by writers. For Paris was a city undergoing rapid transformation in the early nineteenth century. Its population increased from 547,000 in 1801 to 1,539,000 in 1856.[36] This expansion was fuelled not by a rising birth rate, for large cities were dens of high mortality, but from provincials coming in search of work and fortune. Often they concentrated at the margins of the city, outside the gates where tolls were imposed on food and drink brought into the city, so that wine was enjoyed tax free, but where also unhealthy industries such as tanneries, glue factories and slaughter-houses were moved, along with the site of public executions under the July Monarchy.[37] Others packed into the medieval centre of Paris, finding work on the waterfront, in bars, in street trading or rag-picking. Unfortunately, the amount of work available was not enough to sustain the number of hands, thus, at the lower end of society, vegetated a population of casual labourers, tipping into vagrancy, crime and prostitution.

A sharper awareness of the social problems of the capital came with the publication of two major studies. *Prostitution in the City of Paris* by Alexander Parent-Duchâtelet, a medically trained vice-president of the Conseil de Salubrité, was published in 1836, after the author had worked himself to death. Dedicated to issues of public hygiene and social justice Parent-Duchâtelet calculated that while there were only 3,558 prostitutes registered with the Paris authorities in 1832, there were 35,000–40,000 more clandestine ones, often minors exploited by old women posing as midwives or tooth-pullers, posted in bars to bring in custom, concentrated in the narrow streets of the Île de la Cité, where there was one prostitute for every fifty-nine inhabitants. Daughters of workers or peasants who had come from north-eastern France to seek a fortune and failed, often the victims of family abuse or brutality, were sent out to labour in workshops or to help street traders but were often unemployed. 'Only a reproach, a word, an encounter,' observed Parent-Duchâtelet, 'was required to plunge a young girl for ever into an abyss of shame and ignominy.'[38] The second study, *The Dangerous Classes of the Population in the Great Cities*, by H.-A. Fréguier, an administrator in the prefecture of the Seine, was published in 1840. Devoted in fact just to Paris, it examined the fluid frontier between the working and criminal population, suggesting that about a third of the working population lost their jobs in time of cyclical depression. At the bottom of the working hierarchy were the rag-pickers, who were generally alcoholics, homeless youths who hung about markets looking for work or pilfering, prostitutes, pimps and madames, 'rogues, thieves, crooks, fences' constantly supplied by liberated or escaped convicts, using a common argot and operating in gangs. Less humane and more alarmist than Parent-Duchâtelet, Fréguier's analysis was also less sociological and more moralizing. 'As soon as the poor person, abandoned to evil passions, ceases to work,' he argued, 'then he becomes the enemy of society.'[39]

Path-breaking though these works were, they did not have the same impact on social opinion as a fictionalized account of low life in the capital, *The Mysteries of Paris*. This rambling work, serialized for the educated public in the *Journal des Débats* in 1842–3, was the unlikely invention of Eugène Sue, last of a long line of military doctors, who abandoned his career as a naval doctor when his father died in 1830, leaving him a considerable fortune. He became a dandy, haunting the theatre, opera, cafés, salons and the newly founded Jockey Club, until in 1837 he discovered he was ruined. Deciding to write, he was introduced to working-class life in 1841, not in reality but via a play about a poor but honest worker by his friend Félix Pyat.[40]

The Mysteries opens with the descent into the rue aux Fèves on the Île de la Cité of Slasher, abandoned by his parents, working in an abattoir from the age of ten or twelve, doing fifteen years' forced labour for knifing his sergeant in the army, now a docker on the quai Saint-Paul. He forms a brutal relationship with a sixteen-year-old girl known as la Goualeuse or Fleur-de-Marie, also abandoned by her parents, who has been begging from the age of eight for a one-eyed crone called la Chouette. The key figure, who stops Slasher beating up la Goualeuse, is Rodolphe, who poses as the son of rag traders in Les Halles but in fact lives in the Faubourg Saint-Germain, the son and heir of the Grand Duc de Gerolstein. Locked in combat with the underworld, including a family of hereditary criminals and fresh-water pirates, the Martial family, he discovers that la Goualeuse is in fact his own daughter by the Countess Sarah McGregor. In the final scene Slasher loses his life defending la Goualeuse from the Martial family, whose mother is being executed. Describing the people converging on the place of execution as 'a muddy and fetid froth of the population of Paris, this immense crowd of bandits and fallen women who derived their daily bread from crime', Sue cited Fréguier to the effect that 30,000 people in Paris live by crime alone, but his account of the underworld, strangely penetrated and redeemed by a member of high society like himself, was altogether more influential.[41]

The fear that the working population was also the criminal population developed into the fear that the working population was also the insurgent population. In July 1830 and February 1848 popular insurrection which triggered regime change had rapidly been brought under control by the ruling classes, enrolled in the National Guard as the regular military defending the outgoing regimes collapsed. In June 1848, however, the closure of the national workshops that had kept a large proportion of the unemployed in work provoked the June Days revolt. Alexis de Tocqueville, a deputy in the Assembly, argued that the revolt was 'not to change the form of government but to alter the social order. It was not, in truth, a political struggle . . . but a class conflict, a servile war.'[42] On 23 June drum rolls and bugle blasts summoned the propertied classes to the ranks of the National Guard. One of them was Maxime du Camp, his battalion sent to protect the Foreign Ministry. Wounded in the leg, he denounced the 'ferocious and stupid beasts' who threatened 'French civilization'.[43] However, the National Guard held firm, reinforced by volunteers from the provinces, and put paid to the Paris revolt. Tocqueville remembered the arrival of the volunteers from his native Manche, travelling nearly 200 miles across country not yet linked to Paris by rail. 'They were 1500 in number. Among them I recognized with emotion my friends and neighbours, landowners, lawyers, doctors, farmers. Almost all the old nobility had taken up arms and joined the column.'[44]

A Paris redolent of crime and revolt did not befit the capital of a great nation, and when France became an empire once again in 1852, it had to be rebuilt and redefined as an imperial capital. That was the thinking of Georges Haussmann, a career prefect who, as we have seen, ran the Gironde at Bordeaux in 1851 and was offered the prefecture of the Seine in 1853. He lost no time announcing his ambitions at the Hôtel de Ville.

A great city, a capital above all, has the duty to present itself as equal to the role that it plays in the country. When that country is France, when centralization, which is the basis of its strength, has made the capital both the head and heart of the social body, then that capital would betray its glorious mission if, in spite of everything, it became constantly stuck in the ways of superannuated routine.[45]

Building a modern imperial capital meant piercing broad boulevards, cutting long perspectives from one grand monument to the next, including the 'great cross' of the rue de Rivoli, boulevard Sébastopol and boulevard Saint-Michel meeting at the place du Châtelet, increasing the number of avenues radiating from the Étoile from five to twelve, each named after a member of the imperial family or one of Napoleon's victories, and redesigning the Bois de Boulogne to include lakes, gardens, two race-courses and a zoo.[46] In the railway age that was now reaching its apogee it meant driving arterial roads to the main termini, from which railways fanned out to every part of France. 'Everything moves towards Paris: main roads, railways, telegraphs,' Haussmann announced in 1859, 'everything moves out from it: laws, decrees, decisions, orders, officials.'[47] The east of the capital, the popular quarters which formed the heart of any insurrection, were to be penetrated by strategic roads too wide for barricades. Haussmann was delighted to show the emperor the boulevard Voltaire, which would enable troops to take the Faubourg Saint-Antoine from the rear, and to remove the rue Transnonain, macabre centre of the massacre of innocents in 1834, from the Paris map. Last but not least, the very population associated with crime and disorder would be eliminated from central Paris by what Haussmann called 'the disembowelling of old Paris'.[48] Thus the maze of narrow medieval streets around Notre-Dame, the stage-set of Sue's *Mysteries of Paris*, was razed to make way for a few sublime public buildings: the Prefecture of Police, the Palais de Justice, the Tribunal de Commerce, the Hôtel-Dieu, while Les Halles were rebuilt as a modern steel emporium to replace the old den of iniquity.

Most of the Paris populace was driven into the outskirts of Paris, and the population of central Paris actually fell as public buildings, businesses and sites of pleasure and entertainment multiplied. Suburbs such as Belleville, originally semi-rural villages beyond the old city boundary, with a population of 2,800 in 1801, grew into industrious districts with 60,000 inhabitants by the time they were annexed by the city of Paris in 1859–60.[49] However, the shift of popular Paris to the periphery was not uniform. Many workers, needing to stay close to suppliers and clients in the trades they practised, simply crowded more tightly into the lodging houses that remained, or into inner courtyards or attics. Others found temporary accommodation in shanty towns that grew like mushrooms on one development site after another.[50] Haussmann had not dealt with the problem of the revolutionary population of Paris, he had simply moved it. 'Two towns have been created in the capital,' said one commentator, 'one rich, one poor. One surrounds the other. The unruly class is like an immense cordon circling the rich class. It would be a lot better if it were not like that.'[51]

DECENTRALIZATION DEBATED

The Revolution of February 1848 ended the cosy and corrupt alliance between the government and well-disposed notables which had ensured political stability since the mid-1830s and yet closed political life to republicans, Legitimist royalists and all those outside the narrow political class. Suddenly universal male suffrage was conceded and all political groups re-entered the electoral arena. The provisional government replaced prefects by *commissaires*, such as the young Émile Ollivier in Marseille and Toulon, who were supposed to exert some government influence over elections to the National Assembly, but their ability to shape universal suffrage and local interests was limited. Tocqueville, a candidate at Valognes (Manche), led 170 electors, who were either his tenants or members of his local community, on a 3-mile procession to vote at Saint-Pierre-Église on Easter Day 1848, haranguing them on the gravity of their responsibilities, and was certain that all the votes went to him.[52]

Rather than bring together French people under the banner of fraternity, the democracy of the Second Republic had a tendency to drive them apart. This was clear in the elections of 1849 to the Legislative Assembly, under the new constitution, when the country polarized between the republican left, the so-called *démocrates-socialistes* or Montagne, and the Legitimist Right. The Comte de Falloux, who recalled that his grandmother had received Louis de La Rochejacquelein at Angers when the Vendean army occupied the city and was brought up on the *Memoirs* of the marquise, headed a clean royalist sweep of all eleven seats in Maine-et-Loire (Anjou).[53] The Vaucluse divided between the *arrondissements* of Avignon and Carpentras, which had been in the Papal enclave before 1791 and voted royalist, and the *arrondissement* of Apt, which had a French past and voted for the Montagne.[54] The Comte de Montalembert, elected as a Catholic royalist in the Doubs, the core of the Franche-Comté, thanked his supporters, declaring that there were two Mountains, 'an enemy Mountain and a friendly Mountain . . . it is you, the Comtoise and Catholic Mountain, who have chosen me to fight that other Mountain whose doctrine and deeds you detest.'[55]

The question of administrative decentralization had been in the air since the June Days, when, it was argued, France had been saved from another 1793 by stout volunteers from the provinces rushing to Paris to quell the revolt. Tocqueville's cousin, Louis de Kergolay, who had been caught up in the Duchesse de Berry's attempt of 1832, launched a *Provincial Review* in September 1848 in which he argued that under the present centralized system 'a handful of men, an armed coup, is sufficient at any given moment to overturn the government and rule over France by means of the telegraph'. A middle way had to be found between a civil war between the provinces and Paris and a federalism it was feared would fragment France's precious unity.[56] Less squeamish about the term 'federalism', which also stood for the provincial movement against the tyranny of the Montagne at Paris in 1793, a group of Lyon royalists called in January 1851 for a 'Southern federation' that would emancipate French cities and provinces under a restored monarchy.[57] The royalist-dominated Legislative Assembly Campaign engaged with these questions, setting up a commission on decentralization. This proposed to maintain the decree of July 1848 allowing the election of mayors in communes of under 6,000, to widen the powers of municipal councils and *conseils généraux* vis-à-vis prefects, and to equip *conseils généraux* with permanent commissions which would meet outside the rare sessions of the full council.[58]

Louis-Napoleon's coup d'état of 2 December 1851, after which he briefly arrested his royalist opponents, including Falloux and Tocqueville, and crushed the uprising orchestrated by the Montagne, which was especially strong in the south-east of France, put paid to all schemes of decentralization. Louis-Napoleon lost no time in reimposing the centralized administration patented by his uncle in 1800. Prefects were given greater powers to control the press under a law of 17 February 1852, and new police powers to close down political opposition under a decree of 25 March 1852. They were also empowered to appoint police commissioners, JPs, gendarmes, post office officials and now primary school teachers or *instituteurs*. This gave them the ability to mobilize the administration in support of 'official candidatures', the government-sponsored candidates who were now put forward to fight elections, with all the carrots and sticks the regime could muster to see off royalist or republican opposition.[59] Democracy was removed from municipal councils: prefects recovered the authority to appoint mayors in communes of fewer than 3,000 inhabitants under a law of 7 July 1852, while in larger towns and cities this authority was exercised by the central government. Baron Haussmann told the municipal council of Paris when it was enlarged after the annexation of the suburbs in 1859–60 that there could be no question of the sixty councillors being elected by Parisians with narrow Parisian interests since Paris was 'the capital of a powerful Empire, the residence of a glorious sovereign, the seat of all major public bodies, the universal centre of literature, the arts and sciences'.[60]

Alongside the policy of administrative centralization was a policy of economic modernization which would serve to bring the country together in a single market and help to depoliticize it as growing material success took the edge off political passions. At Bordeaux in October 1852, welcomed by Haussmann who was still prefect there, Louis-Napoleon announced that 'we have immense uncultivated territories to make productive, roads to open, harbours to dig, rivers to make navigable. Our railway network remains to be completed.'[61] The Empire, proclaimed in December 1852, presided over and indeed facilitated an immense capitalist boom. After the crisis of credit and confidence in the railway industry in 1847 Pierre Magne at the Ministry of Public Works favoured the merging of competing railway companies in consortia for the purposes of completing the major lines. Thus the struggle for control of the Paris–Lyon–Mediterranean route was resolved by awarding the contract to four bidding companies – a group of British backers and entrepreneurs, the Rothschilds of Paris, the banker François Bartholony, who controlled the Paris–Orléans line, and the Péreire brothers' Crédit Mobilier group – who in 1853 formed the Lyon and Mediterranean Company. Four years later, in 1857, this Company merged with the Paris–Lyon Company to form the famous Paris–Lyon–Mediterranean Company.[62] The fruits of this new policy were quick to appear. Whereas in 1850 there were only 3,000 kilometres of track in France, there were 6,500 in 1857 and 17,500 in use in 1870.[63]

In Paris, the Péreires were heavily involved in financing the rebuilding projects of Haussmann. The Crédit Foncier, founded in December 1852 and, like its twin, able to mobilize savings on a gigantic scale, lent to builders and developers who would then be repaid by the City of Paris. This opened the way to vast private fortunes being made at the expense of city finances, a scandal attacked by the republican Jules Ferry in his 1868 *Fantastic Accounts of Haussmann*.[64] Lyon, linked to Paris by rail from 1845, saw its population grow by 70 per cent under the Empire, and was similarly Haussmannized, with wide boulevards driven through the city, the *quais* rebuilt, passenger and freight stations going up and parks developed. All this drove the city into serious debt, but political opposition was gagged because Lyon was stripped of its elective municipal council in 1852 and was run solely by the powerful prefect of the Rhône, Claude Marius Vaïsse.[65]

Railways stimulated trade, industry and finance; they also underpinned the boom in holiday travel to coastal resorts and spa towns that took place during the Empire. While the Empress Eugénie, of Spanish ancestry, favoured the development of Biarritz as a resort, the Duc de Morny, the emperor's half-brother, who did not like the crowded and chaotic Trouville on the Normandy coast, developed Deauville, further down the estuary, on its own dedicated railway line from Paris, not to mention its own race-meeting, inaugurated on 14 July 1864.[66] The emperor himself preferred spa towns, and gave cachet to Plombières in the Vosges, which he visited in 1858, not least to negotiate secretly with the Piedmontese premier Cavour about Italian unification, and to which a rail link was built in 1860. Under that deal France recovered Nice, which was developed as a winter holiday resort, and Savoy, which included Aix-les-Bains. Aix was visited by 4,150 spa-goers in 1856, but twice that number after the railway link was completed in 1860, rising to 176,000 in 1879.[67]

The attempt of the Second Empire to develop economic activity and leisure in far-flung parts of France along new axes of communication, while retaining the grip of administrative centralization and political paralysis, was a contradictory policy that was bound to fail. The circulation of goods and ideas generated a demand from cities and regions to take their affairs more into their own hands. The traditional regionalist lobby, given a fillip by the June Days but then sidelined by the imperial regime, used regional culture as a way to make a political point. The Association Bretonne, founded in 1843, was closed down in 1859 by the government, which alleged that it was a political vehicle. However, one of its younger leaders, Arthur de La Borderie, had already in 1857 founded a *Review of Brittany and the Vendée*, which celebrated Breton resistance to Franks and French, Breton liberties as defended by the Estates of Brittany before 1789, the Breton language and the Roman Catholic faith which was once more under attack.[68] In Provence Frédéric Mistral interrupted his law studies at Aix after the coup of 2 December and dedicated himself to the development of Provençal literature, certainly as a critique of the centralizing state that used French as its vehicle, but not going as far as to demand Provençal autonomy and indeed exploiting the opportunities afforded by Paris as a literary capital. He went to Paris in 1856 and secured the patronage of the aged Lamartine for his Provençal poem *Mirèio/Mireille*, about a village Romeo and Juliet. This was published in 1859 and was soon made into an opera by Gounod, opening in Paris in 1867.[69]

More weighty than the traditionalists, however, was the liberal and republican lobby which, on the back of the process of modernization and integration, demanded a greater degree of administrative decentralization. Unlike the traditionalists they had no hidden agenda to bring back France's old provinces. They accepted the division of France into departments but wanted more power to be devolved to the *conseils généraux* and to municipal authorities. Their great breakthrough was in the legislative elections of 1863, which showed the limits of the system of official candidates. A Lyon magistrate complained that 'along the railway lines and the banks of the Saône and Rhône it is possible to follow, with the election results, the progress of contagious illness'.[70] Louis Hénon, deputy for Lyon, one of the five republican deputies who had taken the oath to the Empire, denounced the 'virtually irresponsible dictatorship' of the administration in Paris and Lyon, which was neglecting schools and hospitals in favour of 'luxury projects' and opening up boulevards at the expense of private housing, resulting in a doubling of rents. What was required instead, he said, was 'an elected and independent municipal council', emanating from and responsible to the local population.[71] Enthusiasm for a 'municipalism' that would provide an apprenticeship in citizenship and self-government at the lowest level became one of the republicans' main demands.[72] Demands for greater decentralization at both municipal and departmental level were articulated to great effect in the so-called Nancy manifesto published in 1865. Originating with a group of notables from Nancy but endorsed by a galaxy of liberal public figures both royalist – Montalembert, Falloux, Berryer – and republican – Hippolyte Carnot, Jules Ferry, Jules Simon – it declared that 'centralization is stifling us with the abusive interference of the administration in our affairs.' Specifically it wanted to 'emancipate the departments' by giving *conseils généraux* greater powers, more staff and permanent commissions to oversee the work of prefects between sessions. More powers also were demanded for municipal councils, although the signatories were divided on whether mayors should be elected or appointed, given that they were both representatives of the town and agents of the state.[73]

The Nancy group was seen by many republicans as being too dominated by Catholics and royalists, and there was plenty of republican opinion in favour of decentralization but not represented on it. Republican decentralists were concentrated in the large cities, especially Paris, Lyon and Marseille, which massively returned republicans in the elections of 1869. In the popular Paris suburb of Belleville no official candidate dared to run and Gambetta, whose famous Belleville manifesto called for the election of all mayors, beat the moderate republican Carnot. As a result of the republican triumph in the cities the liberal ministry of Émile Ollivier convened a commission on decentralization, chaired by veteran trimmer Odilon Barrot. Opening in March 1870, it came out in favour of permanent commissions for *conseils généraux* and the election of mayors by municipal councils in all communes with the exception of Paris and Lyon. This last recommendation was not acceptable to the government, which passed a law in July 1870 retaining the government's right to appoint mayors.[74] The refusal to recognize that the great cities of the country had the maturity to manage their own affairs was one reason for the municipal revolts of August 1870 and indeed for the Paris Commune.

3

A Divided Society

PEASANTS AND THE STRUGGLE FOR LAND

In *The Peasants* (1844), Balzac presents a peasant community through the eyes of educated outsiders who see it as something alien and violent. 'They are [Fenimore] Cooper's Redskins,' reflects a Parisian journalist, Blondet, 'you don't have to go to America to see savages.' He juxtaposes the château, owned by a count, one of Napoleon's generals, and the tavern, a 'viper's nest' where drunkenness and greed fuel 'the hatred of the proletarian and peasant against the master and the rich man'. The curé, sent like a missionary among the infidel, argues that the French Revolution was a *jacquerie* in revenge for 1,200 years of feudal oppression. At the end of the novel the general is driven out and the peasants divide his estate into a thousand lots which they share between themselves.[1]

This account suggests a tremendous land hunger among the French peasantry which drove them to revolt and savagery. They had a passion to become independent smallholders rather than remain the farmers or labourers of great landlords. There was a common belief in the nineteenth century that before the Revolution the peasantry had been the virtually landless serfs of feudal lords and abbots, and had become landholders as a result of the division and sale of church and noble land at the Revolution. Before 1789, in fact, peasants owned between 22 and 70 per cent of French land, more in the uplands or *bocage* regions of the west, less around large towns where the bourgeoisie bought land.[2] About 10 per cent of all land changed hands at the Revolution, mainly as a result of the sale of church lands, confiscated by the National Assembly as *biens nationaux* in order to solve the state debt crisis, and the sale of lands of nobles who opposed the Revolution and emigrated. At this point it is true that the peasantry gained more land, but not as much as the bourgeoisie and even petite bourgeoisie of traders and artisans, who were better placed to make a killing. In the Nord department, for example, the clergy lost the 20 per cent of the land they held, and the nobility declined from 22 to 13 per cent. The peasantry increased its stake from 30 to 42 per cent, both as smallholders owning less than 10 hectares and as a 'rural bourgeoisie' owning between 10 and 40 or even 100 hectares, but the share of the urban bourgeoisie rose from 17 to 29 per cent, especially around large towns such as Lille.[3] In the Amboise area on the Loire, where 15 per cent of the land changed hands, the peasantry acquired 32 per cent of the land sold, with wine-growers and larger peasant farmers doing particularly well, and artisans and traders such as coopers, innkeepers, butchers and bakers secured 23 per cent; but again the urban bourgeoisie did best with 35 per cent of the land sold.[4] In the Beauce around Chartres, finally, 47 per cent of the buyers were peasants, but they secured only 27 per cent of the land sold, while artisans and traders who were 17 per cent of the buyers obtained 26 per cent of the land, and bourgeois property-owners, liberal professions and civil servants, who also made up 17 per cent of the buyers, obtained 40 per cent of the land.[5]

Even more profound than the land market was the impact of the Revolution on patterns of inheritance. In 1793 the Convention established the equal right of all children to their parents' estate, but this democratic right threatened to break up family farms to a degree that made them unviable, so in 1800 the Consulate allowed parents to dispose freely of part of the estate, while dividing the rest up equally among the heirs. This permitted the family farm to be passed down more or less intact to one main heir, while endowing the other children with dowries or some business capital.[6] While awaiting their inheritance younger sons and daughters generally worked outside the family farms as day-labourers or artisans. Agricol Perdiguier, whose father was a carpenter and winegrower near Avignon, had two elder brothers who wanted to become farmers, one of whom had done eleven years in the revolutionary and Napoleonic wars, so

Agricol was apprenticed at the age of thirteen or fourteen, outside the family, to a carpenter.[7] Marcel Bourgeois, the second son and one of five children of a mountain farmer in Franche-Comté, saw the farm go to his elder brother and was obliged to become a clock-maker in the next commune. As it turned out he married a tradeswoman, his business did well, and in 1847 he was able to buy out the share of his brother in the farm.[8] The heir due to inherit the farm might marry and live and work in the parental household in what was known as a 'pot and hearth' community, but the question of when the inheritance would materialize could become pressing. Arnaud Bouzeran, a ploughman who married Marie Sanson, who was due to inherit the family farm near Montauban, lived with his in-laws under such an arrangement for ten years. He came into the farm but on condition that he pay a pension to Étienne Sanson, his father-in-law, a payment that cancelled out his profits. When in 1827 he fell behind with his payments and Sanson threatened to take him to court, Bouzeran killed him with an axe.[9] This was violence of Balzacian proportions, but it was rare.

The size of a farm was central to whether it could maintain a family. As a general rule 10 hectares of farmland were required for a family to be self-sufficient, but 4 hectares might be enough if they were under vines. In 1862 some 85 per cent of farmers had holdings of less than 10 hectares, and a third of smallholders supplemented what little they owned by renting plots from bourgeois or noble landowners. At the bottom of the pile in 1851 were 900,000 day-labourers and two million *domestiques* or live-in farmhands, some of whom had a future claim on a family farm or inheritance while others made up the rural poor. Louis-François Pinagot, a carter's son of the Perche (Orne), became a clogmaker working in a hut in the forest for a dealer who paid 1 franc a day in 1855, 2 francs in 1867. He escaped military service, which was decided by drawing lots, and married a hemp spinner who was paid only 25 centimes a day. They remained on the margins of the core commu-nity of farmers and though they had eight children only one of his sons, who started as a farmhand, came into property.[10]

Small farms could make a living where the soil was rich, but others, in poor soils and upland areas, obliged farming families to supplement their income by industrial work, either at home or by temporary migration out of the region. Cottage industry operated under a system by which entrepreneurs 'put out' textile work to peasant families in their villages and hamlets, affording cheap labour without overheads for the entrepreneur and the means to remain on the land by access to a little cash income for the peasants. Generally a gendered division of labour applied, with the men continuing in the fields or with their trade and the women spinning or weaving. In the Pays de Caux, the chalk plateau north of Rouen, Rouen merchants put out cotton for spinning until factory spinning killed it off in the 1830s, then they put out spun yarn for handloom weaving. Three-quarters of the 110,000 weavers in the surrounding Seine-Inférieure in 1848 were women, paid at the miserable rate of between 75 centimes and 1.25 francs per day.[11] In the Forez village of Marlhes (Loire), near Saint-Étienne, where 70 per cent of peasants had less than 10 hectares, the local cottage industry was silk ribbon-weaving, and 88 per cent of the weavers were women, 55 per cent of them being single, 38 per cent married and 7 per cent widows in 1851.[12] To the south, in the Velay, lacemaking in silk and linen employed 130,000 country women in 1855, a luxury product marketed by the merchants of Le Puy as far as Germany, Italy, Spain and Britain.[13] To the south-east, in the Ardèche, the peasant populations grew the 'golden tree' or mulberry which fed silkworms, producing either raw silk to be sold to merchants at the markets of Aubenas and Joyeuse or spun in workshops along the Ardèche river, fifty-six of them employing 3,360 workers, almost all women, in 1860.[14] Further west, in the Rouergue (Aveyron) even the mines of Decazeville, developed by the Duc de Decazes and his associates, were worked by peasant miners who owned plots of land and came to the mine only when there was nothing to do in the fields.[15]

THE FORMATION OF A WORKING CLASS

Elsewhere, industry did not come to peasant women but rather men from peasant communities had to go in search of work, migrating seasonally or temporarily. Many if not most industrial workers originated in peasant communities, primarily because 52 per cent of the working population in 1856 was agricultural and only 23 per cent was in mining, manufacturing or building, whereas in Great Britain at the same time only 22 per cent of the working population was agricultural, while 48 per cent was industrial.[16] From the Rouergue, in the south-west of the Massif Central, sawyers went to work during the winter in the forests of the Pyrenees and Catalonia, travelling in teams from the same villages, returning in the spring in time for the harvest and with cash enough to pay taxes or buy land.[17] From the Limousin, on the north-west of the Massif Central, especially the Creuse department, where most peasants had less than a hectare and the soil was too poor even to grow rye, men left in work-teams from the same villages every spring, going to Paris to hire themselves out as masons, returning around St Andrew's Day, 30 November. Leaving from the age of thirteen or fourteen, 34,000 strong in 1846, they were earners of hard currency for the extended family, returning home every third winter, marrying young because they were earning but then leaving their wives in Limousin when spring came round again.[18] Thus Martin Nadaud, schooled as far as his first communion aged thirteen, was equipped with a heavy woollen coat, strong shoes and a top hat, and set out aged fourteen in March 1830 with his father and other comrades from the Bourganeuf area for Paris. Early in 1839, having escaped military service, he married a local girl who provided a dowry of 3,000 francs but he also had to contribute to the 1,200-franc dowry required by his sister, so he went back to Paris after only seventeen days of marriage, returning at the end of 1842 with three bags of a thousand francs each, to repay most of the family debt.[19] Seasonal or temporary migration was not confined to men. Girls also left their homes in the country for a period of work in the city, either in domestic service or in the textile mills. This was generally to save enough money for a dowry and a trousseau in order to marry someone with the prospect of inheriting land, for there was no such thing as a free marriage.[20]

Over time agricultural and industrial populations did draw further apart; the peasantry and the working class became more sharply defined. The development of large-scale, powered and mechanized industry undercut cottage industry, so that first rural spinning and then rural weaving disappeared. Rural populations became less mixed and more predominantly agricultural. In the 1860s, for example, ribbon-weaving in the Loire department shifted to water-powered factories in Saint-Étienne which employed unmarried women only, so that the farmers' wives of upland villages like Marlhes switched to dairy farming, producing milk and cheese for another market.[21] Similarly, rural workers who began by migrating temporarily to the town or city might end up staying permanently, either because they were making a good living in the city or because the prospects of coming into an inheritance at home dwindled. There also emerged the first generation of 'born proletarians' such as Jean-Baptiste Dumay, born in Le Creusot in 1841 to a foreman who died in a mining accident six months before his birth and a seamstress who came from a family of clogmakers in the Nièvre. He was briefly educated in the company school before starting as an apprentice turner making nuts and bolts in the Le Creusot workshops, aged twelve, in 1854.[22]

The formation of a working class also presupposed the development of a working-class solidarity, overcoming differences between different regions or indeed localities. Building workers, especially carpenters, often went as journeymen on a Tour de France lasting several years to learn their trade. It was sustained by a system of *compagnonnage* or brotherhood which gave material and even familial support to the itinerant workers, with a 'Mother' in each town. Although this might have created a sense of solidarity among building workers, in fact it pointed up their differences. Agricol Perdiguier, who went on a Tour de France between 1824 and 1828, was immediately struck by the variety of patois of workers from different towns, starting with those between his native Avignon and those in nearby Marseille and Nîmes, who were not easy to understand. Moreover, *compagnonnage*, rather like freemasonry, was divided between different affiliations allegedly going back to the masters who built the Temple of Solomon. Perdiguier, for example, was a Companion of Liberty or Gavot. These were the sworn enemies of the Companions of Duty or Dévorants, who might rival each other to do the best work but might also resort to violence when they met. Finally, the network of hospitality for itinerant workers was virtually absent in Paris, whose workers, reflected Perdiguier, 'although very skilled and clever, learning every day, have little sympathy for each other, and few ties attaching them to others'.[23] Martin Nadaud, as a mason, was not a *compagnon* and did not go on the Tour de France, but was equally divided as an immigrant worker from the more established Paris workers. The masons lived in boarding houses in their favoured neighbourhood near the place de la Grève, looked down on by Parisians as 'chestnut-eaters', coming from a poor region where chestnut flour was used to make bread. That said, they also fought among themselves, masons from the north of the Creuse called Brulas and those from the south of the department called Bigaros, and woe betide the employer who tried to hire a mixture of them.[24]

Workers were sharply divided not only by place of origin but by level of skill and therefore earning power. Those trained in a trade or craft were much better off than the unskilled who had received no apprenticeship. In the first there was continuity, interrupted only by economic slump or injury, while the second were often in and out of work on a regular basis. Skilled workers had the possibility of progressing in the trade, becoming a master or even entrepreneur, while unskilled workers changed jobs frequently in the hope of finding a better situation, without really getting anywhere.

A comparison of the careers of two workers, Martin Nadaud and Norbert Truquin, will illuminate these differences. Taken by his father, a mason, to Paris in 1830, Nadaud became an apprentice in the trade, earning two francs a day. Two years later he was promoted to *limousinier*, the category which laid the foundations and built the basic walls for three francs a day, before becoming a mason companion proper, paid over four francs a day. Now he headed his own gang and negotiated directly with entrepreneurs such as Georges Duphot, who had started as a mason from the Creuse and became a big property developer. Nadaud was paid 150 francs per month to build a school in 1844 and 180 francs per month to build the town hall of the 5th *arrondissement*, place du Panthéon, in 1847.[25] One of the crowd who invaded the Hôtel de Ville in February 1848 and heard the Republic proclaimed, he was elected deputy for the Creuse to the Legislative Assembly in 1849.

Norbert Truquin, whose brutal and drunken father was briefly the manager of an Amiens woollen mill, received no education and was sent to work at the age of seven in 1840 for a wool-carder for 2 francs 40 a day, removing impurities from the wool with his teeth. After his employer died he took to petty theft, ran errands for prostitutes and joined a pedlar selling haberdashery in Champagne, before grape-picking for a franc a day. Back in his home village, his father sent him to work in a brickyard, then in a knacker's yard. Truquin then went to work in a wool-spinning mill in Amiens, sharing lodgings with mill girls paid 80 centimes to 1 franc 10 a day, but was then laid off and went to Paris where his father was running a wine warehouse, finding work in a woollen-cloth factory. Unemployed during the 1848 Revolution he enrolled in the national workshops and after the June Days tried to make a new start as a settler in Algeria. Unable to make a living there he returned to dig railway tunnels near Lyon before becoming a *canut* or silkweaver in the Croix-Rousse district of Lyon. Often laid off for lack of work he tried to become independent, marrying another silkweaver with 200 francs in savings, borrowing some more and renting lodgings that could hold two looms. Unpaid debts and recession in 1867 forced him to go back as a wage worker, and having become involved with the Revolution of 1871 in Lyon he decided to emigrate to South America, where he was joined by his wife and son. He worked as a charcoal-burner in Argentina to build up his savings and then they moved to Paraguay where he bought a plot of land.[26]

A key factor in the development of a working class was organization, but organization was precisely what government and employers wished to prevent. The Le Chapelier law of 1791 prohibited the association of members of any trade or occupation with a view to collective bargaining, on the grounds that 'there is nothing but the particular interest of each individual and the general interest.' In 1801 Bonaparte introduced the *livret* which every worker was obliged to carry as a record of his employment and to ensure that he repaid all debts to his employer before moving on. Articles 415 and 416 of the Penal Code of 1810 outlawed all 'coalitions' with an intent to raise the price of work by means of strike action as a kind of conspiracy or sedition, and imposed a two- to five-year prison term for leaders of any violation. All this was in the name of the free market, but workers who participated in the July Revolution of 1830 did not take long to prise open the contradiction between the rhetoric of liberty and the reality of exploitation and oppression. The Paris printers, the closure of whose presses had triggered the Revolution, launched their own paper, *The Artisan: Journal of the Working Class*, in September 1830, proclaiming that the working class was 'the most numerous and most useful of society', by the sweat of whose brow other classes made fortunes, but was now discovering a strength in 'association, a means to remedy the misery of the working classes'.[27]

As an organization of the working classes *compagnonnage* was not a good starter at this point. In one sense a charitable organization providing hospitality for young journeymen undertaking the Tour de France, in another it was a monopoly of accredited workers which was dedicated to ensuring that employers paid them a decent wage. A group of *compagnons* were accused of forming a coalition to push up wages and were sent for trial at Saintes (Charente Maritime) in 1812. Although acquitted, the threat of legal procedures continued to haunt them. More serious, the division of the *compagnons* into a number of factions ritually pitted against each other made this an unlikely weapon of the working classes.[28]

More fruitful in the long run as workers' organizations were the friendly or mutual aid societies that developed after the Restoration. Ostensibly dedicated to the health and welfare of their members, and using such names as the Philanthropic Society of Tailors to avoid legal proceedings for coalition, they were in fact nascent trade unions prepared to take on the might of the employers and the state ranged behind them.[29] The first great confrontation of the July Monarchy came in 1831 in Lyon, when the *canuts* or silkworkers, their rates driven down by international competition, organized into a master-weavers' Society of Mutual Duty and a journeymen's Society of Ferrandiers and tried to negotiate a minimum tariff with the silk merchants. Though the prefect chaired a meeting of merchants' and workers' representatives in October 1831 to agree a tariff, the merchants refused to recognize it, going over the head of the prefect to prime minister Casimir Périer for support. Proclaiming that 'the

July sun shone for everybody,' the silkworkers went on strike on 21 November, descending from the Croix-Rousse and other suburbs, clashing with the National Guard (who were essentially the armed bourgeoisie), and briefly seizing control of the Hôtel de Ville. The first round was lost by the workers but mutual-aid societies reformed, including the Society of Mutual Duty of young master-weavers, which organized a successful strike against a pay cut imposed by merchants in February 1834. The government immediately replied with an Associations Law which banned these clandestine unions and sent the strike organizers to trial for illegal coalition. This provoked a demonstration, then an insurrection in Lyon, the silkworkers backed by other trades such as cobblers, tailors and building-workers which had also been trying to form associations. However, the insurrection was put down and the ringleaders sent to Paris, arraigned in the notorious case of the 121, many of them being sentenced to prison and deportation.[30]

Although this kind of conflict with the bourgeoisie and behind them the state helped to shape the consciousness of workers as members of a working class, other factors worked against that class consciousness. The rising of 1834 in Paris, parallel to that in Lyon, had been led by republicans who considered the workers to be an integral part of 'the people', composed of everyone apart from the elite. The Republic proclaimed in 1848 was not particularly committed to workers: only one member of the provisional government and 34 of the 900 members of the National Assembly were workers.[31] The 'organization of labour' was the order of the day and trade associations flourished, but the experiment of national workshops for the unemployed ended in disaster, and the June Days of 1848 witnessed a martyrization of the Paris working class. Norbert Truquin, who saw action on the barricades, spoke of 'a legal massacre of workers'.[32] Workers had a more positive attitude towards the Second Empire, generally enjoying rising wages, with particular enthusiasm among the ironworkers of Lorraine and the miners of the Nord-Pas-de-Calais. The government cultivated the working class in order to wean it away from the republican leaderships.[33] In particular it modified the harsh sanctions of the Penal Code against coalition in a law of 25 May 1864, sponsored by republican deputy Émile Ollivier. While still outlawing picketing in the name of the right to work the law now authorized trade unions which legitimately tried to improve the lot of their members.[34] The government also sponsored an engineering worker, Tolain, to visit the International Exhibition of 1862 in London. He ran as a labour candidate in a Paris by-election of 1863, urging workers not to vote for bourgeois republican politicians. The alliance of Empire and workers was however imperfect. Tolain was inspired by anarchism and led a delegation of French workers to a congress of the International Workers' Association in Geneva in 1866. Some sectors, such as the Lyon textile workers, were never converted to the Empire, and the final years of the regime saw an upsurge of strike action. Although the steel town of Le Creusot was dominated by Eugène Schneider, Jean-Baptiste Dumay, whose career as an ironworker had been interrupted by military service between 1861 and 1867, returned there as a blast-furnace puddler and early in 1870 was involved in an ironworkers' strike over the company's bid to control the benefit fund that was deducted from their wages. The strike spread to the miners employed by the company, and twenty-seven of the ringleaders were sent for trial in April, receiving sentences raging from three months to three years. It seemed that little had changed since 1834, except that the Le Creusot strike became a cause célèbre, and militants of the International Workers Association came to Le Creusot to set up a branch there. Dumay proclaimed: 'We were proud that our cause provoked universal sympathy and when the time comes we will also practise working-class solidarity. In the meantime we loudly proclaim our membership of the great International Association of Workers, that sublime free-masonry of all the workers of the world.'[35]

THE PETITE BOURGEOISIE

One of the characters in Balzac's *Cousin Pons* (1847) is an Auvergnat, Rémonencq, who came to Paris in 1831 and rented a former café to set up as a scrap-metal dealer. He builds up his business to include porcelain and pictures, so that it becomes more like a museum than a junk shop, and exchanges his rough jacket for a *redingote*, guarding his treasure like a dragon. All that he now requires is a wife, and he fastens on Madame Gibot, the tailor's wife, with her 'virile beauty, vivacity and market acumen', although to win her he must slowly poison her husband.

Balzac's Rémonencq is only a caricatured version of the rise of a trader from rural origins to substantial wealth. While the Limousin produced masons and in some cases developers, the Auvergne produced scrap-metal dealers, coal and wine merchants, and by extension café-owners. The presence of an Auvergnat colony in Paris, concentrated around the Faubourg Saint-Antoine, provided the initial contacts, advice and loans for countrymen coming to Paris to make their fortune. The problem of finding a wife who would also be a business partner was generally solved by marrying a girl from home, using her dowry or a mortgage raised on her prospects of inheriting land to expand the family firm, and putting her at the front of the shop to deal with the clientele. Jean-Joseph Lavaissière, who came to Paris from the Cantal, set himself up as a metal dealer, married a local girl whose father had been killed by highwaymen in 1795 and left her a good fortune, bought a house in Versailles and in 1811 started calling himself a *négociant* (merchant). His sons, Jean-François and Guillaume, did even better, marrying outside the Auvergnat milieu into other trading families, and jointly buying a château at Auteil in the 1830s. Jean-François became a colonel in Louis-Philippe's National Guard while Guillaume was awarded the Legion of Honour and a medal at the 1855 Exhibition.[36]

Naturally the streets were not paved with gold for all Auvergnats. Many Auvergnats who came to Paris did no better than to find work as coachmen, working for firms such as the Compagnie Générale des Voitures, and to marry servants.[37] Moreover many shopkeepers rose from a peasant or working-class origin only to return there after a generation or two. Among shopkeepers in the 4th *arrondissement* of Paris between 1835 and 1845 whose fathers had also had their own businesses, only 38 per cent managed to keep their business going for most of their lives. They were more likely to succeed if their grandfathers had also had their own businesses, less likely if those grandparents had been servants or labourers. Similarly their chances of marrying into a small business family were increased if they came from one themselves.[38] That said, there were some extraordinary success stories highlighting the emergence of the department store. Aristide Boucicaut, whose father was a hatter in the Orne, the area that the clogmaker Pinagot never left, came to Paris in 1835 to work as a salesman in one of the new fashion stores, the Petit Saint-Thomas. With his wife Marguerie Guérin, a laundress, he managed to find 50,000 francs to acquire the Bon Marché, which then had twelve employees and a turnover of 450,000 francs. The year Aristide died, in 1877, the store had 1,788 employees and a turnover of 73 million francs, and in 1887, when Marguerite died, the store reopened in the iron and glass palace built by Gustave Eiffel that still stands.[39] Meanwhile Félix Potin, from a farming family in the Paris basin and destined to become a solicitor, abandoned his studies at sixteen to work for a Paris grocer. He founded his own cut-price grocery business in 1844, moving to Haussmann's new boulevard Sébastopol in 1859, which he supplied with groceries from his own food-processing factory in the suburb of Pantin and with wine from a vineyard he acquired in Tunisia. His final coup during the siege of Paris in 1870, when the population was starving, was to purchase one of the two elephants in the Jardin des Plantes and sell that.

The petite bourgeoisie was composed not only of small employers and shopkeepers but also of black-coated workers who made the best use of their elementary education to return to it as *instituteurs*. Under the Guizot law of 1833 every commune in France was required to found an elementary school and provide a teacher's stipend, while each department was to found an École Normale d'Instituteurs or teacher-training college. Most children of rural families attended school, at least in the winter when there was no work in the fields, until they took their first communion at the age of eleven; in the towns the use of child labour made popular education similarly rudimentary. The expansion of the elementary education system created opportunities for the brightest boys from the popular classes. Among trainees at the École Normale d'Instituteurs of Nîmes between 1842 and 1879, for example, 53 per cent were drawn from peasants' families, 23 per cent from workers' or artisans' families and 7 per cent from shopkeeping.[40] Their mission was without brilliance but it was an honourable one, as

Guizot explained in his 1833 letter to *instituteurs*. 'Each family', he wrote, 'requires you to give it back a decent man and the country a good citizen. The sentiments you must develop are faith in Providence, the sanctity of duty, submission to paternal authority, respect due to the law, the king and the rights of others.'[41]

The reality of the *instituteurs*' career was rarely as exalted. The minimum stipend a commune had to pay was 200 francs per year, and this often became a maximum. Families who sent their children to school were expected to pay school fees, but families deemed indigent by the commune did not have to pay and communes were as generous in this respect as they were mean towards *instituteurs*. In 1842 schoolteachers received under 350 francs per year or a franc a day in four departments, between 350 and 700 francs a year or 2 francs a day in sixty-six departments, and over 700 francs in only six departments, including Paris. This was much less than an industrial worker, and on a par with a labourer or domestic servant.[42] The main advantage of the job was exemption from military service, provided that the *instituteur* committed to teach for ten years. It was also a valuable sedentary job for young men who were crippled or otherwise unfit for physical toil. That said, the mayor often required the teacher to undertake a second job, that of secretary to himself and the commune, while the parish priest might insist that he work as choirmaster, sexton or gravedigger. This may have increased his income a little, but the teacher enjoyed no more than genteel poverty and far from being an apostle of civilization in the benighted countryside he was constantly the butt of mayors, priests, parents and the notables who served on the local education committee. A man of the people, the *instituteur* never escaped from serving the people; to go any higher required a secondary education.

COMPETITION FOR PLACE

What marked out the elite of French society was both education and property. The peasantry had a little property, the working class none, and rarely did they have an education past the elementary level. The petite bourgeoisie of small employers had more property and maybe spent a few years in secondary education, but seldom beyond the age of sixteen. The education that led to the elite was secondary education in lycées (one in each department) and colleges (usually one in each *arrondissement*, without a sixth form), for boys only, expensive except for the minority of scholars, based on the classics, leading to the *baccalauréat* at about the age of eighteen which was the passport to the liberal professions. In the Nord department in 1855, sons of landowners, public officials, liberal professions and industrialists made up 83 per cent of the clientele of the prestigious Lycée of Douai in 1855 and 34 per cent of that of the small nearby college of Saint-Amand, where 17 per cent of pupils were sons of shopkeepers, 18 per cent sons of artisans, 24 per cent sons of peasants and 7 per cent sons of workers.[43] At the fictional college of Sarlande, modelled on that of Alès where he was a *pion* or supervisor in 1857, Alphone Daudet described a cohort of 'fifty-odd rascals, chubby mountain-people of twelve to fourteen years old, sons of enriched *métayers* [share-croppers] whose parents had sent them to college to have them made into petits bourgeois for 120 francs a term'.[44] These would never reach the *baccalauréat* and would doubtless return to follow their fathers. The secondary school population was only 50,000–60,000 between 1810 and 1840, after which it expanded to 150,000 in 1880, but it still accounted for no more than one boy in forty-five in 1842, one in twenty-one in 1876. Higher education existed in the form of law and medical faculties which dispensed professional degrees – about 1,000 law degrees and 400 medical doctorates around 1860 – arts and sciences faculties which simply awarded degrees but offered no teaching, and specialized *grandes écoles* to train the military, administrative, engineering and academic cadres of the state.[45]

Education, however, was never enough to access the elite. Success in a chosen profession or the public service required not only qualification but independent resources, usually acquired by a 'good' marriage, together with connections and patronage. In Balzac's *Père Goriot* (1835) the worldly Vautrin advises the ambitious young law student Rastignac:

If you have no patronage you will rot in a provincial court. At thirty you will be a magistrate on 1,200 francs a year ... at forty you will marry some miller's daughter with about 6,000 *livres* in rent. Thank you. If you have a patron you will become a *procureur du roi* at thirty, with 1,000 *écus* [3,000 *livres*] salary and you will marry the mayor's daughter. If you make one or two political gestures . . . you might be a *procureur général* at forty, and a deputy. But I should inform you that there are only twenty *procureurs généraux* in France and 20,000 competitors for the post.[46]

Balzac's analysis, although dramatized, certainly reflects contemporary anxiety about competition for place. A legal training was not an end in itself; it was a passport to public office which offered security and status. Alexandre Dumas, the son of a republican general who fell out of favour with Napoleon and died when he was four, received an education from the Church and was lucky to enjoy the patronage of General Foy in order to obtain a post in the secretariat of the Duc d'Orléans, the future Louis-Philippe.[47] Georges Haussmann, who had a law degree, saw his father's career in the war administration interrupted in 1815 because of his loyalty to Napoleon, and his career in the prefectoral corps interrupted by the death of his patron, the Duc d'Orléans, Louis-Philippe's son, in 1842. Though he married the daughter of a rich Bordeaux businessman he vegetated for nearly twenty years in subprefectures before landing the prefecture of Bordeaux in 1851 and that of the Seine in 1853.[48] Léon Gambetta, on the other hand, the grandson of a Genoese sailor and son of a grocer of Cahors, educated at the seminary, then at the Lycée of Cahors, went to Paris in 1857 to study law, qualifying in 1861. Though he never married he enjoyed the patronage of leading barrister Adolphe Crémieux, by origin a Sephardic Jew from Avignon, deputy for Chinon in the 1840s and minister of justice in 1848, who gave him his big chance of a political trial, defending Delescluze in 1868.[49] Regime change was a job-creation scheme on a large scale and it was the return of the Republic in 1870 that catapulted Gambetta, along with other republican lawyers, into government office.

For the cream of those qualified in the law the fastest route to a top career in the administration was to become an *auditeur* in the Conseil d'État, which drafted legislation. These *énarques* of their day had the best connections. Among the seventy-eight *auditeurs* in 1840, around 20 per cent were related to peers or deputies and 42 per cent were sons of high civil servants, including magistrates and army officers.⁵⁰ Under the Second Empire the proportion of the administrative elite, defined as *conseillers d'État*, permanent secretaries in government ministries and prefects, who were the sons of high civil servants rose to nearly 60 per cent, the rest drawn from the liberal professions and large landowners.⁵¹ Thus while venal office had been abolished by the Revolution a hereditary administrative elite, recalling the *noblesse de robe*, still existed. A good marriage was also required for career success. High civil servants were more likely to marry into the landowning and business classes, with their superior resources, than the daughters of professionals or civil servants. Charles de Franqueville recalled that the income of his father, a technical civil servant at Soissons, was only 12,000–14,000 francs, but that his marriage in the 1840s brought him 6,500 francs a year from government bonds and 10,000 in land revenues, more than doubling his income, so that in 1859 taxes accounted for 12 per cent of his outgoings but 24 per cent went on the house and 6 per cent on carriages.⁵²

In the armed forces the officer corps before the Revolution was confined to those of noble blood while the Revolution opened it to talent, qualified by survival on the battlefield. Napoleon claimed that there was a marshal's baton in every soldier's knapsack, and promotion from the ranks was always an option, but the École Militaire Spéciale he set up in 1802, which moved to Saint-Cyr in 1808, was costly, exclusive and calculated to attract former *noblesse d'épée* back into his service. Louis XVIII hoped to restore noble privilege in the army in full but the Charter of 1814 ruled that 'the French are equally admissible to civil and military employments'. Such endorsements for meritocracy did not make family background and connection redundant, and in 1825 Legitimist nobles were awarded 24 per cent of sublieutenancies. This proportion fell in 1835 to 7 per cent, with 3 per cent going to families ennobled by the emperor, but increasingly what counted for advancement was a military background. Charles du Barail was unable to compete for Saint-Cyr because his Legitimist noble father briefly refused to serve the July Monarchy before resuming his career in Algeria in 1833, obliging his son to interrupt his secondary education. He joined the army in

Algeria as a common soldier, hoping to join the cavalry but finding it 'overcrowded with sons of noble families' therefore joined a less glamorous arm, the spahis. This complaint was disingenuous from a noble who also described himself as 'scion of a race of soldiers'. Rising through the ranks, he took advantage of the fact that Algeria was the only theatre to see fighting in the July Monarchy, and was promoted captain in 1848 and colonel in 1857.[53]

Saint-Cyr and the École Polytechnique were highly competitive schools which provided a specialist training and fast track to military service. The École Polytechnique did not just train for the military; it gave a mathematical and scientific education that led on to further specialist schools such as the École des Mines and the École des Ponts et Chaussées, training state engineers and technical civil servants. Michel Chevalier, born in Limoges the son of a tax official, graduated from the Polytechnique and in 1829 from the École des Mines and became a mining engineer at Valenciennes. Caught up in the 1830 Revolution, he became involved in the utopian socialist and feminist Saint-Simonian movement alongside Pierre Leroux, whose father was a café-owner and who had studied at the Lycée Charlemagne but was unable to accept an offer from the Polytechnique because of the poverty of his family. Although Chevalier spent eight months in prison in 1832–3 following the government clampdown on the Saint-Simonian movement as immoral, he then secured the patronage of Thiers who sent him on a mission to the United States to study its railway system and in 1840 appointed him professor of political economy at the Collège de France. His marriage to the daughter of a rich cloth merchant of Lodève in 1845 gave him the wherewithal to be elected deputy for the Tarn. Meanwhile Leroux, without the benefit of a Polytechnique training, became a socialist thinker and propagandist. He published a *Revue Sociale* at Boussac in the Limousin from 1845 with moral and financial support from George Sand, who was also interested in radical ideas, and was elected to the National Assembly in 1848. Whereas, however, Chevalier rose to become senator of the Second Empire and negotiated a free-trade treaty with Great Britain in 1860, Leroux opposed the coup d'état of 1851 and went into exile in London and Jersey.[54]

A humble background was usually, but not always, a bar to a

brilliant career, and teaching and the Church were the most open to scholarship boys. Victor Cousin was a clockmaker's son whose education at the Lycée Charlemagne, it is said, was paid for by the mother of a young lycéen whom Cousin had protected from bullying. Winning all the prizes at the Lycée Charlemagne he entered the École Normale Supérieure in 1810, himself becoming a lecturer in philosophy there in 1813 and at the Sorbonne after 1815, although between 1820 and 1828 government repression silenced him. Under the July Monarchy he represented the educational establishment and became Thiers' education minister in 1840. More importantly, he was the patron of all *normaliens*, receiving his 'regiment' twice a year to hear their requests and placing them in colleges in Paris and the provinces, all of whose headmasters he knew. Thus Jules Simon, who came from the College of Vannes in Brittany to the École Normale, was placed by Cousin in the College of Caen in 1836, on a salary of 2,900 francs a year, at a time when a third of secondary school masters were paid 1,200–2,000 francs. In 1840, meanwhile, Simon deputized for Cousin as professor at the École Normale for a princely 6,000 francs.[55]

For the bright boy with no resources at all, the obvious avenue was the seminary. This was the only form of Catholic education permitted by the state before 1850, and supplied a need that was far broader than the training of priests. The father of Ernest Renan was a sea-captain who perished when the boy was five, and his mother's grocery business did not long survive. He attended the College of Tréguier, run by secular priests, and envisaged a career in the priesthood that might have finished as grand vicar of Saint-Brieuc. By the good offices of his elder sister Henriette, who was teaching in Paris, in 1839 he was offered a scholarship to the seminary of Saint-Nicolas-du-Chardonnet in Paris, run by the Abbé Dupanloup, who was reputed to be the illegitimate son of an aristocrat and had just won fame by persuading Talleyrand to repent on his death-bed. Renan went on to the seminary of Saint-Sulpice in 1841 to study theology, took minor orders but then lost his faith, threw himself into the study of oriental languages and eventually was appointed to the chair of Hebrew at the Collège de France. He would never have reached such academic excellence had it not been for the Church's system of education; ironically, he then broke with it, becoming an influential critic on scholarly grounds of much of its teaching.

A DIVIDED ELITE

Balzac's Monsieur Grandet, born in 1749, was a cooper in the small town of Saumur, on the Loire, who married the daughter of a timber merchant and acquired his first vineyards during the Revolution, church lands sold as *biens nationaux*. He bought meadows with the profits of white wine sold to the armies of the Republic and became mayor until, under the Empire, he was seen as too 'red'. In 1806, nevertheless, he inherited more vineyards when his wife's parents died, acquired notable status as the biggest taxpayer in the *arrondissement* and was awarded the Legion of Honour. He made a fortune in the bad harvest of 1811, speculating on other people's hardship, bought a château from a marquis forced to sell up and then converted most of his assets into government stock at 20 per cent. When he died in 1827 he left an estimated 17 million francs to his daughter, Eugénie.[56] Jean-Joachim Goriot, born in 1750, was a pasta-maker in Paris whose master's business fell into his hands in the first riot of the Revolution. Essentially a grain merchant, he made a fortune earlier than Grandet by hoarding supplies when others were starving, while protecting himself from mob vengeance by becoming president of his local section, La Halle-aux-Blés. After his wife died he lived in self-imposed poverty, dedicating his fortune to furthering his daughters. Delphine, who loved money, married a banker of Jewish origin, Baron Nucingen, who himself had made a fortune in 1815 selling Grandet's wine to the Allies, while Anastasie, who had 'aristocratic leanings', married the Comte de Restaud. Having married off his daughters, however, Goriot could only see them in secret; as a 'man of 1793' he was *persona non grata* in the society in which they lived. Moreover, as Delphine discovered, money bought entry into the society of financiers and businessmen centred on the Chaussée d'Antin district of Paris; it did not open the world of the old nobility, which centred on the Faubourg Saint-Germain.[57]

'At the present moment, more than at any other time,' reflected Balzac, 'money rules laws, politics and morals.'[58] His reading of French society in the early nineteenth century as dominated by money is painted in vivid strokes, and regrets a world of honour and piety that has passed away. Yet he points out, with much reason, that even in this material world money could not buy everything and that the social hierarchy was also determined by ancestry and connection. Huge fortunes were indeed made in the early part of the century. International trade was greatly disrupted by war before 1815, then by customs barriers, but governments fighting long wars were desperate both for credit and for supplies, so that anyone with capital or goods stood to make great profits. War also stimulated some industries, such as textiles for uniform and iron for armaments, and after peace broke out this ongoing 'industrial revolution' supplied growing urban markets and under-pinned the communications revolution which reached a high point with the railway boom of the 1840s.

Some individuals and some families were able to exploit these opportunities to the full. To do well, a number of strategies were required: a family strategy to mesh personnel and capital; an economic strategy which balanced specialization in sectors where expertise was available with diversification to spread risk and guard against slump in any particular sector; and a political strategy to ensure friends in high places and legislation which broadly favoured the capitalist interest. What could not be legislated for, however, was acceptance of the new capitalist class into the social elite, so that while the Revolution, as Balzac showed, promoted the interests of a rising bourgeoisie in many ways, its association with the Terror permitted its enemies to use it to shut out those who had benefited firstly from politics and then, when that was no longer possible, from polite society.

The capitalist interest was of course not a bloc. There were, first of all, industrial families of local origin who did not expand their investments or political influence outside their home region. The Dollfus family of Mulhouse, headed by Jean Dollfus, who revolution-ized the cotton industry, sent their sons to learn the trade and establish contacts in Great Britain and Belgium but married into other textile families on either side of the Rhine, such as Mieg, Koechlin and Schlumberger, and were not involved in politics beyond the town, Jean Dollfus being mayor of Mulhouse 1863–9.[59] Augustin Pouyer-Quertier, son of a Rouen entrepreneur who put out cotton to rural weavers, married the daughter of a Rouen merchant with a dowry of 58,000 francs, established mechanized and water-powered cotton mills in the Rouen area and was elected deputy for Seine-Inférieure as an 'official candidate' in 1857. He then used his political influence to defend the cause of protectionism after the Empire's free-trade treaty with Britain in 1860, became Thiers' minister of finance in 1871 and married his daughters Hélène and Marguerite to a marquis and count respectively.[60] Another industrialist cultivated by the Empire to counterbalance the influence of loquacious lawyers was Eugène Schneider. A Lorrainer, he began as manager of a woollen mill in Reims but then became involved in iron. He became manager of the Bazeilles ironworks near Sedan, and married the daughter of its owner who was a baron of the Empire and mayor of Sedan. He went into partnership with his elder brother Adolphe, who had married the daughter of the iron master of Fourchambault, Louis Boigues, bringing a dowry of 100,000 francs and an annual income of 60,000, and with a Parisian cloth manufacturer and banker Alexandre Seillière, in order to buy the ironworks of Le Creusot, way outside his native area, in 1836. Adolphe died in 1845, leaving Eugène as sole boss of what became a company town, building arms, ships and locomotives. Eugène became the first president of the Comité des Forges, representing the iron and steel industry, and co-founder of the Société Générale bank in 1864, director of a number of railway companies, 'official' deputy for Le Creusot in 1852 and president of the Legislative Body in 1867.[61]

The richest individuals and families drew their wealth less from industry than from finance and land. Casimir Périer was the fourth son of an entrepreneur involved in the put-out trade in the Dauphiné, who moved into printed cotton goods and banking, lending to Bonaparte's new government in 1800 and becoming one of the founders and first regents (directors) of the Banque de France. Casimir was one of his ten children, who each inherited 580,000 francs on his death in 1801. He set up the Périer Frères bank with his elder brother Scipion, who died in 1821, investing in insurance, sugar-refining, canal-building, the Anzin coal mines near Valenciennes and above all in real estate, buying up the plaine des Sablons outside Paris and selling it in small lots to build out-of-town villas in what became the suburb of Neuilly. He married Pauline Loyer, the heiress of a Lyon magistrate who had been guillotined in the Terror, was elected deputy of the Seine in 1821 and became prime minister in 1831, dealing harshly with the silkworkers' revolt in Lyon, before dying of cholera in the epidemic of 1832, leaving a fortune of 14 million francs.[62]

Other bankers felt that political influence rather than political power suited them better, but they disagreed about investment strategy and risk. Even in the banking world there were aristocrats who proceeded with caution for the greater good of the family and parvenus ambitious to make money fast who sometimes came to grief. James de Rothschild, one of the six sons of Frankfurt banker Meyer Amschel Rothshild, bought gold smuggled out of Britain during the Napoleonic wars which he then resold in Paris and effectively financed the Restoration by arranging loans to the government which had to pay off a war indemnity of 700 million francs. The Rothschild dynasty made a fortune of 109 million by 1828 using the relatively safe strategy of lending to governments and becoming renowned as the bankers of the Holy Alliance. They invested little in real estate, and avoided industry, which was seen as extremely risky. James was challenged by a new species of investment banker, notably the brothers Émile and Isaac Péreire, from a family of Sephardic Jews of Bordeaux whose father lost his fortune when war disrupted international trade and died while they were boys. Moving to Paris and using contacts in the banking world such as Benedict Fould, they foresaw the possibility of fortunes to be made from the nascent railway industry. They persuaded James de Rothschild, rather against his will, to buy shares in the Paris–Saint-Germain railway of 1837 and in the Chemin de Fer du Nord in 1845. They then left him behind with their experiments in conjuring up capital through the Crédit Mobilier of 1852 and the Crédit Immobilier of 1854. There followed a bonanza of investment in railway companies such as the Compagnie du Midi and the Grand Central, a transatlantic shipping company and dockyards at Saint-Nazaire, the rebuilding of Paris and the development of the seaside resort of Arcachon. Isaac was elected to the Corps Législatif as official candidate for Perpignan in 1863. However, Rothschild squeezed out the Péreires from the Chemin de Fer du Nord in 1855, and kept them out of the Paris–Lyon–Marseille railway and from railway concessions in Austria. Then a downturn in the market which drastically cut back their returns forced them to resign from the direction of the Crédit Mobilier and the Crédit Immobilier in 1867, as the Banque de France stepped in. The visit of Napoleon III to Rothschild's Château de Ferrières in 1862 demonstrated that even among Jewish bankers there were kings and there were knaves.[63]

For Balzac all this would be evidence of the rule of money and the decline of the old nobility, whose fortune was based on land. In fact the impact of the Revolution on the landed nobility was limited in material terms: of about 200,000 nobles 1,158 or 0.6 per cent were executed, while 16,500 or 8 per cent emigrated, although this affected perhaps a quarter of noble families, and half of all noble families (12,500 out of 25,000) lost some land. Many families were able to recover land they had lost, or received some indemnification under a law of Charles X in 1825, despite the incumbrance of debt.[64] Landownership still represented a safe investment when war and economic crisis were disrupting markets and the sale of *biens nationaux* confiscated from the Church increased land's attractiveness for non-noble families. Nobles were invariably at the top of the landowning hierarchy. The port of Bordeaux was dominated by a Protestant merchant, Jacques-Henri Wustemberg, but in 1831 he was only the ninth largest taxpayer in the Gironde department, and overall noble landowners were richer than merchants. The richest man was the Marquis de Lamoignan, a robe noble who had emigrated to the London region before returning to his vast estates near Balye, where he was mayor and *conseiller-général*, and was made a peer in 1832. The Duc de Decazes, something of a parvenu, made a peer by Louis XVIII, but of bourgeois origins and founder of a mining company in the Aveyron as a speculative toy in 1826, came in at eighteenth.[65]

The rivalry at the end of the Ancien Régime between old nobles and *anoblis* was sharpened after 1808 with the creation of the imperial nobility. The imperial nobility was the newest version of a nobility of service, a meritocracy of those who worked for the revolutionary and Napoleonic regimes as soldiers or civil administrators. 'Since the soldier of 1793 has become a general and peer of France,' wrote Pierre de Pelleport, 'I have several times been asked by members of an illustrious military family to trace a link between their ancestors and mine. But there is nothing doing: I date only from myself.'[66] Some of the imperial nobility made vast fortunes. Alexandre Berthier, whose father was an *anobli* of Louis XV, became one of Napoleon's marshals, Prince de Neuchâtel and Prince de Wagram. As grand huntsman and vice-constable in the emperor's household he drew an annual income of 400,000 francs, he spent 250,000 a year acquiring landed estates, and he drew another million francs a year revenue from fiefs allotted to him in Germany and Poland; he married the daughter of the Duke of Bavaria.[67]

The fortunes of the imperial nobility were, however, vulnerable to political change, and they were never accepted as equals by the old Bourbon nobility, 80 per cent of whom refused to serve Napoleon and sulked in the Faubourg Saint-Germain or on their country estates, making up for glamour by cultivating honour and ancient lineage. Most of the imperial nobility rallied to Louis XVIII when he was restored in 1814, but the return of the emperor in 1815 faced them with a terrible dilemma: should they rejoin the man who had made them, though Europe was ranged against him, or should they stay with the legitimate monarchy? Berthier dithered, took refuge in Bavaria and died in mysterious circumstances. Ney rallied to the emperor, fought at Waterloo, was captured and tried when the monarchy was restored, and was then shot. Imperial nobles were systematically purged from the army and administration. The loss of their fiefs and offices in an Empire that was no more destroyed their financial position. They made a come-back under Louis-Philippe, whose regime combined monarchy and the revolutionary tradition. Marshal Soult headed the 1832 ministry which also included Victor de Broglie and Guizot, who had begun their careers under Napoleon. A quarter of prefects and 46 per cent of the Chamber of Peers in 1831 were imperial nobles and the return of Napoleon's body to lie in the Invalides in 1840 was in some sense a tribute to their influence.[68]

This political success of the imperial nobility, however, was not echoed by social success in relationship to the old nobility. Between 1789 and 1830 over 75 per cent of marriages of old noble families which had rejected the blandishments of the Empire were with families of the same caste. Noble families who had been at court before 1789 such as the Duc and Duchesse de Duras increasingly sought out provincial families like the La Rochejacqueleins, whose royalist credentials in the Vendean risings upgraded their noble cachet.[69] A similar hesitancy to admit new blood was evident in the salons of Paris which structured the social life of the capital. Some salons allowed an intermingling of different clienteles, such as that of the Comte d'Haussonville, himself a hybrid who had served in Condé's army and been chamberlain to Napoleon, denounced as a 'remade count' by the old nobility, or that of the Comtesse de Flahaut, the daughter of an English admiral who married one of Napoleon's aide-de-camps and whose guests included Casimir Périer, Laffitte, Walewski and Morny.[70] Others, particularly those of the Faubourg Saint-Germain, presided over by the Duchesse de Duras, the Princesse de la Tremoïlle or the Marquise de Montcalm, who ran the salon of her brother, the Duc de Richelieu, were highly restrictive, and used their social exclusivity deliberately to quash the pretensions of mere wealth or exclude those who had any association with the Revolution or Napoleon. 'Conversation there is often and deliberately literary,' said Alfred de Vigny of the time of his election to the Académie Française in 1845. 'It had a religious tone, rendered a little mystical and elegiac by the memory of the ruins of the Revolution of 1789, the pain of exile, the violence of the Terror and the oppression of the Empire.'[71]

French society in this period was clearly in motion, as individuals took advantage of the opportunities offered by economic change and the expansion of the state, to which was geared a developing system of education. Legally, too, careers were open to the talents and could not be confined to any particular caste or corporation. And yet, in many ways, society was becoming more divided. Agricultural populations became more distinct from industrial workers, and though some peasants acquired more land and joined the rural bourgeoisie, the rural hierarchy remained fairly rigid. Industrial progress advantaged urban, factory-based industry over rural industry, which went into decline. Some workers set themselves up as masters or shopkeepers but many workers became locked in class conflict with employers backed by a state that on the grounds of free enterprise refused to allow trade unions to restore any of the restrictive practices of Ancien Régime corporations. In 1831, 1834 and 1848 the state resorted to violence to quell workers' rebellions. The division in the education system between elementary and secondary both reflected and reinforced the division between elite and masses in French society, and though the scholarship system served to promote some individual talent, to acquire a firm position in the administrative, military or judicial elite generally required the right family background and social connections. Within the French elite the landed class was challenged for influence by financiers and industrialists, and the old nobility was challenged by the new imperial nobility. But parvenus generally succeeded best when they aped the manners of the nobility and social divisions were often intensified by political quarrels that went back to the Revolution and the Empire, and became entrenched in marriage patterns and social intercourse.

4

Religion and Revolution

THE CURÉ D'ARS

In 1818 a new priest arrived in the parish of Ars, 35 kilometres north of Lyon on the inhospitable plateau of Dombes, a treeless region, flecked with stagnant pools, the poor population living in clay huts. Religion had scarcely been practised in the parish since the Revolution. The former curé had broken faith by taking the oath to the Civil Constitution of the Clergy, the church was in a state of disrepair, the church bells had been removed and melted down, and Sunday observance was at a low ebb, with the menfolk spending most of the day in the tavern and young people indulging in dances which frequently subsided into orgies.

The priest who arrived in the parish was no callow youth and today he might be called a late developer. Jean-Marie-Baptiste Vianney was thirty-two, but had been ordained only three years previously, in August 1815. Of peasant origin, his parents had a small 12-hectare farm at Dardilly, just outside the north-west suburbs of Lyon. He had worked on the farm from the age of seven, the Revolution having interrupted his prospects of a regular education. After the 1801 Concordat, which re-established organized religion in France, Vianney attended the vicarage school in the neighbouring village of Écully, where the curé saw him as a prospect, and he was confirmed at the late age of twenty in 1807. In 1809 he was called up to fight in Napoleon's armies, but avoided military service first by falling sick, then by going into hiding and lastly by having his younger brother François go in his stead, in return for signing over the 3,000-franc portion of the inheritance due to him. His brother died on campaign in 1813 while Vianney attended the *petit séminaire* and graduated to the *grand séminaire*, but his grasp of Latin was so weak that he was expelled in 1813 and finished his theological education at the feet of the curé d'Écully. The shortage of priests after the Revolution was so severe that Vianney was duly ordained, served as a curate at Écully for three years, and was then sent out to rechristianize the forgotten parish of Ars.

Vianney was not a learned priest and his sermons were cobbled together from theological cribs. However, he set a powerful example of personal piety, at prayer in the church from 4 a.m., was always available for confession, and visited his parishioners in their homes. He was uncompromising in his campaign to impose religious observance in the parish, clamping down on what he saw as the three evils of Sunday: labour, taverns and dancing. He allied himself with a core group of pious women in the parish, spinsters or mothers of priests, and a number of influential families. He trained a body of young girls, recruited into the guild of the Rosary, who recited the chapelet after vespers on a Sunday evening, and sent two of them, Catherine Lassagne and Benoîte Lardet, to train for a year in a community of nuns in order to open a school for girls in the village, which doubled as an orphanage for girls at risk. He mobilized the support of the chatelaine, Mlle Garnier des Garets, known as Mlle d'Ars, aged sixty-four when he arrived and with perfect Ancien Régime manners. Her brother the Vicomte François, who lived in Paris and was childless, became a major benefactor of the parish, rebuilding the church with a number of side-chapels, confessionals and larger choir, having a new bell-tower and bells made, and providing reliquaries, a tabernacle for the holy sacrament, and a dais and banners to carry in processions.

The influence of Vianney was not confined to his parish. In 1823 he assisted the Carthusians of Lyon who were preaching a mission in nearby Trévoux, gaining a reputation as a great confessor, and later that year led a pilgrimage which brought out two-thirds of his parishioners, travelling by boats drawn by horses along the Saône to the chapel of Notre-Dame de Fourvière, on a hilltop above Lyon, to give thanks for the benefactions of the vicomte. The July Revolution, which was in part an anticlerical revolt against the close alliance of Church and reactionary monarchy, affected Ars as elsewhere. A minority on the municipal council tried to unseat him, appealing to the subprefect against the mayor's banning of dancing on the church square on the festival of the village's patron saint. Vianney replied by keeping the young girls in the church after vespers, doing their rosaries as usual, and sabotaging the ball. Despite his campaign against popular vices, he was prepared to make use of popular religion too, especially saint-worship, in order to further his crusade. When Pauline Jaricot, a silk-merchant's daughter known to him in Écully, returned in 1836 cured of her heart condition from the Naples shrine of St Philomena, he begged her for a relic and placed it in a side-chapel at Ars, dedicated to the saint. Of ninety-four girls he baptized between 1836 and 1855, thirty-nine were christened Philomena. Not only the saint cult but also his personal reputation led to pilgrims and penitents coming from all over the region to be confessed and set on the right course by the curé d'Ars. In 1845 there was an eight-day waiting list for the confessional, even though he might be confessing up to fifteen hours a day, and he remained a curé in the same parish until his death in 1859.[1]

The curé d'Ars was exceptional, a parish priest who was beatified in 1905 and canonized in 1925. And yet he was in many ways representative of the parish clergy who were faced by the challenge of rechristianizing France after the Revolution. France was desperately short of priests after a decade of persecution during which virtually no training or ordination had taken place. In 1809 there were only 31,870 secular priests compared to 60,000 in 1789, of whom 10,613 or a third were over sixty, and in 1814 numbers were down to 24,874.[2] In the diocese of Guéret (Creuse department) in 1820, to take one example, they were either old, born before 1770, aged over fifty, or young, born after 1785, and under thirty-five; there were virtually none in the generation born between 1770 and 1785.[3] Whereas priests in the eighteenth century were overwhelmingly of urban and bourgeois origin, in the nineteenth century they were overwhelmingly rural and of peasant or artisan stock. In the diocese of Rennes in the early nineteenth century 84 per cent of the population were of rural origin and so were 82 per cent of the priests, while between 1803 and 1869 in the diocese of Guéret 42 per cent of priests were sons of peasants, 42 per cent sons of artisans or small traders, and only 16 per cent were bourgeois.[4] The abolition of tithes and the confiscation of church lands made the priesthood a far less attractive career than before the Revolution. Under the Concordat priests to the level of cantonal capital or deanery were paid a stipend by the state of 1,200–1,500 francs, but rural curés were paid only 500 francs by the state, rising to 700 francs in 1816 and 800 francs in 1830, the parish or commune being expected to make it up to a living wage.[5] Only for those of rural or peasant origin did the parish priesthood offer any degree of stability or respect; indeed, as in the case of Vianney, it might provide a solution to the question of too many heirs chasing a farm that was too small to be divided further. Yet the *curé de campagne* could exercise great authority as an intermediary between the parish from which many people rarely moved and the outside world, as a notable alongside the notary and doctor but speaking the language, literally, of the peasants, as an ally of the chatelain but not necessarily 'the château's man', as a figure vested with local authority like the mayor but also a spiritual leader, healer and protector of the parish at time of crisis, such as the cholera epidemic of 1832.[6]

The work of Vianney at Ars mirrored what went on to a greater or lesser extent in a thousand parishes. Everywhere the destruction wrought by the Revolution had to be set right. In the diocese of Angers over 200 churches were built or rebuilt in a diocese of about 360 parishes before 1870, with neo-Gothic and stained glass all the rage.[7] The restoration of church bells, slowly under the Empire, faster after 1830, was of immense significance. Ringing the bells of Notre-Dame on Easter Day 1802 to celebrate the Concordat symbolized for many the end of the Revolution. The bell was at the centre of the parish's religious life, although bell-ringing remained an issue between the government and the parish, which constantly tried to multiply the occasions on which bells could be rung, and trusted in them to ward away thunderstorms, disease and evil spirits.[8] The Restoration period saw a vast movement of purificatory missions, preached by a regular clergy back in harness, inviting penitence for sins committed during the Revolution and a return to the true faith in order to recover God's protection of France, culminating in the raising of huge mission crosses, many of which were knocked down by anticlericals after 1830.[9] For nearly a generation after 1792, however, the apparatus of organized religion in the form of churches, parish priests and popular education had been sorely deficient, so that local populations had fallen back on traditional popular practices, many of which smacked of magic and superstition. While pushing forward the official religious revival, parish priests also had to accommodate the popular rites of their flock, as a means of bringing them back to more orthodox practices. So while they did what they could to eliminate the profanity of drinking and dancing, they blessed candles at Candlemas to guard against storms and take dead souls to heaven, blessed box-tree sprigs on Palm Sunday (preferred to palm leaves) to protect homes and stables from illness, and holy water at Easter to sprinkle on beds and in farmyards, led the Fête-Dieu or Corpus Christi procession across the fields to bless the crops and accompanied popular pilgrimages to local shrines which were said to cure one ailment or another, ensuring that they remained orderly and sober.[10]

PRACTISING AND NON-PRACTISING FRANCE

The raw material of Vianney's parish was not promising, and his achievements were exceptional. That said, what most parish priests and the Catholic hierarchy in general could achieve was very much conditioned by the intensity of religious faith in the locality or region, which varied greatly from one part of France to another. Why this varied so much may be debated. One theory is that growing urbanization and industrialization progressively detached the working classes from organized religion, while the backward and traditional countryside remained more religious. Another is more historical and looks to the impact of events such as the Civil Constitution of the Clergy, the ill-fated Church reforms of 1791, for an explanation. A third is geographical and contrasts religious practice in the outlying areas of France with those in the core. A fourth looks to the coexistence of competing religious communities,

Catholic and Protestant, or Catholic, Protestant and Jewish, where rivalry between faiths may have pushed up religious practice. A final explanation brings in the question of linguistic barriers, suggesting that minority languages may have acted as a dam against anticlericalism and impiety carried by the French language.

A study of the population of Paris, published in 1863, seems to provide evidence for the theory that urbanization and industrialization undermined religious practice.

The immense majority of the Parisian working class is Catholic by baptism [but] Catholic ceremonies are a dead letter for the people. Only women and above all children preserve a few feeble ties between the people and the Church ... People are so anticlerical that the few faithful on whom the Church can rely are the targets of sarcasm as much as the few who oppose democracy. The typical Paris worker is an apprentice freethinker.[11]

This explanation blamed not the growing exploitation in large factories or the atomization of communal life in the large cities but politics: the alliance of the Church with reaction. The Revolution of 1848, according to this account, had provided the Church with a great opportunity to link religion and liberty. Initially the clergy had blessed liberty trees and baptized the principles of liberty, equality and fraternity, but then fear had driven them, once again, into 'the camp of adversaries of the Revolution' and the people and religion were forced apart.[12]

This political interpretation suggests that sociological factors were not the most important when it came to explaining religious practice. Indeed, low religious practice was a phenomenon observed not only in Paris but across the Paris basin and central France, not only in urban areas but in rural ones too. 'In the regions near the capital of the kingdom,' noted the bishop of Chartres in 1842, 'religion is practically abandoned by the menfolk; for many, their first communion is also their last.'[13] When Félix Dupanloup was appointed to the bishopric of Orléans in 1850 he greeted it as a 'terrible cure of souls' with '500 indifferent parishes'. 'Faith is declining visibly in this unfortunate region,' reported his archdeacon of Pithiviers, responsible for the Beauce region, where the rate of Easter communion among women was 12.5 per cent and among men 2 per cent.[14] The central

French area of low religious practice extended as far as the Limousin in the Massif Central. The main factor here was the high rate of priests swearing the oath to the Civil Constitution of the Clergy – 75 per cent in the Creuse, 65 per cent in the Haute Vienne, which may have reflected some attempt by priests and their parishioners to find common ground between religion and Revolution.[15] However this attempt failed, ending up with the persecution of priests and the closure of churches and, unlike at Ars, these populations did not return to the churches when they reopened.

If many rural areas were irreligious, there were many industrial areas where religious practice among the working classes was surprisingly high. When coal mines began to be sunk in the Pas-de-Calais, where only 17 per cent of clergy had taken the oath to the Civil Constitution, local clergy worried that religious life would suffer from women dressing up as men and going down mines alongside them, leading to 'the corruption of girls and boys, infidelity among spouses and a diabolical life in households'. However, miners were overwhelmingly of rural origin and retained the religious practice they brought from their home regions, albeit combined with a certain occupational superstition. Thus they crossed themselves before descending the pit, kept the box-tree sprigs from Palm Sunday in the house, celebrated St Barbe, the patron saint of miners, on 4 December, and took funerals extremely seriously.[16] In the Nord, up against the Belgian frontier, religious practice was high not only in the rural, Flemish-speaking part of the department, but in the huge textile towns of Lille, Roubaix and Tourcoing, while the rural south of the department around Cambrai was much less fervent. This was partly because of the rural, Belgian origin of many textile workers, but also because of the experience of the department during the Revolution. The reorganization of dioceses under the Civil Constitution of the Clergy deprived the bishop of Ypres of his parishes in France, and he protested, anathematizing those who took the oath and continuing to appoint priests to French Flemish parishes. Only 15 per cent of the clergy took the oath in the Nord, and only 5 per cent in the Flemish-speaking *arrondissement* of Hazebrouck, and many non-jurors who exercised their ministry from beyond the frontier returned to France in the wake of the Austrian army in 1792.[17]

The proximity of a frontier beyond which there was a strongly practising region offered a good deal of protection to religious practice. Franche-Comté, which like Flanders had been part of the very Catholic Habsburg Empire before 1678, was divided up into three departments and dioceses by the Civil Constitution. The diocese of Besançon (Doubs department) was particularly fervent in its religious practice, and the upper Doubs a fertile area for the recruitment of priests. Only 29 per cent took the oath to the Civil Constitution and the non-juring bishop of Besançon, Mgr de Durfort, organized his non-jurors from the Catholic canton of Fribourg over the border in Switzerland. When he died in 1792 responsibility for French non-jurors was taken over by the bishop of Lausanne, who was resident in Fribourg, and fifty-nine Franc-Comtois priests were ordained in Fribourg during the revolutionary period. The first bishop appointed under the Concordat, the former constitutional bishop of Rennes, Claude Le Coz, remained in place from 1802 to 1815 but had little authority in his diocese.[18] The non-juring priesthood was ready to jump back into harness and the upper Doubs around Pontarlier, perched high in the Jura, where only 18 per cent of priests took the oath, resumed its role as a nursery for priests.[19] Not for nothing did Montalembert, who was elected deputy of the Doubs in 1849, call it the 'French Tyrol'.

Just north of the Franche-Comté, Alsace-Lorraine offered another example of a region that was far from being dechristianized. The working population of the textile town of Mulhouse, which was mainly Catholic, noted Armand Audiganne in 1860, 'has maintained a religious observance which, if it has little influence on their morality, has a powerful hold on their minds. Each Sunday morning men and women crowd into a church which would have been large enough at the beginning of the century but was now thronged by a thousand Catholics.' This religious fervour, which did not prevent them from being dead drunk on Monday morning, may have owed something to the confessional mix of the town, 40,000 or 73 per cent Catholics, 12,000 or 22 per cent Protestants, and 3,000 or 5 per cent Jews.[20] In Strasbourg the confessional mix was more balanced, with 50 per cent Catholics, 46 per cent Protestants and 3 per cent Jews in 1806, and again religious observance was sharpened by religious rivalry.[21]

Catholics were antagonized by the triumphalism of the Protestant celebration of the 300th anniversary of the Reformation in 1817, while Protestants reacted against the Jesuit mission of 1821 and that of 1825, which ended with a 'gigantic cross' being raised near the cathedral. When mixed marriages took place the Catholic clergy insisted that the children be brought up as Catholics, and at Bouxwiller (Bas-Rhin) in 1833 the priest refused to bury a Catholic doctor who had married a Protestant and allowed his children to be brought up as Protestants. The shortage of churches until after 1850 meant that a 'simultaneum' system operated, with the Catholics using the choir and Lutherans the nave at different times of day, but conflicts often arose. At Gundershofen (Bas-Rhin) in 1842, for example, the Catholics erected a balustrade at the entrance to the choir which the Protestants pulled down. Between 1840 and 1870, however, such rivalry stimulated the building of 200 churches, mostly in a powerful neo-Gothic style, and Alsace sustained its reputation as 'the land of organs' with 600 of them in 1844.[22]

The presence of a Jewish minority which was emancipated at the Revolution and had acquired an economic grip over non-Jews stimulated an anti-Semitism which may be interpreted as a kind of religious fervour. Alsace-Lorraine had 26,000 Jews in 1818, which was 79 per cent of the Jewish population in France.[23] Emancipation allowed them to move from village communities not unlike the Polish *shtetl* into the towns, to move from being pedlars, horse- and cattle-merchants and moneylenders to owning land and taking up trades previously closed to them. However, they were now criticized for remaining middlemen and declining the opportunity to exercise 'useful trades' such as crafts or farming, charging extortionate interest to peasants who borrowed from them to buy *biens nationaux*, while continuing to speak a separate 'Judaeo-Alsatian' language and marrying only those of their own faith.[24] A popular hostility to Jewish usury was reported in January 1806 by the prefect of Bas-Rhin at Strasbourg to Napoleon, as he returned from Austerlitz. Napoleon fumed that he 'could not consider Jews who suck the blood of true Frenchmen to be French themselves', and called both a Jewish assembly of notables and a Sanhedrin of rabbis later in 1806 to incite the Jewish population to reform its practices.[25] While the assembly of notables, dominated by cultivated Portuguese Jews from Bordeaux, was conciliatory, the Sanhedrin refused to budge on usury and endogamous marriage, so Napoleon issued his 'infamous decree' of 17 March 1808 protecting Gentiles in debt to Jews, forcing Jewish traders to register each year with the prefect and subjecting them to military service.[26] Such stringent measures headed off popular anti-Semitism provisionally, but in 1832 and 1848 there were pogroms against Jews in Alsace, their neighbours pillaging their homes and attacking them with forks, sticks and axes.[27] Increasingly Alsatian Jews moved out of the villages to the relative safety of the city, and from Alsace to Paris. Jacob Dreyfus, a pedlar from Rixheim (Haut-Rhin), moved to Mulhouse after the pogrom of 1832, and his son Raphael married a butcher's daughter, became a commission agent seeking clients for Mulhouse manufacturers, and in 1862 set up his own cotton mill. After the annexation of Alsace by Germany in 1871 two of his sons, Jacques and Léon, remained at Mulhouse, now part of the Reich, to look after the business, while two others, Mathieu and Alfred, went to Paris to continue their education.[28]

Another area of mixed confessions, and of sharp religious conflict, though here only between Catholic and Protestant, was the Cévennes hills and the lowlands around Nîmes. Here the Protestant population was Calvinist and had been deprived of civil and political rights and persecuted after the Revocation of the Edict of Nantes in 1685. In the early eighteenth century the Calvinists of the Cévennes had risen in revolt, the so-called Camisard wars, which provided them with a myth of resistance. Banned from office and the professions, Protestants turned to trade and a rich bourgeoisie of silk-merchants and bankers, based on Nîmes, emerged. It was this elite which benefited from the concession of civil and political rights at the Revolution, five of the eight deputies of the Third Estate from the Gard in 1789 being Protestant. An attempt by Catholics to prevent them taking over the municipality of Nîmes led to the four-day slaughter of the *bagarre de Nîmes* in June 1790, when the Protestant National Guard, reinforced by Protestant volunteers from the Cévennes, clashed with Catholic irregulars, after which the Protestants established their ascendancy in the administration of Nîmes and the Gard for most of the revolutionary and Napoleonic period.[29]

Hostility to Protestant emancipation was thus a driving force behind Catholic counter-revolution in the region, based on an alliance of landowning nobles excluded from power and poor peasants and workers who felt exploited by Protestant employers and mobilized in irregular militias, the *miquelets*. Their chance of revenge came after the Hundred Days, when Protestant supremacy crumbled with Napoleonic rule, and Catholic royalists unleashed a White Terror to force their way back into power.[30] While the Restoration favoured the Catholics, the July Revolution brought the Protestants back into power. Now there was less violence but the rivalry was just as intense. Emmanuel d'Alzon, from a Catholic noble family in the Cévennes, one of whose ancestors had died in the Wars of Religion and another fighting the Camisards, was originally destined for a military career and when he became a priest dedicated himself to continuing the struggle against Protestants. He set up a Catholic college in Nîmes, even before it became legal under the Falloux law of 1850, staffed by priests belonging to the Assumptionist order he had founded, his intention being to 'batter the Lycée, and gradually to draw off the whole Catholic population', turning the lycée into a Protestant ghetto.[31] Catholic–Protestant competition ensured a high level of religious commitment on both sides, even in industrial towns which might be expected to be less religious. At Lodève, a town in the Cévennes making woollen cloth for the army, Audiganne noted that 'the Catholic religion reigns alone; its practices are observed with a remarkable fervour,' with hooded workers belonging to societies of penitents presiding over funerals and a 'quite extraordinary' cult of St Fulcran, a former bishop of the town.[32] At La Grand'Combe, a mining town further north in the Cévennes, between 30 and 50 per cent of miners took Easter communion in 1880, so that the bishop of Nîmes, Mgr Besson, himself a native of the very Catholic Doubs, reported that the town was one of the most fervent parishes in his diocese.[33]

The west of France, like much of the Midi, was a bastion of Catholic practice. In Brittany there were no religious minorities, and there was an overwhelming opposition to the Revolution, with 83 per cent of non-jurors in the diocese of Rennes (Ille-et-Vilaine department).[34] The diocese of Saint-Malo straddled the western part of Ille-et-Vilaine and the eastern parts of the Côtes-du-Nord and Morbihan and was a laboratory of Counter-Reformation activity. It was abolished under the Civil Constitution of the Clergy, but left its shadow as the part of Upper Brittany where religious practice and the recruitment of priests were highest.[35] A small number of districts did see some attempt to reconcile Catholicism and Revolution. In the district of Quimper, for example, 53 per cent of priests took the oath to the Civil Constitution. This gave rise to a tension between what has been called 'blue Christianity', accepting the principles of 1789 but trying to christianize them, and 'white Christianity', which opposed the Revolution in the name of Church and king, protected the non-jurors and went as far as *chouan* guerrilla warfare against constitutional priests, revolutionary officials and purchasers of *biens nationaux*.[36]

Although it might be imagined that 'white Christianity' corresponded to the Breton-speaking western half of Brittany and 'blue Christianity' to the French-speaking eastern half, in fact this was far from being the case. In the Morbihan, for example, constitutional priests were concentrated in the Breton-speaking west of the department, while most non-jurors came from the French-speaking east, which had belonged to the pious diocese of Saint-Malo before 1789, and left its imprint with a score of only 10 per cent of juring priests. This may suggest that the historic weight of religious practice was more important than language in determining attitudes to the Civil Constitution and the Revolution.[37] It was not, however, that the Breton-speaking areas were less religious. The Lenten address of the bishop of Quimper, Mgr Graveron, born near Brest, highlighted 'the close ties that exist between a people's language and its beliefs, its customs and its morals, its habits and its virtues', and warned that the erosion of Breton by French was bringing impiety.[38] In fact the whole of Brittany was religious, with a quasi-unanimous attendance of both sexes at mass, although some Bretons were more prepared to compromise with the Revolution than others.[39]

The peculiar intensity of religious life in Brittany may in part be attributed to a symbiosis between official Catholicism and popular religion, the former using the latter to underpin official religion rather than attempting to crush it as 'superstition'. Ernest Renan, brought up in Tréguier, in the Breton-speaking west, a town which nurtured the cult of St Yves, noted that there were between ten and fifteen little chapels in each parish which were 'dedicated to a saint who has never been heard of in the rest of Christendom', for whom masses were said once a year. These cults, he said, were 'merely tolerated by the clergy; if they could, they would suppress them.'[40] New saints were being invented right down to the Revolution. The body of a *chouan* victim of the republican armies, known as Le Bonhomme, buried at Le Theil (Ille-et-Vilaine), was exhumed in 1830 and found to be in a remarkable state of preservation. The burial-place became a site of pilgrimage, and a fountain near by was said to cure fevers. The clergy did not suppress the cult but in 1870 built a chapel close by, dedicated to Our Lady of Beauvais, seeking to channel popular piety into the cult of the Virgin Mary which was developing in the nineteenth century as a way to fuse popular and official religion.[41]

The most spectacular example of a popular cult being transformed into official religion was of course at Lourdes. In the Pyrenees, as in Brittany and elsewhere, trees, fountains and stones were widely invested with religious significance, and local shrines, the objects of local pilgrimage and prayer, were thick on the ground. The apparition of a woman in white to a fourteen-year-old shepherdess, the daughter of a ruined miller, on 11 February 1858 at a grotto outside Lourdes was nothing out of the ordinary, except that it happened on a number of occasions and crowds gathered, 7,000 strong on 4 March, to see her fall into a trance as the vision reappeared. People began to bring gifts and started to build a chapel to the Virgin Mary, much to the confusion of the local authorities, who removed the gifts and tried to close the site in the name of public order. The bishop, Mgr Laurence, might have joined the authorities in their reservations, but he was persuaded by the story that on 24 March the apparition had declared, in the local patois, 'I am the Immaculate Conception.' This echoed a doctrine proclaimed by Pope Pius IX in 1854, to the effect that the Virgin Mary was herself preserved from all trace of original sin when her mother conceived her. In 1861 he therefore bought the grotto from the commune and had a Gothic chapel erected above it, which was proclaimed the Basilica of the Immaculate Conception in 1874, while Bernadette, the shepherdess, was removed as a sick pauper into the care of the Sisters of Nevers, dying in 1878. Thus a spontaneous and popular outpouring was taken over by the Church hierarchy and regularized as part of the Marian revival that was paying increasing dividends in the nineteenth century.[42]

INTELLECTUAL WAR

The battle that was fought between religion and Revolution in the parishes was also fought in the media. It was to be won or lost not only on the ground but in the world of ideas. There was a theory prevalent in conservative circles that the Revolution had been caused not by any fundamental crisis in French society or government but gratuitously, by the inflammatory ideas of *philosophes* of the Enlightenment such as Voltaire and Rousseau, which had taken hold of the educated elite and percolated down, in vulgarized and perverted forms, to the people. If therefore the threat of revolution were to be dissipated, it would ultimately have to be done by winning the battle of ideas. Men of religion who wrestled with these issues nevertheless confronted a fundamental problem. Were the ideas emanating from the Revolution to be rejected lock, stock and barrel, or was there a way of christianizing some of those ideas and modernizing religion in order to combat the modern world more effectively? This was an option that was posed each time a revolution shook France, and each time a new generation wrestled with it. The main stumbling block to this strategy, repeatedly manifested, was that the Catholic hierarchy invariably opposed such accommodation, leaving Catholic thinkers to choose between following the logic of their ideas and remaining within the bosom of the Church.

When Chateaubriand returned to France in 1800 he recalled seeing 'only abandoned churches, whose dead had been thrown out, bell-towers without bells, cemeteries without crosses, statues of saints without heads, stoned in their niches'. He wanted to bring France back to religion, and he also yearned for reconciliation with his mother, who had died in 1798 as a result of her imprisonment during the Terror, while he was in exile. He himself had been seduced by the ideas of the Enlightenment, but his mother had written to him, asking him to return to the religion in which he had been brought up. 'I cried, and I believed,' he declared, and wrote the *Genius of Christianity* both as 'a mausoleum to my mother' and as a beacon for the faithful, seeking a way back to 'God's house'.[43]

The task Chateaubriand set himself was to rescue religion from the sarcasm of the *philosophes*, to demonstrate that it was 'neither barbarous, nor ridiculous, nor the enemy of arts and genius'. He argued that the existence of God was proved by 'the marvels of Nature', and that Christianity had inspired art and literature, poetry and music. Forests were 'the first temples of the Divinity', and Gothic cathedrals were like petrified forests. Without Christianity, he wrote, we would be just like the Romans, corrupt, cruel and servile under tyranny: 'Christianity saved society from total destruction by converting the Barbarians.'[44] Published in 1802, the *Genius of Christianity* became the handbook of the Concordat, used by Bonaparte to reconcile the regime with Rome, and Chateaubriand was rewarded with the post of under-secretary at the French embassy in Rome. Chateaubriand later claimed that when he fell from power Napoleon declared that no other work had done more to undermine him.[45] There was, in fact, little political about it, and the generation that came to maturity in 1815 needed something less rhetorical and mystical, a more doctrinal demolition of the principles of 1789.

Félicité Lamennais, fourteen years younger than Chateaubriand, was the son of a shipowner of Saint-Malo ennobled in 1788. His mother died when he was five and he went to live with his uncle, reading Rousseau and other *philosophes* in the library. Sickly and melancholic, he did not find his vocation until the Hundred Days demonstrated how close France was to succumbing again to Revolution, and may thus be considered one of the generation of 1800. 'It is not without a kind of joy that I feel the corrupted and corrupting world shaking under my feet,' he wrote in July 1815. He decided to dedicate himself to 'the victory of the Church and the triumph of its head'.[46] Ordained in 1816 he published the *Essay on Indifference* the following year. This was a direct attack on the Revolution as a narcissistic impulse by which man, 'adoring himself as man', usurped the sovereignty of God and set himself up as sovereign instead. This sovereign man, guided only by his own reason, treated God as a usurper and destroyed the institutions of the Church. Then, when the king was executed, 'society as a whole perished'. 'There is no society and no order without religion,' he stated, and by religion he meant a law, vested in the Church, which defined the relationship between man and God, subject and sovereign.[47] Lamennais defended the Church against the Revolution, but saw the revolutionary attempt to reform it as merely the last episode of the state's attempts at control that could be traced back to Louis XIV. He was thus an ultramontane rather than a Gallican, believing in a universal Church rather than in a series of state Churches. He opposed state control of the Church, but he also saw that the use by the state of the Church as a source of legitimacy and even as a system of police drove away from it those who might otherwise remain in the fold.

The alliance of Church and state, throne and altar, was never closer than under Charles X. It was manifested in his coronation at Reims and in a spate of laws sponsored by the Villèle government: a sacrilege law which imposed the death penalty for stealing chalices and violating the sacred host, a law making it easier for male religious congregations to re-establish themselves, and bills to tighten press censorship. There was a widespread feeling that these laws were inspired by Jesuits, who were formally banned in France yet pulled the strings of the government.[48] After the fall of Villèle a law of 1828 prohibited Jesuits from teaching either in *petits séminaires* or in the secondary schools that were part of the university, a corporation of teachers founded by Napoleon in 1808 that alone could deliver the *baccalauréat* and degrees. Penalizing Jesuits, however, did not solve the problems of the regime. The Catholic Church was felt to legitimate the old Bourbon monarchy so powerfully that when, on 14 February 1831, mass was said in the Paris church of Saint-Germain L'Auxerrois for the Duc de Berry, the Bourbon heir assassinated in 1820, the Paris mob sacked the church and the archbishop's palace next door.

The July Revolution had a great impact on the thought of Lamennais. It became clear to him that by bolstering reactionary regimes in return for their support the Church would only ever attract the backing of reactionaries and provoke the hostility of the mass of people. In August 1830 he published the prospectus of a new paper,

L'Avenir, the motto of which was 'God and Liberty'. On the one hand, he said, 'sincerely religious people have not embraced the teachings of liberty'; 'on the other hand, ardent friends of liberty are darkly defiant of the religion professed by twenty-five million French people.'[49] Events seemed to justify this new credo of meshing religion and liberty. The Belgian revolt of September 1830 against its forced incorporation into the United Netherlands was undertaken in the name of both Catholicism and freedom. The Polish revolt of November 1830 against Russian tyranny was also under the banners of Catholicism and freedom. It was a message that fired a new generation of Catholics, both clergy and lay, born around 1800. Jean-Baptiste Henri Lacordaire, who began a career as a barrister before ordination in 1827, and was a chaplain at the Collège Royal Henri IV, joined Lamennais at his Breton retreat of La Chesnaie in May 1830 and was involved in the *Avenir* project from the start.[50] Charles Forbes René de Montalembert, the son of an émigré who had married into an old Irish-Scottish Catholic family, the Forbes, visited Ireland in 1830 to study the struggle of O'Connell and the Catholic Association against British tyranny and wrote to Lamennais professing his 'love of Catholicism and liberty. I am only twenty.'[51]

Lamennais, Lacordaire and Montalembert became very close friends, as well as being involved in a common enterprise. When Montalembert lost his father in 1831 he told Lacordaire that Lamennais 'promises to act as my father', while Lacordaire wrote to Montalembert, 'Be always good, tender, pious, and pray for me, please, lest I love you too much.'[52] And yet a rupture was in sight. The Church authorities were hostile to the line of *L'Avenir* and the three went on a pilgrimage to Rome to solicit the support of the pope. They were unable to see him and were on their way home, at Munich, in August 1832, when they received the pope's encyclical, *Mirari vos*, condemning *L'Avenir*. Lacordaire and Montalembert tried to persuade Lamennais to reconsider his doctrines, but he became even more radical, publishing *Les Paroles d'un croyant*, in which he argued that Jesus Christ the carpenter's son was betrayed by 'the scribes and the pharisees, the doctors of the law, Herod and his courtiers, the Roman governor and the priests' princes'. It was up to the people, who had always kept faith with Christ, to build the city of God according to the gospel of liberty, justice and love.[53] This was in turn condemned by Rome in June 1835, and Lacordaire and Montalembert were torn between loyalty to their master and obedience to the Church, which tolerated no heresy. 'I would rather throw myself into the sea with a millstone round my neck', Lacordaire wrote to Montalembert, 'than maintain a centre of hopes, ideas, even of good works, next to the Church.'[54] Montalembert in turn wrote to Lamennais, 'I remained faithful to you, and you know with what zeal and love, as far as the frontiers of Catholicism.'[55]

Lamennais crossed the frontiers of Catholicism and broke with both the Church and his disciples. He cultivated a new circle of friends, and eyebrows were raised in Paris at his collaboration with the writer George Sand, who in 1837 published advice to young women in his paper, *Le Monde*.[56] He rediscovered his Rousseauistic origins with his *Livre du peuple* in 1838 which argued that the people had reclaimed their liberty and sovereignty, but it was now necessary to 'spiritualize man more and more', to balance his rights by an understanding of duty, using the gospel's teachings of justice and love.[57] Lacordaire, on the other hand, stayed in the Church and was sought out as an intellectual leader by young Catholics who wanted to debate the role of the Church but did not want to follow Lamennais into heresy. In 1833 Montalembert introduced him to Madame Swetchine, a Russian who had left St Petersburg after converting to Catholicism in 1815 and who presided over the most Catholic salon in Paris. In 1835 she secured the consent of the archbishop of Paris both for a private chapel in her house and for permission for Lacordaire to deliver a series of Lenten sermons in Notre-Dame. This was the society event of its day, attended by 6,000 people, including Chateaubriand, Berryer, Montalembert, Tocqueville, Lamartine and Victor Hugo.[58] In 1838 Lacordaire went even further on his route to orthodoxy. He went to Rome to train as a Dominican friar, took the habit in 1839, and returned to work for the liberty of religious congregations such as the Dominicans to re-establish themselves in France.[59]

Montalembert, meanwhile, from his power-base in the Chamber of Peers, opened a campaign in 1843 for *la liberté de l'enseignement*, the right of Catholics to set up their own colleges independent of the university. Although many of the teaching staff before 1830 were priests, after 1830 the university was heavily laicized and run by a lay clerisy. Montalembert argued that this monopoly violated the principle of liberty proclaimed by the Charter of 1830 and in his publicity campaign he was assisted by an up-and-coming young journalist of humble origins, a cooper's son from near Orléans, Louis Veuillot. A fervent Catholic since meeting the pope in 1838, Veuillot was from 1844 editor of *L'Univers*, a paper founded by Montalembert.[60] This crusade, however, was vigorously opposed by two professors of the Collège de France, of the same 1800 generation: Jules Michelet, professor of history, and Edgar Quinet, professor of foreign languages and literature. Montalembert had in fact tried to involve Michelet in *L'Avenir*, and introduced him to Lamennais in 1831, but since then their ways had parted. In a hugely popular lecture series in 1843 Michelet and Quinet argued that the request for freedom to teach was a trick to allow back the Jesuits, who would soon control all Catholic colleges. The Jesuits, they averred, 'claimed liberty to kill liberty', were the sworn enemies of free thought and intellectual life, were fundamentally opposed to 'the spirit of the French Revolution', and were defenders of divine-right monarchy and, indeed, of 'counter-revolution'.[61]

As the 1830 Revolution had posed the question of whether Catholicism could ally with liberty, so the 1848 Revolution posed that of the alliance of Catholicism and democracy. Initially, the signs were good. Witnessing a liberty tree being blessed by a priest on the Montagne Sainte-Geneviève, Quinet reflected that while the Revolution of 1789 'thought it could save the world by its own spiritual energy', that of 1848 'believed that it could save the world only with the support of the priest'.[62] Lamennais, now close to Michelet, whose book *Le Peuple* in 1846 echoed his own *Livre du peuple*, brought out a paper called *Le Peuple Constituant* which proclaimed 'the French and European masses' deep love of and attachment to an ideal republic, which is synonymous with justice and fraternity'. Lamennais was elected to the National Assembly for Paris on 23 April, with 104,000 votes.[63] Frédéric Ozanam, who as a student in Paris in 1833 helped form the Society of Saint-Vincent de Paul to spiritualize the elite of society through working with the poor, and was now professor of foreign literature at the Sorbonne, joined forces with Abbé Henri Maret, professor of theology at the Sorbonne, and won over an initially reluctant Lacordaire to launch their new paper, *L'Ère Nouvelle*. Their argument was that democracy was 'the work of God', that equality and fraternity were implicit in the gospel's teachings of justice and love, but that democracy and the Republic would have to be Christianized if they were not to go down the same road as the First Republic to the September massacres and Terror of 1793.[64] Ozanam failed to get elected in his home city of Lyon, but Lacordaire was elected in Marseille, one of twenty priests and three bishops to be elected to the National Assembly, and took his place there dressed in his white Dominican robes. Montalembert, also elected, was no part of the new project. He was hostile to democracy which, he thought, would lead only to catastrophe, and became an apologist for the monarchy and aristocracy.

Perhaps Montalembert was right. The project of reconciling democracy and Christianity was dealt a series of blows. When the Assembly was invaded by the Paris mob on 15 May 1848 Lacordaire was so upset that he withdrew from active involvement in the Assembly and in *L'Ère Nouvelle*. During the June Days Ozanam found himself in the National Guard but helped to persuade the archbishop of Paris, Mgr Affre, to go with a white flag to the barricades and negotiate a ceasefire. Unfortunately the archbishop was shot and died the next day, and the workers' uprising was put down by General Cavaignac and the National Guard with great cruelty. 'It is not blood that expiates blood,' Lamennais cried out impotently on 30 June, 'but forgiveness, love.' He attacked the 'butchery' by the military and the imprisonment of 14,000 workers, after which his paper was banned.[65] Ozanam grappled with the reasons for class war, arguing that the materialism of the bourgeoisie that had exploited and impoverished the working classes was driving them to an atheistic socialism. 'The working class will only accept the hopes and consolations of religion', he stated, 'if religion is full of concern for its misery and just towards its legitimate aspirations.'[66] Montalembert, for his part, argued that his former colleagues were entirely wrong to argue that 'Christianity is democracy.' He had fought for twenty years against the doctrine that Christianity meant the Bourbon monarchy, and 'I would fight for another twenty years, if God gives them to me, against this new proposition.'[67] He duly threw himself into the *parti de l'ordre*, which campaigned for the election of Louis-Napoleon Bonaparte as president of the Republic on 10 December 1848.

The alliance of Church and state was now not between Church and monarchy but between Church and Republic, under Louis-Napoleon Bonaparte. It was consecrated by the appointment as education minister of the Comte de Falloux, whose law of 1850 enshrined the *liberté de l'enseignement* for which Montalembert and Veuillot had crusaded, and by the 1849 expedition of French troops to expel republicans from Rome and restore the pope to the Holy City. This recovery of state power by Catholics, however, provoked an equal and opposite reaction from republicans who firmly believed that the Republic should be neutral in matters of religion, not the secular arm of the Catholic Church. They reverted to the argument that Catholicism and liberty were irreconcilable. Victor Hugo opposed French support for the pope in Rome on the grounds that the Papal States were a medieval and barbaric theocracy which had brought back the Inquisition, and denounced the 'clerical party' behind the Falloux law as having 'a history that is written in the annals of human progress, but on the reverse side'.[68] Michelet was at the time writing the passage of his *History of France* that chronicled the attempt by Catholicism and royalism in the Vendée to stab the Revolution in the back.[69] Quinet concluded that Catholicism and liberty were indeed irreconcilable, and set a new agenda to separate Church and state, with the state no longer paying the stipends of bishops and priests, and the separation of Church and school, with religious instruction no longer given there.[70]

Montalembert supported Louis-Napoleon's coup of 1852 which 'routed all the revolutionaries, all the socialists, all the bandits', but soon realized that the Empire was not a friend of liberty in the political sense and refused the offer of a seat in the Senate.[71] In 1859–60, like all Catholics, he was shocked by the support given by the Empire to Italian unification under the leadership of Piedmont, which took place at the expense of the Austrians, the Bourbons of Naples and the Papal States. His ideal, he told Piedmont's first minister, Cavour, was 'a free Church in a free state', which included the independence of the pope himself, based on the Temporal Power, but what he witnessed was 'the Church despoiled in a spoliating state'.[72] Others, such as Louis Veuillot, were even more pronounced in their commitment to the cause of the Papacy. In 1864 Pope Pius IX published the *Syllabus of Errors*, which declared that a whole confection of modern ideas, from control of the Church by the state to liberalism, socialism and nationalism, had led to the disaster in which the universal Church now found itself. There could now be no negotiation between the Church and modern ideas, which were roundly anathematized. Catholics such as Montalembert, who had defended a compromise between Catholics and liberty, were left swinging, while the likes of Veuillot, who had defended orthodoxy against error and held that 'God is the unique truth and the Catholic Church is the unique Church of God', were vindicated.[73]

Lamennais had died in 1854, Ozanam in 1853, but there was now no room for Catholics who argued that Catholicism endorsed democracy. Democracy had led to civil war, then to authoritarian empire. A new generation of republican opponents of the authoritarian Empire, born around 1830, understood that it was not enough to found democracy, but that universal suffrage had to be educated in order to perpetuate the Republic for more than the four years it had lasted after 1848. Rights would have to be balanced by duties in order to ensure a cohesive society and avoid another lapse into violence, but those duties could not be sanctioned by the Church, which had declared itself the enemy of modern ideas. The influence of the Church had to be cut back in state and society, and citizens would have to be educated in a manner fit to underpin a free, equal, fraternal society.

One approach was to separate Christianity from the Catholic Church, to take the example and teachings of Jesus Christ, leaving behind the paraphernalia of magic, mystery and authority. Ernest Renan, who left the Church in 1845 and was appointed professor of Hebrew at the Collège de France in 1861, saw his first lecture course suspended because he denied the divinity of Christ.[74] The lectures were a foretaste of his *Life of Jesus*, published in 1863, and which sold 50,000 copies in French in the first six months. This was not a celebration of the son of God but a biography of the historical Jesus, who came 'from the ranks of the people', inspired a millenarian sect like many others, was 'in some senses an anarchist', had no visions, performed no miracles and was not resurrected but was a spiritual genius who preached that 'the kingdom of God is within you'. 'Jesus planted religion in humanity,' concluded Renan, 'as Socrates planted philosophy and Aristotle science.'[75]

Another approach was to extract from all the great world religions, setting aside different doctrines, the kernel of morality that they all taught. Ferdinand Buisson, a Protestant who parted from the fundamentalist wing of his Church, was a disciple of Quinet, also a Protestant, whom he visited in his Swiss exile and who sponsored him for the post of professor of philosophy at the Academy of Neuchâtel. In 1869 he published a *Manifesto of Christian Liberalism* in which he argued that it was 'a right and a duty to free our piety and moral activity from belief, which is as enervating as it is treacherous, from divine intervention . . . and to secularize religion. We take root in the whole human tradition, without chaining ourselves to the letter of a particular past, be it Jewish, Catholic or Protestant.'[76] This was a moral core that could be used in the schools, separated from the Church, of which Quinet dreamed.

The idea of a residual morality taught by all the great religions was entertained by many freemasons. Jean Macé, a republican teacher who had to go into hiding after the failed Montagnard rising of 13 June 1849 and could not teach in the state sector because he refused to swear an oath to the Empire, took a job in a girls' boarding school in Alsace and promoted the cause of adult education through local libraries. In 1867 he founded the Ligue de l'Enseignement, and used the network of masonic lodges to propagate branches across the country. The task was to educate the people for democracy, a democracy that had been hijacked by the Empire but which at a future date would sustain the Republic. This would require free, compulsory elementary education and would have to be underpinned by a morality that owed nothing to organized religion. In February 1870 Macé described the philosophy of the Ligue as the same as that practised by freemasonry. At the core of all religions was 'a law of voluntary sacrifice to the ideas of human justice and fraternity', 'the fulfilment of a universal duty of love and justice'.[77] This philosophy fed through into the programme of free, compulsory and lay elementary education that was implemented by the Republic in 1881–2 in the hope that this time the Republic would endure.

Two views of the Revolution, as hope and as tragedy.

The Fête de la Fédération of 14 July 1790 reveals a nation united in liberty . . .

. . . while in this hostile cartoon Robespierre is shown executing the executioner after the last citizen has been guillotined.

The revolutionary generation. Clockwise from the top: Madame de Staël, defender of liberty; counter-revolutionary François-René de Chateaubriand; the Marquis de Lafayette, hero of the American and French Revolutions; and ex-bishop Talleyrand, the great survivor of regime change.

Paris old and new: grim alleys imagined by Gustave Doré, and the wide boulevards built by Baron Haussmann, with the new Opéra in the background.

The Romantic generation. Clockwise from the top: liberal politician Adolphe Thiers; painter Eugène Delacroix; writer and prophet Victor Hugo; and Félicité de Lamennais, who attempted to reconcile the Catholic Church with liberty and democracy.

The curé d'Ars, a country priest who worked to restore religious life after the destructiveness of the Revolution, and a peasant family of the kind which bred generations of priests, here from the Auvergne.

Two women with public profiles: Delphine de Girardin, in a painting by Hersent, who declared that 'the first duty of a woman is to be beautiful', and George Sand, the power behind Ledru-Rollin, minister of the interior in 1848.

Private and public society: the salon of Marie d'Agoult, where select writers and politicians networked, and a much more diverse theatre audience that was never shy to voice its opinions.

The Realist generation. Clockwise from the top: scholar and thinker Ernest Renan; novelist Gustave Flaubert; republican politician Léon Gambetta; and revolutionary Louise Michel.

5

'Le Malheur d'être femme'

MARRIAGE AND LOVE

In April 1790 Delphine d'Albémar, recently widowed at twenty-one by the death of a man forty-three years older than she and come into a considerable inheritance, wrote to a poorer cousin, Mathilde de Vernon, to say that she would be delighted to share half her fortune in order to set Mathilde up with the dowry that was necessary to make a noble marriage. Mathilde accepted, asking that the gift remain a secret, and then took it upon herself to criticize Delphine for embarking on a 'wrong path', asking:

Do you think a man would be in a hurry to marry someone who sees everything according to her own ideas, applies her own ideas to her conduct and often scorns received notions? Men who are freest of those truths commonly called prejudices do not wish their wives to be free of any bond. I think it so essential for a woman to pay every respect to opinion that I would advise her in no way to flout it, whether it amounts to superstition (as you would say) or social convention, however puerile it may be.

Delphine replied blithely,

I come into society with a good and true character, wit, youth and fortune: why would these gifts of Providence not make me happy? Why should I torment myself with opinions that are not mine or proprieties I do not know? Morality and religion dictated by the heart have sustained men who have had to follow a path much more difficult than my own: these guides will suffice.

Whether the obedience of a pious young woman to social opinion or that of an independent young woman to the voice of conscience was preferable soon became apparent when they fell in love with the same man, Léonce de Mondoville, who did not defy opinion as men were allowed to do but remained obedient to the aristocratic code of honour. Seeing them both at a soirée he thought that Mathilde sang well but without expression, while Delphine's passionate dancing drew applause from the whole room. He married Mathilde, because that is what his family wanted, and tried to make Delphine his mistress, because the defence of his own honour did not extend to preserving hers.

Delphine's course was always to do what was right in her own eyes and to be loyal to her friends, whatever society thought. She rejected divorce as an option to win back Léonce, not because of his Catholic scruples, but because she would be sacrificing Mathilde's happiness to her own. Soon afterwards Delphine was raped and felt that the only course open to her was to flee the world. She became a nun in an enclosed convent in Switzerland, the superior of which was Léonce's aunt. After Mathilde died in childbirth, however, Delphine decided to break her religious vows, which the Revolution now allowed in France, and met Léonce in Germany. Instead of being delighted finally to be with Delphine, Léonce's sense of honour dictated that he could never marry a woman who had broken her sacred vows, and he went off to join the émigré armies fighting the revolutionaries. Captured at Verdun he was tried and sentenced to death. Delphine visited him in prison, tried to persuade the authorities to spare him, and then took poison. She accompanied Léonce to the plain where he was to be shot, expiring just before he did.

This story was not in fact true but the plot of a novel, *Delphine*, published in 1802 by Germaine de Staël. She was the daughter of the Swiss banker and finance minister to the French crown, Jacques Necker, was hugely privileged in matters of family and wealth, and yet never found happiness in marriage. Originally destined to wed the younger Pitt, she in fact married, in 1786 at the age of nineteen, the Swedish ambassador to the French court, Baron de Staël-Holstein, seventeen years older than she. The love of her life was Louis de Narbonne, said to be an illegitimate son of Louis XV and briefly foreign minister in 1791 before emigrating. She bore him two children, Auguste and Albert. In addition she had a close friendship with Talleyrand and another child, Albertine, by Benjamin Constant, a relationship of the head more than the heart. She separated from her husband in 1800 – he died two years later – and inherited her father's fortune when he died in 1804.[1]

The publication of *Delphine* was remarked as much by English visitors who swarmed to France after an absence of ten years following the Peace of Amiens as by the French themselves. Maria Edgeworth reported that it was originally to have been called 'Le Malheur d'être femme', but that this title had just been snatched up by the French translation of Mary Wollstonecraft's *The Wrongs of Woman*. 'It is cried down universally,' she told her brother, no doubt because it exposed the tyranny of opinion to which women were subjected.[2] One of the critics, Joseph Fiévée, a former royalist and secret adviser to Napoleon, could not tolerate Delphine's commitment to following her own judgement, rather than that of society. She 'speaks of love like a Bacchante, of God like a Quaker, of death like a grenadier, of morality like a Sophist'. For him Mathilde was 'the only person who behaved well in all circumstances; she is the woman whom every man aware of the duties of marriage would desire for his own.'[3] It was an attack not only on a certain image of a liberated woman, whose attempts to find love according to her conscience led ultimately to her death, but also on the female writer who dared to put such subversive literature before the public.

Love and marriage were briefly reconciled in the revolutionary period. Divorce by mutual consent or for incompatibility was introduced by a law of 20 September 1792, and the divorce rate shot up, with 65–75 per cent of divorces in both town and country being requested by women. Control of family property by wives as well as husbands was allowed for by the Convention, and a law of 2 November 1793 declared 'there are no more bastards' in respect of inheriting family property, opening the way to paternity suits being filed by abandoned mothers or natural offspring.[4] A conservative reaction set in, however, soon after Thermidor, as much in public opinion as from the authorities, as the family unit and family property under patriarchal control was felt to be the basis of a much needed stable social order.[5] Several versions of a Civil Code were drafted before that finally endorsed by Napoleon Bonaparte on 21 March 1804. Its article 213 announced, 'The husband owes his wife protection, the wife owes her husband obedience.' The Code retained divorce, but mutual consent no longer sufficed; it was now a sanction for defined transgressions, namely criminal conviction, cruelty, and adultery – by the wife, counting against the husband only if he kept his mistress in the family home. The control of family property by husbands alone was restored and Bonaparte announced, 'society has no interest in recognizing bastards,' who once again were prevented from laying claim to the family inheritance. Divorce, however, did not outlast the Empire: the royalist Chambre Introuvable passed a law of 8 May 1816 which provided only for legal separation, allowing spouses to live apart and property to be divided, but prohibiting remarriage.[6]

This restrictive legislation did little more than reflect prevailing opinion among the families of the social elite. Family alliances and the accumulation of patrimonies from which an independent income could be drawn came before any notion of romantic love. A man could not marry until he had established himself in a situation or inherited property. For a young woman to make a 'good' marriage with someone of sufficient standing she required firstly virginity, which was ensured by a closely supervised and pious convent education, and secondly a dowry from her own family large enough to suggest equivalent wealth. It was thus not uncommon for women under twenty to marry men over forty. Once married, a woman was regarded as subordinate to the family, her sole duty being to see to its welfare. Finding happiness in love or fulfilment or recognition in a career were simply not considerations. While a married man might pursue relationships outside marriage with impunity, such behaviour on the part of a married woman brought dishonour and even catastrophe. And yet the system which married off teenage virgins to much older men for dynastic reasons was, as Balzac observed in his 1829 treatise, The Physiology of Marriage, a time-bomb waiting to explode. Young wives married to ugly old men characterized essentially by 'nullity' would be laid siege to by at least three highly sexed bachelors who had not yet established a situation for themselves that would permit them to marry and thus had to choose between frequenting prostitutes and adultery. Balzac postulated that a woman subjected to an arranged marriage would suffer a build-up of unhappiness such that thirty was the optimum age at which she would take a young lover, cuckolding her old husband.[7] Unsurprisingly, his novel *La Femme de trente ans*, serialized in the *Revue de Paris* in 1832, explored precisely this predicament.

How French women in fact charted a course for themselves can be examined through the lives of three women born in the years 1804 and 1805, Delphine Gay, Marie d'Agoult and George Sand. These were drawn from the noble or upper bourgeois elite and were untypical in that they all had a public profile, but their experiences and reflections upon them shed a great deal of light on the predicament of women from their class in the early nineteenth century.[8] Delphine Gay was a young and talented poet to whom Madame de Staël was said to have passed her quill pen as she lay on her deathbed in 1817. Her mother, Sophie Gay, was married in 1791 at the age of fifteen to a banker twenty years older than she, ran a salon in the Chaussée d'Antin under the Directory, and fell in love with a soldier who had returned from the Egyptian expedition, Sigismond Gay, by whom she had a daughter before she divorced and married him in 1803. Moved by Madame de Staël's *Delphine*, which she defended in print, she named the new daughter she bore Sigismond in 1804 after the heroine. Sigismond became an imperial functionary, appointed receiver-general at Aix-la-Chapelle, but his wife's mordant wit upset the authorities and he lost his office in 1811, reverting to banking. Sophie published novels herself and launched Delphine in the Faubourg Saint-Germain as a young writer. Her reputation, however, was initially made by her beauty rather than her pen. Lamartine recalled seeing her, aged eighteen, the year of her father's death, at Terni in Umbria, leaning on a parapet and watching the waterfalls. 'A painter', he wrote, 'could not have chosen an attitude, expression or day that better matched her grandiose beauty.'[9] That painting was in fact executed by Louis Hersent, and became the pose that was her trademark. Thus Théophile Gautier said of the first night of *Hernani* in February 1830, 'When she entered her box and leaned over to see the crowd, her beauty – *bellezza folgorante* – momentarily calmed the tumult and provoked a triple round of applause. The beautiful girl was wearing the blue scarf of the Hersent portrait and, with her elbow resting on the edge of the balcony, she involuntarily reproduced the famous pose.'[10]

Sophie's ambitions for her daughter also included marriage and Delphine was courted by an habitué of her mother's salon, Émile de Girardin, the illegitimate son of an imperial general made doubly ambitious by his sense of inferiority. He fought in the courts to secure the right to use his father's name, de Girardin, and with loaded pistols to defend his honour against slurs in the press. In 1836 he launched *La Presse*, a popular newspaper which attracted a new clientele by means of the serialized novel or *feuilleton*. Delphine's great coup was to win over Balzac, whose *La Vieille Fille* was soon serialized in *La Presse*. Her marriage to Émile was not happy personally, although she did make it work for her professionally. Émile soon went back to a childhood sweetheart, an illegitimate daughter of the banker Ouvrard, with whom he had been brought up in the same foster-home, while Delphine had an affair with a young dandy addicted to gambling, who subsequently committed suicide.

In the winter of 1826 Delphine was introduced to Marie d'Agoult in the Faubourg Saint-Germain; Delphine excelled at poetry, Marie at the piano. Marie's origins were fully aristocratic, as the daughter of a royalist émigré, Alexandre de Flavigny, who returned to France with his German wife in 1809, settled in Touraine, and died in a hunting accident when she was not yet fourteen, in 1819. Marie was sent to a convent school, married off in 1827, at the age of twenty-one, to Charles-Louis-Constance d'Agoult, first equerry to the Duchesse d'Angoulême, daughter of Louis XVI, and presented to Charles X. She later said of the arranged marriage:

for a young lady of the nobility there could be no question, in the period I am speaking about, that she might listen to her heart for a single minute when it came to choosing the husband to whom she was to entrust her entire destiny. Only what was called the marriage 'of convenience' was admitted in principle. Birth, fortune, situation, alliances, 'expectations' – that is to say the presumed inheritance, more or less imminent, depending on the age of the parents and grandparents – those were the 'conveniences' between which it was permitted to hesitate and choose.

After the marriage, she continued, the husband disappeared as quickly as possible from the home and savoured society on his own. Society hostesses did not like to receive husbands with their wives – 'it was said to freeze conversation. Wit, the desire to please, flirtatiousness, verve and spicy provocation', she observed, 'were killed off by the insipid commerce of conjugal habit.'[11]

Marie d'Agoult founded her own literary salon, and frequented the world of Romantic musicians where she found greater inspiration. In 1832 she met Franz Liszt, six years younger than she, and left her husband. For the sake of discretion she travelled abroad with Liszt to Switzerland in the summer of 1835, and bore him a daughter, Blandine. Two years later, after a visit to Italy, she had a second child by him, Cosima, then a son, Daniel. In 1835 Liszt introduced Marie d'Agoult to George Sand, with whom he had had a brief affair. George Sand's background was more mixed than Marie's: her father, Maurice Dupin, was Murat's aide-de-camp in Spain in 1808 and died in a riding accident that year, when she was only four; her mother was the daughter of a billiard-hall proprietor and canary-seller in Paris and had herself been a prostitute. Aurore Dupin, as she was then, was brought up by her father's authoritarian mother, Marie-Aurore Dupin de Francueil, herself the illegitimate daughter of Louis XV's military commander, Marshal de Saxe. Aurore was sent off to a convent school, but out of school on her grandmother's estate at Nohant in Berry she enjoyed horse-riding, for practicality in men's clothes. After her grandmother died in 1821 Aurore returned to her mother in Paris, but soon found an escape by marrying a rather boorish sublieutenant, Casimir Dudevant, who promptly resigned his commission to live off her inheritance of 500,000 francs, which he controlled under French law, permitting her an allowance of 3,000 francs per year.[12]

Aurore had an affair in 1830 with a young novelist, Georges Sandeau, left her husband, and began a series of relationships which ran the gamut of Romantics of both sexes in Paris: Marie Dorval, the mistress of Alfred de Vigny, Prosper Mérimée, Alfred de Musset, six years younger than she, with whom she went to Italy, and the republican lawyer Michel de Bourges who secured her legal separation from her husband in 1836. She idealized her father and wrote that 'had I been a boy and lived twenty-five years earlier, I know and sense that I would have acted and felt in all things like my father'.[13] From 1831, to secure her financial independence, she worked on *Le Figaro* – the only woman on the staff – and dressed as a man in a greatcoat, in order to move freely around Paris and not least in order to sit in the stalls at the theatre (women were confined to the boxes). Publishing her first novel, *Indiana*, which related the loves and dreams of a Creole woman unhappily married to a Napoleonic officer, in 1832, she abbreviated the name of her first lover as her pen-name, George Sand.

George Sand and Marie d'Agoult were both fascinated by and rivalrous with each other. Marie d'Agoult envied George Sand her literary success, while George Sand was jealous of Marie's pure aristocratic pedigree. 'I am burning to challenge you for literary glory,' wrote Marie. George replied, 'For me, at present, you are the ideal of the fairy-tale princess, artistic, loving, gentle in manners, speech and movement, like kings' daughters in epic times'; her only criticism was that she was 'devilishly too intelligent'.[14] After her separation had been finalized, George Sand invited Marie and Liszt to spend the summer of 1837 with her at Nohant. The two women went out for early-morning rides, savouring nature, and conversed in the evening. Yet the rivalries were too powerful. George Sand found Marie cold, Marie found George like a spoiled child, and indiscriminate in her affections. They confided their regrets to friends in ways that got back to the other – George's portrait of the superior, frigid Marie found its way into Balzac's characterization of Béatrix in his 1839 novel of that name. Meanwhile Marie was convinced that George was trying to rekindle her relationship with Liszt, and may well have done so before she found her own enduring Romantic hero in Frédéric Chopin, likewise six years younger than she, with whom she began a relationship in 1838. What might have been a powerful friendship between two exceptional women became a silent hatred that lasted from 1838 for well over a decade. In 1847 George Sand broke up with Chopin and in many ways her most fulfilling relationship was the quizzical, ironic, platonic one she sustained with Gustave Flaubert. Having met at Magny's, the Paris restaurant where the literary and artistic elite gathered in the 1860s, they embarked on a long playful correspondence in which he would address her in the masculine as 'cher maître' or even 'cher bon maître adoré', while she would sign off 'Ton vieux troubadour'.[15]

If marriage was so closely defined socially and unlikely to lead to personal happiness, one option was to remain unmarried. The proportion of women at fifty who had not married rose from 12 per cent of those born in 1821–5 to 14 per cent of those born in 1836–40.[16] Of course this might condemn women to a life of poverty, while doing nothing for their happiness. Spinsterhood was said to predispose to madness in the nineteenth century and half the patients confined in Paris's Salpêtrière hospital as mad in 1838–48 were unmarried.[17] One solution which combined spinsterhood with integration into a community and a degree of social support was, as Madame de Staël's Delphine discovered, to become a nun. Instead of regarding spinsterhood as a social stigma, taking the veil consecrated virginity as the highest state woman could achieve. Of every hundred women who did not marry in the 1850s, twelve became nuns. Being a nun, however, was different after the Revolution, which had dissolved religious orders and prohibited perpetual vows as a violation of natural liberty. Cloistered communities as experienced by Delphine and before her by Simone Simonin, Diderot's fictitious *Religieuse*, who was deprived of her dowry and confined to a convent because she was illegitimate, were a thing of the past. The new congregations that sprang up like mushrooms – six per year between 1820 and 1860 – were unenclosed and dedicated to the service of the community, either by nursing or by teaching. They were overwhelmingly women's congregations – only one male congregation a year was founded in 1810–60, for male orders like the Jesuits were seen as a political threat and the Church as reconstituted by Napoleon was that of the secular clergy. Lastly, rather than a way of removing unwanted upper-class girls from sight the female congregations were highly democratic, with 22 per cent of their founders of noble origin in the early nineteenth century, 43 per cent bourgeois, 18 per cent from artisanal or shopkeeping families, 14 per cent of peasant origin and 4 per cent from the working classes.[18]

One example of this new kind of nun was Jeanne Jugan, born into a large Breton family outside Cancale in 1792. Her father, a fisherman, joined the navy to fight the English in 1798 and never returned. While her two elder sisters and younger brother married, Jeanne at twenty-five became a nurse in the hospital of the recently founded Soeurs de la Sagesse, in nearby Saint-Servan. She spent six years there, caring in particular for an invalid priest, then became the maid of a local lady whose brother had been a priest and who left Jeanne a small legacy when she died in 1835, at which point Jeanne shared lodgings with a former priest's housekeeper who had a similar small legacy, continuing to work as a domestic but now also looking after the poor of Saint-Servan. The key relationship in the foundation of any new congregation was that between a pious woman like Jeanne Jugan, the local priest, who in this case was the curé who arrived in 1840, and a benefactor, here a prosperous Saint-Servan shopkeeper, Mlle Doynel, who bought the nuns a house that had belonged to an old convent. The Little Sisters of the Poor, as they called themselves, bound by simple (not perpetual) vows, were constituted in 1842, and by 1850 had founded houses at Rennes, Dinan, Nantes, Angers, Tours and Paris. In fact Jeanne Jugan, now Sister Mary of the Cross, ill educated as she was, served as superior for only one year, but in 1845 was awarded the Prix Montoyon of the Académie Française, presented to 'a poor French person who has done the most virtuous act', cited as one of 'those helpful souls who, themselves without any possessions other than a loving heart and a strong arm, have nonetheless managed to become the good angels of their fellows'.[19]

WOMEN AND EMPLOYMENT

For women, whether married or unmarried, there were few career options for most of the nineteenth century. The professions and state service were restricted to those with a classical education leading to the *baccalauréat*, and this kind of education was not available to women. Women's education was increasingly controlled by congregations of nuns – who in 1850, for example, taught 73 per cent of girls in the Rhône department (around Lyon) and 94 per cent of those in the Loire department (around Saint-Étienne)[20] – was not very academic and concentrated on the shaping of future wives and mothers, if not future nuns. State service was a function of government patronage, but the only official posts that were available to women were those of local postmistresses (*receveuses des postes*), in which role they were often preferred to former NCOs from the 1840s, if they could claim, for instance, that they were the orphaned daughter of an army officer or widow of a civil servant. Accommodation was attached but the pay was meagre – from 800 francs per year to 1,300 at retirement age in the 1860s – and although they were not barred from marriage, 58 per cent of them were spinsters in 1880.[21]

The domination of girls' teaching by nuns and the absence of state secondary schools for girls before 1880 meant that there were very few teaching options for lay women. One exception was the career of Marie Pape-Carpentier, whose father, an NCO in the gendarmerie, was killed by *chouans* in the Sarthe before she was born. She was entrusted to her grandmother at Alençon to learn lacemaking, but by dint of independent study she became head of the *salle d'asile* – a cross between a nursery school and crèche to keep poor children off the streets – first at La Flèche in 1834–9, then at Le Mans. She achieved a wider reputation with a handbook on running *salles d'asile*, published in 1846 and awarded the Prix Montoyon of the Académie Française, and in 1848 was appointed head of a new training school for nursery school teachers in Paris. She married a captain of the Paris National Guard in 1849, but he died in 1858, leaving her to raise two daughters, so that her salary of 3,000 francs was essential. In 1862 she wrote a series of articles in the *Économiste Français* on the need to open careers such as teaching, the civil service and pharmacy to women, and was invited by education minister Victor Duruy to give five lectures on *salles d'asile* in the Sorbonne during the Universal Exhibition of 1867, after which she was appointed general inspectress of *salles d'asile*. That said, she forged her career in the face of opposition from the Catholic Church for promoting a sector over which they did not have control, and was even suspended in 1874–5 by the Moral Order regime of the Third Republic before the republicans took office.[22]

Henriette Renan, four years her senior, was also confronted by difficulties arising from her father's death and competition from the Church. Her father, a Breton sea-captain of Tréguier, was drowned when she was seventeen, leaving substantial debts, and her mother's grocery was not enough to keep the family. Essentially self-taught, she was unable to make a living as a primary school teacher in Brittany where the nuns enjoyed a virtual monopoly, so in 1835 she went to Paris to teach in a private girls' boarding school, where she was worked sixteen hours a day, then became governess to an aristocratic Polish family living in Warsaw and Vienna. She declined an offer of marriage and dedicated what she earned to furthering the career of her brother Ernest, twelve years younger than she, whom she brought to Paris to be educated at the seminary of Saint-Nicolas-du-Chardonnet. Fiercely sceptical herself, she persuaded Ernest not to become ordained, and set him up with an annual allowance in 1845 so that he could study independently to become an academic, a sum that he called 'the corner-stone of my life'.[23] From 1850 she lived with him in Paris, was hugely grieved when he married, but followed him on his expedition to Syria in 1860–61, where she copied out and commented on his drafts of the *Life of Jesus*. She died there of malaria in 1861, a woman who in another age would have been an academic herself but whose final accolade was Renan's dedication of the *Life of Jesus* 'to the pure soul of my sister Henriette'.[24]

Women's careers were frustrated by a combination of interlocking factors: the absence of state education provision leading to the *baccalauréat*, the effective closure of the professions, the Church's virtual monopoly of women's education, and a social prejudice that the education of women was to be geared not to any career but to their calling as wives and mothers. Julie Daubié, the first woman to pass the *baccalauréat*, in 1861, under the pseudonym of C. de Sault, followed her success with a treatise on *The Poor Woman in the Nineteenth Century* in 1866, arguing that women who wanted to teach outside the Church were condemned to private boarding schools, a third of which were lay establishments in 1864, but were paid a mere 200–400 francs a year, or to private tuition, paid as little as 25 centimes an hour as piano teachers. The only solution, she said, was state secondary education for girls and ultimately the opening of the Académie Française to women: the award of the Prix Montoyon to women for a work 'most useful for morality' was not enough.[25] When education minister Victor Duruy attempted a compromise measure in 1867, the opening of 'secondary courses' taught by secondary school masters to girls attending private boarding or convent schools, a broadside was opened up by the Catholic Church which saw this as an attack on its monopoly and a mistaken attempt to train *femmes savantes*. 'What I want', wrote Mgr Dupanloup, bishop of Orléans, who led the attack, 'is not *femmes savantes* but what is necessary for their husbands, children and homes – intelligent, judicious, attentive women instructed in that which they need to know as mothers, housewives and society ladies'.[26] Whole areas of the country controlled by the Church boycotted the courses, which were attended by only a couple of thousand girls, often daughters of teachers or civil servants, usually chaperoned by their mothers. Access to higher education was even more controversial. When a young widowed mother, Madeleine Brès, obtained permission from the Empress Eugénie in 1866 to enrol in the Paris Medical Faculty, a public debate broke out about whether women doctors would be able to amputate limbs, dissect corpses or examine male genitals. Not least perhaps to skirt round this criticism, Mme Brès wrote a doctoral thesis on breastfeeding and devoted herself to the care of mothers and children.[27] Thus, even when they penetrated the professions, women were pushed into spheres where they could put to special use their qualities as wives and mothers.

The logic of the bourgeois marriage as the path of least resistance becomes clear. The opportunities for women here should not be ignored: for some, marriage, work and wealth were attainable together. Pauline Motte-Brédart was both mother and manager of the family cotton factory at Roubaix, the French Manchester, because her husband was not interested in the business. When her second son Louis Motte-Bossut built a famous 'giant mill' in 1843 she was able to nip through the hedge and help him with the accounts, but while her eldest daughter Adèle Danzin-Motte inherited her head for business, her younger daughter Pauline Delfosse-Motte and three daughters-in-law opted out of business matters or were excluded from them by their husbands. Instead, the second generation of mill-owners' wives based themselves on the home, running the house-hold, organizing dinner parties, sending the children to Catholic schools, building the family alliances that underpinned the business empire, and developing charities to control and civilize the working classes, such as acting as *dames patronesses* for *salles d'asile* to look after the chil-dren of women working in the mills or setting up workshops for young working women who risked falling into prostitution.[28]

To be a bourgeois woman increasingly meant not working outside the home, but further down the social scale working women were fully part of the family enterprise. A baker, for example, not only required his wife to run the shop and cultivate the clientele while he (by night) baked the bread, but relied on marriage to supply the capital to buy the business in the first place. Jean-François Baulme, for example, was an employee in a baker's shop in Lyon until in 1835, aged twenty-eight, he more or less simultaneously married and bought a shop of his own. He stumped up 1,800 francs himself (of which 1,000 francs came from his father, a peasant farmer in the Ain), while his wife advanced 3,000 francs (including a 1,500-franc inheritance from her mother). Bakers could not do without wives – who were more often of more urban origin, adept at managing social relations – to front the business, and generally remarried quickly if they lost them. In an exception to the Civil Code's restrictions on married women's control of property, article 220 permitted a married woman in trade to keep and run the busi-ness in her name in the event of the husband's death, which explains the frequency of 'veuve' in the names of businesses. That said, widowed *boulangères* tended to remarry within a couple of years in mid-nineteenth-century Lyon, if they wished to continue the busi-ness, because they could not do without the baker in his *fournil*.[29] In the countryside, the need to maintain the family farm intact meant that, as in the upper classes, romantic love had to take second place to family considerations. Marriages were often arranged by a go-between, and a good marriage involved pooling property or the promise of inheritance, and a robust relationship between a healthy, hard-working couple. Courtship might take the form of squeezing hands until the knuckles nearly broke, in order to test the strength of the intended, and beauty was actually seen as a negative quality.

'A girl tall and beautiful is like half of the devil' ran one Breton saying; 'A woman without an apron is anybody's' ran another. The married couple observed a strictly gendered division of labour. The man's tasks included cutting wood, ploughing and planting the soil, scything the grain, tending the vines, looking after the horses and oxen used in production, and extracting manure from the stables. The woman's jobs included fetching the water used for cooking, washing and cleaning, feeding both humans and animals, milking the cows, looking after the farmyard and kitchen garden, knitting, sewing and weaving if it were for the family's own needs, and bringing up the children. There was never any question of farmers' wives contesting these age-old conventions.[30]

Rural society was hierarchical, and day-labourers without the expectation of land could not expect to marry. Girls without the expectation of a dowry might go to the city to work as domestic servants, hoping to accumulate enough for a trousseau in order to return to the village and make a decent marriage. Often they came from poorer regions of the country such as Brittany, Auvergne or the Morvan. Having domestic servants was another sign of a bourgeois family, and the number of domestic servants increased during the century to a high point of 1,156,000 in 1881, some 70 per cent of them women. 'Domestique' covered a range of conditions from milkmaids at the bottom to ladies' companions and governesses in rich families at the top, and in between shop assistants, barmaids and the cleaning staff of colleges, convents, hospitals and asylums, as well as cooks, chambermaids and valets in private homes.[31] Cleaning in a hospital was often the first job after arriving from the country, paid about 12 francs a month in the 1840s because the main perk was accommodation; the next stage would be service in a private household, paid at 35 or 40 francs a month.[32] Saving for a dowry was not easy in these circumstances, and in addition the work was insecure. Servants were seen as easy prey by employers and their sons and becoming pregnant led immediately to dismissal. Single mothers were totally rejected by society and little stood in the way of the descent into prostitution. Up to a half of prostitutes in Paris had started work as domestic servants.

Industrial work for women offered scarcely more money or more security. The right bank of Paris was the centre of luxury trade, where women made so-called *articles de Paris* – costume jewellery, perfumes, fans, gloves, umbrellas, artificial flowers and feathers – or were employed as milliners, dressmakers or embroiderers, for 2 or 3 francs a day. Suzanne Voilquin (née Monnier) was the daughter of a hatter from Nîmes who had moved to Paris during the Revolution but whose business failed. As a girl she went to work with her sister in an embroidery shop in the rue Saint-Martin, starting work at 7 a.m. and regularly being accosted after work by men who saw them as no better than prostitutes. After her mother died and her father left Paris she became the girlfriend of a medical student who promised to marry her but never did.[33] As such she was typical of the *grisettes*. These young workers in the luxury trade might become the girlfriends of middle-class students, who helped them to pay the rent but soon abandoned them when it was time to settle down. In fact working-class girls rarely married at all. Marriage was about the acquisition and inheritance of property, and they had none. It required the written permission of parents, which was difficult to obtain when the girl had migrated from one part of France to another, and documents drawn up at great expense by a notary. Living in 'concubinage' as it was called also had advantages: if the relationship broke up the woman, not the man, acquired control of the children and another relationship could not be deemed adulterous.[34]

Industrial work was highly gendered, and patterns of female labour differed sharply between textile towns and those where mining and metallurgy predominated. Working-class families observed a traditional division of labour. In the cotton town of Roubaix (Nord), textiles provided plenty of employment for women. Nearly 55 per cent of female workers were in textiles in 1872, as against 15 per cent in commerce and dressmaking, and 15 per cent in domestic service. Eighty-one per cent of women worked if they were unmarried, although only 17 per cent of married women did so. In the south of the same department, in the mining town of Anzin, underground miners were all men, though some girls were employed to sort the coal and carry baskets. Of those women who did work, 15 per cent ran bars and cafés and 34 per cent were seamstresses, but most tended the garden and raised animals like a farmer's wife, since the miner's wage was good enough to keep the family.[35]

Textiles and the clothing industry relied on female labour, and conditions were generally harsh. In Lyon girls were recruited from the age of eleven or twelve from peasant or artisan families all over the south-east of France to work twelve hours a day in the silk mills, virtual industrial convents under the eye of nuns, housed in dormitories from which they were rarely allowed home, and paid 15 centimes an hour (1.8 francs a day). Nearly 2,000 of these ovalists as they were called went on strike in Lyon in June 1869 in pursuit of a ten-hour day paid at 2 francs. The employers refused to meet them so they petitioned the prefect, alluding to the fact that they had to supplement their wages by recourse to prostitution. They joined the International Association of Workers, which applauded their strike at its Basle congress in September 1869, though it was already over. Under the settlement the working day was reduced to ten hours but the rate remained the same, 15 centimes an hour, with overtime paid at 30 centimes.[36]

In this context prostitution was often resorted to out of a simple need to make ends meet. Alongside the regulated prostitution of *maisons de tolérance* or of girls working independently was clandestine or irregular prostitution practised outside the official system. The clearance of traditional haunts of the trade such as the Île de la Cité by Baron Haussmann brought about a shift from *maisons de tolérance* to the clandestine trade of girls living in the suburbs or who descended each night to do business on the boulevards. A survey of 1878–87 in Paris showed that clandestine prostitutes, much as registered ones, were recruited from dressmakers and other workshop employees, shop assistants, barmaids or domestic servants. Most telling was the fact that 29 per cent were orphaned of both parents, 34 per cent had lost their father and 19 per cent their mother. They did not have the support of a family either to launch them or on which they could fall back in hard times.[37] Of course there was a hierarchy among prostitutes, as there was in any trade, and those who acquired some protection generally did better. At the top were the courtesans, re-created as cultivated ladies and able to choose their lovers, who contributed lavishly to their upkeep. Marie-Anne

Detourbey, for example, born near Reims in 1837, lost her carpenter father and became a bottle-washer in a champagne house. Moving to Paris to be initiated into *la vie galante* she was cultivated by Alexandre Dumas *fils*. She asked him to find her a teacher in order to penetrate society and her tutor was none other than Sainte-Beuve, who called her the 'madonna of the violets'. She was launched as an actress at the Théâtre de la Porte Saint-Martin, but was not a success, and eventually became the mistress of Prince Jérôme-Napoléon, cousin of the emperor. In 1870 she acquired a fortune and a title from the Comte de Loynes, who subsequently disappeared to England, leaving her as the Comtesse de Loynes to preside over her own salon, and in turn to launch the literary career of her lover Jules Lemaître.[38] Few prostitutes, however, ever reached this degree of fame and fortune.

WOMEN AND POLITICS

The French Revolution saw a brief flurry of feminist activity. Olympe de Gouges, the daughter of a butcher from Montauban who came to Paris as a playwright, published a Declaration of the Rights of Women in 1791, in which she argued that since women had the right to mount the scaffold they should have the right to contribute to public debate. A Society of Revolutionary Republican Women was set up in 1793 by chocolate-maker Pauline Léon and actress Claire Lacombe, to press for radical measures against counter-revolutionaries and hoarders. Unfortunately the involvement of women in politics during the Ancien Régime had been discredited by the influence of the mistresses of Louis XV and of Louis XVI's Austrian wife Marie-Antoinette. The French Republic was constructed as a republic of brothers who alone were citizens and subscribed to the male virtues of dedication to the public good, whereas the role of women was to ensure order in the home. In the autumn of 1793 the Society of Revolutionary Republican Women was closed down and both Marie-Antoinette and Olympe de Gouges were guillotined.[39]

If women achieved political influence it was generally behind the scenes, promoting the careers of men, as the hostesses of salons which often had a political as well as a literary function, and as writers, though usually under assumed names. Germaine de Staël was thrown into her role as a salon hostess by the illness of her mother when her father, Jacques Necker, was a minister in 1788–90, his brief dismissal on 11 July 1789 provoking the storming of the Bastille. She exerted influence behind the scenes to establish her lover Narbonne as minister of war in 1791 and Talleyrand as foreign minister in 1797, and to further the political career of Benjamin Constant. In 1800 she published a study of *Literature and its Relations with Social Institutions*. Before the Revolution, she argued, women who wrote had to fear appearing ridiculous, now they simply provoked hatred for drawing attention to themselves; genius and renown were for men only. Although the influence of women might 'calm men's furious passions', she wrote, 'since the Revolution men have thought it politically and morally useful to reduce women to the most absurd mediocrity. They have no more occasion to develop their reason, but morals, for all that, have not improved.'[40] The book was not well received in the current climate. Sylvain Maréchal, who had taken part in a republican conspiracy in 1796, published a pamphlet in 1801 entitled *Bill to Prohibit Teaching Women to Read*. He argued that 'reading leads to adultery' as well as to women wanting to write and participate in politics. 'A woman poet is a little moral and literary monstrosity,' he wrote, 'a woman ruler is a political monstrosity.'[41] The advent of Bonaparte was even more tragic for Germaine de Staël. He hated her novels, which placed independent-minded women centre-stage, and saw her salon stoking liberal opposition to his regime. In 1803 he banned her from Paris and she spent most of the next decade either on her father's Coppet estate near Lake Geneva or wandering from one European country to another.

Napoleon's idea of a public role for women was charity. In 1810 he revived the Society for Maternal Charity and placed it under the patronage of his new queen, Marie-Louise. Through this organization, which spread from Paris to provincial towns, women of the social elite both raised money for charitable works such as nurseries and homes for fallen women, and supervised the institutions they funded. The presidents of the different branches were generally the wives of the mayor, prefect or highest magistrate, and they undertook in the realm of care and relief what their husbands were undertaking in the realm of public order. The Society exhibited the social order, for the presidents were invariably noble. The bourgeoisie mimicked them, and in 1860 the wife of the cotton king and deputy Augustin Pouyer-Quertier was invited to assume the presidency of the Rouen branch of the society. The charitable sector, in which the maternal role and morality found expression outside the home and in some sense domesticated society, was regarded as entirely fitting for women of society.[42]

Some women, of course, were not content with such a role and demanded greater involvement and recognition in the public sphere. Marie-Madeleine Poutret de Mauchamps ran a salon under the July Monarchy and, alongside her husband, edited the *Gazette des Femmes*. In 1837 the *Gazette* published a petition to the Académie Française requesting that women artists be allowed to compete for the major prizes in painting, sculpture, architecture and music, and the following year another was submitted to the king and Chamber of Deputies requesting that women be admitted to university courses and become eligible to qualify as doctors and lawyers. This campaign to open doors to educated women provoked a backlash against what was termed the bluestocking, who was attacked for sacrificing her femininity and indeed family to her thirst for knowledge. Daumier's series of cartoons of *Les Bas-bleus* in the *Charivari* of 1844 ridiculed women who left their husbands to feed the baby and mend their own trousers, suggesting that infidelity was around the corner.[43]

The jibes of Daumier were one thing, but the campaign of the *Gazette* did not even command full support among women who were making their mark in public debate. Delphine de Girardin, whose husband owned *La Presse*, wrote a column for it under the pen-name of the Vicomte Charles de Launay. This 'Courrier de Paris', which ran between 1836 and 1848, retailed the gossip and social issues that revolved around her salon and elsewhere. Her success, said Gautier, was due to 'a very feminine finesse of observation and a rather virile common sense'.[44] In 1844, however, she responded impatiently to one of the petitions demanding that women be eligible for chairs at the Académie Française. 'Why should women have a chair in a country where they cannot sit on the throne? Why would you give them a pen when you refuse them a sceptre?' She continued, six months later, 'Today we declare that the first duty of a woman is to be beautiful.'[45]

Marie d'Agoult, who, tired of travelling with Liszt, returned to Paris in 1839 to develop her salon, wrote an *Essay on Liberty* under the pseudonym of Daniel Stern. In this she rejected arguments that women were inferior, incapable, even perverse, which condemned them, according to their social class, to be either 'a useful servant or a gracious slave'. Her answer, however, was not legal or political emancipation. Society was not ready for this. 'Flirtation', she asserted, 'is the revenge of weakness.' In her opinion women achieved ascendancy not by demanding degrees and jobs but by using their femininity to the best advantage. 'In all civilized societies,' she wrote, 'flirtation has become a science as profound as the science of politics. Since society leaves them outside real action, they have easily learned to make use of a man's desires to make him, at least temporarily, her slave.'[46]

Other women under the July Monarchy were more assertive in their demand for rights. Most significant were the mainly lower-class women who were involved in the Saint-Simonian movement of utopian socialism. Désirée Véret, a seamstress, Jeanne Deroin, a shirtmaker, who was studying to take her teacher's certificate, embroiderer Suzanne Voilquin, married to a man who turned out to be syphilitic, and Eugénie Niboyet, a mother and writer from an intellectual Protestant family, were attracted by the Saint-Simonian project to reorganize society on the basis of dividing labour according to aptitude and talent and remuneration according to work. In practice this meant the emancipation of workers, 'the most numerous and poorest class', and of women. However the movement's charismatic leader, Prosper Enfantin, saw the emancipation of women coming essentially from free love and set up a commune at Ménilmontant on the outskirts of Paris as cholera raged there in 1832. Politically, he announced, women were still minors and could not take part in the mission: their calling was that of 'muse and madonna'. The free-love commune resulted in Enfantin being condemned to a year in prison for immorality in August 1832, while his female followers were consternated. 'Your caresses and kisses have brought me back to life,' Désirée Véret wrote to him, 'but you have caused a real anarchy within me, just as it is in society.'[47]

The Saint-Simonian women broke away to found their own journal later in 1832, *La Femme Libre*. The liberty they demanded would come not from free love, they argued, but from the possibility of divorce, greater educational opportunities for women (Jeanne Deroin secured her teacher's certificate after several attempts) and the opening of professions to women. Characteristically, however, they based their demands for emancipation on their qualities as mothers. 'Women, rely on your title of mother to reclaim your equality from men,' wrote Suzanne Voilquin in 1834. 'Motherhood is our most beautiful quality.'[48] Marriage and motherhood, in fact, soon slowed down the campaign. Jeanne Deroin married the bursar of a retirement home in 1832, Désirée Véret went to England in 1833–4 and married Jules Gay, who translated Robert Owen into French. On the other hand Suzanne Voilquin separated from her husband in 1833, went to Egypt in 1834 to seek a spiritual Mother for their cause, and subsequently qualified as a midwife.

Perhaps the Mother or Female Messiah of whom Enfantin had spoken was, in the short term at least, Flora Tristan. At the age of fifteen she discovered that she was the illegitimate daughter of a Peruvian aristocrat who had died when she was four, and travelled to Peru in order to recover her inheritance. Her uncle fobbed her off with a small allowance, which he stopped after she exposed the imprisonment in Peruvian convents of women abandoned by their lovers in her 1838 *Peregrinations of a Pariah*. Before that she had worked as a colourist in a lithographic shop, married her employer, had two sons and was pregnant with a daughter when she fled the home. She battled in the courts for control of the children and petitioned the Chamber of Deputies in 1837 for the restoration of divorce; the following year her husband shot and wounded her in the street and was sentenced to sixteen years' hard labour.

At this point, like the Saint-Simonians, she decided that the emancipation of women workers must accompany that of workers, another pariah class, and that such women needed to mobilize workers as their allies. In 1843 she launched a Workers' Union scheme to build workers' palaces in every town, providing work, education and training for male and female workers and accommodation for old and sick ones. 'What education, what teaching, what direction, what moral or physical development does the woman of the common people receive?' she asked. 'None.' 'I demand rights for women because I am convinced that the ills of the world come from this forgetfulness and scorn that until now have been inflicted on the natural and imprescriptible rights of the female,' she declared, and implored the workers to 'free the last slaves who still remain in French society'.[49] Unfortunately, as she toured the country to rally support, she discovered that the working classes did not live up to her ideal as allies. *Compagnonnage* was fragmented and deeply sexist, acknowledging only its own mothers in each town. And while the workers of Paris and Lyon had some education, of the weavers of Roanne and ribbon-makers of Saint-Étienne she complained, 'They all speak patois and wear clogs . . . They are quite simply peasants from the mountains, with the stupidest expression on their faces.'[50]

The question of the political rights of women was not really posed until the Revolution of 1848 proclaimed universal suffrage, but for men only. On 18 March 1848 the provisional government announced, 'Dating from this law there are no more proletarians in France. Every Frenchman of mature age has political citizenship. Every citizen is an elector. Every elector is sovereign.' This provoked an immediate response from Jeanne Deroin and Eugénie Niboyet, who set up a Committee for the Rights of Women and headed a delegation to the mayor of Paris on 22 March to insist that if women were not given the vote there would still be seventeen million proletarians in France.[51] Deroin and Niboyet backed up their campaign with a paper, *La Voix des Femmes*, in which Niboyet couched the claim to be citizens in the duties of motherhood. 'The mother, natural educator of the child, devoted to her family,' she wrote, 'must participate in the common progress by dedicating herself to the Fatherland, to the Republic.'[52]

To heighten their profile *La Voix des Femmes* approached George Sand to run on their behalf as a candidate in the elections to the National Assembly. There was a frosty response. Sand claimed not to know any of the radical women of the clubs and papers and did not want to become 'the ensign of a feminist coterie'. She did not think the time had come for women to take part in politics; first they had to secure the civil rights that marriage confiscated from them. At the same time, however, by her connections with the republican elite, notably the interior minister Ledru-Rollin, she was anonymously drafting proclamations to the people in the *Bulletin de la République*. 'Here I am,' she boasted to her son, now the mayor of Nohant, 'already busy like a statesman.'[53] Marie d'Agoult did not even use her connections to seek influence, convinced that politics was not for women. In her *History of the Revolution of 1848* she dismissed both the 'mere agitation' of George Sand and the 'legion of women of doubtful morals' who 'failed to take account of dominant attitudes, clashed head-on with usage and custom instead of trying to persuade minds ... rather than advancing step by step, prudently, as opinion came round, they indulged in impolitic gestures, noisily opening clubs which immediately became the target of ridicule ... publishing papers that nobody read'.[54]

Marie d'Agoult's reference to opinion might have come from Madame de Staël's *Delphine*. There was no point in demanding rights if society was not yet ready for the political woman. Many of the prejudices about the inferior nature and subordinate role of women voiced by Maréchal at the beginning of the century were still current or being reworked by a new cohort of sexists, appalled by the agitation of the viragos of 1848, and it was against these prejudices that women now had to fight. Jenny d'Héricourt, a Protestant from Besançon, who had separated from her husband, been secretary to the Society for the Emancipation of Women in 1848 and trained at the Paris Medical Faculty as a midwife, wrote an article in the Turin journal *La Ragione* in 1855, denying that 'nature made men rational and women emotional; it is education and morals that made them thus.'[55] She continued her campaign in the in-house journal of a philosophical circle she attended, the *Revue Philosophique et Religieuse*, which was aimed squarely at Pierre-Joseph Proudhon who had famously argued in 1846 that, while the husband's sphere was production and exchange, that of the wife was saving and consumption: 'housewife or courtesan, I see no middle way.'[56] His marriage in 1849, while in prison, to a working-class girl who bore him three daughters did not change his ideas. He responded in 1858 with his *De la justice dans la Révolution et dans l'Église*, in which he reiterated his position on 'the physical, intellectual and moral inferiority of woman'. 'Woman is a receptivity,' he continued, 'unproductive by nature, inert, without industry or understanding, without justice or shame, she needs a father, brother, lover, husband, master, a man.' He went on to attack women who by stepping outside their allotted sphere became men. George Sand, for instance, was 'no longer even of her sex, she wears men's clothes and retains of womanhood only that which serves for making love'.[57]

This tirade provoked a double response, both from Jenny d'Héricourt and from a young, unhappily married woman who frequented the philosophical circle, Juliette La Messine née Lamber. For two months, she noted, 'I shut myself in my room at night, alone with my daughter, while my husband was more occupied with one of the servants than me,' and penned *Les Idées anti-Proudhoniennes*.[58] She rejected the prejudices that women were physically, intellectually or morally inferior to men. She argued that women had a calling outside the home as doctors to women and children and *mairesses* supervising wet-nurses, crèches, nurseries, schools and charities. More than that, she argued that 'the civilization of a society is proportional to the role, influence and moral dignity of women in that society', for the history made by men was nothing but 'battles, massacres, rivers of blood, oppression, injustice, treachery'.[59] This splash led to her becoming the protégée of Marie d'Agoult, to leaving her husband, and to setting up her own salon in 1865. For her part Jenny d'Héricourt counter-attacked with *La Femme affranchie* in 1860, announcing to Proudhon that 'I am raising the standard under which your daughters will one day shelter, if they are worthy of the name they bear.' She argued that the inferiority of women imposed by society in fact 'undermined our modern civilization', not least by causing women to abandon the revolutions of 1789 and 1848 that had granted them no rights and had then failed. Marriage, she insisted, was an association of equals and there was no possible objection to women becoming doctors, chemists or mathematicians.[60] Still not done, Proudhon published his *La Pornocratie ou les femmes des temps modernes* in which he saw marriage as 'the union of strength and beauty', pronounced that women had smaller brains and that 'all women who dream of emancipation lose, *ipso facto*, a healthy soul, a lucid mind and the virginity of the heart'.[61]

In practical terms, Marie d'Agoult was correct that the time was not right to demand political rights for women. Her own tactic, and that of Juliette La Messine, was to preside over salons where male political figures met and to seek to influence events through them. During the 1850s the republican opposition to the Second Empire was split between those who refused to take the oath to the regime and therefore could not run for parliament, and those who were prepared to take the oath in order to acquire a parliamentary platform to press for liberal reforms. The star of Marie d'Agoult's salon was Émile Ollivier, who married her daughter by Liszt, Blandine, in 1857, and therefore leaned more to those who wanted to liberalize the Empire from within; the salon of Juliette La Messine, by contrast, became the haunt of intransigent opponents of the Empire, including a former journalist of *Le National*, Edmond Adam, whom she married in 1868, and indeed the launch-pad for the career of Gambetta.[62] An alternative tactic was to link moderate demands for women's rights to the freemasonry network. For though freemasons were a men-only movement, individual freemasons sympathized with women's struggle. Thus Maria Desraismes, who had been left a fortune by her father and decided not to marry in order to retain greater independence, made a political alliance with Léon Richer, a former solicitor's clerk on the Paris–Orléans railway and a journalist with a column on the *Petit Parisien*. She was invited to Sunday 'philosophical conferences' organized by the Grand Orient when political meetings were authorized in 1868, funded and contributed to the *Droit des Femmes* paper that Richer launched in 1869 and with him founded the Society for the Amelioration of Women's Condition, which held a first feminist banquet on 11 July 1870.[63] One of their enthusiasts was Julie Daubié, who brought Elizabeth Garrett to Paris to undertake the doctorate she was barred from doing in London and Edinburgh, and who secured a degree herself in 1871.[64]

In 1870 the lives of women of the social elite were still dominated by the arranged marriage, although lower down the social scale where property was less of an issue relationships were often freer, if less secure. Divorce was still illegal, separation was a second best, for it did not permit remarriage, and adultery was an inevitable part of the system. Women did more than their fair share of unpaid and paid work; the burning issue was whether they could acquire secondary and higher education and begin to challenge for the professions. Politically, the demand for emancipation moved from Saint-Simonianism and radical journalism to seeking to influence male politicians through the salons over which society women presided and masonic lodges with which they might ally. Significantly, however, the demand for equality was couched not in terms of individual rights but in terms of the civilizing influence that women could exercise over society as a whole.

6

Artistic Genius and Bourgeois Culture

ROMANTICS, WRITERS AND REPUTATIONS

It was in 1801, with the publication of *Atala*, recalled Chateaubriand, that 'the noise I make in this world began. I ceased to be a private person and my public career began.' The story of a graceful Indian girl, untouched by civilization in the virgin forests of the New World, was quite different from the classical literature of the Consulate and Empire, and critics were unsure whether to categorize it 'among monstrosities or beauties; was it the Gorgon or Venus?' It inaugurated the Romantic era, catching the public's enthusiasm, with the characters from the novel exhibited at the annual Salon of the Academy of Fine Art, reproduced in engravings hung in coaching inns, moulded into wax dolls sold on the *quais* of Paris, or done up in feathers in the boulevard theatres.[1] This public recognition was not only artistic. Along with the impact of the *Genius of Christianity* the following year, it propelled Chateaubriand towards a diplomatic career, election to the Académie Française in 1811, a peerage in 1815 and the Ministry of Foreign Affairs in 1822. He became the model of literary success and wider public acclaim that was to be the envy of aspiring writers and artists who followed him.

Although Chateaubriand cultivated the Romantic style of the melancholy genius, misunderstood by and ill at ease in the world, literary or artistic success in fact required both the knitting together of patronage and connections and the manipulation of public opinion. There was no possibility of an artistic career outside Paris, and in Paris it was necessary to frequent salon society and to negotiate support among publishers, theatre directors and academicians. Romantic artists also needed a direct rapport with the public, to show themselves to be divinely inspired, although this might in fact involve begging support from the critics and mobilizing *claques* to lead the applause in the theatre.

The first generation of artists to follow in Chateaubriand's wake, born around 1800, were in some sense sons of giants, either aristocrats who had survived the Revolution or Napoleonic generals. The fall of Napoleon in 1815 created opportunities for artistic careers to take off but it also left many feeling that with the collapse of France's European power life would never be as exciting again. Alphonse de Lamartine's father served in the royal bodyguard and was wounded defending the Tuileries on 10 August 1792, the day the monarchy fell, and Lamartine himself joined the royal bodyguard in 1814. After his love affair with the young wife of the seventy-year-old perpetual secretary of the Académie des Sciences was cut short by her death in 1817, he cultivated a solitary melancholy and published a volume of poems, *The Meditations*, in March 1820. They had 'an unheard-of and universal success', he told a friend.[2] It provoked a 'universal inebriation', said Théophile Gautier, artist and chronicler of the Romantics. 'Young people and women were enthusiastic to the point of adoration ... Lamartine was not just a poet, but poetry itself. His chaste, elegant and noble nature seemed to rise above the ugliness and triviality of life.'[3] This apparent unworldliness as far as his public were concerned sat with a very worldly pursuit of prospects and a career. In June 1822 he married an English heiress with a dowry of £10,000, to which his father added a château and town house in Mâcon, and embarked on a diplomatic career in Naples and Florence. He frequented the salon of Charles Nodier, librarian of the Arsenal, a crossroads for Romantic writers and nexus of contacts. In 1825 he was invited to write a poem in honour of the coronation of Charles X, which led to the award of the Legion of Honour, and he was elected to the Académie Française in 1829, just before the July Revolution caused him, as a Legitimist, to resign from the diplomatic service.[4]

In 1816, at the age of fourteen, Victor Hugo wrote in his journal, 'I want to be Chateaubriand or nothing.'[5] He had a row with his father, a former general of Napoleon, who wanted him to enter the École Polytechnique, and he wrote poetry in praise of the restoration of the statue of Henri IV to its plinth on the Pont Neuf that won prizes. He frequented the salon of Sophie Gay in the Chaussée d'Antin, where Chateaubriand dubbed him 'the sublime child' and he married very young. He was also an habitué of Charles Nodier's salon, where he established his reputation alongside Lamartine as one of the 'two gods of poetry'.[6] Nodier put Hugo forward, like Lamartine, to write an ode for the coronation of Charles X, and the award of the Legion of Honour reconciled him with his father. At Nodier's he met Baron Taylor, the Brussels-born Englishman who was director of the Comédie Française, and used the connection to promote his play, *Marion Delorme*. Unfortunately, it portrayed a weak Louis XIII in a chaotic kingdom and was banned by Charles X, despite Hugo's mission to the palace of Saint-Cloud in a bid to make the king change his mind.[7] On the positive side, however, Hugo had a tame critic, Sainte-Beuve, who from 1827 created the myth of Hugo 'born into the camps, brought up amid our warriors, criss-crossing Europe behind our flags', now fighting battles and seeking glory through the arts.[8] When he finally had a play, *Hernani*, set more tactfully in Charles V's Spain, performed in February 1830 at the Comédie Française, a veritable 'Romantic army' of supporters was organized to mobilize applause and shout down those who opposed the liberties taken by the Romantics with the classical conventions. These were led by the former schoolfriends Gérard de Nerval, a young poet who had translated Goethe's *Faust* in 1827, and Gautier, then a long-haired *rapin* or apprentice in an artist's studio and undecided between painting and literature.[9] Sainte-Beuve, true to form, told Hugo, 'You will have your Austerlitz, your Jena. Perhaps *Hernani* is already Austerlitz.'[10]

In fact *Hernani* had been preceded by another dramatic break-through of the Romantic generation, *Henri III and his Court* by Alexandre Dumas. Dumas, like Hugo the son of a Napoleonic general, was greatly inspired by the Paris tour of a troupe of English players – Kemble, Kean, Macready and Harriet Smithson – who performed Shakespeare with extended sword-fights and death scenes in 1827. He was one of the inner circle of the Nodier salon, with a place laid for him every Sunday night, and he persuaded Baron Taylor to commission his play, a story of adultery and murder revolving around the Duc de Guise, his wife and her lover, for the Comédie Française. When it opened in February 1829 Louis-Philippe, Duc d'Orléans, in whose secretariat he worked, turned up with his aristocratic coterie and guaranteed a positive reception.[11] After the July Revolution he had an even greater success with *Antony*, which transposed the drama of adultery and murder to modern times, and abandoned the rather mannered actors of the Comédie Française in favour of the more passionate actors of the Porte Saint-Martin Theatre, the darkly menacing Pierre Bocage in the title role and Marie Dorval, then the mistress of Alfred de Vigny, as the mistress he stabs to death. 'Never before had applause swept so directly from the audience to the actors,' wrote Dumas, 'and what an audience! The fashionable audience of dandies, the audience in the boxes, and the audience that does not normally applaud shouted itself hoarse and split their gloves with clapping.'[12]

Fame, of course, was rarely enduring and the competition for esteem was sharp. Lamartine never repeated the success he had with his *Meditations*. A woman in her thirties, reading his *Harmonies* in 1837, noted, 'it does not have the same effect on me as the meditations. That was rapture, ecstasy; I was sixteen, how beautiful it was.'[13] After *Hernani*, Hugo switched to the novel, publishing *Notre-Dame de Paris* in 1831. Mixing the religious and the pagan, the beautiful and the ugly, it confused those who expected something more uplifting from a novel set in a cathedral. Sainte-Beuve reminded Hugo that Lamennais had said that it was 'not religious enough' and described it himself as 'lit from below by the grates of hell'.[14] One reason for Sainte-Beuve's cooler critique was his love for Hugo's wife, Adèle, while Hugo was himself infatuated by the actress Juliet Drouet, who played in his *Lucrèce Borgia* at the Porte Saint-Martin in 1833.[15] Dumas also took to writing historical novels, hoping to become a French Fenimore Cooper or Walter Scott, publishing *The Three Musketeers* in 1844 and *The Count of Monte Cristo* in 1844–5. In order to maintain an impossible tempo of research and writing he relied on a friend of Gérard de Nerval who made a living as a teacher at the Collège Royal Charlemagne, Auguste Maquet. In

1845 he was accused by a certain Eugène de Mirecourt of running a 'novel factory' that turned out thirty-six volumes in 1844 and promised twice that in 1845; how could that be all his own work? Mirecourt argued that he was still the copyist who had worked in Louis-Philippe's office, a *dégrossisseur* of what others wrote for him.[16] Dumas sued Mirecourt and had him sent to prison for a fortnight. He was riding a wave of literary and financial success. He signed a contract for his complete works for 1.5 million francs in 1843, built the château of Monte Cristo at Le Port-Marly near Versailles in 1844 and a Théâtre Historique on the boulevard du Temple to stage his plays, beginning with *La Reine Margot* in 1847.[17] He was at the pinnacle of his career and it did not matter to him if Delacroix, putting down *Monte Cristo*, sighed, 'When you've finished reading it, you've really read nothing at all.'[18]

Some writers, acknowledged as kings of the canon now, had a much lesser impact on the public at the time. Henry Beyle, better known as Stendhal, fitted uneasily into the Romantic generation. Born in 1783, his career was too closely linked to the Napoleonic era to afford him the right contacts. Between 1815 and 1821 he lived in Italy and London, making a career as a critic and writing about Italian music and painting. In 1821 he returned to Paris, forming a close friendship with Prosper Mérimée and frequenting the salon of Baron Gérard, the king's painter, where Delacroix was a regular, and that of Madame Ancelot, which was known as 'a local branch of the Académie Française'.[19] He was not invited to the salon of Sophie and Delphine Gay, because he was considered too rude, and preferred the nocturnal salon of the Italian actress Madame Pasta, where the Milanese exiles met.[20] He did not find state employment again until the July Monarchy looked more favourably on those with a Napoleonic pedigree, when he was made consul at Civita Vecchia near Rome. He was there when his novel *Le Rouge et le noir* came out in December 1830. Based on a true-life story of a young seminarist who became the lover of the mistress of the house where he was a tutor and then killed her, it managed only two editions of 750 copies each and was a resounding flop. Even Mérimée asked him, 'Why did you choose such an impossible character? Read the late Boileau's *Art of Poetry*.'[21] Stendhal wrote to a friend ironically in 1831 that Simón Bolívar had died. 'Do you know from what? From envy at the success of the *Rouge*.'

Balzac's struggle for recognition was also tough but more rewarding. He had a brief career as a notary's clerk, set up a printing business that collapsed in 1828, made no money from his 1829 novel *The Chouans* nor from his treatise on *The Physiology of Marriage*, and fell and concussed himself trying to get elected as deputy for Chinon in 1832. What he earned came from reviews and articles for the various journalistic enterprises of Émile de Girardin.[22] His first literary success came with *La Peau de chagrin* (*The Magic Skin*) in 1831, a story revolving around an ass's skin which grants wishes but shrinks with each wish made. Sainte-Beuve described it as 'fetid and putrid, witty, corrupt, inspired, sparkling, marvellous in the way it threads tiny elements and makes them ring like a clinking of atoms'.[23] Balzac began to appear on the town as a dandy, with a turquoise-pommelled cane, seen at the Opéra with other men of fashion such as Eugène Sue and lionized in the salon of Delphine de Girardin. Yet he did not have the stylistic qualities of Hugo, and his studies of modern mores did not usurp the public's passion for the historic or the exotic. 'Despite the popularity he was starting to enjoy with the public,' wrote Gautier, 'he was not acclaimed as one of the gods of Romanticism, and he knew it.'[24] Neither did Balzac have the facility for production that Alexandre Dumas had. He struggled to build a vast interlocking *Comédie humaine* that would articulate the structure of modern society. Crisis point was reached in 1846, when the serialization of his *Peasants* in *La Presse* was interrupted to make way for that of Dumas' *La Reine Margot*, which was about to be published.[25] Costume drama had more appeal to the bourgeois reader than dark rural tensions, and Balzac himself now spent more time with his admirer and mistress, the Polish Countess Anna de Hanska, than with his books.

THE READING PUBLIC, PUBLISHING AND THE PRESS

Between the Restoration and 1870 the market for books, newspapers, plays and music achieved a certain consistency and uniformity, which might be characterized as a bourgeois market. At the beginning of the century there was a wide gap between the small, elitist market for high culture and the mass market for popular culture. One market was extremely literate, fashionable and rich, the other semi-literate, traditional and poor. There was often an overlap between genres, with themes from popular culture being taken up and reworked for high culture, and vice versa, but the overlap of publics was much less. Developments over the next few decades however, such as urbanization, faster communications and the spread of elementary education, led to the growth of a market for the middle classes, in which both the elite and ordinary people could participate. The reading public, defined as literate people over the age of fourteen, grew from about 4.6 million men and 2.7 million women in 1801 to 9.8 million men and 8.0 million women in 1871. This was a highly positive development for the production of books, the number of which published in France rose from 2,547 in 1814 to 13,883 in 1866.[26] It did not, however, necessarily mean a wider circulation for great works of literature, for the enthusiasm of the wider public was not necessarily for the novels of Stendhal and Flaubert, which goes a long way to explaining the frustration of writers with the undiscriminating taste of the bourgeois public.

'There are only two hundred people in France who buy new novels,' wrote Émile de Girardin around 1830, 'and eight hundred *cabinets de lecture* which monopolize the distribution of books.'[27] Under Napoleonic legislation all printers and booksellers had to have a *brevet* or licence, and in 1867 there were still only 4,000 bookshops for 36,000 communes. In the first part of the century novels were published in small runs of only a few hundred and cost 7.5 francs a volume. Since two octavo volumes was the minimum for a novel, a new novel cost at least 15 francs, about ten days' wages for an average worker in 1827.[28] Newspapers were similarly expensive. In 1824 there were thirteen main political dailies in Paris, with a combined circulation of 60,000. They were circulated to subscribers, who paid 80 francs a year for the privilege. The flow of political opinion, information and literary pleasure was thus restricted to an elite living in the major cities. This did not mean that the populations of small towns and the countryside were deprived of reading material, only that it was made available on an entirely different circuit. In the absence of bookshops *colporteurs* or chapmen travelled from town to town and village to village carrying a pack of pious works, almanacs, treatises of magic and tiny bestsellers covered in blue sugar-paper, reworkings of traditional epics, romances and fairy-tales, such as *The Four Sons of Aymon*, *Robert the Devil* and *Geneviève of Brabant*. To these were sometimes added the so-called '4-sou novels' of hacks such as Guillaume Ducray-Duminil, derived from the Gothic horror novels of Ann Radcliffe. The *colporteurs* generally originated from the high Pyrenees, making a better living travelling the roads than on the mountain pastures, covering northern France in the summer, southern France in the winter. The books they sold, called the Blue Library on account of their covers, were produced by specialist publishers in the Champagne city of Troyes.[29]

Ways of bringing these two circuits together developed after 1830. On the demand side, the *cabinets de lecture* to which Girardin referred were commercial reading rooms which held all the newspapers and doubled as lending libraries. There were over 400 of these in Paris in the Restoration period, with the same number outside the capital. It was possible to borrow a single newspaper to read at home for 5 centimes a day or 2 francs a month, or read all the newspapers in the *cabinet*, on the spot, for 20 centimes a day. For 30 centimes books as well as newspapers could be read, and for 3 francs a month books could be borrowed.[30] This clearly increased access to books and newspapers many times over. Newspapers were also sent out to the provinces by mail-post, to a radius in 1832 of 250 kilometres after one day, 400 kilometres after two days, reaching cities such as Bordeaux, and arriving in Marseille on the third day. Although there was always a local press, with three political papers of different political persuasions in the Dordogne in 1832, for example, news-paper reading was generally limited to the urban bourgeoisie in northern and eastern France.[31]

On the supply side changes in publishing also increased the avail-ability of newspapers. Political caricature exploded after the fall of the monarchy in 1830 and Charles Philippon, a former apprentice in Baron Gros' studio, launched the weekly *Caricature* (November 1830), with a lithograph folded into the paper, and the daily

Charivari (December 1832), whose prints were integral to the text. These were still quite expensive, the first at 52 francs a year with 600–1,000 subscribers, the second at 60 francs with 1,000–1,400 subscribers in 1834, but copies were available in fifty *cabinets de lecture* and 130 cafés in 1835, waging a war of ridicule on the regime with the help of artists such as Daumier who famously portrayed Louis-Philippe's face as a pear; and both publications were constantly harassed by the press laws until forced to close after the September laws of 1835.[32] Responding to that political clampdown Émile de Girardin, the husband of Delphine Gay who nevertheless permanently struggled for fortune and recognition, founded *La Presse* in 1836. Selling at 40 francs a year, half the price of the existing dailies, it dealt more in business than in politics, tapped a new income stream by selling advertising space, and above all launched the *roman-feuilleton* or serialized novel, taking Balzac's *La Vieille Fille* as its first serial.[33] This brought new novels to the attention of the non-book-buying public and boosted newspaper circulation, turning women for the first time into newspaper readers. Sainte-Beuve observed that Balzac's works appealed in particular to women aged between twenty-eight and thirty-five, exploring as Balzac did the question of the arranged marriage. However he also condemned as 'industrial literature' what he saw as the perversion of writing for what was in effect the contemporary equivalent of the soap opera.[34] The practice of the serialized novel was imitated by other papers, which competed for the most popular writers. Eugène Sue's *Mysteries of Paris* was serialized in the *Journal des Débats* between June 1842 and October 1843 for a fee of 26,500 francs while after a bidding war his *Wandering Jew* went to Véron's *Le Constitutionnel* for 100,000 francs, boosting its circulation from 3,600 in 1844 to 25,000 in 1845–6.[35]

Despite the success of *La Presse* it did not become the paper with the widest circulation. It had the reputation of being on the side of the government, especially after Girardin, challenged on the subject of his illegitimate birth during a circulation war, fought a duel with the republican Armand Carrel, editor of *Le National*, on 22 July 1836, and killed him.[36] *Le Siècle*, with a circulation of 34,000 in 1845–6, as against *La Presse*'s 22,000, was more radical and anticlerical in tone, and circulated in cafés where popular opposition to the government was fomented and which became the bases for political banquets in 1847 and political clubs in 1848. It educated the crowd that Tocqueville witnessed invading the National Assembly on 15 May 1848 and whom he called Montagnards. They spoke a curious jargon, he observed, that was 'neither the French of ignorant people nor that of the educated', using 'swear words but also grandiloquent expressions . . . a constant stream of abusive and jovial comments . . . I think they have developed their attitudes in cafés and sharpened their wits on newspapers alone.'[37]

A THEATRE FOR ALL SEASONS

In the theatre, as in the publishing market, there was a hierarchy of genres, and this was formalized by Napoleon for political reasons. The function of the theatre was to entertain, but it was also a vehicle for political comment and criticism. During the Revolution the politics of the theatre had often run out of control and Napoleon reasserted order with a decree of 1807 which arranged the theatre according to type of production and placed it under close supervision.[38] At the top of the pile was the state-subsidized theatre, the Théâtre Français, otherwise known as the Comédie Française, where classical tragedy and the great comedies of Molière were played, the stage of tragic actors such as Talma and Mlle Mars.[39] The Odéon performed Molière's prose plays, such as *Le Bourgeois Gentilhomme*, and added Shakespeare in 1827. Below these were the tolerated popular houses, each allotted its own genre. The Porte Saint-Martin Theatre was allowed to perform melodramas, the Théâtre de la Gaïté pantomimes, watched by 'fat, good-humoured market women, laughing fit to burst and fanning themselves with six-sous fans they had bought at the theatre itself',[40] while the Variétés and the Vaudeville were given over to farces. At the very working-class Funambules mime king Jean-Gaspard Bureau played Pierrot in harlequinades six times a day and nine times on Sundays, for 4 sous a throw.[41] The flea-pits of the popular quarters of Paris were at the bottom of the heap, strung out along the boulevard du Temple, commonly known as the boulevard du Crime on account of the dark gallows humour of its repertoire and the amount of blood shed on stage.

The strict hierarchy devised by Napoleon was gradually subverted by the evolution of genres and the changing tastes of the public. The mannered, declamatory style of the Comédie Française was not adapted to the passion of the new Romantic plays and fell out of favour with writers and the public. Juste Olivier, a budding Swiss man of letters visiting Paris in 1830, saw *Hernani* there, and found Mlle Mars 'a little too old, at fifty-one' to play the leading lady.[42] Alexandre Dumas, frustrated with the failure of Mlle Mars to give him the expression he wanted for the adulterous wife in *Antony*, moved his play to the Porte Saint-Martin and hired the thirty-three-year-old and more passionate Marie Dorval.[43] The Porte Saint-Martin, whose public of shop-assistants had hounded out the English touring company performing *Othello* in English in 1822, throwing apples and coins, now became the preferred venue for Dumas and Hugo. It steadily became more bourgeois, attracting a mixed audience from the beautiful ladies of the Chaussée d'Antin, hiding behind their fans, via the middle classes to a section of the literate working classes.[44]

There was much circulation of material and actors between the different theatres and there was a downgrading or trickle-down effect whereby material from the elite theatres was reworked for the more popular ones. Pastiches of Hugo's *Hernani* were being performed at the Vaudeville and Variétés in 1830, poking fun at the Romantics, within a very short time of the first performances for which the Romantic army was mobilized.[45] Similarly an actor such as Frédéric Lemaître went from the Porte Saint-Martin to the Folies Dramatiques on the boulevard du Crime in 1834 to star as gentleman crook and popular hero Robert Macaire. 'He parodied himself,' wrote the theatre critic Jules Janin, 'and the public applauded the wit of this man who now repudiated his glorious past.'[46] There was also, however, a capillary action by which material and actors moved up to more respectable theatres. Marie Dorval, who had played opposite Lemaître at the Porte Saint-Martin, went on to play *Phèdre* at the Opéra-Comique in 1842, a tragic role for which she was however ill suited. Henri Monnier, a pupil of Gros who had excelled in artists' studio productions, invented and played the character of Monsieur

Prudhomme, the quintessential bourgeois, for the Vaudeville in 1831, and took it revamped as the *Grandeur and Decadence of Monsieur Prudhomme* to the Odéon in 1853. It was a caricature of the bourgeoisie for the bourgeoisie itself. Prudhomme, for Gautier, was 'the synthesis of bourgeois stupidity. How his fat lips drop leaden aphorisms which make one terrified of common sense.'[47]

The *embourgeoisement* of the theatre reached its climax in the middle of the century. The theatres of the boulevard du Crime were demolished in 1862 during the Haussmannization of Paris, an attack on a genre which was always feared for its ability to nurture violent emotions. The Comédie Française struck back after 1838 with the discovery of a brilliant tragic actress, Élisa-Rachel Félix, known simply as Rachel, the daughter of a Jewish pedlar from Switzerland who made her debut playing Hermione in Racine's *Andromaque* and pursued a vertiginous but brief career.[48] 'Racine and Corneille were revived among us as during the great century of Louis XIV,' recalled Dr Véron, director of the Comédie Française, 'a feverish popularity surrounded the young tragedian and old tragedy.'[49] Rachel's greatest role was Racine's *Phèdre*, 'the mere announcement of this tragedy,' noted one critic, 'no matter how frequently repeated, sufficing to attract half the playgoers of Paris to the doors of the Théâtre Français'.[50] Exhausted by tours of the United States and Egypt, she died in 1858 aged only thirty-seven.

Much of the other half of the Paris public, meanwhile, would be at the Gymnase Theatre, where Rachel had begun her theatrical career in 1837. This had been founded in 1820 and was known as the Theatre of Madame because it received the patronage of the Duchesse de Berry, whose husband was assassinated that year. The theatre was dominated by the talent of Eugène Scribe, a silk-merchant's son who wrote 182 plays for the Gymnase Theatre, 107 in the 1820s and 68 between 1830 and 1848, accounting for 40 per cent of its productions. Like Dumas, he employed a number of collaborators to achieve this vast output, characterized by a tight plot, witty interaction and a fast pace. There was no political content but only gentle social satire, portraying the ambitions, rivalries and foibles of different elements of contemporary society.[51] 'The whole middle class and the distinguished part of society does not dream of anything better,' wrote Sainte-Beuve in 1840. 'One emerges neither too moved, nor too disoriented, as befits our contemporary passions and our affairs.'[52] Scribe represented what was best about bourgeois theatre, offering a mirror for bourgeois society but offering no criticism, providing entertainment rather than literature.

FROM POPULAR MUSIC TO GRAND OPERA

The musical world also had its own hierarchy. At the popular end, in the first half of the nineteenth century, were the working-class singing clubs or *goguettes*, of which there were 300 in Paris in 1818 and 500 in 1836. A few, like the Lice, were closed to women, others were more familial, places where the populace went to drink, laugh and sing. Often the songs were political – republican, Bonapartist or socialist in sympathy – those of Béranger being particular favourites. His popular song, 'Le Drapeau', for example, celebrated the tricolour flag of the Revolution and Empire that was banned after the Restoration. *Goguettes* flourished in the revolutionary ferment of 1848 but after that the authorities clamped down, authorizing only sixty of them in 1849.[53]

More salubrious, but equally successful, were the popular concerts that took off in Paris under the baton of French rivals of Johann Strauss. While high society danced at the Opéra or in the gardens of the Tuileries palace, Philippe Musard presented winter waltz nights at the Salle Valentino in the rue Saint-Honoré from 1833 and promenade concerts in a marquee on the Champs-Élysées from 1837, with an entry fee of 1 franc to keep out the rabble. Facing competition from Strauss in Paris he plied most of his trade in London after 1838. Meanwhile the director of concerts at the Turkish Garden was Louis-Antoine Jullien, whose father had been music director of the Papal Guards and who had been both a sailor and a soldier before undergoing a brief training at the Paris Conservatory and launching his concerts with the quadrille from *The Huguenots*. Where Musard was buttoned up, Julien was a showman, with seductive moustache and yellow gloves, an inveterate duellist and always in debt. Like

Musard, he pursued his career in London after 1840, opening a space for Jacques Offenbach, who had written walzes for Jullien and made his reputation with operetta in the Second Empire.[54]

Until then, French comic opera was dominated by Eugène Scribe, who was not only a playwright but also a librettist, writing for the composers Daniel Auber and Adolphe Adam. Auber synthesized the Italian and French traditions and had a particular success in 1830 with *Fra Diavolo*, about the Neapolitan friar–bandit who had given Bonaparte's forces such a hard time. 'M. Scribe has created a kind of comic opera that is his alone,' wrote Gérard de Nerval in 1844. 'M. Auber sets this kind of literature to a fitting music which everyone is sure to like, and this witty and harmonious partnership brings forth a host of pleasant successes which will cease only when one of them dies.'[55] In fact Scribe's collaboration with Adam was equally successful, with such hits as the 1836 *Postillon de Longjumeau*, for which Jacques Offenbach played in the orchestra as a cellist. A third composer with whom Scribe worked was Giacomo Meyerbeer, of German-Jewish origin, who came from the Milan opera to stage *Margaret of Anjou* at the Opéra-Comique in 1826. Together Scribe and Meyerbeer developed a French grand opera, characterized by rich historical settings, lavish production and massive orchestration, produced not at the Opéra-Comique but at the more prestigious Opéra. *Robert the Devil*, staged in 1831, took a traditional folk story and made it into a vast medieval pageant, complete with dancing nuns, while *The Huguenots*, a Protestant–Catholic *Romeo and Juliet* set at the time of the St Bartholomew massacre, was put on in 1836. Combining material and musical extravagance, grand opera appealed to a broad bourgeois public. *Robert the Devil* completed 500 performances in 1868, and *The Huguenots* reached the same landmark in 1872.[56]

PAINTING AND POLITICS

Fine art, like the theatre, had a political dimension. The state was the most powerful patron of architecture, sculpture and painting, using them to dramatize its legitimacy. It was not a free medium, but was constrained by the artistic conventions laid down by the Academy of Fine Arts. In general this body required high-quality drawing, heightened colour and impeccable finish. It subscribed to an eternal and universal concept of beauty which could best be explored by taking models from the Ancient world or Ancient mythology. The artistic equivalent of the Opéra or Comédie Française was the Salon or exhibition held annually in the Louvre, an arena in which the great battles of artistic schools and individual reputations were fought out. The selection of works of art for the Salon was made by a jury, the composition of which was also a battlefield. During the Revolution access to the Salon was supposed to be equal, but even the artists demanded some kind of selection. Under the Empire the government took a leading role, then selection was devolved on to the Academy of Fine Arts, chaired until 1830 by the director of the Musée du Louvre. The public flocked to the Salon, especially for the opening. In 1830 Balzac described the 'immense crowd' around two paintings exhibited by an artist fresh from studying in Italy. 'People were almost killing each other to get to the front. Speculators and great lords offered piles of gold coins, but the artist obstinately refused to sell, or to permit copies.' Daumier caricatured the throng of the bourgeoisie in a number of lithographs. The critics also had their say, publishing their verdicts on the winners and losers in a wide range of reviews and newspapers.[57]

Under Napoleon the Salon was almost eclipsed by the permanent exhibitions in the Louvre, which displayed for his own glory and the edification of the public the artistic treasures that he had sent back to Paris in baggage trains during his various conquests, from Italy to Germany and Spain. In order to legitimate his new Empire he secured the support of Jacques-Louis David, who had signed Louis XVI's death-warrant and choreographed the festivals of Robespierre's Republic, and commissioned him to execute a series of huge paintings for his palaces, depicting his coronation in Notre-Dame and the distribution of eagles of victory to his troops. The first was exhibited in the Salon of 1808, the second in that of 1810, and David was paid a fee of 77,000 francs. After Austerlitz Napoleon marked his victories by having a triumphal arch built at the Carrousel, at the entrance to the Tuileries, starting the Arc de Triomphe at the Étoile, which remained unfinished at his fall, and erecting a column on the model of Trajan's column in the place Vendôme, in honour of the Grande Armée, unveiled on his birthday, 15 August 1810.[58] To define his leadership and represent his military prowess and domination of Europe Napoleon harnessed the talent not only of David but of his pupils. David had painted *Napoleon Crossing the Great Saint-Bernard* in 1801, but his pupil Antoine-Jean Gros followed Bonaparte's Army of Italy in 1796 and submitted the portrait of *Bonaparte at Arcola* to the Salon of 1799. Gros portrayed Napoleon as a king with a healing touch in *Napoleon in the Pest-house of Jaffa*, exhibited in 1804, and as a great military leader in his 1808 *Battle of Eylau*, foregrounded by the frozen bodies of men and horses. François Gérard provided the first portrait of Napoleon in imperial robes in 1805, and he triumphed with his *Battle of Austerlitz*, exhibited in the Salon of 1810. In the same Salon, from which Napoleon bought twenty paintings for 47,000 francs, Girodet exhibited the ferocious *Revolt of Cairo*, showing French soldiers putting down Mameluke rebels. Ten years younger than this cohort of David's pupils, Ingres nevertheless worked alongside them, producing his own portrait of the emperor in imperial garb in 1806, before winning the Prix de Rome and going to work in Italy.[59]

Under the Treaty of Vienna the art treasures plundered by Napoleon had to be returned to their place of origin. The Prussian army occupying Paris in July 1815 organized the return of art works to the German states, Metternich took care of Italy and the Duke of Wellington acted on behalf of the new Kingdom of the Netherlands. Even the restored King of Spain wanted his Murillos back. So upset was the director of the Louvre that he resigned in October 1815.[60] The Louvre had to fall back on French painting, and in any case for political reasons the restored monarchy was keen to demonstrate the continuity of national art since 1789 and powers of royal patronage equal to those of Napoleon. Military painting was frowned upon as too gruesome, recalling the generation of war that was now over. David was exiled as a regicide to Brussels in 1816 and died in 1825, but his pupils Girodet, Gérard and Gros reinvented themselves as painters of the glories and sufferings of the monarchy and for the time being dominated the jury of the Salon. For the Salon of 1817, for example, Gérard exhibited *The Entry of Henri IV into Paris*, foreshadowing the restoration of the statue of Henri IV to its plinth on the Pont-Neuf in 1818, while Gros submitted his *Departure of Louis XVIII for Ghent*, marking the moment when the king learned of Napoleon's return from Elba. Gros was made a baron not by Napoleon but by Charles X.

This continuity and national perspective did not go unchallenged. Artists committed to Bonapartism celebrated the heroism of the National Guard who had defended Paris against the advancing Allies in 1814 and that of the soldiers of Waterloo. Nicolas-Toussaint Charlet, who had been one of those national guardsmen, depicted a *Grenadier of Waterloo*. Horace Vernet organized a private exhibition after his *Barrier of Clichy*, showing the same defence of Paris by the National Guard, and his *Soldier of Waterloo* were rejected by the Salon of 1822. The use of lithography meant that these iconic pictures could be reproduced on a mass basis and sold to veterans of Napoleon's armies. Closely associated with these Bonapartist circles was Théodore Géricault, who returned from two years in Italy to produce a powerful lithograph of *The Retreat from Russia* in 1818. The following year, moved by the scandal of a shipwreck caused by a reckless noble captain bound for Senegal and the cutting adrift of survivors on a raft, Géricault submitted his dramatic *Raft of the Medusa* to the Salon. Representing a few desperate survivors among a pile of corpses on the raft waving at a passing sail, echoing the Last Judgements of Michelangelo and Rubens, it was variously heralded as a work of genius and a gratuitous descent into horror.[61] The Salon of 1819 indeed marked a turning point. There was a breakthrough of 'young artists who wanted to dethrone David and overthrow his school', said the art critic Delécluze, himself a former pupil of David, 'the nude was proscribed, the beautiful rejected, and the choice of subjects from Antiquity absolutely condemned.'[62] Prompted by Romantic poets and writers such as Lord Byron and Walter Scott, artists turned to the Middle Ages for an inspiration that was chivalric and religious. The so-called Troubadour school was in vogue, epitomized by the acclaim received by Louis Hersent for his *Abdication of Gustave Vasa*, a poignant rendering of a good

Swedish king enjoining his people to preserve the unity he has built up. Even Ingres broke with the Antique in the period 1812–26, inspired by Raphael and enjoying success with his *Vow of Louis XIII*, exhibited in the Salon of 1824, recalling the moment in 1637 when the king committed France to the protection of the Virgin Mary in the hope of being granted an heir.

The Romantic offensive continued through the 1820s. An artistic revolution was under way, as Romantic painters preferred life and movement to precise drawing, individual character and local colour to eternal beauty, and real historical context to the world of Antiquity and mythology. The movement was spearheaded by Eugène Delacroix. Delacroix, who was inspired by Géricault and mortified by his early death in 1824, painted not to display beauty but to express physical and mental anguish, his paintings full of movement, sensuality, exotic colour, executed with bold brushstrokes rather than the conventional fine finish. He owed much to Byron, and to contemporary events such as the Greek struggle for independence against the Turks with which Byron was involved. His *Scenes from Massacres at Chios*, exhibited in the Salon of 1824, portrayed the death and enslavement of Christian Greeks. The Salon of 1827 saw a head-on clash of Romantic painters and the classical school, the flame of which was now taken up by Ingres. Ingres exalted the Ancient world in his *Apotheosis of Homer*, in which his beloved Raphael and classical writers Corneille, Racine, Molière and La Fontaine paid homage to the great storyteller. Delacroix on the other hand exhibited a powerful painting drawn from Byron of the Assyrian king Sardanapalus waiting for death, surrounded by his harem, slaves and horses who are about to be engulfed in a funeral pyre.[63]

In art as well as in literature, the Revolution of 1830 represented a triumph for Romanticism. Delacroix combined allegory and contemporary event in his *Liberty Leading the People*. He threw himself into a series of pictures inspired by Dante, Shakespeare, Goethe, Walter Scott and Chateaubriand. The jury that controlled the Salon, dominated by lesser-known artists of the generation of David's pupils, were keen, however, to defend the canons of the classical school against the Romantics. In 1836, for example, they rejected Delacroix's *Hamlet*, which was pointedly bought by the heir to the throne, the Duc d'Orléans.[64] Reviews such as *L'Artiste* dedicated themselves to campaigning on behalf of the Romantic school.[65] In time, however, the tide moved against the Romantics. In 1841 Ingres returned from Rome, where he had been director of the French school at which winners of the Prix de Rome studied, to preside over a revival of interest in harmonious line and beauty, articulated now less by reference to classical Antiquity than to mythology and the Orient. Whereas the Oriental themes of Delacroix were executed with passion, the odalisques or slaves in Turkish harems painted by Ingres were an excuse to study nudes that were both sensual and serene.

The July Monarchy was keen to move beyond the battle between classical and Romantic art, preaching a *juste milieu* between order and movement, monarchy and the heritage of the French Revolution, and a national greatness that was articulated by a succession of regimes, royal, republican and imperial. Louis-Philippe converted the Château of Versailles into a national museum, with the motto 'To all the Glories of the Fatherland' over the entrance. The Hall of Battles was given over to paintings of fifteen centuries of French glory, from the victory of Clovis on the battlefield of Tolbiac (496) to the triumph of Napoleon at Wagram (1809). Romanticism and classicism were reconciled by inviting Delacroix to paint the battle of Taillebourg (1242) and Gérard to submit his *Entry of Henri IV into Paris* as well as a study of *Austerlitz*. Horace Vernet, a rebel after 1815, was tamed by Charles X with the Legion of Honour in 1825, and became Louis-Philippe's artist of choice. He was entrusted with the last three battles of Jena, Friedland and Wagram, and also brought to the Hall his Bouvines and Fontenoy, painted for Charles X.[66] When the French armies enjoyed a rare bout of glory after 1815 by subduing the Algerian leader Abd-el-Kader, Vernet was called upon to represent this victory in a vast panorama 21 metres long, exhibited in the Salon of 1845. The *juste milieu* of the July Monarchy was also expressed by an eclectic style that combined the best of classical and Romantic. The talking point of the Salon of 1847 was *The Romans of the Decadence*, another monumental painting, nearly 5 metres by 8, by Thomas Couture, a pupil of Gros. Its theme was classical and it was highly composed, but its subject was not the glory of Rome but its decline, a salutary tale for the French bourgeoisie, and the forms of some of the draped bodies echoed those on the *Raft of the Medusa*, albeit in languid ecstasy rather than death. Ingres and Delacroix, wrote one critic, 'are no longer the young generation . . . They have established their style; we must bow to them and pass them by.'[67]

THE ARTS, POLITICS AND MARKETS IN THE SECOND EMPIRE

The Second Empire censored the political press and took a broad view of the need to protect public order and public morals. The economic boom with which it coincided and which it tried to foster by railway building, urban development and free trade, was designed to have a depoliticizing effect on a bourgeois public which had more disposable income but less patience and preferred to be entertained rather than challenged. Political repression and bourgeois philistinism bred a frustration in a new generation of writers who wished to challenge the narrow and materialist values of the bourgeois society that was now dominant. However, artists challenging dominant mores ran the risk of provoking the ire of the state, which did not hesitate to prosecute writers who were held to transgress these norms.

Alexandre Dumas *fils* came up against the authorities with his *Dame aux camélias*, the story of a courtesan, Marguerite, who falls in love with one of her lovers, Armand. First published as a novel, it was adapted as a play but was censored by the interior minister of the Second Republic, which was then dominated by royalists. Dumas went with his father to try to secure an audience with the minister, but to no avail. The situation improved when the Duc de Morny, one of the masterminds of the coup d'état of 2 December 1851, himself became interior minister. He took a much less censorious view, and the play opened at the Vaudeville Theatre in Paris on 2 February 1852. In fact, the play did not really challenge social norms but rather reinforced them. Marguerite is visited in Act III by her lover's father, who tells her that she is a 'dangerous person' who cannot marry his son. He has two children to marry, and his daughter, 'young, beautiful, as pure as an angel', is due to marry into 'an honourable family which wishes that everything in my family is honourable too'. Besides, a marriage between his son and Marguerite 'would have neither chastity for foundation, nor religion for support, nor a family as its fruit'.[68] Rather than threaten bourgeois hypocrisy, Marguerite sacrifices herself, dies, and releases Armand for a successful career and traditional marriage.

The challenges posed by Charles Baudelaire and Gustave Flaubert were considered more serious. Baudelaire was in revolt against his own family as well as against society. His father, a civil servant under the Empire, died when he was five, and his mother remarried an establishment figure, a major-general and ambassador who was appointed an imperial senator in 1853. Charles contracted venereal disease at eighteen, dropped out of the law faculty at nineteen and having attacked his stepfather at a dinner party was put on a ship for Calcutta. Coming into his father's inheritance at twenty-one, in 1842, he pursued the life of a writer in Paris, calling Sainte-Beuve his uncle, and becoming a disciple of Théophile Gautier (whose reputation as a poet was made with his 1852 *Émaux et camées*) and a friend of Maxime du Camp.[69] Gautier admired his almost British reserve and called him 'a dandy lost in bohemia',[70] He established himself as an art critic, and was a great admirer of Delacroix. Covering the Salon of 1846 he judged that while Hugo was a worker, Delacroix was a creator. 'His works are poems,' he wrote, 'naively conceived, executed with insolence, shaped by genius . . . while the one takes only the skin, the other snatches the entrails.'[71] In 1857 Baudelaire buried his stepfather and published *Les Fleurs du mal*. Gautier remarked that it betrayed a sense of the 'original perversity' of man but that 'more than once, with a powerful movement of the wings, rises towards the bluest regions of spirituality'.[72] Other did not agree, and the authorities took the view that the work was immoral, obscene and irreligious. Baudelaire was brought before the Tribunal de la Seine and fined 300 francs, one and a half times his monthly income. Fortunately, he had contacts in high places and on appeal to the empress his fine was reduced to 50 francs.[73] After this he gave more time to art criticism, defending the work of Delacroix and Manet.

One writer who sympathized deeply with what Baudelaire was

attempting was Flaubert. Flaubert congratulated him on rejuvenating Romanticism and said he was 'like nobody else'. 'You celebrate the flesh without loving it, in a sad and detached way I like. You are as hard as marble and as penetrating as an English fog.'[74] Flaubert, son of the chief surgeon at Rouen hospital, and the same age as Baudelaire, also dropped out of law studies in Paris, after failing in his first-year examination. In 1843 he met Victor Hugo, and was disappointed to find the great man so ordinary. That same year, after a carriage accident, he began to suffer epileptic fits. His closest friend from his brief student days, Maxime du Camp, said that 'this illness ruined his life, making him solitary and wild'.[75] Following his father's death in 1846 he came into his inheritance, and was able to spend most of his time on the family's country property at Croisset in Normandy.[76] With du Camp he toured Brittany in 1847 and undertook a *voyage en Orient* taking in Egypt and Turkey in 1850, after which he hesitated between writing something exotic, such as *Une Nuit de Don Juan* or '*Anubis*, the story of a woman who wants to be seduced by God', and something that explored provincial bourgeois life in all its ordinariness.[77] His *Madame Bovary* was serialized in *La Revue de Paris*, which du Camp edited, in the autumn of 1856. The novel explored the dreams and frustrations of a doctor's wife in Normandy, and rather than dress up sex or death in any distant or invented setting it laid it bare in the heart of the French bourgeoisie. As with *Les Fleurs du mal* some passages were deemed an affront to 'public and religious morality' and Flaubert was brought before the courts by the government. The prosecution argued that the book glorified Madame Bovary's adultery and elided her sexual desires and religious yearnings. The defence argued that it was a work of social criticism, demonstrating what happened to a farmer's daughter who was educated above her station and was married for reasons of social advancement rather than for love. The prosecution said that the book would corrupt female readers, the defence that Madame Bovary's death would serve as a warning to them. Some critics also thought that the novel was too brutal in its realism. 'The son and brother of distinguished doctors,' wrote Sainte-Beuve, 'Flaubert wields his pen as others wield the scalpel. Anatomists and physiologists seem to be everywhere.'[78] Many readers, on the other hand, using the same metaphor, were moved by the truthfulness of Flaubert's portrayal of the predicament of contemporary women. 'I have not stopped crying since yesterday about this poor woman and have not been able to sleep at night,' wrote Mlle Leroyer de Chantepie of Angers. 'Monsieur, where did you gain this perfect understanding of human nature? It is like a scalpel applied to the heart, to the soul. Alas, it is the world in all its ugliness.'[79] Flaubert was acquitted, he was acclaimed as the leader of the Realist school, and *Madame Bovary*, now published in hardback by Michel Lévy, became an instant success.[80]

Writers who attacked the moral and religious basis of the Empire might still be socially acceptable to it. In an attempt to avoid trial, Flaubert mobilized contacts in high places including the poet Lamartine, the emperor's cousin 'Plon-Plon' (Prince Jérôme-Napoléon) and ladies-in-waiting to the empress. In the 1860s he was a guest at the leading literary and artistic salon, presided over by another cousin of the emperor, Princess Mathilde, who was separated from her husband Prince Demidov and had found a new calling as a patron of the arts. The Goncourt brothers, Edmond and Jules, who had also been tried on an obscenity charge in 1853, recorded that at the empress's in January 1863 they and Flaubert 'formed an odd-looking group; we were almost the only three people there without decorations and the government of the Emperor, whom we could almost touch with our elbows, had dragged all three of us through the police courts for outraging public morals. The irony of it all.'[81] In fact they were happier in the cafés and restaurants of Paris which provided a more democratic if male-dominated form of sociability. In 1862 the Goncourt brothers founded a dining society of Realist writers that met on Sunday nights, twice a month, at Magny's restaurant. It included Sainte-Beuve, now happy to denounce Victor Hugo as a 'charlatan', Turgenev, Taine, Renan and Flaubert. George Sand was invited on a few occasions but said little and told Flaubert, 'You are the only person here who does not frighten me.'[82]

The social connections that linked the writers of the Realist movement did not, however, necessarily bring public recognition. George Sand may have been shy in the restaurant but she enjoyed a wider public. In 1869 Flaubert published *L'Éducation sentimentale*, featuring a mirror-image of one of Balzac's heroes, 'a man of every weakness', who blends perfectly into the bourgeois milieu by dint of education, manners and fortune, but fails to pursue a career and fails to win the woman he loves, while the tumultuous events of 1848–51 simply pass him by. The novel was at best widely misunderstood and at worst condemned by the critics as an attack on bourgeois ideals. There were only two isolated voices of praise. Émile Zola defended Flaubert by underlining his 'nervous analysis of the smallest facts, a notation of life that is both meticulous and alive'.[83] George Sand argued, positively, that it was the fault of contemporary society if it was 'in fact mediocre, ridiculous, condemned to see its aspirations continually aborted'.[84] However, she was a friend and had the delight at the same time of seeing her play, *L'Autre*, become a box-office success at the Opéra-Comique. Flaubert, who saw it himself early in 1870, told Sand, 'what a pretty work, and how one loves its author!'[85] The fact that a masterpiece was damned by the critics while a play of which nothing has since been heard was praised to the rooftops says a great deal about the bourgeois society that was the market for literature, drama and music in the nineteenth century.

It was not that Flaubert lacked a good publisher for his novels, rather that the eye of publishers in the Second Empire was on the expanding demand for information and entertainment. The careers of the Lévy brothers and Louis Hachette demonstrate the dramatic changes that took place in book publishing after 1840. Simon Lévy was a Jewish pedlar from Alsace who came to Paris in 1826, selling theatre programmes and the texts of plays running in Paris before opening a *cabinet de lecture* in 1836. His son Michel set up as a music publisher in his own right in 1845 and, having taken the side of Alexandre Dumas against accusations of running a 'literary factory', secured the right to publish the complete works of Dumas, which appeared as thirty-eight volumes at 2 francs each in 1847. The success of that year led to Michel and his brothers Calmann and Nathan putting 50,000 francs each into a family publishing business, and they acquired rights to the works of both George Sand and the playwright and librettist Eugène Scribe in 1855. In 1857 they published Flaubert's *Madame Bovary* in a first edition of 6,000, at 1 franc each, and a second edition in 1858, but their all-time bestseller was Ernest Renan's 1863 *Life of Jesus*, which sold 140,000 copies in the first year and a half and made them enough money to open a new bookshop on the place de l'Opéra in 1871.[86] For his part Louis Hachette, having dropped out of law studies, developed a publishing niche in school textbooks for the expanding school system and soon became king of the textbook, publishing fifty-four titles in 1833–9. Another sector of his market was the publication of dictionaries, culminating in Littré's dictionary of 1863. In 1851 he visited the Great Exhibition in London and returned to Paris determined to establish himself as the French W. H. Smith. Just as the main railway system was being completed and with the powerful patronage of the Duc de Morny, with whom he co-owned a paper-manufacturing business, he negotiated an exclusive right with railway companies to set up station bookstalls. He developed a whole library of colour-coded paperbacks as train-journey reading, retailing at between 50 centimes and 1 franc 50, avoiding anything political or immoral and including the popular children's stories of the Comtesse de Ségur. Hachette also acquired the right to distribute newspapers through station bookshops, and by the time of his death in 1865 newspaper sales were bringing in more than book sales.[87]

The press likewise responded quickly to the commercial and communications revolutions. The heavy censorship of the political press after the 1848 Revolution encouraged press barons to develop a more informative, entertaining kind of newspaper. Hippolyte de Villemessant, the illegitimate son of an aristocratic mother who sought redemption in Legitimism and commercial success, acquired *Le Figaro* in 1854, and turned it into the society paper of the Second Empire which 'relates Paris to Paris'.[88] When press censorship was relaxed in 1867 he successfully merged the literary-gossip dimension with American-style political reportage, and the paper had a healthy daily circulation of 47,000 in 1868.[89] One of his journalists, Henri Rochefort, the son of a Legitimist marquis who was introduced to republicanism by his father-in-law, broke with Villemessant and in 1868 launched his own paper, *La Lanterne*, in response to the more liberal press laws. Satirical and scurrilous, it caught the mood of growing opposition to the Empire in Paris and sold 125,000 copies on its second Saturday, before the government clamped down. He had already fled to Belgium to take refuge with the Hugo family, who dubbed him 'the proud archer', before the government sentenced him to a year in prison.[90]

Very different from both these papers was *Le Petit Journal*, launched in 1863 by Polydore Millaud, who originated in the Sephardic Jewish community of Bordeaux and sought his journalistic fortune in Paris after 1836. Tabloid in design, selling for a mere 5 centimes, *Le Petit Journal* was distributed along the railway network and expedited to towns and villages by a network of itinerant paper-sellers who replaced the *colporteurs*, killed off by government restrictions since 1849. It not only served a popular audience in town and country that was no more than semi-literate but taught it to read. Non-political, it provided a wealth of information and entertainment from stock-market prices to reviews and reports of criminal trials, with *faits divers* or human-interest stories a new selling point. Its editorialist, who went under the trade name of Timothy Trimm, provided comment on the issues of the day from Easter celebrations to military service, answered readers' letters and was careful to avoid a Parisian focus. The novels it serialized were far from high literature, concentrating on Rocambole, the mysterious righter of wrongs of Ponson du Terrail's *Drames de Paris*, and the Monsieur Lecoq detective stories of Émile Gaboriau. The line between fact and fiction was not always closely drawn, and news, human interest and the detective story came together with the Tropmann affair, the case of a murder of parents and six children in the Paris suburb of Pantin. Circulation was 357,000 on 23 September 1869, the day the crime was announced, and rose when each body was found and the culprit apprehended, reaching 594,000 on 15 January 1870, the day of his execution.[91]

In the musical world the Second Empire was keen to eliminate any political opposition and to encourage pure entertainment. The *goguettes* were closed down and effectively replaced by the *café-concerts*, which multiplied after 1850 and reached their apogee around 1865. Making money out of the drinks they sold, they attracted a varied clientele of students, bohemians, the elegant and foreign tourists. Politics was replaced by sex, in terms both of the sauciness or obscenity of the songs sung and of the prostitution that was plied there. Some of the *café-concert* singers acquired star status, such as Thérésa, a former seamstress with a brief acting career who sang at the Alcazar and Eldorado. She competed for fame with the great actress of the day, Hortense Schneider, claiming that Schneider 'was called the Thérésa of the theatre, while I was called the Schneider of the *café-concerts*'.[92]

In the theatres the public of the Second Empire began to tire of the pompous extravagance of Meyerbeer's grand opera, favouring instead the smaller-scale, lyrical and intimate. Charles Gounod, who had fallen under the spell of Lacordaire when he won the Prix de Rome in 1839, became director of the Foreign Missions church in Paris and was briefly a seminarist at Saint-Sulpice in 1847–8. Now he turned from sacred music to opera and had *Faust*, based on Nerval's translation, performed at Léon Carvalho's Théâtre-Lyrique in 1859. It found itself in competition with Meyerbeer's latest work, *The Pardon of Ploërmel*, with a Breton and religious theme, at the Opéra-Comique. Georges Bizet, who saw both productions, thought Meyerbeer's 'rather boring' and *Faust* 'splendid. Gounod is the most complete of French composers.'[93] It was no easy task to judge the taste of the opera-going public. Bizet won the Prix de Rome in 1857 but his *Pearl Fishers*, produced at the Théâtre-Lyrique by Carvalho in 1863, was regarded as too Wagnerian and had to be alternated with Mozart's *Marriage of Figaro* to keep up box-office receipts. Even more of a flop was Berlioz's *Trojans*, which he could not get accepted by the Opéra and which became another Carvalho production in 1863, but lasted for only twenty-one performances.[94]

The career of Offenbach beautifully illustrates the way in which popular music was upgraded and grand opera subverted in order to produce a new genre, the operetta, which exactly matched the musical taste of the French bourgeoisie in the Second Empire. The son of a bookbinder and synagogue cantor from the Rhineland, Offenbach came to Paris in 1833 for Conservatory training, worked his way up through the orchestras of the boulevard du Temple and the Opéra-Comique, and became leader of the Comédie-Française orchestra in 1850. The Paris Exposition of 1855, which brought five million visitors to the capital, prompted him to write to the minister in charge, Achille Fould, asking for permission to open a theatre putting on 'a show in good taste, where until now there have been only more or less uncouth parades'.[95] The outcome was the small-scale Théâtre des Bouffes-Parisiens, which enjoyed the backing of *Le Figaro* newspaper, and made an impact with a send-up of *The Huguenots*, *Ba-Ta-Clan*, in 1856.[96]

More success came with *Orpheus in the Underworld* which parodied Greek myth and with it the court of the Second Empire, and opened at the Bouffes in 1858. Offenbach now moved on to the Opéra itself, with a ballet called *Papillon* in 1860, but the forum of his greatest triumphs, after theatres were accorded far more freedom in 1864, was the Théâtre des Variétés. *La Belle Hélène*, another spoof of Greek myth, starring Hortense Schneider, was described by *La Vie Parisienne* as encapsulating 'the present, our society, us, our beliefs, taste and gaiety', confident enough in itself that it could poke fun at the Ancients.[97] The Paris Exposition of 1867, which attracted eleven million visitors, was a showcase of French industrial progess as well as French culture. Two Schneiders were in view. Eugène, who announced that a French locomotive had been bought by the British, and Hortense, who played the lead in *The Grand Duchess of Gérolstein*, a story of love and war set in a diminutive German state which became the talk of the town and was attended by Napoleon III, the Prince of Wales, Bismarck and Tsar Alexander II.[98] Gérolstein was familiar as the duchy of Rodolphe, hero of Sue's *Mysteries of Paris*, and illustrated how Offenbach was taking over popular tropes just as the somewhat violent boulevard theatres were being demolished by Haussmann. At the same time, however, the witty and playful operetta displaced heavyweight opera as the favourite genre not only of the bourgeoisie but of high society, fantasizing about soldier Fritz, General Boum, Baron Puck and the Grand Duchess just as an altogether more militaristic Germany was about to bring Parisian gaiety to an end.

The great event of the artistic season, during the Second Empire as before, was the annual exhibition of the Paris Salon. The jury drawn from the Academy of Fine Arts mediated between the government and the bourgeois public, excluding any works that went against an aesthetic canon which favoured paintings that were religious, historical, mythological, pastoral or sentimental, inspired by classical or Renaissance art, and more recently by the Orient. Whereas the movement to keep out in the 1830s was Romanticism, in the 1850s it was Realism, the portrayal of modern life in all its grimness, and depicting peasants and workers rather than aristocrats and bourgeois. The defeat of the Revolution of 1848 destroyed the illusions of many artists and drove them to examine the reality of the world around them that had brought dreams of social emancipation to nothing.

Gustave Courbet had enjoyed no success under the July Monarchy, with only three of the twenty-two pictures he submitted accepted by the jury. At the Salon of 1849 he won a gold medal for his *After Dinner in Ornans*, and as a medal-winner he now gained the right to exhibit every year, bypassing the jury. In 1850 he provoked controversy with the unyieldingly severe *Stone-breakers* and *Burial at Ornans*. The art critic Champfleury, who took up the defence of Realism, asked, 'Is it the artist's fault if material interests, small-town life, sordid egoism, provincial narrowness have clawed their faces, dimmed their eyes, furrowed their brows, made their mouths stupid? Many bourgeois look like that. M. Courbet paints bourgeois.' A contrary view was put by the aged Delécluze, who wrote, 'Never, perhaps, has the worship of ugliness been so openly practised.'[99] Again, at the Salon of 1853, Courbet exhibited his *Bathers*, which portrayed not nymphs in some ethereal glade but flesh-and-blood women of generous proportion climbing out of a river. At a private view the empress thought they looked no different from the plough-horses exhibited in the next painting. The authorities had their revenge at the Paris Exhibition of 1855. Courbet submitted his *Burial at Ornans* but had no special privilege for this festival. He was turned down, and erected a tent for his own private show, under the banner, 'Realism. Gustave Courbet'.[100]

The artists who were favoured by the Academy at this moment were those who continued the classical school such as Jean-Léon Gérôme and William Bouguereau. Bouguereau won the prestigious Prix de Rome in 1848 and studied in Italy for four years, while Gérôme travelled in Italy in 1843–4 and after 1857 made several journeys to Egypt. Under the Empire Bouguereau accepted commissions to decorate public buildings, churches and town houses, typically with allegorical figures representing music and love. His paintings, of a photographic realism and highly finished, were nevertheless of purely imaginary mythological idylls, featuring nymphs and fauns moulded like Greek statues. Gérôme's first paintings were in a neo-Greek style but after he discovered the Orient he specialized in slave-markets and Arab street scenes, and painted a series imagining Bonaparte's 1798 campaign in Egypt.[101]

In 1863 there was another challenge to this school of painting. For the Salon of that year Gérôme presented three paintings which were all accepted: *Greek Comedians*, *A Turkish Butcher in Jerusalem* and a historical work, *Molière Breakfasting with Louis XIV*. Édouard Manet, however, presented *Le Déjeuner sur l'herbe*, which subverted paintings such as Raphael's *Judgement of Paris* by moving the scene from a mythological setting to a modern river bank and putting his carefree nude in the presence of dressed men. His new style of painting depicted modern life in the form of cafés, the theatre, bullfights, railway stations, street-scenes, the racetrack and the seaside, rather than beauty or ideals clothed in some timeless and escapist form. The composition was sometimes randomly cropped at the edges and used a rougher surface rather than the perfect design and glossy finish beloved of the Academy. So many paintings of this kind were rejected by the Salon jury in 1863 that the emperor exceptionally authorized a 'Salon des Refusés' to be arranged to show them.[102] The artists whose works were turned down were not social misfits or social rebels but of bourgeois background, possibly even more exalted than Gérôme, a jeweller's son from Vesoul, and were formally trained at the École des Beaux Arts. Manet was the son of an official in the Justice Ministry, while Édouard Degas was the son of an Italian banker and American mother, who, like Baudelaire and Flaubert, had abandoned his law studies. Socially, although Gérôme was a regular at the salon of Princesse Mathilde while Manet met the likes of Baudelaire and Émile Zola at the Café Guerbois in the Grande rue des Batignolles (now the avenue de Clichy), Manet had also toured Italy where he met up with Émile Ollivier, whom he caricatured in 1860, and was visited in his workshop by the Goncourt brothers. Generationally, the painters of modern life were a decade younger that the academic artists, but the main source of antagonism was aesthetic and political.

The new artists had an ambivalent relationship with the Salon, for they could not afford to forgo the recognition it provided. Manet's *Olympia*, which was accepted by the Salon of 1865, poked fun at the stylized nude of paintings such as Titian's *Venus of Urbino* by painting a reclining prostitute, accompanied by a black cat and black servant, obviously awaiting a client. In 1866, however, more of Manet's pictures were rejected from the Salon and Zola took up his cause. In a series of articles in *L'Événement* in April–May 1866 he defined the works of Manet and his circle as 'a corner of creation seen through a temperament'.[103] By the end of the Second Empire Manet's pictures called into question not only the canons of the Salon and the Academy, but the politics of the regime. While Gérôme hailed the establishment of a French empire in Indo-China for the Salon of 1865 by painting a line of Siamese ambassadors crawling to the thrones of Napoleon III and Empress Eugénie, Manet chose to depict *The Execution of Maximilian*, the ill-fated prince the French government tried to impose on the Mexican people, who expressed their thanks by shooting him. The thanks of the regime naturally went to Gérôme, who was sent as one of the official party for the opening of the Suez Canal in 1869, while Manet was told that his *Execution* would be rejected by the Salon of 1869 if it were submitted.

7

The French in a Foreign Mirror

The French reached the apogee of their military power in 1812, their domination of Europe reaching as far as Moscow. After that, their power collapsed, leaving France with a long road to recover great-power status. The French people's image of themselves was never purely conditioned by military power. They saw their superiority in terms of being bearers of liberty and culture, which might be but did not have to be propagated by cannon or bayonets. But they never lost confidence in themselves as a great power, a major player in Europe and the world. As they travelled, the French judged each nation by the liberty, culture or power to which it could lay claim. Some had culture but no liberty or power, some had power but no liberty or culture. Each nation held up a different image of the French to themselves, and made them think about their own identity, but none in their eyes could achieve that unique blend of liberty, culture and power that was French.

ITALY: RUINS AND BEAUTY

Stendhal began *The Charterhouse of Parma* (1839) with the entry of General Bonaparte into Milan on 15 May 1796, after his victory at Lodi, expelling the Austrians who occupied Lombardy, and 'in a few months awoke a people who had fallen asleep'. The French soldiers were all under twenty-five; Bonaparte, at twenty-seven, was said to be the oldest man in the army. Italy was taken by a storm of youth and 'suddenly found itself inundated with light'. The only opposition to the arrival of the French came from the monks who had preached that learning to read was a waste of time and if the Lombards simply paid their tithes and confessed their sins they would earn their place in heaven.[1]

This novel was in a sense autobiographical. Stendhal himself ended the account of his painful childhood, *The Life of Henri Brulard*, during which he had battled against his father and the priests hired to educate him, with his entry into Milan on 10 June 1800, attached to the French army and aged seventeen, when the French army again expelled the Austrians after the battle of Marengo. He later said of the Italians that 'Marengo moved on the civilization of their country by a hundred years, just as another battle [Waterloo] stopped it for a century'.[2] On another occasion he argued that the Italians had known modern civilization only between 17 May 1809, when Napoleon introduced the Civil Code into Italy, and April 1814, when the French were themselves forced to abandon that country and when the Kingdom of Italy, which Napoleon had set up and of which he had been crowned king in 1805, came to an end.[3]

What Stendhal meant by civilization was something decidedly modern: political unity, a free society under the rule of law, and the Enlightenment. Italy may have been the cradle of ancient civilization, but that was now dead, and the Italians were gripped by political divisions, foreign rule, petty despotisms and the spiritual and temporal domination of the Roman Catholic Church. This perception was not peculiar to Stendhal but was a commonplace among French visitors to Italy. Chateaubriand, who arrived in Rome in June 1803 as secretary to the French legation there, and stood at the other end of the political spectrum from Stendhal, was delighted to find that the pope was reading his *Genius of Christianity*, but saw the city 'slumbering in the middle of ruins'. The Tiber, he said, separated two glories that were now past, 'Pagan Rome, sinking deeper into its tombs, and Christian Rome, descending once more into the catacombs from which it came'. The deadness of the city affected even its inhabitants, who seemed to be dying of hunger but did not work, preferring to live from the charity of the Church.[4] Madame de Staël, who went to Italy in 1804–5, wrote in her novel *Corinne, or Italy* that Italy was a 'country of tombs' and 'tired of glory'. Divided into small states and occupied by foreign powers it had no centre of enlightenment like Paris and liberty was there in mourning. What it did have was artistic genius: the country of Petrarch and Dante and of popular energy manifest at Carnival. 'Our only glory', Corinne tells Oswald, the Scottish lord she admires, 'is the genius of the imagination', and she herself excels as a poet, musician, actress and dancer, crowned with laurels on the Capitol. Corinne inspires Oswald with her genius, but this does not make her marriageable: Italy is dominated by conservative social conventions, imposed both by Italians and by visiting Britons and Frenchmen, so that Oswald marries her half-sister and does not realize his mistake until Corinne dies broken-hearted.[5]

After the departure of the French in 1814–15 there were restorations of Austrian rule in the north, Vatican rule in the Papal States in the centre and Bourbon rule in Naples and Sicily. Stendhal, who was out of favour with the French Bourbons, lived from 1814 to 1821 in Milan, for him 'the most beautiful place on earth',[6] hating the stifling political atmosphere but arguing that there was no better environment for music or love. While France was a nation state dominated by its capital, Italy was divided into a myriad of small states, each with their courts and 'eight or ten ministers without the workload of a [French] prefect between them', with nothing better to do than to vex the population. The peoples of the different city states, he said, all spoke different dialects and hated each other. He saw this as a 'legacy of the tyrannies of the Middle Ages and a great obstacle to liberty'. Rome, under papal rule, was a despotism which refused to countenance any new ideas. There was scarcely any middle class to serve as a vehicle of progressive ideas and the nobility made common cause with the people in their support of reaction. The small number of Italians who desired liberty and unity, members of the *carbonari* secret society, risked being put to death in the cruellest way in the Papal States if they were caught. And yet for Stendhal La Scala was the greatest opera house in the world. 'Only music is alive in Italy,' he said. 'If you are a citizen you will die of melancholy . . . the only thing to do in this beautiful country is to make love.' He estimated that of a hundred French women in the Bois de Boulogne scarcely one was beautiful, whereas in Italy thirty would be over made up, 'fifty would be beautiful, but with nothing more than an air of voluptuousness, while the twenty others would be of the most ravishing classic beauty'.[7]

Attempts were made by liberals and patriots to shake off Austrian, papal and Bourbon rule, but without success. An uprising in Bologna, once part of the Napoleonic Kingdom of Italy but now ruled by the papal bureaucracy, was put down with the help of Austrian troops. Edgar Quinet, visiting Italy in 1836, was horrified to find Austrian troops still occupying Bologna, as well as Milan and Venice. 'At that moment,' he confessed, 'I hated Germany for all the ill it has done to Italy. No, no, it cannot go on. The white uniforms must disappear, the prickly cavalry must go back over the mountains ... let them return to the valleys of the Danube, the Elbe and the Spree, and harness their feudal ploughs.'[8] Flaubert, travelling in Italy a decade later, in 1845, saw Milan as a place of transition between Italy and Austria, and was fascinated by the variety of uniforms of the Austrian and Hungarian regiments. Like Stendhal, he remarked on the paradox of political lifelessness and clerical despotism on the one hand and cultural life and emotional excitement on the other. 'I entered La Scala with a religious emotion,' he wrote, 'because there human thought ... seeks to escape reality and people come to cry, to laugh or to marvel.' At an open-air theatre in Genoa, he was fixated by 'the most beautiful woman I have ever seen' and 'contemplated her as one drinks a wine of exquisite taste'.[9]

In 1848 Quinet urged the Italians 'not to resurrect a nation but TO CREATE ONE'. An Italian nation had to end Austrian domination but could not, as some Italians advised, found one around the reactionary leadership of the Papal States. Although the French had themselves occupied Italy, they should be trusted to liberate it.[10] In 1859–60 Italy was duly liberated and united by a French army which, in alliance with Piedmont, drove out the Austrians from Lombardy and triggered a national movement which ultimately deprived the pope of the Papal States and toppled the Bourbons of Naples. At the beginning of the campaign Napoleon III told his troops that as they passed the former battlefields of Lodi and Marengo they would be 'marching on a sacred road, amid glorious memories'. Liberating the Italians was what the French were good at, and they had little fear that a united Italian nation would turn its force against them.

Hippolyte Taine, travelling in Italy in 1864, called it 'a backward France, like a younger sister who is growing up and closer to its elder sister'.[11] Under French patronage, Italy was receiving the gift of modern civilization from the French seventy years after their Revolution, transforming 'a feudal people into a modern people', the educated and commercial bourgeoisie on the side of progress, the old nobles and the clergy on the other, fighting for the loyalty of the peasantry. The new Italian state was creating a new army, a national guard, a new system of justice, and above all schools to unite and enlighten the population, with old rivalries between cities and provinces dissolving in the solvent of fraternity. The main area of resistance to change, the former Kingdom of Naples, where monks had been thrown out of their monasteries, where the feudal nobility sulked behind closed doors and where peasants took to the hills as brigands to avoid conscription into the new army, was just like an Italian Vendée, but would soon be brought under control.[12]

GERMANY: FROM DREAMS TO AWAKENING

The relationship of the French with Germany was never so easy. While for Stendhal, crossing the Alps to Milan was joy, for Madame de Staël, crossing the Rhine on a cloudy and cold day in 1803, anxious about her small children in tow, was a penance.[13] Admittedly, she was going into exile at the command of Napoleon, but Germany was always much stranger to the French visitor than Italy, and the French were much less able to patronize it. Although the French were inclined to use the same rhetoric of bringing liberty and civilization to Germany as they were to the Italians, Germans promptly took it up to use as a weapon against the French, at the service of the German nation and German culture.

Despite her reluctance to go to Germany, in 1813 Madame de Staël published *On Germany*, the single most influential account of Germany for the French reader in the first half of the nineteenth century. Germany, she explained, was a young civilization, much of it still buried under forests and uninhabited. Whereas France and Italy were marked by the Roman Empire, Germany was shaped by the Middle Ages: it was Gothic, feudal, chivalrous. The 'spirit of chivalry' had been destroyed in France by Richelieu and replaced by a 'spirit of vanity' which sought to ruin the reputations of women; in Germany, it remained, and the honour of women was safe. The persistence of feudalism meant that 'the separation of classes was more pronounced in Germany than elsewhere', but this went along with the 'pre-eminence of the military state' and habits of obedience to government. The great difference between France and Germany was thus liberty. 'The love of liberty has not developed among the Germans,' said Madame de Staël. 'They have not learned how dear it is either by enjoying it, or by having to do without it.' This did not mean that there was no intellectual life in Germany. On the contrary, there was, but the thinking of intellectuals was not directed to calling into question the feudal or militaristic political system, rather it was confined to philosophical speculation and literary creation. There was no German Voltaire or Rousseau, but there was Kant, and there were Goethe and Schiller. She quoted one German writer to the effect that 'the English had the empire of the sea, the French the empire of the land and the Germans the empire of the air'.[14]

Like Italy, the Germany that Madame de Staël knew was divided up into a multitude of small states, controlled by secular or ecclesiastical rulers, or cities enjoying a great deal of autonomy. This meant that just as there was little love of liberty, there was little love of the fatherland. Germans were divided among themselves, belonging not only to different states but to different religions, and these divisions were often exacerbated by foreign powers becoming mixed up in German affairs. 'This division of Germany, fatal for its political strength,' she explained, 'is very conducive to all kinds of experiments that genius or imagination might attempt.' Because there was no capital city where society congregated, like Paris, the pressure to conform to a certain accepted taste was much less powerful. 'Most writers and thinkers work in solitude, or surrounded only by a small circle that they dominate.' In that way, though Germany lacked national strength, it was a hive of cultural activity.[15]

Madame de Staël's work may have been influential, but it did not agree with the views of Napoleon, whose police minister had the first edition of the work seized in 1810. The explanation given was that the French had no cause to look for models elsewhere and that the book was thus anti-French. Napoleon may have had a point: there is no mention in *On Germany* of the country's transformation under French authority after his military victories: the absorption of a mass of free cities and prince-bishoprics into secular states such as Prussia and Bavaria in 1803, the alliance of sixteen German states of western and southern Germany in the Confederation of the Rhine in July 1806, or the dissolution of the Holy Roman Empire the following month, as the Austrian emperor realized he had no more authority over the German states. Napoleon may well have taken the view that he had brought liberty and civilization to the feudal, church-encrusted, small-state Germany that Madame de Staël described but which he was busily modernizing. He might also have taken offence at her suggestion that at least in Germany writers were free to write and women were treated with dignity, neither of which, she would claim, obtained in Napoleon's France.

Whereas the French could claim to be patrons of liberty in Italy after the restoration of 1814–15, the liberty that was appropriated by the Germans in 1813 was turned against French power in an attempt to found a free and united people. The restoration of 1814–15 reimposed Austrian power in Germany through thirty states gathered in the German Confederation, but the dream of a free united Germany now haunted the German educated class. Edgar Quinet, who studied at Heidelberg in 1826–8, noted in 1831 that the Germany of Madame de Staël, 'a country of ecstasy, a continuous dream . . . no centre anywhere, no ties, no ambition, no public spirit, no national strength', was now gone. While the invasion of 1814 had induced a desire for peace and reconciliation in France, in Germany it had created 'the love and taste for political action'. Austria, traditional and Catholic, based on the Danube and Italy, had lost influence to Prussia, which prided itself on helping defeat Napoleon at Waterloo and was troubled by an 'irritable and angry nationalism'. The French Revolution of 1830 had echoes in certain German states which were forced to concede constitutional government, but more significant was a growing desire for the 'territorial unity of the German nation'.

The Prussian government had not itself conceded a constitution but the 'demagogic party' had made a tacit agreement with the government 'to postpone liberty, and together augment the fortune of Frederick [the Great]'. Most worrying of all for France, popular nationalism criticized the Prussian government for not having taken Alsace and Lorraine, lost to France in 1648, back again in 1815.[16]

Earlier than most Frenchmen, Quinet spotted that the Germans, far from being able to sponsor liberty and national sentiment in their own country, would use liberty and nationalism to challenge France for great-power status in Europe. France itself felt constrained by the limits imposed on it by the Treaty of Vienna, and its subordination to British, Russian and Austrian power. Then, in 1840, during the diplomatic crisis in the Near East, demands arose in France for a recovery of the Rhine frontier lost in 1815 and Prussia mobilized its troops on the Rhine, which it had been granted as a barrier to French expansion in 1815. France suffered another diplomatic defeat, and Quinet ranted, 'The Revolution surrendered its sword in 1815; it was thought that she would take it up again in 1830, but it was not so.' Now, in 1840, the monarchy had blustered but been humiliated. The only chance, in Quinet's view, was for France to become a republic, and on that basis assert its national strength against Germany.[17]

Despite Quinet, there was an enduring sense in France that the Germany of Madame de Staël was not dead, that it was still a country of small states and cosmopolitan ideas. The journalist Edmond About wrote in 1860 that the German philosophy of Kant and Hegel was taught in French schools, that Goethe, Schiller, Lessing and Heine were admired writers, that French scientists prided themselves on corresponding with Liebig or Graefe, that Haydn, Gluck, Mozart and Beethoven were considered gods of music. Wagner's *Tannhäuser* was booed three performances in a row when it was staged in Paris in March 1861, but less because Wagner was German than because it was felt to be imposed on the Paris Opéra by the wife of the Austrian ambassador, Princess Metternich; if there was a political dimension, it was felt that this was revenge for Austria's defeat in Italy. Edmond About had no objections to German unification under Prussia, and indeed saw it as a triumph of 'religious reformation, commercial progress and constitutional liberalism' over Catholic, feudal, divine-right Austria. The only provisos were that Prussia should itself choose constitutional government over divine-right monarchy, and that it should not claim French territory, in particular Alsace-Lorraine. 'We keep what belongs to us,' he said, 'we ask no more.'[18] Unfortunately for the French, Germany under Bismarck, who became Prussian minister-president in 1862, was united by 'blood and iron', a series of wars against Denmark in 1864, against Austria in 1866 and, finally to eliminate French influence in south Germany and to recover Alsace-Lorraine, against France in 1870. Liberty and culture were sacrificed to despotism and militarism. 'Germany was my mistress,' recalled Renan in 1871. 'Think how much I suffered when I saw the nation that taught me idealism forsake all ideals, when the fatherland of Kant, Fichte, Herder and Goethe decided to pursue only the goal of an exclusive nationalism ... A nation that confines itself to pure self-interest has no further universal role.'[19]

GREAT BRITAIN: NO FREEDOM, NO EQUALITY

France, of course, was locked in a struggle for European supremacy with Great Britain long before it had to worry about Germany. Peace almost broke out between France and Britain in 1800, after Bonaparte came to power, and survived for just over a year under the Peace of Amiens in 1802, but mutual suspicion, rivalry, fears for security and the sense that Europe was not big enough for both powers led to the resumption of war in 1803.

With war came propaganda. Napoleon hired a royalist journalist who had rallied to the new regime, Joseph Fiévée, to cross the Channel and write some *Letters from England* which would blow away the pro-British sentiments that persisted in some liberal circles and among royalist émigrés who had found refuge in England during the excesses of the French Revolution. Fiévée was keen to use England as a foil to exalt French liberty and French civilization. England was not free because there was no representative government, so corrupt was the system. There were three kinds of elections, 'those that are bought, those that are given, and those that are contested'. The people thought they were sovereign, but only because they were plied with free drink at election time. As for civilization, England was not civilized because money tarnished everything. While France had a warrior nobility, a younger son of an English noble could trade without losing status. The only criterion of status was money: honour was 'a French idea that had never fully been adopted into English customs'. Englishmen were not civilized because they disliked the company of women. They preferred to drink on their own after dinner, while their wives yawned upstairs in the drawing room. Worst of all, Fiévée unearthed the myth that an Englishman was entitled to put a rope around his wife's neck and take her to market to sell her.[20]

The victory of Great Britain in 1815 obliged the French to take the military and naval power of their rival seriously, but observers were quick to point to the price that had to be paid in terms of a Promethean work ethic. The economist Jean-Baptiste Say explained how Britain's sea-power had enabled it to confiscate the trade of other countries and establish a virtual commercial monopoly, while its wealth enabled it to command vast amounts of credit to supply not only its own armies but those of its allies. On the other hand to create this wealth the British were condemned to ceaseless work. 'There are no cafés filled with the idle from morning to night, and promenades are deserted every day except Sunday ... those who slow down in the slightest are promptly ruined,' and whereas 'the greatest shame in France is to lack courage, in England it is to lack money'.[21] Stendhal, visiting London in 1821, joked that the ceaseless work to which the English were condemned 'avenges us for Waterloo'. Though he was enthralled to see Kean playing *Othello* at Covent Garden he said that most English people were obsessed by the fear of wasting time and reluctant to read anything not related to making money. In this sense the English were 'the most obtuse, the most barbarous people in the world'.[22]

Long before Marx and Engels, French visitors were aware that British wealth and power was derived not only from hard work but from the exploitation of one class by another sharpened by the industrial revolution.[23] Describing a visit in 1810, Louis Simond reported that while the gun-makers of Birmingham were comfortably off, living in small three-bedroomed houses, Scottish cotton-workers suffered 'extraordinary distress', driven off the land by sheep-farming and earning a quarter of what they did twenty years before, while prices had doubled.[24] Travelling in Britain in the early 1820s, Édouard de Montulé noted that while Liverpool was booming like an American town, in Manchester there were 'a hundred thousand slaves of need, who breathe fetid air all the year round'.[25] French observers were often keen to enter into dialogue with British experts on the social question. In 1835 Tocqueville debated with Nassau Senior whether the livelihood of the poor had been sacrificed to the wealth of the rich, with Senior defending the wages of industrial workers as adequate and Tocqueville arguing that 'in England the rich have gradually monopolised almost all the advantages that society bestows upon mankind'.[26] In 1843 the French political economist Léon Faucher visited the East End of London with the public health reformer Dr Southwood Smith and found that the French Huguenot weavers of Spitalfields were 'in some ways the moral aristocracy of the area' but that the Irish weavers of Bethnal Green had a child-labour market, 'something not yet seen in a civilized country'.[27] In 1840 the feminist and utopian socialist Flora Tristan was particularly struck by the young prostitutes on the Waterloo Road, and calculated that 80,000–100,000 girls were driven by poverty to live by prostitution in London.[28] Stendhal, adrift in London in 1821 with a couple of Frenchmen, took a rather different view, visiting prostitutes on the Westminster Bridge Road.[29]

If working-class poverty and exploitation struck French visitors at one end of the social spectrum, at the other they were impressed by the dominance of the aristocracy, both socially and in political terms. They were keen to draw a distinction between Britain as an aristocracy and France, following the French Revolution which had abolished the corporate privileges of the French nobility and sold much of its land, as a fundamentally democratic society. Baron d'Haussez, a Norman noble who had been navy minister in 1829 but was forced to flee to England after the July Revolution, argued that primogeniture and entails, now unknown in France, ensured the continuity of large landed fortunes, and that these were translated into aristocratic influence and corruption which ensured that the landed classes controlled not only the House of Lords but the Commons too.[30] Léon Faucher observed that the Reform Bill of 1832 had made little difference, since the middle class aped the aristocracy and gentry rather than acting as a revolutionary class, as it had in France in 1789, and that 1832 witnessed a compromise between 'the lower classes, the middle class and a part of the aristocracy'.[31]

What French observers were not able to fathom, however, given the gross inequalities of British society and the aristocratic nature of its constitution, was why Britain was not more vulnerable to revolution than France. Part of the answer may have lain in the British relationship with sport, something that aroused some confusion in the French. Flora Tristan, for example, noted that social hierarchy was upheld even at the races, with the queen, aristocracy and lower classes all in their rightful places. She went as far as to suggest that whereas in France women were the most honoured creatures, in England it was the horse.[32] What she failed to register, however, was that horse-racing was a sport that brought together all levels of British society in a common spectacle. The other British sport that obsessed the French was one unknown in France: boxing. While the upper classes settled differences among themselves with the sword or pistol, an English gentleman who was offended by a man of the people would resort to fisticuffs, so that boxing for Édouard de Montulé was a means to 're-establish social equilibrium'.[33] The socialist Louis Blanc, in exile in England under the Second Empire, and remarking that it 'sweated aristocracy from every pore', attended a boxing match in December 1862 between the American champion John Heenan and the English champion Tom Sayers. He was appalled that men could fight only for money, whether prize money or bets, and that the public included MPs and ministers of the Church, so that the fight brought together 'the vices of the upper class and the vices of the lower class'. The social significance of the fact that boxing was 'a passion that has invaded all classes' and that a colonel told him that he preferred boxing to the opera, however, seemed to pass him by.[34]

THE UNITED STATES: DEMOCRACY AND SLAVERY

In the spring of 1791, on leave from the French army, Chateaubriand sailed to the United States, landing at Baltimore and visiting Philadelphia, New York, Albany and Niagara Falls before returning to France that winter. On the strength of his acquaintance with the Mohawk country in 1801 he published his novel *Atala*, about an Indian girl of that name, portrayed as a noble savage, living in the virgin forests of the New World. The following year he published *René*, the story of a melancholy Frenchman who takes a ship for the French colony of Louisiana in 1725, hears the story of Atala from an old Indian, Chactas, and dies fighting for the Natchez tribe of Louisiana against the French. These hugely popular works conveyed an image of America still in a state of nature, beloved of Romantics fleeing the modern world. Yet they were pure invention. Chateaubriand never travelled down the Mississippi, and the Natchez had long been dispersed by French settlers and soldiers.[35]

Louisiana itself, a vast area of land west of the Mississippi, stretching west to the Rockies and north to Canada, had been ceded by France to Spain in 1763 in return for Spain's part in the Seven Years War against the British. Napoleon recovered it from Spain in 1800, hoping to restore France's colonial empire, but when he realized that he would be unable to defend it he sold it in 1803 to the Americans, 838,000 square miles for 60 million francs, in order to fund the war against Britain.[36] Thomas Jefferson, the American president, offered the governorship of Louisiana to his old friend and comrade in the struggle for American independence, Lafayette, but Lafayette turned down the offer, saying that while liberty was safe in America, it was threatened in a Europe under Napoleonic despotism, and it was his duty to remain in the Old World to work for its restoration.[37]

America, for the French, was thus on one hand the virgin forests peopled by noble savages of Chateaubriand, and on the other the land of liberty to which they themselves, and especially Lafayette, had contributed. America was the model of the free government they craved but had been unable to realize as the Revolution lurched from Robespierre's Terror to Napoleon's despotism. Jefferson's message to Lafayette was always that free institutions needed long maturing and that Lafayette's sudden switch in the Hundred Days to hope for a 'national insurrection' under Napoleon to restore the gains of the Revolution was folly. He had advised Lafayette to compromise with the king to secure constitutional monarchy in 1789 and he proposed the same in 1815. As if to justify French views of liberty, Lafayette constantly reminded Jefferson that slavery in the Southern states, which was spreading out to new states formed after the Louisiana Purchase, such as Missouri, was a 'wide blot on American philanthropy . . . ever thrown in my face when I indulge my patriotism'.[38]

In 1824–5 Lafayette toured the United States at the invitation of President Monroe. He visited twenty-four states in twelve months, including the tomb of Washington at Mount Vernon on the Potomac and the battlefield of Yorktown, and embraced his old friend Jefferson at Montebello. There he was concerned that like all planters in Virginia Jefferson farmed his vast property with slave labour. In the deep South he was also concerned about treaties being forced on the Indians obliging them to withdraw west across the Mississippi, which did not compare with the crimes of violence used by the British against their Asian subjects, but would probably nevertheless result in their destruction. All this, however, was forgotten at the final banquet offered to him in Washington, when Lafayette announced how happy he was 'to see the American people daily more attached to the liberal institutions which they have made such a success, while in Europe they were touched by a withering hand'.[39]

Matters of American democracy, the treatment of Indians and slavery were thus not new issues when Tocqueville set sail for the United States with his friend Gustave de Beaumont, in 1831. Aged only twenty-five, he had decided against taking an oath to the July Monarchy required of him as a young magistrate, but secured a commission to study the American prison system. He obtained a letter of introduction from Chateaubriand, to whom he was distantly related, while Beaumont asked for one from Lafayette, whom Tocqueville considered a 'vain and dangerous demagogue'.[40] Tocqueville had been seduced by the idea of the inexorable rise of democracy thanks to Guizot's lectures on civilization in Europe which he had attended in 1829–30, and was keen to see what must come to Europe working in the democratic laboratory of the United States. He learned English from an American girl on the ship that sailed from Le Havre and arrived in New York on 14 April 1831. He was immediately impressed that 'the whole of society seems to have melted into a middle class. No one seems to have the elegant manners and the refined courtesy of the high classes in Europe . . . But at the same time no one is what in France one might call ill-bred.'[41]

This impression was elaborated in the first volume of *Democracy in America*, published in 1835, as the 'equality of conditions' explained on the one hand by the abolition of the English law of primogeniture in favour of equal inheritance by the American revolutionaries, and on the other by the general level of education enjoyed by all American citizens.[42] This equality of conditions helped to sustain democracy as a political principle, by which he meant the sovereignty of the people. But in France the sovereignty of the people had been used in turn to justify popular revolution and Napoleonic despotism. In Boston the Reverend Jared Sparks, a Unitarian minister and newspaper editor, provided Tocqueville with an account of the workings of self-government in Massachusetts. Key to maintaining free government, Tocqueville realized, were free institutions such as administrative decentralization and autonomous town councils, a powerful judiciary and jury system, associations dedicated to civic initiatives and a free press, together with sentiments which underpinned liberty such as the desire to participate in political life, a religious spirit and a willingness of individuals to help each other out. It was not a case of the French copying American laws and morals, but unless they cultivated free institutions and habits they would find themselves under 'an equal tyranny for all'.[43]

Tocqueville and Beaumont, however, did not sidestep the two issues that made the American model less glorious than it might be. They visited Albany and Utica in the Mohawk valley, but did not find the noble savages of Chateaubriand, only Indians wearing dirty linen and drunk on liquor, taking, as Beaumont wrote, 'but the vices of civilization and the rags of Europe'.[44] In *Democracy in America*, Tocqueville chronicled the expulsion of Indian tribes beyond the

Mississippi, blaming the greed of white settlers and the tyranny of state legislatures in the South, describing the silent passage of the Mississippi by a troop of Choctaws, dragging with them their children, their sick and their aged.[45] Likewise he described the slavery of the South which sustained the only aristocracy that survived in the country, an evil not only for the slaves but for the masters too. Thus on the north bank of the Ohio river the population of the state of Ohio, without slaves, was industrious and prosperous, building roads, canals and factories, while on the south bank, in Kentucky, where slavery existed, the white man 'living in idle ease, had the habits of idle men . . . he is less interested in money than in excitement and pleasure, hunting and war are his delights.'[46] Southerners, he found, did not talk to outsiders about slavery, but to his mind it was condemned to disappear, attacked by both political economy and religion, and if it were not abolished legally a black revolution would destroy it by force. Beaumont tackled the question head-on in his 1835 novel *Marie ou l'esclavage*. Ludovic, a French traveller like himself, meets a beautiful girl in Baltimore, who rejects his love. He discovers that she and her brother George have been 'tainted by a drop of black blood' and live in fear of being exposed. 'America is the classic soil of equality,' reflects Ludovic, 'but no European country has so much inequality.' George is thrown out of a New York theatre as a black man and dies in the Carolinas defending Indian tribesmen who have been driven out by land-hungry Southern states. Marie and Ludovic find solace in the virgin forests of Saginaw, on the banks of the Great Lakes, where she too dies. Twenty-five years before the American Civil War Tocqueville and Beaumont acquainted the French public with the deep contradictions of American democracy.[47]

RUSSIA: LIBERATOR OR TYRANT?

The most likely contact an ordinary Frenchman had with Russia in the early nineteenth century was as one of Napoleon's multinational army of 600,000 which invaded Russia in June 1812. Napoleon's forces entered Moscow in September, abandoning it to pillage and fire, but the most gruelling experience was the retreat from Moscow and the crossing of the River Beresina on 27–28 November 1812, under fire from Russian batteries, which left terrible carnage. But just as the French made up only a part of an army composed of Italians, Poles and Germans, so some French soldiers were serving not the French emperor but the Russian tsar. The Duc de Richelieu, who emigrated during the Revolution, fought for Catherine the Great against the Turks in 1789–92 and then served Tsar Alexander in preference to Napoleon. His younger cousin, the Comte de Roche-chouart, also had a commission in the Russian army, and was appointed aide-de-camp to Tsar Alexander in 1810. Having fought against the Turks until 1812 he was with the Don Cossacks on the Beresina, witnessing the carnage, and at the town of Studianska, mostly burned by the French, he occupied a room over the door of which was written the name of his childhood friend, the Baron de Mortemart. The same room, he reflected, 'had been occupied by a Mortemart, aide-de-camp to the Emperor of the French, and then by a Rochechouart, aide-de-camp to the Emperor of Russia'.[48]

The relationship of French and Russians was at best ambiguous. Were the Russians to be regarded as allies or enemies, as liberators or oppressors, as Europeans or Asians? The Comte de Rochechouart was with Tsar Alexander, the Prussian king and the Austrian gener-alissimo Prince Schwarzenberg for their victory parade in Paris on 31 May 1814, the night before they decided not to negotiate with Napoleon but to guarantee the integrity of France. During the parade Rochechouart recalled that 'a young woman contrived – how I do not know – to raise herself onto the stirrups of the Tsar, and shouted frantically in his ear, *Vive l'Empereur Alexandre!*'[49] On the other hand the historian Lavisse, born in 1842, often heard his grandmother, a native of Picardy, talk of 'the *time of the enemy*, escapes into the woods where hiding places had been made ready, of the joy of victories, the rout of Waterloo, and of the arrival of the Cossacks who occupied the country in 1815'.[50]

The victories of 1814–15 against Napoleon made Russia, as much as Great Britain, the European great power to be reckoned with. Russians occupied large areas of north-west France until 1818. The Russian Empire dominated Europe from St Petersburg, from Poland, of which the tsar was now king, and from Odessa, from which it threatened the Mediterranean. Édouard de Montulé, who visited Russia and published his account of it in 1825, observed that liberty was enjoyed only by serf-owning Russian nobles who defended serfdom by saying that without it the land would remain untilled and packed insubordinate serfs off to serve in the army for decades. And yet, he thought, 'despite the disasters they have experienced, Russians and French have not contracted a national hatred for each other'. Much of this he attributed to the fact that educated Russians spoke French and cultivated French manners and that Russian noblewomen were charming and better educated than their French counterparts.[51]

The most influential account of Russia in this period was written by the Marquis Astolf de Custine, whose *Russia in 1839* was published in 1843. By the age of four he had lost both his father, French ambassador in Berlin, and his grandfather, a general who had surrendered the city of Mainz to the Prussians in 1793, during the Terror, and his own reputation was gravely affected by a homosexual scandal in 1824. Soon after the publication of *Democracy in America* he met Alexis de Tocqueville at Madame Récamier's salon and, envious of the achievements of a man fifteen years his junior, decided to do for Russia what Tocqueville had done for America.[52]

There was much about Russia that did not seem strange to Custine. The world of the Russian nobility was that of the French nobility before the Revolution. At Yaroslavl, north of Moscow, he found that the wife of the governor had been brought up by a French governess who had followed the Polignac family into exile in Russia during the Revolution. 'The noble simplicity of her bearing reminded me', he wrote, 'of the manners of the old people I knew when I was a child. The traditions of the court and high society were what was most seductive about a time when our social superiority was uncontested.'[53] But while the pre-eminence of the French nobility had been destroyed by the Revolution, in Russia it had never existed. Peter the Great's Table of Ranks established a military and bureaucratic hierarchy which recognized not birth but only service to the state as a criterion of nobility. Russia, like France, 'lacked a social hierarchy' in the sense of a nobility with its own independent power-base.

However, 'without aristocracy there can only be tyranny in monarchies, as in democracies'.[54] Where Tocqueville warned of the danger of the tyranny of the majority in democracies, Custine warned of the danger of autocracy in monarchies. For Custine 'Russian government was camp discipline substituted for the order of the city, the state of siege become the normal state of society.'[55]

The lack of an independent nobility in Russia was accompanied by the absence of an independent Church. Custine himself observed that while the Catholic Church was generally a bastion of liberty in western European states, the Orthodox Church prevailing in Russia after the schism had fallen into the hands of the state and thus become just another instrument to enslave the Russian people. All this had consequences for the balance of power in Europe and a forthcoming struggle between civilized Europe and backward Russia. Custine feared that so-called civilized Europe was becoming weakened by democracy which replaced a military aristocracy by self-serving politicians and would not be able to resist a Russia which decided to test its strength. 'One day the sleeping giant will raise itself and force will put an end to the reign of words. In vain, then, will defeated democracy summon the old aristocracy to defend liberty. The weapon, taken up too late by hands too long inactive, will be powerless.' Scions of old noble families, excluded from power by the Revolution, would no longer be able to help.[56]

There was a common perception in France that Russia was an autocratic and arbitrary power, very different from Europe apart from St Petersburg but a real military threat. Alexandre Dumas had an enduring fascination for the noble officers of the Guard, many of whom had imbibed constitutional ideas while frequenting liberal circles in France in 1814–18, and who seized the opportunity of the death of Alexander in December 1825 to impose a constitution and civil code in Russia. The so-called Decembrist revolt was put down with great severity by Nicholas I, and over a hundred officers were sentenced variously to death, forced labour or exile in Siberia. Informed of this by a fencing master who had been in Russia, Dumas published a novel about it, *Memoirs of a Master-at-Arms*, in 1840. It concentrated on the suffering of one of the noble officers, and of his French wife who made the journey to Siberia through packs of wolves to share his exile.[57] The publication came to the attention of Nicholas, and Dumas was denied entry into Russia during the lifetime of the tsar. Nicholas died in 1855 during the Crimean war, when France and Great Britain successfully challenged the ambitions of Russia to undermine the Ottoman Empire from the Danube and the Balkans to the Caucasus, and precipitated a crisis in the autocratic, militaristic state.

In 1858–9, after peace returned, both Dumas and the poet and critic Théophile Gautier undertook tours of Russia. Dumas returned to the question of the Decembrist revolt, and quoted the words of the brother of one of the rebels, interrogated by the tsar: 'the emperor has complete power of life and death, and the people has no law against him.' 'His thirty-year reign was a continuous watch,' said Dumas, 'which not only gave the signal that revolutions were approaching, but kept itself at the ready to smother them, whether at home or abroad.' Dumas reported that hearing of Russia's imminent defeat Nicholas took poison. He wrote a study of serfdom in Russia, relating that like petty tsars lords made serfs work from 4 a.m. to 9 p.m. on their lands, three days a week, thought nothing of giving them a hundred lashes and sent recalcitrant serfs off to the army for twenty-five years. Although Dumas was not present to witness the effects of the emancipation of the serfs in Russia, he announced that 'the Emperor Alexander has signed one of the greatest and most humane acts ever accomplished by a sovereign. He has restored liberty to twenty-three million people.'[58]

The account of Gautier, who went to Russia to prepare a volume on the treasures of Russian art, which never materialized, was less backward-looking. Like Custine, he found that there was much that was European about Russia. St Peterburg was 'a northern Venice'. Alexander II, whom he espied at the Winter Palace, was quite unlike his father, with 'an expression of majestic firmness lit up from time to time by a graceful smile'. Shakespeare was playing at the theatre with the black American actor Ira Aldridge playing Othello and Lear. In some sense the influence of Europe was deleterious. There was no Russian school of painting, and the most famous modern Russian canvas, *The Last Days of Pompeii*, was by Karl Briullov, who trained in Italy. Observing that the Kremlin was constantly being repainted, Gautier observed that 'like people who are still naive, the Russians like what is new, or at least seems so.' Otherwise Russian art was the Byzantine art of the Orthodox Church, 'a hieratic, priestly, changeless art, where nothing is left to the fantasy or originality of the artist. Its formulae are as rigid as dogma. In this school there is neither progress, nor decadence, nor even period.' Even then, reflected Gautier, the capital of Byzantine art was not Moscow but Mount Athos.[59]

THE *VOYAGE EN ORIENT*

The Orient exercised a fascination over the French. Napoleon Bonaparte, pursuing his dream of becoming a new Alexander the Great, invaded Egypt in 1798, defeated the local Mameluke forces at the battle of the Pyramids on 21 July and entered Cairo in triumph. Unfortunately the blow that he hoped to deliver to British and Russian power by taking control of Egypt served only to provoke his rivals into a second coalition against France. Nelson attacked and sank the French fleet in Aboukir Bay on 1 August, the Ottoman Turks and Russians declared war and the Russian fleet entered the Mediterranean. Bonaparte moved north with his army to conquer Syria, but was defeated at Acre by the Turks and a British force under Sir Sidney Smith. The French fell back on Egypt and Bonaparte left almost at once to seize power in France. Under the Treaty of Amiens in 1802 Egypt was evacuated by both British and French.[60]

The French failed to found an empire in Egypt but the army of archaeologists, antiquarians, historians and scientists who took part in Bonaparte's expedition presented their findings in a twenty-three-volume *Description de l'Égypte*, published between 1809 and 1828. Meanwhile, driven by curiosity rather than the thirst to conquer, French writers, poets and artists regularly undertook a journey to the Orient, by which they generally meant that part of the Mediterranean, from Greece and the Balkans to Constantinople, Syria and Lebanon, and to Egypt, Tunisia and Algeria, which was still in the hands of the Ottoman Turks or, more usually, their vassals. They were not always in search of the same things, but in different ways the Orient was always a mirror which reflected what was individual about France and the French identity.

Chateaubriand, having broken with Napoleon and forfeited his diplomatic post in Rome, set off from France in July 1806, sailing from Venice to the Peloponnese and Constantinople, returning via Egypt and Tunis, to see the ruins of Carthage, to Spain and France in May 1807. He was bitterly hostile to the Turkish presence in Europe, and searched in Greece for the relics of Ancient Greek liberty and patriotism, and in Constantinople for the sophistication of the Byzantine Empire, under the yoke imposed by the Turks. The goal of his journey was Jerusalem, which he visited as a pilgrim and as a crusader, recounting the epic of the crusaders' recovery of the tomb of Jesus Christ in Jerusalem in 1099, which they held on to for eighty-eight years. At stake, he said, was the question of 'which would triumph on earth, a religion that was the enemy of civilization, promoting ignorance, despotism and slavery, or a religion that had revived the genius of learned antiquity among modern peoples and abolished servitude'. Of the persecution of the Christian monks who guarded the tomb of Jesus Christ he used the term 'Oriental despotism'.[61]

Twenty-five years later, in 1832, Alphonse de Lamartine, having resigned from the diplomatic service in opposition to the Revolution of 1830, hired a brig and sailed off with his wife and daughter less, as he put it, like Chateaubriand's pilgrim and crusader, more as a 'poet and philosopher'. Greece was now liberated but he was not impressed by the country as it descended into civil war, seeing it as 'the shroud of a people'.[62] What struck him above all was his first encounter with the Lebanon, approached from the sea.

Never did the sight of mountains impress me so much. The Lebanon has a character that I have not witnessed either in the Alps or in the Taurus. It is the combination of the imposing sublimeness of the lines and peaks with the grace of detail and variety of colour. Like its name it is a solemn mountain: the Alps under an Asian sky.[63]

Lamartine's view of Jerusalem was completely different from that of Chateaubriand. The Church of the Holy Sepulchre had burned down in 1808 and been rebuilt by the Greek Orthodox Church, but control was contested by the Catholic Church and in the light of their squabbles Lamartine saw the Muslims as 'the only tolerant people'. At Constantinople he reflected that, far from being despotic and cruel, the Turks were 'a people of philosophers. They draw everything from nature, they relate everything to God.' His concern was that politically the Ottoman Empire was crumbling. He foresaw that a congress of European powers might have to divide up the Empire into a series of protectorates, but he was concerned that the role of the Turkish people should be preserved. 'They are a people of patriarchs, of meditators, of worshippers, of philosophers,' he said, 'and when God speaks for them, they are a people of heroes and martyrs.'[64]

In fact the main threat to the Ottoman Empire was the viceroy of Egypt, Mehemet Ali, who owed allegiance to the Ottoman sultan but wanted to establish himself as an independent, hereditary ruler of Egypt, and secure a hereditary governorship of Syria for his son Ibrahim. In July 1839 he defeated the sultan's forces and forced the Ottoman fleet to surrender. In some circles Mehemet was vaunted as the creation of Mathieu de Lesseps, sent as consul to Egypt by Talleyrand after 1798 to select someone from the Egyptian army who could bring order to the delta.[65] Now the French government under Adolphe Thiers decided to back the cause of Mehemet Ali against the sultan in order to acquire an influence in the region by proxy. Unfortunately the British were unwilling to countenance either the challenge of France's power or the break-up of the Ottoman Empire that would go with it. They marshalled Prussia, Russia and Austria into a London agreement (15 July 1840) which backed the sultan and gave Mehemet Ali twenty days to accept a hereditary governorship of Egypt as the limit of his ambitions. On 11 September the British made their point by bombarding Beirut and Alexandria. Thiers proposed to reject the treaty and mobilize nearly 100,000 men for war if that was necessary. The nationalist press joined the fray, arguing that this was the moment to throw off the restrictions imposed on France by the treaties of 1815 and to recover its rank among European powers.[66] At the last moment, however, the French blinked. King Louis-Philippe was not prepared to risk war and Thiers resigned, to be replaced by his arch-rival François Guizot, French ambassador in London, who smoothed over the situation. France's dream of an empire in Egypt was again in tatters.[67]

The only part of the Ottoman Empire in which France was able to build an empire was Algeria, where its ambitions were not contested by other European powers. Algiers had been seized by French forces in 1830, the last gasp of the Bourbon monarchy before it fell, and was inherited by the July Monarchy as something of a poisoned chalice. In 1834 the patriotic press was quick to equate brutal military measures used to quell insurrection in Paris and Lyon with military measures used to quell resistance by Arab forces in Algeria.[68] In fact French aggression provoked the emergence of an Algerian leader, Abd-el-Kader, who began to impose a centralized state on the disparate tribal aristocracies, with the ability to raise taxes and troops, and forced the French back to enclaves around Algiers and Oran in 1837. However, a lobby in favour of the conquest of Algeria and its colonization by well-armed settlers gained strength. In 1840 General Bugeaud was appointed governor-general of Algeria by Thiers who, perhaps fearing that the Egyptian adventure might not come off, argued that rather than fighting each other all European powers were now moving in on 'barbarian peoples', the British in China, the Russians in the Caucasus.[69] After a visit to Algeria in 1841 Tocqueville argued that if France did not hang on to Algeria other powers would move in and France would descend to the second rank of powers, leaving European affairs to be decided by others. The regime of Abd-el-Kader, whom he described as 'a kind of Muslim Cromwell', was destroyed by the military force of General Bugeaud, but for lasting domination this had to be backed up by French settlers colonizing the region, grouped in fortified villages.[70]

While French forces were battling with Abd-el-Kader in Algeria, unable to force his surrender until 1846, French travellers continued to visit the Orient, but at the other end of the Mediterranean, which continued to exercise a historic or aesthetic fascination even though France had no military power there. Those who followed in the path of pilgrims or crusaders to Jerusalem after 1840 were generally more sceptical than their predecessors. Many were less impressed by the natural beauty of the Orient, like Lamartine, than aware of the modernization it was undergoing in response to European challenges. At the same time what was increasingly explicit was the Orient as a site for exotic and erotic fantasies, the Orient of the *Arabian Nights*.

In January 1843 the poet Gérard de Nerval, recovering from a nervous breakdown, set sail from Marseille to Alexandria, progressing to Beirut and Constantinople. Rather than regarding Arabs as barbarian, he confessed that 'I am the barbarian, a coarse son of the North.' In Europe, he said, where modernization meant that physical force was less important, 'women have become too strong'. He thus came to Cairo to indulge his fantasies about Oriental women, declaring, 'I am right in the middle of the *Arabian Nights*.' However, he soon came face to face with the inaccessibility of Muslim women behind the veil and his travelling companion Soliman-Aga explained that while Muslim men protected their women, European women were anybody's. Nerval consoled himself with the thought that even behind the veil 'a few days have taught me that a woman who senses that she is being looked at allows herself to be glimpsed, if she is beautiful,' but he then succumbed to Soliman-Aga's advice that he should find a wife. He went to the slave market where Nubian women predominated but bought a Javanese girl, the type familiar from Dutch paintings, for 625 francs. He stayed with her in Cairo for eight months, but she felt humiliated to be with a man Muslims considered to be of inferior race, while when he took her to Beirut the Catholic Maronite clergy were scandalized and he therefore left his wife in the care of a Catholic convent. By this time Nerval had spent all the time and money he should have devoted to a trip to the Holy Land, and was obliged to return to Europe.[71]

As sexual tourists Gustave Flaubert and Maxime du Camp, who left Marseille for Egypt in November 1849, were more fortunate. Having smoked a pipe contemplating the Sphinx and visited the battlefield of the Pyramids they sailed up the Nile to Wadi Halfa where they were entertained by dancing girls who provided pleasures all night long, while objecting to Flaubert's moustache. At the same time he wrote to his mother, 'Every morning I read a little Homer in Greek and Maxime reads the Bible. We go to bed at 9 p.m.'[72] At Damascus Flaubert was struck by the beauty of boys aged eighteen to twenty and joked that if he were a woman he would come to the city on a pleasure trip. While Nerval did not even get to Jerusalem,

Flaubert did but felt himself 'emptier than an empty barrel. This morning, in the Holy Sepulchre, a dog would have been more moved than I was.' He was struck by the rivalry of the churches at Jerusalem, Catholic, Greek Orthodox and Copt, a rivalry that he found repeated in the Lebanon between the Maronites and Druzes. 'If the Druzes burn two of their villages, the Maronites burn two of theirs and sometimes four.'[73] And yet the Orient was becoming rapidly westernized. 'Soon the Orient won't exist any more,' he told Théophile Gautier, 'perhaps we are its last observers . . . I have seen harems passing in steam-boats.'[74]

Flaubert returned to the Orient in 1858, this time travelling alone to Tunis and Carthage to research his new novel *Salammbô*. 'Bovary has left me disgusted with bourgeois morals for a long time,' he wrote to Mlle Leroyer de Chantepie. 'For a few years I am going to find a splendid subject far from the modern world with which I am heartily fed up. What I am undertaking is senseless and will have no public recognition. Who cares? You have to write for yourself first. It's the only chance to do something beautiful.'[75] *Salammbô* portrays a sumptuous, opulent, decadent Carthage built on war and plunder, turned on by its barbaric mercenary forces. Salammbô, daughter of the Carthaginian commander Hamilcar, representing the mysterious and sensual Oriental feminine, is coveted by the Libyan mercenary chief Mâtho, but both are doomed in a war which sets Carthaginians against mercenaries. Published in 1862, *Salammbô* in fact generated something of an artistic cult, culminating in the empress's commanding of a Carthaginian ball at court.

Not all French travellers in the Orient were obsessed by sex and violence. Certainly not Ernest Renan, who came to the Holy Land in 1860 to research his *Life of Jesus*. He was accompanied by his new wife but also by his elder sister, Henriette, who was in a real sense his mentor and companion, nothing if not jealous of his pretty wife. Édouard Lockroy, who had been with Garibaldi in Sicily, engaged by Renan's publisher Michel Lévy to accompany them, said that everything about Renan suggested the priest while Henriette, 'more mother than sister', was really 'the man of the family'.[76] Henriette was as much struck by the squalor of Beirut as by the beauty of the Lebanon, itself tarnished by the sorry sight of women who had survived the civil war between Maronites and Druzes. She observed that 'the role of the woman in the Orient is exclusively that of the housewife, and in her house seems to be only the first servant,' although she recognized that they were charming hostesses and that their real status came from being mothers.[77] Henriette remained in the Lebanon with her brother as his secretary after his wife returned to France, and died there in September 1861.

French interest in the Orient seemed to be divided between a military and colonial presence in Algeria and a literary and artistic fascination with Egypt and the Lebanon, where the British and Russians conspired to prevent the French from exercising real power. The way out of this impasse was technology, or technology facilitated by diplomacy. Returning to the East in 1864, Renan was met at Alexandria by Ferdinand de Lesseps and for three days shown the works on the Isthmus of Suez, where thousands of Indians and Chinese labourers were at work 'right in the desert, in the middle of endless plains of sand'. He even took a railway from Suez to Cairo, unable to comprehend how the Egyptians had adapted to the technology. 'To see these precision machines in the hands of the Arabs is something extraordinary. It is difficult to see why the thing doesn't derail or blow up.'[78]

The Suez canal had been a long time in the making. Ferdinand de Lesseps had first come to Egypt, where his father was consul, as a twenty-six-year-old consular student in 1832. He became the friend of Mehemet Ali's son Saïd, whom he taught to ride, and also became acquainted with the 1798 plan of Napoleon's engineer Lepère to build a canal across the Isthmus of Suez. Ferdinand was sent by Lamartine, foreign minister in 1848, to be ambassador in Madrid, then Rome, but when Saïd succeeded as viceroy in 1854 de Lesseps secured a firman from him (30 November 1854) authorizing him to form a company to build the canal. The diplomatic outlook seemed good, with France about to enter the Crimean war in alliance with Great Britain, and de Lesseps enlisted the support of Cobden in London to widen backing for the Suez Canal Company. The British, however, had not forgotten 1840 and were perfectly aware of the military and diplomatic significance of the canal. Britain's long-serving ambassador in Constantinople, Stratford Canning, who had great influence over Ottoman foreign policy, managed to stonewall ratification by the sultan of the viceroy's firman until by chance Napoleon III met the Ottoman grand vizir in Marseille in 1865. The canal, on which building work had already begun, was completed in 1869 and was opened in the presence of the Empress Eugénie on 17 November that year.[79] De Lesseps realized the dream of Napoleon to establish French influence in Egypt. When in 1884 Renan welcomed de Lesseps into the Académie Française he said, 'You were king. You had all the trappings of sovereignty. I saw your kingdom in the desert.'[80] Ironically, eighteen months before, the British had occupied Egypt and driven out the French.

PART TWO

France, 1870–1914

8

War and Commune, 1870–1871

Between the high summer of 1870 and the late spring of 1871 France suffered a series of interrelated crises which all but undid the work of rebuilding the country that had taken place over seven decades since 1799. War against Prussia brought about the collapse of the Empire and ushered in the Republic for the third time since 1792. Northern France was occupied by German forces and Paris besieged, leaving the southern half of the country more or less independent, a pattern that would in many ways be reproduced in 1940. The republican attempt to continue the war against German forces failed and an armistice was agreed, but whereas in 1940 the Germans occupied Paris without encountering resistance, in 1871 the population of the beleaguered city refused both to give up the fight against the Germans and to be disarmed by the republican government. The result was the insurrectionary Paris Commune and a civil war that cost at least 20,000 lives. The Commune was at one and the same time a class war, a war between Paris and the provinces, a war against organized religion and a revolution in gender roles that left deep scars in French society which would not be healed until the eve of the Great War.

The Franco-Prussian war of 1870 began as a dynastic and religious war and finished as a national war. Since Prussia's triumph over Austria at the battle of Königgrätz or Sadowa in 1866 France felt that it had lost its leading rank among European powers, and the sense of humiliation was compounded by Bismarck's attempt to encircle it by placing a Hohenzollern prince on the throne of Spain. Asking the Legislative Body for war credits on 15 July 1870 Napoleon's chief minister, Émile Ollivier, said that ministers would go to war 'with a light heart' because France's honour had been impugned and its greatness must be recovered.[1] The population of Paris was massively behind the war, coming out on to the streets on the nights of 13, 14 and 15 July, crying 'Vive la France! Vive la Guerre! À bas la Prusse! À Berlin!' After the triumph of the plebiscite on the constitution of a Liberal Empire in May, said one report, 'This war will generate wide enthusiasm and rally the whole of France behind the Napoleonic dynasty; this war will deal the final blow to the republican cause in France.'[2]

Unfortunately, France did not have the military organization to back up its puffed-up patriotism and grandiose aspirations. Military reform had been debated since 1866 but France did not go down the Prussian route of universal conscription and three years' service in the regular army followed by extended readiness in the reserve. It preferred a 'professional' army of hardened soldiers, 'the *grognards* of the First Empire' praised by generals of the Second Empire like Trochu, selected by lot and overwhelmingly of peasant stock because those with money could always purchase their 'replacement' by the poor.[3] A reform of 1868 increased military service for the minority who were conscripted from seven years to nine, but for everyone else there was only a fortnight's training a year, after an initial military service of five months, to qualify them for the National Mobile Guard. In 1870 this Mobile Guard existed little more than on paper, and chaotic mobilization meant that the Rhine army that invaded Germany under the personal command of Napoleon III on 2 August was only 202,000 strong instead of 385,000. Forces under Marshal Bazaine were defeated at Wissembourg on 4 August and at Forbach on 6 August, while on the same day a cavalry charge at Froeschwiller under the orders of General MacMahon was decimated by Prussian gunfire. On 9 August, as news of these defeats reached Paris, a crowd of 10,000–30,000 demonstrated outside the Legislative Body urging deputies to declare the Empire finished. They secured the resignation of Ollivier, his political career now over at the age of forty-five, but the Empire remained intact. Panic spread through the country at large and republicans risked being attacked as fifth-columnists in the pay of Prussia. At a fair in the Dordogne village of Hautefaye the mayor's son, who shouted 'Vive la République,' was set upon by a group of locals and murdered. 'We killed him to save France,' one of the killers explained at his trial. 'Our Emperor will save us in return.'[4] In fact, the Rhine army was besieged in Metz, and the army sent under MacMahon to relieve it was defeated at Sedan on 1 September. Napoleon III, a sick man, surrendered to the Prussian King William on 2 September and was escorted to the Belgian border while over 100,000 French soldiers became prisoners of war.[5]

War destroyed the dynasty, and it also plunged the Catholic Church into crisis. French Protestants were accused by bishops of supporting Protestant Prussia, and Alsatian Protestants in particular of facilitating the Prussian invasion. More than that, the victory of Prussia, condemned by Catholic journalist Louis Veuillot as 'Europe's sin' because of its identification not only with Protestantism but with atheism, was seen in Catholic circles as a divine punishment for France's apostasy from the Catholic religion, dating from Voltaire and the Revolution and culminating now in the withdrawal from Rome, where they had defended the Papacy since 1849, of French troops in order to fight the Germans.[6] The way was now clear for Piedmontese forces to occupy Rome and complete Italian unification, which they did on 20 September 1870. Only a few thousand papal zouaves, among whom were loyal French Catholics such as the division commanded by a descendant of the Vendean leader Charette, defended the Holy City until told by the pope to lay down their arms. These became heroes and martyrs for the Catholic Church, the more so because France now fell into the hands of godless republicans.

On 4 September 1870 crowds invaded the Legislative Body and demanded that it now proclaim the Republic. The speaker, Eugène Schneider, president of the Comité des Forges, was obliged to suspend the session as the deputies elected for Paris, led by Léon Gambetta and Jules Favre, but without the Orleanist Adolphe Thiers, went to the Hôtel de Ville. 'The Republic was victorious over the invasion of 1792. The Republic is proclaimed,' they announced, and formed a provisional government which they called the Government of National Defence.[7] 'Let the lion of 1792 draw itself up and bristle,' declared Victor Hugo, returning from exile in Brussels to Paris. 'Let us make war day and night, war in the mountains, war on the plains, war in the forests.'[8] Gambetta, as minister of the interior, mobilized the Paris National Guard that had been disbanded by Louis-Napoleon after his coup of 1851 and by the end of September had built it up to a force of 134 battalions and 400,000 men. These supported the 60,000 regular troops and 100,000 Mobile Guards who were commanded by General Trochu, now military governor of Paris and president of the Government of National Defence, whom Juliette Adam hoped would be 'our Washington'.[9]

Unfortunately, 1792 did not materialize in 1870. Paris was surrounded by German armies after 19 September and cut off from the rest of the country. On 7 October Gambetta left Paris by balloon to take command of a delegation of the Government of National Defence that had been set up at Tours on the Loire, as minister of war as well as of the interior. He took the engineer Charles de Freycinet as his right-hand man to build up a Loire army of 200,000 regular troops for the relief of Paris and appealed to citizens of all French departments on 9 October to launch a 'national war' in which national guardsmen, mobile guards and irregular units of *francs-tireurs* would take part, enrolled into an Auxiliary Army with the same rank and pay as regular soldiers on 14 October.[10] *Francs-tireurs* defended Chateaudun, west of Orléans, attacked by the Germans on 18 October, and provoked German reprisals against surrounding villages. What for the French was the highest manifestation of the nation-in-arms was for the Germans resort to unlawful guerrilla warfare, and it bred a fear of the hidden enemy, civilian rather than soldier, which returned to haunt them during later occupations after 1914 and 1940.[11]

In fact, Gambetta's 'people's war' was not generally supported by the Government of National Defence. Having told European governments on 6 September that France would not cede 'an inch of her soil or a stone of her fortresses', foreign minister Jules Favre visited Bismarck in James de Rothschild's pastiche Renaissance château of Ferrières, east of Paris, on 19–20 September, to learn that Prussia would not return Alsace-Lorraine, placed under German administration on 26 August. Between 12 September and 12 October Thiers, at the request of the government, toured the European capitals from London to Vienna and from St Peterburg to Florence, trying to convince the powers to intervene on France's side, but to no avail, so he came to Tours to urge peace. Neither could Gambetta rely on the commanders of the regular army, who were Napoleon III's appointees, had no love for the Republic and feared that Gambetta's patriotic war would lead to social revolution, as in 1793. Bazaine, besieged in Metz, surrendered with 100,000 troops on 28 October, a gesture that was condemned by Gambetta as a 'sinister epilogue of the military coup of December [1851]'.[12] At his court martial in 1873 Bazaine argued that the army was the 'palladium of society' and must be kept intact for the maintenance of social order as much as for the defence of the frontier.[13] Trochu, far from being a French Washington, refused to make use of the Paris National Guard on several occasions when sorties were made in an attempt to break through the Prussian ring round Paris. He later claimed that a tenth of the National Guard was made up of criminals and professional revolutionaries indulging in 'armed demagogy' and attacked Gambetta for being obsessed by 'the military tradition of 1793'.[14]

The German occupation of northern France had a traumatic effect on the French people. 'I do not know how I am not dead, I have suffered so much for the last six weeks,' Flaubert wrote to George Sand on 11 October. 'The Prussians are now twelve kilometres from Rouen and there is no order, no command system, no discipline, nothing, nothing.'[15] The system of administrative centralization set up in 1800 buckled and the country threatened to fragment into its constituent cities and departments. With Paris surrounded by nearly 250,000 Prussian and other German troops, southern France began to separate from the north. Republican feeling in cities such as Marseille, Lyon, Bordeaux and Toulouse had given a majority of 'no' votes in the plebiscite of May 1870, and military setbacks now opened a political breach for republicans. In Marseille the town hall was invaded by republican hotheads, led by a young Jewish lawyer, Gaston Crémieux, at the news of the first imperial defeats on 8 August. Municipal elections held on 27–28 August put moderate republicans in charge of the city, but on 5 September, the day after the Republic was declared in Paris, Crémieux and his friends occupied the prefecture and set up a departmental commission, rivalling the city hall. As minister of the interior Gambetta sought to regain control of the country by purging the prefectoral administration and appointing his own men to eighty-five of the eighty-nine prefectures in the ten days to 14 September. His nominee for Marseille was Alphonse Esquiros, a Montagnard deputy of 1849 who had gone into exile after the coup of 1851. Unfortunately for Gambetta, Esquiros went native and on 18 September set up a Ligue du Midi which federated thirteen departments in the south-east of France, from Marseille to Lyon and from Nice to Montpellier. Its declared ambition was to raise forces to save the One and Indivisible Republic, but this was also the rhetoric of the federalist movement of 1793 which defended the interests of the cities and departments against Paris. Gambetta was forced to dismiss Esquiros and send a more reliable Montagnard of 1849, Alphonse Gent, to wrest control of the Marseille prefecture from Crémieux's commission on 2 November and preside over new elections which returned Bory to office. Lyon constituted another challenge for Gambetta. It declared the Republic on 4 September ahead of Paris and established a committee of public safety in the town hall which introduced itself to Gambetta's prefect, Challemel-Lacour, as 'the government of Lyon'. Municipal elections on 15 September returned a combination of moderate republicans and members of the committee of public safety to the city council, under the sensible hand of Louis Hénon, a professor at the Medical School and one of the five republicans elected in 1857 to take the oath to the Empire. On 28 September the town hall was again invaded, this time by a band led by the Russian anarchist Bakunin and Albert Richard, leader of the Lyon silkweavers and local architect of the International Workers' Association founded in 1866. They proclaimed the abolition of the state and called for a federation of communes across the country to set up 'committees for saving France', taxing the rich and raising volunteers, but Richard panicked and Bakunin and his crew were soon ejected by the Lyon National Guard. Cities such as Lyon and Marseille wanted not social revolution or the abolition of the state but a decentralizing republic that would merely allow them to enjoy municipal autonomy.

The most serious problem for the Government of National Defence, nevertheless, was Paris itself. While Gambetta ruled from Tours, the rest of the government, including Jules Ferry, was still based at the Paris Hôtel de Ville. Yet almost immediately after 4 September the revolutionary currents which had been dammed by the Empire, wholly until 1868, then partially, broke free. The bookbinder Eugène Varlin had organized a Paris Chamber of Workers' Unions in December 1869, which joined the Paris federation of the International. These workers followed the teaching not of Marx, who believed in the dictatorship of the proletariat and the nationalization of industry, but of Proudhon, who had died in 1865, but believed in a stateless society of trade unions, co-operatives and communes freely associating. Moreover, although the Paris International had been devoted to international socialism before the fall of the Empire, on 4–5 September, much to the dismay of Marx, it sent an address to the German people quoting article 120 of the constitution of 1793, 'the French people . . . does not make peace with an enemy occupying its territory,' and calling on them to 'recross the Rhine!'[16] Based at the place de la Corderie du Temple, the Paris International was behind the setting up of vigilance committees in the twenty *arrondissements*, each of which maintained surveillance of their own municipal council and mayor, in order to ensure that they remained radical and patriotic. Varlin was a key figure in the vigilance committee of the 6th *arrondissement*, dyeworker Benoît Malon in that of the 17th. That of the 18th *arrondissement*, Montmartre, was the power-base of the red schoolteacher Louise Michel, who made it her business to extract food from hoarders during the siege and distribute it to the poor.[17] In December the twenty vigilance committees elected a central committee, the Delegation of the Twenty Arrondissements, which also sat at the Corderie and maintained a 'dual power' opposite the Government of National Defence, intending to fight any sign of 'bourgeois reaction'.[18]

Vying with the Internationalists for radical and patriotic influence were the professional revolutionary Auguste Blanqui and his followers. Blanqui launched *La Patrie en Danger* on 7 September 1870, or 20 *fructidor* Year 78 according to the revolutionary calendar it resurrected. It was bitterly critical of the failure of the Government of National Defence, Gambetta as well as Trochu, to pursue the war and contain reaction. ''92 saved the Revolution and founded the

Republic, but the Hôtel de Ville is destroying them,' he declared on 30 October/9 *brumaire* Year 79.[19] The formation of a revolutionary, all-Paris Commune, on the model of that set up on 10 August 1792, when the monarchy was overthrown, was a frequent demand in clubs which mushroomed in halls and cafés all over the capital. 'If you had the Commune,' said an orator at the Club Reine-Blanche, Montmartre, on 4 November, 'you could act like revolutionaries. You could send emissaries to stir up the shit in the departments.'[20] The battalions of the National Guard, which elected their own officers, were also forums of revolutionary debate, although they remained fairly autonomous until the formation of a republican federation of battalions of the National Guard at the end of February, with a central committee that was to be the guiding force behind the insurrection of 10 March 1871.

Paris in the autumn of 1870 was defined as much by the siege as by the rising revolutionary temperature. Madeleine Brès, the first French woman to enrol in the Paris Faculty of Medicine, was taken on as an intern at the Hôpital de la Pitié, although only for the duration of the siege. Juliette Adam rediscovered her expertise as a doctor's daughter and organized a hospital for wounded soldiers in the Music Conservatory in the 9th *arrondissement*. 'All day I am with the wounded who moan, are dressed, amputated, whose tortures afflict me,' she wrote, although she was still in a position to maintain something of a salon in the evening, not least because her husband Edmond was prefect of police.[21] Despite the hardships Paris society still existed to a limited extent. Jules de Goncourt died in 1870 but his brother Edmond hosted Tuesday literary dinners at Brebant's restaurant, attended by Théophile Gautier, Ernest Renan, the chemist Marcellin Berthelot, Auguste Nefftzer, editor of *Le Temps*, and later Louis Blanc, with his 'priest's physique and his Levite's frock coat ... secretly bitter that his name, so popular in '48, has so little weight with the masses'.[22] At the other end of the spectrum, reported the writer Francisque Sarcey, 'Victor Hugo is finally having the day he has awaited for eighteen years,' his attack on the Second Empire, *Les Châtiments*, being read to 3,000 spectators at the Porte Saint-Martin Theatre, before transferring to the Comédie Française. The Popular Sunday concerts of Pasdeloup began their autumn season on 23 October and the Folies Bergère was still frequented by Parisians who wanted to 'smoke a cigar and have a good joke, which is the nature of every *boulevardier*'.[23]

The wit and resourcefulness of Parisians could not disguise the fact that the situation was becoming increasingly desperate. Frustration with the Government of National Defence, which seemed to prefer surrender to using the energy of the armed people to lift the siege of Paris, came to a head with news of the capitulation of Marshal Bazaine at Metz on 28 September and the decision of General Trochu to abandon Le Bourget outside Paris on 30 October. On 31 October the Hôtel de Ville was invaded by revolutionaries led by Blanqui and Flourens, who commanded the Montmartre and Belleville (20th) National Guard, taking the Government of National Defence hostage. Leaping on to a table, Flourens proclaimed the formation of a committee of public safety that was to include Blanqui, Delescluze and Victor Hugo, to oversee the election of a Commune. In the event, the government was liberated by loyal National Guards led by Jules Ferry and Edmond Adam. A deal was reached with the insurgents under which there would be no arrests, but a referendum would take place testing support for the Government of National Defence. In addition elections would be held, not for a Commune, but for new municipalities in the twenty *arrondissements*. This appeal to the electorate marginalized the revolutionaries. The Government of National Defence was acclaimed by 90 per cent of the vote on 3 November, and municipal elections on 5/8 November returned radical mayors to only two town halls in north-east Paris, Delescluze to the 19th and the Blanquist woodworker Gabriel Ranvier to the 20th. To offset them Jules Ferry was appointed mayor of Paris.

The survival of the Government of National Defence did nothing to relieve the military situation. The Army of the Loire, sent to liberate Paris, captured Orléans but was driven out again on 4–5 December. The Army of the North took Saint-Quentin on 18 January, but was forced out the next day. The government retreated to Bordeaux as the so-called artists' battalion of the National Guard built a huge snow statue entitled *Resistance* above the city defences of the 19th *arrondissement*.[24] Conditions in Paris, however, were making resistance difficult. An attempted breakout to Champigny on 30 November ended in disaster two days later. Food prices rose astronomically: a chicken worth 3 francs before the siege was sold for 15 francs, ham went up from 2 francs 50 to 16 francs a kilo. Eggs were a franc each when a worker's wage was 4 francs a day if he was in work, but only 1 franc 50 if he was a national guardsman.[25] The poor were reduced to eating dogs and cats, the bourgeoisie to eating wildlife and zoo animals. Juliette Adam served camel's hump on 23 December and a portion of the elephant Castor, partner of another called Pollux, on New Year's Day 1871. On 14 January Edmond de Goncourt ate a blackbird he had shot in his garden. Trees in the Bois de Boulogne were stripped and wooden fences knocked down for firewood.[26] On 27 December the Prussians opened up an artillery bombardment, clearing the Avron plateau, and began a bombardment of Paris itself on 5 January. 'The barbarians,' wrote Juliette Adam, 'more than three thousand bombs fell around the Jardin des Plantes and the Luxembourg . . . One woman returning home found her two children in shreds.'[27] A final breakout attempt to the west of Paris on 19 January came to grief at Buzenval. This triggered another attack on the Hôtel de Ville on 22 January, orchestrated by the Delegation of the Twenty Arrondissements, which ended with the opposing sides for the first time shooting at each other. Trochu was finally dismissed as governor of Paris but this was not to steel Parisian defences. On 26 January Jules Favre went to discuss an armistice with Bismarck, who was now chancellor of the German Empire that had been proclaimed in the château of Versailles on 18 January.

The armistice agreed on 28 January might have restored France to peace and order. France was to pay Germany an indemnity of 5,000 million francs for starting the war, to disarm its regular army and to forfeit Alsace and Lorraine. German forces still encircled Paris, although people and supplies could now cross the lines. Elections to a National Assembly, to meet in Bordeaux, were held forthwith in order to endorse the armistice. The elections of 8 February 1871 restored the country as a political unit and the conservative countryside and small towns swamped the radicalism of Paris and the large cities. Of 768 deputies, 400 were royalists, including two sons of Louis-Philippe, the Duc d'Aumale and the

Prince de Joinville. This did not mean that a restoration of the monarchy was imminent: the vote was for peace and order against war and disorder. The Legitimist Comte de Falloux, now re-elected, had no wish for a monarchy restored by a foreign power, as in 1814 and 1815, and was prepared to wait for the Republic to destroy itself.[28] In Paris the International put up forty-three candidates for the forty-three seats on offer but failed to have any of them elected. Those elected for Paris included Gambetta, Henri Rochefort, Victor Hugo, Louis Blanc and Edmond Adam; Juliette was delighted to leave Paris for Bordeaux, where the Assembly met on 11 February. The Assembly elected Adolphe Thiers head of the executive power, inevitably, some said, as a longtime opponent of the Empire but also of the war, having warned Ollivier against it on 15 July 1870. Thiers, an Orleanist by nature, added the words 'of the Republic' to his title: as in 1850 he thought the Republic was the regime that divided French people least, permitting the reconstitution of a 'party of order' of royalists and moderate republicans, and isolating the revolutionaries.

To ensure that the armistice was indeed ratified, German troops marched into Paris on 1 March, paraded in the Bois de Boulogne and were reviewed by the German emperor on the Champs-Élysées; when terms were duly ratified, they withdrew on 3 March. In protest against the surrender of their provinces the deputies of Alsace-Lorraine together with Gambetta, Rochefort and Victor Hugo walked out of the Assembly, but this was not the moment for thoughts of *revanche*. The obstacle to the armistice was not the Assembly but Paris. The revolutionary movement had fought for months against what Blanqui called 'the alliance of reaction with Bismarck' and was not prepared to stop now.[29] It had a particular hatred of Thiers, the quintessential bourgeois held responsible for the massacre in the rue Transnonain in 1834 and declared enemy of the 'vile multitude', the 'dressing-gowned Cavaignac of the Third Republic' (after the general who put down the insurrection of June 1848), in the opinion of journalist Jules Vallès.[30]

Thiers, however, could not regain control of Paris, where 300,000 armed national guardsmen were still at large. On 18 March 20,000 regular troops were sent into the city to seize artillery and to disarm the National Guard. A confrontation between the government and the people of Paris threatened, as in the June Days of 1848, but this time the people were armed and organized, and also keen to exact vengeance. General Clément Thomas, despatched to Montmartre to remove cannon, was remembered as 'having behaved with incredible ferocity towards the defeated insurgents' in June 1848, and was murdered along with another general, Lecomte, by an angry crowd.[31] Georges Clemenceau, mayor of Montmartre since November 1870, tried to intervene, but was too late. This was the signal for a general insurrection, orchestrated by the Central Committee of the National Guard with the support of the Delegation of the Twenty Arrondissements. Jules Ferry tried to hold on to the Hôtel de Ville, but there was no question of negotiation, as on 31 October. His October 'fix' was now seen to be a trick, with Blanqui and Flourens, promised amnesty, now under sentence of death, and during the siege he had gained a reputation as 'famine Ferry'. Rejected by the Paris electorate on 8 February, he was instead elected deputy of his native Vosges and represented the desire of the provinces to smother the capital. Ferry was forced to abandon the Hôtel de Ville at 10 p.m. on 18 March and tried briefly to rally the mayors of the bourgeois *arrondissements* in the town hall of the 1st *arrondissement*. However crowds outside were crying 'Mort à Ferry!' and he escaped through the church of Saint-Germain L'Auxerrois to reach Versailles, where the government and Assembly were now located, the next day.

The insurrection of 18 March 1871 was revenge for June 1848. It was also a re-run of 10 August 1792, when the monarchy was toppled and an insurrectionary Commune was formed in Paris which for nearly two years dictated the pace of revolution to the Convention parliament elected the following September. The revival of their own city government, instead of the dictatorship of the prefect of the Seine and the prefect of police, ending the division of power between what *Le Grand Colère du Père Duchesne* called 'a heap of mayor-of-*arrondissement* buggers', was what the people of Paris demanded.[32] There was one attempt at negotiation, on 19 March. Clemenceau and some of the twenty mayors obtained the authority of the Central Committee of the National Guard, now sitting in the Hôtel de Ville, to request permission from the National Assembly, now sitting in Versailles, to elect a unitary city government, the Commune. This was refused by Versailles, so the central committee unilaterally called elections to the Commune on 22 March. Much of the bourgeois population had left Paris after the siege and many others did not vote: the abstention rate was 52 per cent, higher in the richer *arrondissements*. The mayors put together a moderate list but it took only fifteen out of ninety-two seats and these members soon resigned in the face of the overwhelming presence of revolutionaries. Seventeen of those elected, including Eugène Varlin, Benoît Malon, Édouard Vaillant and Charles Beslay, were members of the Paris section of the International, professing federalist and Proudhonian ideas, and most of these had come up through the vigilance committees. In their general orbit were the like of the journalist Vallès and the painter Courbet. About thirty were Jacobins, such as Gustave Flourens and Charles Delescluze, a veteran of 1848 and in many ways the Robespierre of the Commune. A dozen were Blanquists (although Blanqui himself had been arrested just before the insurrection), including Émile Eudes, Théophile Ferré, Raoul Rigault and Gustave Tridon, historian of the Hébertistes who had dominated the Commune of 1792–4.

Marx called the Commune a proletarian government, the first example of the dictatorship of the proletariat. Others have pointed out that many members of the Commune were not authentically working class but middle-class *déclassés* such as Vaillant, a notary's son who had studied at Heidelberg university, or Flourens, a young professor at the Collège de France with a private income of 30,000 francs. But the members of the Commune had made their reputation in the direct democracy of the sections and unions of the International, in the radical clubs and press, in the municipal vigilance committees and battalions of the National Guard, so that they were in the truest sense representatives of the people. Many measures were taken by the Commune of a socialist nature: nightwork in bakeries was abolished, valuable objects were returned from pawnshops and abandoned workshops were handed over to workers' co-operatives. Some hotheads complained that the deserted apartments of the rich had not been requisitioned for slum-dwellers, although Thiers' house was pulled down on 11 May, and Beslay stood guard over the vaults of the Banque de France, to ensure that the National Guard would be paid. It was nevertheless clear to Edmond de Goncourt, one of the few bourgeois who remained in the city, that 'what is happening is very simply the conquest of France by the workers and the enslavement under their despotism of the nobles, the middle class and the peasants'.[33]

The Paris Commune did its best to trigger other communes across the country. Unlike in 1793, it promised in its address to the French people on 19 April that it would not seek to impose a red dictatorship on France. It called for the autonomy and self-government of all communes, towns and villages, free of the grip and interference of the central administration, and for them to show solidarity with the Paris Commune in its struggle against the militarism, clericalism, bureaucracy and exploitation incarnated by Versailles. Communes were proclaimed in sympathy on 23 March at Lyon and Marseille, on the 24th in the industrial towns of Le Creusot and Saint-Étienne and at Narbonne, with Toulouse following on the 25th, but attempts to declare communes at Limoges and Bordeaux failed. While some towns and cities wished to regain their municipal liberties, the inauguration of the Republic was felt to be enough to guarantee that autonomy. In Lyon, mayor Hénon and his deputy Désiré Barodet were able to convince extremists that to all intents and purposes Lyon already had a commune, and a rising in the working-class suburb of La Guillotière on 30 April was easily put down. In Marseille power was again seized at the prefecture by Gaston Crémieux, and three representatives of the Paris Commune arrived on 28 March, but Crémieux was opposed by Bory's municipality which was able to rely on the National Guard and regular forces under General Espivant to restore order on 3 April. Thiers was determined to make an example of Crémieux, who was tried and shot on 30 November.

'Thank God the civil war has begun,' wrote Edmond de Goncourt on 2 April, as the army directed from Versailles began to bombard Paris.[34] A desperate attempt to reach a compromise between the Paris Commune and Versailles was made on 29 April by a body of freemasons, who went to parley with a freemason general of the Versailles army, Leclerc, on the bridge at Courbevoie, but to no avail. Within Paris the Commune divided over whether to set up a committee of public safety with supreme authority. The Jacobins and Blanquists were in favour and won the vote on 1 May, the anti-Jacobin Internationalists were against, and lost. The Internationalist minority resigned from the Commune on 15 May, although not from the fight. Delescluze, appointed war delegate on 10 May, declared that 'if your breasts are exposed to bullets and shells of the Versaillais it is for the prize that you have promised yourselves, the liberation of France and the world, the safety of your home and the lives of your wives and children. Long live the universal Republic! Long live the Commune!'[35]

The Versailles forces closed in, taking the outlying forts of Issy on 8 May and Vanves on the 14th. The finalization of the peace treaty, following on from the armistice, by Jules Favre at Frankfurt on 10 May enabled French prisoners of war to be released and returned to reinforce the Versailles army, which numbered 55,000 in April but 120,000 towards the end of May. Thiers, scoffed Marx, 'hounds on the prisoners of Sedan and Metz by special permission of Bismarck'.[36] These were pumped up with extra pay, double drink rations and propaganda to the effect that the rebels were the criminals, pimps, spies and alcoholics of the *classes dangereuses* in order to steel them for the work of repression.[37]

Versailles forces broke into Paris proper through the Porte de Saint-Cloud on Sunday 21 May, and the week that followed became known as the Semaine Sanglante. 'The hour of revolutionary war has struck,' announced Delescluze. 'To arms, citizens, to arms!'[38] Some lukewarm revolutionaries like Henri Rochefort slipped away before things became too hot, while women organized in the Union des Femmes and the Légion des Fédérées of the 12th *arrondissement* took up arms to replace them, defending their own barricade on place Blanche on 23 May.[39] The participation of women in the defence of Paris was later caricatured as the use of petrol-bombs to set fire to the city, while they were attacked as 'unworthy creatures who have taken it upon themselves to become an opprobrium to their sex'.[40] Hostages were taken and executed on both sides. The Communards arrested the archbishop of Paris, Mgr Darboy, in order to barter him for Blanqui, held by the Versaillais under sentence of death. When no exchange was forthcoming, they shot him together with a batch of Dominican monks. The Church did not forgive the Communards for this act, but was also keen to make religious capital out of it. 'God is victorious,' wrote Veuillot, who himself remained in Paris editing *L'Univers* until 12 May. 'He has taken martyrs, we will have miracles, we are saved!'[41]

The Commune was forced to abandon the Hôtel de Ville on 24 May and took refuge in the town hall of the 11th *arrondissement*. Delescluze donned his scarf of office and climbed on to the barricade at the place du Château d'Eau to meet a hail of bullets. Last stands were made on the Buttes Chaumont and in the Père Lachaise cemetery on 27 May, where captured fighters were machine-gunned and rolled into an open ditch. Belleville gave out on 28 May and Varlin was captured and shot in rue des Rosiers. Perhaps 10,000 Parisians died in the fighting and another 10,000, seized with weapons in their hands, were taken to barracks in various parts of the city and summarily executed *en masse*. Edmond de Goncourt observed columns being taken into the Lobau barracks near the Hôtel de Ville.

Almost at that instant there is an explosion like a violent sound enclosed behind doors and walls, a fusillade having something of the mechanical regularity of a machine-gun. There is a first, a second, third, fourth, a fifth murderous *rrarra* – then a long interval – and then a sixth, and still two more volleys, one after the other.[42]

Less than two weeks later, on 10 June, Goncourt had lunch with Gustave Flaubert, who had come up to Paris to do more work on his *Temptation of St Anthony*. Flaubert's house at Croisset had been occupied by the Prussians in the autumn, but they had done no damage, and left his study untouched. He wrote to George Sand:

The smell of bodies disgusts me less than the miasmas of egoism breathed from every mouth. The sight of ruins is nothing compared to the immense Parisian stupidity. One half of the population wants to strangle the other, and the other has the same desire. You can read it in the eyes of passers-by.[43]

Paris was calm, but France was in a state of dislocation and shock. It had been defeated and humiliated, toppled from its great-power status, no longer certain of the superiority of its civilization.

Revolutionary violence had broken out again, stirring up painful memories of 1793 and June 1848, and that in a modern democracy where universal suffrage was supposed to replace violent by peaceful change. The national territory had broken up: the government had been driven out of Paris, Alsace and Lorraine were lost, provincial cities and departments had attempted to reclaim their independence. A society that preached careers open to talent and held together by ambition had fallen victim to class war. The long march of rechristianization undertaken since the Concordat in 1802 faltered as priests, including another archbishop of Paris, were murdered and churches desecrated. Women, who were supposed to impart religious teaching from one generation to another, were now throwing petrol-bombs into Paris apartments. Perhaps only literature, Goncourt and Flaubert might have reflected as they lunched on 10 June, had survived the descent into anarchy, but their literature was of no interest to the mass public that was now emerging. Much work was required if France was to regain political stability, national consensus and great-power status.

9

Consensus Found: French Politics, 1870–1914

Few in 1871 would have predicted that the Republic proclaimed on 4 September that year would still be in place in 1914, let alone last until 1940. Its legitimacy was contested both by Bonapartist apologists of the Empire, who as late as May 1870 had claimed the endorsement of 7.3 million votes, and by both species of monarchist, Legitimists faithful to the Bourbons of 1814 and Orleanists faithful to the July Monarchy of 1830. Yet beneath the quarrels over regimes seethed another issue: fear of popular revolution manifest in 1793, the June Days of 1848 and now in the Paris Commune. There was an underlying pressure on the political class to sink its ideological differences and rally behind the regime most likely to defend the supremacy of the propertied and educated. 'The masses, sheer numbers, are always stupid,' wrote Flaubert to George Sand; 'what we need above all is a natural and therefore legitimate aristocracy.' 'Let us cure ourselves of democracy,' said Renan. 'Civilization began as an aristocratic creation, the work of a small number of nobles and priests ... and its preservation is an aristocratic task too.'[1]

A REPUBLIC FOR REPUBLICANS

Although France was a republic in 1871 the National Assembly elected in February that year was dominated by a 'party of order' of royalists and conservative republicans very like the one which had controlled the Legislative Assembly of 1849. Many of those elected in 1871 had indeed served in that of 1849. Unlike in 1849, however, there was no president of the Republic elected by universal suffrage who might threaten to dissolve it. The Assembly elected Adolphe Thiers president of the executive power, a tribute to his opposition to the authoritarian and bellicose Empire in the name of 'necessary liberties'. Having vanquished the Commune he was promoted president of the Republic by the Assembly on 31 August 1871, but made responsible to it for his actions and therefore always liable to be overturned by the Assembly.

Thiers was in fact threatened from three different quarters: republican, Bonapartist and royalist. Gambetta, leader of the republicans, who had stormed out of the Assembly over the abandonment of Alsace-Lorraine and went briefly into exile in Spain, was returned to the Assembly in a by-election in July 1871 and began a long campaign to dissociate the republicans from their violent image. Like the republicans of 1848 he put his faith in the power of universal suffrage which, although it had been manipulated for eighteen years by the Empire, playing on the ignorance of the peasantry, was 'the strength of numbers and power enlightened by reason'. In a tireless tour of French towns Gambetta argued that the republicans would complete the work of the French Revolution, which was characterized not by violence but by the delivery of political and civil equality, private property, universal education and freedom of conscience.[2]

For the Legitimist royalists, the Comte de Falloux wrote to Thiers after the collapse of the Commune urging him to restore the monarchy, since 'in France we will never prevent the Empire from signifying and inviting despotism, the Republic signifying and inviting disorder, and the Bourbon monarchy signifying and inviting representative government.' In 1872 the Orleanist Duc Albert de Broglie resigned the London embassy where Thiers had placed him and returned to France to attack the Republic as 'the reign of ill-educated men'.[3] The Bonapartists were discredited by association with despotism and defeat, but they argued that the declaration of the Republic on 4 September 1870 by a caucus of Paris deputies had itself been a coup d'état, violating the plebiscite of the previous May which had massively endorsed the Empire. Paul de Cassagnac, heir to his father's Bonapartist fief of the Gers in south-west France, a journalist whose newspaper, Le Pays, was banned for its denunciation of the republican coup, founded an Appeal to the People

Committee in 1872 in which he argued that another plebiscite must be held and that the deeply Bonapartist masses would once again restore the Empire.[4]

Thiers' strategy was to commit himself to the Republic as the *de facto* regime and the one that divided Frenchmen least, while establishing his credentials as a man of order. Around this he hoped to build a consensus of the ruling class. His ministers were drawn from the so-called centre-left, like himself former Orleanists who had rallied to the Republic such as foreign minister Charles de Rémusat and interior minister Auguste Casimir-Périer, son of the man of order who had put down the revolts of 1832. A law was passed by the Assembly on 14 March 1872 criminalizing membership of the International, which was held responsible for the Paris Commune, leading to the round-up of large numbers of socialists and anarchists.[5] At the opening of the parliamentary session on 13 November 1872 Thiers announced that 'the Republic will be conservative or it will not be,' but royalists and Bonapartists increasingly considered him a hostage of hard-line republicans.[6] The breaking point was a by-election in Paris on 27 April 1873 when the government candidate, Charles de Rémusat, was defeated by Désiré Barodet, who had been mayor of Lyon until the government abolished the city-wide mayoralty on 2 April 1873 for alleged sympathy with the Paris Commune. Barodet was adopted by the radical republicans to take their revenge in Paris, and for Albert de Broglie his triumph signalled that 'the conservative republic was toppled by the radical republic . . . it was like witnessing the resurrection of the Commune.'[7] On 24 May 1873 de Broglie duly tabled a vote of no confidence in the government for failing to impose a 'resolutely conservative' strategy which was passed by the opposition by 360 votes to 344, and forced the resignation of Thiers. Marshal MacMahon, a career soldier who had served monarchy and Empire in Algeria, the Crimea and Italy and during the Franco-Prussian war was elected president of the Republic by the conservative majority in the Assembly.

The fall of Thiers ushered in a 'new monarchical dawn' for the Comte de Falloux.[8] Thiers' attempt to bed down a conservative republic had failed and the road was now open for the royalist majority in the Assembly to bring back the king. Why France did not achieve a restoration of the monarchy in 1873 is one of the great ironies of its history. At first everything seemed to be going smoothly. The problem that there were two pretenders, the Comte de Chambord, grandson of Charles X, and the Comte de Paris, grandson of Louis-Philippe, was overcome by the latter paying a visit to the former at Frohsdorf castle near Vienna, where the Bourbon court was in exile, on 5 August 1873. The Comte de Paris surrendered his claim to the throne on the understanding that after the death of the childless Comte de Chambord the title would revert to the Orleanist branch, and the 'fusion' of the two houses would thus be complete. A commission of nine royalists, including right-wing Legitimists known as 'the light horse', moderate Legitimists who followed the Comte de Falloux, and Orleanists such as the Duc d'Audiffret-Pasquier now drafted terms under which the Comte de Chambord would be restored. For though a minority of so-called 'light horse' Legitimists simply wanted to turn the clock back to the Ancien Régime, the majority of Legitimists and the Orleanists wanted the king as the best guarantee of a constitution enshrining 'necessary liberties' and parliamentary government in their hands as the ruling class, for which they had battled under the Empire and which they were not prepared to forsake under the monarchy. The division between these views was symbolized by the white flag of the Bourbons: since it signalled the neo-absolutist monarchy of Charles X the majority of Legitimists were prepared to accept only the tricolour of the Republic, Empire and July Monarchy under which French armies had fought for sixty-nine of the previous eighty-four years. On behalf of the commission the moderate Legitimist Pierre-Charles Chesnelong visited Frohsdorf in October 1873 and returned with the triumphant news that the terms had been agreed by the Comte de Chambord. On 27 October, however, the Comte told Chesnelong that he would not after all give up the white flag, concede constitutional guarantees or become 'the legitimate king of the Revolution'. D'Audiffret-Pasquier, who argued that the pretender must 'respect the opinions of those who would form the indispensable majority' and should have accepted the tricolour as Henri IV had accepted the mass, declared, 'We are lost.'[9] Monarchical restoration had failed and the Assembly made another attempt to establish the conservative

Republic by voting a seven-year presidential term or Septennate on 10 November 1873 to Marshal MacMahon, who brought back Albert de Broglie as chief minister.

As the monarchist threat evaporated, however, a new threat to the Republic appeared from a surprising quarter, Bonapartism. The Bonapartist cause had collapsed after the defeat of the Empire in 1870 and only nineteen Bonapartist deputies were elected to the National Assembly in February 1871. The death of Napoleon III in exile at Camden Place, Chislehurst, on 9 January 1873 was a severe blow to the cause. However on 16 March 1874 his son the prince imperial celebrated reaching his majority at eighteen with a reception at Camden Place, attended by seven thousand delegates from Bonapartist organizations in France, at which he announced that an *appel au peuple* or referendum should be held and 'if the name of Napoleon emerges an eighth time from the popular vote, I am prepared to accept the responsibility imposed on me by the national will'.[10] Bonapartist candidates now won a string of by-elections, beginning with the victory of the Baron de Bourgoing in the Nièvre on 24 May 1874, and the neighbouring department of the Yonne, where Louis-Napoleon had been elected to the National Assembly in June 1848, was flooded by Bonapartist photographs and pamphlets supporting the claim of Napoleon IV, so that, reported *La République Française*, 'it was as if the Septennate existed only at Versailles and the Yonne was an annexe of the principality of Chislehurst'.[11]

It was in fact the Bonapartist threat that drove together the centre ground of the Orleanists and moderate republicans in the National Assembly to agree the constitution of what was to become the Third Republic. This was managed not by revolution but by negotiation and compromise. After the vote of the Septennate Gambetta's *La République Française* had commented, 'Ah! We know it is the side door . . . we are far from the admirable ideal of the poet who speaks somewhere of the new generations of French democracy entering the Republic and passing "Under the great sky-lit door / Of the dazzling future". But perhaps this is the mysterious fate of the republicans of our day.'[12] The Orleanist Duc de Broglie argued that if France were to be a republic then the only solution was 'to surround this republic which we will have created and stamped with conservative institutions'. His fervent wish was to get rid of universal suffrage and revert to the limited suffrage of the July Monarchy, but since universal suffrage had been hallowed by over twenty years' prescription he demanded a largely appointed second chamber, full of civil servants, magistrates, generals and admirals, 'the representation of intelligence and interests opposed to the crude representation of numbers'.[13] This proposal was rejected on 16 May 1874 by an unholy alliance of Legitimists and republicans and de Broglie fell from power. Initiative now passed to the centre-left of men close to Thiers. Édouard Laboulaye, professor of comparative law at the Collège de France and an expert on Tocqueville and the United States, argued for 'a republic that resembled a parliamentary monarchy like two peas, a republic that was only lacking a king'. It might be inferior to a constitutional monarch, he joked, 'but you have not got one!'[14] His amendment was lost by 26 votes but on 30/31 January 1875 Sorbonne history professor Henri Wallon, who had called in his 1873 history of *The Terror* for 'the union of all decent men' against revolution, secured a 353–352 majority for his amendment that 'legislative power is divided between two assemblies, the Senate and Chamber of Deputies; the president of the Republic is elected for seven years'.[15] How the Senate would be elected was now brokered in talks between the Orleanist spokesman d'Audiffret-Pasquier and the centre-left spokesman Auguste Casimir-Périer, whose political differences were attenuated by the fact that they were brothers-in-law and lived in adjoining mansions on the Champs-Élysées. The compromise reached was a Senate of 300, whose members had to be over forty and would serve for nine years; 225 would be elected indirectly by electoral colleges of deputies, mayors and local councillors, and 75 would be life senators chosen by the National Assembly before it dissolved.

Elections to the Senate produced an elite of republican notables, three-quarters of whom had previous parliamentary experience and who occupied the political centre ground. The life senators included twenty royalists such as the Orleanist d'Audiffret-Pasquier and fifty-five republicans, weighted to the centre-left with Édouard Laboulaye and Casimir-Périer but also including left republicans close to Jules Ferry such as Jules Simon and Gambettists like Auguste Scheurer-Kestner. Senatorial elections held in January 1876 returned a list headed in Paris by Victor Hugo, whose 1874 novel *Quatre-vingt-treize*, set in the Vendée in 1793, celebrated the 'ideal republic' that showed mercy against the 'absolute republic' committed to destroying its enemies. The centre-left again did well, with senators drawn from the economic and intellectual elite and often from 'la haute société protestante' such as the industrialist and Cambridge blue William Waddington (Aisne), Léon Say, son of the economist Jean-Baptiste Say and editor of the *Journal des Débats* (Seine-et-Oise), and Charles de Freycinet, Gambetta's technical right-hand man during the war of 1870 (Paris). However Albert de Broglie was elected senator in Normandy and, overall, conservatives – both royalist and Bonapartist – had a majority over republicans.[16]

By contrast elections under universal suffrage to the Chamber of Deputies in February 1876 produced a republican triumph of 340 seats out of 533, against 155 conservatives (royalists and Bonapartists). Their success was explained in part by spin and in part by networking. Gambetta delivered key speeches such as that at Auxerre in June 1874 selling the republican party as committed to the principles of the French Revolution yet standing not for social revolution but for the hardworking 'new social strata' of smallholders, industrialists, shopkeepers and white-collar workers who together increased the economic and intellectual capital of the country.[17] Under pressure to grant an amnesty to the Communards from radicals such as Alfred Naquet, who ran against him in Marseille in February 1876, and Henri Rochefort, who had escaped from New Caledonia but was not yet allowed back into the country, he said that public opinion was not yet ready for such a measure, provoking Rochefort to label him an 'opportunist'.[18] He recruited brilliant young men to service the republican press, such as Joseph Reinach who joined the staff of *La République Française*.[19] To make political alliances he haunted the Wednesday salon of Juliette Adam, taking the advice of her husband Edmond that 'you can be in opposition from the cafés but you can only be in government from society.'[20]

The victory of the republicans did not mean that President MacMahon invited them to form a government. On the contrary, the principle of ministerial responsibility to a majority in the Chamber of Deputies had yet to be established and MacMahon did everything in his power to keep them out. He appointed as premier Jules Simon, who announced that he was 'resolutely republican and resolutely conservative'. Gambetta wounded him by denouncing his links with political Catholics – 'clericalism, there is the enemy!' – and MacMahon dismissed him on 16 May 1877 for his failure to contain the left, unleashing the so-called Seize Mai crisis. The Duc de Broglie was again brought back as premier and used the constitutional mechanism whereby the president, if he had the support of the Senate, could dissolve the Chamber of Deputies and call new elections. The Chamber was duly prorogued for a month on 18 May and dissolved on 25 June. There were echoes of the crisis of July 1830. Political legitimacy now passed squarely to the republican camp: a broad church of 363 republican deputies who acquired heroic status, from the centre-left and republican left of Jules Ferry, deputy of the Vosges, to Gambetta's republican union and Louis Blanc's extreme left, passed a vote of no confidence in the government for its 'violation of the law of majorities, which is the principle of parliamentary government'. In the campaign for the new Chamber they fought a propaganda war against the Seize Mai as a coup d'état and counter-revolution against a sovereign people who had repeatedly declared in favour of the Republic.[21] Despite administrative purges, official candidates and recourse to censorship the government could not prevent another republican victory in the elections of October 1877. The leaders of the Republic of 1848 which had established universal suffrage were now commemorated as founding fathers. Both at the funeral of François Raspail in January 1878 and while unveiling a monument to Ledru-Rollin on the thirtieth anniversary of the Second Republic, 24 February 1878, Louis Blanc paid homage to their advocacy of universal suffrage which embedded the Republic not by riot but by a fraternal popular will.[22]

The final breakthrough in the slow republican ascent to power was the 'town hall revolution' of January 1878 which swept republicans into the *mairies* of thousands of towns and villages. Since mayors were the bedrock of the colleges that elected senators, republicans gained a majority in the Senate in the elections of January 1879. Without any base of support MacMahon resigned and the deputies and senators elected the first republican president of the

Third Republic, Jules Grévy, who had been speaker of the National Assembly in 1871. Even this, however, did not mean that Gambetta took over as premier. The ministry Grévy appointed was headed by William Waddington and included Léon Say (Finances), Charles de Freycinet (Public Works) and Jules Ferry (Education). The great tribune Gambetta remained speaker of the Chamber of Deputies, and was said to exercise an 'occult power' over the ministry, but he was kept out of the government until 1882.

THE REPUBLICAN RULING CLASS UNDER SIEGE

Although the republicans had come to power by democratic means and ruled under democratic principles, it was important for the stability of the regime that what amounted to a republican ruling class be constituted. The president of the Republic, Jules Grévy, was obliged to appoint a president of the council (prime minister) who formed a ministry that had to command a majority in the Chamber of Deputies. The Chamber of Deputies was entitled to 'interpellate' the ministry on questions of policy and if it secured a majority for its challenge the ministry was forced to resign. This resulted in a rapid turnover of ministries – 108 between 1870 and 1940 – but the fall of a ministry did not trigger a general election, which was programmed every four years. Another ministry would be reconstituted by 'replastering', that is including as ministers politicians from the victorious majority but carrying over old faces from the previous team. In the period 1879–93 a pool of six or seven dominant republican figures formed the basis of almost every ministry and Charles de Freycinet was president of the council four times.[23]

This republican political elite found Gambetta frankly an embarrassment. He was seen to be a great tribune but tending, after his moment of unchallenged power in 1870–71, towards a 'bourgeois dictatorship'.[24] When his followers triumphed in the elections of 1881 Grévy was obliged to appoint him president of the council, but more moderate republicans such as Freycinet, Ferry and Léon Say refused to serve under him and his ministry lasted a mere sixty-seven days (10 November 1881–26 January 1882). He was brought down over his project to change the electoral system from single-member constituencies, which tended to become the fiefs of independent-minded local notables, to a *scrutin de liste* which obliged parties to put together a slate of candidates for each department and was intended to produce a disciplined republican party under his control. By the end of the year, as a result of a shooting accident and appendicitis, Gambetta was dead, aged forty-four. It was not that the likes of Jules Ferry opposed political reform: indeed, it was during Ferry's ministries of 1880–81 and 1883–5 that press freedom, compulsory free lay education, the right to form trade unions, the abolition of life senators and indeed the *scrutin de liste* were conceded. As he told the Chamber at the beginning of his two-year ministry in 1883, however, 'Yes, we have received a mandate to reform from the country, and we are fulfilling it, but the country requires us at this time, with no less energy, to administer, to govern, to root the republic.'[25]

The moderate republicans who exercised power in the 1880s endeavoured to establish themselves as a ruling class. They were determined to avoid tearing themselves apart in fratricidal struggle, as had their predecessors in the First Republic, or being swept away by royalists and Bonapartists, as had their predecessors in the Second Republic. Whereas the ruling republicans of the Directory failed to win elections and had to resort to coups d'état, the republicans of the Third Republic devoted huge amounts of time and resources to nurturing their contacts and constituencies. Deputies were paid an allowance of 9,000 francs a year whereas their expenses in the form of election campaigns, travel, publicity and correspondence, receptions and *la vie mondaine* to nurture connections and support might be five or ten times as much. No deputy could be without a local newspaper which sang his praises, from his achievement of office to obtaining permission for branch lines in the department. Three preconditions of success were an independent income, a good marriage and involvement in business. Overwhelmingly deputies enjoyed independent incomes – 48 per cent of deputies were in the liberal professions, 18 per cent in state service, 15 per cent in commerce, industry and finance and 8 per cent landowners in

1871–85. Their earnings were often supplemented by membership of the boards of banks and large companies investing in transport, utilities and industry at home and abroad. This could lead to what was known as *affairisme* – the use of government influence to facilitate business success and vice versa – and lay deputies and ministers open to accusations of corruption.[26] A good marriage bringing in a substantial dowry was essential, and the core republican aristocracy was closely related by marriage. Jules Ferry, Charles Floquet, who was president of the council in 1888–9, and life senator Auguste Scheurer married three sisters, respectively Eugénie, Hortense and Céline, of the Alsatian Protestant industrialist Kestner family, who brought substantial dowries and entry into the upper bourgeoisie. It is significant that Clemenceau, whose proposal of marriage had been rejected in 1864 by Hortense Kestner who later married Floquet, led the radical opposition to this ruling group, while Gambetta, though he had a mistress, Léonie Léon, never married. As a result of these strategies, 49 per cent of ministers who died before 1914 left fortunes of between 100,000 and one million francs, which was true of less than 2 per cent of French people who died in 1907, while 29 per cent left fortunes of over a million francs, which was true of only 0.1 per cent of the population.[27]

All these resources were put to good electoral purpose. Whereas the political bases of politicians such as Gambetta were in the great cities of Paris, Lyon and Marseille, those of the ruling group were in the provinces. Jules Ferry's fief was Saint-Dié in the Vosges, where he was elected in 1876. Jules Méline, his minister of agriculture, was deputy for Remiremont, also in the Vosges. René Waldeck-Rousseau, his interior minister, was deputy for the Breton capital Rennes. They were keenly aware of the need to anchor the Republic not only in the towns but in the countryside, hitherto controlled by conservatives. To achieve this Méline introduced a tariff in 1885 to protect the peasantry, in the throes of agricultural depression, from the threat of cheap grain imports and Ferry proclaimed, in the election campaign that year, 'we have conquered the universal suffrage of the countryside: let us retain it, not trouble it or weary it . . . It is by a spirit of conservation and love of stability that the French peasant has become the firmest support of the French Revolution,' which gave him land.[28]

The access of the republican ruling group to dynastic alliances, business opportunities, electoral success and ministerial office stoked the resentment of their political opponents, who were both on the right – royalists or Bonapartists – and on the left – radical republicans or socialists. Although the constitution of 1875 had been made by an alliance of moderate republicans and Orleanists, Orleanist and Bonapartist support for the Seize Mai coup enabled republicans to argue that they were the enemies of the Republic and should never be allowed to regain power. A convention arose that no ministry could rely on the votes of the right to sustain it if it could not command the support of a republican majority. The death of the Comte de Chambord without an heir in 1883 deprived Legitimists of their leader and Napoleon III's son, the prince imperial, died fighting the Zulus as an officer of the British army in 1879. In a speech at Le Havre in 1883 Jules Ferry announced that 'the royalist threat no longer exists: it is buried beneath two tombs . . . but another threat has replaced it and we have to consider it squarely in order to confront it with the only cure, the only barrier: the ever closer union of those republican forces that are capable of forming a government.'[29]

In fact Ferry underestimated the ability of the royalists and Bonapartists to continue to pose a threat. Royalist and Bonapartist managers who had historically been more hindered than helped by the pretensions of their respective pretenders looked now to achieve a majority of conservatives within the Republic, and their royalist–Bonapartist 'Union of the Right' headed by the Baron de Mackau won 176 seats to the republicans' 127 in the first round of the October 1885 election. This was explained in part because moderate republicans, who now considered the main enemy to be radical republicans, had run against them as well as against conservatives. In the second round the moderate and radical republican wings were obliged to sink their differences, under the slogan of 'republican concentration', under which the worst-placed republican candidate, of whatever tendency, retired in favour of the best-placed one. In this round they won 244 seats to the conservatives' 25, achieving a total of 383 republicans to 201 conservatives.[30]

What stood between the moderate republicans on the one hand

and the radical republicans and socialists on the other was the ghost of the Paris Commune. Since 1871 survivors of the Commune were either vegetating in New Caledonia, to which they had been deported, or were living in exile in London or Geneva. Their solidarity and anger was forged by the memory of the Semaine Sanglante in which they claimed 30,000 of their number had been massacred. For them class conflict was not just an ideology but a reality. The revolutionary Commune group, for example, set up in London in 1874 and including Blanquists such as Émile Eudes and Ernest Granger, together with Édouard Vaillant, dreamed of a 'future Commune' that would rekindle 'the great battle between the bourgeoisie and proletariat' and establish a 'Communard Republic'.[31] How they aimed to bring about the new socialist Republic differed in line with the rival factions on the Paris Commune of 1871. The Blanquists urged a seizure of power, although they conceded that elections could be used to raise awareness. Thus Blanqui, in prison at Clairvaux, ran as a candidate in a Bordeaux by-election in 1879. The Jacobin tradition represented by Delescluze, who had died on the barricades in May 1871, was taken up by Jules Guesde, who had been in exile in Switzerland but returned clandestinely to France in 1876 and was converted to Marxist socialism in Paris by German émigrés. He founded *L'Égalité* in 1877 and the Marxist Parti Ouvrier at a congress of workers in Marseille in 1879. On Sunday 23 May 1880 and each succeeding year Jules Guesde led his Parti Ouvrier on a pilgrimage to the Mur des Fédérés in Père Lachaise cemetery – where during the Semaine Sanglante the last Communards had made a final stand and been summarily shot – in order to maintain a revolutionary class consciousness.[32] Ten weeks later his Parti Ouvrier boycotted what they called the 'bourgeois fête' of 14 July, arguing that 'its Bastilles were still to be taken'.[33] The anti-authoritarian or Proudhonist tendency, hostile to any dictatorship including that of the proletariat and favouring direct action to bring about a federation of autonomous workers' associations and communes, was represented by Benoît Malon and Paul Brousse, in exile in Switzerland and affiliated to the so-called anti-authoritarian International of Bakunin.

Within France, radical republicans such as Georges Clemenceau, Paris municipal councillor and deputy in the 18th *arrondissement*

(Montmartre), who had tried to mediate between the Paris Commune and Versailles on 19 March 1871, campaigned ceaselessly for an amnesty for the Communards. But the Commune was vilified by the likes of Maxime du Camp who argued that 'the events of the Commune were nothing to do with politics but only about criminality' and that 'an amnesty would bring back traitors, incendiaries and assassins to the country whose destruction they have sworn.'[34] Moderate republicans such as Ferry, who had himself narrowly escaped the violence of the Commune on 18 March 1871, steered a course between placating conservative opinion and achieving the union of all republicans when public opinion was ready, which earned them the name of 'Opportunists'. A bill of 1879 tried to confine amnesty to Communards who had not been convicted of criminal acts, only political deeds, but this pleased neither right nor left. Eventually, under pressure from Gambetta and in an attempt to steal the thunder of the left, a full amnesty was proclaimed on 10 July 1880, ahead of the celebrations of republican union on 14 July, and the likes of Henri Rochefort and Louise Michel returned home.[35]

There was little possibility of insurrection in 1880s France but the return of the Communards brought about the emergence of socialist parties and reinvigorated radical republicans who did not believe in social equality but desired a far more democratic republic than that provided by the constitution of 1875. For the elections of 1881 Jules Guesde went to London to meet Karl Marx and his son-in-law Paul Lafargue, in order to draft a 'minimum programme' of social reforms as the manifesto of the Parti Ouvrier. Guesde's initiative did not persuade all revolutionaries. After the death of Blanqui in 1881 his disciples Eudes, Granger and Vaillant founded their own Central Revolutionary Committee, and Vaillant as 'candidate of the social Republic' was elected to the Paris municipal council in 1884. Brousse opposed the 'Marxist authoritarianism' of Guesde's centralized party which was obedient to London and planned a dictatorship of the proletariat, and broke from him at a socialist congress in Saint-Étienne in 1882 to found the Fédération des Travailleurs Socialistes de France.[36] Brousse believed in the right of local socialist federations to set their own agenda and interpreted the anarchist philosophy of direct action as achieving power at municipal level first. In 1887 his Possibilists, as they were known, won nine seats on the Paris municipal council and took control of the Paris Bourse du Travail, the city-funded body which federated all the trade unions in Paris.

Socialists formed a minority on the Paris municipal council, which was the power-base of radical republicans. The council made clear its commitment to the French Revolution by unveiling a statue of the Republic, capped by a Phrygian bonnet, on the place de la République, on 13 July 1883, a ceremony that was attended neither by President Grévy nor by premier Ferry. In 1887 it commissioned a statue of Danton, portraying him (to placate moderate opinion) as the patriot of 1792 and champion of popular education. Alexandre Millerand, a young lawyer who worked on Clemenceau's paper *La Justice*, was elected to the Paris council in 1884 and obtained funding from it to found a chair in the history of the French Revolution at the Sorbonne, the first incumbent of which in 1886 was Alphonse Aulard. Clemenceau himself was the terror of the moderate republicans in the Chamber of Deputies. His reform programme was to abolish the Senate and presidency of the Republic in favour of a sovereign National Assembly, on the model of that of 1848 or the Convention of 1792. He helped to topple Gambetta for defending the Senate in January 1882 and mobilized opposition to the government's colonial policy to overturn Freycinet in July 1882 and Ferry in March 1885. After the elections of October 1885 the moderate republicans no longer held a majority, but were only 239 strong, squeezed between 201 conservatives and 144 radicals. From now on the republican governing class was under siege.

THE BOULANGIST MENACE

In the face of the challenge from radicals and socialists, the long-term project of the republican governing class was to make common cause with the right against them. However, this strategy was hampered by the principle of republican legitimacy, which since 16 May 1877 held that republican ministries should not rely for their parliamentary majority on royalist or Bonapartist votes, and by the reflex of 'republican concentration' which dictated that they should build a left-wing alliance of all republicans, moderates and radicals, when the Republic was in danger. However, radical republicans and socialists were often reluctant to fall into line behind the republican oligarchy, preferring to attack the 'bourgeois Republic'. This opened the way to the possibility that radicals and socialists might, for short-term advantage, themselves make common cause against the republican oligarchy with royalists and Bonapartists. This is precisely what happened in the Boulanger crisis of 1886–9, the first major political crisis that the Republic had to weather after 1877.

Under the rules of governmental majorities, the moderate republicans were obliged after the 1885 elections to open the ministry to radicals or their nominees, and in 1886 the radical leader Clemenceau put forward as minister of war General Boulanger, a contemporary of his at the Lycée of Nantes who had a reputation for being both patriotic and reforming. Keen to demonstrate these credentials Boulanger struck from the army list officers belonging to the Orleanist or Bonapartist former ruling houses, while after an extravagant wedding reception given by the Comte de Paris for his daughter which seemed to reconstitute the Orleanist court the radicals forced through a law of exile in June 1886 banning members of former ruling houses from French soil.

In order to check these radical initiatives the moderate republicans challenged the convention whereby ministries should not rely for their survival on the votes of the right. A coalition of moderate republicans and Baron Mackau's Union of the Right overturned the ministry in which Boulanger was war minister in May 1887, and the Union supported the new ministry headed by Maurice Rouvier, Ferry's former minister of commerce. Boulanger was sent off to take charge of the XIII Army Corps well out of the way at Clermont-Ferrand, but his departure from the Gare de Lyon on 8 July 1887 was marked by a massive demonstration in his support organized by Blanquists and Paul Déroulède's patriotic and radical Ligue de Patriotes. While radicals like Millerand attacked the Rouvier ministry as 'the protégé of the right', Jules Ferry made a speech at Épinal in the Vosges declaring that 'a well-constituted republic needs a conservative party. To temper, contain, and moderate democracy is a noble thing.'[37]

The radicals, however, were far from finished. A scandal was uncovered revealing that President Grévy's son-in-law, Daniel Wilson, was selling honours from his office in the Élysée palace. Since the president was not himself constitutionally responsible to the Chamber Clemenceau interpellated the Rouvier government on the question in November 1887 and rallied a majority of radicals and the right to topple the ministry. Grévy, who had always favoured moderate republican ministries, was still the target of newspapers from Rochefort's *Intransigeant* to the conservative *Figaro*, and the tactical refusal of ministers including Clemenceau to form a new government forced Grévy to resign. The obvious candidate to replace him was Jules Ferry, but Ferry was the *bête noire* not only of the radicals but of the right, who did not forgive his attacks on church schools. Demonstrations on the place de la Concorde on 2 December 1887, organized by the Ligue des Patriotes and Blanquists and opposing the candidature of Ferry, turned to riot. Deputies and senators met at Versailles on 3 December to elect a new president and in order to defeat Ferry radicals gave their votes to Sadi Carnot, a compromise candidate from a great republican dynasty. A week later a mad Lorrainer who thought Ferry unpatriotic approached him in the Palais-Bourbon and tried to kill him, two bullets lodging in his side and chest.

Boulanger now became the vehicle of a campaign, orchestrated by both radicals and the conservatives, to dissolve parliament and to revise the constitution in a way that would permit the election of the president of the Republic not by the deputies and senators but by universal suffrage. For the radicals this would brush away the Republic of notables and fixers and subordinate the executive to the sovereign people; for the Bonapartists direct presidential elections would open the possibility of a repeat of 1848, when Louis-Napoleon was elected president, while the Comte de Paris was now ready to fall back on the hope of a restoration of the monarchy by plebiscite.

The dismissal of Boulanger from the army on 15 March 1888 provoked the formation of a Republican Committee of National

Protest headed by radicals such as Henri Rochefort, Paul Déroulède and Alfred Naquet. The tactic adopted was to run Boulanger in all by-elections, the magic being that under the *scrutin de liste* adopted in 1885 a whole department rather than one constituency turned out to vote. Within months the country was rocked from one end to the other by this electoral steeplechase. In the midst of economic recession Boulanger was supported by the weavers of Amiens in the Aisne (25 March 1888), the miners of Anzin and metalworkers of Valenciennes in the Nord (15 April), but also by the Bonapartist peasants of the Dordogne (8 April). A meeting of Boulangist organizers with Émile Eudes sealed an alliance with the Blanquists, but the socialists were divided, Lafargue keen to harness the revolutionary potential of Boulanger's popular support against the bourgeois republic, but Guesde seeing the dispute as one between rival sections of the bourgeoisie and warning, 'between cholera and the plague there is no choice.'[38]

While the left provided the organization, unbeknown to them it was the right that provided most of the funding. Bonapartists were divided between those such as Paul de Cassagnac who demanded the return of the hereditary Empire or nothing and others like Georges Lachaud who argued that successive elections had endorsed the Republic but that the parliamentary Republic had to be replaced by a national or plebiscitary republic based on direct presidential elections. On 2 January 1888 Bonapartist manager Georges Thiébaud, who was in the second camp, paid a visit to the pretender, Napoleon's cousin Prince Jérôme-Napoléon, at his Prangins estate in the Swiss Vaud, to obtain approval for their backing of Boulanger. On the royalist side the key player was Count Arthur de Dillon, who won over the Comte de Paris and the Baron de Mackau. Generous funding was provided by flamboyant royalists such as the Duchesse d'Uzès, who was indebted to Boulanger for allowing her when he had been minister of war to hunt in the forest of Rambouillet.

Despite the sound and fury the Boulangist threat petered out. In the first place its challenge to the Republic was an electoral one and, when it materialized, the division between radical and moderate republicans which had allowed it to develop closed up under the banner of republican concentration. In particular Clemenceau, who had initially promoted Boulanger, began to fear the Caesarist threat he posed and in May 1888 founded the Société des Droits de l'Homme et du Citoyen which grouped moderate republicans, radicals and socialists, to oppose the general. Second, Boulanger was always a man of style rather than substance. He took his seat in the Chamber on 12 July 1888, immediately demanded its dissolution, and provoked a duel with premier Floquet. Unfortunately he came off worse, wounded in the neck. The moment for action arrived on 27 January 1889 when he was elected in Paris by a combination of opponents of the government on left and right. A crowd of Ligue des Patriotes and Blanquists gathered in front of the Café Durand on the place de la Madeleine where Boulanger was hosting a victory dinner, but he could not be prevailed upon to seize the moment and march on the Élysée palace. Instead he panicked and fled over the border to Belgium. Third, the Republic showed itself to be far more decisive in the face of this kind of threat than it had been in 1799 or 1851. It mobilized the legal, judicial and administrative weapons of the Republic to defeat Boulanger and his associates. The electoral conditions that had made Boulangism possible were terminated by legislation of 1889 which abolished the *scrutin de liste* and banned candidates from standing in more than one constituency. The Ligue des Patriotes was dissolved and its leader Déroulède sent for trial. The Senate fulfilled its role as the 'fortress of the Republic' by sitting as a high court on 14 July 1889 to try Boulanger, Rochefort and Dillon *in absentia*. In the general elections of October conservatives ran as Boulangists in seats they could not hope to win under their own colours, but interior minister Ernest Constans used every weapon in his armoury to secure the return of 366 republicans against 168 of the right and 42 Boulangists. The young Maurice Barrès was returned as a Boulangist for Nancy, but the election of Boulanger in the 18th *arrondissement* of Paris was quashed. Fourth, the Republic used the occasion of the 100th anniversary of the French Revolution in 1889 to proclaim its legitimacy. A banquet for 13,000 mayors was laid on at the Palais de l'Industrie and a preliminary, plaster-cast version of a monument entitled *The Triumph of the Republic*, sculpted by Dalou, was unveiled by President Carnot on the place de la Nation on 21 September 1889. In September 1891, two months after the death of his mistress (and bankroller) Marguerite de Bonnemain, Boulanger shot himself on her grave in Brussels.

The republican oligarchy could not be displaced by Boulangism, but a new weapon emerged in the form of political anti-Semitism to dislodge much of the republican ruling group in 1893. Anti-Semitism had the ability to mobilize popular emotions and leap class barriers in a way that Boulangism had failed to do. 'It is hatred, simply hatred, that is first and foremost expressed by this anti-Jewish senti-ment,' wrote Barrès in *Le Figaro*.[39] The rumour was spread that the regime had won the elections of 1889 only with the help of Jewish gold, provided in particular by the Rothschilds. On the left Henri Rochefort denounced 'the triumph of Juiverie' while a French Anti-Semitic League was founded in September 1889 by Édouard Drumont, author of the 1886 bestseller *La France juive*, together with the Marquis de Morès, a hugely wealthy speculator of Spanish noble descent.[40] In 1892 Drumont's new press weapon, *La Libre Parole*, exposed the fact that bribes had passed between the Panama Canal Company, headed by Ferdinand de Lesseps, and certain republican politicians whose influence had been needed to pass a 1888 law authorizing the Company to float a share-issue. It delighted to point out that the intermediaries between the Company and the politicians were the German-Jewish banker Jacques de Reinach, uncle and father-in-law of Joseph Reinach, who committed suicide, and the German-Jewish promoter Cornelius Herz. The link between repub-lican politics, business and Jewish influence destroyed the careers, at least in the short term, of moderate republicans such as Rouvier and Joseph Reinach and radical republicans such as Clemenceau, defeated in the elections of 1893.[41]

THE RETURN OF CLASS WAR

After the Boulanger Affair socialists were forced to reconsider their strategy. The demagogic hold of Boulanger on much of the working class had seduced some socialist leaders, until it became clear that he wished to use popular support only for his own ends. The new faith of anti-Semitism was also seductive, and leaders like Rochefort mobilized it to attack what was seen to be Jewish control of the rich and powerful in the Republic. A third siren was that of moderate and radical republicans, who repeatedly called on socialists to rally in defence of the regime against its enemies of the right. After all, the Republic was democratic and the possibility existed that socialists might at some future date conquer a majority under universal suffrage and achieve power by legal means.

The clear message for socialist movements confronted by these false routes was in fact to turn back to the working class and to organize it as a labour movement for specifically socialist ends. In this respect 1890 and the years immediately following it were a turning point, when class struggle was squarely back on the agenda and memories of the Paris Commune acted both as an inspiration and as an object lesson that caused socialists to rethink how they would achieve a more equal society. There was, however, no single model of socialist opposition.

On the Proudhonist wing, Paul Brousse and the Possibilists had taken the path of defending the Republic against Boulangism, and benefited by meeting the democratic challenge, both locally and nationally. They had a powerful voice on the Paris municipal council and returned two deputies to parliament in 1889. The rank and file of the movement, however, considered that the Possibilist leaders had become bourgeois politicians and lost touch with the movement. A challenge to Brousse's leadership was launched by Jean Allemane, a printworker, veteran of the Commune and former deportee to New Caledonia at the Châtellerault congress of the Fédération des Travailleurs Socialistes de France in October 1890, using the slogan that 'the emancipation of the workers must be the task of the workers themselves'. Breaking away from the Broussists they set up a Parti Ouvrier Socialiste Révolutionnaire and took control of the Paris Bourse du Travail.[42] The Bourses du Travail, employment centres that also provided office space for all trade unions in a given town, spread across the country and formed a Fédération des Bourses du Travail at Saint-Étienne in 1892. Although funded by republican city councils, often as a reward for labour support in local elections, they might constitute a threat to the republican regime. In July 1893 the Paris Bourse du Travail was closed down by the government and remained closed for nearly three years.

Possibilists and the Guesdist Parti Ouvrier – the French Marxists – vied with each other to be the dominant socialist party in France. In 1889 they hosted two separate congresses in Paris of the International Socialist movement, which was starting up again after the collapse of the First International in the early 1870s, this time representing only bona-fide socialist parties from each country. What the rival congresses agreed on, however, was that from 1890 May Day should be celebrated by labour movements in Europe, on the model provided by the USA since 1886, agitating for a straight-forward reform, the eight-hour day, and enabling socialist parties to secure a grip on the labour movement.[43] The Guesdists dominated the Fédération Nationale des Syndicats after 1886 but were keen to wean it away from open-ended strike action over which it had no control. Governments were not happy with what amounted to a one-day strike and demonstration and on 1 May 1891 the police opened fire on the May Day demonstration in the woollen town of Fourmies (Nord), killing nine and wounding thirty, including many children. The heavily industrialized Nord, with its large-scale textile factories and exploited textile workers, was one of the power-bases of the Parti Ouvrier, and Paul Lafargue, one of its leaders, was arrested for instigating the demonstration. He was defended at his trial in July at the Douai Assize Court by Alexandre Millerand, radical republican deputy for Paris XII who was trying to introduce socialist ideas into republicanism and steer socialism towards reformism. Sentenced to a year in prison Lafargue was elected deputy of Lille in November 1891 and released.[44] The following year Guesdists conquered a number of municipalities including Roubaix, the textile town adjacent to Lille. The reality of class struggle was feeding into the electoral success of a socialism that was revolutionary only in rhetoric.

Strike movements and democratic socialism operated in tandem in other parts of France. In the small mining town of Carmaux (Tarn), the miners' union launched a strike in pursuit of higher wages in March 1892 and took control of the municipality in May. The secretary of the miners' union, Calvignac, who was elected mayor, was refused two days a week leave to discharge his mayoral functions by the mining company and sacked. The miners left the pits, 1,500 soldiers were sent in, and the town became a focal point for socialists demanding nationalization of coal mines. Most influential was Jean Jaurès, brought up in nearby Castres, a graduate of the École Normale Supérieure in Paris who had returned to teach history at the university of Toulouse, contributed to the *Dépêche de Toulouse* and was elected a republican deputy for the Tarn, aged twenty-six, in 1885. Defeated at Castres by Baron Reille, chair of the Carmaux board in 1889, while another board member, the Marquis de Solages, was elected at nearby Albi, Jaurès was converted to socialism by the librarian of the École Normale, Lucien Herr, and wrote a thesis on *The Origins of German Socialism*. He saw socialism as a fulfilment of the revolutionary credo of liberty, equality and fraternity which had been confiscated by the republican bourgeoisie, and was as much about justice as about material decency. In October 1892 the mining company capitulated, Calvignac was reinstated as mayor, the Marquis de Solages resigned from parliament, and Jaurès was elected in his place in the by-election of January 1893. He called himself an independent socialist like Millerand, but he appeared with Guesde at the Tivoli Vauxhall Gardens that January to launch a united socialist front for the 1893 elections while Millerand took possession of *La Petite République*, which became the mouthpiece of French socialism. Nearly fifty socialist deputies were elected to the Chamber in 1893, including Jaurès (Albi), Guesde (Roubaix), Vaillant, Millerand and the latter's secretary Viviani in respectively the 20th, 12th and 5th *arrondissements* of Paris.[45] However, whereas Guesde, born in 1845 and personally marked by the Paris Commune, found it difficult to give up the rhetoric of revolutionary class war, even when participating in elections, Jaurès, Millerand and Viviani, born around 1860, subscribed to the notion that the Commune had been a premature revolution and that socialists would not take power until a long preparation of the working classes in party and trade unions had been completed.

Not all leftist opponents of the regime went down the socialist road. On 1 May 1891, while textile workers were being shot at Fourmies, a group of anarchists infiltrated the demonstration at

Clichy, in the northern suburbs of Paris, brandishing the black flag, and exchanged shots with police. After these were arrested and sent for trial, anarchists launched a campaign of terror in retaliation. François-Claudius Ravachol, hitherto little more than an armed robber, set off bombs in the flats of judges who had sentenced the Clichy anarchists. Singing revolutionary songs and calling for vengeance before he was guillotined on 11 July 1892, he became a folk hero. The following year, on 9 December 1893, a casually employed worker Auguste Vaillant (no relation to Édouard) hurled a bomb into the Chamber of Deputies, killing no one but throwing the parliamentary Republic into shock. He was executed on 5 February 1894. A week later, taking the bourgeoisie in general for his target, Émile Henry, the son of a Communard who had himself failed the examination for the École Polytechnique, threw a bomb into the Hôtel Terminus at the Gare Saint-Lazare, killing one person and wounding twenty. He was executed on 21 May 1894. President Sadi Carnot, who had refused to pardon all these terrorists, was himself stabbed to death by an Italian anarchist Santo Geronimo Casiero in Lyon on 24 June 1894.[46] The government reacted decisively, pushing a series of laws through the Chamber to criminalize all those associated with or defending terrorism, the so-called *lois scélérates*. Leading anarchists were rounded up and what became known as the Trial of Thirty, including the shoemaker Jean Grave, editor of *La Révolte*, Émile Pouget, editor of *Le Père Peinard*, Sébastien Faure, editor of *Le Libérataire*, who had been entrusted with the care of Vaillant's daughter, and the art critic Félix Fénéon, took place at the Assize Court of the Seine in August 1894. The prosecution failed to establish links between them and all but three were acquitted, but the tactic of terrorist attacks was clearly no longer the way for anarchism.[47]

The most promising road ahead was a hybrid of anarchism and trade unionism known as anarcho-syndicalism or revolutionary syndicalism. Fernand Pelloutier, the son of a post office employee, expelled from the *petit séminaire* of Guérande for writing an anticlerical novel, contributed briefly to Barrès' anti-establishment *La Cocarde* paper of 1894–5, for which the future royalist Charles Maurras also wrote.[48] More important was his association with Aristide Briand, whose father was a wine merchant and café-owner of Nantes, who qualified as a lawyer in Paris then returned to practise at Saint-Nazaire and was elected as a radical to the municipal council in 1888. Repeatedly defeated when he ran for the Chamber, after 1889 Briand moved towards anarchist circles in Paris. In 1892 he and Pelloutier founded a Bourse du Travail at Saint-Nazaire and hit on the strategy of the revolutionary general strike as the way for workers to reclaim control of their own destiny from socialist politicians by direct action. As delegates of the Saint-Nazaire Bourse they challenged Guesde for control of the Fédération Nationale des Syndicats when it held its congress at Nantes in September 1894, and won a majority. This opened the way to the formation of a new trade union umbrella, the Confédération Générale du Travail, in 1895. In that year Pelloutier became secretary of the Fédération des Bourses du Travail, which he was keen to keep separate from the Confédération, although they adopted similar strategies of direct action. He wrote a seminal article in Grave's *Temps Nouveaux* urging anarchists to infiltrate the labour movement, educate the working classes and, linking up with the Proudhonian libertarian and federalist tradition, use the general strike as a tool to found a socialist society, 'the free association of free producers'.[49]

THE REPUBLICAN ELITE ON
CONSERVATIVE CRUTCHES

The red peril of socialism and anarchism had a profound impact on the political configuration of the Third Republic. The strategy of republican concentration which allied moderate and radical republicans was practised in the elections of 1893, but became increasingly irrelevant as the threat from the left outweighed that from the right. Between November 1895 and April 1896 there was a short-lived experiment of a radical ministry with socialist support. The prime minister, Léon Bourgeois, subscribed to a notion of 'solidarism' whereby those who did well out of society should be required to put more back in, notably through a progressive income tax to pay for benefits such as compensation for industrial accidents, medical cover and pensions. This policy was seen by the ruling class as a frontal attack on private property. Since the ministry had a majority in the Chamber of Deputies the Senate was mobilized to pass votes of no confidence in the ministry and finally to reject its budget. Nothing remained of the Bourgeois programme except the bill on accident compensation which became law in 1898.[50]

The Bourgeois ministry was in fact an aberration from the new shape of the governing coalition, which was a moderate republican government, now called Progressist, ruling against radicals and socialists with a majority provided by conservative votes in the Chamber. Although it was strictly against the rules of republican legitimacy laid down in 1877 for a republican ministry to rely on conservative support, two things had happened. First, the red peril had divided republicans along class lines, so that moderate republicans, representing the ruling class, had more in common with conservatives, also representing the ruling class, than with radicals or socialists; and second, after 1890 many conservatives decided to fight no more for the restoration of monarchy or Empire but under what was called the Ralliement to embrace the republic as the *de facto* regime and work within it to make it more conservative, as it were, more Tory.

The shadow of this new moderate-republican–Tory-right coalition appeared first on the question of protective tariffs. Confronted by the collapse of farm prices and global manufacturing competition, agricultural and industrial lobbies converged in favour of protective tariffs and achieved a majority of the Chamber elected in 1889. Sponsored by Jules Méline, who had taken through a previous agricultural tariff in 1885, this tariff on the import of agricultural and certain industrial goods was passed 386–105 on 29 December 1891: there were 242 republicans and 144 conservatives in favour with 80 republicans and 25 conservatives against, and the bill passed into law on 11 January 1892.[51] The configuration also appeared outside parliament, in pressure-groups set up to explore social reform as an antidote to socialism. The ramifications of the social question, from factory conditions and poor housing to tuberculosis and alcoholism, which helped to foster socialism, could equally be alleviated by reforms carried out by ruling groups of all political persuasions. Such a pressure-group was the Musée Social, founded in 1894 and including 'rallied' monarchists such as the Comte de Chambrun, the Prince d'Arenberg and Albert de Mun, moderate republicans such as Jules Méline and René Waldeck-Rousseau and radical republicans such as Léon Bourgeois. Many of these had business interests, such as d'Arenberg, who was president of the Suez Canal Company, and Émile Cheysson, a former director of the Le Creusot steelworks and lecturer at the École Libre des Sciences Politiques, who was deeply committed to social engineering.[52]

The bombing of the Chamber on 9 December 1893 had the effect of converting the coalition into a government. The president of the council, Jean Casimir-Périer, son of Auguste, framer of the 1875 constitution, grandson of Louis-Philippe's minister and himself a director of the Anzin mining company, sometimes seen as the unacceptable face of capitalism, lurched to the right, enjoying the support of 'rallied' conservatives such as the Prince d'Arenberg.[53] He rushed through the *lois scélérates* against terrorists and was elected president of the Republic on 27 June 1894, after the assassination of Sadi Carnot, but he was unable to wield the power he wished to and resigned on 15 January 1895. He was replaced by Félix Faure, a businessman of Le Havre who had been close to Gambetta but defined himself as above party and had voted against the expulsion of the princes in 1886 and therefore benefited from the support of conservatives.[54]

The governmental manifestation of the moderate–conservative coalition was exemplified by the ministry of Jules Méline, which held office between April 1896 and 1898. Ushered in by the Senate coup against the Bourgeois ministry, it brought in a number of significant younger republicans such as Louis Barthou, lawyer and deputy for Oléron in the Basque country, who became minister of the interior.[55] Inside the Chamber it relied on the support of conservatives, much to the anger of radicals and socialists, the latter denouncing the fact that 'the Méline ministry has a majority of republicans against it; it is saved only by votes from every shade of the right, rushing to support this embattled opportunism.'[56] Outside the Chamber, it had the support of business leaders keen on protection and social defence. These were solicited and corralled by the Association Générale du Commerce et de l'Industrie, headed by René Waldeck-Rousseau, who had reverted to making money as a commercial lawyer after electoral defeat in 1889, although he was parachuted in as senator for the Loire in 1894.[57] All seemed set for a moderate–conservative victory in the elections due in May 1898. This new ruling class might have taken powerful root had not a momentous event intervened.

THE DREYFUS AFFAIR: EMBATTLEMENT AND REPUBLICAN DEFENCE

In December 1894 a General Staff officer of Alsatian-Jewish origin, Captain Alfred Dreyfus, was court-martialled for passing French military secrets to the German army. After a ceremonial degradation in the courtyard of the École Militaire on 5 January 1895, when his emblems of rank were torn from his tunic and his sword broken, he was sent as a traitor to Devil's Island off French Guiana. Little sympathy surrounded him: writing in *La Justice* on Christmas Day 1894 Clemenceau criticized the lightness of the punishment which would have been much harsher for an ordinary soldier, and demanded the death penalty.[58]

Almost two years later a small group of individuals began to suspect that Dreyfus had been framed by his superior officers in order to cover the guilt of a Gentile officer who was much more closely integrated into the patronage system of the army. This group was partly Jewish – Alfred's brother Mathieu, the former Gambettist and editor of *La République Française*, Joseph Reinach, the anarchist Bernard Lazare and the lawyer and intellectual Léon Blum. It was also partly Alsatian, and thus marginal but keen to demonstrate its patriotism. Colonel Picquart, head of the army's Intelligence Service, who had taught Dreyfus at military school, began to suspect Major Ferdinand Esterhazy, a flamboyant nationalist, and reported his concerns to his superiors and Méline's war minister, General Billot. Rather than explore that line they posted Picquart to Tunisia in January 1897. Granted a short leave in June 1897 Picquart returned and made contact with a lawyer who had been his contemporary at the Lycée of Strasbourg, Louis Leblois. On 13 July 1897 Leblois met the patron of all Alsatian republicans and Protestants, Auguste Scheurer-Kestner, who was immediately converted to the possibility of a miscarriage of justice. Scheurer-Kestner went straight to the top, calling on President Faure, General Billot and premier Méline. None of them wanted to have anything to do with his concerns and claimed that he had no evidence warranting a fresh look at the case. Méline announced to the Chamber on 4 December 1897, 'There is no Dreyfus Affair.'[59]

More than that, the rumour began to spread in the autumn of 1897 that this troublemaking, designed only to bring the army into disrepute and weaken the nation, was the conspiracy of a 'Jewish syndicate'. This story was spread not only by hardline anti-Semites such as Drumont but by Catholic leaders such as Albert de Mun who denounced the 'occult power' behind the campaign and by left-wing nationalists like Henri Rochefort who, parodying Maupassant, dubbed Joseph Reinach 'Boule de Juif'. The weight of opinion against the 'syndicate' pulled socialists along in its wake. Alexandre Millerand told Joseph Reinach, whose uncle had committed suicide during the Panama scandal, to rehabilitate his own family before he tried to rehabilitate Dreyfus, and fought a pistol duel with him.[60] Although Jaurès was inclined towards Dreyfus, Jules Guesde and Édouard Vaillant told socialists on 19 January 1898 that they should ignore both sides in what they termed a 'bourgeois civil war'.

In fact Esterhazy was brought to court martial on 10–11 January 1898, a ploy by the military to clear the air, for he was promptly acquitted. This triggered a second phase of the Affair: an open letter to the president of the Republic, entitled J'accuse, penned by the novelist Émile Zola, and published on 13 January 1898 in L'Aurore by Clemenceau who, as over Boulanger, had changed his mind in mid-course. Zola denounced the cover-up by the military, naming war minister General Mercier, chief of General Staff General de Boisdeffre and Commandant du Paty de Clam as the officers concerned, issued warnings about military despotism, and perorated on the inevitable triumph of truth and justice.[61] He was supported by a manifesto of intellectuals, among whom were Anatole France and Marcel Proust, published on 14 January, by Charles Péguy, a graduate of the École Normale Supérieure, who spread the word from his Bellais bookshop in the rue Cujas, and by avant-garde journals such as *La Revue Blanche*, run by the art-critic Natanson brothers.[62] These intellectuals, however, remained a small minority. Of the fifty-five daily newspapers in January and February 1898, forty-eight were anti-dreyfusard.[63] Zola was sent to trial on 7 February 1898 for defamation and sentenced to a year in prison, although he managed to escape to England. Outside the courtyard hostile crowds were orchestrated by Jules Guérin and his newly formed Ligue Anti-Sémitique, composed mostly of butchers' boys from the abattoirs of La Villette.[64] Henri Rochefort, who was sentenced to a mere five days' gaol for libelling Reinach, was carried shoulder-high by the crowds on his way to Sainte-Pélagie.[65] Anti-Semitic riots broke out in the main cities of France, degenerating in Algiers into a veritable pogrom.[66] The only response of note on the dreyfusard side was the foundation of the Ligue des Droits de l'Homme, primarily by freemasons, Jews and Protestants, who had themselves been persecuted before the Revolution, in order to fight for human rights and tolerance.[67]

Intellectuals without electoral concerns might join the highly exposed Dreyfusard camp. Politicians with elections to fight in May 1898 did not. In those elections the Dreyfus Affair was not an issue: to mention it was electoral suicide. Any politician suspected of favouring Dreyfus was unceremoniously abandoned: thus not only Joseph Reinach but also Jean Jaurès and Jules Guesde lost their seats, although the latter's defeat may be explained by the revenge of the Roubaix textile magnate, Eugène Motte. The election saw the return of twenty-two self-confessed anti-Semites, notably Édouard Drumont in Algiers, where the Ligue Anti-Sémitique had been his electoral agents. The main result of the elections was defeat for Jules Méline as opinion shifted to the left, and a radical, Henri Brisson, was appointed premier. The move to the left however, did nothing for the case of Dreyfus. Brisson's war minister, Godefroy Cavaignac, told the Chamber on 9 July 1898 that he had irrefutable proof of Dreyfus' guilt. The son of the republican dictator of 1848, he saw himself as a soldier in all but name, while Reinach described him as 'the Robespierre of patriotism', determined to put the national interest above individual rights.[68] His certainty about Dreyfus' guilt was punctured by the *Preuves* published by Jean Jaurès, and suspicion for framing Dreyfus now fell on Colonel Henry of the Intelligence Section. Arrested and confined in the fortress of Mont-Valérien, Henry slit his throat on 31 August 1898, evidence of his guilt for dreyfusards and of his martyrdom for antidreyfusards.

Antidreyfusards now had the wind behind them. The defeat of the moderates around Méline removed the plank along which the 'rallied' royalists and Bonapartists sought to return to power. There had always been royalists and Bonapartists critical of the Ralliement; now the initiative shifted to them as it seemed that they would never gain control of the parliamentary Republic, so it must be destroyed. In the autumn of 1898 anti-parliamentary leagues gathered shape and momentum, putting the parliamentary Republic in danger. The royalist pretender, now the Duc d'Orléans, saw the possibility of using the popular fighting-force provided by the Ligue Anti-Sémitique as a route back to power. Jules Guérin and a selection of his butchers' boys were introduced to the duke in his Brussels exile on 24 January 1899, and royalist money for the Ligue was channelled by Boni de Castellane, who had married the American heiress Anna Gould, and by André Buffet, son of the Orleanist Louis Buffet, who had been a Moral Order premier in 1875.[69] The Ligue des Patriotes, dissolved after the Boulanger Affair, was reconstituted in September 1898 by Paul Déroulède, who was elected deputy for Angoulême in 1898. Resistant to pressure from his militants to embrace anti-Semitism, he was if anything Bonapartist, and was looked to by Bonapartist leaders such as Gustave Cunéo d'Ornano, deputy for Charente, who coveted less the Empire than the Consulate of 1799–1804 as the model of a plebiscitary republic, under which the president would be elected by universal suffrage. Déroulède's moment came on 23 February 1899, the day of the state funeral of President Félix Faure, who had died in the arms of his mistress. Déroulède, at the head of his Ligue, tried to seize the bridle of General Pellieux, who was leading the funeral procession, in order to march on the vacant Élysée palace and take power. But Pellieux refused to co-operate, and the coup d'état was bungled.[70]

More bourgeois and respectable, less plebeian and streetwise, was the Ligue de la Patrie Française founded in January 1899 by two secondary school teachers, Henri Vaugeois and Gabriel Syveton.

Their ambition was to bring over a majority of the Académie Française in order to demonstrate that not all intellectuals were dreyfusards, and they began with the poet François Coppée and the playwright and critic Jules Lemaître. Maurice Barrès delivered a keynote lecture to them, arguing that France had been desiccated and divided by a cerebral, Jacobin notion of the *patrie* peddled by philosophy teachers and that a deep and unifying nationalism had to be generated by a cult of the soldiers of 1870 who lay in graves in Alsace, now part of Germany, the cult of *la terre et les morts*. The high point of the Ligue came with the municipal elections of 1900, when several of them were voted on to the Paris municipal council, which was now captured by conservatives.[71] Even before then Henri Vaugeois had branched off to join the left-bank journalist Maurice Pujo and Provençal regionalist Charles Maurras to found an Action Française Committee (April 1898), then an *Action Française Bulletin* (July 1899). Maurras had converted to monarchism during a visit to the eastern Mediterranean in 1896 when he realized how little influence republican France had in comparison to the monarchical empires of Great Britain, Germany and Russia. The Dreyfus Affair convinced him that the Republic had fallen into the hands of the 'four confederate states' of Jews, Protestants, freemasons and foreigners, and that only a restored monarchy could bring back a strong state, a united nation and national greatness. His approach to monarchism was theoretical rather than sentimental and his relationship with the Duc d'Orléans and his staff was decidedly ambivalent. Unlike the Ligue de la Patrie Française, Action Française had no truck with elections but communicated its ideas through its publications and street demonstrations and put its faith in a *coup de force*.[72]

The turning point of the Dreyfus Affair came in the summer of 1899. On 31 May Déroulède, charged with attacking state security on 23 February, was acquitted by the Assize Court of the Seine. On 1 June Colonel Marchand, who had confronted British forces at Fashoda on the Upper Nile but been recalled by the government, made a triumphant procession through Paris.[73] On 3 June the Cour de Cassation decided that the case for revising the Dreyfus conviction had to be answered, and referred the matter back to the court martial.

The next day right-wing demonstrators assaulted the new president Loubet, who was thought to favour reopening the case, at the Auteuil races, and knocked his top hat off. Loubet now summoned Waldeck-Rousseau to form a government of so-called 'republican defence' that would bring together broad support for the regime and defuse the Dreyfus Affair. His ministry of 22 June 1899 was composed of former supporters of Méline who now broke with him over his refusal to deal with the Dreyfus Affair, and was the first government to include a socialist. His finance minister was Joseph Caillaux, son of an Orleanist Moral Order minister who joined the elite Inspection des Finances, inherited the family constituency at Mamers (Sarthe) as a moderate republican in 1898 and had Maurice Rouvier as a patron.[74] In the difficult post of war minister Waldeck placed General Gallifet, who had fought with the Versailles forces in 1871 but had been a confidant of Gambetta. Most significantly, to draw in the left wing he appointed Alexandre Millerand as trade minister, the first time a socialist had held government office. Waldeck pushed through a raft of reforms including an Associations Law of 1901 which permitted trade unions to own property collectively, a factory act which limited the working day first to eleven hours and later to ten, and a pensions bill that did not become law till 1910.

Waldeck's government acted fast to secure the regime. The arrest of Jules Guérin and his royalist backer André Buffet was ordered for threatening state security. Guérin holed up with his Ligue in their offices in the rue Chabrol, near the Gare du Nord, and police were sent in for what became known as 'the siege of Fort Chabrol'. The retrial of Dreyfus by court martial was conducted for security reasons outside Paris, in Rennes. Had he been acquitted General Mercier and the military top brass would have been liable to prosecution for obstructing the course of justice, and might have resorted to a coup d'état, but on 9 September the court again found Dreyfus guilty, by a majority vote, 'with extenuating circumstances', whatever they might be. This opened the way to a pardon being granted by President Loubet on 19 September, which did nothing to satisfy the dreyfusards, who dreamed of a formal acquittal and punishment of the guilty generals. 'Once again it is up to us poets', Zola wrote to Madame Dreyfus, 'to nail the guilty to the eternal pillory.'[75] Only the right-wing civilian conspirators were charged with conspiracy and effectively dealt with. The Senate sat as a high court from November 1899 till January 1900, condemning Guérin to ten years in prison and Déroulède and Buffet to five years' exile.[76] As if to mark this success the final, bronze-cast version of Dalou's *Triumph of the Republic* was unveiled on 19 November 1899 on the place de la Nation in the presence of President Loubet and premier Waldeck-Rousseau.[77] Finally, in June 1900 Waldeck secured the Chamber's approval of a bill to amnesty all those implicated in the Affair, cunningly quoting what his first political master Gambetta had said about amnestying the Communards. '"When disagreements have divided and torn apart a country,"' he repeated, '"all men of political wisdom understand that the time comes when these need to be forgotten." Messieurs, I think that the hour of which Gambetta spoke has arrived.'[78]

BETWEEN REPUBLICAN CONCENTRATION AND *APAISEMENT*

The Dreyfus Affair split the political class that had been plastering over its differences in the 1890s in order to deal with the threat of socialism and anarchism. The renewed threat to the parliamentary Republic, even to the Republic itself, provoked a throwback to republican concentration in defence of the regime that had characterized the 1870s and 1880s. The rhetoric of the French Revolution was once more in the air: Aulard's *Political History of the Revolution*, which saw it as the inevitable victory of national sovereignty, appeared in 1901. The dominant party until 1940 was the Republican, Radical and Radical-Socialist Party, founded in 1901 as a party that 'rallies all the sons of Revolution, whatever their differences, against all the partisans of counter-revolution'.[79] These Radicals were constantly alert to the militarist and clerical threat from the right that had manifested itself during the Dreyfus Affair, but they had no truck with socialism and were resolute defenders of private property. They represented France's *petites gens* – small businessmen, artisans and shopkeepers, small farmers, the salaried lower-middle class of government employees, *instituteurs*, post office workers, the employees of banks, insurance firms and railway companies, very much the 'nouvelles couches sociales' whose advent Gambetta had proclaimed in 1874. These had their 'hearts on the left and pockets on the right', subscribing to the principles of 1789 and hostile to monopoly capitalism but believing that people should make their way by hard work, saving and education. They were led by small-town and rural notables: doctors, lawyers, teachers and businessmen, who nurtured the single-member constituencies by obtaining concessions and favours from the government: new schools, roads and branch lines, jobs and scholarships in the public gift, exemption from military service or legal proceedings.[80] The increase in deputies' allowances to 15,000 francs in 1906 made it possible for less wealthy men to envisage a parliamentary career. In the Palais Bourbon, those they might disagree with politically belonged to the same 'république des camarades', who 'sit on benches that touch, receive their constituents and mistresses in the same salons, use the same offices, the same library, the same headed paper and the same café'.[81] Between 1906 and 1913 the president of the Republic, Armand Fallières, with his white beard and taste for good living, symbolized a period of pacification after political struggle in what became known as 'the Republic of Monsieur Fallières'.[82]

The threat from the right was in fact squarely dealt with. Those who had conspired against the army were punished, although the officer corps had not been fully republicanized and was still a stronghold of Catholic and conservative opinion. The Catholic Church, in particular certain teaching congregations, was dealt with by eliminating it from the education system. Although the Church remained powerful in society it ceased to be a political threat. In 1902 Albert de Mun founded a Catholic party, the Action Libérale Populaire, but it was not on the same scale as the German Centre Party or the Italian Partito Popolare. Like other reactionary leagues, the Ligue de la Patrie Française became an electoral body of little significance, and petered out in 1904. Action Française was a thorn in the Republic's side, attacking its leaders as traitors to French interests, and the Camelots du Roi, who sold the daily *Action Française* on the streets, organized demonstrations such as that of 4 June 1908 when Zola's ashes were reburied in the Panthéon and pot shots were taken at Dreyfus.[83] The main right-wing party, however, were antidreyfusard Progressists who followed Méline into the Fédération Républicaine (1903), while the dreyfusard Progressists followed Waldeck-Rousseau into the Alliance Démocratique. The performance of the right, including the Fédération Républicaine, Action Libérale Populaire, royalists and nationalists, declined steadily in elections from 246 seats in 1902 to 167 in 1906, 148 in 1910 and 121 in 1914.

The serious political threat came not from the right but from the left, from socialist parties and the anarcho-syndicalist penetration of the labour movement. Guesde and Vaillant issued a manifesto on 14 July 1899 condemning the acceptance of office in a bourgeois government by the so-called socialist Millerand and announced a return to revolutionary class war. The unveiling of *The Triumph of the Republic* was interrupted by demonstrators waving red and black flags and shouting 'Vive la Commune'. Jaurès, by contrast, argued that 'since reaction has formed a bloc, the Revolution must form a bloc.'[84] For him the revolutionary seizure of power was a 'hallucination' that would lead only to bourgeois repression, as in 1871. In 1900 he and Guesde locked horns in debate at Lille. Jaurès conceded that society was divided between capitalists and proletarians, but argued that the 'return of forces from the past' such as the Church and the army sometimes obliged the proletariat to join the defence of the Republic and democracy. In a democratic republic, he said, socialists could come to power legally, by winning a majority, if necessary in alliance with other left-wing parties, and indeed this is what all socialists practised. Guesde, by contrast, argued that Millerand as a minister was a hostage of Waldeck's bourgeois government and that Jaurès was tying the proletariat to 'the tail of the imprisoning bourgeoisie, which had the shooting bourgeoisie of 1871 behind it'. The proletariat, he stated, must remain united around the principle of class war and never lose sight of the goal of revolution.[85] As a result at the Paris congress of December 1900 the socialists divided over the question of participating in bourgeois governments into a Guesdist Parti Socialiste de France and Jaurès's Parti Socialiste Français.

Both Guesde and Jaurès disliked strike action, over which the parties had no control, and in 1902 Jaurès came into conflict with

Aristide Briand who, while moving from anarchism to socialism, still believed in the legitimacy of the general strike.[86] This was more than ever the strategy of anarchists who penetrated the labour movement. Pelloutier, secretary of the Fédération des Bourses du Travail and author of *What is the General Strike?* (1895), died of tuberculosis in 1901 at the age of thirty-three and his Fédération was merged with the Confédération Générale du Travail the following year. At its 1904 congress in Bourges, under the influence of Émile Pouget, who was very much Pelloutier's heir, the CGT espoused the tactic of the general strike in pursuit of a popular goal, the eight-hour day, and launched such a strike on 1 May 1906.[87] There followed two years of virtual class war, involving the miners of the Pas-de-Calais and metalworkers of Hennebont (Morbihan) in 1906, shoemakers of Fougères (Ille-et-Vilaine) and Raon l'Étape (Vosges) and the wine-growers of the Midi in 1907, post office workers and *instituteurs* whose aim to unionize and affiliate to the CGT was opposed by the government, and electricians who plunged the Paris Opéra into darkness. Then in 1908 strikes moved into the unskilled sector when the sand-quarriers of the Seine were fired on by troops, provoking another general-strike call on 3 August that year.[88]

Waldeck's attempt to construct a broad government of republican defence was frustrated by the elections of April–May 1902. In a Bloc des Gauches which won 350 seats his supporters took only 100 seats against 200 Radicals and 48 socialists. He was obliged to resign and died of cancer in 1904. To form the next ministry Loubet invited Émile Combes, a medical doctor and mayor of the small town of Pons in the Charente-Inférieure, and senator, founder and leader since 1891 of the Gauche Républicaine, the equivalent of the Radicals in the Senate. Combes' finance minister, back after his disgrace in the Panama scandal and a career in banking, was Maurice Rouvier, placed there to reassure the markets. On the other hand, though Combes included no socialist in his ministry the government majority was held together in the Chamber by a Délégation des Gauches dominated by Jaurès, now re-elected to the Chamber. Since losing his seat in 1898 he had worked on his *Socialist History of the French Revolution*, in which he concluded that though the Revolution was bourgeois it had proclaimed the universal rights of man which it was up to the proletariat to fulfil in a socialist society.[89] Revolution, he told the 1902 congress of the Parti Socialiste Français, was not a means but an end, not barricades and bullets but the gradual transformation by social reform from capitalism to collectivism.[90]

Despite promises of income tax reform and the nationalization of railway companies the main obsession of Combes was to deal with the Catholic teaching congregations and the army. The former were dissolved by switching the Associations Law from protecting trade unions to eliminating religious congregations that had not been properly authorized. Files on the private lives of army officers included information provided by masonic lodges in order to ascertain who attended mass and used Catholic schools, with the aim of preferring more secular-minded and republican officers for promotion. This was exposed by *Le Figaro* in October 1904, and in the Chamber on 4 November war minister General André was slapped by Gabriel Syveton, treasurer of the Ligue de la Patrie Française and deputy for Paris.[91] This *affaire des fiches* led to the fall of the Combes ministry, and to the death of Syveton – whether by murder or suicide was unclear – but even before then Combes had lost his supporters on the left.[92] 'I could never imagine that any government could limit the horizon of its ambitions to the struggle against the religious congregations,' Alexandre Millerand told the Chamber in March 1904, denouncing the failure to undertake any social reform and in particular the delays to his pensions bill. In August Jaurès faced criticism from the International Socialist Congress, meeting in Amsterdam, where the German Social Democratic Party secured a majority against 'revisionist' tactics in favour of revolutionary rhetoric, and forced him to abandon Combes.[93] In 1905 Jaurès joined Guesde in a united socialist party committed to Marxist principles, the Section Française de l'Internationale Ouvrière (SFIO).

Between 1906 and 1909 the dominant figure in French politics was Georges Clemenceau, who after the Panama scandal returned to parliament in 1902 as senator for the Var. Minister of the interior in March 1906, he finally became president of the council in October 1906, at the age of sixty-five. Never himself a member of the Radical Party he maintained its hold on power while saying of the Fédération Républicaine, 'I do not claim the right to excommunicate them from the republican party.'[94] Picquart, hero of the Dreyfus Affair, became minister of war. Poincaré, who had been finance minister under the previous government, declined to serve under him, so he offered the finance portfolio to Joseph Caillaux, who soon became frustrated by Clemenceau's refusal to countenance his projects of progressive income tax and railway nationalization. Louis Barthou, of the same generation as Poincaré and Caillaux, now in their mid-forties, took over Public Works. Aristide Briand, who had run unsuccessfully for the Chamber since 1889, was elected deputy for Clermont-Ferrand in 1902. He had honed his legal and diplomatic skills negotiating the Separation of Church and state in 1905 and been groomed for society in the salon of Madame de Caillavet, muse and mistress of Anatole France.[95] Now appointed education minister he was released from his membership of the SFIO by Jaurès, who did not wish a second Millerand Affair. Like him, René Viviani, who was given the new Ministry of Labour, resigned from the SFIO.

The elections of May 1906 gave another sixty seats to the Bloc des Gauches and reduced the grip of the right, which failed to make political capital out of the Separation of Church and state. The battle was no longer with them but with labour. As interior minister Clemenceau had sent 20,000 troops into the coal basin of the Pas-de-Calais in April 1906 to deal with a miners' strike that followed a pit disaster in which 1,100 miners had died. He then dismissed 300 post office workers who went on strike, in order to stop public servants forming trade unions. On 1 May 1906 the CGT brought 200,000 workers on to the streets to support a general strike in favour of the eight-hour day. Clemenceau declared a state of siege, sent in the troops and arrested the labour leaders. 'Your means of action is disorder,' he declared, 'my duty is to ensure order.'[96] The scourge of government in the 1880s had become the 'strike-breaker' or 'first cop in France'. Aristide Briand, now Clemenceau's accomplice as a man of order, was violently criticized for his volte-face by Jaurès in a two-day speech in May 1907. This came as troops fired on demonstrating winegrowers on the Mediterranean coast at Narbonne and Montpellier, although in Béziers the soldiers mutinied, refusing to fire on demonstrators. Finally, on 2 June police fired shots on striking building workers holed up in a café at Vigneux, killing two of them.

The 'fusillade de la salle Ranque' became a cause célèbre, triggering a CGT demonstration at Villeneuve-Saint-Georges on 30 July. Clemenceau had the CGT leaders arrested, which provoked a general strike on 3 August.

When Briand became president of the council in July 1909 his aim was to break away from the tyranny of the Bloc des Gauches and to seek accommodation with Catholics and conservatives, a strategy that had not been attempted since before the Dreyfus Affair. His ministry left out Caillaux and was dominated by moderates: Barthou at the Justice Ministry, Millerand at Public Works, Viviani at Labour. In a keynote speech at Périgueux on 20 October 1909 he spoke of 'apaisement' and 'détente' and called for 'union in the Republic of all French people who understand that struggle and strife offer no real prosperity . . . Our secret is to make people love the Republic.' He urged electoral reform to replace the 'stagnant pools' of single-member constituencies which favoured the Radicals by a system of proportional representation that would allow all political currents to have a voice and, he hoped, would strengthen government authority.[97] In favour of making workers stakeholders in the system rather than rebels and to win over moderate trade unionists he and Viviani finally carried through the workers' pensions law. The elections of April–May 1910 brought in a new generation of deputies, who approved Briand's ministry by 404 to 121, only the 75 socialists and extreme right against him. Even Albert de Mun and the Action Libérale Populaire were keen to embrace the new premier. When the railway workers went on strike in October 1910 Briand demonstrated his new hostility to the general strike and forced on his cabinet a law drafting strikers into the army for a period of twenty-one days and thus subjecting them to military law. Barthou, Millerand and Viviani opposed the decree as *ultra vires*, but it was approved by the Chamber by 329 votes to 183, with socialists and left-wing Radicals voting against.[98] At their Rouen congress of October 1910 the Radicals denounced Briand's 'policy of reactionary compromises which throws the republican idea into confusion', the first time a Radical congress had attacked a ministry.[99] Briand resigned and formed a new ministry on 4 November. Ironically, since Barthou, Millerand and

Viviani refused to serve, he was forced back on to the Radicals and *apaisement* came to a sudden stop.

THE *UNION SACRÉE*

After 1911 the reins of power were shared between one segment of the generation of 1860, which had originated in the socialist fold, including Briand and Millerand, and another segment, which had originated on the right, composed of Caillaux, Barthou and Poincaré. The latter were linked by their careers and even their private lives: both Caillaux and Barthou were vice-presidents of the Alliance Démocratique and went on holiday to Egypt together with their partners in the winter of 1910–11, Alice Barthou having introduced Caillaux's future second wife, Henriette Rainouard, to him.[100] Poincaré, for his part, was a witness at Caillaux's wedding to Henriette in October 1911.[101] Yet they were divided by political ambition and political style and were all the more savage because they knew the details of each other's private lives. Caillaux became president of the council in June 1911, but did not include Barthou in his cabinet because Barthou was a former Briandist and Caillaux rejected Briand's policy of *apaisement*. Besides, Caillaux – who according to his protégé Émile Roche, 'with his shiny bald head, precise gestures, monocle, elegant dress, imperturbable confidence, was something of a Balzacian dandy', a republican aristocrat with all the privileges of birth and education – considered Barthou, whose father was an ironmonger, to be 'vulgar from head to toe, both morally and physically'.[102] Barthou had his revenge in January 1912 when he sat with Poincaré on the parliamentary commission which investigated the Franco-German treaty that Caillaux had secretly negotiated to defuse the Morocco crisis and toppled Caillaux for selling France's national interests short. Poincaré was invited to form the next government and with a view to continuing *apaisement* he offered Briand the Ministry of Justice and Millerand the Ministry of War. When the presidency of Armand Fallières came to an end in January 1913 the succession was about both principles and personalities. Clemenceau assumed the role of grand elector and pushed the cause of a

Radical-Socialist senator Jules Pams. Raymond Poincaré, the rival candidate, who had been writing a biography of Adolphe Thiers that was never published, was promoted by Millerand and enjoyed the support of moderates and Catholics.[103] Indeed he did a secret deal with Catholic leader Albert de Mun that if he won he would solemnize his civil marriage in church. Poincaré was elected with this conservative support and relaunched the policy of *apaisement* in his choice of premiers: Briand in January 1913, Barthou in March. Barthou announced a ministry of 'détente, union and republican conciliation', the centrepiece of which would be an increase in the duration of military service from two years to three, duly approved by parliament in July 1913.[104]

France might have gone into the First World War on the basis of this *apaisement*, but the issue of the Three-Year Service Law provoked a massive backlash on the left. The CGT and SFIO mobilized against the proposed law in the spring and summer of 1913. Jean Jaurès made a speech to a crowd of 150,000 on the Pré-Saint-Gervais on the north-eastern outskirts of Paris on 25 May 1913, and a petition sponsored by the SFIO garnered 700,000 signatures. The antimilitarist movement gained a hold in the universities and lycées, as at the time of the Dreyfus Affair, drawing on a group of militants born around 1890. They included Raymond Lefebvre and Paul Vaillant-Couturier, who had graduated from the Lycée Janson-de-Sailly in Paris to the Sorbonne and were deeply moved by Jaurès' famous speech.

The Three-Year Law was voted by parliament in July 1913 but the revival of the left was exploited by Joseph Caillaux who, smarting from his defeat at the hands of Barthou and Poincaré, was in search of a coherent majority to force the gates of power. He managed to get himself elected leader of the Radical-Socialist Party at its Pau congress of October 1913 and on 30 November attacked Briandists as 'those who sent people to sleep and were of no party because they wished to subjugate all of them'. On 2 December he toppled the Barthou ministry by ridiculing its plans to pay for the Three-Year Law by a public loan rather than by espousing his more radical scheme of a progressive income tax. Briand attacked Caillaux in his turn as a 'plutocratic demagogue' who 'shook his fist at wealth while making a fortune with scandalous ease'.[105] President Poincaré delayed the moment when he would be obliged to offer the premiership to Caillaux by offering it to the Radical-Socialist deputy of the Gard Gaston Doumergue, who made Caillaux his finance minister. Elections were due in April–May 1914 and while Barthou forged a Fédération des Gauches to stop Caillaux, Caillaux entered into talks with Jean Jaurès about a joint Radical–SFIO ministry should they win. After the elections Caillaux controlled 300 Radical and Socialist seats against 178 in Barthou's centre and a mere 121 on the right. In order to prevent a cartel of the left which would abrogate the Three-Year Law Poincaré invited Viviani, who was committed to the law, to form a government, which was approved by the Chamber on 16 June.

To finish off Caillaux, his personal life was exposed. From Caillaux's first wife, Berthe Guydan, Barthou obtained love letters between Caillaux and Henriette which was evidence that he was having an affair with her during his first marriage, and these he passed on to Gaston Calmette, editor of *Le Figaro*. Advised that legal proceedings could not stop publication of her correspondence Henriette went to the *Figaro* offices on 16 March 1914 and shot Calmette dead. Although she was acquitted on 28 July 1914 her husband's claim to the presidency of the council was in tatters.[106] It was the outbreak of war that finally achieved political *apaisement* in what Poincaré called the 'Union sacrée'. On 26 August Millerand returned as minister of war, and Briand as minister of justice. Included as minister without portfolio was not Jean Jaurès, cruelly assassinated on 31 July 1914, but Jules Guesde.

10

Reconciling Paris and the Provinces

The war of 1870–71 had a dramatic effect on the supremacy of the French centralized state and the integrity of the French nation. French armies were defeated and German troops occupied the north-east of France and laid siege to Paris. The French government fled first to Tours, then to Bordeaux, tracing a path of shame that another government would take in 1940. Departments, thrown back on their own devices, joined forces in federations such as the Ligue du Midi. Towns and cities reclaimed the freedom to elect their own mayors and run their own affairs. Revolutionary communes were set up not only in Paris but in Marseille, Lyon, Le Creusot, Saint-Étienne, Toulouse and Narbonne. Inspired by the federalist ideas of the late Pierre-Joseph Proudhon, the Paris Commune issued a Declaration to the French People on 19 April 1871 denouncing 'despotic, stupid, arbitrary and onerous centralization' and calling for a new political unity based on 'the voluntary association of all local initiatives'.[1] Under the Treaty of Frankfurt of 10 May 1871 which ended the Franco-Prussian war France was amputated of the provinces of Alsace and Lorraine, which it had ruled respectively since 1648 and 1766, and the population of those areas were given just over a year to decide whether they wished to become French and leave or German and stay. These events thrust open old debates about the centralization or decentralization of the administration, and about the loyalty of the mosaic of populations that composed a French nation which since 1789 had been conceived in terms of political unity rather than of ethnic or linguistic uniformity.

WEBS ADMINISTRATIVE AND POLITICAL

For the republican government, confronted by German occupation and the disintegration of the country, there could be no alternative to taking up the threads of administrative centralization bequeathed by the Second Empire and drawing them as tightly as it could. Léon Gambetta, who had preached the virtues of local democracy in his Belleville manifesto of 1869, acted as a virtual dictator when he became minister of the interior in September 1870, appointing new prefects in eighty-five departments, postponing municipal elections and setting up republican municipal commissions where necessary, avoiding the election of a National Assembly which he feared would be dominated by royalists and Bonapartists. Adolphe Thiers, who had preached in favour of 'necessary liberties' in 1864, as head of the executive power scuppered a project in the National Assembly to permit the election of all mayors. He warned of the threat of the 'demagogic party' in the large cities, citing not only Paris but Marseille, where he alleged 500 sailors had attacked the prefecture with axes, and declared, 'You want us to maintain order and at the same time you deprive us of the means!'[2] The law of 14 April 1871 thus gave the government the authority to appoint mayors in all towns with a population of over 20,000 and strict control over municipal budgets and decisions. Paris was not accorded an elected mayor and fell back under the control of the prefect of the Seine and prefect of police. Gaston Crémieux, who had headed the commune in Marseille after the exploits of the axe-wielding sailors, was sent before the firing squad on 30 November 1871. In Lyon the republican municipality under Hénon and his deputy, Désiré Barodet, kept a revolutionary commune at bay by arguing that they had all the autonomy the city needed. This did not prevent Thiers from abolishing Lyon's city-wide mayoralty on 4 April 1873, leaving nothing between the prefect and the thirty-six wards, a measure which backfired when Barodet defeated Thiers' foreign minister in the Paris by-election of 27 April and terminated Thiers' presidency. The Duc de Broglie, largely responsible for the fall of Thiers, although the grandson of that champion of liberty, Madame de Staël, extended government control even further under the Moral Order regime to keep out the republicans with a law of 20 January 1874 which gave the government the right to appoint all mayors, down to the smallest commune.

The reflex of the government, to deal with revolution in Paris and other towns by tightening the hold of central over local administration, was nevertheless challenged by a rival argument. This was that the best antidote to a seizure of power by the reds in Paris who would use the apparatus of the centralized administration to try to spread revolution over the whole country, in 1871 as in 1848 and 1793, was to permit administrative decentralization, giving greater autonomy to the departments and cities. The argument had been forcefully put in the Nancy manifesto of 1865 and largely endorsed by Émile Ollivier's commission on decentralization, whose conclusions had not in the end been acceptable to Napoleon III. In 1871 as in 1848, revolution in Paris had been snuffed out by volunteer forces recruited in the provinces. The Communards blamed their defeat on Breton Gardes Mobiles led by General Trochu and on Catholic–royalist Vendeans, led by the grandsons of the Vendean leaders of 1793, Henri de Cathelineau and Athanase-Charles-Marie Charette de la Contrie, seeking revenge for the Terror, although in fact many more volunteers had been drawn from eastern provinces such as Lorraine and the Vosges.[3] Reward for their loyalty in the form of administrative decentralization was championed in conservative quarters. Arthur de Gobineau, following Alexis de Tocqueville, whose *chef de cabinet* at the Foreign Ministry he had been in 1849, since when he had written the notorious *Essay on the Inequality of Human Races* and had become Legitimist *conseiller-général* of Chaumont-en-Vexin (Oise), argued that France's centralized bureaucracy and Paris's tentacular strength were perennially at the disposal of revolutionaries who seized the Hôtel de Ville.[4] Similarly the Catholic historian Henri Wallon argued in his book on the Terror that its driving force had been the Commune of 1793, which intimidated the elected Convention and massacred 'federalists' in the departments who rose to defend liberty; he subtitled his study *France Defeated by the Paris Commune*. 'And today,' he warned, 'if the vanguard of the Jacobins (for there are always Jacobins), if the *anarchists* as they were called in 1793 . . . seize power, what would France do, I ask you?'[5]

The Republic, in time, did bring in measures of administrative decentralization. A law of 10 August 1871 responded to conservative fears by giving more power to the *conseils généraux* or elected assemblies in the departments, indeed implementing the recommendations of the Ollivier commission. Republicans triumphed in the municipal elections of 1878 and 1881 and demonstrated that they were not red revolutionaries. Although Paris was considered too dangerous to have its own mayor until 1977, Lyon recovered its city-wide mayor in 1881. A law of 28 March 1882 restored to all municipalities, except Paris, the right to elect their own mayors, and a further law of 5 April 1884 transferred more powers to municipalities from the central administration. The Republic took immense pride in its mayors as representatives of the regime in the 36,000 communes of France. They were fêted at great banquets in Paris, 1,119 of them attending on 14 July 1888, and 11,000 on 18 August 1889, on the occasion of the Universal Exposition and centenary of the French Revolution. On 22 September 1900, for the next Exposition, 20,777 mayors lunched in four hectares of tents in the Tuileries gardens, President Loubet sitting beside the mayor of Lyon, the largest commune, and that of the smallest, with only seventeen inhabitants, the youngest mayor and the oldest.[6]

The controversy over the appointment of mayors arose because they were the smallest cog in the centralized administration as well as the basic cells of democracy. Whereas under the Second Empire the grounding of the regime in the localities was provided essentially by the administrative system, which appointed mayors and senators and organized the election of 'official candidates' as deputies, under the Third Republic the webbing was provided above all by the political system, with deputies and senators key mediators between Paris and the provinces. They often began their political careers as mayors and members of the departmental *conseil général*, following a *filière* or path that led to the Palais Bourbon or the Luxembourg.[7] A good deputy had what was called the 'bras long', a long reach to the goodwill of ministers on whom he hoped to prevail to obtain advantages for his constituents such as funding for new roads, bridges and schools, a decision to have a planned railway line pass through his town, scholarships, exemption from military service or jobs in the administration. He was on good terms with the prefect who would use his patronage and influence to facilitate the deputy's re-election, and under the Republic a powerful deputy could have an uncooperative prefect moved to another post. Canvassing was done mainly in cafés, and on election days the wine flowed freely, with barrels even finding their way into the polling station.[8] The deputy disposed of a local newspaper to record the agricultural shows he opened and school prize-givings he addressed, and to sing the praises of the ministry whose favour he enjoyed. *La Dépêche de Toulouse*, run by Maurice Sarraut, backed the election of Jean Jaurès to the Chamber in 1893 and of his brother Albert Sarraut in 1902, but it was the paper and networking agent of the Radical-Socialist Party in general and in 1905 the joke ran that it was necessary to be a southerner to succeed in Paris.[9] Good management and publicity made the *arrondissement* into a deputy's fief, and challengers who did not have access to power found it very difficult to shift him. The introduction of the *scrutin de liste* in 1885–9 inhibited the cultivation of the fief and the proportion of former deputies in the 1885 legislature fell to 57 per cent, but this rose again where the *scrutin d'arrondissement* was restored in 1889 and the proportion of former deputies rose to 70 per cent in the legislature of 1906.[10]

Senators were often even more embedded in local life than deputies. Gambetta called the Senate the 'grand council of the communes of France'. Unlike deputies, senators were elected not directly by the individual citizens but indirectly, by colleges in each department composed of other elected representatives: the deputies of the department, members of the *conseil général*, and delegates from each commune, usually the mayor. The composition of colleges was heavily weighted in the direction of mayors from rural communes and small market towns. Large towns were grossly and explicitly under-represented, in order to limit the influence of latterday Jacobins. In the Bouches-du-Rhône, for example, Marseille, with 500,000 inhabitants, had twenty-four delegates in the college, but so did seventeen other towns with a combined population of only 30,000.[11] Although elections took place at the departmental level, senatorial seats by convention 'belonged' to certain districts within each department. Thus when two seats needed to be filled in the Nord in 1906, one went to an industrialist from Douai in the south, the other to a candidate from Dunkerque in the north, son of the deceased senator, boss of the port.[12] Early in the Third Republic the *filière* of local government was less important: Pierre-Edmond Teisserenc de Bort, on the board of the Paris–Lyon–Marseille railway and a large land-owner in the Limousin by marriage, elected to the National Assembly in 1871 and frequently minister of commerce or agriculture in 1872–7, failed to win election to the *conseil général* of Haute-Vienne but served as its senator from 1876 to 1892.[13] More typical for the embedded republican regime was Émile Combes, an ex-seminarist who taught in Catholic colleges in Nîmes and Pons (Charente) before he married in 1862, then requalified as a doctor, using his practice as a rural GP to cultivate an electoral clientele. He was elected to the municipal council of Pons at the age of thirty-four, in 1869, became its mayor in 1878, and claimed to know the name of every one of its 1,200 electors. He was elected to the *conseil général* of Charente in 1879, and to the Senate in 1885, and though he became president of the council in 1902 he declared himself 'provincial to my fingertips. I adored my Saintonge and, with the Saintonge, my little town of Pons.'[14]

ALSACE-LORRAINE, DECENTRALIZATION AND REGIONALISM

The loss of Alsace-Lorraine in 1871 was not simply an amputation of territory but a test of citizens' loyalty. The government of the newly united Germany gave the population of its recovered provinces until 1 October 1872 to decide whether they would accept German nationality and stay with their houses and property or opt for French citizenship and leave with no more than they could carry. Edmond About, a Lorrainer by birth and Alsatian by choice, argued in 1873 that 1.1 million out of 1.6 million of the population opted for French citizenship, and described the emigrants' hurried sale of their prop-erty, to Jews happy to oblige, before piling their furniture on to carts and joining a 'pitiful procession' into France.[15] Scholarly research has massively reduced these figures. In fact, only 164,000 people, 10 per cent of the population of annexed Alsace-Loraine, opted for French citizenship, a third of them young men fleeing German military service, to whom should be added 362,000 natives of Alsace-Lorraine living in other parts of France, 7,000 in other European countries and 16,200 living outside Europe.[16]

The choices of the population of Alsace-Lorraine were widely debated in French literature, sometimes from a patriotic perspective, sometimes with a greater understanding of the private and local priorities. Alphonse Daudet wrote a tear-jerking short story in 1872 describing the last lesson of a French schoolteacher in his Alsatian school. He tells his pupils that they must not forget French, the language of liberty, makes them copy out 'France, Alsace' into their books and writes 'Vive la France' on the board before leaving them to their incoming German teacher.[17] The irony is, of course, that while the teacher from the French-speaking educated stratum leaves, his pupils, whose dialect is Germanic, stay. The literary team Erckmann and Chatrian took very different views of the Alsatian dilemma. Chatrian, in Paris and writing for the stage, regarded Alsatians who remained in Germany as little better than traitors and had a play banned by the government in 1880 as too anti-German. Erckmann, on the other hand, driven out of Phalsbourg by the Prussians in August 1870 and angry at their razing of its defences in 1871, nevertheless sympathized with those who stayed.[18] In his 1872 *Story of the Plebiscite* the miller and village mayor Christian Weber stays in order to keep the land he has 'paid for by the fruit of [his] labour', while his cousin Georges Weber, the innkeeper, marries his daughter to a stone-merchant in anticipation of plenty of rebuilding work.[19] Two further Erckmann stories, *Brigadier Frédéric* and *The Banished*, relate the fortunes of the forest guard of Saverne, Brigadier Frédéric, who abandons his job and property and goes to France rather than swear an oath to the King of Prussia, his daughter having been beaten to death by Prussian soldiers, but later returns in search of his grandmother's grave and daughter's ghost before dying in the garden of his old house.[20]

More reassuring for the French public was *Le Tour de France par deux enfants*, by Augustine Fouillée, published in 1877, which sold three million copies by 1887 and six million by 1901. It tells the story of two boys, aged fourteen and seven, who leave Phalsbourg after it falls to the Prussians and their father is killed, go in search of their uncle in Marseille and decide to become French. On their travels through France they discover the variety of its regions, economies and cultures, but each one combining harmoniously to form a single France. They admire its beauty but also its fertility and the incessant work of its peasants and artisans. They realize that their mission is to work the French soil and to contribute to France's prosperity and greatness. Their uncle buys them a farm in the Orléanais, and the younger boy, 'in the joy he felt finally to have a fatherland, a house, a family, as he had so often wished', shouts 'J'aime la France!'[21]

Though the French 'of the interior' wanted passionately to believe in the patriotism of Alsatians and Lorrainers, the population of the 'lost provinces' made decisions on practical grounds and set more store by the liberty, faith and prosperity of their provinces than by an abstract French or German nationalism. Raphael Dreyfus, a cotton manufacturer of Mulhouse, which was occupied by German troops in September 1870, went to Carpentras to join his daughter Henriette, who had married a Jewish fabric merchant there. He opted for French citizenship, as did his son Alfred, who went to school in Paris, entered the École Polytechnique in 1877 and graduated as a sublieutenant in the French army in 1882. His elder brother Jacques, by contrast, who fought in the French army in 1870, went back to Mulhouse, now German, to run the family business.[22] The *Reichsland* of Alsace-Lorraine was put under German military and bureaucratic control, the mayors of Strasbourg, Metz and Colmar were removed and Jesuits and other religious orders were expelled in the anti-Catholic *Kulturkampf* of 1873, leading to republican and Catholic protesters winning the provinces' fifteen seats in the Reichstag in 1874. However the grant of a territorial assembly and the realization that Alsace-Lorraine was escaping the Third Republic's attack on Catholic schools led to the success in the Reichstag elections of 1879 of 'autonomists' who were happy to accept the Reich so long as local liberties and religion were respected by Berlin. After this there was no sense that the population of Alsace and Lorraine had any desire to become French again.[23]

The loss of Alsace-Lorraine and the sense that the German dialect spoken there had weakened loyalty to the French nation stimulated a movement in the French administration to eliminate minority languages such as Flemish and Breton, and to attack the many patois spoken in different parts of France. A survey of 1863 showed that in twenty-four of the eighty-nine departments, south of an arc from Bordeaux to Metz, together with Brittany and Flanders, the population in half the communes did not speak French.[24] On 7 June 1880 the Ministry of Public Instruction announced unequivocally that 'only French will be used in schools'.[25] It was not just a question of patriotism: French was seen as the vehicle of liberty and civilization which was to be spread with missionary zeal. In 1888 the official in charge of primary education in the Nord, where Flemish was widely spoken, asked, 'is it not shameful that a part of the Nord population still does not know French? By uprooting people from their local tongue we are freeing them from a kind of prison where air, sun and life are wanting, where progress does not penetrate, and where souls atrophy in age-old routine.'[26]

The crusade against non-French languages was in some sense counter-productive. Rather than dissolve local loyalties and identities it often served to strengthen them. Frédéric Mistral, who retired to his Provençal village of Maillane in 1872, relaunched the Félibrige, his movement dedicated to defending Provençal culture, with new statutes at an inaugural banquet there in May 1876. Provençal liberties were for him a barrier against the 'revolutionary virus' spreading out from Paris to Lyon and Marseille and the Provençal language, that of the medieval troubadours, was a way to root people in their local communities, trades and faith. A Catholic and a royalist by instinct, he hoped to achieve many of the same goals by preaching the revival of provincial life rather than that of the Church and king. In the spring of 1884 he went to Paris to promote his new work, *Nerto*, a celebration of the Avignon papacy of the fourteenth century, and at the Félibrige festival demanded 'a small place for the maternal tongue alongside French in the schools'. He denied that Provence had any separatist ambitions, but the loss of Alsace-Lorraine sensitized French intellectuals and politicians to the political dangers of local languages, and Edmond de Goncourt denounced Mistral as a 'separatist troubadour'.[27] Speaking in Avignon in 1888, Mistral again deplored the ban on local languages in schools. Respect for Provençal in schools, he reiterated, was 'not a retrograde or anti-French idea. On the contrary it is the only way to preserve and spread ... that provincial and local attachment and enthusiasm which alone gives life to the province, as it once gave liberty to Switzerland, independence to America and the Renaissance to Italy.'[28]

Mistral, it is true, had no desire to give Provence or other French provinces any political form: his interest was literary, historical, folkloric. He had, nevertheless, disciples in the Félibrige movement whose ambitions were more political, and politically different. Xavier de Ricard joined the Félibrige at Montpellier in 1877 but his formative experience was the Paris Commune, after which he fled to Switzerland. Far from having royalist sympathies his vision was to bring back the federative republic dear to Proudhon. Where Mistral loved the Avignon of the popes, Ricard sympathized with heretical resistance to the Catholic Church, so potent in Languedoc, whether that of the medieval Cathars or the Cévennes Protestants persecuted by Louis XIV in the seventeenth century, and he told Mistral in 1878 that he was 'a Huguenot of the will'.[29] Most significantly, he was impatient with Mistral's obsession with the Provençal language, dress and dancing. 'I believe that the *langue d'oc* will never be fully revived until the country where it is spoken is liberated,' he wrote to Mistral in 1879; 'it is absolutely necessary that we acquire or reconquer our political and national autonomy.'[30]

Xavier de Ricard was not the only dissenter. In 1892 a young generation of Félibres, born around 1860, parted company with Mistral not because they disagreed with his Catholic and conservative views but because, like Ricard, they believed that the cultural defence of local languages and customs had to be fortified by political action to reverse centuries of administrative centralization and to restore real power not to the departments, but to the historic provinces of the French monarchy. Where Mistral was concerned only with Provence, the younger generation believed that all French provinces should recover their historic liberties. At a meeting of Parisian Félibres at the Café Voltaire on 2 February 1892, two Provençals, Frédéric Amouretti and Charles Maurras, read a manifesto announcing,

We are fed up with keeping quiet about our federalist intentions. We can no longer confine ourselves to demanding the rights and duties of freedom for our language and writers; that freedom will not achieve political autonomy but will flow from it ... We demand liberty for our communes ... We want to release from their departmental cages the souls of provinces that are still used everywhere by everyone: Gascons, Auvergnats, Limousins, Béarnais, Dauphinois, Roussillonnais, Provençaux and Languedociens ... We want sovereign assemblies in Bordeaux, Toulouse, Montpellier, in Marseille or Aix. These assemblies will run our administration, our courts, our schools, our universities, our public works.[31]

They were duly expelled from Mistral's Félibrige and set up their own Paris school of the Félibrige. The Republic was increasingly sensitive to the question of decentralization, and an extra-parliamentary commission was set up to examine it in 1895, but after 1898 Maurras marginalized himself by his insistence on political autonomy for the Ancien Régime French provinces, and conversion to the idea that only a restored monarchy would provide the necessary authority to pursue France's 'national destiny', devolving 'to communes matters that are properly municipal, to the provinces matters that are properly provincial'.[32]

In the 1890s pressure to decentralize the French administration built up in a constituency far wider than the disciples of Mistral, and more generally across the political spectrum. Maurice Barrès, a native of that part of Lorraine that remained French, and grandson of an officer in Napoleon's army, had a profound disdain for the parliamentary Republic which subordinated public to private interest and was elected a Boulangist deputy for Nancy in 1889. After the failure of Boulangism he refined his critique of the Republic, which he called 'dissociated and decerebrated'. The parliamentary regime, he argued, was headless: ministers were beholden to deputies who could topple them on the most trivial issues, and deputies were beholden to constituents, whom they had to bribe and flatter to get re-elected. Both disposed of a centralized administration reduced to the task of managing the elections by patronage and funding a partisan press, and both were corrupted by private financial interests seeking political sanctions for their speculative schemes. Allied to the politicians were the schoolteachers of the republican school system, in which Catholic education was replaced by a state philosophy to which all citizens had to subscribe, based on an abstract duty to fellow citizens, the task of which however was simply to legitimate the shoddy regime. Barrès' answer to this was a charismatic leader like Boulanger who would sweep clean the Augean stables, and propagate a morality much closer to home which taught the young to love the soil of their own province and to listen to the voices of their ancestors. Barrès spread these ideas in the short-lived *Cocarde* newspaper of 1894–5, and the even shorter-lived Ligue Nationale de la Décentralisation, but much more influentially in bestselling novels such as *Les Déracinés* of 1897. *Les Déracinés* traces the fortunes of a group of young men, uprooted from their native Lorraine by their philosophy teacher at Nancy, M. Bouteiller, a 'son of reason' who becomes a republican politician. It follows their careers in Paris where they discover that parliamentary politics are controlled by German-Jewish financiers such as the baron Jacques de Reinach. Two of the band, deprived of the salutary influence of family and province, descend into murder, leading to the guillotine, but the others are redeemed by rediscovering the message of 'la terre et les morts' derived from contact with Lorraine.

Barrès differed from Maurras in that he believed that the energy of the provinces could be released within the Republic. 'The federalist doctrine is consonant with the deepest tradition of France and the Revolution,' he told an audience in Bordeaux in 1895. 'Between 1789 and 1793 the Revolution was federalist; it was the Jacobins who centralized us decisively in June 1793 . . . to deal with the temporary crises in the Vendée and on the Rhine.'[33] For him the Jacobin Republic was an aberration, a more federal republic truer to French history. Similar ideas were upheld by Félibres who followed Xavier Ricard, indebted to Proudhon rather than to Mistral. Jean Charles-Brun, a young academic from Montpellier who took the *agrégation* in Paris in 1893 and was true to Mistral through his

work on troubadours, joined Maurras' Paris school of the Félibrige
and argued in 1896 that 'the felibrean idea gives patriotism a much
more active sense; people dislike notions that are too abstract, and
as Charles Maurras has said, a corner of sky or a wall are the surest
road to nationalism.'[34] He parted company with the Félibrige movement in 1897, considering that talk of restoring Ancien Régime
provinces risked marginalizing decentralizers as reactionaries. Instead
he favoured the notion of the region, a modern concept based on
economic, geographical and historical ties. In 1900 he founded the
Fédération Régionaliste Française, the ambition of which was to
gather the energies of all 'decentralizers, regionalists or federalists'
who were opposed to the Jacobin over-centralization of the Republic
and believed in the 'management of communal affairs by the municipality, regional affairs by the region and national affairs by the state'.
It proclaimed itself resolutely above political parties and in 1904
included on its honorary committee men as diverse as Xavier de
Ricard, Maurice Barrès, Charles Beauquier, radical deputy of the
Doubs, and the socialist Charles Longuet. Originating in the south
it was keen to build bridges to other areas where regionalists were
active. Among organizations which affiliated to it were the Comité
Flamand de France of Camille Looten, professor at the Catholic
university of Lille, and the Union Régionaliste Bretonne, founded by
the academic and writer Anatole le Braz in 1898 but soon taken
over by the Marquis de l'Estourbeillon, deputy of the Morbihan.[35]

CONTAINING SOCIALIST
MUNICIPALITIES

One of the fears provoked by the Paris Commune was that decentralization would play into the hands of revolutionaries who would
sow a string of communes across the country. For this reason Paris
was not allowed a mayor of its own, only a municipal council, each
of the twenty *arrondissements* of central Paris and suburban
communes having their own mayors and municipal councils. Other
towns and cities benefited from the decentralization measures of
1882 and 1884, and in places where industrial workers were

concentrated socialist parties soon began to make gains. In 1882 socialists won control of the mining town of Commentry in the Allier, and ex-miner Christophe Thivrier became mayor. Later elected a deputy, he was proud to wear his workers' overalls over his frock coat. In 1884 Saint-Amand (Nord) and Vierzon (Cher) fell to the socialists, as in 1888 did Saint-Étienne and the Paris suburb of Saint-Ouen. Eighteen-ninety-two was a breakthrough year, in which socialists took control of sixty towns including the textile town of Roubaix (Nord), the mining town of Carmaux (Tarn), Montluçon (Allier), the Paris suburb of Saint-Denis, busy with railway yards, engineering and chemical industries, and the ports of Marseille and Toulon. These industrial towns often returned socialist deputies too, with Jules Guesde elected at Roubaix and Jean Jaurès at Carmaux in 1893.

Some of the socialist municipalities behaved defiantly. The Blanquists elected at Saint-Denis in 1892 banned religious processions, expelled the police from the police-station and put the likes of Jean-Baptiste Clément, author of the revolutionary song 'Le Temps des cerises', on the municipal payroll.[36] Others acted more sensibly. Roubaix council, under former weaver, Guesdist socialist and mayor Henri Carette, implemented a wide programme of social welfare, including crèches for working mothers, free school meals, clothing and school equipment for poor children, cheap public restaurants, and assistance to old and sick workers, which both offered protection to the working class and consolidated a clientele.[37]

There were in fact limits to how much revolution a socialist municipality could achieve. Municipal liberty was confined by the centralized state – municipal decisions could be overruled by prefects or the Conseil d'État. Christophe Thivrier was suspended as mayor of Commentry in 1888 for alleged 'political correspondence', sending a message of support to a trade union conference in Bordeaux, while in 1893 the prefect of the Nord annulled the decision of the Roubaix council to set up a municipal pharmacy offering cost-price drugs to the public.[38] The Conseil d'État permitted the municipalization of water services as contributing to the public good, but ruled against that of bus and tram services in 1897 and of gas works before allowing Marseille to go ahead with gas municipalization in 1907, on the grounds that private enterprise would be more efficient and did not drain public finances.[39] Struggles against monopoly capitalism were not always won by socialist councils. A project of the socialist municipality re-elected at Saint-Étienne in 1900 to municipalize the electricity supply from the Alps monopolized by the Edison Electrical Company, in order to provide cheap electricity for the machines of ribbon workers in their homes, was frustrated by the Edison Company and the Conseil d'État, which stuck rigidly to free-market principles in this case.[40]

Many municipalities did not have the resources to spend as they wished, dependent as they were on the *octroi* or excise and unable to derive much from rates because of poor housing. Some working-class towns remained faithful to industrial feudalism, which provided for their needs. The steel town of Le Creusot was controlled by Henri Schneider from 1871 to 1896 and thereafter by his son Eugène Schneider II, who responded to strikes and unionization in 1899–1900 by organizing a lockout and sacking militants.[41] Socialists, once in power, were frequently defeated at a subsequent poll by right-wing parties representing financial or industrial interests. In 1902 the Roubaix socialists were defeated by cotton magnate Eugène Motte, chair of the Roubaix-Tourcoing Chamber of Commerce and of the board of the Northern Railway, although he was obliged to develop his own social welfare policies to retain support.[42] The same year the socialist municipality of Marseille, whose ambitious social welfare policies and support for a dock strike which closed the port for forty-three days in 1901 nearly ruined the city, was ousted by conservatives fronting the powerful Chamber of Commerce.[43] More successful was the Lyon municipal council under mayor Victor Augagneur, a professor of surgery at the Lyon Medical Faculty who moved towards socialism as a result of the Dreyfus Affair and built a republican bloc, including socialists, which captured the city hall in 1900. He sorted out municipal finances by replacing the traditional *octroi*, which fell mainly on the food of the poor, with a range of property rates and taxes on horses, cars and entertainment, borne mainly by the rich, and undertook a programme of municipalization of water and lighting, abattoirs, and nursing and social services hitherto provided by religious congregations who were now expelled.[44] In

1905 he was appointed governor of Madagascar but had groomed as his successor Édouard Herriot, history master at the Lycée Ampère who had become politicized by the Dreyfus Affair, a Radical-Socialist who disliked the *Communist Manifesto*'s idea of class struggle, wrote theses on the friends of liberty Madame de Staël and Madame Récamier, and hated the Terror which in response to the federalist revolt of 1793 had declared, 'Lyon is no more.' In these capable hands Lyon was governed, except during the occupation, from 1905 to 1957.[45]

GRANDE PATRIE, PETITE PATRIE

Just as the French state was forced to negotiate with socialist municipalities, so it had to deal with local communities whose first language was not French. The law after 1880, as we have seen, was that French only was to be taught in schools, but central to the education of children was the catechism class in preparation for first communion, which after 1882 was eliminated from publicly funded schools and was generally delivered by the parish priest in the vicarage. In northern Flanders and western Brittany, Flemish and Breton were preserved as the language of instruction for the catechism, and indeed for sermons in the church, not only because they were the mother tongue but because they were felt to be a powerful medium of the faith, whereas French was seen to be the vehicle of modern, irreligious ideas. As the archbishop of Cambrai, whose diocese included Flanders, said in 1882, 'Flemish is the language of heaven.'[46]

Where to draw the line between French as the official language and minority, private languages, even in Flanders and Brittany, was not always clear. In their dark coats, *instituteurs* or primary school teachers assumed the role of 'black hussars of the Republic', bearers of French and republican values from large cities to isolated communes, and they were frequently rivals of the parish priest, whose mission was to defend the faith. In 1900 an incident flared up at Killem in Flanders where the *instituteur* demanded that his son be taught the catechism for the first communion in French, whereas diocesan practice was that in Flanders it should be taught in Flemish.

The education authorities in the Nord discovered that in twenty-three Flemish communes the catechism was taught in both languages and in twenty in Flemish only, and were worried that Flemish was being used to encourage anti-French feeling. The republican authorities used the sanction they wielded against the clergy under the Concordat, namely to suspend their stipends if the local mayor did not certify that they taught the catechism in French. Seeking a compromise, the archbishop of Cambrai explained that 'French is studied in school but at home, in the street, at work and at play people speak Flemish instinctively.' The Flemish, like Bretons, Basques and Provençals, he added, 'love both their great and little *patries*'; affection for one did not undermine loyalty to the other.[47]

The Republic did not back down from its commitment to French and when Émile Combes became president of the council he issued a decree on 29 September 1902 forbidding the use of non-French languages in catechism classes and in church sermons. 'The Bretons will only be republicans when they speak French,' he declared.[48] This stirred up particular trouble in Finistère, where the bishop of Quimper reported that over two-thirds of the population could not understand a sermon in French, and only in five of his 210 parishes were sermons given uniquely in French. However, the Radical government in Paris was out of step both with local republican deputies, who argued that the Breton tongue could convey republican as well as reactionary sentiments, and with the prefect of Finistère who feared that such brutal legislation would provoke an anti-republican backlash at the next elections. The government nevertheless insisted on suspending the stipends of sixty-seven parish priests who refused to undertake to preach and teach in French. In the end a compromise was found. Clergy continued quietly to teach catechism and give sermons in Breton and Flemish until, after the Separation of Church and state in 1905, the state no longer had the weapon of suspending clerical salaries. The elections of 1906, which produced an even more convincing republican majority, demonstrated that local people could at one and the same time defend their local language and be loyal to the Republic.[49]

The notion that affection for the *petite patrie* did not threaten affection for the *grande patrie*, and could indeed nurture it, had in fact been developing for some time in French educational circles. The *Tour de France par deux enfants* explored each region of France in turn, praising the beauty of the countryside, listing the variety of trades in which people were engaged, and recalling the names and deeds of local heroes. Visual education or 'l'enseignement par l'aspect' became popular, so that geography was taught to primary school children less out of books, more on school walks to inspect local industry or agriculture, waterways and railways, and local historical sites such as battlefields. Hachette, which found a mass market in schools, circulated maps of the local department which highlighted notable sites and, through the new technology of the slide show, lent 3,548 collections of slides to schools in 1895–6, of which 57 per cent were geographical.[50] Although Lavisse's *History of France* was standard in all schools, the study of local history was now seen as complementary. In the preface of an 1891 *History of Brittany* the historian Charles Langlois wrote,

France is one and indivisible, but it is composed of parts which each have a unity. We are French, but we are also Bretons, Normans, Picards, Flemish, Lorrainers, Burgundians, Provençals, Languedocians, Gascons. Each of us has a *petite patrie* of whose familiar landscape, customs, costumes and accent we are proud. In order to strengthen our love of France, our common fatherland, nothing is more legitimate, more natural, more proper than to love this *petite patrie*.[51]

Local geographical societies were founded in Normandy in 1879, the Nord in 1880, the east in 1882 and Brittany in 1889, nearly half of whose members were *instituteurs*. Many of these were also secretaries to the *mairie* and used local knowledge and archives to write the history and geography of their commune for a national competition in 1900. By 1911 the republican government had changed its tune and Briand's education minister Maurice Faure was complaining that 'most pupils and too many French people are almost entirely ignorant of the history and geography of their commune, of the department in which they were born and the old province to which the department belonged before the Revolution,' although 'love of our native soil, as I told the Chamber of Deputies, is the strongest foundation of our love of the fatherland.'[52] He duly set up a Society for Local Studies in Public Education which was headed by historians Lavisse and Langlois and geographer Vidal de la Blache, together with Charles Beauquier, deputy of the Doubs and vice-president of the Fédération Régionaliste Française.[53]

The legitimation of the *petite patrie* was echoed by a greater acceptance of the need for decentralization in mainstream republican circles. Although it was still being preached by Félibres around Mistral and by monarchists around Maurras, after 1900 decentralization was no longer identified with reaction. One reason was the achievement of Jean Charles-Brun, whose Fédération Régionaliste Français of 1901 popularized the geographical notion of the region rather than the historic one of the province and sought to attract all political schools to the cause. Another was the Republic's survival of the crisis provoked by the Dreyfus Affair and the arrival in political circles of a generation of activists who had not been shaped by the republican–reactionary contests of the 1870s and 1880s but had a less ideological and more sociological approach to organizing the Republic. They included Joseph Paul-Boncour, a brilliant young lawyer who professed independent socialist ideas and argued in his law thesis on economic federalism that strong trade unions and co-operatives should be developed alongside regionalism, and a young diplomat André Tardieu, both of whom were recruited to Waldeck-Rousseau's political office in 1899 and met Charles-Brun in 1900.[54]

In response to the centralizing thrust of Émile Combes in 1903, these young republicans triggered a debate on the question of decentralization. Paul-Boncour argued against the reactionaries that the Republic had a long and honourable decentralizing tradition, including the laws of 1871, 1882 and 1884, and reminded Radicals that decentralization had long been part of their manifesto, along with the election of judges and the abolition of the presidency of the Republic.[55] André Tardieu backed him up by arguing that 'while decentralization is not opposed to the Republic it is irreconcilable with Radical-socialism', for 'nothing is more odious to the Jacobin spirit now in control of France than these [historical] diversities.'[56] Georges Clemenceau, replying for the Radicals, claimed at first to agree with Paul-Boncour that 'we have to be done with Napoleonic

centralization that has fallen into the hands of anonymous bureau-
crats whose routine stifles all initiative and responsibility.' However,
after the intervention of Charles Maurras who argued that the
Republic was incapable of decentralizing because it relied on the
centralized administration of ministers, prefects and mayors to 'make'
elections in the interest of the ruling republican party, Clemenceau
warned, 'interrogate these wild decentralizers and you will soon find
that their aim is to decentralize not liberty but reaction.'[57] Administrative decentralization found its way back on to the government
agenda under Briand in 1909–10, but even he was too dependent
on Radical support to achieve anything concrete.

TOURISM AND THE REDISCOVERY
OF THE PROVINCES

The development of tourism took huge strides forward with the
advent of the railway network and then, at the turn of the century,
of the motor car. Paris and the provinces were brought closer together
in terms of time and ease of transport. However, a study of guide-
books published to help the traveller suggests that little was done
to undermine long-held stereotypes about the inhabitants of far-flung
parts of France.

Paul Joanne's guides to France were geared to the railway traveller
and were readily on sale in the railway kiosks owned by Hachette.
The 1892 guide to Brittany proposed two possible itineraries, the
Chemin de Fer d'Orléans leaving the Gare d'Austerlitz and reaching
Nantes in eight hours, or the Chemin de Fer de l'Ouest leaving the
Gare Montparnasse and reaching Brest in between fourteen and
twenty hours. This was a good deal faster than the three days and
nights it took Victor Hugo to reach Brest by mail-post in 1834.
Prices from Paris to Brest were 82 francs first class, 55 francs second
class. Joanne recommended a travel budget of 12 or 15 francs a day
for 'young people who travel in threes and fours, go some of the
way on foot and can carry their own baggage. For a woman, who
may never carry her own luggage, daily expenditure may rise to an
average of 20–25 francs.' When travelling on foot, Joanne advised

the tourist seeking his or her way from a peasant always to ask for the 'bourg' or 'parish' of a village since 'Breton communes are generally vast and are composed of a centre, or parish, with the church and numerous scattered hamlets.' Curiously, the guide's descriptions of the Bretons who might be encountered differed little from descriptions current in the days of Hugo or Balzac.

The Bretons descend from a mixture of Celts and Kymris, nations of Indo-Germanic origin ... The Breton is stubborn, and loves his native soil passionately. The charm of the Breton environment acts just as powerfully on their children, since most of them have not transformed it by labour or opened their minds by study. That is why Bretons removed from home are often overtaken by nostalgia. Enclosing their thoughts in memories of their homeland they are dead to what surrounds them and they die without having escaped from the grip of their dreams.[58]

Within twenty years the advent of the motor car made provincial France even more accessible. The tyre manufacturers André and Édouard Michelin were among the founders of both the Touring Club de France, founded in 1890 and boasting 104,000 members in 1906, and the more exclusive Automobile Club de France, founded in 1895. The Touring Club published its first handbook in 1891, listing its members, approved hotels and mechanics. The first Michelin red guide was published in 1900, a 400-page book with thirteen city maps, indicating train stations and post and telegraph offices by symbols, and listing hotels by price range. The 1900 edition had a print run of 35,000; that of 1912, with 750 pages and 600 town maps, sold 86,000 copies. After 1907 the guide included seventy-two pages of maps for planning trips. The Touring Club, with the help of the Ponts et Chaussées department, produced its own maps for motorists and cyclists after 1897, and in 1908 produced a series of forty-seven maps of France, 1 centimetre for every 2 kilometres, folding concertina-style, priced at a franc each on paper, 2 francs on cloth.[59]

The availability of maps and guides did not necessarily break down the barriers between Paris and the provinces. The first touring maps to be produced were for the Paris region, Lyon and the Riviera; others followed. Asking directions from local people, many of whom spoke patois, was to be avoided. To this end Michelin sponsored a petition which in 1912 gathered 200,000 signatures, at a time when there were 125,000 cars on the road, for the government to number roads, erect signposts and paint the road numbers and distances from towns on milestones. Presented to the government at the Paris air-show in November 1912, it became the official policy of the Ministry of Public Works in 1913.[60] The Touring Club guidebook on Brittany 1901 argued that with the spread of French the Celtic language would have vanished in a hundred years, or be spoken only by 'a few old people'. Local fashions such as men with shoulder-length hair, wide felt hats and embroidered waistcoats would also go, although women's lace headdresses would be slower to disappear, since women were 'more tenacious, more conservative than their husbands, fathers, brothers and sons'. The Breton character was sturdy, but it was about to be destroyed not by schools or roads or the market, but by drink.

The soul of the Breton-speaking Breton echoes the grey stones, dark by day, sinister by night, under the watery moon, the granite outcrops, the moorland, the old oaks, the mist, the rain, the sighing sea, all that pessimistic nature. He is sad like his moor and his mist, sometimes stormy, like the sea, always tenacious like his rocks. He dreams and he acts. He is a poet and warrior, but above all a man of the sea. But now error, injustice and the abomination of solitude have had their effect. Honesty, uprightness, the spirit of sacrifice, devotion, fidelity, honour, passive courage and active bravery, will, faith, the flower of poetry, all this perishes and dies under the tap of barrels of alcohol.[61]

11

Class Cohesion

PEASANTS: CHANGE AND RESISTANCE

Echoing Balzac's *Les Paysans*, Émile Zola set the peasants' greed for the land at the centre of his novel of 1887, *La Terre*. The Fouan family, former serfs living in the Beauce, had struggled for 400 years to defend and extend their property, 'with an obstinate passion that father bequeathed to son'. The old patriarch Fouan, rather like King Lear, is about to divide his 50 acres between two sons and two daughters, and there is not enough to go round. One daughter, Lise, has married her thuggish cousin, Buteau, who has been working as a farmhand in the Orgères district, from which during the Revolution a notorious band of brigands terrorized the peaceful farmers of the Beauce. Buteau and Lise confront another daughter, Françoise, in a field. Buteau rapes her, Lise attacks her, and in the ensuing struggle Françoise falls on a scythe and dies. Fouan has observed this scene and is likely to disinherit Lise and Buteau, so Buteau beats him to death in his bed and sets fire to the house, to make it look like an accident. Only the great worker earth, observes the seed-sower Jean, Françoise's intended, remains impassive in the sight of 'our engaged-insect quarrels, taking no more notice of us than of ants'.[1]

Zola was a city-dweller from Avignon who bought a house in the country at Médan on the Seine in 1878. Émile Guillaumin, by contrast, was brought up on his grandparents' farm of Neverdière in the Bourbonnais, where his father, Gilbert, had married the old couple's daughter and worked on the farm. In 1892 Gilbert inherited his own father's farm, Les Vignes, to which he became the sole heir

311

after the death of his brother. Although the father had come into his own, Émile Guillaumin was reluctant to move and the fate of the peasant, displaced repeatedly from one plot to another, sometimes to inherit but more often evicted by some rapacious landowner, was one of the themes of his 1904 novel, *The Life of a Simple Man*. Schooled until first communion aged twelve and thereafter self-taught, Guillaumin tells the story of Étienne Bertin or 'Tiennon', a *métayer* or sharecropper whose lot was to put capital into a farm alongside the landowner's contribution and share the produce and profits, although without enjoying security of tenure. Tiennon rented his first farm, Les Craux, when he married, aged twenty-two, and eight years later his second farm, La Creuserie, large enough to require him to employ two farmhands, an agricultural labourer for the summer, and a servant girl. However after twenty-five years he was evicted by a landlord who declared '*métayers* are like servants; with time they become bold and have to be changed.' At fifty-five he rented a third farm from which he was evicted six years later on the death of the landowner, and at sixty-one he was left with a 'little plot with three cows, about the same size as that with which I started at Les Craux'. Ever rehearsing the cycle of the seasons, *The Life of a Simple Man* also teaches that a peasant's life is also cyclical, with little hope of making progress.[2]

France was in many ways a peasant democracy, a country of small farms rather than sharply stratified, as in eastern and southern Europe, between large landowners and peasants with little or no land. In 1892, the year Guillaumin's father inherited his own farm, 75 per cent of French farms were owner-occupied, that is owned by the peasants who worked them, the others being rented as farms or, in certain areas like the Allier, from which Guillaumin came, under *métayage*. Farms, whether owned or rented, were small, 53 per cent between 1 and 5 hectares, 23 per cent between 5 and 10 hectares in 1892.[3] There was a general tendency towards an increase in the number of and area covered by small farms and the erosion of large estates. In the village of Mazières-en-Gâtine (Deux-Sèvres), studied between the wars by Roger Thabault, the proportion of farms under 5 hectares increased from 67.5 per cent in 1860 to 70.5 per cent in 1913, while that of farms between 5 and 10 hectares grew from 13.3 to 16.3 per cent. The largest estate in the village, owned by the Vicomte de Tusseau, was gradually sold off in 1881–6, the biggest portions picked up by a bourgeois landowner of Niort and a Paris lawyer who was a deputy of the Deux-Sèvres. 'In spite of the growing prosperity of farmers in the commune,' noted Thabault, 'none of them was rich enough to become involved in this sale of a property that had belonged to local notables for at least three centuries.'⁴ In the Beauce, where Zola set his novel, small properties (under 19 hectares) which accounted for 40 per cent of the land in 1820–30 developed to cover 49 per cent of the land in 1914, while in the same period large properties (over 30 hectares) lost 18 per cent of the land. Within that group, large properties owned by nobles shrank from 46 to 36 per cent over the century, the Duc de Luynes being left with 3,540 hectares in the Marchenoir region in 1914 compared to 4,200 held by his ancestors in the 1820s.⁵ In winegrowing areas, the division of land was even more intense, landholdings being often just plots providing a supplementary income to artisans and industrial workers. In Courson (Aude) in 1911, alongside wine barons employing agricultural labourers, 24 per cent of landholders owned between 1 and 5 hectares, but 24 per cent owned under 1 hectare.⁶

The world of the peasant was not unchanging, as some fantasies of rural life believed, and at the end of the nineteenth century the challenges facing the countryside were greater than ever. Industry which for so long had provided handwork for seasonally employed peasants was increasingly based in the towns, powered by steam and then electricity. Rural industries collapsed, destroying the balance between agricultural and industrial incomes that had sustained so many rural communities, so that what was now a surplus of rural labour moved to the towns. The rate of migration to the towns rose from 85,000–100,000 per annum in 1881–91 to 100,000–130,000 in 1891–1913. The rural population, defined as living in communities of under 2,000 inhabitants, declined from 69 per cent of the total population in 1872 to 56 per cent in 1911. The proportion of the working population employed in agriculture fell from 53 per cent in 1856 to 49 per cent in 1876 and 41 per cent in 1911.⁷ Those who left were not so much farmers as rural artisans such as coopers, wheelwrights, basket-makers, clogmakers and saddlers, together with farmhands and agricultural labourers, often the sons and daughters of farmers, who saw more employment possibilities in the towns than in the countryside. Young Bretons used to seek additional income by going to harvest in the Beauce and Normandy. They were charged only on the outward trip by railway companies and were paid 5 francs a day. They took the steamer in the autumn in gangs of twenty to sell onions in the south of England. After 1880 they went to work in the arsenals of Brest, on the transatlantic steamers of Le Havre, and above all in the railway yards and the tanning, gas and chemical factories of the heavily industrial Paris suburbs, such as Saint-Denis, becoming permanent immigrants. Breton girls, former lacemakers or farm servants, also went to Paris to work as maids, hoping to save enough to return home with a dowry to marry a farmer, but often staying for good.[8] That said, France remained an agricultural country in a way in which many other European countries had ceased to be by the Great War. The proportion of the working population employed in agriculture in 1909–11 was only 9 per cent in Great Britain, 23 per cent in Belgium and 37 per cent in Germany, with France's 41 per cent only a little lower than Ireland's 43 per cent.[9]

Even more powerful as a challenge was the development of steamships and the penetration of the railways that created a global market for agricultural produce and threatened the traditionally unspecialized and somewhat autarkic French farm. The opening up of the wheat plains of the Ukraine and American Midwest resulted in a glut of grain, and a 20–25 per cent fall in cereal prices in the early 1880s, confronting French farmers with the alternative of specializing in cash crops that were in demand or facing bankruptcy. Cereal farming remained the staple of the central plain of France, but became more efficient, with mechanical innovations such as reapers, reaper-binders and threshing machines replacing agricultural workers who were now scarcer and became 30 per cent more expensive in 1890–1910, and also with the use of chemical fertilizers, the consumption of which doubled in France between 1890 and 1900 alone.[10] The demand for meat and dairy produce from growing towns encouraged a shift from arable to pasture for cattle in Normandy and Brittany, Poitou and the Charentes, with a supporting acreage of fodder crops.

Normandy developed a network of dairies to make cheese and a meeting of fifty cheesemakers at Lisieux in 1911 established a cartel to defend their monopoly of true Camembert cheese.[11] The Nord and Pas-de-Calais concentrated on sugar beet, known as 'the vine of the north', which supplied not only industrial sugar production but also fodder for increased cattle production. Étienne Lantier, hero of Zola's *Germinal*, arrives at the mine near Valenciennes where he is seeking work 'across fields of beet', which grew denser under the impact of price rises and booming production in 1897–1914.[12] Meanwhile in the south of France wine production became less of a facet of polyculture than a regional monoculture, serving the growing wine consumption of the urban French. The problem with specialized cash-crops is that years of boom were too often followed by years of slump, when the crop failed or the bottom fell out of the market. In the Midi, phylloxera – a yellow aphid attacking the vine roots – spread across the vineyards from the 1870s. Thousands of small winegrowers went out of business, their plots acquired by the wine barons who were able to replant at great cost with undamaged vines from California. Failed winegrowers returned to work as agricultural labourers, who in 1892 formed 17 per cent of the agricultural population in the Midi compared to a national average of 9 per cent.[13] Catastrophe, however, struck again after 1900 when bumper harvests, combined with the import of wine from Algeria and the switch from wine to beet to distil alcohol, caused wine prices to collapse. The price of table wine in particular fell from 23–24 francs per hectolitre in 1871–5 to 10–11 francs in 1902–6.[14]

French peasants had a reputation for being solitary and individualistic, dedicated to holding on to their plot and increasing its yield. However, in the face of these challenges peasants were forced to organize themselves. The cost of fertilizer and machines and the need to secure fair prices for cash crops encouraged the formation of co-operatives. Mazières in the Deux-Sèvres, which was linked to the railway system in 1886 and was shifting to dairy cattle, set up a dairy co-operative in 1895 under the initiative of the republican mayor, while the purchase of fertilizer was organized by the agricultural union, run by his conservative political rivals, after 1901.[15] Trade unions were permitted under legislation of 1884 and in the countryside agricultural unions tended to be less the instruments of peasants against landowners than the instruments of landowners to control peasants while providing them with benefits such as co-operatives. These tended to be run in the west of France and Massif Central by Catholic conservative landowners, as a legitimate vehicle for their royalist politics, but were challenged by competing unions of republican notables. Hervé Budes de Guébriant, a royalist land-owner of Saint-Pol, became president of the Office Central des Oeuvres Mutuelles Agricoles du Finistère in 1911 and with the help of the clergy kept Breton peasants on a tight leash down to the Second World War.[16] Trade union legislation was exploited for class purposes on the other hand by landless or near-landless peasants. The woodcutters of the Cher and Nièvre in central France, whose product faced competition from iron for building and coke and coal for smelting and heating, saw the rates paid by wood merchants more than halve in the 1880s, founded woodcutters' unions after 1890 and organized strike action in 1903.[17] Near by, in the Allier, Émile Guillaumin was involved in founding a union of *métayers*, the Federation of Landworkers, in 1905, to improve their ability to negotiate with landlords.[18] In Languedoc-Roussillon unions of the landless workers in the wine industry were founded in the 1890s, linked in 1903 into the Federation of Agricultural Workers of the Midi, 15,000 strong, based at Béziers, and launched a general strike in 1904. This was unsuccessful, because those who suffered from the glut were not just landless labourers but small and larger wine-growers, indeed whole communities. A new phase was opened in 1907 by Marcellin Albert, winegrower and café-owner of Argilliers, and Ernest Ferroul the Radical-Socialist mayor of Narbonne, who was also a Félibre and friend of the 'red Félibre' Xavier de Ricard. In May and June 1907, using the rhetoric of the Albigensian revolt against the tyranny of Paris, they organized huge demonstrations, hundreds of thousands strong, from Perpignan, Carcassonne and Narbonne to Béziers, Montpellier and Nîmes, and orchestrated the mass resignation of municipalities – 76 per cent in the Hérault, 53 per cent in the Aude, 44 per cent in the Pyrénées Orientales – leaving such notices as 'closed because of misery' or 'free commune'. In late June Clemenceau, as premier, was forced to send in the army, which killed five demonstrators in Narbonne but, made up of conscripts as it was, mutinied at Béziers. Marcellin Albert, summoned to Paris to negotiate, was discredited by accepting a hundred francs for his fare home, and a law of 29 June 1907 restored some order to the wine industry.[19] The 'revolt of the vignerons' was community activism rather than class struggle and, despite the drama, was limited to one corner of Mediterranean France.

ORGANIZING THE WORKERS

On 21 February 1884 a miners' strike broke out at Anzin in the Nord. Émile Zola interrupted his work on *La Terre* to go to the scene, escorted by Alfred Giard, professor at the Science Faculty of Lille and republican deputy for Valenciennes. He met the miners' leader, Basly, and was permitted to go down a pit 675 metres deep. He returned to Paris to complete research into mining matters and to write *Germinal*, which was serialized in *Gil Blas* between November 1884 and February 1885, and published in book form in March 1885. In the novel Étienne Lantier, sacked from the railway workshops in Lille, arrives at Anzin to find the aged miner Bonnemort, who had 'worked for fifty years at the pit, of which forty-five were underground'. Becoming a leader, and later addressing a meeting of 3,000 striking miners, he exhibits Bonnemort and exclaims, 'is it not terrible: a people dying at the coal-face from father to son, in order to bribe ministers and allow generations of great lords and capitalists to give parties or grow fat at their fireside!'[20]

Zola's image of a race of miners, whose families had been exploited for generations, is powerful but far from the experience of most miners. The annual turnover rate for miners in the Valenciennes area was 8 per cent in 1896, rising to 14 per cent in 1906 and to 34 per cent in 1914. Some who left went to the newer mines of the Pas-de-Calais, where wages were better, while still more abandoned the mine for jobs in the steel industry with local firms such as the Company of Furnaces, Forges and Steelworks of Denain-Anzin.[21] Most miners, especially in the mines flanking the Massif Central, were recruits from the countryside, initially with their own plots of land, and leaving the pit each evening and each summer to work in the fields. Mining companies had to work hard to force miners to live near the pits, providing them with back-to-back accommodation as an incentive, and to discipline them to a full working day, winter and summer. The Carmaux mine was beginning to recruit second-generation miners or 'born proletarians' by the 1890s, but the turnover rate was still daunting. In order to retain one miner the Carmaux company had to hire between one and two miners in 1890–92, but between four and five miners in 1900–1901 and sixteen or seventeen miners in 1911–12.[22]

The number of industrial workers in France fell from 3,151,000 in 1876 to 3,056,000 in 1886, because of economic depression in those years, but it grew to 3,303,000 in 1906 and even more rapidly to 4,726,000 in 1911.[23] Such growth could not be supplied by the urban working classes themselves because of high death rates but required the influx provided by rural depopulation, as we have seen, by increasing the proportion of women in work from 25 per cent of women in 1866 to 39 per cent in 1911,[24] and now by foreign immigration. The nationality law of 1889 was fairly flexible, making French nationality automatic for children of foreigners who were themselves born in France, and optional when the foreign parents had been born abroad, so that by 1911 foreigners accounted for 2.8 per cent of the population, 3.3 per cent including naturalized foreigners. There had long been seasonal migration of Belgians over the border to help with the beet harvest, but 40 per cent of the textile workers in the textile boom town of Roubaix were Belgian in 1904 and the Lille suburb of Wazemmes was known as 'little Belgium'. The development of large-scale wine production in Languedoc-Roussillon after the phylloxera epidemic sucked in Spanish migrant labour, whose numbers rose from 62,000 in 1872 to 105,000 in 1911. Italians, who had hitherto been familiar in the shops of Marseille, were increasingly visible as warehousemen in the southern ports, and as navvies building railways, tunnels and dams in south-eastern France. In 1894 they provided blackleg labour to break a miners' strike in Rive-de-Gier, above Saint-Étienne. The previous year, after the assassination of President Carnot by an Italian anarchist, twenty Italian workers were set upon and killed at Aigues-Mortes (Gard). After 1908 Italian labour was recruited by the Comité des Forges to work in the orefields and steelworks of French Lorraine, where they numbered 14,000 by 1913. Finally, Russian and Romanian Jews fleeing pogroms arrived in Paris, concentrating around the Marais and Montmartre, where they were the mainstay of the garment industry as tailors and capmakers, and prominent as cabinet makers.[25]

The working classes had never formed a bloc, sharply divided as they were by differences between regional economies, local and national origin and gender. A huge skills gap separated the working-class aristocracy of artisans who had undergone an apprenticeship, and organized legally or illegally to ensure a closed shop for the trade and payment at a good price, and the unskilled labourer, competing for work with the rest of the 'industrial reserve army' and taken on seasonally or casually at whatever wage was dictated by the economic cycle. These divisions were changing, however, in the later nineteenth century, and a more homogeneous working class was emerging. Production was moving from the countryside to the town, into large factories powered by steam or electricity, where labour discipline was imposed by long days and close surveillance. The *canuts* or handloom silkweavers of Lyon were displaced by power looms in factories in the city suburbs or along the Isère valley, where hydro-electric power was harnessed. By the eve of the First World War a third of Lyon workers were employed in the engineering industry, including car manufacture, and chemicals, while only a quarter were left in textiles.[26] At Saint-Chamond near Saint-Étienne domestic artisanal ribbon-weaving gave way to factory braidmaking. The stocking makers of the Troyes region no longer worked in their homes, scattered over the Champagne countryside, but were concentrated in the hosiery mills of Troyes itself.[27] Mechanization was making progress in trades hitherto requiring precise manual skills. Sewing, stitching and lasting machines transformed shoemaking from an artisanal to an industrial process, undertaken in factories such as those of Fougères in Brittany. The introduction of the Siemens oven after 1878 revolutionized glass production and undermined the skilled glass-blowers of Rive-de-Gier, outside Saint-Étienne.[28] Meanwhile the file-forgers of nearby Le Chambon-Feugerolles were said to be 'boiling over' in 1899. 'A company has been established at Trablaine for the mechanical manufacture of files and this has resulted in a great anger among the workers. According to them,' reported a local paper, 'the number of workers is going to be reduced, they will be deprived of their skill and reduced to misery.'[29] Printers who came to Paris for the 1900 Exhibition were, in the words of one worker, Jeanne Bouvier, 'shattered to see the linotype compositing machine which they thought would reduce their salaries and throw many of them out of work'.[30] Machines degraded the expertise of the skilled artisan since they could be operated by semi-skilled workers who were cheaper and now more efficient. Closed shops were broken open and apprenticeship fell into disuse. The profile of the working class now shifted, with a growing body of semi-skilled workers at its heart, displacing the elite of skilled workers and throwing the unskilled into the 'industrial reserve army' of the unemployed.

The working classes challenged these developments by strike action. Strikes were launched first by the skilled workers trying to protect their skills monopoly and conditions during the boom that coincided with the republicans' arrival in power in 1878–9 and held out hope of a 'social republic'. They were followed by the 'big battalions' of miners and textile workers, initially trying to take advantage of the rising market to push up wages and reduce hours, then, as depression bit in 1883–6, defending against wage-cuts and lay-offs. The Anzin miners' strike of 1884 witnessed by Zola was mirrored by other miners' strikes at Carmaux in 1883 and Decazeville in 1886, when an engineer was thrown out of a window and killed.[31] Forty thousand textile workers went on strike in Lille, Roubaix, Tourcoing and Armentières (Nord) in April 1880. 'Striking France', asserts Michelle Perrot, 'was above all textile France, capital Roubaix.'[32] On 9 March 1883 thousands of unemployed workers, under the leadership of building workers, marched and demonstrated in Paris, the first of many such events in the 1880s.[33]

The thinking in governing circles was that ordinary workers were interested only in jobs and pay, and that strike action was fomented by agitators, often from outside the working-class community, drunk on half-baked socialist ideas. In *Germinal* Étienne Lantier is portrayed in this way, while Maheu, a solid miner with a large family to feed, is to begin with not interested in militant action. The republican government took the view that if workers were allowed freely to form trade unions, to negotiate legitimately to defend their economic interests, they would no longer be vulnerable to the political blandishments of socialist agitators. This was the purpose of the law of 21 March 1884, sponsored by the government of Jules Ferry, who declared in 1887, 'the strike is industrial war, the union is social peace.'[34]

In the event workers were fairly slow to form trade unions, with only 9 per cent of the industrial workforce unionized in 1891.[35] The skilled trades, which had a long tradition of *compagnonnage* or illegal workers' associations, were the quickest to respond. In 1901 some 60 per cent of miners were unionized, as were 31 per cent of printers and 21 per cent of metalworkers, but only 9 per cent of textile workers were unionized, explained in part because women formed a large proportion of the workforce, while unskilled workers such as the Bretons of the chemical and tanning factories of Saint-Denis or Italian workers in the Lorraine ironfields were largely unorganized.[36] Employers were reluctant to recognize trade unions and in company towns where the employer was the main service provider they were able to resist dealing with them. At Saint-Chamond near Saint-Étienne, with one big employer, the Company of Naval Steelworks, and jobs secured by orders for warships, the local steelworkers helped to elect Aristide Briand their deputy in 1902 and supported him even when he broke the railway strike of 1910.[37] In 1913 only 1,064,000 or 10 per cent of the industrial workforce was unionized in France, as against 3,023,000 or 26 per cent in Great Britain and 3,317,000 or 63 per cent in Germany.[38] Perhaps Waldeck-Rousseau and Ferry were correct, and it was the lack of unionization in France that explained the upsurge in strike action after 1906.

Trade unions needed to federate in order to prevent divide-and-rule tactics by employers and the government. Two options were available: either to form national federations of workers in the same trade, or to found local federations, based on the same town, of workers in different trades. It was a characteristic of the French labour movement that national federations were less successful than local federations, that France lacked the powerful national federations of miners, railwaymen or engineers found in Great Britain and Germany. The French labour movement remained essentially regional.

National federations, it is true, were set up in the skilled trades, by hatters in 1880, printers in 1881, building workers in 1882. Railway workers set up a national federation in 1890 but the skilled engineers and firemen had their own union and were reluctant to co-operate with it, severely undermining the railwaymen's strike of 1898.[39] A national textile union was founded in Lyon, although 30 per cent of the members of the founding congress came from Lyon.[40] Most eloquent, however, was the story of the national miners' union. A national union was founded at Saint-Étienne in 1883 by Michel Rondet, a miner from La Ricamerie, but his reformism brought him into conflict with the revolutionary Marxist miners of the Loire basin, led by Gilbert Cotte. Matters came to a head in 1888 when the Loire miners went on strike, opposed by Rondet who was the same year elected to the Saint-Étienne municipal council. Rondet was expelled from the Loire miners' union but remained general secretary of the national miners' union. He made common cause with the miners of the Nord and Pas-de-Calais, controlled by Émile Basly. Basly was less a militant than a power-broker, who saw the best strategy for his miners not as strike action but as building a local power-base and cultivating relations with those who mattered in Paris. On the strength of the Anzin strike he was elected deputy for Paris in 1885-9, then fell back on the Pas-de-Calais, elected deputy for Lens in 1891 and mayor of Lens from 1900 to his death in 1928. Rondet and Basly refused to affiliate the miners' union to the Confédération Générale du Travail, which was dominated by anarcho-syndicalists, from 1895 until 1908. Indeed, when the national miners' union called a general strike in October 1902 Basly broke the united front and kept his Pas-de-Calais miners out of it.[41]

Much more successful were the local federations of unions. These came under the umbrella of the Bourses du Travail, which were to begin with simply labour exchanges to deal with the pressing problem of unemployment in the 1880s. They were funded by republican municipalities, generally as a reward for the electoral support of workers in delivering republican victory in municipal elections.

However, they provided much needed venues for local trade unions accustomed to meet in the back rooms of cafés, and trade unionists used the contact with unemployed workers to encourage them to join the union if it found them a job. Bourses du Travail were set up at Marseille in 1885, Paris in 1886 and Lyon in 1891, and a Saint-Étienne conference of 1892 set up a federation of Bourses du Travail. Local solidarity proved much more effective in promoting the cause of labour, as in 1893 when powerful support for the striking metalworkers of Rive-de-Gier came from the glassworkers of the town.[42] As in agriculture, local loyalties were generally more powerful than class solidarity.

A WIDENING PETITE BOURGEOISIE

The processes of industrial concentration and mechanization did not mean the disappearance of the artisan or *petit patron*, employing a small number of workers, from the French economy. The number of firms in fact peaked in 1906 and while some industrial sectors, such as mining, metallurgy and textiles, were given over to large enterprises, in others the small firm continued to exist. A survey of 1907, for example, showed that the average number of workers employed was 2.4 in the joinery trade and shoe industry, 2.1 in the female garment trade and 1.4 in the case of tailors, 1.1 for bakers and 0.8 for *charcutiers*.[43] Competition from large-scale industry drove many small firms out of business, but it also created a demand for specialist suppliers. Thus in Paris there were thriving small workshops which provided spare parts for larger engineering firms, and 'articles de Paris' such as artificial flowers, imitation jewellery, vanity bags and umbrellas were made in workshops that had moved from the centre of Paris to the suburbs, while demand for fashion goods from department stores provided work for subcontractors who had orders made up in sweatshops or at home by women now using sewing machines.[44]

Just as large factories competed with small workshops, so department stores competed with small shops. In Zola's *Au bonheur des dames* an orphaned Denise comes from Normandy to work in her uncle's crumbling draper's shop, Au Viel Elbeuf. There is no place for her there so she goes to work as a sales assistant in a department store painted by Zola as a brightly lit cathedral of commerce, whose only aim is to seduce the fashionable ladies of Paris. Mocked as a country girl by more urbane staff, worked off her feet from 8 a.m. to 9 p.m., she nevertheless ends up marrying Octave Mouret, the owner of the store.[45] This happy end is perhaps the only fanciful element in Zola's book, which might have been modelled on the career of Jules Jaluzot, the son of a notary of the Nièvre who dropped out of Saint-Cyr, became head of the silk department at Bon Marché, married a rich heiress and set up Printemps in 1865. After a fire he rebuilt it in the style of a cathedral, complete with nave, in 1881-5, lit by electricity, and was elected to the Chamber of Deputies in 1889.[46] Of course the department stores squeezed out the small shops of central Paris which had sold the same products, provoking more militant shopkeepers to form a Ligue Syndicale du Travail, de l'Industrie et du Commerce in 1888, attacking the German-Jewish bankers they saw funding the big stores.[47] However, many shops moved to the suburbs where they catered for the working-class and white-collar clienteles who lived there. While the number of small grocers in the central 1st *arrondissement* fell from 131 to 60 between 1860 and 1914, in the popular Belleville 20th *arrondissement* they multiplied from 196 to 456.[48] Auvergnats continued to exploit their niche in wine stores, cafés, hotels, ironmongery and coal provision. Only about 30 per cent enjoyed business success, but those who did returned to the Auvergne in the summer on 'Bonnet trains', named after Louis Bonnet, owner of the *Auvergnat de Paris*, who negotiated special rates with the railway company. There they showed off their gold watches, cigars and silk dresses, dominated conversation in the café and teased the country-folk who stayed in the villages for their backwardness.[49] Lastly, although the countryside lost rural artisans, it gained shops which moved in to meet the rising living standards of the farming clientele. Mazières-en-Gâtine for example had one grocer in 1850 but three in 1880, selling coffee, sugar, soap, candles and matches, needles and thread, and one café in 1850 but six in 1880. A wine merchant and beer shop arrived in 1896, the butcher and *charcutier* were joined by a fishmonger in 1911, and a second baker set up in 1906 as peasants stopped making their own bread.[50]

Denise's career in *Au bonheur des dames* was in many ways typical of those who moved not upwards, out of the petite bourgeoisie, but sideways, from the 'old lower-middle class' of shop or workshop, which required some capital but little formal education, to the 'new middle class' of white-collar workers, which required no capital but some education and a polite and subservient manner. In 1911 the twelve largest Parisian department stores had 11,000 employees. They were recruited not from the countryside, which supplied domestic servants, but from Paris and provincial towns, and were not working class but came from a retailing or white-collar background.[51] The development of global markets, expanding communications and urbanization created new opportunities for clerical workers in banks, in railway and insurance companies, and in utility companies supplying water, gas and electricity. The state was extending its responsibilities into education and social services, not least with the expulsion of religious congregations from schools, while developing postal, telegraph and telephone services and, at the local level, as we have seen, taking over some provision of utilities. The white-collar population of Paris grew from 126,000 or 16 per cent of the working population in 1866 to 353,000 or 21 per cent in 1911, the proportion of women increasing from 15 per cent to 31.[52] They behaved differently from the working class: not necessarily earning more money but having more education, as the elementary education system added extra classes up to the age of sixteen, to provide the necessary numeracy and good handwriting.[53] The director of the École Turgot in Paris was proud to announce in 1875, 'the principal goal of the great majority of both pupils and parents is office employment.'[54] Office workers tended to marry later and have fewer children, regarding children as a hindrance to social mobility. They were savers rather than spenders, paying into sickness and pension schemes provided by the firm or mutual aid societies.

That said, white-collar workers, like manual workers, were subjected to long hours and bullying by superiors, and in 1889 they set up a Federal Union of Employees. In the public sector post-office workers formed two unions in 1900, and claimed that two-thirds of workers were members by 1903. The state, however, forbade public servants from forming trade unions, and sacked several hundred post-office workers after a strike in 1906, which provoked another strike in 1909.[55] Some *instituteurs* or primary school teachers felt similarly about their situation. 'We educate the children of the people by day,' proclaimed the manifesto of syndicalist teachers in 1905, 'what could be more natural than thinking of meeting men of the people in the evening?'[56] *Instituteurs* waged war with the government in 1907 about the right to form trade unions, but had little thought of going on strike. Of those training to be *instituteurs* at the École Normale of Douai in the Nord in 1893–1914 only 15 per cent were sons of industrial workers; 35 per cent were sons of peasants, artisans or shopkeepers, while 21 per cent were sons of other white-collar workers, 19 per cent sons of *instituteurs*, and 9 per cent from property-owning, professional or business backgrounds.[57] Most regarded themselves as secular priests with a mission to modernize France and root the Republic in the towns and villages, not to undermine it.[58]

COMPETITION FOR THE PROFESSIONS

In *Les Déracinés* of 1897, Maurice Barrès explored how seven young students from Nancy who went to Paris to make brilliant careers came up against intense competition for success.

As I write these lines there are 730 graduates in arts and sciences who are looking for jobs in education; they regard their qualification as a guarantee from the State. While waiting, over 450 have become school supervisors in order to live. And how many jobs are there? Six per year. This situation discourages neither the young people, nor the secondary education system. There are 350 scholars taking degrees and the *agrégation*. That is to say that the State makes 350 new commitments when it has only six places already fought over by 730 individuals who will become 1,080 and increase to infinity . . . if they do not become angry with the government they will attack society. In 1882–1883 a particular class is taking shape under our eyes: a student proletariat.[59]

Of the students, four had the advantage of family resources. Henri de Saint-Phlin, of noble stock, studied for an arts degree. François Sturel, also from a landed background, and Georges Suret-Lefort, whose father was a businessman, began law degrees. Maurice Roemerspacher, a doctor's son, attended the Paris Faculty of Medicine. Three were not so well provided for. Antoine Mouchefrin, a scholar at the Lycée and a photographer's son, started medical studies but ran out of money and dropped out. Honoré Racadot, the son of a peasant who did well out of selling livestock to the Germans during the 1870 war, became a notary's clerk in the hope of later buying a notarial office, for which no legal qualification was required. Alfred Renaudin, who had lost his father, a tax inspector, hoped to make a living as a great journalist, but was reduced to being a humble reporter.

After 1889 competition became even more intense when the new military service law, introducing a universal three-year period, exempted from the army those with arts or science degrees, doctorates in law or medicine, or diplomas from a *grande école*. Henri Bérenger, in his 1901 study of *Intellectual Proletarians in France*, complained that 'a host of young men who previously would have gone into commerce or industry, have thrown themselves into university to escape military service.'[60] The university population rose from 11,200 in 1876 to 42,000 in 1914, fuelling a great debate at the turn of the century about the *déclassement* of young people from the lower classes seeking to escape menial occupations, the ballooning of higher education which turned out larger numbers of young people with useless degrees, the intense competition for places in the professions and government service that would leave many of them dissatisfied, and the political danger posed by half-educated intellectuals.[61]

The obvious path for young people of academic ability who lacked family resources was the teaching profession. Bouteiller, the grey eminence of *Les Déracinés* who taught the young men at the Lycée de Nancy before being appointed to Paris, was described as 'the son of a Lille worker who was picked out at the age of eight for his precocious and studious intelligence, and won scholarships all the way up to the École Normale [Supérieure] from which he graduated at the top of the list'.[62] Teachers in secondary schools were more and more qualified during the Third Republic, the elite securing an *agrégation* from the École Normale Supérieure and obtaining the best posts in the lycées or competing for university positions, the mass of teachers in lycées and municipal colleges (which did not have a sixth form) now having a degree from an arts or science faculty. Such was the demand for posts, however, that many were reduced to serving time as *répétiteurs*, commonly known as *pions* or pawns, who were not allowed to teach but supervised homework, playgrounds and dormitories. In 1876 only 7 per cent of *pions* had degrees; in 1898 it was 35 per cent, in which year only 3.4 per cent of them secured a permanent teaching post in a college.[63] Secondary school teachers had cultural but not social capital: among those teaching in 1900–1914, around 9 per cent were sons of industrial workers, 39 per cent sons of peasants, shopkeepers and artisans, 19 per cent sons of *instituteurs* and secondary school teachers, 13 per cent sons of other white-collar workers, and only 11 per cent sons of professional and businessmen, a profile that differed little from that of the École Normale d'Instituteurs of Douai.[64] Even among academics, the social origin of professors in French universities was sharply inferior to those teaching in German universities in 1870–1930, with 35 per cent of French arts professors from teaching backgrounds and 35 per cent of science professors originating in the petite bourgeoisie or working class.[65] In some cases teachers might succeed by acquiring connections and marrying into wealth. Édouard Herriot, the son of a soldier who was educated at the École Normale Supérieure, began his career training candidates for the École Normale at the Lycée Ampère of Lyon. However, during the Dreyfus Affair, through his involvement in the Ligue des Droits de l'Homme, he acquired the patronage of the mayor of Lyon, Victor Augagneur, married the daughter of a doctor (who was president of the *conseil général* of the Rhône) and granddaughter of a senator of the Rhône, and was thus launched on a political career that took him to be mayor of Lyon from 1905 to 1940, senator in 1912, minister in 1916, deputy in 1919 and prime minister in 1924–6 and 1932.[66] More of a struggle was experienced by Jean Guéhenno, the son of a shoeworker of Fougères in Brittany, who was obliged to leave the local municipal college when his father became ill, and work as an office-boy in a shoe factory. He swotted for the *baccalauréat* on his own, in order to 'become a Monsieur', and then won a scholarship to the Lycée of Rennes to compete for the École Normale Supérieure. He saw himself as a 'strange candidate, who knows neither Latin nor Greek', and he failed the examination first time, after which his father died. He succeeded the second time in 1911, this time from the prestigious Lycée Louis-le-Grand in Paris, but felt 'ridiculous' compared to the sons of 'kings and leaders' there and was embarrassed to return to Fougères, wanting his determinedly working-class mother to wear a hat. Among recruits to the École Normale Supérieure between 1868 and 1941 in arts subjects, only 3.4 per cent came from the working class and 8.6 per cent from artisans, peasants and shopkeepers, as against 34 per cent from business, professional and higher official families, but those with a teaching background from higher to primary levels and therefore with cultural rather than social capital were overrepresented, accounting for 32 per cent of the entry.[67] Nevertheless, Guéhenno had a successful teaching career, preparing students of the top Paris lycées for admission to the École Normale, becoming a writer and left-wing intellectual, and succeeding to Herriot's chair at the Académie Française in 1962.[68]

Medicine was another profession in which competition was severe. There were 2,629 medical students in France in 1876, and 8,533 in 1914, over half of them in Paris and 10 per cent of them women.[69] Until 1892 qualified doctors did not even have a monopoly of medical practice, but had to compete with so-called health officers such as Charles Bovary in Flaubert's novel, who were supposed to increase medical provision in the countryside but did not even have a secondary education. The latter were effectively killed off by the military service law of 1889 which required them, unlike medical students, to do three years in the army, and by the monopoly legislation of 1892.[70] That said, in 1901 Henri Bérenger calculated that of 2,500 doctors in Paris, 1,200 earned less than 8,000 francs, and made ends meet as 'beaters' finding clients for more successful doctors and surgeons, by running VD clinics or doing back-street abortions.[71] As with teachers, a good marriage and connections were essential. Georges Clemenceau, a doctor's son from the Vendée who qualified in 1865, married a wealthy American, Mary Plummer, whom he met on a trip to the United States. More crucial for him, however, was the support of the leading republican Étienne Arago, who when he was mayor of Paris in September 1870 appointed Clemenceau mayor of Montmartre, and allowed him to begin his political career.[72] The increasing status of doctors under the Third Republic was reflected in their greater political profile: doctors accounted for 9 per cent of deputies in 1885 and 12 per cent in 1893, while they provided 8 per cent of senators in 1885 and 14 per cent of senators in 1900.[73] Election to the Chamber or Senate was an accolade for a country doctor who had done well through contacts he had made for himself. About half the 10,000 doctors in the provinces earned little, according to Bérenger, but they had more opportunity to cut a figure and marry well in local society. Émile Combes, for example, a weaver's son from Rocquemaure in the Tarn, was seminary-educated and taught in the 1850s at the *petit séminaire* of Castres, the famous Assumptionist College of Père d'Alzon in Nîmes and the diocesan college of Pons (Charente), before marrying the daughter of a draper, whose uncle was a banker. The dowry and loans enabled him to requalify as a doctor in 1868 and he set up comfortably as a GP in Pons, using his network of clients to launch a political career and being elected a senator in 1885.[74]

The law was an equally competitive profession, but one where the rewards were potentially greater, since it was the royal road to government office. The 5,239 law students in 1876 became 16,465 in 1914, with 46 per cent of them in Paris but only 149 or 0.05 per cent of them women.[75] Bérenger was equally scathing about the rat race of the legal profession, arguing that of 3,000 barristers in Paris few earned anything before their early thirties and only 200 earned over 10,000 francs. To succeed they needed family resources and, as usual, connections. The law was an obligatory training for government bureaucracy, and 94 per cent of prefects in 1876–1918 were legally trained.[76] The appointment of prefects was generally influenced by the deputies from the area they would serve, so political patronage was important. The Cambon brothers, Paul and Jules, lost their father, who owned a tanning factory at Avallon, when they were young, but their uncle was bishop of Langres and as law students in Paris they were close to Jules Ferry. Paul Cambon escaped with Jules Ferry, then prefect of the Seine, when the Commune broke out, and at thirty, in 1873, was appointed the youngest prefect of France, at Troyes. There he met and married a general's daughter, and became prefect at Lille in 1878, a post to which his brother succeeded in 1882. Paul was promoted minister-resident of the new Tunisian Protectorate, while Jules became governor-general of Algeria in 1891. From colonial administration the Cambon brothers moved into diplomacy, Paul ambassador at Madrid and Constantinople before going to London in 1898, Jules ambassador in Washington and Madrid before going to Berlin in 1907.[77]

While lawyers from humbler backgrounds might finish up as professors in law faculties, the plum posts in the *grands corps* such as the Cour de Cassation, Cour des Comptes or the Inspection des Finances, an elite body of public service accountants who went on to run the Ministry of Finances or the private offices of ministers, were colonized by lawyers whose families enjoyed hereditary wealth as well as political influence. In 1900 the Cour des Comptes recruited 27 per cent of its members from landowning, banking or business circles, and 31 per cent from administrative dynasties and political families, whereas 40 per cent of professors in law faculties came from the petite bourgeoisie.[78] The father of Joseph Caillaux, for example, had been minister in the Moral Order regime and was brought up in Versailles with a son of a Moral Order foreign minister, the second Duc de Decazes. Educated at the Jesuit college on the rue des Postes in Paris and at the Law Faculty, he became an *inspecteur des finances* in 1888, deputy of the Sarthe as a republican in 1898 and minister of finance in 1899. Caillaux's wealthy background gave him leverage into the republican mandarinate, and his jettisoning of royalist for republican ideas enabled him to become a minister.

A UNITED ELITE

There was a danger, under the Third Republic, that the republican official and political elite would remain divided from the royalist or Bonapartist social elite, dangerously compromising stability. In fact, while politically sensitive posts such as prefectures were reserved for genuine republicans, other posts, notably in the diplomatic corps and the army, could still be accessed by those uneasy in the Republic, and over a long career they were inclined to rally to it. Pierre de Margerie, educated by the Jesuits at Lille and at Lille's new Catholic University, where his father was dean, was reluctant to take an oath to the Republic before sitting the examination for the Quai d'Orsay, until his father explained to him that it meant only that he would not conspire against the regime. In 1891–8 he was secretary to Paul Cambon when the latter was ambassador at Constantinople, and he became convinced that the Republic could satisfactorily defend French interests. He helped to further a career that took him to Madrid, Bangkok and Peking by marrying the daughter of the assistant mayor of Marseille, Amédée Rostand, and becoming the brother-in-law of the writer Edmond Rostand.[79] The army, which was held to be a bastion of royalist and Bonapartist power, became less of an aristocratic caste: 38 per cent of divisional generals were noble in 1876, but only 19 per cent in 1901.[80] At the time of the Dreyfus Affair there was still a fear that Catholic and conservative officers, recruited from the Jesuit college in the rue des Postes, were capable of conspiring against the Republic, but after the Affair care was taken to promote republican generals such as Joffre. Just as important for the coherence of the ruling class was the possibility of marriage between the republican official and political class on the one hand and the older families who controlled the economic and social capital of the country on the other. In 1859 for example, Cécile Anspach, daughter of a high official in the Cour de Cassation, married Gustave de Rothschild of the great banking family. A generation later, in 1895, the aspiring politician of modest means Louis Barthou married Alice Mayer, whose father was a successful businessman with large investments in railways, utilities and Paris property as well as being on the *conseil général* of Seine-et-Oise, setting him on course to become prime minister.[81]

'It is difficult to dispel the excessive love the French have of *fonctionnarisme*,' commented Bérenger in 1901. 'We lack industrialists, agriculturalists and colonists while administrative offices are battled over furiously.'[82] In fact, other pathways were opening to ambitious young people in the world of industry, commerce and banking. The first industrial revolution, based on textiles, coal, iron and railways, which was losing momentum in the 1870s, was supplemented at the end of the nineteenth century by a 'second industrial revolution' based on steel, engineering, chemicals and electricity. The family firm, which had dominated for so long in the nineteenth century, was overtaken by the joint-stock company, in which the ownership of shareholders was separated from the running of the business by trained and salaried managers. The growing dependence of industry on advanced science and technology increased the demand for *ingénieurs*, graduates from the archipelago of *grandes écoles* which paralleled the traditional university faculties, heralded in 1880 as the 'kings of the epoch'.[83]

The most prestigious of these schools, the École Polytechnique, for a long time regarded itself as too exclusive to provide graduates for industry. Its alumni moved into the army, into high civil service posts such as the Inspection des Finances, and via supplementary training in the École des Mines and École des Ponts et Chaussées, into services developing the country's infrastructure. Only from the 1890s did substantial numbers of graduates from the Polytechnique go into industry, to work on such ambitious projects as the development of electrical grids to light Paris and to power the metro.[84] Less prestigious but more effective as far as industry was concerned was the École Centrale de Commerce et de l'Industrie. Gustave Eiffel, the son of a military administrator, whose mother made the family fortune by supplying coal to iron-furnaces in the Haute-Marne, went to Centrale only because he failed the examination for Polytechnique. He worked for the Chemin de Fer de l'Ouest and then set up his own engineering firm at Levallois-Perret outside Paris in 1866, building bridges and viaducts for railways, providing the steel frame for the Statue of Liberty, and for the Paris Exhibition of 1889 building the tower that bore his name.[85] At the turn of the century the French tyre and car industry was essentially developed by graduates of Centrale. Armand Peugeot, trained at Centrale, switched the family business in Montbéliard from making springs for the watchmaking industry to making bicycles in 1886 and cars in 1896.[86] André Michelin, another Centralien, and his brother Édouard, who had a law degree, took over a failing family firm in Clermont-Ferrand and hit success with the manufacture of the detachable pneumatic tyre in 1891, with which they won the Paris–Brest cycle race that year, and were employing 5,000 workers by 1914.[87] Ironically, one of the greatest car manufacturers, Louis Renault, failed the examination to Centrale. He refused to follow his father, a Paris draper and button-seller, developing models in the garden of the family's out-of-town property at Boulogne-Billancourt. In 1898 he and his two brothers each put 30,000 francs capital into a car factory, expanding the old-fashioned way by ploughing back profits, winning contracts to provide taxis for the Paris and London markets in 1909, and became the biggest French car manufacturer, employing 4,440 workers in 1914.[88]

Family firms still existed but the largest of them drew heavily on outside finance and their heads were very much part of the French economic and social elite. Henri Schneider of Le Creusot moved into arms manufacture in 1875 and aspired to become the French Krupp. His business interlocked closely with that of de Wendel, sharing the same bankers, Demachy-Sellière, and dominating the Comité des Forges steel cartel. When much of the de Wendel empire found itself annexed by Germany, Schneider helped to develop a French site for the de Wendel business at Jouef in French Lorraine. Socially, Schneider behaved less like a steel magnate and more like a grand seigneur. He acquired a château in the Sologne, which was prized hunting country, and, using the shooting to develop contacts with aristocratic neighbours and business partners, married his son Eugène II and four daughters into aristocratic families.[89]

Finance was traditionally closer to the aristocracy than was heavy industry. It was less tarnished by grime, and gained cachet from lending money to governments and the social elite. After the economic recession of 1882 which brought down a number of banks, Henri Germain, founder of the Crédit Lyonnais, decided to cease investment in industry, concentrating on the property market, insurance, public utilities and lending to home and foreign governments.[90] This aristocratic sheen did not mean that it was impossible for ordinary people to make a successful career in banking. Émile Mercet, whose parents were both in domestic service and who had no formal qualification, became an employee at the Crédit Lyonnais, charged with founding its Constantinople branch in 1876, heading its St Petersburg branch from 1879 to 1881, and finishing as president of the Comptoir d'Escompte in 1904.[91] In other ways, though, banking circles were growing closer to the nobility. The family strategy of the Rothschilds, for most of the nineteenth century, had been characterized by endogamy, with cousins marrying cousins. At the end of the century, however, their practice was to marry out. In 1878 Marguerite de Rothschild, for example, became the second wife of the Duc de Gramont, Napoleon III's ill-fated foreign minister of 1870, and hosted immense society balls at their house in the rue de Chaillot.[92]

By the same token, the French aristocracy became less choosy about new wealth, and keen to make alliances with the super-rich from finance and industry. This tendency was encouraged by the fall in land values and land rents that followed the agricultural depression of the late 1870s and 1880s. Landed families now invested more of their resources in banks, railways, insurance companies and even industry, and to protect their investments accepted places on the boards of directors of large companies and trusts. The president of the Suez Canal Company was the Prince d'Arenberg, and in 1914 five of the seven directors of the Comité des Forges were noble. At the same time the reconciliation of many noble families with the Republic through the Ralliement meant that the divisive influence of the French Revolution, which had turned the nobility of the Faubourg Saint-Germain into a caste, became attenuated. Aristocratic families married their daughters into money as never before, promoting a plutocratic super-elite that was both noble and grand bourgeois, part landed and part monied. The Catholic and royalist aristocrat Albert de Mun married each of his daughters into a wine family and at the turn of the century American heiresses were all the rage. In 1893 Winaretta Singer, heiress to the sewing-machine fortune, married Prince Edmond de Polignac, son of the last minister of Charles X, while in 1895 Anna Gould married Boni de Castellane only to divorce him in 1906 and marry his cousin, the Prince de Talleyrand-Périgord. And while under the Third Republic the nobility forfeited political influence, having no more than 5 per cent of ministerial appointments in 1879–1914, their profile in the Chamber of Deputies falling from 23 per cent to 9, they remained the rulers of society. Aristocratic hostesses of the Faubourg Saint-Germain held the best salons to which every aspiring politician or artist sought admission. One of the most brilliant was hosted by the Comtesse Élisabeth de Greffulhe, known to Proust as the cousin of his friend Robert de Montesquiou, the model for the Duchesse de Guermantes in *À la recherche du temps perdu*.[93]

French economy and society demonstrated a number of weaknesses before 1914. Agriculture faced the challenges of glut and depression, and saw its strongest sons and daughters leave for a better life in the cities. Industrial development was held up by the prevalence of the family firm, but in large-scale industry class conflict was rife. Those who secured secondary education competed for jobs in the professions and public sector, fuelling fears of *déclassement* and *fonctionnarisme*. On the positive side, however, were many factors which contributed to a high degree of social cohesion in pre-war France. The proportion of those working in agriculture remained high in comparative European terms and private property was widely disseminated in the form of farms, shops and workshops. There was a high degree of mobility both geographical and social together with a widening of the petite bourgeoisie which defused class conflict, and in any case workers tended to be organized on local rather than occupational lines. State-building and the development of education offered wide possibilities for employment in the public sector, but the growth of managerial capitalism created opportunities in the private sector also. Finally, the French elite was increasingly interconnected, both in terms of land, finance and industry, and between the republican political and official elite and the non-republican social elite. The *apaisement* that was apparent in politics in the Belle Époque was thus also reflected in the social order.

12

Secularization and Religious Revival

SIN AND REPARATION

The events of 1870–71 dealt a triple blow to the Catholic Church. First, the few French forces protecting the pope in Rome since 1849 were withdrawn to fight the Prussians, and in September 1870 Rome was occupied by the Piedmontese army to complete the work of Italian unification. An elite of French Catholics such as the Vendean volunteers led by Athanase-Charles-Marie de Charette de la Contrie fought to defend the Holy City until instructed by Pius IX to lay down their arms, then returned to France where they fought in the Army of the Loire with volunteers of western France, taking part in the charge at Patay near Orléans on 3 December.[1] Second, France, regarded by Catholics as the eldest daughter of the Church, was defeated by Prussia, which for Catholics was seen as the incarnation of both the Protestant Reformation and the Enlightenment, since Voltaire had been 'trumpeter and adviser' to Frederick the Great. It was divine justice, according to Louis Veuillot, writing in *L'Univers*, that France should be punished for its sins against God – the Enlightenment and the Revolution – by the power that represented 'the sins of Europe'.[2] Lastly, the Paris Commune, which sacked churches, murdered the archbishop of Paris and other clergy, and set fire to the city, was for Catholics such as Veuillot who remained in the capital until the end of April 1871 the apocalyptic culmination of the atheistic revolution that had shaken France since 1789. Only the restoration of the pope to his Temporal Power and the restoration of Henry V to the French throne could save the situation for Veuillot and his readers.[3]

Catholics argued that France had been punished for its revolt against God. The only way it could redeem itself and recover God's protection was to undergo a process of reparation to expiate its sins. The period of so-called Moral Order in the early 1870s, when France indeed came within a whisker of royalist restoration, was a period of intense Catholic activity to bring France back to the fold. To begin with, there was a boom in the pilgrimage movement, sponsored by the Assumptionist fathers of the Père d'Alzon. A national pilgrimage movement was orchestrated by d'Alzon's disciples, Père François Picard and Père Vincent de Paul Bailly, who had set up an Assumptionist house in Paris and had been hunted during the Commune. These harnessed the support of aristocratic ladies such as Madame de la Rochefoucauld, grouped in Notre-Dame de Salut, and of a new congregation of nuns, the Petites Soeurs de l'Assomption, who accompanied the pilgrim trains. In 1872 they organized a pilgrimage to La Salette in the French Alps, where a weeping Virgin prophesying disaster had appeared in 1847, followed by one to Lourdes in 1873. Other pilgrimages headed by the conservative nobility and royalist deputies went in June 1873 to Paray-le-Monial in Burgundy, where Marguerite-Marie Alacoque had received divine instruction in 1689 to have France put under the protection of the Sacred Heart, and to Chartres, where Mary's veil was said to be kept and the cult was devoted to the pregnant Virgin.[4] That same summer the royalist-dominated National Assembly approved a request from the archbishop of Paris that a site at Montmartre, high point of the Paris Commune, should be acquired in order to build a 'church of the national vow to the Sacred Heart of Jesus'. A provisional chapel was blessed there in 1876, and 500,000–600,000 pilgrims per year over the next thirty years bought *cartes du Sacré Coeur* divided into bricks, a full card representing a donation of 127 francs, raising 60 per cent of the total of 40 million francs that the basilica of Sacré Coeur ultimately cost.[5] An equestrian statue of Joan of Arc by the sculptor Frémiet was unveiled on the place des Pyramides off the rue de Rivoli in 1874, on the site where she had been wounded during the Anglo-Burgundian siege of Paris, marking a new stage in the cult of the heroine who was venerated for liberating French soil from foreign occupation and restoring France to the Church.[6] During this period, finally, a huge effort was made by the Church to extend its grip on national education. The control of girls' education by nuns reached a peak in 1878, when the number of those in female congregations, which had been 66,000 in 1850, rose to 135,000. In 1875 the National Assembly passed a law permitting Catholic universities, although their students still had to take their degrees in state faculties, and Catholic universities were opened in Angers and Lille, the former funded by the Catholic nobility, and the latter by the Catholic employers of the textile industry.[7]

THE REPUBLICAN OFFENSIVE

The renewed grip of the Catholic Church on the education and social life of the country was seen by republicans as a massive threat. Loyalty to the Papacy, evidenced by campaigns in Catholic quarters to demand the restitution of the Papal States to the pope, was seen to undermine loyalty to France. The *Syllabus of Errors* published by Pius IX in 1864 delivered a frontal attack on modern ideas of liberalism, democracy and nationalism. The Church, moreover, was seen to have supported reactionary regimes, the monarchy or the Empire, and always to have attacked the Republic. The failure of the two previous republics was felt very much to have been the work of the Church. It was intolerable that religious congregations should be free to undermine the Republic, that schools maintained by municipalities, departments and the state should so often be staffed by teaching brothers and nuns, inculcating Catholic thought and prejudices. The education of citizens for the Republic required that state education should be dispensed by lay teachers and that religious education be eliminated from the classroom. The programme of the republicans, the generation of 1830 that acquired power in the late 1870s, was clear, but their rhetoric was always sharper than their bite. Republicans were fully aware that much of the French population was more likely to accept the Republic if it were allowed to practise its own faith; it was entirely possible to be both republican and Catholic. Therefore, while there were always republicans of anticlerical and freethinking disposition demanding more and more extreme measures against the Church, republicans in power were generally keen to maintain some kind of working relationship between Church and state in order to retain the loyalty of the Catholic majority.

In his Belleville manifesto of 1869 Gambetta committed himself to free, compulsory, lay education, and to the abolition of the Concordat, that is to the Separation of Church and state. Addressing a republican banquet at Saint-Quentin in November 1871 he said:

> I desire from the bottom of my soul not only the separation of Church and state but the separation of the Church from schools. *(Loud applause.)* Because people have abandoned the Church and the Church has forfeited much of the respect that was once due to the clergy, we have seen the clergy cease to be apostles and become instruments of power under the most corrupt and conservative regimes. *(Applause.)* The message of the Syllabus … is the greatest threat to the society of 1789 of which we are the heirs and representatives. The main aim of the society of 1789 was to base the political and social system on reason instead of grace, to assert the superiority of the status of the citizen over that of the slave … For eighty years two world views have been present, dividing minds and fomenting conflict, a desperate war in the heart of society. The lack of unity in education means that we have been continually thrown from revolt to repression, from anarchy to dictatorship, without any chance of stability.[8]

The previous month the Ligue de l'Enseignement had launched a petition for free, compulsory education, to which lay education was later added under pressure from the republican press. In June 1872 and January 1873 successive versions of the petition were presented to the National Assembly, with 119,000 signatures in favour of compulsory education only, 410,00 for compulsory free education, and 388,000 for compulsory, free and lay education, 917,000 signatures in all. Unfortunately, after the fall of Thiers in May 1873 and the inauguration of the Moral Order regime, there was no chance of the petition being heard. However, when the republican but Catholic premier Jules Simon seemed unable to check a campaign by Catholic clergy and laity in favour of restoring the pope's Temporal Power, Gambetta warned the Chamber on 3 May 1877 that 'clericalism is the enemy,' infiltrating the army, bureaucracy, education system and ruling class.[9] President MacMahon, dismissing Jules Simon on 16 May 1877, provoked the crisis that forced him finally to accept a republican administration and with it an anticlerical programme.

Pressure for anticlerical legislation came from the radical wing of the republican party, to which Gambetta again appealed in his speech at Romans in September 1878 in which he attacked a spirit that was not only clerical but 'Vaticanesque, monastic, congregational and Syllabist'.[10] Anticlericalism was also closely linked to masonic lodges and to free-thought societies, the main function of the latter being to organize civic burials for their members, predominantly artisans, *instituteurs* and the owners of cafés where they tended to meet. In 1873 the prefect of the Rhône required civic burials in Lyon to be held at night, provoking student accusations that the council was being run by the Jesuits, and comments that 'we need another '93 to purge France of that black band.' In 1882 a League for the Separation of Church and State was set up under the leadership of Jules Steeg, a former Protestant pastor and deputy of the Gironde, and Désiré Barodet, former mayor of Lyon and deputy of Paris, with ninety-six deputies or senators from the left of the republican party on its books.[11] Anticlericals also had an influential presence on municipal councils which fell massively into republican hands in 1878 and 1881. Victory was often crowned by expelling the Christian Brothers or Marists from municipal schools. For example at Alès, a mining town in the Cévennes, the Christian Brothers rejected the prize-day books provided by the new republican municipality in 1879 as antireligious, provoking the municipality to expel them and appoint lay *instituteurs*. At Martigné-Ferchaud in Upper Brittany, the republican municipality expelled the Christian Brothers in 1878 as a small crowd demonstrated, crying 'Long live the Republic! Down with the *chouans*, down with the monks!'[12] On 30 May 1878 radicals on the Paris municipal council and the republican left linked up with intellectuals such as Émile Littré and Ernest Renan to organize a celebration of the centenary of the death of Voltaire, a riposte to a celebration of the death of Joan of Arc at Notre-Dame and a wreath-laying at the Frémiet statue.[13] Since the government banned a public procession in honour of Voltaire, festivities took place in the Théâtre de la Gaîté, under the famous bust of the *philosophe* by Houdon. Victor Hugo, aged seventy-six, recalled Voltaire's defence of the Protestant merchant Calas who was broken on the wheel in 1761 for allegedly killing his son who had converted to Catholicism, and his intervention on behalf of the Chevalier de la Barre, who had his tongue ripped out and hand cut off before he was burned at the stake in 1776 for insulting a church procession. With his pen, 'he defeated the feudal lord, the Gothic judge, the Roman priest,' declared Hugo. 'He defeated violence with his smile, despotism by sarcasm, infallibility by irony, obstinacy by perseverance, ignorance by truth.'[14]

When the republicans took power they were in a position to enact their anticlerical programme, but also had to take the balance of power into account. Gambetta, as we have seen, was speaker of the Chamber, but the ministry of February 1879 was headed by the centre-left premier Waddington and was dominated by the centre-left finance minister Léon Say and minister of public works Freycinet, with the moderate republican Jules Ferry as minister of education. Five of the nine ministers, including Waddington, Say and Freycinet, were Protestants and Ferry was married to one, and while Protestants were keen to pin back the influence of the Catholic Church they also sought religious peace.[15] Moreover, Waddington, Say and Freycinet were all senators, and the Senate was wedded to the middle ground. The first piece of anticlerical legislation was designed to prohibit religious congregations that had not been properly authorized to teach. This was rejected by the Senate and the measure was therefore executed by government decrees on 29 March 1880, one to dissolve the Jesuits, who had crept back to refound colleges in France after 1850, the other to dissolve a number of other congregations. Freycinet, who became premier in December 1879, opposed the extension of the decree to other congregations, and resigned. Ferry, who took over as premier (September 1880), exempted female congregations which were not regarded as a political threat and educated not future citizens but future wives and mothers, for whom piety and virginity were seen as essential even by republican fathers. No attack, it should be underlined, was planned on the secular clergy, the bishops or parish priests. Paul Bert, professor of physiology at the Sorbonne

and deputy of the Yonne, one of the least practising of French departments, echoed the slogan of the French revolutionary armies, 'peace
to the cottages, war on the châteaux', by proclaiming at a republican
banquet in August 1880, 'peace to the curé, war on the monk'.[16]

In power, the republicans legislated for free elementary education
on 16 June 1881 and for compulsory lay education in state schools
on 28 March 1882. Paul Bert was chair of the parliamentary
commission that reported on lay education. The doctrine of *laïcité*
dictated that the state school was a neutral space in which liberty
of conscience prevailed and no religion was taught. Religious education would be provided by the curé, in the church or vicarage, and
school time was set aside on Thursdays for this to take place.
Protestants and Jewish children would have their religious education at the same time. This did not mean that no morality was
taught in school, but it was an 'independent' morality that, rather
than relying on religion for guidance or sanction, used such secular
notions as fraternity and solidarity. Protestants such as Ferdinand
Buisson, who had lived in exile in Switzerland during the Second
Empire and published a *Pedagogical Dictionary* of 1878, were
powerful inspirers of this new teaching, and Buisson oversaw its
introduction as inspector-general of primary education.[17] Alongside
moral education would be taught civic education, the training of
the future citizen in democratic principles. Naturally these were
also republican principles, inspired by the Revolution of 1789. As
Paul Bert said, 'we want, the country wants, the millions of voters
who gave us power to be educated to ensure that the principles of
the Revolution triumph over their adversaries.'[18]

The Catholic Church could not of course accept these new provi-
sions. Mgr Freppel, bishop of Angers and deputy for Finistère,
denounced 'the oppression of the majority by a minority' and what
he called 'the atheistic school, the godless school' that was now being
hatched.[19] In the Tarn, to give one example, the archbishop of Albi
in 1883 ordered parish priests to refuse first communion to children
attending lay schools and holy communion to their parents and
teachers, in order to boost attendance at private schools where
catechism could still be taught. The pretext was the putting on the
Index, the Vatican list of banned books, of a number of new works

343

of moral and civic instruction, including a 1880 textbook by Gabriel Compayré, a native of Albi who now taught at the ladies' teacher-training college of Fontenay-aux-Roses and was republican deputy of the Tarn.[20] Jules Ferry, education minister and premier, stood up to Mgr Freppel, saying that neutrality in school was 'important for state security and future republican generations'. Republicans had a duty not to leave education to those like Mgr Freppel who had declared that 'the principles of 1789 are the negation of original sin.'[21] On the other hand he also wrote a letter to *instituteurs* in 1883 instructing them not to say anything in class that would offend the religious sensibilities of any family. Likewise when the stipends of fifty priests in the Tarn were suspended for their sanctions against families who patronized lay schools and the archbishop of Albi was condemned by the Conseil d'État, Ferry told the new pope, Leo XIII, via the French ambassador in Rome, that despite previous republican commitments the French government had no intention of dismantling the Concordat, of separating Church and state. As he put it,

I believe strongly that the practising Catholic population of this country is not a party, that the majority of it voted for republican candidates, that it is attached to its traditional religion but is also impregnated by the principles and laws of the French Republic, that while it is faithful it is not clerical, as some say, and in case of conflict between the civil and spiritual powers it would oppose those who took it upon themselves to denounce the Concordat.[22]

For Ferry, the Concordat which had governed the church of the majority of French people since 1802, and in particular its relationship with bishops and priests, was a fixed point. Separation, he declared to a republican meeting in 1888, would be 'absolutely contrary not only to the beliefs of a great number of French people but to something much stronger than beliefs, to the habits and traditions of the French people, to popular instinct itself. Separation, Messieurs, would mean religious war.'[23]

After the elections of October 1885 moderate republicans around Ferry lost their dominance and were forced to bring radicals into the cabinet to defend against a powerful showing by the Union of the Right. There was a new burst of anticlerical legislation, in particular a law of 30 October 1886 which required all teaching congregations to leave municipal schools within five years in the case of boys' schools, without time limit in the case of girls' schools. Nothing decisive could be attempted for girls for a number of reasons. While communes tended to own the boys' school and could dispose of it as they wished, they were often reluctant or too poor to build an additional girls' school, so these were often owned by the Church or a private benefactor, and the commune would have to build a new girls' school to compete with the nuns. Lay female teachers were also in short supply, because although teacher-training colleges for *instituteurs* had been mandatory in every department under the Guizot law of 1833, similar colleges for *institutrices* were not required till 1879 and were only just beginning to turn out teachers. Many communities in any case disliked the prospect of single, educated lay women in their midst and preferred to entrust the education of girls to nuns. Between 1880 and 1900 the proportion of girls educated by nuns was reduced in the departments of the Gard and the Nord from 62 per cent to 46 and 45 per cent respectively, but in the Upper Breton department of Ille-et-Vilaine virtually no impression was made at all, and the proportion was squeezed from 86 to 80 per cent.[24]

THE TENACITY OF RELIGIOUS PRACTICE

Jules Ferry was correct that a great many of the French population were practising Catholics, but this was not a uniform pattern. One of the main stimuli of religious practice was the coexistence of faiths, Catholic and Protestant, Catholic and Jewish, although areas that were almost totally Catholic, such as Brittany, could also be extremely pious. Other factors worked against organized religion, notably the revolutionary tradition and growing urbanization and industrialization, which were seen to detach the popular classes from the grip of the Church. However, these factors did not play as straightforwardly as might be imagined.

In the company town of Montceau-les-Mines, near Le Creusot,

the biggest employer, Léonce Chagot, was also the mayor, and he believed in disciplining his workforce by entrusting the local schools to the Marists and the nuns. In 1882 Chagot lost control of the town hall to a republican, but responded by tightening clerical control, obliging miners' families to attend mass and sacking troublesome miners who were denounced by the Marists and nuns. The miners responded by celebrating the feast of the Assumption, 15 August 1882, by setting fire to the nuns' school and chapel and blowing up a statue of the Virgin Mary. This suggests that the working class were essentially irreligious, not because they were abandoned by the Church but because they felt that the Church had allied with political reaction and capitalist exploitation.[25]

Industrial workers were certainly parting company with organized religion, although the pattern was not uniform. In the Nord the glassmakers of Anor were described by one cleric in 1899 as 'a sad, sad, sad population for the Nord, which is a country addicted to pleasure, dancing and onanism'. In the mining basin around Anzin a quarter of children were not baptized and 41 per cent of burials in 1911 were civic, refusing the intercession of the priest. In the north of the department, in the textile conurbation of Lille, Roubaix and Tourcoing, where much of the workforce was French Flemish or Belgian Flemish, religious practice was much higher, up to 75 per cent of the population taking Easter communion.[26] This was, however, also a stronghold of Guesdist socialism which, once it took control of local town halls, worked hard to build a counter-culture of trade unions, co-operatives and support for the children, the old and the sick of working-class families. Despite Guesde's strictures that anticlericalism was a waste of time, since the Church as an ally of capitalism would disappear with it, the sentiments of the Guesdists of the Nord were clearly expressed when in February 1899 the body of a pupil of the Christian Brothers was found dead in their school complex in Lille and traces of blood and sperm were discovered in the bed of the Flemish Christian Brother Flamidien. Although Flamidien turned out to be innocent, the anticlerical backlash involved students as well as workers, moderate republicans as well as socialists. Socialist militant Paule Minck addressed a huge audience on the use of the confessional by clergy to persuade women to denounce the revolutionary activities of their husbands, and the refrain of a song popular with the workers of Roubaix ran 'The social Republic / Is that of humanity / It will give us back our liberty / In spite of the clerical plague.'[27]

Not all industrial areas were in large towns and not all cities were industrial, so whether urbanization had an impact on religious practice has to be examined in its own right. In Paris in 1909–14 Sunday mass was well attended in the posh bourgeois *arrondissements* – 46 per cent in the 7th and 31 per cent in the 16th, but in the working-class and lower-middle-class *arrondissements* of eastern Paris mass attendance fell to 6 per cent in the 20th and 4 per cent in the 11th.[28] Similarly civic burials in Paris accounted for 20 per cent of burials in 1903 but rose to 39 per cent in the popular 20th *arrondissement*.[29] That said, immigrant populations from regions with high religious practice kept up their religion in order to preserve their identity in the large city. A club founded in 1897 for Bretons at Montparnasse, the Paris terminal for trains from Brittany, and run by Abbé Caduc, had 15,000 members by 1907.[30] Low levels of religious practice, meanwhile, were not confined to large cities. The largely rural dioceses of the Paris basin were among the most dechristianized in France, especially in the case of men. The proportion of those who took their Easter communion was under 4 per cent of men and 20–21 per cent of women in the dioceses of Soissons (1905) and Châlons-sur-Marne (1911–13), 2.6 per cent of men and 17 per cent of women in the diocese of Sens (1912) and a mere 1.5 per cent of men and 15 per cent of women in the diocese of Chartres in 1909.[31] In the Limousin, the industrial town of Limoges has been described as the 'regional capital of free thought', under the influence of Émile Noël, founder of *Le Libre Penseur du Centre*. Religious processions in the town were banned in 1880, the number of civic burials rose from 6 per cent in 1899 to 28 per cent in 1910, and in 1911 and 1913 Noël's daughters were married civilly in red dresses, red cockades on the breast and crowns of red eglantines. Yet these practices were not confined to Limoges itself. A quarter of rural communes in the Haute-Vienne banned religious processions after 1900 and there were eight or nine free-thought societies in the small towns of the Haute-Vienne and up to fifty in the Creuse, recruiting a counter-priesthood that would preside over civic burials. 'The peasant, long credulous, no longer wants to be duped,' it was reported from Beissat (Creuse) in 1907. 'Honour be to those who cleave to reason instead of the enigmatic revelation of which the men in black wish to guard the secret. Let us shake off the monastic and clerical yoke and thus become free men again.'[32]

More intense religious practice was often stimulated by the rivalry between two different religions. This was certainly the case at the other extreme of the Massif Central from the Limousin, in the Cévennes, where Catholic and Protestant had struggled since the sixteenth century. In 1887 a monolith was raised in memory of the Camisard revolt at Fontfroide, near Florac in the Lozère, the site of a Camisard battle. Addressing a crowd of 4,000 Pastor Vigié of the Paris Theology Faculty paid tribute to 'the heroism of our martyrs' but declared that 'on the very site of fratricidal conflict we wish to lay a stone like a seal of peace to close for ever the cursed era of hatred and civil war.'[33] This area of mixed faith certainly stimulated healthy religious rivalry. A group of cantons bordering the Ardèche, Haute-Loire and Lozère supplied 'a larger contingent to the regular and secular clergy than some French provinces', reported Eugène-Melchior de Vogüé in 1893. 'Large families, almost all from the mountains, send some of their boys and girls to Le Puy, the ecclesiastical capital of the region. These children divide between the noviciates, seminaries and convents which make Le Puy a little mountain Rome. The boys are taught Latin and prepared for the priesthood, while others are sent to the Christian Brothers. The girls take the veil with the Sisters of Charity or join congregations of *béates*, which are so numerous on the soil of the Vélay.'[34] Indeed, despite the wishes of Pastor Vigié, the rivalry could sometimes degenerate into violence. For the elections of 1902 the mixed canton of Saint-Agrève (Ardèche) was moved from one Tournon constituency to another to deliver its Protestant votes to the anticlerical government candidate, who won. This provoked accusations of electoral fraud and fears of 'a St Bartholomew', as the local press indicated:

Protestants of the plateau of Saint-Agrève saw, exhibited in their honour, old instruments of torture used against their ancestors. The tocsin of religious war was rung in several communes. At Rochepaule more than two hundred people armed with guns, axes and knives went to the curé to receive the order to massacre heretics. For two days the gendarmerie of Saint-Agrève had to stay put to safeguard Protestants from a crowd of fanatics drunk with rage and hatred . . . We thought that the wars of religion were over, and that people today shrank in horror from deeds done in the past for the same reason, but it seems that some individuals want to bring back those terrible times and revert to barbarism.[35]

By the end of the nineteenth century rivalry between Catholic and Protestant had almost, although not entirely, been overtaken by the rivalry between Christian and Jew. After the annexation of Alsace-Lorraine by the Reich, Alsatian Jews, like other Alsatians, had to decide whether to keep their property and remain under German rule, or abandon their property and move to France. Some families like the Dreyfuses, as we have seen, had it both ways, Jacques staying in Mulhouse to manage the family textile business, Alfred going to Paris where in 1890 he entered the École de Guerre as an artillery captain. Alfred married Lucie Hadamard, civilly in the *mairie* of the 9th *arrondissement*, then in the synagogue of the rue de la Victoire, where Grand Rabbi Zadoc Kahn officiated.[36] Alfred Dreyfus thus joined the elite of assimilated French Jews commonly called Israélites who often practised their religion in private but partook fully in French culture and made a mark for themselves not only in business but in the professions, civil service and even the army. Among the most successful at the turn of the century were Joseph Reinach, a protégé of Gambetta on *La République Française* and deputy of Digne (Basses-Alpes), Arthur Meyer, editor of the *Gaulois*, who in fact converted to Christianity, the publisher Calmann Lévy, the Natanson brothers of *La Revue Blanche*, the lawyer and critic Léon Blum, who became prime minister of the Popular Front government of 1936, Émile Durkheim, professor of sociology at Bordeaux, and Henri Bergson, professor of philosophy at the Sorbonne. From the 1880s, however, these assimilated Jews were joined by Russian and east European Jews fleeing pogrom and persecution, about half of them settling in Paris before the First World War. There they formed only 17 per cent of the total Jewish population of 50,000 – the Jewish population of France being 80,000 at the turn of the century – but they had a distinctive profile, living in their own

neighbourhoods like the Pletzel in the Marais, Belleville and Montmartre, mostly artisans in the garment business, jewellers and
cabinet-makers, speaking Yiddish, with their own Yiddish newspapers, theatres and clubs.[37] These 'Juifs' were perceived as very
different, even by the assimilated Israélites. Bernard-Lazare, a
Sephardic Jew of Nîmes, the son of a cloth merchant who was
educated in the French system and became a literary critic in Paris,
gave a public lecture in Paris in 1890 on 'Jews and Israelites' in
which he asked, 'What have I in common with those descendants
of Huns?', and attacked the philanthropic Alliance Israélite Universelle
for 'bringing these despicable people into a country that is not theirs
and cannot feed them and assisting their conquest of it'.[38] At this
point nothing separated Bernard-Lazare from an anti-Semite, but the
development of anti-Semitism would encompass not only immigrant
but also assimilated French Jews and cause the likes of Bernard-
Lazare to engage with this new barbarism.

A CATHOLIC OFFENSIVE

French Catholics at the end of the nineteenth century faced a double
challenge. On the one hand they needed to respond to the republican
attack which eliminated teaching congregations and religious instruction from the state and municipal school system. This tended to
provoke a high level of rhetoric against the godless school and masonic
Republic. On the other hand, Catholics had to respond to the alienation of the mass of industrial workers and much of the urban
population from organized religion. This alienation was to some
extent a reaction against the perceived alliance between the Church
and the dominant landed and capitalist class and provoked a searching
in some Catholic circles for a more 'social Catholicism' or even
Christian democracy, rekindling attempts to reconcile the Church to
the modern world begun by Lamennais, Montalembert and Ozanam.
This challenge suggested to some Catholics that their energies might
best be concentrated on social issues rather than on attacking the
Republic and indeed that working within and even with the Republic
to achieve their ends might be the best way forward.

The career of Comte Albert de Mun provides one illustration of this change in Catholic thinking. De Mun was an aristocratic, Jesuit-educated and Legitimist army officer who had served in Algeria, was taken prisoner at Metz by the Prussians in 1870 and as a prisoner at Aachen heard of the work done among the Rhineland working classes by Bishop Ketteler of Mainz. He fought with the Versailles forces under General Gallifet to suppress the Paris Commune but believed that the Commune had been provoked in part by 'the apathy of the bourgeois class', led by Thiers, which wanted only to exploit workers.[39] In 1872 he launched a scheme of Catholic workers' circles to attract a working-class elite away from socialism back into the Catholic fold, founding circles in Paris, Lyon, Marseille, Bordeaux and Toulouse. His vision was of a monarchical and Christian social order. Laying down his commission, he was elected as a royalist deputy for Pontivy in Brittany in 1876 and 1877. He fell in with the Vendean leader Charette who wanted to use 40,000 members of workers' circles to restore the monarchy and de Mun announced at a pilgrimage of workers' circles to Chartres in 1878, 'we are the irreconcilable counter-revolution.'[40] The death of the Comte de Chambord in 1883 was a sharp blow to de Mun, as he had no love for the Orleanists. He lobbied the republican government to legislate to permit associations of employers and workers and to protect the workforce from undue exploitation and began to think in terms of making use of republican legislation on trade unions to further his Catholic goals.[41]

Permission for Catholics to accept the Republic came from Pope Leo XIII who, at loggerheads with the anticlerical government of a united Italy, was looking to another European power to save him from diplomatic isolation. Exploiting the fact that for the French republican government anticlericalism was not for export but the French Church abroad was a pillar of its colonial enterprise, the Papacy primed Cardinal Lavigerie, archbishop of Algiers since 1866, founder of the missionary White Fathers, apostolic administrator of Tunis, where the French established a protectorate in 1881, and from 1884 primate of Africa, to offer a toast to the Republic at a dinner for French naval officers of the Mediterranean fleet in Algiers on 12 November 1890.[42] This opened the way to the Ralliement of

Catholics and royalists such as de Mun to the Republic, although they remained a minority. De Mun was one of an international Catholic lobby including Bishop Ketteler and Cardinal Manning which obtained the encyclical *Rerum novarum* from Pope Leo XIII in 1891, urging the ruling classes to charitable action and governments to social measures in order to combat atheistic socialism, and in parliament he supported the law of 2 November 1892 limiting the working day of women and children to eleven hours. After the Union des Droites burned its fingers supporting Boulanger and the republican leadership was disgraced by the Panama scandal, de Mun and Jacques Piou, deputy for the Haute-Garonne, saw an opportunity to build a new majority of moderate republicans and conservatives who accepted the Republic, displacing the radical republicans and their socialist fellow travellers. In 1893 Piou announced the formation of the Republican Right, 'a Tory party bringing together under the constitution all men of goodwill who are tired of the abuses and excesses of the party in power' and working for 'an open, tolerant and honest republic'.[43] The Republican Right needed moderate republican partners, but these were all too few as the moderate and radical republicans again fought the 1893 elections together under the banner of 'republican concentration'. In 1894, after the new socialist municipality of Saint-Denis banned religious processions and an anarchist bomb was thrown into the Chamber of Deputies, minister of education Eugène Spuller, once a confidant of Gambetta, proposed a 'new spirit' in republican relations with the Church. The announcement by Leo XIII that year that Joan of Arc was 'venerable', the first step on the road to sainthood, encouraged Joseph Fabre, republican senator of the Catholic Aveyron department, to table a bill to establish a national Joan of Arc day in May to commemorate the liberation of Orléans. This initiative was nevertheless unable to reconcile the Catholic version of Joan's story, that she had heard angels, restored France to her divine mission and been burned by the English, with the republican version that Joan was a popular national heroine betrayed by the king and burned by the Church. The bill was passed by the Senate but rejected by the Chamber, confirming the narrowness of the middle ground that still existed between Catholic conservatives unhappy with the Republic and anticlerical republicans still suspicious of Catholic conspiracy.[44]

Much more powerful than social reform as a way to building a bridge between Catholic conservatism and a popular base was anti-Semitism. Édouard Drumont, whose father had been an official at the Hôtel de Ville and early in the Second Empire the boss of Henri Rochefort, was a journalist who was increasingly unhappy with the opportunist Republic and with the influence over it of the Rothschilds and Reinachs. In 1886 he published *La France juive*, which sold over 100,000 copies in its first year alone and made his fortune. Singlehandedly, he transformed anti-Semitism from a socialist ideology that had been peddled by Proudhon and certain Blanquists, which attacked the Jews as usurers and capitalists, into an all-embracing condemnation of Jews for the evils of the modern world. They were said to embody parasitic finance capital, promoting large department stores at the expense of small shopkeepers and lending to peasants at extortionate rates. They were exposed as the power behind the republican political class, as bankers, newspaper magnates, publishers, members of the Académic Française, the theatre, schools and universities, who were increasingly divorced from and shamelessly exploited and deceived real, popular, eternal France. Ever since they crucified Christ they had ceaselessly attacked the Catholic Church, hatching freemasonry to launch the French Revolution. The divorce law of 1884 was the work of one Jew, Naquet, the law of 1880 introducing lay education for young women that of another, Camille Sée. Most of Drumont's ideas were entirely ridiculous – the defeat of 1870 was said to be a conspiracy of German Jews to take over France, Gambetta was a Jew from Genoa, Protestants were half Jewish – but the idea of a Jewish plot behind all contemporary misfortunes was highly seductive. Reviewing *La France juive* the socialist Benoît Malon pointed out that 'the proletariat and petite bourgeoisie suffer from capitalism as a whole, whether it is Jewish or non-Jewish.'[45] And yet *La Croix* argued in 1894 that 'the social question is, fundamentally, the Jewish question.'[46]

Drumont gave focus to anti-Semitism in his slogan 'La France aux Français' and in the arguments which were broadcast even more widely by the paper he founded in 1892, *La Libre Parole*. His ideas were taken up by other movements, not least by Catholics seeking to broaden their appeal and to find new weapons against the Republic. *La Croix*, founded by the Assumptionists in 1880 and edited by Vincent de Paul Bailly, became a daily in 1883 and by 1895 had eighty-six departmental editions, most of them weeklies. It was aimed not at the bourgeoisie but at the lower clergy and a popular clientele; *La Croix du Nord* had a circulation of 23,000 in 1899 and was read among others by textile workers, miners, small tradesmen and peasants. It embraced anti-Semitism in 1889 and the following year proclaimed itself 'the most anti-Jewish paper in France, because it is emblazoned by Christ, mark of horror for the Jew'. Sales rose from 60,000 in 1888 to 160,000 in 1892 and 200,000 in 1899. Echoing *La France juive*, it blamed Jews for the capitalism that was destroying hard-working, traditional France, the liberalism that eased them into positions of power, and the Jewish press and education system that was undermining religion. In order to structure their support in the regions the Assumptionists set up Comités Justice-Égalité after 1896. When Dreyfus was arrested in 1894 it came as no surprise to the Assumptionists: Vincent de Paul Bailly described him as 'the Jewish enemy betraying France'.[47]

Attempts to bridge the gap between Church and people became more common and more committed in the 1890s as socialism increased its hold on the working class and republican politicians showed no sign of relaxing anticlericalism. One such initiative was undertaken by the so-called *abbés démocrates*, local clergy who drew their populist ideas in part from *Rerum novarum*, in part also from the anti-Semitic press. They were democratic in that they wished to free the Catholic Church from its association with the rich and political reaction and inspired by the gospel took the side of ordinary people – peasants, artisans, shopkeepers, industrial workers – recognizing their right to form trade unions and even to strike, and sometimes coming into conflict with their bishops. They were democratic in that they endorsed popular sovereignty and developed a popular press or popular movements or ran in elections against not only republican anticlericals but also Catholic conservatives. Here they were particularly successful in fervently Catholic areas where peasant democracy was strong and landowners weak. The Abbé Lemire, born into a Flemish peasant family and teaching at the seminary at Hazebrouck, was inspired by *Rerum novarum* and decided to 'embrace modern society to bring it back to the Church'.[48] In 1893 he was elected deputy for Hazebrouck against General de Freschville, a conservative ally of Jacques Piou who was also supported by the archbishop of Cambrai. The Abbé Gayraud, a former Dominican, was elected in 1897 at Brest against the royalist Comte Louis de Blois and opposed by the bishop of Quimper.[49] These *abbés* were, however, populist rather than democratic in their espousal of anti-Semitic ideas as a way to cultivate their popular base. Significantly the Abbé Naudet, who founded *La Justice Sociale* in 1893, appealed to those who wanted to 'free our country from freemasonry and Jewry' and set 'Religion, Family and Property at the head of our manifesto'.[50] The Abbé Garnier, of Norman peasant stock and a former papal zouave, worked on *La Croix* until he left it to found *Le Peuple Français* in 1893. In this he argued that the aim of Jews was 'not only to ruin France but to destroy the Church of which France is the strongest support . . . The Jewish question arises because we have chased Jesus Christ from our midst: it is a punishment for our impiety.' Garnier founded a Union Nationale which had committees in thirty-five departments, mainly in Lyon and the south-east, whose task was to rechristianize France by fighting socialism, freemasonry and Jews. It used Drumont's slogan 'La France aux Français' and supported Drumont's Anti-Semitic League in Paris in the elections of 1898; and in 1910 *Le Peuple Français* merged with *La Libre Parole*.[51]

THE DREYFUS AFFAIR AS A RELIGIOUS WAR

The clamour from the end of 1897 that Captain Dreyfus had been the victim of a miscarriage of justice and that his case should be reopened was a direct challenge to those Catholics who believed that France could be saved only by eliminating the influence of Jews, Protestants and freemasons. At the head of those fighting for a judicial review were Dreyfus' brother Mathieu and Joseph Reinach, former associate of Gambetta and deputy of Digne, Bernard-Lazare and Léon Blum, which gave some substance to the Catholic accusation that the campaign was led by a 'Jewish syndicate'. Zola, if not a Jew, was denounced by Barrès as a 'deracinated Venetian'.[52] The involvement of leading Protestants such as the Alsatian Auguste Scheurer-Kestner provoked parallel attacks on Protestants who were considered half-Jews by Drumont – rich, clever, cosmopolitan and therefore traitors to the national interest. Polemics such as Pierre Froment's *Protestant Betrayal* and Ernest Renauld's *Protestant Peril* in 1899 argued that Protestantism had stood for 'continuous revolution' in France since 1789, that Protestants had conquered all the top posts in state and society, that the godless school was an instrument of 'Protestant dechristianization' and that Protestants supported Germany and Great Britain as Protestant powers against Catholic France.[53] Charles Maurras launched an attack against the Monod family of formerly Swiss Protestant pastors and professors, a 'state within a state' who were corrupting French universities with their Germanic science and had thrown themselves into 'the hystero-epilepsy of dreyfusism'.[54] Freemasons too were subjected to attacks, since the whole masonic enterprise was thought to be a Jewish invention, notably by Jules Lemaître of the Ligue de la Patrie Française in his 1899 *Franc-maçonnerie*.

To begin with, the big blows were struck by the antidreyfusard camp. Émile Zola was put on trial for libel and found guilty. Outside the courtroom Jules Guérin's Anti-Semitic League fomented trouble and beat up Joseph Reinach. In the elections of 1898 Reinach failed to get re-elected at Digne whereas Drumont was returned at Algiers and twenty-two anti-Semitic deputies took their place in the Chamber. At a prize-giving at the Dominican college of Arcueil Père Didon defended the army as 'the guardian of law, the spotless knight of justice'.[55] Six weeks later, when Colonel Henry slit his throat in Mont-Valérien prison and Joseph Reinach suggested that he had framed Dreyfus, Drumont's *La Libre Parole* opened a subscription 'For the widow and orphan of Colonel Henry against the Jew Reinach', to pay for her widowhood and for libel proceedings against Reinach.[56] The Dreyfus case was finally reopened in 1899, sitting out of the way in Rennes. Attending it, Maurice Barrès visited the nearby château of Combourg, where Chateaubriand had been raised, and observed, 'that Dreyfus is capable of treachery, I know from his race.'[57] Dreyfus was again found guilty, albeit with 'extenuating circumstances'.

'Writers, scholars, artists, professors! . . . this penetration of "intelligence" filled us with joy,' Léon Blum later wrote of the Affair, which for many historians saw the birth of the French intellectual, committed to a public cause.[58] More powerful at the time, however, was the dreyfusards' sense of being a small group of apostles, persecuted for their commitment to truth and justice, ready if necessary to sacrifice themselves as martyrs to the cause. 'I hope that from my first article', wrote Zola, 'I became one of the band.' 'Whoever suffers for truth and justice', he told the jury at his trial, 'becomes august and sacred.'[59] They saw themselves fighting against both prejudice and lies, called by Anatole Leroy-Beaulieu 'the doctrines of hatred', and against the arbitrary power of the army and for many months the state.[60] They were refighting the battles of the French Revolution, setting up the Ligue des Droits de l'Homme at the time of the Zola trial, but they also identified with Voltaire's battles against the intolerant Catholic Church, the single religion of the absolutist state before 1789. Raoul Allier, professor at the Protestant Theology Faculty of Paris, revisited the Calas affair as a previous miscarriage of justice in a study of 1898.[61] A statue of Chevalier de la Barre, hero of freethinkers, was provocatively erected in front of the basilica of Sacré Coeur, which had been completed in 1891, during a convention of the national congress of freethinking societies in Paris in 1903.[62] Other dreyfusards went back to medieval times to find parallels of religious persecution. Camille Pelletan denounced the Dominican Père Didon as 'truly the heir of those ferocious *dévots* whose order was founded to massacre heretics and in the Middle Ages put the south of France to fire and sword', adding that he had forged 'a holy alliance between habit and plume, between sabre and holy-water sprinkler'.[63] Going back to Biblical times the Protestant Ferdinand Buisson, one of the founders of the Ligue des Droits de l'Homme, condemned 'Phariseeism, which is worse than anti-Semitism . . . the clerical, military, judicial or political Phariseeism that says: there is no Dreyfus Affair'.[64]

Eventually the republican state stepped in to deal with the Catholic and anti-Semitic assault that was deemed to threaten not only Jews, Protestants and freemasons but the Republic itself. The Waldeck-Rousseau ministry was formed under the banner of 'republican defence' and Waldeck had recourse to law to impose restrictions on the Catholic Church. Since the expulsion of the Jesuits in 1880 the Assumptionists were considered the most powerfully organized, influential congregation, the engine behind the antidreyfusard attack. Waldeck denounced '*ligueur* monks and business monks' and the Assumptionist order was dissolved in 1900.[65] The Associations Law of 1 July 1901 was used not only to authorize trade unions but to regularize the position of religious congregations that had been set up during the nineteenth century without formally requesting permission under the Concordat. As a republican from Nantes and former deputy for Rennes, Waldeck-Rousseau understood that Catholic populations like the Bretons would vote republican so long as their religion was safeguarded. He therefore intended to apply the Associations Law discriminately, and to ask the advice of communes in which teaching congregations had schools before giving or refusing permission.

Feeling among anticlericals was nevertheless running high. Masonic lodges and freethinking societies were among those organizations which set up the Radical Party in 1901, and this party emerged as the dominant force in the 1902 elections. Waldeck-Rousseau was obliged to resign and Émile Combes, who had been *rapporteur* of the Associations Law in the Senate, was invited to form a government. Combes decided to apply the law in a completely different way, rejecting requests for authorization from congregations as a whole, female congregations included, without regard to how popular they were in individual towns and villages. While teaching brothers ran only a minority of boys' schools and enjoyed little popularity, *les bonnes soeurs* as they were known ran most girls' schools and provided a range of services including nursing, crèches and nurseries, and were very popular in many areas. The people of Finistère, for example, set great store by the Filles du Saint-Esprit, often local girls who would otherwise have migrated as maids to Paris, who instead provided childcare for women working in the sardine factories and free medical care in a region where doctors were scarce. Demonstrations were organized and the local Radical deputy Georges Le Bail, whose windows were broken, intervened on their behalf, but to no avail, and he almost lost his seat in the 1906 election.[66]

In Catholic circles Combes was regarded as a Jacobin, sectarian and political freemason. He regarded himself as a 'spiritualist *philosophe*' who thought that all congregations, 'under a veil of piety and charity . . . cultivate a hatred of modern society, its institutions and its laws'.[67] As a former teacher in the Assumptionist College of Nîmes he clearly had views on the subject and one of his models was Ernest Renan, another man of religion turned freethinker, a statue to whom he unveiled in 1903 in Renan's home town of Tréguier in Brittany. Combes himself was from the southwest, and Waldeck's former *chef de cabinet*, Joseph Paul-Boncour, saw him as a heretic taking revenge on the Catholic Church for the crusades against the Albigensians.[68]

Combes not only closed down the teaching congregations, he also terminated diplomatic relations with the Vatican in 1904 after Pope Pius X protested against the state visit of President Loubet to Italy. He had plans to revise the Concordat in ways that would have tightened state control over the Church but he fell from power before he could impose them. The parliamentary commission charged with redefining Church–state relations was chaired by a Protestant, Ferdinand Buisson, and included Paul Grunebaum-Ballin, the Jewish *chef de cabinet* of Aristide Briand who, as secretary of the commission and representative of the new political generation born around 1860, wished to stake out a reputation as the architect of religious peace. The commission proposed to separate Church and state, or rather Churches and state, since the Protestant Church was also regulated under the Concordat and would recover its freedom, and this became law on 9 December 1905. Separation meant that clergy would no longer be paid by the state, but in return the state would no longer appoint bishops or control their relations with Rome, and bishops would be allowed to have their own assembly, which had not been permitted under the Concordat. The main stumbling block was the ownership of churches, seminaries and vicarages which, under the Concordat, were publicly owned. The law provided for lay associations which would take possession of church property, and this solution was initially welcomed by French bishops. However, visitations by public authorities to undertake inventories of the furniture and sacred vessels held in churches was regarded in some communities as a prelude to confiscation, and in Catholic areas such as the west of France, Massif Central, Brittany and Flanders the faithful barricaded themselves into churches to stop inventories taking place. Moreover the pope regarded the lay associations set up to manage church property as an attack on the hierarchy and, just as his predecessor condemned the Civil Constitution of the Clergy in 1790, so he rejected the Separation in 1906. Deadlock ensued until in 1907 the government ruled that the clergy could use churches albeit 'without legal title', a makeshift situation that persisted until the pope authorized diocesan associations in 1924.[69]

RELIGIOUS REVIVAL AFTER THE SEPARATION

The deputies who voted the Separation law were returned *en masse* in May 1906. Catholics were unable to make political capital out of the dissolution of the teaching congregations or the Separation of Church and state. Albert de Mun claimed that the mantle of liberalism now fell on those who wanted to 'defend religion persecuted by sectarians and the country threatened by cosmopolitans', but the Action Libérale Party he set up won only seventy-eight seats in the 1902 Chamber elections and, rechristened the Action Libérale Populaire, sixty-four in the elections of 1906.[70] There was a great exodus of teaching brothers and especially nuns from France, to countries such as Belgium or Canada where they would be welcome. Catholic schools could survive only if former brothers or nuns discarded the habit and acquired 'letters of secularization' from their superior, and moved to a different school. Increasingly Catholic schools fell back on curates or a lay staff, usually women, for whom financial prospects were precarious indeed. While state schools were free, school fees had to be charged in Catholic schools but covered only a fraction of the cost. In order to populate Catholic schools at the expense of state schools, bishops launched a new offensive against 'godless schools' in 1909, targeting not manuals of moral and civic education, as in 1882, but history textbooks placed on the Index which praised the Reformation and Revolution and denigrated France as the eldest daughter of the Church. This had some success in heavily practising areas such as the Côtes-du-Nord, where the Catholic school population rose by 29 per cent in 1908–12.[71] Young priests threw their energies into the foundation of youth clubs or *patronages* aimed at those who had just left school, providing hobbies, amateur dramatics, gymnastics and football alongside religious education.[72] In 1908 a congress of young women's clubs under diocesan supervision which federated in 1904 sang 'Despite the hell, we wish that France / Returns by thee Jesus, to thy law,' and the beatification of Joan of Arc in 1909 gave a great boost to young female religiosity.[73] Pilgrimages to Lourdes reached a peak in 1908, on the fiftieth anniversary of Bernadette's visions, with over a million pilgrims travelling there.[74] All these efforts had little effect, however, on the anticlerical majority in parliament. Just before the third elections after the Separation the archbishop of Rennes regretted that 'those who are Christians in their private life contradict themselves lamentably in public life. They attend church, claim to be good parishioners, and would not willingly defy divine teaching. Yet when the elections come they lose all idea of things Catholic and sometimes leave mass to vote for the worst enemies of religion.'[75]

One effect of the Separation was to involve the laity much more closely in the work of the Church, and here youth movements were particularly important. Albert de Mun had set up the Association Catholique de la Jeunesse Française (ACJF) in 1886, to group former college students of the Jesuits and other expelled congregations; it was somewhat conservative, and closely supervised by bishops. Rather different was the Sillon, founded in the wake of the Dreyfus Affair by Marc Sangnier, a graduate of the Catholic Collège Stanislas in Paris and the École Polytechnique. Rather than constantly sniping at the Republic and seeking to inoculate the converted against its evil influence, he accepted that republican democracy was here to stay but argued that the Republic did not have to be sectarian, that 'democracy has a thirst for Christianity.'[76] In March 1905 he engaged in debate with the Marxist Jules Guesde at Roubaix, arguing that the Church was not the capitalists' gendarme and that the working classes had to be emancipated spiritually as well as economically.[77] His enemies on the right were even more intractable. At Easter 1905 challenges passed between the ACJF congress meeting in Quimper and the Sillon congress meeting in Saint-Brieuc. Although the Sillon had 640 groups and 10,000 militants Sangnier accused the ACJF of using the hierarchy to seek to monopolize Catholic youth.[78] In 1906 Charles Maurras accused him of being a 'Christian anarchist' and in 1910 Pope Pius condemned the Sillon.[79] The comment was made at the time that like Lamennais he had gone too far from the Church, and like Lamennais had been condemned.[80]

Although progressive Catholics found it difficult to take the Church with them, much less stood in the way of young people who had been brought up in the lay republican system converting on an individual basis. The Separation of Church and state dissipated the shadow of the state Church with pretensions to impose some uniformity of belief in France, while the policy of Combes and his ilk suggested that persecution was now the style of the Republic. The period before the war indeed saw the conversion of a number of high-profile, educated young people who were advised by influential Catholic writers.[81] The writer Léon Bloy suffered a spiritual crisis after his father's death in 1877 and began to visit La Salette, becoming obsessed with the Virgin crowned with thorns and weeping for humanity. He and his family lived a life of pious poverty on Montmartre, values which he exalted in *La Femme pauvre* (1897). He had a huge influence on a group of Sorbonne students who came from prominent republican families. These included Jacques Maritain, grandson of Jules Favre, Ernest Psichari, grandson of Ernest Renan, who both frequented the Bellais bookshop of Charles Péguy in the Latin Quarter, and together with Péguy attended the lectures of Henri Bergson, which celebrated intuition over analytical reason, at the Collège de France. In 1904 Maritain married Raïssa, a Jewish girl whose family had fled the pogroms in Russia, who read *La Femme pauvre* and made contact with Bloy. Two years later, under the guidance of Bloy, who became their godfather, Jacques and Raïssa Maritain were baptized, had their marriage blessed, and went on pilgrimage to La Salette.[82] Ernest Psichari, rejected by Maritain's sister Jeanne and fearing that his grades would not be good enough for the academic career to which his family had destined him, had a breakdown in 1903. He became a soldier, serving in Africa, and converted under the guidance of Maritain in 1913, a model for the new generation of muscular Christian youth celebrated by another contemporary, Henri Massis, who co-wrote *Les Jeunes Gens d'aujourd'hui* under the pen-name Agathon.[83]

More difficult was the trajectory of Charles Péguy, who sought to reconcile Catholicism with his dreyfusard and even socialist roots but was not fully accepted by Catholic converts. Péguy broke with the left in 1903 when he saw socialists like Jaurès using the dreyfusard cause, to which he had been devoted, for purely political reasons, to legitimate the Bloc des Gauches. He denounced the radical republicans for seeking to impose an irreligous state philosophy. In 1908 he announced, 'I have recovered my faith, I am Catholic,' and in 1910 published *La Mystère de la charité de Jeanne d'Arc*.[84] For this he was claimed for the Catholic right by a chorus of Barrès, Maurras and Drumont, who regarded this as a political coup, and he was forced to reply in *Notre Jeunesse* that while antidreyfusards like them had sought only the temporal salvation of France, dreyfusards like him had sought its eternal salvation, refusing to leave it in a state of mortal sin.[85] Catholics like Maritain, whom Péguy had long considered a younger brother, were not so convinced. Maritain argued that Péguy's Joan was too wilful, too ambitious, instead of being the passive vessel of God's grace, and was concerned that Péguy refused to have his marriage solemnized or his children baptized. 'You still have far to go,' Maritain told him, 'in order to become a faithful Christian.'[86] The division between anticlerical republicans and Catholics remained clear, and would require another factor to bridge it: patriotism.

13

Feminism and its Frustrations

MARRIAGE IN QUESTION

In 1883 a new play, *Around Marriage*, opened in Paris. The heroine, Paulette d'Hautretan, aged twenty, is engaged to marry a thirty-six-year-old man, Monsieur d'Alaly. In the smoking room he tells his friends, 'I will mould her as I wish and assert an influence over her from the beginning that I shall keep.' Her mother warns Paulette that 'from tomorrow, you will have to obey him . . . Your husband will have every right over you . . . He could ask anything of you.' But in response to the question suggested by this, 'Would you like to have children, Paulette?', Paulette blithely replies, 'Not right away. You see, mother, I will tell you frankly, I am getting married to have fun.'[1]

Paulette is at once naive and capricious, inclined less to flout convention than to see it as irrelevant to her. On honeymoon, she asks her husband to change his name – 'Joseph is a ridiculous name' – and tells him after their wedding night, 'If I thought it was going to be worse, I also thought it would be more fun.' When her husband reprimands her for reading *Things of Love* she ripostes, 'I didn't get married to read Walter Scott,' and she antagonizes him by using slang, playing tennis, wearing swimming costumes that show off her legs, and going riding in male attire, all in the company of male admirers. 'You are a terrible flirt [*coquette*],' he complains, to which she replies,

But it's unconscious – unconscious!! . . . God knows, they did everything to make me an accomplished little lady, eyes cast down, sweet, submissive, banal and insignificant, with simple desires and an imperious need to meet a guide (or several) in life, absolutely unable to do anything thoughtless.

But it didn't work, as you see, and I don't think that you will succeed where others failed.[2]

At the end of the play Paulette decides to leave her husband and goes to find a lawyer who, taking her for a *cocotte*, or lady of easy virtue, makes a pass at her which, incredulous, she rejects. The sequel, *Around Divorce*, was staged in 1886, after divorce had become possible again in 1884. Paulette reads up on it herself in law books, conjures up a story of her husband's shaking her arm at a ball in order to qualify for one of the conditions of divorce – brutality – and goes through with a theatrical trial. The life of a divorced woman, she finds, however, is not all fun. She is besieged by her former male companions who want to become her lovers but who now just annoy her, and she becomes jealous of her former husband flirting with other women. In the end she confesses, 'perhaps I had happiness to hand and passed it by,' and goes back to him.[3]

Reviewing *Around Divorce*, Jules Lemaître welcomed Paulette as 'the most modern feminine type', feminine in her prettiness, nervousness and illogicality, masculine in her boyish allure, dress and lack of sentimentality. She is irreverent, even 'a revolutionary' in her almost unconsidered defiance of 'certain proprieties and certain prejudices which are still powerful' in her society, but she never falls from grace in a way that would exclude her from it. She is a *coquette* without ever being a *cocotte*. 'This immoral little creature', concluded Lemaître, 'remains virtuous.'[4]

Paulette was the creation of Gabrielle de Riqueti de Mirabeau, Comtesse de Martel de Janville, 'the last of the Mirabeaus', who wrote under the punchier pen-name Gyp. Like her heroine she too was the product of a highly conventional upbringing whose codes she dared to subvert. Her parents separated the year after she was born and she scarcely knew her father, Arundel-Joseph de Riqueti de Mirabeau, great-nephew of the orator Mirabeau, who died fighting in the Papal zouaves against Italian unification at Castelfidardo in 1860. She was brought up in Nancy by her mother, Marie Le Harivel de Gonneville, and by her grandfather, a colonel who had been a counter-revolutionary, then served in the imperial and royal armies till 1830, who interested Gabrielle in toy soldiers and riding. She married a Norman noble, Roger de Martel de

Janville, at the age of twenty, in 1869, but disgraced herself by fraternizing with the Prussians both in Normandy and in Nancy. She came to Paris in 1879, living in the rich suburb of Neuilly, where she began to make a career as a writer, her first books being serialized in *La Vie Parisienne* and published by Calmann-Lévy. Her pen-name, Gyp, 'is "gyno" gone wrong', one historian has suggested, combining both feminine and masculine elements. Her true identity was not revealed until *Around Marriage* was staged, after which, she wrote, 'the entire Faubourg [Saint-Germain] side of the family shunned me.'[5]

The mixed reception encountered by Paulette suggests that a 'modern' woman was emerging but that society was not yet fully ready to embrace her. Marriages were still family alliances centred on property for which under the Civil Code parental consent was needed, even if the intended were over twenty-one. This was relaxed in 1896 by a law sponsored by Abbé Lemire, which required the consent of one parent only, and parental consent for non-minors was no longer required after 1907. Love was much more a factor in marriage, although there was still great pressure at all levels of society to marry within one's social class, and 'expectations' were influential. Thus in 1881 a textile worker of Crémieux (Loire) preferred to abort her pregnancy rather than marry an agricultural labourer 'for fear of a *mésalliance* angering the bachelor uncles from whom we were hoping to inherit'.[6]

Virginity was a precondition for marriage, because a man had to be quite sure his inheritance was going to his own blood, and young women were brought up to be ignorant of sexual matters before they married.[7] The catastrophe of premarital sex was highlighted by Paul Bourget's novel of 1883, *Irreparable*, in which the rich and beautiful Noémie de Hurtrel, who has just come out into society, is raped by a playboy. This renders her unfit to marry the man of her dreams, Sir Richard Wadham. She agrees to marry a man who is 'perfectly educated and perfectly insignificant', but shoots herself immediately after the wedding.[8] Twenty-five years later Léon Blum, who had made a mark for himself during the Dreyfus Affair, wrote a treatise *On Marriage*, in which he argued that the obligation on women to marry, as virgins, men who had been allowed to experiment sexually and had arrived at the 'monogamous period' of their lives was at the root of marital unhappiness and infidelity. Women were now marrying at the age of twenty-five rather than eighteen or twenty, as at the beginning of the nineteenth century, but he advised that they should marry at thirty, after a period of sexual experimentation, and that the double standard should cease.[9] This view did not, naturally, command universal approval, and Blum conceded that his argument was aimed only at the rich or middle class. There is indeed evidence of a growth in premarital sex, particularly in the large cities, in northern France, and among the working class.[10] The risk, however, was always that pregnancy would lead to the relationship being broken off, leaving the girl abandoned and under pressure to abort, kill or abandon the child. Prospects were, it is true, becoming gradually easier for women in this condition: after 1900 midwives accused of abortion were treated more leniently by the courts, half the women brought to trial for infanticide were acquitted, and shelters for poor and pregnant women or single mothers were set up in Paris by the Catholic Church (1866) and the municipal council (1886).[11]

Even within marriage, there were plenty of taboos against sexual pleasure, whether from the Church, from the medical profession or from the fear of unwanted pregnancy. Undressing before one's partner was rare – when in Zola's novel *Nana* the Comte de Muffat sees Nana in her dressing room Zola comments that 'He, who had never even seen the countess put on her suspenders, was observing the intimate details of a woman's toilette' – and kissing on the mouth did not become accepted until the 'American kiss' became fashionable between the wars.[12] Yet in some ways marriage was becoming eroticized. The Church fought a long war against what it called 'conjugal fraud', by which it meant contraception, since it admitted sex only in the service of procreation. The most common form of contraception, *coitus interruptus*, was denounced by a former naval doctor, J.-P. Dartigues, who argued in his 1887 *Experimental Love or the Causes of Female Adultery* that withdrawal left the woman dissatisfied and could drive her to nymphomania and infidelity. 'The husband', he warned, 'must never forget that his wife has just as much right as he to the voluptuous sensations of love, and that it is in this way that the chastity of the home is preserved.'[13] For Dartigues the guarantee of a happy marriage was the female orgasm. Contraception was promoted on a much wider front, although not only in the interest of sexual pleasure. The League for Human Regeneration founded by the socialist teacher Paul Robin in 1896 thought birth control the solution to working-class misery, although other socialist leaders argued that the workers needed to breed fighters for the future proletarian revolution. In 1898 the demographer Arsène Dumont registered the spread of birth control among the middle classes, although he linked it to the desire for social mobility – the need for ambitious families to travel light.[14]

The orthodoxy of the virginal bride and chaste wife was in part a defence against female sexuality, which was feared as a threat to marriage and the family. This was well illustrated in 1872 by the Dubourg affair. Convent-educated Denise MacLeod, aged nineteen, though in love with M. de Précorbin, a clerk at the Prefecture of the Seine, was obliged for family reasons to marry Arthur Dubourg, twenty-nine, whose father had a château in Normandy. Miserable and suicidal, she was briefly confined to a mental hospital. She then tried to instigate separation proceedings, which Dubourg resisted. She resumed her relationship with Précorbin until in April 1872 Dubourg followed her to the flat where they met and attacked her with a sword-cane and dagger; she died three days later. The court rejected the accusation of premeditated murder and Dubourg was sentenced to five years in prison, but there was much public feeling in favour of his acquittal. Alexandre Dumas *fils* sold 50,000 copies of a tract entitled *The Man-Woman*, in which he played on fears of the bestiality lying under the skin of women, as evidenced by the *pétroleuses* of the Paris Commune and the tribe of adulteresses.

Every day in the street we pass redskins tinted pink, negresses with plump, white hands, real cannibals who, unable to eat man raw, prepare to gnaw him alive, as civilized women should, with marriage or pleasure sauce, plates, serviettes, forks, mouth-washes, sacraments and legal protection.

If the law would not protect a man from his wife, Dumas concluded, he had only one piece of advice for husbands: 'Kill her.'[15]

This fear of female sexuality was exploited by Zola in his *Nana* of 1880, in which the prostitute–actress, set up as a courtesan by a general's son and practising Catholic the Comte de Muffat, takes her revenge on him and Paris high society, devouring inheritances, destroying reputations and spreading syphilis. Alongside the main plot, however, is the story of the count's straitlaced wife Sabine. She was seventeen when he married her nineteen years previously, but was rejuvenated by an affair she had with one of the young bloods, Fauchery, before, 'in a supreme fit of madness, she ran off with a manager of a great department store, a scandal which soon gripped Paris'.[16] In the world of prostitution, in fact, the bog-standard brothel gave way to *maisons de débauche* offering all sorts of attractions to a male clientele in search of ever more refined erotic pleasures. Meanwhile inadequately kept married women made themselves available, alongside widows, divorcees, out-of-work actresses and shop assistants, in *maisons de rendez-vous*. Very popular after 1890, these were set up like bourgeois apartments, conveniently close to the department stores, and the hostesses were permitted to choose their own clients. When the Bazar de la Charité burned down in 1897 many husbands were delighted and yet bemused to see their wives, who they thought had been shopping there, return from the dead.[17]

In fact only 4 per cent of women who came before the courts as adulteresses were bourgeois ladies, while a quarter of male adulterers were bourgeois. This did not prevent a veritable obsession at the turn of the century with the question of female adultery.[18] In his 1891 *Physiology of Modern Love* Paul Bourget, reworking Balzac, suggested that 'out of every hundred virtuous women there are only five or six honest ones.' He ventured a typology of three basic types of adulteress: first, women of 'temperament', who behaved with a masculine sensuality in love; second, women of the heart, for whom romantic love alone counted; and lastly, women of the head, the 'true modern mistress'. These were driven by curiosity, by the desire to play a role, as in a novel, by vanity and social-climbing, by rivalry and the need for social domination.[19] In novels and the theatre there appeared a new character, *la déserteuse*, the married woman who abandons the family home. *Maman Colibri*, in Henri Bataille's play first staged at the Vaudeville in 1904, deals with the boredom of Irène, long ago subjected to the 'Zulu ceremony' of an arranged marriage with a Belgian industrialist, the Baron de Rysbergue, and falling at the age of forty for a friend of her son Richard, who talks to her about Balzac. 'I have accomplished my duty to you,' she tells her son, 'my task as a mother is finished . . . life is so short. I am a spring late.' Although de Rysbergue had had a few affairs of his own, he declares, with a nod to Dumas, 'I am not the kind of husband who kills his wife,' and simply says, 'be gone, then!' She goes with her lover to Algiers and the Côte d'Azur, until her money runs out. Then she wishes to come home but her husband will not have her, confessing that his ideas are simply not modern enough. 'Our religious past, prejudices, old and much loved customs cannot erase from our memory this conception of the pure and chaste wife, of the one love, faithful to the family home.'[20]

Unhappy marriage might lead to adultery, but with or without adultery an exit from marriage was once again provided by the reintroduction of divorce in 1884. Divorce was one of the main demands of the new wave of bourgeois feminism led by a generation born around 1830, contemporary with the founders of the Third Republic, notably Maria Desraimes and her political partner Léon Richer. The divorce bill was sponsored by Alfred Naquet, a radical republican of Jewish origin, who separated from his wife when she insisted on baptizing their son. While the conservative republican senator Jules Simon argued that indissoluble marriage protected women from abandonment, Naquet replied that there were nearly 3,000 legal separations a year, of partners who could not remarry, and who therefore multiplied the number of illegitimate children. The law of 19 July 1884 was a compromise measure: it stopped short of divorce by mutual consent, which had been possible between 1792 and 1804, and reverted to the regime of 1804, making divorce available on the grounds of adultery, violence or criminal conviction. The marriage of adulterous couples was finally legalized in 1904, while divorce after three years' separation at the request of one of the partners became legal in 1907.[21]

The divorce rate more than tripled from 3,880 per year in 1885–8, representing 52 in every 100,000 couples, to 13,655 per year in 1909–13, representing 164 in every 100,000 couples.[22] Women initiated 63 per cent of divorce suits in 1886–95, and 86 per cent of separation proceedings. In 1897 women sued on the grounds of their husband's adultery in 683 cases, while husbands divorced their wives for adultery in 1,344. Women tended to cite brutality, which provided grounds for 8,014 or 77 per cent of divorces in that year. About 30 per cent of divorced women remarried, as against 35 per cent of men, but the author of a 1905 law thesis on this subject concluded very positively that 'divorce benefits women.'[23]

Women were now empowered to get rid of their adulterous husbands, as the aristocratic playboy Boni de Castellane found when he married America's richest heiress Anna Gould in 1895 and assumed that he could continue his affairs. To Boni's dismay he lost his wife, children and fortune in 1906 while she married his bachelor cousin and became a princess.[24] On the other hand the possibility of divorce and remarriage did not always get the better of social conventions. Henriette Rainouard, who divorced her theatre-critic husband and married the leading Radical politician Joseph Caillaux in 1911, found that revelations about her affair with Caillaux before their marriage could threaten not only his career but her own social standing. She feared that being 'dishonoured' as an adulteress would result in her father cutting off her inheritance, the impossibility of her marrying off her nineteen-year-old daughter by her first marriage, and in her exclusion from Paris society.[25] Although she behaved in a virile way by shooting dead the editor of *Le Figaro*, which was about to publish these revelations, her defence in July 1914 was based on the old prejudice of the irrationality of women, now dressed up in the language of the unconscious. 'The case of Madame Caillaux', explained her lawyer, Maître Labori, who had defended Dreyfus, 'is a typical case of subconscious impulse, together with a complete splitting of the personality as a result of an intense and continuous emotional state during which the patient has neither rational control of her acts nor a clear notion of their implications and consequences.'[26] Henriette was duly acquitted, and her marriage survived, but at the price of a murder portrayed as the act of a hysterical woman.

THE GENDERING OF WORK

The prospects of women were shaped, of course, not only by questions of love and marriage, but by educational possibilities and the labour market. The presence of women in the workforce became even more marked as the century progressed – 25 per cent of women were in paid work in 1866, but 39 per cent in 1911. Marriage was not a bar to paid employment: on the contrary, 40 per cent of married women were in work in 1866, but 49 per cent in 1911.[27] This was to a large extent a response to global economic competition which sharpened incentives to reduce costs by mechanization, employing less skilled labour and paying lower wages to a workforce that was 'docile' and not organized into unions. In all these respects women fitted the bill as the ideal worker. This 'feminization of labour' did not escape the notice of contemporaries, whether social reformers or labour leaders.[28] It threatened traditional models of motherhood at precisely the time when the demographic deficit, in comparison to countries like Germany, increased anxieties about women producing too much, and reproducing not enough.[29] Social reformers brought forward legislation in order to increase protection for women in work. Ironically, however, the main effect was simply to move working women out of the factory or workshop back into the home, beyond the reach of factory inspectors, where they were simply exploited more.

Female industrial workers remained confined to labour ghettos where the conditions of work and pay were poorest. After a law of 1874 banned women and girls from working underground in mines, the proportion of women employed in mining fell from 9 per cent in 1866 to 2 per cent in 1911, while at the same time the proportion of women employed in textiles rose from 45 to 56 per cent, in clothing from 78 to 89 per cent, in the food industry from 11 to 19 per cent and in agriculture from 26 to 38 per cent.[30] Working women who married miners or metalworkers in towns like Saint-Étienne were fairly comfortable, as the heavy work was left to the man, while they ran a quarter of the shops in the quartier du Soleil around 1900 – not as butchers or bakers, which were family affairs, but as café-owners, grocers and haberdashers, enterprises which women managed on their own.[31] At Roubaix, by contrast, two wages from the textile industry were required to provide the 22–24 francs a week required to sustain a family of five in the 1870s, and 83 per cent of female textile workers were married to semi-skilled workers or labourers.[32] Within the textile and clothing industries work was sharply gendered. Thus at Troyes, the centre of the hosiery industry, *bonnetiers* were skilled male stocking-knitters, the aristocrats of the trade, while *bonnetières* were employed in the workshop doing tasks to service them, such as bobbin-winding, hooking the fabric on to the machines or repairing flawed goods; their reputations gained nothing from association with men in the workplace.[33]

The career of one female worker, Jeanne Bouvier, highlights the transitory, insecure and exploited nature of female labour at the end of the nineteenth century. Her father worked as a navvy on the Paris–Lyon–Marseille railway until he inherited a small farm in the Drôme, but his vines were ruined by the phylloxera epidemic and the family moved to the outskirts of Lyon. With her father unemployed, Jeanne went to work after her first communion in 1876 at the age of eleven in a silk-mill, doing a thirteen-hour day for 50 centimes (although under a labour law of 1842 children under twelve could work no more than eight hours). The father then left the family, which returned to the Drôme: Jeanne worked in the fields in the summer and in a silk-mill in the winter, boarding in a dormitory with other country girls from Sunday night to Saturday night, bringing her own food and eventually being paid 1.25 francs a day. In 1879 her mother found work in Paris with a shaving-brush manufacturer and brought Jeanne with her; in one year Jeanne was employed in turn as a servant by a brush merchant, a paint merchant, a grain merchant, an ironmonger and a doctor who was married to one of Proudhon's daughters. Though her mother soon returned home and Jeanne dreamed of returning to the country to raise hens and rabbits, she stayed in Paris and went into the clothing industry. The pay was so poor that she knew one girl who committed suicide at twenty-two and others who went on to the street as prostitutes. Jeanne began as a hatmaker, paid 45 francs in a good week but 15 out of season, before the firm went broke, then for a corset-maker earning 2 francs a day, then as a *midinette* or dressmaker in the Opéra district, starting at 2.5 francs a day but later 5 francs a day, supplemented with work at home for personal clients.[34]

Bouvier hoped that the labour law of 1892, which limited the working day of women to eleven hours, would bring some relief. However the law exempted 'family workshops', and in the face of global competition this resulted in a massive increase in women working as sweated labour. This was work at home for a subcontractor who could respond quickly to changing demands without having to worry about overheads. True, the expansion of homework made it easier for women to combine earning a living and raising a family, but it was under the most atrocious of conditions. Making artificial flowers was one of the 'articles de Paris' that traditionally employed a female labour aristocracy, but competition from the German and American markets forced prices down and 38 per cent of women in this sector were working at home for subcontractors by 1906.[35] The clothing industry was increasingly subjected to homework, facilitated by the arrival of the sewing machine. In the Paris suburbs of Belleville and Ménilmontant women specialized in shirt-making, while wives of shop-assistants, clerks and *petits fonctionnaires* earned extra family income by making lingerie at home.[36] In the west of France, women might earn between 2.5 and 4.5 francs a day in the shoe factories of Fougères, but the Cholet region confronted international competition by developing a niche market in slippers, employing women at home for 1.50 or 1.75 francs a day.[37]

Since labour legislation served only to drive exploitation underground, women had to take matters into their own hands. Although one attraction of female labour was its docility, women workers did occasionally go on strike. The sugar-workers of Paris struck in 1892, the corset-makers of Limoges struck for 108 days in 1895, the sardine-workers of Douarnenez, who were paid 1.5 francs for every thousand sardines cleaned and made a typical wage of 22 centimes an hour, struck in 1905, and a quarter of the striking shoeworkers at Fougères in 1907 were women.[38] Jeanne Bouvier went to the Paris Bourse du Travail to join the union of dressmakers in 1897, and recalled that 'at that time there were always debates about revolution, the general strike, expropriation, the abolition of capitalism and wage-labour. I didn't really understand what it meant, but to appear a good trade unionist I applauded as vigorously and with as much conviction as those around me.'[39] Few women actually joined trade unions, only 101,000 in 1911, in comparison to 1,029,000 men.[40] In part this was because they put family before work and because they were less militant. They also faced great opposition on the part of male workers. Though working women made an indispensable contribution to the family budget, male trade unionists feared that women, working for lower wages, threatened not only their jobs but also their traditional role as breadwinners. 'Women are beginning to invade the workshops,' warned a delegate at the 1892 metalworkers' congress. 'If this continues, the heads of the family will be doing the cooking while the wife and children go out to work.'[41] These fears were not totally without foundation. The introduction of linotype in 1895 led to an increase in the number of female typesetters, some of whom were used to break a print-workers' strike at Nancy in 1901. At the printworkers' congress in 1910 the general secretary, Auguste Keufer, took the Proudhonist view that 'men's wages must be sufficient for women to remain in the private realm and fulfil their natural function of mother and family educator.'[42] Thus, when the printworkers Emma and Louis Couriau came to Lyon in 1912 and asked to join the printworkers' union, Emma was refused entry and her husband, who had already joined, was expelled. Although Emma's cause was supported by the South-East Feminist Federation, Parisian feminists and a number of revolutionary syndicalists, the union would not budge.[43] The labour movement rallied to spokesmen of both the bourgeoisie and the Catholic Church who opposed female labour in theory, if not in practice.

One way out of the trap of low-level employment in agriculture, industry or domestic service was to pursue an education, and the education of women took important steps forward at the end of the nineteenth century. Overall, the proportion of French departments which educated all girls aged six to thirteen rose from 58 per cent in 1872 to 88 per cent in 1881, when elementary education for that age cohort became compulsory and free, and to 99 per cent in 1906. Whereas for Jeanne Bouvier the end of schooling was signalled by first communion, increasingly it was marked by taking the *certificat d'études*. Only 25 per cent of girls took this exam in 1876, but 45 per cent did so by 1907, and in that period their pass rate increased from 70 to 85 per cent. Beyond that was the option of taking the *brevet*, which was awarded to 5,769 girls in 1876 and 18,194 in 1882.[44] Such a qualification opened up the possibility of white-collar work for women which was more secure and respectable if not paid much more. In commerce and banking women had 25 per cent of the jobs in 1866 but 39 per cent of them in 1906, as the male clerk was replaced by the female typist or secretary.[45] Even more attractive was the possibility of employment as *dames employées*, first in the telegraph service after 1877, away from the public, then after 1892 in the post office. This provoked a certain amount of resistance from male clerks, and debate about whether ladies should be working face to face with the public. Successful candidates were well qualified. As many as half of them had the *brevet*, perhaps even ten years' experience as assistants to rural postmistresses or telegraphers, but they were paid a mere 800 francs per year, raised to 1,000 francs in 1892. In the first wave 86 per cent of the employees were unmarried, but many, particularly in Paris, married simply in order to pool two salaries.[46]

The most obvious career opened by the *brevet* was elementary school teaching, which offered great opportunities for young lay women, as nuns were excluded after 1882 first from publicly maintained schools, then from private ones too. Écoles Normales or teacher-training colleges for *institutrices*, present in only major cities before then, were set up in every department under a law of 1879. The number of lay *institutrices* increased from 22,000, or 34 per cent of the elementary teaching body, in 1872, to 78,000, or 94 per cent, in 1906.[47] A few teachers had brilliant careers. Pauline Kergomard, the daughter of a primary school inspector in Bordeaux, was brought up by her uncle, Jacques Reclus, a Protestant pastor, two of whose sons were exiled after Louis-Napoleon's coup d'état of 1851. She graduated from the École Normale d'Institutrices of Bordeaux, went to Paris in 1861, moved in republican, liberal Protestant and feminist circles, married one of Garibaldi's Thousand volunteers who had liberated Sicily and

Naples, and was appointed chief inspector of nursery schools in 1879, a post she held until 1917, revolutionizing nursery education in France. In general, however, the career of *institutrice* was thankless and not well paid. They received 700–900 francs a year in 1875, rising to 1,200–2,000 francs in 1905, but significantly less than an *instituteur* and between 3 and 5 francs a day when a milliner might earn between 5 and 20 francs a day. Even more difficult was life in an isolated village, especially where nuns had formerly run the village school. Lay teachers might see the priest refuse to take their pupils for first communion, village children would jeer 'la laïque' or 'la communale' at them, or the locals would refuse them wood or groceries. Sometimes parents petitioned the authorities, alleging that the teacher called their children dirty, or thieves, or bastards, while allegations were made that the teacher was the mistress of the postman or living with a younger man. At worst, the lay teacher was considered a witch. 'Her gifts are wickedness and ambition,' complained parents in Normandy in 1881. 'She is evil towards anyone who does not think like her.'[48] In 1897 a public debate was triggered after a review of Léon Frapié's *Provincial Schoolteacher*, which highlighted the sufferings of Louise Chardon, sent as an *institutrice* to a village in Berry where the local population, deprived of their *bonnes soeurs*, took their revenge on her. Now teachers wrote in with their tales of woe. One complained that the mayor, while drunk, had tried to kiss her and when she resisted suggested that she was a lesbian.[49]

Career possibilities were further extended by the development of state secondary education under a law sponsored by Camille Sée in 1880. The girls' lycées and colleges now set up did not break the older grip of the Catholic Church on the education of young bourgeois ladies, and recruited above all the daughters of teachers and civil servants who were still criticized as bluestockings. Most took the *brevet* to qualify for teaching, but an elite took the *baccalauréat*, which required Latin and Greek until an alternative combining Latin and modern languages was introduced in 1902.[50] To staff these lycées and colleges a new profession emerged, that of the secondary school mistress. In the period 1880–1900 these originated not from bourgeois families who would have been able to provide them with a dowry to make a 'good' marriage, but from the milieu of teachers, civil servants, the military, or white-collar workers; 10 per cent of them (18 per cent at the teacher-training college for secondary-school women teachers, the École Normale de Sèvres) were indeed orphans. A quarter were drawn from the primary sector and the majority had the *brevet supérieur*; if they acquired the *agrégation* it was in post. A schoolmistress in Paris, with the *agrégation*, earned a respectable 3,000 francs at the beginning of her career, and 4,700 at the end, though less than the 3,200 and 8,000 respectively for a schoolmaster in the same position. Only 40 per cent of schoolmistresses married, and when they did they had the reputation of marrying 'badly', which was not necessarily the case if they came from the lower-middle class. Nevertheless they tended, if they did marry, to marry other teachers. Although or perhaps because the nuns were their rivals, they modelled themselves on the sobriety and decorum of nuns, and were expected to do so in the towns where they taught. Marguerite Aron, who graduated from Sèvres with the *agrégation* and went to teach in a provincial girls' lycée, was told by her teachers 'to behave at the age of twenty-four as a sedate woman of thirty', only to be teased by the father of one of her pupils as being a member of an 'authorized congregation'. There was, however, no place for scandal. One headmistress was dismissed for wearing trousers on a climbing holiday; the townsfolk complaining that they did not want a 'George Sand'.[51]

Very few women gained a university education in France before the *baccalauréat* reform of 1902. Even when they did, they were sharply over-represented in arts faculties, where in 1914 they formed 35 per cent of the student body. At that point women made up only 10 per cent of the students in medical faculties, 9 per cent of those in science faculties, and a mere 0.09 per cent of law students.[52] Significantly, 43 per cent of those students were foreign, 54 per cent of them in the medical faculties. Two of those were Bronya Sklodovska, who came from Poland to study medicine in Paris, and her sister Manya, who followed her in 1891, studied science at the Sorbonne and married a physics lecturer, Pierre Curie, in 1895. Marie Curie, as she now called herself, passed the *agrégation* in 1896 and taught at the École de Sèvres while undertaking research to isolate radium, defending her doctoral thesis in June 1903 and winning the Nobel prize with her husband that December. Ironically, it was only as a result of the death of Pierre, who was run over by a horse-drawn cab in 1906, that it was possible for her, although with the inferior title of 'course director', to succeed to his chair of physics on a salary of 10,000 francs a year. As a woman she was rejected by the French Academy of Sciences in 1911, just before she won the Nobel prize for the second time, and was regularly attacked as a Russian, German, Pole or Jew who had come to Paris like an intruder and usurper.[53]

The medical world was similarly well defended against women. 'They want to become men!' proclaimed one doctor in 1875, but they did not have the 'virile qualities' to perform dissections without fainting at the sight of blood. He was hostile to the enrolment of Elizabeth Garrett Anderson who was accepted by Paris having been refused enrolment in London and Edinburgh and became the first qualified woman doctor in Britain. Madeleine Brès, the first French woman to enrol in a medical faculty, was taken on as a provisional clinical intern at the Pitié hospital during the siege of Paris in 1870–71, but was turned down for a permanent internship after the siege ended. Women were not permitted to compete for clinical training as externs until 1881 and as interns until 1885. The number of women medical students in Paris duly crept up from five in 1870–71 and forty in 1881–2 to 114 in 1887–8, although of these 114 twenty were Polish, seventy Russian, eight English, and only twelve French. When women doctors did qualify they were forced into specializations where the advantage of motherly or female skills could be demonstrated, or into areas which were notoriously unpopular, such as mental health. A staunch opponent of women training as doctors was Professor Charcot of the Paris Medical Faculty who was best known in the 1880s for his experiments on hysterical women at the Salpêtrière hospital, which were also a theatrical display of the subjection of irrational females by the male scientist. One of his students, Blanche Edwards, nevertheless passed the examination for clinical training in 1886, and chose the option of specializing in children in care. She married a doctor and succeeded him on his death as director of the nursing school at the Salpêtrière.[54] Madeleine Pelletier, the daughter of a fruit and vegetable seller in

Les Halles, and educated by nuns till the age of twelve, studied on her own for the *baccalauréat*. She passed in 1897 and obtained a scholarship from the Paris municipal council to study at the Faculty of Medicine. She chose the specialization of mental health, obtained a doctorate in 1903, and worked as a medical assistant for the social services, dealing with very poor patients, until she was allowed to compete for clinical training in psychiatry, and worked at the Villejuif mental asylum.[55]

Nursing was another area of medicine where women were allowed to contribute. Anna Hamilton, the daughter of an Irish Protestant father who speculated his fortune away, passed her *baccalauréat* at Chambéry and submitted her thesis on nursing reform at Montpellier in 1900. She saw herself as a French Florence Nightingale, who would sweep away the rustic and illiterate staff of French hospitals labouring under the eye of unscientific nuns, and replace them with highly trained young women. She secured the help of the mayor of Bordeaux to set up a nursing school at Tondu hospital, Bordeaux, in 1904. This new model was adopted by Blanche Edwards at the Salpêtrière hospital, but was otherwise resisted by conservative doctors and communities of nuns who demonstrated greater competence in retaining control over hospitals than they did in respect of schools.

Slowly, women penetrated the liberal professions, but even more slowly in law than in medicine; in 1914 there were only eight female barristers. And yet even a limited change provoked an outcry against this new model of bluestocking who sacrificed love and family life to knowledge and the pursuit of a career. Catching the mood were the novels of Colette Yver. In *Les Cervalines* (1902) a young doctor who wishes to marry complains that his problem is not with men-hating feminists who start to look like men but with female doctors and teachers who 'remain charming but who . . . having let their life-blood flow to the brain, have no need of love'. Similarly, in *Princesses de science* (1907) an eminent doctor's daughter, Thérèse Herlingue, marries a fellow medical student but refuses to give up her career. She builds up a respectable clientele but her own child, abandoned to a nurse, falls ill and dies. Her husband, finding the house cold and deserted, takes to drink and eats out. Finally, on the brink of losing him, she has a change of heart and declares, 'I am all yours now. You will always find me here. You will love your home again. You have work to accomplish, Fernand, I will help you; you will triumph.'[56] Whatever the achievements of women, the dominant opinion expressed in such works was that the traditional model was still the norm, and would win out in the end against female emancipation.

WOMEN'S RIGHTS, POLITICS AND OPINION

In the pursuit of civil and political rights, as in the battle for education and careers, women had to contend with the weight of opinion behind the dominant model of the wife and mother, which was defended not only by most men but also by many women. The Third Republic saw the emergence of organizations dedicated to women's rights, but the suffragette was a marginal and uncomfortable figure. There was no militant suffragette movement in France on the scale of the Women's Social and Political Union in Great Britain. The peculiar nature of French feminism was its attempt to put forward the demand for civil and political rights in a language that did not depart from the cult of motherhood, the family and indeed of femininity, and femininity did not sit well with physical force.

In 1872 Maria Desraismes of the Society for the Amelioration of Women's Condition issued a firm riposte to Alexandre Dumas *fils*, whose pamphlet *The Man-Woman* urged men to reassert control over their wives, killing them if they committed adultery. She argued, as Jenny d'Héricourt had, that it was not the emancipation but the servitude of women that was a threat to society and civilization, and that the new Republic should grant rights to women.[57] Despite the failure of the First and Second Republics to grant those rights, Desraismes took the view that the Third Republic offered new hope and should therefore be defended at all costs. The banning of her society by the conservative Moral Order regime in 1875, and its reauthorization by the republicans in August 1878, indicated that she might be correct. Neither was she prepared to move faster than republican opinion would take. In this she came up against a young rival, Hubertine Auclert, an orphan who had cut her anticlerical teeth in a series of convent schools and who tried to raise the question of female suffrage at the Women's Rights conference organized by Desraismes and her colleague Léon Richer in July–August 1878. When this was rejected as premature she broke away to found her own Society for Female Suffrage, sustained after 1881 by a paper called *La Citoyenne*. She followed the line of most French feminists that women's rights would strengthen and moralize the nation. However, she was not prepared to wait for the vote and sought publicity for her cause by trying to register to vote, refusing to pay taxes (until the bailiffs arrived to take her furniture) and by organizing a demonstration with a banner wreathed in black at the place de la Bastille on 14 July 1881.[58]

Three times as many feminists stayed with Desraismes and Richer than followed Auclert. Desraismes made it a priority to defend the Republic from the right, and turned her Pontoise country estate into committee rooms for the republican cause in the elections of 1881 and 1885, and her Paris salon into a headquarters against Boulangism. She chaired many of the meetings of the Anticlerical Congress in 1881, believing that women had urgently to be freed from the grip of the Church. Richer, who set up the French League for Women's Rights (LFDF) in 1882, was also of the opinion that 'it is enough for us to have to struggle against reactionaries of the masculine sex without giving to these partisans of defeated regimes the support of millions of female ballots subject to the occult domination of the priest, their confessor.'[59] In the meantime, Hubertine Auclert had tried to harness the re-emerging socialist movement to her cause, perhaps remembering the attempts of Flora Tristan to do the same in the 1830s. Auclert attended the first socialist congress since the Commune at Marseille in October 1879, and obtained a resolution from it in favour of women's social and political equality. But a year later the Le Havre socialist congress fully committed itself to Marxism, and subordinated women's rights to the class struggle. Louise Michel, returning from exile, might have become an ally of Hubertine, but preferred to take the socialist line. Declining to run as a candidate she said that 'Women in the Chamber would not prevent the absurdly low pay of women's work and the prison and the pavement would continue no less to vomit, one on to the other, legions of unfortunates.'[60] The only leading figure to take Auclert's side, paradoxically, was Alexandre Dumas *fils*, who had undergone a strange and sudden transformation, arguing that women could vote in elections for school boards in New York and thus that 'there should be women in the Chamber of Deputies. France owes the civilized world the example of this great initiative.'[61] Hubertine Auclert married a government official and followed him to Algeria when he was posted there in 1888. The following year, coinciding with the centenary of the French Revolution, Richer and Desraismes presided in triumph over the Women's Rights Congress which brought together middle-class and professional women such as Blanche Edwards, to make such moderate demands as equal pay for women teachers, the opening up of the professions to women, control of their earnings by married women, and the abolition of regulated (and thus legalized) prostitution, which humiliated working women and endorsed the infidelity of their husbands.[62]

The French feminist scene received a new boost in 1897 with the conversion to the cause of Marguerite Durand. Thirty-six years younger than Desraismes and twenty-six years younger than Auclert, Durand, one of the generation born around 1860, was the illegitimate daughter of a general, fled her convent school to become an actress at the Comédie Française, married the politician Georges Laguerre who moved from radicalism to Boulangism, and became the 'Madame Roland of Boulangism'. She divorced in 1891, and wrote a column in *Le Figaro*, by which she was sent to write a witty article on the Amazons attending the congress of the 1896 French League for Women's Rights. In the event she was converted, and launched her own women's newspaper, *La Fronde*, making a bid to become a new Delphine de Girardin. *La Fronde* brought together a galaxy of women writers including Séverine, who wrote 'Notes of a Frondeuse', Clémence Royer, who had translated Darwin, Avril de Sainte-Croix, the leading campaigner against legalized prostitution, Pauline Kergomard, the chief inspector of nursery schools, and Maria Vérone, a law student who wrote the paper's legal column and became in 1907 only the fifth French woman admitted to the bar.[63] The great achievement of Durand was to combine feminism with femininity, and indeed to use femininity for political ends. She espoused the cause of women who wanted to emerge from the private sphere without risking the accusation that they were becoming mannish, bluestockings or *cocottes*. She later wrote,

I was not much more than thirty when I founded the *Fronde*. The fact of seeing a woman who was still young and not totally out of favour, who made her life seem easy, who was interested in the lot of other women and who made that her preoccupation . . . all this was at first astonishing and then interesting. Feminism owes a lot to my blonde hair.[64]

Durand's feminism was bourgeois and dreyfusard and did not command universal support. One of her ambitions was to encourage women to improve their lot by joining trade unions, and Jeanne Bouvier was introduced to the dressmakers' union by a private client who read *La Fronde*.[65] But the International Women's Rights Congress which Durand sponsored in September 1900 was divided over whether maids should be given a whole day off a week. The Feminist Socialist Group of Élisabeth Renaud, the widow of a printworker who had worked in a Jura watch factory and as a governess in St Petersburg and now kept a boarding house in Paris, and a seamstress, Louise Saumonneau, who defended the maids' holiday, clashed with the wife of the mayor of the 18th *arrondissement* who declared, 'So I'm to cook lunch for my maid? I'm not a saint!'[66] On another front, Durand broke with Gyp who was engaged to provide a drawing a week for *La Fronde*, until Durand objected to their anti-Semitic nature. Gyp became an outspoken campaigner for the antidreyfusard cause, called as a witness to give evidence at Déroulède's trial in the high court in 1899 and famously giving her occupation as 'anti-Semite'. Similarly Durand fell out with the editor of the anti-Semitic *La Libre Parole*, Gaston Méry, when she refused to give money to help the widow of Colonel Henry and he accused her (possibly alluding to her liaison with Baron Gustave de Rothschild) of being 'a bad mother, a prostitute with Jewish lovers'.[67]

Not all French feminism in the Belle Époque was so colourful. One of the powerful streams it emerged from was religious philanthropy, whether Catholic, Protestant or Jewish. A leading light of

Protestant philanthropy was Sarah Monod, from a great family of Protestant academics and churchmen, whose main commitment was to fight social injustice, but who also sought 'a definition of feminism which would reconcile the demand for rights with an edifying conception of the *femme au foyer*'.[68] She chaired a congress on Women's Charities and Institutions in June 1900 which dealt with the social issues of prostitution, alcoholism and access to higher education for women, and also favoured the extension of sweated labour as a way of helping working mothers to combine work and motherhood. In 1901 she became chair of the National Council of French Women (CNFF), the French branch of the International Council of Women founded in Washington DC in 1888. Its leading lights were Protestant – Sarah Monod, Julie Siegfried – or Jewish – Madame Weill, Madame Salvador – and it was still basically philanthropic, with some interest in civil, but not political, rights. Catholics, troubled by the domination of women's movements by Protestants, Jews and freethinkers, went their own way, but still tried to combine social action with the cult of the home and family. Marie Maugeret, who founded a periodical called *Christian Feminism* in 1896, wrote in 1899, 'the fact that a woman develops her mind with all sorts of serious matters does not make her any less able to be her husband's companion and child's educator. The Christian woman respects her husband's authority as head of the family and takes the place that is rightly hers in the home.' Catholic women did become involved in politics after the Dreyfus Affair, but in the context of defending the Catholic family and education. Baroness Reille, who was among the founders in 1902 of the Ligue Patriotique des Françaises, whose watchwords were 'Fatherland, property and liberty', was against contraception, abortion, the godless school imposed by freemasons and the takeover of the country by the Bloc des Gauches. She was not interested in campaigning for female suffrage but told an audience at Toulouse in 1903, 'Be honest, ladies, if you do not drop a ballot in the box, you guide the hand that does.'[69]

In the teeth of the pressure of family values and social reform a limited suffragette movement did take shape in the years before 1914, but it failed to get the better of a more sedate suffragism, which entrusted itself to the regular political process and parties and made very little headway. The suffragette movement was led by Hubertine Auclert, who had returned to Paris from Algeria after her husband died there in 1892 and recruited a knot of younger militants including Caroline Kauffmann, an unhappily married child-labour inspector, and Madeleine Pelletier, now a psychiatrist at the Villejuif asylum. Symbolically, in 1904 when the centenary of the Civil Code, which in so many ways imposed the constitutional inferiority of women, was being officially celebrated, Auclert led a procession of fifty feminists to the statue of Napoleon in the place Vendôme where they tore out pages from the Code. In May 1908, during municipal elections, Auclert, Kauffmann and Pelletier marched into a polling station in the 4th *arrondissement*, overturning a ballot box, then threw stones at the windows of another. Auclert was sent for trial but the authorities decided not to make a martyr of her; the hostility of public opinion was already doing the job. Pelletier wondered why the feminists did not follow them, and concluded, 'Marching in the streets seemed vulgar to them; this was suitable for working-class women. A respectable woman should stay at home.' To see how suffragettes managed it in Britain, she attended a 500,000-strong demonstration in Hyde Park on 21 June 1908, and later wrote, 'If I had Pankhurst's troops, I would certainly attempt a violent demonstration.'[70]

Just as the suffragette movement picked up militancy in Great Britain, however, so it lost it in France. Emmeline Pankhurst herself was no stranger to France. The daughter of a Manchester calico-printer who did much business in France, she was educated in the 1870s in a boarding school on the avenue de Neuilly, Paris, and her best friend was Noémie Rochefort, 'daughter of that great Republican, Communist, journalist and swordsman, Henri Roche-fort', in exile in New Caledonia following the Commune. She gained an entrée into French literary circles and almost married a French man of letters, but her father would hear nothing of foreign husbands and dowries and summoned her home to marry an Englishman. Women dressed as Joan of Arc figured prominently in processions organized by the Women's Social and Political Union, which she founded in 1903; her daughter Christabel fled to Paris in 1912 to avoid arrest after the campaign of smashing shop windows in the West End, and edited the *Suffragette* from there; and after Emmeline was sentenced to three years' hard labour in 1913 for setting fire to Lloyd George's country home her suffragette supporters left the Old Bailey singing the Marseillaise. This militancy, however, did not rub off on French feminists. The British state did not avoid confrontation with suffragettes. Arrests led to trials from which political capital was made, imprisonment led to hunger-strikes and renewed militancy. In 1912 the WSPU launched a campaign of violence, pouring acid into postboxes, cutting telephone cables, slashing paintings in art galleries, setting fire to public and private buildings. In 1908, however, Hubertine Auclert, aged sixty and ten years older than Emmeline Pankhurst, attended a meeting of the National Congress of Civil Rights and Universal Suffrage that was designed to federate all movements seeking reform of the Civil Code and votes for women. Publicly, to a standing ovation, she apologized for her use of violence, which had achieved nothing. She had no successors in terms of militancy. The initiative now shifted to the suffragists around Jeanne Schmahl, a doctor who had just piloted through parliament a law of 1907 giving married women control of their earnings and who launched the French Union for Women's Suffrage (UFSF) in 1907. This was the French equivalent of the National Union of Women's Suffrage Societies, set up in 1897 by Millicent Garrett Fawcett, the sister of Elizabeth Garrett Anderson, which limited itself to constitutional agitation.[71]

The progress of suffragism by legal means depended of course on obtaining the sponsorship of a major party. Here French suffragists faced the same problem as their British allies, who were blocked by the ruling Liberal Party and unable to persuade the Labour Party to place votes for women ahead of the votes for all adults, disfranchised workers included. After the separation of Church and state in France in 1905 the anticlerical work of the Radical Party was complete and hope for a series of reforms was pinned on the new premier, Aristide Briand, a former socialist turned moderate.[72] Schmahl went to see him in October 1909 about votes for women, but he was clear: the country was not yet ready for it.[73] No more help was forthcoming from the socialists.

Madeleine Pelletier lobbied Jaurès and spoke to the SFIO congress at Nancy in August 1907, but they still insisted that class came before the concerns of educated women.[74] Marguerite Durand then hit on the publicity stunt, which was not endorsed by the UFSF, of high-profile feminists running in the parliamentary elections of 1910 in Paris: she in the 9th *arrondissement*, Auclert in the 11th, Pelletier in the 5th. In the event, Pelletier was offered a nomination by the SFIO, not in the 5th but in the unwinnable 8th, the fief of royalist deputy Denys Cochin. In this respect French campaigners were ahead of their British counterparts, who did not stand themselves but campaigned to unseat MPs of the Liberal Party, such as Winston Churchill in Manchester in 1908. They were divided, however, by the issue of femininity. The former suffragettes felt ill at ease on the election platform in the company of Durand, who flaunted her beauty. Auclert was critical of her 'regiment of lovers', while Pelletier, who cropped her hair and wore masculine dress, complained, 'I do not understand how these ladies don't see the vile servitude that lies in displaying their breasts. I will show off mine when men adopt a special sort of trouser that shows off their . . .'[75] The women candidates in Paris secured about 4 per cent of the vote. The only success story, with 27 per cent of the vote, was that of Élisabeth Renaud, standing at Vienne (Isère), who was supported by socialists strong in the town council as well as feminists, particularly the local union of *institutrices* seeking higher pay. Ironically, she was removed from the Group of Socialist Women in 1913 by her former comrade Louise Saumonneau, who wanted to orientate the group towards a 'proletarian feminism' closely tied to the SFIO.[76]

Feminist politics was defeated in the end by opinion. The more feminists demanded, and the more aggressive their political tactics, the more they found themselves isolated, not only from French men, but also from women who saw themselves as wives and mothers, and even from feminists who did not want to sacrifice their femininity. Marguerite Durand fell out with Hubertine Auclert and Madeleine Pelletier on the issue of femininity, all these were isolated from Protestant and Catholic feminists who would put a toe in the water only if marriage and the family were not called into question, while men, who controlled the political citadel, were not minded to lay down their defences. With some poetic licence, Georges Clemenceau wrote in 1907, 'If the right to vote were given to women tomorrow, France would all of a sudden jump back into the Middle Ages.'[77]

14

Modernism and Mass Culture

The successful writer, artist or musician at the end of the nineteenth century had access to three indispensable resources. The first was connections and patronage, which could further a career, and might be provided by an influential salon in Paris or official recognition in the annual Salon sponsored by the Académie des Beaux Arts or by the prizes and membership of the Académie Française. The second was the dialogue, comradeship and support that could be offered by fellow writers and artists, who often met in favourite cafés and restaurants and reviewed each other's work in journals and newspapers. Conflict between different approaches was common, a sense of betrayal was rife, and friendships often came to a bitter end, but all this was grist to the mill of literary, artistic and musical innovation. The third was public recognition and a market for their work in the growing consumer society. Not every writer or artist had access to all three resources. Official recognition in the Salon or Académie Française was generally confined to those who subscribed to the classical French canon as laid down by those institutions and did not seek radical or avant-garde approaches. Avant-garde writers and artists scorned official institutions and canons, or at least affected to do so. They also affected to scorn the demands of the mass market, which they denounced as ignorant and philistine, although they could not entirely eschew the oxygen of publicity and the income to live. For a mass culture was developing, which was something different from both elite culture and popular culture: a culture demanded by a largely urban society, shaped by mass education and craving instruction and entertainment more than cultivation, and supplied by a mass media of books, newspapers, universal exhibitions, music halls, cinemas, sports stadiums and race tracks. Classical and avant-garde or modern art and the mass consumer society were locked in a tension, but the art, literature and bohemian lifestyle of Paris were themselves becoming national assets, widely commented upon in Europe and America and drawing in foreign writers, artists and tourists.

MODERNISM AND CLASSICISM

Princesse Mathilde, Napoleon III's cousin, returned to Paris from exile in Brussels a fortnight after the suppression of the Commune, assured by head of government Thiers that despite her ties with the fallen Empire she was not a political threat and would be left alone. She reconstituted the Wednesday salon which had been so influential under the Empire and continued to be so under the Third Republic. The older Romantic generation of her faithful, born around 1800 – Sainte-Beuve, Gautier, Mérimée – had died, as had Jules de Goncourt of syphilis at the age of forty in 1870, and the salon was dominated by the generation born around 1830 – Edmond de Goncourt, Taine and Renan, Flaubert, Alexandre Dumas *fils*, Alphonse Daudet, author of the *Lettres de mon moulin*, along with the painter Gérôme and the composer Gounod. Zola she could not abide and he was not a regular.[1]

Princesse Mathilde's salon was home to the Realist school of writers, but these also had other venues for meeting. From 1874 Flaubert organized monthly dinners, suceeding those at Magny's restaurant in the 1860s, for 'the Five' whose novels may have been successful but whose plays had been shouted down by theatre audiences. 'We were all gourmands,' recalled Alphonse Daudet, 'with as many gourmandises as temperaments and provinces of origin. Flaubert wanted Normandy butter and Rouen ducks, Zola demanded seafood, Edmond de Goncourt ordered ginger delicacies while Turgenev tasted caviar. Ah! We were not easy to feed and the Paris restaurants remembered us. We often had to change the venue.'[2] After Flaubert's death in 1880 the group was kept together by Daudet who held his own salon on a Thursday in the avenue de l'Observatoire, presided over by his wife Julia, while in 1885 Edmond de Goncourt refurbished the loft at Auteuil where his brother Jules had died, done up with Japanese art, and visited with some trepidation by the Princesse Mathilde the following year. Zola bought a villa at Médan on the Seine in 1878 with the royalties from *L'Assommoir* and held meetings of his own young protégés such as Guy de Maupassant and Joris-Karl Huysmans, son of a Dutch father and French mother. In 1880 they published a collection of short stories, *Les Soirées de Médan*, which served as a manifesto for the Naturalist school and included Maupassant's *Boule de suif*, a short story set during the war of 1870 about a prostitute who is persuaded by her bourgeois travelling companions to sleep with a Prussian officer so that the coach can move on, and described by Flaubert as a masterpiece.[3] Naturalism, depicting humanity as determined by hereditary and environmental laws and reduced almost to bestiality, in fact drove a wedge between Zola and his circle on the one hand and Goncourt and Daudet on the other. In 1887, after the publication of Zola's *La Terre*, an attack on his work's 'indecency and filthy terminology' was published in *Le Figaro*, which Zola believed to have been inspired by Goncourt and Daudet.[4]

Close links had been established before this break between the Realists and the Impressionists. Both challenged the literary and artistic establishment with their treatment of modern life, warts and all, and were often marginalized by it. Monet and Degas held court in the Café Guerbois in the Batignolles district, then in the more refined Café de la Nouvelle Athènes, which were also frequented by Zola. Nana, the prostitute who appears in *L'Assommoir* before having a novel to herself in 1880, was painted by Manet, a picture rejected for the Salon of 1877, while Zola tried to defend Impressionism through his treatment of the struggling artist in *L'Oeuvre* of 1886. Huysmans was launched as an art critic by Zola, attacking the academic art of the Salon and preaching the virtues of Manet and Degas. 'A painter of modern life is born,' said Huysmans of Degas in 1880, painting the flesh of ballet dancers lit by gaslight or the pale glow from courtyards, completely different from the classical school of Bouguereau's *Birth of Venus*, a 'badly pumped-up windbag, without muscles, nerves or blood. A single pinprick in the torso and it would collapse.'[5] That said, Zola and

Huysmans found other Impressionists such as Monet and Pissarro guilty of 'indigomania' and Gauguin argued that Huysmans liked Degas and Manet only because their work was figurative: 'it is naturalism that gratifies him.'[6]

In the 1880s a breach opened up between Realists and Impressionists on the one hand, who were committed to the representation of modern life, and other artists whose ambition was to flee it, to search for meaning in some essence or ideal that lay behind the mask presented by reality, and were inspired by the primitive or the exotic, by myths and legends, by the spiritual and religious, symbols which seemed to permit access to an inner or unconscious world. Their art was modernist in form but was a critique of modernity – the materialistic world of urbanization, industrialization, science, secularization and mass education.[7] It was avant-garde, grouping like-minded intellectuals seeking new literary forms and sometimes challenging bourgeois conventions by a bohemian lifestyle. One of their early haunts was the salon of Nina de Callais, who had been painted by Manet in 1874 as *The Woman with the Fan*. The poet Paul Verlaine, who had been a clerk in the Hôtel de Ville before the Paris Commune, met the sixteen-year-old Mathilde Mauté there in 1869 and married her in order to escape military service. She later admitted that she was 'overcome by pity for a poor being with disgraceful appearance and who seemed sad'.[8] In fact he was a spoiled child, alcoholic and violent. Obsessed by the brilliant young poet Arthur Rimbaud who arrived in Paris in the autumn of 1871, he tried to strangle his wife, threw his three-month-old baby against the wall and ran away to Brussels with Rimbaud. In 1873 he shot Rimbaud in the hand during another row and spent two years in a Belgian prison, after which his wife separated from him and Rimbaud went to Africa to trade in ivory or guns, according to the rumour. Briefly reforming himself, he published a collection of his own work and that of Rimbaud and Mallarmé, *Les Poètes maudits*, in 1883, which for the first time put this new generation of Symbolist poets on the map. He was then jailed again for an attack on his mother and spent much of the last years of his life in hospital.

For Symbolists the most important meeting-place was the salon of Stéphane Mallarmé. Mallarmé, who made a living teaching

English in a succession of lycées in the provinces and Paris, organized his own literary salon on Tuesdays at his house in the rue de Rome. From 1885 it became the focal point for young writers of a new generation born around 1860 who experimented with elegant but opaque and suggestive forms of language. Where Verlaine destroyed bourgeois domesticity, Mallarmé incarnated it, although as poets they had the same ambitions. 'The wife and daughter embroider under a dim lamp,' wrote one of his disciples, Paul Valéry. 'He smokes a pipe in a rocking-chair, eyes half closed, voice very low. Then suddenly his eyes are wide open and he raises his voice, panting. He becomes a *savant* in a moment, now epic, now tragic.'[9] Other disciples of this rarefied salon were Jules Laforgue, who died of tuberculosis aged twenty-seven in 1887, Henri de Régnier, Félix Fénéon, Maurice Barrès, the musician Claude Debussy, the novelist André Gide, the German poet Stefan George and 'the execrable Oscar Wilde who should have grasped from our mute reprobation', said another disciple, 'that one did not come to Mallarmé's to make speeches'.[10]

One of the greatest advocates and interpreters of the Symbolist movement was Huysmans, whose novel of 1884, *À rebours* or *Against the Grain*, documented the life and obsessions of a decadent, aristocratic artist, Des Esseintes. Withdrawing from the urban, industrial, materialistic and mechanistic contemporary world, seeking meaning in narcotically inspired dreams, erotic fantasies and memories of lost civilizations, he discovers Mallarmé, 'that poet who in a century of universal suffrage and lucre lived apart from the world of letters, sheltered from surrounding stupidity by his disdain, dedicated to the surprises of the intellect and the visions of his mind, which he grafted with Byzantine finesse, fixing them with the lightest touches that an invisible thread scarcely linked'.[11] The book was an attack on the Naturalism of his former master Zola, which he thought squeezed all psychological complexity out of his characters and made them mere puppets of instinct and environment. Huysmans was taken to task by Zola in a country lane near Médan in the summer of 1884, and the rupture was complete.

Disciples of the new school who followed Huysmans from decadence to religion attracted the name of Decadents, but they preferred to call themselves Symbolists and had a powerful publicity machine working for them. Jean Moréas, a writer of Greek origin, published a Symbolist manifesto in *Le Figaro* in 1886 which announced that 'symbolist poetry seeks to clothe the Idea in sensible form.' They regarded the external, material world as merely a veil over the ideal or spiritual world. They trusted in emotions rather than sensations, in what would soon be called the unconscious, and they sought to release deeper meanings by exploring myths and legends, primitive cultures and different manifestations of mysticism and religion. The review *La Plume*, which published much of their work, sponsored Symbolist evenings on a Saturday night at the Soleil d'Or café on the place Saint-Michel, at which Verlaine would arrive late, already the worse for wear. Maurice Barrès set the tone in the Latin Quarter by reinventing the decadent dandy that Baudelaire was supposed to have been, adopting 'several souls', well dressed and polite on the outside, sensuous and immoral in his inner life.[12]

Symbolism, or the search for a more spiritual art, shaped not only the poetry and literature of the *fin de siècle* but also painting, drama and music. As a reaction against the contemporary world, it could end up either in retreat from the world or in criticism of it. The death of Manet in 1883 dealt a blow to Impressionism, which embraced modern life and fixed the impressions it made, and artists took new directions. In 1886 Gauguin discovered Brittany, with its heaths and rocky coves, little chapels and traditional costumes. 'There I find the savage and primitive,' he wrote, and by 1888 he had gathered a group of artists of the 1860 generation at the fishing village of Pont-Aven. These included Émile Bernard, who perfected the *cloisonné* method of painting, with blocks of colour divided by black lines, as in stained glass, and Paul Sérusier, whose rendering of a landscape on the lid of Gauguin's cigar box became the talisman of the group.[13] Linked to them was Maurice Denis, who took an oath on All Saints' Day 1884 to remain always a Christian and announced in 1886 that 'even the purest realism and naturalism cannot satisfy . . . we must make an effort, a great effort, to bring Art back to its great master, who is God.'[14] After Gauguin sailed to Tahiti in 1891 in search of more primitive societies, this group became the core of the Nabis, including Pierre

Bonnard and Édouard Vuillard. For them Denis wrote a manifesto stating that 'before it becomes a war-horse, a nude woman or some anecdote, a painting is essentially a flat surface covered with colours assembled in a certain order.'[15] The Nabis were keen to apply their techniques to other decorative arts, such as tapestries and stage sets, and Denis had been at the Lycée Condorcet with avant-garde theatre director Aurélien Lugné-Poë. Lugné-Poë and the Nabis shared a studio in the rue Pigalle and after 1893 the Nabis designed sets and programmes for the north European idealist drama at the Théâtre de l'Oeuvre, notably *Pelléas et Mélisande* by the Belgian Symbolist Maeterlinck and a string of Ibsen plays from *Rosmersholm* and *An Enemy of the People* to *The Master Builder* in 1893, with not a single French play until 1894.[16]

The search for a more spiritual art could lead squarely to religion. Huysmans only flirted with Decadence after his break with Naturalism. He was embraced by the Catholic writer Léon Bloy who argued that everyone had to decide 'whether to guzzle like the beasts of the field or to look upon the face of God', and dined frequently with the Abbé Mugnier, 'confessor of duchesses'. Attracted by the aesthetic dimension of Catholicism he went on pilgrimages to La Salette and Lourdes, undertook a retreat with the Trappists and died in 1907 in the robes of a Benedictine oblate.[17] Maurice Denis had always been devoted to the Italian Primitivist Fra Angelico, 'the only really Catholic painter', and in 1898 went on a pilgrimage to Rome with André Gide, where he discovered Raphael and 'the theory of ideal, absolute beauty'. He broke with Nabis like Vuillard who espoused dreyfusism, reverted to painting the Virgin Mary and Joan of Arc and decorated the Chapel of the Holy Virgin at Le Vésinet. In his search for classicism and order he even joined Action Française.[18]

Modernist criticism of the modern world was, however, as likely to end up on the extreme left of the political spectrum as on the extreme right. Just as the Pont-Aven group gathered around Gauguin, so another cohort of the 1860 generation, the painters Georges Seurat and Paul Signac and the critic Félix Fénéon, gathered after 1886 around Pissarro. Seurat and Signac introduced Pissarro to the new technique of *pointillisme*, which involved dividing tones into dots from which new forms and colours were built. They painted scenes from modern life, such as circus artists and bathers, notably Seurat's 1885 *Sunday at La Grande Jatte*, but also bleak industrial suburbs on the outskirts of Paris and peasants toiling in the fields. They considered the Pont-Aven school to be reactionary and Pissarro denounced Symbolism as part of a conspiracy to 'restore to the people their superstitious beliefs'. 'Impressionists have the true position,' he said, 'they stand for a robust art based on sensation, and that is an honest stand.'[19] He attacked the Exhibition of 1889 as a capitalist extravaganza, produced a print of the sun of revolution rising behind the Eiffel Tower in his *Turpitudes sociales* series, and joined forces with Louise Michel, Benoît Malon and the anti-militarist Lucien Descaves in the Club of Social Art. In 1891 Seurat died aged thirty-one while Signac wrote an article on 'impressionists and revolutionaries' in *La Révolte*, published by the anarchist Jean Grave. Félix Fénéon, who defended their cause both artistically and politically, finished up in the dock alongside Jean Grave during the infamous trial of anarchists, the Procès des Trente, in 1894, while Pissarro fled to Brussels to avoid arrest.[20]

These Symbolist and modernist experiments were a reaction against the classical art of the bourgeois world, which was also that of the political mainstream. One of its platforms was the salon of Juliette Adam, which had been home to Gambetta and the republican opposition under the Empire, before she broke with the great man over his policy of rapprochement with Germany. From 1879 she published a *Nouvelle Revue* in which she promoted the work of aspiring writers, notably the *Crime de Sylvestre Bonnard* by Anatole France in 1881, the poetry of Jules Lemaître, and *Pêcheur d'islande* by the naval officer Pierre Loti in 1886, a poignant story of the impossible love between a Parisian girl and a Breton fisherman divided by class, culture and the long voyages of the seafarers to the Icelandic fishing banks. 'I can still hear', recalled Julie Daudet, 'the old Count Beust [former Austrian chancellor] playing an outdated waltz, Gounod singing a dramatic Breton legend, the poetry readings of that ardent poet and admirable patriot Paul Déroulède. The salon was active and lively, the *Nouvelle Revue* was published not far away, Paul Bourget was brought in, Pierre Loti was discovered and Léon Daudet [Alphonse's son] published his first timid volume there.'[21]

Juliette Adam secured the election of Pierre Loti to the Académie Française in 1891, while other protégés of hers moved on to even more influential salon hostesses, both artistically and amorously. When Madame Léontine Caillavet first invited Anatole France to her salon in 1883 she found him shy and stammering, but within five years they had become lovers. France divorced his wife and Madame Caillavet overcame his diffidence by shutting him up on her rural estate of the Gironde until he had finished *Le Lys rouge*, a study of contemporary jealousy, in 1894.[22] France had attacked both Zola's *La Terre* as 'a scurrilous Georgics' and the Symbolists for torturing the French language.[23] Now Léon Blum declared that 'M. Anatole France is the principal writer of our time. One rediscovers in him the classical beauties of the language; he united the richest currents of the French spirit: the fluidity of Renan, the sure and difficult taste of the Parnassians, the courageous freedom and natural sensibility of Diderot, the precise and delicate elegance of Fénelon or Racine, always the abundant and sustained irony of Montaigne or Rabelais.'[24] Anatole France was duly elected in his turn to the Académie Française in 1896.

In 1885 Jules Lemaître went on to the salon of the Comtesse de Loynes, which included the aged Taine and Renan, Dumas *fils*, Maupassant and Georges Clemenceau. Lemaître and the countess soon became lovers, he thirty-two, she fifty. Both had risen from humble origins. Lemaître was the son of an *instituteur* from near Orléans, while the countess was an illegitimate textile worker from Reims who became a courtesan under the Empire and numbered Prince Jérôme-Napoléon or Plon-Plon among her clients. She was educated in the ways of society by Dumas *fils* and Sainte-Beuve and had an unsuccessful career as an actress, but inherited a fortune from the son of a minister of the Empire who was killed in 1870 and acquired a title from marrying the Comte de Loynes, who soon disappeared. The countess lunched theatre directors until she found one, that of the Odéon, to stage Lemaître's first play, *Révoltée*, in 1889.[25] With these connections Lemaître was elected to the Académie Française in 1895, and defended classical French art through his theatre criticism. He welcomed Rostand's *Cyrano de Bergerac*, which opened at the Porte Saint-Martin in 1897 and ran throughout the

Dreyfus Affair, as 'a recapitulation, or if you prefer it, a culminating efflorescence of a form of art which dates back three centuries'. Taking a sideswipe at the Symbolists he attributed the success of *Cyrano* to 'the degree to which the public has been wearied and surfeited with so many studies of psychology, so many trifling tales of Parisian adultery, so many productions by feminists, socialists and Scandinavians ... [It has] set on foot a revival of nationalism in France.'[26] 'The symbolist nightmare is fading,' echoed another critic, 'the northern fog has been holed and dissipated by this glorious flambée of Provençal sunshine which has restored France to herself, to her genius.'[27]

While this classical, mainstream art enjoyed success during the Dreyfus Affair, at a time when France felt uneasy about its standing as a nation, it did not manage to stifle new waves of avant-garde art in music and drama which made a huge impact in the so-called Belle Époque leading up to the First World War. Even at this late date and at the experimental end of art the patronage of the salon hostess could still be important. Winaretta Singer, who had inherited her father's sewing-machine fortune, had her marriage with one French aristocrat annulled in 1891 because of her lesbianism and in 1893 married Prince Edmond de Polignac, son of Charles X's last minister, a relationship which flourished on their joint homosexuality and love of music. The salon of the Princesse de Polignac, as she now became, had a music room designed by the poet, aesthete and patron Comte Robert de Montesquiou, who inspired Huysmans' Des Esseintes and Proust's Baron de Charlus. For the opening ceremony she dreamed of bringing together Gabriel Fauré, choirmaster of La Madeleine church whose Requiem had been performed there in 1888, and the now very sick Paul Verlaine. This ambition was not fulfilled, although Fauré, enjoying the hospitality of her palace on the Grand Canal in Venice, set a number of Verlaine poems to music as *Five Melodies from Venice*. Claude Debussy was another habitué of the princess's salon. He also set Verlaine to music, and although his love of Wagner's *Parsifal* was not shared by the Prince de Polignac, it was the inspiration for his only completed opera *Pelléas et Mélisande*, based on Maeterlinck's play, which was performed in 1902. Most important, musically, however, was the princess's promotion of the

Russian ballet of Serge Diaghilev which took Paris by storm in successive seasons after 1909. With his choreographer Fokine, designer Benois and leading dancer Nijinsky, Diaghilev made a ballet of Debussy's *Après-midi d'un faune* in 1912, in which Nijinsky simulated an orgasm, and also launched Stravinsky on to the Paris scene with the *Firebird* ballet in 1910 and *Petrushka* in 1911. The opening night of the *Rite of Spring* at the Théâtre des Champs-Élysées on 29 May 1913 was so revolutionary it nearly caused a riot and Debussy covered his ears, but by the end of the season Stravinsky had become a hero.[28]

Modern art as well as music enjoyed a heady phase in the years before 1914. After a few visits from Spain Pablo Picasso settled definitively in Paris in 1904, joining a colony of artists living on Montmartre. His key contacts were the poet and critic Guillaume Apollinaire, who was born in Rome of a Polish mother and claimed to be an illegitimate son of the pope, the patrons Gertrude and Leo Stein, a German-American-Jewish couple, and the German-Jewish art dealer Kahnweiler. Picasso did not like to exhibit and sold directly to his dealer and patron. Gertrude Stein, whom he painted laboriously in the winter of 1905–6, claimed that 'I was the only person to understand Picasso at the time.'[29] After his pink period, painting circus folk and their families, he launched out in 1907 with he *Demoiselles d'Avignon*, five female nudes, possibly in a brothel, each seen from a different angle. Even his friends were confounded. Gertrude Stein saw it as 'too awful', Leo as 'a horrible mess', Kahnweiler as 'mad or monstrous'. Matisse himself thought it 'an audacious hoax'. It lay under wraps and was not sold until 1924.[30] Picasso found a way out through his association with Braque. Together they launched Cubism, rendering first landscapes, then still lifes, in more and more abstract forms. They were assisted financially by Kahnweiler and promoted in the literary press by Apollinaire, who wrote experimental poetry for his own reputation and pornography in order to make a living. Still Picasso refused to exhibit, but Cubist followers such as Robert Delaunay and Fernand Léger did, at the salon of independent artists. At the salon of 1910 Apollinaire announced that the new school had completed the 'rout of impressionism', with Matisse in particular seeking 'not to imitate nature but to express what he sees and feels through the very matter of the picture'.[31] In 1911 Apollinaire was wrongly arrested for stealing the *Mona Lisa* from the Louvre, but hit back by gaining control of the *Soirées de Paris* review in 1913 in which he sang the praises of Picasso, Braque and Matisse, the writers Alfred Jarry, creator of Ubu Roi, and Max Jacob, and, from the world of popular literature, the Fantômas detective series.[32]

The pinnacle of modernism came with the publication in 1913 of the first volume of Proust's *À la recherche du temps perdu*. Its birth had not been easy and acclaim was not immediately forthcoming. Proust, the son of a successful doctor and Jewish mother, was received into the salon of Madame Caillavet in 1889 and called Anatole France 'the first of my masters', although France once quipped, 'Life is too short and Proust is too long.' He was invited to the salon of the ageing Princesse Mathilde and after 1894, through his friendship with Robert de Montesquiou, became a regular at the salon of Montesquiou's cousin, Comtesse de Greffulhe, the leading society beauty of the Faubourg Saint-Germain.[33] Living on family income and contributing occasional literary pieces to *Le Figaro*, he wrote and rewrote his great work in the Grand Hôtel of Cabourg and in the cork-lined bedroom of his Paris apartment. The novel was a social panorama on a scale not attempted since Balzac, but he was not content to observe characters from the outside. 'Our social personality is a creation of others' opinions,' he wrote, of fantasies about their pasts and the worlds they live in.[34] He examined the conversation and gestures of his characters in order to understand the rules governing the relationships between aristocrats and intellectuals, Jews and Gentiles, married partners, mistresses and their lovers, and homosexuals. These relationships changed over time, so that rich and cultivated Jews who were assimilated into high society were cast out of it as a result of the Dreyfus Affair, and passion and jealousy waxed and waned according to 'the intermittence of love'. While most authors projected their heroes forward in time and followed their adventures, Proust wished to understand the secrets of life and love which were merely experienced the first time. Meaning was given to them only when memories surged up unexpectedly from the unconscious or when lost worlds were recaptured by the genius of the artist who could draw together sensations, associations and memories.

Proust found it almost impossible to publish his novel. He dedicated it to Gaston Calmette, editor of *Le Figaro*, but Calmette rejected it for serialization in his paper and failed to deliver a contact he promised with another publisher, Fasquelle. The *Nouvelle Revue Française*, founded in 1909 by André Gide and his friends and published by Gallimard, also rejected it, regarding Proust as 'a snob, a literary amateur, the worst possible thing for our magazine'. Eventually Proust published it with Grasset at his own expense, and Calmette grudgingly published a review in *Le Figaro*, three months before he was shot. The book was not a commercial success, selling only 2,800 copies in the first year, but it was a literary event. Belatedly, Gide told Proust that 'the refusal of this book will always be the gravest mistake the NRF ever made, and . . . one of the most stinging regrets, nay, remorses, of my whole life.' Gallimard now recovered the rights from Grasset, publishing a full and revised version in 1922, and in 1919 the second volume of *À la recherche*, *À l'ombre des jeunes filles en fleurs*, won the Goncourt Prize it had been denied in 1913. 'And I thought I was unknown,' Proust wrote to Grasset, as a hundred newspapers covered the event.[35] He died recognized, but as the quintessential modernist artist who had no regard for mass culture and no resonance with it.

MASS CULTURE

Avant-garde culture was in tension with classical bourgeois culture, as epitomized by the likes of Anatole France, Jules Lemaître and Edmond de Rostand, but as a rule both were defined against mass culture. This was the culture generated by a mass market of a largely urban but also rural population that was literate but not bookish, and wanted to be informed and entertained rather than educated. It was fed by the mass production and distribution of media, a mass scale that was also sensitive to different markets, such as the female market, which had long existed, and new markets, such as that of adolescents. Just as avant-garde and bourgeois culture cross-fertilized literature, art and music, so mass culture also produced crossovers between books, the theatre and new media such as the cinema, as well as between the press and sport. Despite their fundamental opposition, however, there could nevertheless be interaction between mass culture and more elitist forms of art. Thus some writers and artists found a wider audience through media such as the *café artistique*, while some popular literary forms, such as the comic cartoon, were beloved of students.

Books and bookshops catered essentially for a bourgeois audience, although reading matter was produced in new and more accessible forms for the mass market. A book in this period cost 3 francs 50, a good day's wage for most workers, and the production of titles reached a high point of 15,000 in 1889, then fell to 11,500 in 1912. The novels of Zola were bestsellers, with *L'Assommoir* selling 40,000 copies in 1878 and *Nana* 80,000 in 1880. In 1892 *Le Figaro* calculated that the 120,000 copies of *La Débâcle* sold to date, if piled on top of one another, would rise eleven times as high as the Eiffel Tower.[36] Zola's readership in 1887, however, as gauged by those who wrote to him, was almost entirely middle class, with hardly any artisans, shopkeepers, peasants or servants, although perhaps these may have been readers but not letter-writers.[37] Much more popular were authors not now part of the classical canon. Jules Verne's *Around the World in Eighty Days* was serialized in *Le Temps* in 1872, published by Hetzel in 1873, and also adapted as a play for the Théâtre de la Porte Saint-Martin in 1874. Complete with special effects and a live elephant, it was as much circus as fiction and enjoyed huge success, with a run of 1,550 performances down to 1898, while the book itself sold 108,000 copies before 1904. By then, taken together, Jules Verne's works had sold a million copies.[38]

It was not that the mass public did not read, just that they did not go into bookshops. Plenty of other media existed for reading material to reach a mass public, some developments of traditional *colportage* or hawking, others using and at the same time promoting the popular press. *Romans-feuilletons* or novels serialized in the press, at the bottom of the first page and sometimes page three as well, appealed in particular to a female readership. Many women cut out the serials and sewed them into little books, or used special binders provided by the newspaper, and swapped them with friends. Stories with pacey plots, heroes and villains, about wronged innocence finally redeemed, were republished in popular editions or adapted for the stage, as was the immensely popular *Porteuse de pain* of Xavier de Montépin in 1884, the story of a widow wrongly accused of arson and gaoled, staged at the Théâtre de l'Ambigu in 1889.[39] Alongside female audiences a new public was emerging among adolescents. These generated a new genre of adventure stories featuring American heroes such as Nick Carter or Buffalo Bill but also homegrown masked lords of crime with their own gangs of 'apaches' who flouted work, and were addicted to drink and violence, pursued but never caught by their police inspector nemeses. From 1909 to 1913 *Le Matin* serialized the adventures of Zigomar, written by a failed dramatist Léon Sazie. These were later sold as 'little novels', in instalments, once or twice a week, for between 1 and 2 sous (5 and 10 centimes), the price of a newspaper, and sold not by bookshops but by grocers, stationers and street criers.[40] The Zigomar stories sold a million copies a time and were imitated by other dubious heroes, notably the masked bandit Fantômas invented by Marcel Allain and Pierre Souvestre and launched in 1911. Meanwhile the gentleman thief and detective Arsène Lupin, with his plebeian father and aristocratic mother, a redresser of wrongs echoing some of the characters of Eugène Sue, was created in 1905 by Maurice Leblanc. After their original incarnations as serials Fantômas and Arsène Lupin were published as 'popular books' by Joseph Arthème Fayard, who was repackaging old favourites such as the *Porteuse de pain* but also the new detective and thriller genres for adolescents.[41]

The popular newspapers that carried serialized novels entered an era of mass circulation at the end of the nineteenth century, fuelled by a growing urban population, universal suffrage and the liberal press law of 29 July 1881. *Le Petit Parisien*, founded in 1876, was taken over in 1888 by Jean Dupuy, senator of the Hautes-Pyrénées, and its circulation rose from 100,000 in 1884 to 555,000 in 1894 and 1,453,000 in 1914. It overtook *Le Petit Journal* at the turn of the century, but these two Paris dailies together with *Le Matin* and *Le Journal* had a combined circulation in 1914 of 4.5 million copies, controlling 75 per cent of the Paris daily market and 40 per cent of the provincial market. Powerful regional dailies such as *La Dépêche de Toulouse* and *L'Écho du Nord* also had wide circulations, selling 180,000 copies a day in 1914, while *Le Progrès de Lyon* topped 200,000. This circulation went far beyond the middle classes to the petite bourgeoisie, working class and some elements of the peasantry. News information was provided for these newspapers by agencies such as Havas, which also managed their advertising, and also became involved after 1889 in the sale of Russian bonds through the press. New technology and marketing gimmicks constantly expanded the readership. From 1903 *Le Petit Parisien* published photographs and also ran competitions with large prizes. Alongside the news, information was provided about stock exchange prices, food market prices, racing prices, trial proceedings and crime. *Faits divers* or human-interest stories including crime, accidents, suicides, fires and rescues took up between 10 and 20 per cent of *Le Petit Parisien* in 1894–1914, with a whole proletariat of reporters hanging around police stations and even conducting parallel investigations in order to provide material, the reportage drawing on and in turn fertilizing the contemporary taste for crime and detective fiction.[42]

The press and popular novels were not the only ways of reaching a mass public. Popular hunger for up-to-the-minute news and comment was fed by fast-selling pamphlets, songs and cartoons, supplied by a multitude of printers – perhaps 1,500 in Paris – and sold by *camelots*, the heirs of the *colporteurs*, particularly during dramatic events such as the Dreyfus Affair. Answering Zola's *Letter to France* of 7 January 1898, which had sold 47,000 copies, Léon Hayward, otherwise known as Napoléon, printed a *Reply of All French People to Émile Zola*, which sold 200,000 copies. This was a continuation of the Grub Street literature of the Revolution which involved the labouring classes, unemployed and immigrants in political debate.[43] Of the more substantial illustrated magazines, *Excelsior* had a circulation of 100,000 in 1910, while one of the successes of the Offenstadt brothers was the youth press, comics with titles like *L'Épatant* thriving after 1908 on the back of Louis Foulon's cartoon strip, the Pieds-Nickelés, featuring the subversive and inventive heroes Croquignol, Filochard and Ribouldingue, and using speech bubbles for the first time. Jean-Paul Sartre, born in 1905, recalled not only 'reading the concluding pages of *Madame Bovary* twenty times' but dragging his mother to the kiosk at the corner of the boulevard Saint-Michel and the rue Soufflot to buy the weekly copy of *L'Épatant*.[44]

Mass culture was generally blended in with entertainment and thus drew on other resources such as drink, music and sex. A law of July 1880 removed the Empire's police control over cafés, requiring owners simply to register them rather than seek permission. The number of cafés in Paris ballooned from 22,000 in 1870 to 42,000 in the mid-1880s, falling back to 30,000 in the Belle Époque, and were the social space of a broad mixture of classes. In 1867 the theatres' monopoly of putting on shows had ended, leading to a great expansion of *café-concerts* such as the Alcazar and Eldorado which had developed under the Empire, a 'democratized theatre' or 'theatre of the poor' which generally charged only for food and drink, not for the show. In the working-class districts the tradition of communal, participatory singing carried over from the *goguettes* was common, but in central Paris the tendency was to greater refinement and sophistication. The *cabaret artistique* or literary café was aimed at a bohemian, intellectual clientele and launched the careers of poets and singers. Émile Goudeau, a low-level functionary in the Finance Ministry, founded the Hydropathes in the Latin Quarter in 1878, which boasted the humorist Alphonse Allais on the bill. Later Allais moved to Le Chat Noir, a cabaret on Montmartre decked out in mock Louis XIII style, where writers such as Maupassant and Huysmans, who generally moved in literary circles, could find a wider audience. Le Chat Noir was bought in 1885 and renamed Le Mirliton by Aristide Bruant, a bourgeois whose education had been cut short by his father's death. He was apprenticed to a jeweller, fought in the Franco-Prussian war and was a clerk in a railway office before going into show business. An excellent publicist and self-publicist, Bruant commissioned posters from Toulouse-Lautrec, was deliberately rude to his clients, and celebrated the criminals and pimps of Paris in songs the vulgarity of which for Edmond de Goncourt provided 'warning signs of the approaching end of the bourgeois age'.[45]

Another upgraded version of the *café-concert* was the music hall, which developed after 1890. These were sumptuous variety theatres like the Moulin Rouge, which opened for the Exposition of 1889, and the Folies Bergère, draped in red and gold, lit by gas or electricity. These charged at least 2 francs entrance, 3 francs standing and 4 or 6 francs for a seat after 1900 when the Comédie Française cost 2½ francs, which put them beyond reach of the *petit peuple*. These had to be content with downmarket *guingettes* such as the Moulin de la Galette, which charged 50 centimes for men and 20 for women and combined entertainment with clandestine prostitution. Music halls put on circus acts such as trapeze artists, fairground spectacles such as the Pétomane whose act was a symphony of farts, and dancing girls such as the Barriston sisters from America. Music and comedy were central to the routine and stars of the music hall emerged such as Yvette Guibert, whose father died when she was nineteen and who worked as a sales girl in Printemps before being spotted and launched as an actress. She made her career as a singer and comedienne, starting at Eldorado in 1889, moving to the Moulin Rouge, but was also popular in the open-air *cafés chantants* such as the Ambassadeurs, unmistakable in her long black gloves and iconized by Toulouse-Lautrec. The buttoned-up American writer Rupert Harding Davis found her songs and sketches 'neither funny, witty, nor quaint, but simply nasty and offensive. The French audiences of the open-air concerts, however, enjoy these, and encore her six times nightly.' Other audiences also appreciated the star, who made successful tours of Europe and America.[46]

At the turn of the century the new medium of cinema began to emerge. It separated itself from the fairground and theatre only with difficulty. The Lumière brothers from Lyon who manufactured photographic products demonstrated the first film in Paris in 1895 and for the Exposition of 1900 they projected a twenty-five-minute show on to a giant screen 21 by 18 metres. For the 5,000 viewers at a time who saw it the effect of the film was not unlike the panoramas they were already used to, created by a large drum of painted scenes revolving round the audience, showing Madagascar or the trans-Siberian railway. After Georges Méliès bought the theatre of the conjuror Robert Houdin in 1888 and developed special effects such as the guillotined man reluctant to lose his head, it was a short step to the fantastic films he made at his Montreuil studio after 1897, such as *Cinderella, Bluebeard* or Jules Verne's *Round the Moon*, which also used special effects. Charles Pathé, who sold Edison phonographs and cylinders of popular songs in fairgrounds, built his own studio at Vincennes in 1905 and made melodramatic films for a fairground audience such as *The Story of a Crime* in 1901. More revolutionary were the comic films he made after 1905 with actor Max Linder, a precursor of Charlie Chaplin, such as *Max's Holidays* and *Max's Wedding*, which created the first film star, fêted from Barcelona to St Petersburg in the years before 1914. Meanwhile filmmaker Victorin Jasset engineered the crossover between adolescent fiction and film with his *Nick Carter, King of Detectives* in 1908, *Zigomar, King of Bandits* in 1911, and, inevitably, *Zigomar against Nick Carter* in 1912.[47]

Alongside cinema, a new dimension to mass culture at the turn of the century was sport. Until then, sport had meant essentially horse-racing, with the track of Longchamp in the 1870s attracting 200,000 visitors a year (generally punters), 500,000–600,000 in the 1890s. It also meant gymnastics in the German or Swedish style that took off in the wake of the defeat of 1870, with a Union of French Gymnastic Clubs set up in 1873, in an attempt to make the young male population fitter for war. Parallel to this developed athletics clubs, such as the Racing Club de France, which after 1892 organized Sunday races in the Bois de Boulogne, with runners wearing jockey colours and caps, sometimes carrying whips, and bet upon as though they were themselves horses in a flat race. Rugby and football penetrated from England, the first extended along the wine-trade route into south-west France, the second into Channel ports such as Le Havre, into Paris and the northern industrial towns following other business connections. When the Le Havre Athletic Club won the French championship in 1899, six of its players were English. Football and rugby clubs were generally set up by alumni of elite secondary schools, and provided winter activity for those doing athletics in the summer. The development of athletics was furthered by Pierre de Coubertin, a Jesuit-educated noble who studied at the Paris Law Faculty and the École Libre des Sciences Politiques, was worried by the neglect of physical education and character-building in French lycées and believed that England's enthusiasm for team games helped to fortify its ruling class against revolution and underpinned its empire-building. In 1889 he founded the Union of French Athletic Societies and on 20 March 1892 refereed a football match in the Bois de Boulogne between Stade Français and Racing Club de France in front of a crowd of 2,000. In this period athletics, along with the football and rugby that grew out of it, retained a somewhat bourgeois and English profile. As one sports paper noted in 1891, 'The Grand Prix de Longchamp attracts over fifty thousand, a football match hardly five hundred.'[48]

Much more French and much more popular was cycling. It was the product of a technological revolution that brought down the price of cycles from 500 to 100 francs in the 1890s, so that there were 3.5 million of them in France in 1914. The French Cycling Union set up in 1881 had 44,000 members by 1893, and acted as a formidable lobby, persuading the Paris municipal council and other town councils to fund cycle stadiums as popular race-courses in the 1890s to match those of the rich at Auteuil and Longchamp. In time road-racing became even more popular, with big prizes and accolades for rival manufacturers to be made in the Bordeaux-to-Paris and Paris-to-Brussels races. These gave opportunities to young men of working-class origin, such as Charles Terront, the son of a railway mechanic of Saint-Ouen and a former errand-boy for Havas, to win fame and money. It was however the intervention of the press that made cycling into a sport of mass appeal. This was the work of one man, Henri Desgranges, who gave up a career in the law to become manager of the Parc des Princes cycle stadium in 1897 and three years later took control of a new sports daily financed by the Comte de Dion, *L'Auto*. In 1903 he boosted the fortunes of both cycling and *L'Auto* by launching the Tour de France, with prize money of 20,000 francs. *L'Auto* pumped up the Tour, inventing heroic stories such as that of 'the Old Gaulois' Christophe, who in 1911 carried his machine with a snapped fork down the Pyrenees to have it repaired by a blacksmith before he continued his route. Circulation of *L'Auto*, which had a monopoly of the coverage of the Tour, went from 20,000 to 120,000 in 1913, with 332,000 during the Tour in July 1914.[49] This supreme amalgam of racing, journalism and advertising epitomized the versatility and success of mass culture.

15

Rebuilding the Nation

The defeat of 1870 precipitated France into the lower rank of the great powers, below Germany, Great Britain and Russia, above Italy but at about the same level as the Habsburg Monarchy, itself defeated by Germany in 1866. Defeat and occupation led to civil war in 1871 and a country profoundly divided, not least on whether the army should be used to defend France's frontiers or suppress revolution at home. In addition, defeat demoralized France as a nation and demonstrated the fragility of its national identity. Three challenges therefore confronted France. First, whether it could escape from diplomatic isolation and through military feats, outside Europe, regain a place among the great powers. Second, whether it could rebuild national unity and in particular recover the confidence of the nation in its army. Lastly, whether it could define and propagate a coherent and confident national consciousness to underpin its diplomatic and military endeavours.

IMPOSSIBLE *REVANCHE*

The Treaty of Frankfurt which ended the war of 1870–71 dictated not only the loss of Alsace-Lorraine but the obligation to pay reparations to the new German Empire while German forces occupied part of France. President of the Republic Adolphe Thiers paid the final instalment on 5 September 1871 and German troops marched out of Verdun and across the border on 13 September. A League for the Deliverance of Alsace-Lorraine had been set up after the Treaty by the Alsatian industrialist and deputy to the National Assembly,

Scheurer-Kestner, but when Chancellor Bismarck objected it was dissolved and Jules Grévy, president of the Assembly, told him that France must renounce Alsace. 'Do not believe the madmen who tell you otherwise and who have aggravated our misfortunes by espousing a hopeless cause.'[1]

Despite France's massive humiliation a huge public turned up to watch a military review at Longchamp in June 1871, when 120,000 French soldiers marched past, headed by Marshal MacMahon, commander at Sedan the previous September, who was embraced by Thiers.[2] The defeated army had regained some of its lustre by suppressing the Paris Commune, but this had also discredited the army and called into question what kind of an army France should have. Old republicans such as Edgar Quinet deplored the army having 'its eyes fixed on the interior, obsessed by civil war, and not destined for distant wars'. He argued that it should be drawn from the entrails of the nation like the Prussian *Landwehr* of 1806, with all citizens doing three years' military service, the vehicle of national revival.[3] The nation-in-arms, however, reminded Thiers too much of Gambetta's *levée en masse* of 1870 which had led to the Commune and which would be like 'putting a gun on the shoulder of every socialist'.[4] His alternative was to divide the population of military age into two, to make the first serve under the colours for five years, becoming Napoleonic *grognards*, while the other half would do only six months' service, and go into the reserve. Although military service was compulsory, seminarists, trainee teachers and most students were exempted.[5] This semi-professional army may have been insulated against revolution but it did nothing to rebuild national unity.

Revanche (revenge) against Germany in the sense of a war to recover Alsace-Lorraine was simply not an option in the years after 1870. France had no allies and no stomach for a fight. Although Gambetta had walked out of the Assembly in protest against the Treaty of Frankfurt Bismarck considered that Catholic ultramontanes were more likely to start a war to recover the pope's lost territories than republicans were to regain Alsace-Lorraine. Seeking to escape his reputation as a warmonger, Gambetta told a republican audience at Saint-Quentin in November 1871, 'never speak of the foreigner, but let it be understood that we are always thinking of him.'[6] There is some evidence that Bismarck provided financial help for the republicans in the 1877 elections that followed the Seize Mai crisis, on condition that they abandon all references to revenge.[7] When Gambetta and his mistress Léonie Léon toured Germany in the autumn of 1881 there were rumours that he had visited Bismarck on his country estate of Varzin, but as Bismarck would not relax his grip on Alsace-Lorraine a meeting would have been pointless. That said, Gambetta's abandonment of the idea of revenge terminated his relationship with the salon hostess Juliette Adam who had sponsored his rise to power for a decade.[8]

SHAPING A NATIONAL CONSCIOUSNESS

While France's fight with Germany was taking place on the battlefield in the autumn of 1870 a debate was also taking place in the universities, as historians argued about whether Alsace-Lorraine should be properly French or German. Theodor Mommsen, history professor at Berlin, stated that a nation was defined by its language, which expressed the soul of the people, and thus Alsace and the Moselle department, which predominantly spoke a German dialect, had legitimately been recovered by the Reich. Fustel de Coulanges, who had been a history professor at Strasbourg between 1860 and 1870, argued that a nation was based not on language or race but on 'a community of ideas, interests, sentiments, memories and hopes'; in a word, *'la patrie* is what you love.' 'If Alsace is and remains French,' he concluded, 'it is uniquely because it wishes to.'[9] After the war, only 10 per cent of the population of Alsace-Lorraine opted to remain French, but this was in large part explained by the fact that to remain French they had to leave their province and their property.[10] The view of French intellectuals was nevertheless that even those Alsatians and Lorrainers who stayed in the Reich remained French in memory and aspiration, and thus Alsace-Lorraine became a model for French thinking about nationhood.

In a seminal lecture at the Sorbonne in 1882 Ernest Renan argued against the Germanic idea that the nation was a *Volk* defined by a single language and race. 'France is Celtic, Iberian and Germanic,'

Paris under siege and Paris in revolution, 1870–71. Above, national guardsmen hold off an invisible Prussian enemy; below, they build barricades against a defeatist and repressive government.

The generation of Rejuvenators, who shaped the Republic of the Belle Époque.
Clockwise from the top: Aristide Briand, anarchist turned peacemaker; Alexandre Millerand,
socialist turned nationalist; Joseph Caillaux, 'plutocratic demagogue'; and Henriette Caillaux,
here shooting the editor of the *Figaro* to defend her honour.

Belle Époque France at ease with itself. The middle classes holiday at Trouville, while Louis Renault races one of his new machines.

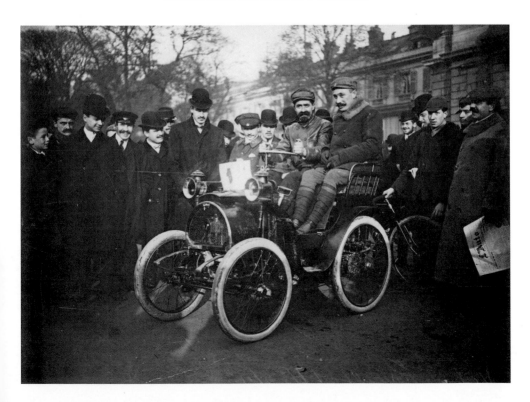

Two faces of French feminism: former actress Marguerite Durand, who claimed that 'feminism owes much to my blonde hair', and Madeleine Pelletier, a grocer's daughter and psychiatric doctor who defended women's right to abortion and campaigned with British suffragettes.

103 *CHANTILLY.* — *Rendez-vous de Chasse.* — *LL.*

Despite these images of a divided society – the social elite hunting in the forest of Chantilly, and button-makers on strike in the Paris region – French society was becoming increasingly cohesive around a broad middle class.

The generation of Sacrifice, which brought together patriotism, faith and social conscience. Clockwise from the top: Charles Péguy; Marc Sangnier, leader of republican Catholic youth; Ernest Psichari, the model Catholic soldier; and Raïssa Maritain, a Jewish refugee whose conversion to Catholicism was much acclaimed.

Faces of French nationalism. Clockwise from the top: national heroes Joan of Arc and Vercingétorix imagined together by sculptor Chatrousse for the Salon of 1872; colonial proconsul Lyautey in France's Moroccan protectorate; and Big Bad Wolf Britannia confronts Red Riding Hood France at Fashoda on the Nile in 1898.

Peace and War. Socialist tribune Jean Jaurès addresses an antimilitarist rally on the outskirts of Paris in 1913, while in 1914 Renault taxis are used to transport troops to the battle of the Marne, where the German offensive was checked.

he declared, while 'Germany is Germanic, Celtic and Slav.' While the United States and England spoke English and Spain spoke Spanish, he continued, Switzerland spoke three or four languages but was still a nation because nationality was a question of will. He continued,

A nation is a soul, a spiritual principle. This is made up of two things which are really only one. One in the past, the other in the present. One is the collective ownership of a rich legacy of memories, the other is the present consent or desire to live together, the will to continue to develop the inheritance it has received intact ... The nation, like the individual, is the culmination of a long past of striving, sacrifice and dedication. The cult of ancestors is of all cults the most legitimate; ancestors have made us who we are. A heroic past, great men, glory (I mean the real kind) are the social capital on which the national idea is based. To have common glories in the past and a common will in the present; to have done great things together and to wish to do more of them, that is the prerequisite of a people. We love in proportion to the sacrifices we have agreed to, to the evils we have suffered. Indeed, collective suffering unites more than joy. As far as national memories are concerned, mourning is more important than triumph, because mourning imposes duties and dictates a collective effort ... The existence of a nation is, if you will excuse the expression, an everyday plebiscite, as the existence of an individual is a perpetual affirmation of life ... It is never in the real interest of a nation to annex or keep a country in spite of itself. The will of a nation is in the end the only legitimate criterion and the one to which we must always return.[11]

After the war was over the French indeed concentrated not so much on *revanche* as on rebuilding a national spirit that had been demoralized by defeat and was now deeply divided by political and religious conflict. A first step was to devise an 'official history' that would underline the continuity of the national struggle and the coherence of its identity over and above its sufferings and divisions. Ernest Lavisse, who succeeded Fustel de Coulanges at the École Normale Supérieure in 1876 and began to lecture at the Sorbonne in 1880, derived a sense of the ever-present past from his grandmother, who recalled the occupation of Picardy by Cossack forces in 1815.[12] Beginning his Sorbonne lectures in 1881 he invited historians to 'give the children of France that *pietas erga patriam* which must be founded on an understanding of their country'. Over and above the quarrel between the monarchical past and republican present, they must teach 'the notion of solidarity that unites the present to the past, the living to their ancestors', and nurture 'that national pride that is the solid foundation of patriotism'.[13] He launched a *History of France* that was written over the next forty years by his former pupils who were at the École Normale Supérieure in the 1870s, nine volumes preceding the Revolution, nine volumes after. At the same time he wrote school textbooks such as that of 1884 which ended by explaining that France had been defeated in 1870 because the French loved peace too much and had forgotten how to fight. 'Our disasters teach us that we must not love those who hate us, that we must love our *patrie* France first, and humanity after.'[14]

If the story of common glories and sufferings was taken care of by Lavisse and his acolytes, the cult of France's great ancestors was undertaken in a series of public commemorations. After the liberation of French territory in 1873 particular focus fell on previous heroes and heroines who had united the country, resisted foreign invasion, and sacrificed themselves in the attempt. Exalted above all were Joan of Arc, who in 1429 steeled the indecisive Charles VII at Chinon to fight the English, raised the siege of Orléans, and had the king crowned at Reims before attacking Paris and being burned at the stake at Rouen. Alongside her was Vercingétorix, the Gallic chief who had defeated Julius Caesar at the battle of Gergovia in 52 BC before succumbing to him at Alésia and being taken in chains to Rome for execution. These two heroes, imagined hand in hand for the Salon of 1872 by the sculptor Chatrousse, symbolized an eternal France that went back to ancient Gaul and a united France, despite the battles that took place between rival political and religious factions to 'own' their memory. Joan was claimed both by the republican followers of Michelet, who saw her as a 'girl of the people' who saved France despite the incompetence or treachery of king, nobles and clergy, and by the Catholic Church which saw her as sent by God to restore France to its divine mission and as a candidate for sainthood. In fact there was now some convergence in the interpretations. Dupanloup, bishop of Orléans, calling for Joan to be made a saint in 1869, described her as a 'daughter of the people' inspired by a double love, 'the love of God and of her country'. Meanwhile, at the unveiling of the famous Frémiet statue on the place des Pyramides in 1874 poems were read by the republican patriot Paul Déroulède.[15] On this model the epic journey of Joan of Arc was commemorated in towns and cities that erected equestrian statues to her at the end of the nineteenth century, from Chinon and Rouen to Orléans and Reims.

The cult of Vercingétorix was embedded in the landscape rather than the city, but the site of his defeat at Alésia was disputed between partisans of Alise-Sainte-Reine (Côte d'Or), which raised a great statue to him there in 1865, and those of Alaise (Doubs), each side sponsoring frantic excavations. The sculptor Bartholdi exhibited an equestrian statue of Vercingétorix in the Salon of 1870, and a group of Gallic chiefs galloping over a fallen Roman at the Salon of 1878. In an overlapping dispute about the origins of the French nation, Fustel de Coulanges took the view that the defeat of Vercingétorix by Caesar in 52 BC had allowed France to be civilized by the Romans, while only the baptism of the Frankish king Clovis had made France the eldest daughter of the Church. On the other hand, Albert Réveille, who became professor of Celtic studies at the École Pratique des Hautes Études in 1876, defended the Gallic point of view that the chieftain 'fought and died not for a canton, nor for an overlord, nor for a dynasty, but *pro patria*, for the Gallic fatherland, which is still ours'.[16]

COLONIALISTS AND THEIR ENEMIES

After the defeat of 1870 there was very little for ambitious young soldiers to do except to further the colonial ambitions of France. Joseph-Simon Galliéni, who had joined the marines from Saint-Cyr at the age of twenty-one in 1870 and, captured at Sedan, spent six months as a POW in Germany, was sent by the governor of Senegal in 1879 to explore the upper Niger. He concluded a treaty the following year with Ahmadou, sultan of Ségou, establishing a French protectorate and trading rights on the Niger in return for guns and money. Received as a hero on his return in 1882, he married a rich heiress, published *Voyage to the Soudan* in 1885, and returned there as commander of French Sudan in 1886. Five years younger than Galliéni, Jesuit-educated Hubert Lyautey graduated from Saint-Cyr in 1875 and was involved in Albert de Mun's workers' circles before serving in Algeria, where he learned Arabic and championed direct relations between French soldiers and tribal chiefs rather than the expansion of the civil administration. This anticipated a distrust between colonial soldiers and the French administration and politics which persisted throughout the Third Republic.[17]

Ambitious young soldiers stuck in Europe were equally frustrated. Vicomte Eugène-Melchior de Vogüé, who was also taken prisoner at Sedan, became attaché at the embassy of St Petersburg at the age of twenty-nine in 1877. He was present at the Congress of Berlin in 1878 when the great powers pinned back Russian ambitions in the Balkans, and Great Britain managed to obtain Cyprus from the Ottoman Empire. Vogüé noted that France had no more weight than Italy and that the French 'returned from Berlin and those satiated giants with such a sadness that you could almost hear the collapse of our old foreign policy. Oh Spain!'[18] In fact at Berlin Bismarck and the British foreign secretary Lord Salisbury gave France a green light to further its colonial ambitions in Tunisia, Salisbury as a *quid pro quo* for Cyprus, Bismarck because he wanted to take France's thoughts off Alsace-Lorraine. The only other power that had an interest in Tunisia that France could offend was Italy, and when it was offended it jumped straight into Bismarck's arms in the form of a Triple Alliance with Germany and Austria. The government of Jules Ferry used the pretext of an attack by Krumir tribesmen in the south of the country to impose a protectorate on the Bey of Tunis under the Treaty of Bardo in May 1881. Ferry defended his action as 'the triumph of civilization over barbarism' and argued that 'France was not lightly resigned to play the part of a greater Belgium in the world', while Gambetta declared, 'France is recovering its rank as a great power again.'[19]

Catastrophe, however, almost immediately followed in Egypt, where the French had built the Suez Canal before 1870. The khedive of Egypt was maintained in power by foreign loans he could no longer pay off, and British and French interference was deeply resented by the local population and military. After riots in Alexandria on 12 June 1882 had killed sixty Europeans, the British and French planned a joint intervention. The Freycinet government, however, was fiercely attacked in the Chamber of Deputies by Georges Clemenceau at the head of radical opinion, who questioned the wisdom of the expedition. As a result the Chamber refused credits for military action, the ministry was toppled on 29 July 1882, and British forces marched into Cairo alone on 15 September. 'This country', observed Vogüé, who had just resigned from the diplomatic service, 'has as many reserves of virility as a eunuch.'[20] Once the enormity of the decision became clear, the Chamber was eager to recover some honour, and when the naval captain de Brazza returned from the Congo with a treaty signed with King Makoko the Chamber and Senate endorsed it emphatically, on 22 November 1882, triggering another phase in the 'scramble for Africa'.[21]

France's bid to become a colonial power was fiercely opposed by radicals who argued that the country was wasting men and resources that needed to be husbanded for a future war on the Rhine, whenever that came, and that by scrambling for Africa it was simply doing the bidding of Bismarck. At the time of the Berlin conference of 1884 which partitioned Africa Clemenceau called Ferry 'the protégé of M. Bismarck'.[22] Another leading anti-colonialist was Paul Déroulède, who resigned from a commission on military education in 1882 when it became clear that Ferry favoured only gymnastics in schools, not a basic military training, and founded the Ligue des Patriotes. This demanded the revision of the Treaty of Frankfurt and the recovery of Alsace-Lorraine and in the meantime 'the liberation of the soul of France which is still occupied and oppressed by the foreigner' – this liberation to be furthered by a 'patriotic and military education by means of books, songs, shooting and gymnastics'. At a prize-giving for the first national shooting championships in 1884 Déroulède declared, 'I have said it before and I repeat that before going to plant the French flag where it has never flown, we should replant it where it has flown before, where we have all seen it with our own eyes.'[23]

As he spoke France was becoming embroiled in a colonial war

with China. In what is now Vietnam French power was being built out from Cochin-China in the south to Annam in the centre and Tonkin in the north. Jules Ferry, who oversaw the campaign, defended French strategy as designed to gain control of the Red River and gain access to a market of 400 million consumers in China, while Freycinet endorsed the policy of 'indirect *revanche*'.[24] However, Chinese forces drove back the French from Langson and when Ferry asked the Chamber on 30 March 1885 for another 100,000 francs to avenge Langson, to defend their grip on Indo-China and 'for our honour in the entire world', he was exposed to another scathing attack from Clemenceau. 'Is there not enough scope here for human ambition,' he asked, 'and is not the idea of increasing the sum total of knowledge, prosperity, liberty, law, and organizing the fight against ignorance, vice and poverty a better use of social energies and enough challenge for a politician or party?'[25] 'Ferry the Tonkinois' was overthrown and Clemenceau and the Ligue des Patriotes lobbied for the promotion to the War Ministry of the republican General Boulanger, who promised to turn the army more into the nation-in-arms and take a firm line against Bismarck. Unfortunately, as in 1870, Bismarck proved a master of political manipulation. Unable to push through the Reichstag the bill that provided seven years of credit for the German army, he made a violent speech to it on 11 January 1887, stating in no uncertain terms that Boulanger meant war. He then dissolved the Reichstag, sent 75,000 reservists to Alsace-Lorraine, secured a governmental majority and had the military credits voted. French republicans were now faced with the possibility of a war of revenge and backed down. The government in which Boulanger was war minister was overturned by a combination of moderate republicans and conservatives on 16 May 1887, and Boulanger was sent to take up a provincial command in Clermont-Ferrand, seen off in style at the Gare de Lyon by the Ligue des Patriotes.

Although Boulanger enjoyed a brief popularity, this did not suggest that the French were warmongers. His opposition to the republican political class was the main reason for his success. There was indeed a growing hostility to the army as it had been organized in 1872, with long-term service for some and exemption for others. Around 1890 there was a spate of anti-militarist novels, written by men of the generation born around 1860, who had not been marked by the defeat of 1870 as their fathers had, and who criticized the harsh conditions of barrack life. Lucien Descaves, a great admirer of Louise Michel and Pissarro, wrote *Sous-offs* (NCOs) in 1889, a barely fictionalized account of brutality, drunkenness, disease and prostitution set in garrison towns where he had served for four years. This led to a prosecution of the author and editors brought by the Ministry of War. It was followed by Georges Darien's *Biribi* (1890), a story based on his experiences in a disciplinary battalion in Tunisia, and Georges Courteline's *Train de 8h47* (1891), a reaction to his conscription after drawing a short straw.[26] Much criticism was aimed at the semi-professional army which since Louis-Napoleon's coup of 1851 and the suppression of the Paris Commune was regarded in left-wing circles as the vehicle of political reaction and social order more than national defence. The military service law of 1889 introduced compulsory service for three years and reduced exemptions, moving much closer to a national army. However, the effect was not felt immediately. On 1 May 1891 French troops fired on demonstrating textile workers at Fourmies in the Nord. Marcel Cachin, a student in Bordeaux, recalled that he had joined the socialist party in 1891 on hearing of the Fourmies massacre. The Marxist leader Paul Lafargue, accused of provoking the incident, was defended by the socialist deputy Alexandre Millerand who was a critic of the army then, but as minister of war twenty years later would have a very different attitude to militarism.[27]

THE FRANCO-RUSSIAN ALLIANCE

For twenty years France had been diplomatically isolated as Bismarck locked Austria-Hungary and Italy into the Triple Alliance and Austria-Hungary and Russia into the Dreikaiserbund. Tsar Alexander III was no fan of French ministries with Jacobin generals who expelled members of former French ruling families: 'your government is no longer the Republic,' he told the French ambassador, 'it is the Commune.'[28] Relations between the two countries were improving, however, on a course that would lead to a Franco-Russian alliance in 1894. Juliette Adam had long been a friend of Russia. She visited it in 1882, accompanied by Melchior de Vogüé. De Vogüé had witnessed the turn-out of 100,000 people for the funeral of Dostoevsky in 1881, and this moved him to publish his bestselling *Russian Novel* (1886), which brought Dostoevsky along with Gogol, Turgenev and Tolstoy to the attention of the French reading public as voices of suffering in a noble and passionate country.[29] In 1886 Paul Déroulède, a regular of her salon, went to Russia and met Panslav leaders such as Katkov, who preached a forward policy in the Balkans to free Slav peoples under Austrian or Ottoman domination. Juliette Adam founded a Franco-Russian Artistic and Literary Association in 1888, which also popularized Tchaikovsky, and a Society of Friends of Russia in 1890.[30] French enthusiasts for Russia were not only literary. In 1888 German bankers lost out to their French counterparts in the battle to offer loans to the Russian government and Russian industry. The so-called 'Russian loans' floated in the French money markets were immensely attractive to French investors, mainly in mining and iron and steel industries stimulated by the building of the trans-Siberian railway. At the outbreak of the First World War 25 per cent of all French foreign investment was in Russia, and 38 per cent of new French investments since 1882, as against 13 per cent of German and under 3 per cent of British investment.[31] Diplomatic and military ties followed behind. The Reinsurance Treaty of 1887, by which Bismarck tried to tie in Russia after the lapse of the Dreikaiserbund, itself lapsed in 1890 on Bismarck's fall from power, leaving Russia open to new allies. The arrest of Russian anarchists in France that year persuaded Alexander III that the Republic was a respectable government after all, and in July 1891, when a French squadron visited the Russian naval base of Kronstadt, the tsar stood bareheaded while the Marseillaise was played. Under a military convention of August 1892 France and Russia pledged themselves to a defensive alliance against German aggression, and following a return visit of the Russian fleet to Toulon in 1893 a special train took Russian dignitaries to celebrations in Paris and Versailles, at which Juliette Adam was resplendent.[32] A Franco-Russian alliance was formally agreed on 4 January 1894, and a bridge over the Seine was built in honour of Alexander III, which was opened by the new tsar, Nicholas II, when he visited France with the Tsarina Alexandra in 1896.

SHOWDOWN AND ENTENTE WITH GREAT BRITAIN

After 1890 France's principal enemy appeared to be not so much Germany as Great Britain. In July that year Great Britain concluded a treaty with Germany giving the latter the North Sea island and naval base of Heligoland in return for Germany renouncing its claims to Zanzibar and Uganda and recognizing the Nile valley as a British sphere of influence. The following month France relinquished similar claims to Zanzibar and the Nile valley in return for a free hand in annexing Madagascar. This was regarded as a sell-out in French colonial circles which now began to organize and agitate. A Committee for French Africa was set up in 1890 under the Prince Auguste d'Arenberg and journalist Harry Allis to support French claims as widely as possible in Africa. The French Colonial Union of 1893 under Joseph Chailley-Bert, a lawyer and professor at the École Libre des Sciences Politiques, was a business lobby which pressed the government to develop railways, mines and settlements in Africa and Indo-China. A Colonial Group formed in the Chamber of Deputies in 1892, ninety strong, rising to 120 after the elections of 1893. One of its leaders was Eugène Étienne, born in Oran to a soldier serving in Algeria, educated in Marseille, a champion of the Marseille–Oran shipping business and elected deputy for Oran in 1881. The other was Théophile Delcassé, the son of a minor legal official in the Pyrenean department of the Ariège who had a career in teaching and the Gambettist press before marrying the widow of a former deputy of the Ariège and winning a seat in the same department in 1889. These leaders soon acquired ministerial influence as under-secretary of state for colonies, Étienne in 1887 and 1889–92 and considered an unofficial colonial minister even when out of office, Delcassé in 1893 and a fully fledged minister for colonies in 1894–5. About the same ages as Galliéni and Lyautey, old enough to be marked as young men by the defeat of 1870, they formed a nexus dedicated to restoring French greatness. Étienne was indeed the patron of General Galliéni, who served in Tonkin with his second-in-command Lyautey and was sent to Madagascar as commander-in-chief and resident-general in 1896, again with Lyautey, on a mission to pacify it.[33]

The ambition of the French colonial party, notwithstanding the treaties of 1890, was to prevent Britain building a string of colonial possessions from the Cape to Cairo and instead forge a French empire from Senegal in the west to Somaliland in the east. This would mean sending a military expedition to beat the British forces in Egypt in a race to the headwaters of the Nile. Securing the upper Nile would have the added advantage of putting pressure on the British in Egypt and reopening the question of their unilateral occupation of the country in 1882. The French African Committee put together an expedition commanded by Captain Jean-Baptiste Marchand which was approved by the French government in November 1895 and left from Marseille in August the following year.

Matters came to a head in 1898. Marchand arrived at Fashoda on 29 August and declared himself high commissioner for the French government in the upper Nile and the Bahr el Ghazel. The British army under Lord Kitchener, pushing south into the Sudan, defeated the Mahdist state at Omdurman on 2 September and challenged Marchand on 19 September. France was at that point in the grip of the Dreyfus Affair. Since Zola's *J'accuse* the French military command had been attacked in dreyfusard circles as dominated by Jesuit-trained officers who were more exercised by the influence of Jews, Protestants and freemasons in the Republic than by the idea of restoring French greatness. The antidreyfusard camp, on the other hand, argued that the army was the bearer of French honour and greatness and must be shielded from the attacks of the 'Jewish syndicate' that were demoralizing it and undermining its ability to stand up to its enemies. Paul Déroulède, who had been condemned by the high court for his involvement in the Boulanger conspiracy, relaunched his Ligue des Patriotes on 25 September 1898, denouncing those who ignored the fact 'that the army has been the honour of France for twenty centuries, its holy bayonets, as Michelet said'.[34]

British tactics for dislodging the French from Fashoda were

two-pronged, first psychological, then military. Lord Kitchener sent extracts from the French press to Marchand's camp, revealing the attacks of the dreyfusards on the French army. 'The ten officers were trembling and weeping,' wrote Marchand in a letter that was published by *Le Figaro* on 20 November. 'We learned then and there that the terrible Dreyfus Affair had been opened with its dreadful campaign of infamies and for thirty-six hours not one of us was able to say anything to the others.'[35] 'Nothing can give an idea of the moral disorganization of this country,' de Vogüé wrote to Lyautey.[36] In Paris there was huge agitation by nationalists demanding that the government stand up to the British. 'No! the only response worthy of France,' proclaimed *Le Matin* on 5 October.[37] The sea-port cities of Marseille and Bordeaux were more inclined to compromise, however, and the government did not want to fall into the same trap as in 1870, fully aware that the French navy was in no position to fight a war. Delcassé, now foreign minister in the Brisson government, was keen on a negoti-ated settlement and on 12 October concluded a deal with Great Britain which involved the withdrawal of Marchand. This provoked a nationalist demonstration on 25 October and the fall of the Brisson government. Lord Salisbury decided on a show of force and on 28 October mobilized the Mediterranean fleet and sent the Channel fleet to Gibraltar. In the new ministry formed on 1 November Delcassé was reappointed foreign minister and two days later the recall of Marchand was ordered.[38]

As dreyfusards and antidreyfusards tore each other apart, his-torian Ernest Lavisse, who was working on the Louis XIV volume of his *History of France*, joined forces with Lyautey in January 1899 to issue an Appeal to Union.[39] The situation was effectively saved by the moderate republican Waldeck-Rousseau, who formed a government of national defence in June 1899 and reappointed Delcassé foreign minister. His war minister, General Gallifet, was supposed to purge the top ranks of the army of officers hostile to the Republic, but the amnesty law of 20 December 1899 in fact removed the threat of court martial from the army's top brass and with it the threat of a military coup. Waldeck-Rousseau had good relations with General Galliéni and his right-hand man Lyautey, and was keen to support the colonial army even if the army at home was open to criticism. Returning to France from Madagascar in 1899–1900 Galliéni visited the Exposition of 1900, where the Madagascar pavilion was prominent, and he and Lyautey undertook lecture tours, addressing colonial and geographical societies and chambers of commerce on the benefits and virtues of the French Empire and colonial army.[40] A law of July 1900 sponsored by Gallifet gave organizational autonomy to the colonial army, so that it had its own general staff and colonial commands were reserved to officers with colonial experience. In this way it was better insulated against metropolitan politics.[41]

Under the premiership of the Radical Combes, relations with both the Church and the army and indeed navy deteriorated. The government and its war minister General André were much exercised by the weight of Jesuit-trained officers in the army who were assumed to be disloyal to the Republic. Not only the police but also the masonic lodges were mobilized to spy on officers, and files were kept on whether they or their wives attended mass and whether they sent their children to Catholic schools. If they did, they were liable to be passed over for promotion in favour of republican officers or ambitious NCOs. This *affaire des fiches* exploded in October 1904 when *Le Figaro* published clear evidence that the Grand Orient masonic lodge was influencing promotions.[42] Combes entrusted the Navy Ministry to the outspoken Radical Camille Pelletan, who set France resolutely against joining in the naval race engaged in by Great Britain and Germany. He cut back the battleship programme, downsized the Mediterranean fleet on the grounds that officers spent most of their time on the Riviera, and allowed shipyard workers to form a union and affiliate to the CGT.[43] The final military legacy of the Combes ministry was the military law of 21 March 1905, which reduced universal military service from three years to two. A victory for those who wanted more of a nation-in-arms, it was severely criticized as not giving enough scope for proper military training.

This was not to say that French patriotism and French national interests were neglected. Émile Combes lent his weight to the ongoing definition of French national identity by unveiling the huge equestrian statue of Vercingétorix by Bartholdi on the main square of Clermont-

Ferrand on 10 October 1903.[44] On the colonial side, the governor-general of Indo-China, Paul Doumer, organized an exhibition in Hanoi in the winter of 1902–3 to showcase the capital of newly conquered North Vietnam, highlight the commercial potential of the region and celebrate Western understanding of the East through an International Congress of Far East Studies.[45] Meanwhile relations with Great Britain improved by default as Britain became obsessed by Germany's battleship programme and evidence of German support for the Boers in South Africa. Following a visit of Edward VII to Paris and of President Loubet to London in 1903 twenty years of resentment over Egypt were finally resolved by the Entente Cordiale of 8 April 1904, under which France recognized Britain's claim to Egypt and Britain gave France a free hand in Morocco.[46] The colonial party lost no time in taking advantage of this opening. A French Morocco Committee was formed by the French African Committee, and Étienne, as informal colonial minister, encouraged Lyautey to extend French military influence into Morocco from the Algerian border. This risked provoking conflict with Spain and Germany, both of which had interests in Morocco, but when Delcassé and the Combes government told Lyautey to pull back in July 1904 he called on the support of Étienne and threatened 'a second Fashoda'.[47]

RIVALRY WITH GERMANY

This Fashoda came not from Britain but from Germany. On 31 March 1905 Kaiser William II landed unexpectedly in Tangier and challenged France's attempt to control Morocco by declaring the independence of the sultan and demanding equal rights for all the powers. The German government held Delcassé responsible for France's bid to gain control of Morocco and issued an ultimatum demanding his dismissal. The Rouvier ministry of which Delcassé was foreign minister panicked and dropped him on 6 June.[48] The great powers met in conference in Algeciras in January 1906 to decide what to do about Morocco. The Germans tried to bully France into abandoning its claim, but Great Britain regarded this as a first test of the Entente Cordiale and stood firm behind France. In March it was the German chancellor Bülow who suffered a diplomatic defeat, followed by a heart attack. Because Germany was not prepared to go to war over Morocco it was forced to recognize that France had the upper hand there.

For many on the French left the Moroccan crisis demonstrated an upsurge of militarism and colonialism that had brought France to the brink of war, and an antimilitarist backlash followed. The French national interest had nothing to do with the working class for Gustave Hervé, a schoolteacher from Sens, who declared at a socialist meeting in April 1905, during the Morocco crisis, 'Our country is our class.' In the event of an attack on France, 'without thought of who the aggressor is', he continued, 'we will answer the call to arms by a general strike of reservists.'[49] An International Antimilitarist Association (AIA) was founded at Amsterdam in June 1904 and in October 1905 the French branch led by Georges Yvetot, secretary of the Fédération des Bourses du Travail, Miguel Almereyda of the anarchist paper *Libertaire*, and Gustave Hervé launched a poster campaign for the benefit of the new cohort of conscripts. It read,

When you are ordered to shoot at your brothers in poverty, workers, tomorrow's soldiers – as has happened in Chalon, Martinique or Limoges – you will shoot, but not on your comrades. You will shoot at the braided stooges who dare to give you such orders. When you are sent to the frontier to defend the capitalists' strong-boxes against other workers as exploited as you are, you will not march. All war is criminal. You will answer the mobilization order by an immediate strike and insurrection.[50]

Antimilitarists argued that, whether they were repressing French workers or killing indigenous populations, armies were the instruments of capitalism and were driven to further their interests by war. A 1905 study of *Colonialism* by the socialist Paul Louis argued that colonies had been founded since 1880 to provide 'new sources of exploitation of wealth' for 'the industrial and commercial bourgeoisie'. Colonialism, he said, was disguised by the rhetoric of greatness and the civilizing mission but it massacred native populations and imposed slavery, increased the servitude of the proletariat at home and led inevitably to an arms race and war between industrial powers.[51]

The government came down hard on these antimilitarists. Twenty-eight members of the Antimilitarist Association were sent for trial in December 1905, and all but two received prison sentences, including four years for Hervé and three for Yvetot and Almereyda. Amnestied in 1906, Hervé and Almereyda continued to broadcast their views in *La Guerre Sociale*. The antimilitarists, however, were not representative of the mainstream left, which fell back on the revolutionary patriotism of the Volunteers of 1792, who at Valmy had defeated the Austrian and Prussian invaders intent on crushing the French Revolution. They disliked standing armies but embraced a patriotism which held that France was the cradle of liberty and must defend itself not only for France but for the universal cause of liberty. 'It is impossible to announce in advance', said Jean Jaurès during the trial, 'that one will not defend oneself by military force against the invasion of a foreigner who threatens us, our republican liberties, and is the agent of international reaction.'[52] Jaurès took on the antimilitarists at the SFIO congress of Nancy in 1907. He rejected such slogans as 'down with the Republic', for the Republic was the site that gave the proletariat the freedom to undertake its revolutionary work. If France were 'threatened, invaded or brutalized, the duty of the socialist and revolutionary would be to defend the independence of the nation'. Otherwise, he claimed, 'Tsarist Russia could invade and subjugate socialist Germany with impunity or imperial Germany could subjugate republican France.'[53] To reconcile hostility to standing armies, which he called praetorian or caste-like, with a love of national independence, he advocated a 'New Army' of armed citizens, who would defend the frontier but not shoot workers or start colonial wars, and would eventually bring about a federation of free nations.[54]

Other figures on the left also embraced patriotism at this juncture. As a former dreyfusard, Charles Péguy had a profound suspicion of the praetorian army, but he rallied to the nation when it was challenged by Germany in the Morocco crisis. Breaking with Hervé whom he had known as a schoolteacher, and rejecting his notion that the country did not belong to the working class, he argued in *Notre patrie* that the French people were revolutionary but also patriotic, and peace-loving but also instinctively warlike where necessary. For Péguy the French were a chosen people with a universal mission to spread liberty and civilization. They must respond to German aggression with a defensive war, not only for France but for humanity, to defeat the oppression and barbarism that Germany represented.[55] This was a patriotism that went back to the Republic of 1792 and to Michelet's notion of France as the vessel of humanity, and closely paralleled the thinking of Jaurès, even though Péguy had broken with Jaurès over what he saw as the latter's hijacking of dreyfusism for party-political purposes. This patriotism – open, generous, republican, at the service of humanity – was very different from the nationalism of the antidreyfusards, which was inward-looking, defensive, hostile to the Republic and exalted French traditions, although in the wake of 1905 there was increasingly convergence between them.

The Morocco crisis was widely seen to have engendered a 'revival of national sentiment' in France, a new sense of its worth as a nation and willingness to defend it by war if necessary.[56] Whereas at the time of the Dreyfus Affair nationalism had been a stick with which to beat the Republic of Jews, Protestants and freemasons, now nationalism and nationalists in general supported the Republic. Paul Déroulède, who had been exiled to Spain in 1900 by the Senate sitting as a high court for his attempted coup of 1899, returned to Paris in November 1905, but did not return to his old *frondeur* ways. Defeated in the elections of 1906, he abandoned politics in favour of regular pilgrimages of the Ligue des Patriotes to sites of heroic combats during the siege of Paris in 1870–71: the plateau of Châtillon in September, Le Bourget in October, Champigny in November, Buzenval in January. At these gatherings he banned all slogans apart from 'Long live the Army!', 'Long live France!', 'Long live the Republic!', and on the twenty-fifth anniversary of the founding of the Ligue des Patriotes in 1907 declared that 'we applaud the foreign policy of the state, the work of Delcassé, against that eternal stranger and enemy, Germany.' The threat to government interests was no longer from the nationalists but from the antimilitarists. 'It was to fight against this anarchist and revolutionary agitation', Déroulède announced, brazenly rewriting history, 'that the Ligue des Patriotes was already Boulangist in 1887 and nationalist in 1897. In 1907 it will be traditionalist.'[57] On the other hand, he was keen to rescue the cult of Joan of Arc for the Republic from the extreme right and the Church. In the winter of 1908–9 the Camelots du Roi, who sold Action Française's paper and stewarded its meetings, broke up the Sorbonne lectures of Amédée Thalamas, who had called into question Joan of Arc's divine mission and virginity. When Joan was beatified by the pope on 18 April 1909 in Rome, 40,000 French pilgrims wept. Déroulède, however, speaking at Orléans for the commemorations of May, paid homage to her 'as the Christian patriot I have always been and the Catholic republican I shall always be'.[58]

A few nationalists such as Charles Maurras and Action Française continued to use nationalism to attack the Republic and demand the restoration of the monarchy that alone could restore France's greatness, but they were isolated even on the right. Maurice Barrès broke with Maurras in 1900, arguing that the Republic had been great, especially during the Revolution, and that the nation should be brought together not around one regime or another but around a cult of the dead and the lost provinces of Alsace-Lorraine. From the 1890s he had gone on a pilgrimage every August to the battlefields of the war of 1870 in Alsace, the climax of which was the visit to Reichshoffen, site of the last charge of the cuirassiers.[59] At the time of the Dreyfus Affair he developed a cult of French soldiers buried in what was now German soil in order to promote a sense of solidarity with the lost provinces and an idea of a French nation rooted in *la terre et les morts*. 'At Chambière,' outside Metz, where 7,200 French soldiers from the war of 1870 were buried, he told the Ligue de la Patrie Française in a lecture of 1899, 'where the sand is mixed with our dead, our heart persuades our mind of the great destiny of France and imposes on all of us a moral unity.'[60] In 1905–9 he published a cycle of novels entitled *Les Bastions de l'Est* which reinvigorated the question of Alsace-Lorraine as a central trope of French nationalism. In one of them, *Colette Baudoche* (1909), the heroine, a young woman in occupied Metz, is engaged to a German schoolmaster Asmus until she follows the annual pilgrimage to Chambière and to the annual mass for the souls of those who died in 1870 in the cathedral of Metz. There the lessons of *la terre et les morts* persuade her to break off her engagement and espouse France.[61]

Barrès was very much the *maître à penser* of young French nationalists of the generation born around 1890. One of his disciples,
Ernest Psichari, was won over not only from his erstwhile guide,
Charles Péguy, and his dreyfusard friends, but from the whole university milieu which was congenitally hostile if not to patriotism then
to militarism and nationalism. Psichari was the grandson of Ernest
Renan, stalwart of the generation of 1830, who had lectured in 1882
on *What is a Nation?* Renan's daughter married a linguist of Greek
origin who taught at the Sorbonne and was an ardent dreyfusard.
Psichari, who studied philosophy at the Sorbonne, was expected by
his family to follow an academic career. Instead, after a nervous
breakdown in 1903, he joined the new colonial army and took part
in an expedition up the Congo to Lake Chad in 1906–7. Not entirely
forgetting his literary inheritance, he wrote an account of his adventures, *Lands of Sun and Sleep*. In this he praised Africa as 'one of
the last refuges of national energy' and war itself as 'an unspeakable
poem of blood and beauty'. He provided legitimation for the colonial
project in national rather than material terms and a new role model
for young men bored with endless examinations who craved a life
of action and excitement in the service of France. The book was sent
to Barrès, who was fiercely opposed to the family over the Dreyfus
Affair but recognized Psichari as 'an admirable man' and obtained
a literary prize for him. Colonial ambitions thus rebuilt a patriotic
bridge that had been severed by the Affair.[62]

Although nationalist agitation in support of colonies and Alsace-
Lorraine ceased criticizing a republic whose national interests were
satisfactorily protected by the likes of Delcassé, foreign minister from
1898 to 1905, Georges Clemenceau, who had repeatedly unseated
ministries in the 1880s over colonial questions, was still reluctant to
let the colonial party and its military protégés such as Lyautey have
their heads if there was any danger of risking a war. When he
was president of the council in 1906–9 the front line was on the
Algerian–Moroccan border, from which Lyautey was keen to push
towards Fez, although this would inevitably provoke Spain and
Germany. After Clemenceau fell, Lyautey occupied Fez in May 1911,
and Germany responded by sending a gunboat to Agadir on the Atlantic
coast of Morocco to force France to negotiate. Joseph Caillaux, who

became French premier in June, asked the chief of the General Staff Joffre whether France had a 70 per cent chance of winning a war and was told that it did not. Caillaux therefore looked for a deal and on 4 November Germany recognized France's claim to Morocco in return for cession of slices of the French Congo, enabling Germany if it wished to build a railway from the Cameroons to East Africa. This agreement was ratified by the Chamber of Deputies but severely criticized by nationalist opinion which accused the government of selling out. The Senate was more obstinate and on 10 January 1912 Caillaux was summoned before its foreign affairs committee where he remembered Clemenceau, now reincarnated as a defender of the French Empire, and Poincaré 'huddled in a corner, whispering to each other, sneering'.[63] Caillaux was accused of using secret diplomacy via his banking contacts in Germany and of dismantling the Empire, and was forced to resign as premier.

This was a turning point in French diplomacy and military thinking. For forty years *revanche* had been relegated to the realms of fantasy or forgetting; now it was a real possibility. Poincaré became president of the council in January 1912. Under the Treaty of Fez signed on 30 March 1912 the sultan of Morocco agreed to a French protectorate over his country. Alexandre Millerand, who twenty years previously had been defending strikers and antimilitarists, became minister of war and took a series of measures which greatly increased French colonial power and military discipline. He telephoned Lyautey, then garrisoned in Rennes, to ask him to serve as resident-general of Morocco with authority to put down any anti-French disturbances. General Joffre as chief of the General Staff was given supreme control over the French army. 'All the powers of the military establishment finally became concentrated in my hands,' he wrote. 'It was the first time that any such authority had been confided in a single man.'[64] To eliminate any remnants of antirepublican sentiment in the officer corps Millerand banned officers from founding any political or religious associations in the army. He organized military parades in garrison towns, Napoleonic style, to dramatize the force and beauty of the military. Finally, to eliminate antimilitarism in the ranks of the army he pushed through a law of 30 March 1912 giving him the authority to send not only criminals but also antimilitarists and strike leaders, when conscripted for military service at the age of twenty, to disciplinary battalions in North Africa, the so-called Bat' d'Af.[65]

A Bat' d'Af in Tunisia had been the destination of 589 soldiers of the 17th Infantry Regiment which had mutinied in the face of a winegrowers' demonstration at Narbonne in June 1907, of whom fifteen died.[66] Regiments were recruited in specific regions, so a refusal to fire on demonstrators who might be from the soldier's town or village was a certain risk. In fact the 17th Regiment, like others, was recruited from the south-west in general rather than from Narbonne, Béziers or the Aude specifically, so the mutinies of 1907 remained exceptional. In the pre-war period fewer that 1 per cent of conscripts were disciplined, and that for offences such as rudeness to officers, theft and absence without leave, rather than for mutiny. For most young men conscription was a significant rite of passage to adulthood, and was celebrated in the community. Only those who were not 'bons pour le service' were exempted and those who were selected by the military board marked the event by a charivari of conscripts, marching with trumpet and drum to the local town, where they were fêted by the mayor, and returned home to kiss the girls before they left for barrack life.[67]

The harshness of the Millerand law provoked an attempt at bridge-building to conscripted soldiers from antimilitarists nationally. Primary school teachers meeting in conference at Chambéry in August 1912 voted the 'Soldier's Penny' by which teachers would send a 5-franc coin to teachers who had just been conscripted, to keep them in touch with civilian life. Since many teachers were followers of Gustave Hervé and had a reputation for antimilitarism, even anti-patriotism, there was a public outcry against teachers who were now 'sans patrie' as well as godless, and the education minister clamped down on teachers' trade unions, which were illegal.[68] In fact, however, some teachers followed the model of Maurice Vincent, hero of Psichari's second novel, *The Call to Arms*, published in 1913. Vincent, the son of an antimilitarist teacher of the generation of those 'who had witnessed the defeat as frail innocent children and forgotten it', falls under the spell of a Captain Nangis who hunts pheasant in his home region of Brie and believes that 'understanding the former destinies of our races helps us to live in the present and above the contingencies of social life'. Vincent is converted to army and Church by visits to the battlefield of Champigny and the Benedictine Abbey of Jouarre. He recognizes himself as one of the new generation which 'did not witness the defeat, but remembers it', and joins up. Psichari dedicated this book to his former adviser Charles Péguy, whom he now saw as embodying 'the soul of France'. Through Psichari Péguy learned to bring his craving for spiritual values down to earth and see that the soldier 'measures the quantity of land where a language is spoken, where morals, a soul, a religion, a race hold sway . . . the quantity of temporal land that is *the same* as the spiritual land and intellectual land'.[69] Psichari himself became the symbol of the generation of 1890, one of the key interviewees in a survey of 1913, *Les Jeunes Gens d'aujourd'hui*, by his friend Henri Massis of Action Française and the sociologist Alfred de Tarde. Like *The Call to Arms* this contrasted the decadent, intellectual generation born around 1860 with the young men of 1910 who loved sport, machines and action, were building the Empire and in a year or so would be leading men out of the trenches of northern France.[70]

In the autumn of 1912 war broke out in the Balkans, and in January 1913 French national unity and nationalism moved into another phase when Raymond Poincaré was elected president of the Republic by the votes of right-wing parliamentarians such as Albert de Mun as well as those in the centre. 'A nation can only be peace-loving', he told the assembled deputies and senators, 'if it is always ready for war. A France exposed to challenges and humiliations by its own fault would no longer be France.'[71] The Action Française argument that only a king would restore French greatness was made redundant. Charles Péguy argued that Poincaré had been raised to power by 'a deep popular movement, a new leap of national energy', which responded to moments of crisis and eliminated *rois fainéants*. The Merovingians, Carolingians and Capetians had been cast aside because they had been too weak, but 'the Republic was the fourth dynasty, strong in its youth.'[72] A second Balkan war in the summer of 1913 resulted in the expansion of Serbia, posing a powerful threat to Austro-Hungarian interests. Germany, allied to Austria-Hungary, passed an army bill on 30 June 1913, massively increasing the size of its armed forces. In order to expand French forces Poincaré replied with a law of 19 July 1913 which increased military service from the two years decreed in 1905 back to three years. This provoked riots in the garrison towns of eastern France – Toul, Belfort and Nancy – when conscripts learned that they would have to serve for another year, and meetings that were addressed by antimilitarists such as Yvetot. The CGT called a massive demonstration against the Three-Year bill on 13 July 1913, and the SFIO and Radical-Socialists under their new leader Joseph Caillaux made opposition to the law the central plank of their programmes. At the traditional march-past of 14 July 1913 at Longchamp, however, the military significance of the French colonies was amply demonstrated as President Poincaré presented tricolour flags to twenty-five new regiments of colonial or mixed colonial and French recruits – ten Moroccan, five Algerian, three from each of Senegal, Indo-China and Madagascar, and two from Chad and Gabon. If conscripts from France were wavering, those from the Empire were ready to fight.[73]

The crisis was not over because in the elections of April–May 1914 radicals and socialists won a majority. To redeem the situation Poincaré appointed as premier a socialist who was committed to the Three-Year Law, René Viviani. Antimilitaristic hostility to the Three-Year Law and the struggle for peace did not, however, mean that socialists and trade unionists would stand in the way of national defence if France were attacked. At an extraordinary congress of the SFIO on 15–16 July 1914, three weeks after the assassination of Archduke Franz Ferdinand at Sarajevo and a week before Austria's ultimatum to Serbia, a motion was passed endorsing a general strike, not however to trigger revolution or desertion but to persuade governments to defuse the situation by international arbitration. 'Whatever our enemies say,' declared Jaurès' paper, *L'Humanité*, on 18 July, 'there is no contradiction between making the maximum effort to ensure peace and, if war breaks out in spite of us, doing the maximum to ensure the independence and integrity of the nation.'[74] As the crisis deepened, international workers' solidarity dissolved. CGT leader Léon Jouhaux met the leader of the German trade-union movement, Karl Legien, in Brussels on 27 July, and was convinced that German unions would not take part in an international general strike against war. The CGT was itself afraid that its leaders, listed in the Interior Ministry's notorious Carnet B, would be arrested as soon as war broke out and on 31 July it concluded a deal with the ministry: there would be no call for a general strike and no arrest of CGT leaders.[75] That evening, Jean Jaurès was assassinated by a nationalist fanatic who considered him a traitor, and socialist resolve to fight growing war fever fell apart.

For two weeks of the crisis President Poincaré and premier Viviani were on the high seas, sailing to St Petersburg and back both to urge restraint on Russia and to ensure the solidity of the Franco-Russian alliance if it came to war. On their return to France on 29 July they were greeted by a demonstration organized by the Ligue des Patriotes. Paul Déroulède, its president, had died in January, but Maurice Barrès had succeeded to the post. Gustave Hervé now admitted that 'he had always had a weakness for Déroulède,' and declared that if German unionists and socialists reneged on the international class struggle, then French unionists and socialists would 'return to the revolutionary patriotism and idea of national defence that had been favoured by bourgeois democracy and working-class socialism since 1793'. He promptly changed the name of his newspaper from *La Guerre Sociale* to *La Victoire*.[76] Russia mobilized in defence of Serbia on 31 July and Germany declared war on it on 1 August. The previous day Germany had pressed France to remain neutral but Joffre threatened to resign if France did not mobilize, which it did on 1 August. On 3 August Germany declared war on France and invaded Belgium. Great Britain declared war on Germany the following day.

This was the moment at which the French nation was put to the severest test. Unlike in 1870, it was not diplomatically isolated. It fulfilled its commitment to the Franco-Russian alliance, and Great Britain made concrete the Entente Cordiale. It had strengthened its army under the Three-Year Law and despite the antimilitarist opposition this had provoked it remained intact. There was very little resentment of the call to arms: citizens who joined up did so not from a desire for greatness or to recover Alsace-Lorraine but because they felt the object of German aggression.[77] France was a proud and confident nation once again, buoyed up by a national consciousness that had been formed steadily since 1870. There was a sense of a historical continuity going back a thousand years, whatever the dynasty, whatever the regime. The French were inspired by 'great ancestors', some thinking of Joan of Arc, others of Vercingétorix. The myth of the Volunteers of 1792 that had given heart to the embattled Republic in 1870 was once again a potent resource, locking into the nation those who might have been swayed by anarchist or Marxist antipatriotism. 'If Jaurès were still here,' said CGT leader Jouhaux at his open grave on 4 August, 'he would tell you, comrades, that above the national cause, in the harsh struggle that is beginning, you will be defending the cause of the International, and that of civilization, of which France is the cradle.'[78]

Conclusion: 1914

The great fear in 1914 was that there would be a catastrophic repeat of 1870. German troops drove into Belgium and northern France and by 2 September were within 30 miles of Paris. As in 1870 the government left the capital for Bordeaux and half a million Parisians took to the roads in a flight which prefigured the exodus of 1940. Then, on 3 September, came the news that instead of driving on to Paris the German First Army under von Kluck had turned south in order to encircle the city from the east, exposing its right flank. The commander-in-chief General Joffre now gave the order to the French Fifth and Sixth Armies to attack, and the battle of the Marne was engaged.

Charles Péguy was a lieutenant in the 276th Reserve Infantry Regiment, part of the Sixth Army. On 5 September, near the village of Villeroy close to Meaux, the regiment advanced on the German lines, resplendent in red trousers. The company captain, Pierre Guérin, aged thirty-two, a veteran of Morocco, was killed, followed by Lieutenant Cornillère. Victor Boudon, a commercial traveller in civilian life and a member of the Ligue des Droits de l'Homme, takes up the story:

Péguy was still standing up, in spite of our shouts of 'Get down!', a glorious fool in his bravery. He drew himself up, defying the machine guns, as if inviting the death he had glorified in his poetry. At that very moment a deadly bullet pierced his noble forehead. He fell on his side, without a cry, with a low groan, having had the ultimate vision of a victory so much longed for and finally near. And when, a few metres further on, leaping like a madman, I glanced behind me, I saw the body of our dear, brave lieutenant, on the hot and dusty earth, amid broad green leaves, a black and red blotch among so many others.[1]

The battle of the Marne lasted until 12 September, at which point the German armies were in retreat. Two hundred and fifty thousand Frenchmen were killed in the battle, but Paris was saved and the government soon returned there to direct the war effort. More than that, the spectre of another 1870 had been exorcized, and the French Republic and nation had held together under fire. 'Our troops, as well as those of our Allies, are admirable in morale, endurance, and ardour,' Joffre telegraphed the minister of war, Alexandre Millerand, on 13 September. 'The Government of the Republic may be proud of the army which it has prepared.'[2]

The death of Péguy symbolized the meeting of a multiplicity of strands in French politics, society, religion and culture that in 1799 had plunged France into civil war and defeat but by 1914 had come together to ensure a consensus around the Republic and the strength and unity of the nation. Maurice Barrès, who had fought Péguy over the Dreyfus Affair and had been unable to win him over to the right in 1910 when Péguy published *La Mystère de la charité de Jeanne d'Arc*, now hailed him as a national icon. 'His sacrifice heightens the importance of his work,' he wrote. 'He celebrated the moral greatness, abnegation and exaltation of the soul. It was given to him to prove the truth of his work in a single minute. He is now sacred. Dead, he is a guide, who will be more active than ever, and is more than ever alive.'[3]

Péguy, for Barrès, brought together the man of the people and the intellectual, the provincial and the Parisian. 'This grandson of a peasant who entered the École Normale', said Barrès, 'was always thinking of his fields, that is of his *Cahiers de la Quinzaine*, which had to be dug over, fertilized and extended . . . In his brief career as a man of letters he gave expression to the virtues of a peasant expanding his domain, of a shopkeeper counting and recounting his money, of a printer producing beautiful work, of a curé preaching to his flock and of a line officer leading his men into battle.'[4] In his final incarnation as an officer, echoed Victor Boudon in his tribute to Péguy, he defended Paris with a company composed of 'workers of Belleville and Bercy, and peasants of Seine-et-Marne . . . More than any other he recognized and used the rugged independence of these workers from the Paris suburbs, these farmers of Crécy and

Voulangis, and to see them in a noble light.' In the 19th Company of the 276th Regiment Péguy was nicknamed 'the schoolmaster' or 'the *pion*', but Péguy replied, 'Joke, joke, my friends, but you wait till you see him at work, your *pion*.' Having earlier in the fighting been sent forward into Lorraine when he could overlook the Moselle, he met Ernest Psichari by chance just before Psichari was killed, and may well have wanted to imitate the other man's embrace of a life of action and death for the *patrie*.[5]

Péguy, for Boudon on the left, as for Barrès on the right, was 'at the confluence of our traditional and revolutionary forces'. He was a republican, dreyfusard and socialist but also a Catholic and attached to the values of old France, nourished by Joinville and Joan of Arc, embodying the medieval 'loyalty of man to man, and truth to the faith'.[6] As a native of Orléans he was especially drawn to the story of Joan of Arc, writing *Joan of Arc* in 1897, returning to her with the *Mystère* in 1910 and going on a pilgrimage to Orléans in 1912 to pray for a child of his who was sick. When in 1914 he saw the cathedral of Senlis bombarded by the Germans he exclaimed, 'the savages,' and made a monk, Roussel, both chaplain to the company and his private chaplain. After his death one of Péguy's friends wrote to Barrès, 'we have lost a saint,' and his wife and children later converted to Catholicism.[7] As a patriot, Péguy argued that France had two missions, one old, one new. The old one was the divine mission that France honoured as the 'eldest daughter of the Church' to defend Christian civilization. The new one was the revolutionary mission incumbent on France as the cradle of liberty since 1789, to defend liberty wherever it should be threatened. The cult of Joan of Arc went hand in hand with the cult of the Convention of 1792 that had declared that France was the friend of all peoples struggling for their freedom.

For most of the nineteenth century France was torn between forces which embraced the Revolution of 1789 and those that opposed them. Each generation wrestled with the legacy of the Revolution, marked by it but also contributing to the long process of laying to rest the ghosts of division and destruction and recovering what was constructive and unifying about it. By 1914 Revolution no longer evoked civil war or anarchy but was a source of legitimacy for the

Republic founded in its name, preached up in school textbooks and ritually commemorated in monuments and on occasions such as 14 July. Revolutionaries and counter-revolutionaries were marginalized by a republic of the centre, acceptable to as broad a political spectrum as possible. Even those tempted by the extremes of anti-militarism and royalism, however, answered the call to arms in 1914 and ensured the survival of the Republic through the Great War, which finally fused republic and nation into a single entity.

The Revolution established France as the One and Indivisible Republic, which then collapsed into the chaos of provinces, cities and departments seeking autonomy, before unity was reimposed by Napoleon's iron cage of administrative centralization. Over the next century the French learned to combine the benefits of centralization with a growing appreciation of the geographical, linguistic and cultural diversity of the country. Decentralization was made more acceptable by being articulated in terms of regionalism rather than a return to the provinces of the Ancien Régime. French was imposed as the lingua franca in the public places of the Republic, such as schools and town halls, but minority languages were tolerated in private places, including in churches for religious instruction. By 1914 the *grande patrie* of the French nation had come to coexist harmoniously with the *petites patries* to which French men and women were so attached.

France's economy, which for long had been criticized as backward, embraced agricultural and industrial modernization without doing irreparable damage to its social structure. The weight of agriculture in the economy and in rural life provided ballast against over-rapid change and loss of equilibrium. Small farms and small businesses were disseminated more widely in 1914 than at the beginning of the nineteenth century, and if the old lower-middle class of artisans and shopkeepers was threatened by proletarianization a new lower-middle class of white-collar workers expanding at the end of the century maintained a social balance between the rich and poor. The thickness of this stratum of *classes moyennes* defused the danger of class struggle which was more pronounced in countries that were more industrialized, such as Great Britain or Germany, or less so, as in Russia. Tensions within the social elite were also reduced. While earlier generations were divided between Ancien Régime and Napoleonic nobilities and between landed and capitalist wealth, in later generations economic developments brought together landed, financial and industrial wealth. Moreover the republican office-holding class was careful to build bridges to the traditional social elite which had been reluctant to embrace the Republic, by a combination of social intercourse and intermarriage, so that a ruling class emerged that was more united than ever before.

Religious struggles that were reignited by the French Revolution continued throughout the nineteenth century and only gradually was religious peace negotiated. Attempts to reconcile religion and liberty were long frustrated by revolutionaries' distrust of religion as counter-revolutionary, and by the Napoleonic system of state control for churches at the price of state funding. The solution to the first problem was the invention of the principle of *laïcité*, under which religion was eliminated from state-run schools, replaced by a moral and civic education appropriate to citizens of the Republic, while parish clergy were not troubled. The solution to the second problem was the Separation of Church and state in 1905. The state ceased to fund the Church but also ceased to persecute it. Catholics were obliged to fall back on their own resources, but Catholicism was able to flourish socially, culturally and intellectually. Anticlericals such as Péguy spoke the same language of admiration for Joan of Arc as Maurice Barrès, who hailed the victory of the Marne in which Péguy died as a miracle worked by Joan of Arc, as he threw himself into a campaign that resulted in her canonization and her nomination as patron saint of France after the war.

Women were initially liberated by the Revolution, then excluded from the public sphere by revolutionaries who associated political women with the court intrigue of the Ancien Régime and perfected a model of the male citizen and soldier and the female wife and mother. Women gradually fought back for emancipation, but they anticipated republican fears that Catholic women would bring back the monarchy if they were given the vote and concentrated on securing civil rights: divorce, control of their property, education, and the opening up of the professions. When they did start to demand the vote they had no time for the civil disobedience of British suffragettes.

As women demanded emancipation, society expressed fears of female sexuality, a falling birth rate, family break-up, over-educated blue-stockings grown mannish and female voters bringing back the Ancien Régime. French women may have gained less than their British counterparts, but they negotiated an emancipation that was tempered to the demands of femininity, family, society, Republic and country.

In the cultural sphere, there was a tension between the creativity of the artist, the control and patronage of the state, and the demand of the market. Successive generations of avant-garde artists and writers, Romantic, Realist and Symbolist, challenged both artistic and social conventions. Their excesses, however, were balanced by writers and artists who kept faith with the classical canon and more easily pleased audiences. Beneath both of these the growing demand of a mass semi-educated urban market stimulated the beginnings of a mass media which included serialized novels, detective fiction and thrillers, the 1-sou press, comics, the popular theatre and the cinema. Avant-garde creativity was not self-contained but drew on the powerful popular inspirations of myth, folklore and religion, and also sought the public recognition afforded by attention-grabbing manifestos, reputable dealers and publishers, and literary prizes. It was also international in status. What went on in Paris salons and opera-houses, on Montmartre or in Montparnasse, branded Paris as the European, even Western, capital of art.

How France fared on the great-power stage was nevertheless more important to most French people than its cultural standing. The revolutionary generation saw France as the Grande Nation, then the Grand Empire, dominating Europe from the Atlantic to the Urals and from the Mediterranean to the Baltic. It developed an ideology first of bringing liberty to oppressed peoples, then of bringing civilization in the form of the rule of law and enlightenment. All this came to an end in the snows of Russia, the mountain gorges of Spain and the farmland of Belgium. Successive generations through the nineteenth century struggled to reconstruct France's national greatness and, to sustain it, a national identity. They looked anxiously around to assess which countries enjoyed more liberty or more civilization than France. Hopes that the revolutions of 1830 or 1848 would relaunch French armies to liberate Europe came to nothing.

A revival of French power under the Second Empire was checked by the defeat of 1870, the amputation of Alsace-Lorraine, and the loss of great-power ranking to Germany, Great Britain and Russia. France's greatness was painstakingly rebuilt in the colonies, from Indo-China to sub-Saharan Africa and the Maghreb. Officers who saw action in the colonies and indigenous troops recruited into French units played a significant role in the war effort of 1914–18. At the same time the pain of defeat was used to rebuild French national identity. The cult of Vercingétorix and Joan of Arc, the soldier–citizens of 1792 and Napoleon served to create a coherent national consciousness and confidence. It inspired the *jeunes gens d'aujourd'hui*, who went to the front as young officers, and the peasants from Brittany to the Alps who became the *poilus* of the trenches, and who together left a million and a half bodies on the battlefields of France and Belgium to defend the French Republic and French nation.

Notes

INTRODUCTION: THE CHILDREN
OF THE REVOLUTION

1. Karl Mannheim, 'The Problem of Generations', in *Essays on the Sociology of Knowledge* (London, Routledge & Kegan Paul, 1952), 276–320
2. Alan B. Spitzer, *The French Generation of 1820* (Princeton, Princeton University Press, 1987), 3–34
3. Edgar Quinet, *Histoire de mes idées* (Paris, 1878), 21, 108, 142. See also *Edgar Quinet: The Story of a Child*, translated with introduction and notes by Rosemary and Peter Ganz (London, Duckworth, 1995), 18, 66, 84
4. Alfred de Musset, *Confessions d'un enfant du siècle* (Paris, Garnier, 1968), 1–5
5. Claude Digeon, *La Crise allemande de la pensée française, 1870–1914* (Paris, PUF, 1959). Digeon explores the impact of the defeat of 1870 on several generations of French writers and thinkers, with a periodization of generations differing slightly from my own.
6. Agathon [Alfred de Tarde and Henri Massis], *Les Jeunes Gens d'aujourd'hui* (Paris, Plon, 1913)

CHAPTER 1: REVOLUTION OR
CONSENSUS? FRENCH POLITICS,
1799–1870

1. Richard Cobb, *Reactions to the French Revolution* (London, Oxford University Press, 1972), 181–211; Michel Vovelle, *Ville et campagne au 18e siècle (Chartres et Beauce)* (Paris, Éditions Sociales, 1980), 299–303

2. Henri Pirenne, *Histoire de la Belgique*, IV (Brussels, La Renaissance du Livre, 1974), 157–8

3. T. C. W. Blanning, *The French Revolution in Germany* (Oxford, Clarendon Press, 1983), 289–300

4. Howard G. Brown, *Ending the French Revolution: Violence, Justice and Repression from the Terror to Napoleon* (Charlottesville and Paris, University of Virginia Press, 2006), 163–8

5. Bernard Gainot, *1799: Un Nouveau Jacobinisme: La Démocratie représentative, une alternative à brumaire* (Paris, Ministère de l'Éducation Nationale, 2001)

6. Report of Bureau Central, 28 prairial An VII/16 June 1799, in Alphonse Aulard, ed., *Paris pendant la Révolution thermidorienne et sous le Directoire*, V (Paris, 1902), 567–8

7. Howard G. Brown, 'Revolt and Repression in the Midi toulousain, 1799', *French History* 19/2 (2005), 234–61

8. Quoted by F.-A. Aulard, *L'État de la France en l'an VIII et l'an IX* (Paris, 1897), 15

9. P.-J.-B. Buchez and P. C. Lavergne-Roux, *Histoire parlementaire de la Révolution française*, XXXVIII (Paris, 1838), 122–3

10. Quoted by Alan Schom, *Napoleon Bonaparte* (New York, HarperCollins, 1997), 208

11. Buchez and Roux, *Histoire parlementaire de la Révolution française*, XXXVIII, 201–20

12. Claude Langlois, 'Le Plébiscite de l'an VIII ou le coup d'état du 18 pluviôse an VIII', *Annales Historiques de la Révolution Française*, 44 (1972), 43–65, 231–46, 390–415

13. Jean Thiry, *Le Sénat de Napoléon (1800–1814)* (Paris, Berger-Levrault, 1932), 39–49; Isser Woloch, *Napoleon and his Collaborators: The Making of a Dictatorship* (New York and London, Norton, 2002), 46–52

14. Woloch, *Napoleon and his Collaborators*, 27, 76–9. See also Count of Las Cases, *The Memorial of Saint-Helena* (London, 1823), I, 1st part, 347–9, entry for 18 Dec. 1815

15. Napoleon 1st, *Correspondance*, VI (Paris, 1860), 574, letter of 7 Sept. 1800

16. Chateaubriand, *Mémoires d'outre-tombe* (Paris, Gallimard Pléiade, 1951), I, 308–439, 492–3

17. Cynthia Cox, *Talleyrand's Successor: Armand-Emmanuel du Plessis, Duc de Richelieu, 1766–1822* (London, Arthur Barker, 1959), 51–69

18. L. de la Sicotière, *Louis de Frotté et les insurrections normandes, 1793–1832* (Paris, 1889), 469–501

19. G. Lenôtre, *Georges Cadoudal* (Paris, Grasset, 1929), 70–81

20. Frédéric Bluche, *Le Plébiscite des Cent-Jours* (Geneva, Droz, 1974), 37

21. Jean-Victor Moreau, *Discours prononcé au tribunal criminal spécial du département de la Seine* (Paris, 1804), 1–4. See also Louis de Villefosse and Janine Bouissounouse, *L'Opposition à Napoleon* (Paris, Flammarion, 1969), 248–50

22. Chateaubriand, *Mémoires d'outre-tombe*, I, 534

23. Lazare Carnot, *Discours prononcé au Tribunat, 11 floréal An XII* (Paris, 1804), 4–8

24. David Chanteraine, *Le Sacré de Napoléon* (Paris, Tallandier, 2004); Laurence Chantal de Brancion, *Le Sacré de Napoléon* (Paris, Perrin, 2004)

25. Jean-Roch Coignet, *The Notebooks of Captain Coignet* (London, Greenhill, 1998), 95–102, 117–23, 133–9

26. Jean Tulard, *Napoléon et la noblesse de l'Empire* (Paris, Tallandier, 1979), 93–8

27. Quoted by Natalie Petiteau, *Élites et mobilités: La Noblesse d'Empire au XIXe siècle (1808–1914)* (Paris, La Boutique de l'Histoire, 1997), 211

28. Georges Six, *Les Généraux de la Révolution et de l'Empire* (Paris, Bordas, 1947), 24–8

29. Charles Durand, *Les Auditeurs au Conseil d'État de 1803 à 1814* (Aix-en-Provence, La Pensée Universitaire, 1958), 16–38; Marquis de Noailles, *Le Comte de Molé, 1781–1855* (Paris, 1922), I, 13–174; Victor de Broglie, *Souvenirs, 1785–1870* (Paris, 1886), I, 2–111

30. Joanna Richardson, *Stendhal: A Biography* (London, Methuen, 1912), 105–234

31. George Whitcomb, 'Napoleon's Prefects', *American History Review* 79/4 (1974), 1089–1118

32. Madame de Rémusat, *Mémoires, 1802–8* (Paris, Tallandier, 1979), 97–104

33. Duchesse d'Abrantès, *Histoire des salons de Paris* (Oxford, Oxford University Press, 1989), 209–12

34. Schom, *Napoleon*, 617–27; Graham Robb, *Victor Hugo* (London, Picador, 1997), 12–41

35. Germaine de Staël, *Choix de lettres, 1778–1817*, ed. Georges Solovieff (Paris, Klincksieck, 1970), 443–72, letters to Bernadotte, 25 Mar., 11 Sept., 11 Oct. 1813, and to Moreau, 12 Aug. 1813

36. Jean Tulard, *Joseph Fouché* (Paris, Fayard, 1998), 226

37. Talleyrand, *Mémoires 1754–1815*, ed. P. L. and J.-P. Couchod (Paris,

Plon, 1982), 636; Jean Thiry, *Le Sénat de Napoléon, 1800–1814* (Paris, 1932), 325–50; 38. Alexis Eymery, *Dictionnaire des Girouettes* (Paris, 1815); Alan B. Spitzer, 'Malicious Memories: Restoration Politics and a Prosopography of Turncoats', *French Historical Studies* 24/1 (2001), 37–61

38. Tulard, *Fouché*, 297–8; Thiry, *Le Sénat de Napoléon*, 377–9. On the reconciliation of imperial titles in general see Gordon K. Anderson, 'Old Nobles and *Noblesse d'Empire*, 1814–1830: In Search of a Conservative Interest in Post-revolutionary France', *French History* 8/2 (1994), 151–3

39. Charles de Rémusat, *Mémoires de ma vie* (Paris, Plon, 1959), I, 152

40. François Guizot, *Mémoires pour servir à l'histoire de mon temps*, I: *1807–1816* (Clermont-Ferrand, Paléo, 2002), 7

41. A. Philippe, *Royer-Collard: Sa vie politique, sa vie privée, sa famille* (Paris, 1857), 51, 67–8, 71

42. Benjamin Constant, *Oeuvres complètes*, IX/1: *Principes de politique et autres écrits, juin 1814–juillet 1815* (Tübingen, Niemeyer Verlag, 2001), 160–61; Alain Laquièze, 'Le Modèle anglais et la responsabilité ministérielle selon le groupe de Coppet', in Lucien Jaume, ed., *Coppet, le creuset de l'esprit libéral* (Paris and Aix-en-Provence, Economica-PU Aix-Marseille, 2000), 157–76

43. Lazare Carnot, *Mémoire adressé au roi en juillet 1814* (Brussels and London, 1814), 14; Marcel Reinhard, *Le Grand Carnot* (2 vols, Paris, 1950)

44. Jean Vidalenc, *Les Demi-solde: Étude d'une catégorie sociale* (Paris, Rivière, 1955), 9–14

45. Marshal Macdonald, *Recollections*, ed. Camille Rousset, trans. Stephen Louis Simon (London, 1893), 371; Henri Welschinger, *Le Maréchal Ney, 1815* (Paris, 1893), 12–15

46. Count of Las Cases, *The Memorial of Saint-Helena* I, 1st part, 316–17, entry for 10–12 Mar. 1816

47. Welschinger, *Ney*, 28–52; Harold Kurtz, *The Trial of Marshal Ney* (London, Hamish Hamilton, 1957), 127–33

48. Guizot, *Mémoires*, I, 95–6, 98

49. Noailles, *Le Comte de Molé, 1781–1855*, I, 205–32

50. Benjamin Constant, *Mémoire sur les Cent Jours* [1819], in *Oeuvres complètes*, XIV (Tübingen, 1993), 213–14

51. Bluche, *Le Plébiscite des Cent-Jours*, 37

52. Talleyrand, *Mémoires*, 757; Robert Alexander, *Bonapartism and Revolutionary Tradition in France: The Fédérés of 1815* (Cambridge, Cambridge University Press, 1991), 97–8

53. Comte de Villèle, *Mémoires et correspondance* (Paris, 1888), 318
54. Marquise de Montcalm, *Mon journal* (Paris, 1936), 202
55. Broglie, *Souvenirs*, I, 325–33; Welschinger, *Ney*, 314
56. Welschinger, *Ney*, 317–18
57. Montcalm, *Mon journal*, 184–5, entry for 4 Sept. 1816; Robert Gildea, *The Past in French History* (New Haven and London, Yale University Press, 1994), 23
58. Ernest Daudet, *Louis XVIII et le Duc de Decazes, 1815–1820* (Paris, 1899), 19–59; Roger Langeron, *Decazes, ministre du roi* (Paris, Hachette, 1960), 23–30, 63–6
59. Daudet, *Decazes*, 250
60. Chateaubriand, 'De la monarchie selon la Charte', in *Écrits politiques, 1814–1816* (Geneva, Droz, 2002), 462
61. Guizot, *Mémoires pour servir à l'histoire de mon temps*, II: *1816–1830* (Clermont-Ferrand, Paléo, 2003), 9–43
62. Ephraïm Harpaz, *L'École libérale sous la Restauration: Le 'Mercure' et la 'Minerve', 1817–1820* (Geneva, Droz, 1968)
63. Paul Thureau-Danguin, *Le Parti libéral sous la Restauration* (Paris, 1888), 84–9
64. Daudet, *Decazes*, 402
65. Chateaubriand, *Mémoires d'outre-tombe*, II 12
66. Villèle, *Mémoires*, 370
67. Vidalenc, *Les Demi-solde*, 176–89; Robert Alexander, *Rewriting the French Revolutionary Tradition* (Cambridge, Cambridge University Press, 2003), 144–9
68. Bernard Ménager, *Les Napoléon du peuple* (Paris, Aubier, 1988); Sudhir Hazareesingh, *The Legend of Napoleon* (London, Granta, 2004)
69. Jean Touchard, *La Gloire de Béranger* (Paris, Colin, 1968); Albert Cim, *Le Chansonnier Émile Debraux, Roi de la Goguette, 1796–1831* (Paris, Flammarion, 1910); F. L'Homme, *Charlet* (Paris, Allison, 1892)
70. Gustave Geffroy, *L'Enfermé* (Paris, 1904)
71. Guizot, *Mémoires*, II, 134
72. Charles de Rémusat, *Mémoires de ma vie*, II, 146
73. J. P. T. Bury and Robert Tombs, *Thiers, 1797–1877: A Political Life* (London, George Allen & Unwin, 1986), 6–13
74. Guizot, *Histoire de la Civilisation en France* (Paris, Didier, 1846), 202–8; Pierre Rosanvallon, *Le Moment Guizot* (Paris, Gallimard, 1985), 212–14
75. Thiers, *Histoire de la Révolution française* (10 vols, Paris, 1823–7), I, 136, II, 7–8, III, 435

76. Fabrice Boyer, *Martignac (1778–1832)* (Paris, Éditions du Comité des Travaux Historiques et Scientifiques, 2002)

77. Vincent W. Beach, *Charles X of France: His Life and Times* (Boulder, Col., Pruett, 1971), 294

78. Guizot, *Mémoires*, II, 175

79. Lafayette, *Mémoires*, VI (Paris, 1838), 389

80. Bury and Tombs, *Thiers*, 35

81. Guy Antonetti, *Louis-Philippe* (Paris, Fayard, 1994), 590–92

82. *Le National*, 6 Aug. 1830

83. Guizot, *Mémoires*, III: *La Révolution de 1803* (Clermont-Ferrand, Paléo, 2003), 24

84. Madeleine Bourset, *Casimir Périer: Un Prince financier au temps du Romantisme* (Paris, Publications de la Sorbonne, 1994), 213–79. On the Lyon revolt see below, pp. 99–100

85. Chancelier Pasquier, *1830: Un Ministère de défi. La Révolution. Procès des ministres de Charles X* (Paris, Plon, n.d.)

86. Chateaubriand, *De la nouvelle proposition relative au bannissement de Charles X et de sa famille* (Paris, 1831)

87. Cited by Thureau-Danguin, *Le Parti libéral sous la Restauration*, 97

88. Frederick A. Deluna, *The French Republic under Cavaignac, 1848* (Princeton, Princeton University Press, 1969), 14–29; Geffroy, *L'Enfermé*, 4–45; Roger Merle, *Armand Barbès: Un Révolutionnaire romantique* (Toulouse, Privat, 1977); Marcel Dessal, *Un Révolutionnaire jacobin: Charles Delescluze, 1809–1871* (Paris, Rivière, 1952), 9–17

89. Jill Harsin, *Barricades: The War of the Streets in Revolutionary Paris, 1830–1848* (New York and Basingstoke, Palgrave, 2002), 124–44

90. Louis Blanc, *Histoire de dix ans, 1830–1840* (Paris, 1848), IV, 338. The session was on 15 December 1834.

91. Pierre Jacomet, *Avocats républicains du Second Empire* (Paris, Denoël, 1933), 30–34

92. Geffroy, *L'Enfermé*, 77ff; Harsin, *Barricades*, 124–44

93. Charles de Rémusat, *Mémoires de ma vie*, IV, 42

94. Georges Duveau, *Raspail* (Paris, PUF, 1948), 33–7

95. *Le Réformateur*, 10 Jan. 1835

96. Alphonse de Lamartine, *Histoire des Girondins* (Paris, 1847), VII, 60

97. Victor Hugo, *À ses concitoyens* (Paris, 1848)

98. Dessal, *Un Révolutionnaire jacobin*, 52–4; Émile Ollivier, *Journal, 1846–1869* (Paris, René Julliard, 1961), I, 19–20

99. Comte de Falloux, *Mémoires* (Paris, 1925), I, 265–7; Charles de Rémusat, *Mémoires de ma vie*, IV, 292

100. Georges Duveau, *1848: The Making of a Revolution* (London, Routledge & Kegan Paul, 1967), 155–6

101. Pierre-Joseph Proudhon, *Les Confessions d'un révolutionnaire* [Oct. 1849], *Oeuvres complètes*, VII (Paris, Rivière, 1929), 168–70

102. Comte de Falloux, *Mémoires*, I, 320

103. Louis-Napoleon Bonaparte, *Les Idées napoléoniennes* (Paris, Paulin, 1839), 1, 14–15, 31, 44–9; *Les Fragments historiques*, in Napoleon III, *Oeuvres*, I (Paris, 1869), 342, cited by William H. C. Smith, *Napoléon III* (Paris, Hachette, 1982), 68, 93

104. Charles de Rémusat, *Mémoires de ma vie*, IV, 358–60

105. *La Fraternité*, 8 June 1848, cited by H. Forestier, 'Le Mouvement bonapartiste dans l'Yonne', *Annales de Bourgogne* 21 (1949), 120

106. André-Jean Tudesq, *L'Élection présidentielle de Louis-Napoléon Bonaparte* (Paris, Colin, 1968), 186

107. Charles de Rémusat, *Mémoires de ma vie*, IV, 385

108. Frédéric Barbier, *Finance et politique: La Dynastie des Fould, XVIIIe–XXe siècle* (Paris, Colin, 1991), 135–61; Robert Schnerb, *Rouher et le Second Empire* (Paris, Colin, 1949); Vincent Wright, *Le Conseil d'État sous le Second Empire* (Paris, Colin, 1972), 29–31

109. Adolphe Thiers, speech of 13 Feb. 1850, *Discours parlementaires*, VIII (Paris, Calmann-Lévy, 1880), 609

110. Victor Hugo, *Actes et paroles: Avant l'exil, 1841–1851* (Paris, Michel Lévy, 1875), 330

111. Jean-Marie Rouart, *Morny: Un Voluptueux au pouvoir* (Paris, Gallimard, 1995)

112. William H. C. Smith, *The Bonapartes* (New York and London, Hambledon & London, 2005), 141–2

113. Honoré Farat, *Persigny: Un Ministre de Napoléon III, 1808–1872* (Paris, Hachette, 1957)

114. General du Barrail, *Mes souvenirs* (Paris, 1913), I, 437–8

115. Matthew Truesdell, *Spectacular Politics: Louis-Napoleon Bonaparte and the Fête Impériale, 1849–1870* (New York and Oxford, Oxford University Press, 1997), 58–67

116. Sudhir Hazareesingh, *The Saint Napoleon: Celebrations of Sovereignty in Nineteenth-Century France* (Cambridge, Mass., Harvard University Press, 2004)

117. J. M. and Brian Chapman, *The Life and Times of Baron Haussmann* (London, Weidenfeld & Nicolson, 1957), 5–68; Bernard Le Clère and

Vincent Wright, *Les Préfets du Second Empire* (Paris, Colin, 1973), 24–71, 195–205

118. Roger Price, *The French Second Empire: An Anatomy of Political Power* (Cambridge, Cambridge University Press, 2001), 99

119. Eric Anceau, *Dictionnaire des Députés du Second Empire* (Rennes, Presses Universitaires de Rennes, 1999), 302–3, 365–6, and appendix

120. Alexis de Tocqueville, Letter to J.-B. Roussel, 14 Dec. 1851, in *Oeuvres complètes*, X (Paris, Gallimard, 1995), 561–2

121. Duc de Broglie, *Mémoires*, I (Paris, Calmann-Lévy, 1938), 255

122. Ollivier, *Journal, 1846–1869*, I, 291, entry for July 1857

123. Juliette Adam, *Mes premières armes littéraires et politiques* (Paris, 1904), 71, 101–3

124. See below, pp. 189–90

125. Geffroy, *L'Enfermé*, 231–4; Jean-Baptiste Duroselle, *Clemenceau* (Paris, Fayard, 1988), 51–3

126. Guizot, letter to Mistress Austin, in *Lettres à sa famille et à ses amis* (Paris, 1884), 328

127. Nassau William Senior, *Conversations with Distinguished Persons during the Second Empire, 1860–1863* (London, 1880), II, 112

128. Émile Ollivier, *L'Empire libéral*, VI (Paris, 1902), 224–47; Pierre Guiral, *Adolphe Thiers* (Paris, Fayard, 1986), 301–6

129. Henri Allain-Target, *La République sous l'Empire* (Paris, Grasset, 1939), 185

130. Cited by Smith, *Napoléon III*, 315

131. William Smith, 'La Constitution de 1870 et la cerise Hohenzollern', in Anne Troisier de Diaz, ed., *Regards sur Émile Ollivier* (Paris, Publications de la Sorbonne, 1984), 207–23

132. Jacques Gouault, *Comment la France est devenue républicaine* (Paris, Colin, 1954), 25

CHAPTER 2: DISCOVERING FRANCE

1. Victor Hugo, letter to Léopoldine, 8 Aug. 1834; letter to Louis Boulanger, 24 June 1836, *Voyages: France et Belgique, 1834–1837*, ed. Claude Gély (Grenoble, Presses Universitaires de Grenoble, 1974), 86, 191–2

2. Rick Szostak, *The Role of Transportation in the Industrial Revolution: A Comparison of England and France* (Montreal and Kingston, McGill-Queen's University Press, 1991), 71

3. Jacques Godechot, *Les Institutions de la France sous la Révolution et l'Empire* (Paris, PUF, 1968), 588–96; Isser Woloch, *The New Regime: Transformations of the French Civic Order, 1789–1820s* (New York and London, Norton, 1994), 54–9, 109–10, 127–33

4. Marie-Noëlle Bourget, *Déchiffrer la France: La Statistique départementale à l'époque napoléonienne* (Paris, Éditions des Archives Contemporaines, 1989), 139

5. Ibid., 66–75

6. Ibid., 207–8

7. Jacques Cambry, *Voyage dans le Finistère, ou état de ce département en 1794 et 1795* (Paris, Year VII), I, 88

8. Ibid., 70–71, 185–7, II, 258, 288–93

9. Jacques Cambry, *Description du département de l'Oise* (Paris, Didot, 1803), I, 3, 260; Bourget, *Déchiffrer la France*, 150–51

10. Alexandre Dumas, *Impressions de voyage en Russie* (4 vols, Paris, 1865–6), III, 121

11. Francis Borrey, *La Franche-Comté en 1814* (Paris and Nancy, Berger-Levrault, 1912); Nicholas Richardson, *The French Prefectoral Corps, 1814–1830* (Cambridge, Cambridge University Press, 1966), 68

12. Roger Grand, *La Chouannerie de 1815* (Paris, Perrin, 1943), 43, 165, 230

13. Marquise de La Rochejacquelein, *Mémoires* (4th edn, Paris, Michaud, 1817), 44

14. George Sand, *Histoire de ma vie* (Paris, Calmann-Lévy, 1876), III, 122–7; Jean-Clément Martin, *La Vendée de la mémoire (1800–1980)* (Paris, Seuil, 1989)

15. Gwynne Lewis, *The Second Vendée: The Continuity of Counter-Revolution in the Department of the Gard, 1789–1815* (Oxford, Oxford University Press, 1978), 185–210

16. Daniel P. Resnick, *The White Terror and the Political Reaction after Waterloo* (Cambridge, Mass., Harvard University Press, 1966), 3–36

17. Brian Fitzpatrick, *Catholic Royalism in the Department of the Gard, 1815–1852* (Cambridge, Cambridge University Press, 1983), 61–75

18. Auguste Johanet, *La Vendée à trois époques, de 1793 jusqu'à l'Empire, 1815–1832* (Paris, Dentu, 1840), II, 217

19. Christine Guionnet, *L'Apprentissage de la politique moderne: Les Élections municipales sous la Monarchie de Juillet* (Paris, L'Harmattan, 1997), 101

20. Laurence Wylie, ed., *Chanzeaux: A Village in Anjou* (Cambridge, Mass., Harvard University Press, 1966), 37–51

21. Jean-Yves Guiomar, *Le Bretonisme: Les Historiens bretons au XIXe*

siècle (Mayenne, Société d'Histoire et d'Archéologie de la Bretagne, 1987), 121–52

22. Théodore Hersant de La Villemarqué, *Barzas-Breiz: Chants populaires de la Bretagne* (Paris, 1839), xviii

23. Théodore Hersant de La Villemarqué, *L'Avenir de la langue bretonne* [1842], republished by *Le Terroir Breton* review (Nantes, 1904), 11–12

24. Théophile Gautier, article on 'Voyages littéraires', 6 Jan. 1837, in *Fusions et eaux-fortes* (Paris, Charpentier, 1880), 37. See also Stephen Gerson, 'Paris Littérateurs, Provincial Journeys and the Construction of National Identity in Post-revolutionary France', *Past & Present* 151 (1996), 141–73

25. François Caron, *Histoire des chemins de fer en France, 1740–1883* (Paris, Fayard, 1997), I, 48–70, 131, 171–91

26. Balzac, *Les Chouans* (Paris, Garnier Frères, 1957), 24, 39

27. Michelet, *Tableau de la France* [1833], from *Histoire de France*, II, part 1 (Paris, 1949), 7–18, 41–54

28. Ibid., 92–4

29. Michelet, lecture of 26/30 Apr. 1838, in Paul Viallaneix, ed., *Cours au Collège de France, 1838–1851* (Paris, Gallimard, 1995), I, 98

30. Michelet, *Histoire de la Révolution française* (2nd edn, 1869), III, 477

31. Prosper Mérimée, *Notes d'un voyage dans le Midi de la France* (Paris, 1835), 132

32. Stendhal, *Mémoires d'un touriste*, I: *Oeuvres complètes*, XV (Paris, Levallois-Perret, Cercle du Bibliophile, 1968), 104–6, 281, 285

33. Stendhal, *La Vie de Henri Brulard* (Paris, Gallimard, 1973), 223

34. Gustave Flaubert, *Voyages*, I, ed. René Dumesnil (Paris, Les Belles Lettres, 1948), 52–5, 66–81

35. Gustave Flaubert, *Par les champs et par les grèves: Touraine et Bretagne* [1847], *Voyages*, I, 285–7. See also Maxime du Camp, *Souvenirs littéraires,* I (Paris, Hachette, 1883), 351–5

36. Louis Chevalier, *La Formation de la population parisienne au XIX siècle* (Paris, PUF, 1950), 284

37. John Merriman, *The Margins of City Life: Explorations on the French Urban Frontier, 1815–1851* (New York, Oxford University Press, 1991), 13, 17–18, 46

38. A. J. B. Parent-Duchâtelet, *De la prostitution dans la ville de Paris* (Paris, Baillière, 1836), I, 35, 61–96, 506, 583–5

39. H.-A. Fréguier, *Des classes dangereuses de la population dans les grandes villes* (Paris, Baillière, 1840), I, 6–7, 27, 34–5, 104–10, 185–96, 205–63. See also Louis Chevalier's classic study, *Labouring Classes*

and Dangerous Classes in Paris during the First Half of the Nineteenth Century (London, Routledge & Kegan Paul, 1973)

40. Jean-Louis Bory, *Eugène Sue* (Paris, Hachette, 1962)

41. Eugène Sue, *Les Mystères de Paris* (Paris, Éditions Hallier, 1977–81), IV, 246

42. Tocqueville, *Souvenirs*, in *Oeuvres complètes*, XII (Paris, Gallimard, 1964), 151

43. Maxime du Camp, *Souvenirs de l'année 1848* (Paris, Hachette, 1892), 293–5

44. Tocqueville, *Souvenirs*, 177

45. Baron Haussmann, *Mémoires*, II: *Préfecture de la Seine* (Paris, 1890), 32

46. David P. Jordan, *Transforming Paris: The Life and Times of Baron Haussmann* (New York, Free Press, 1995), 192–208; Colin Jones, *Paris: Biography of a City* (London, Allen Lane, 2004), 344–68

47. Haussmann, *Mémoires*, II, 202–3

48. Haussmann, *Mémoires*, III: *Grands Travaux de Paris* (Paris, 1893), 54; Jordan, *Transforming Paris*, 188–98

49. Gérard Jacquemet, *Belleville au XIXe siècle du faubourg à la ville* (Paris, EHESS, 1984), 25

50. Jeanne Gaillard, *Paris: La Ville, 1852–1870* (Lille, Université de Lille III, Atelier de Reproduction des Thèses, 1976), 192

51. Anthime Corbon, *Le Secret du peuple de Paris* (Paris, Pagnerre, 1863), 209. See also Gaillard, *Paris*, 210–11; David Harvey, *Consciousness and the Urban Experience* (Oxford, Blackwell, 1985), 145–6, 186; Merriman, *Margins of City Life*, 26–7

52. Tocqueville, *Souvenirs*, 114

53. Comte de Falloux, *Mémoires d'un royaliste* (Paris, Perrin, 1888), I, 2–13; Jacques-Guy Petit, 'Grégoire Bordillon et la République romantique (1848–1849)', in Jean-Luc Marais, *Les Préfets de Maine-et-Loire* (Rennes, Presses Universitaires de Rennes, 2000), 239

54. Philip Vigier, *La Seconde République dans la région alpine* (Paris, PUF, 1963), II, 184–6, 212–14

55. Montalembert, speech of 30 Aug. 1849, in *Discours*, III: *1848–1852* (Paris, Lecoffre, 1860), 237

56. *La Revue Provinciale*, 15 Sept. 1848

57. *L'Étoile du Midi*, 18 Jan. 1851

58. Baron Charles de Larcy, *La Décentralisation de 1789 à 1870* (Paris, 1870), 18–19

59. Bernard Leclère and Vincent Wright, *Les Préfets du Second Empire* (Paris, Colin, 1973), 37–68

60. Haussmann, *Mémoires*, II, 197

61. Napoléon III, *Oeuvres*, III (Paris, 1856), 343–4

62. Caron, *Histoire des chemins de fer*, I, 211–18

63. Roger Price, *An Economic History of Modern France, 1730–1914* (London and Basingstoke, Macmillan, 1981), 21–5, 134

64. Harvey, *Consciousness and the Urban Experience*, 77–120; Jules Ferry, *Les Comptes fantastiques d'Haussmann* [1868] (Neuilly-sur-Seine, G. Durier, 1979)

65. William B. Cohen, *Urban Government and the Rise of the French City: Five Municipalities in the Nineteenth Century* (Basingstoke, Macmillan, 1998), 10, 225–6; Françoise Bayard and Pierre Cayez, eds, *Histoire de Lyon des origines à nos jours* (Le Coteau, Horvath, 1990), 275–9, 293–4

66. Alain Corbin, *The Lure of the Sea: The Discovery of the Seaside in the Western World, 1750–1840* (Cambridge, Polity, 1994), 275; Pierre de Régnier, *Deauville* (Paris, Émile-Paul Frères, 1927), 10–11

67. Douglas Peter Mackamen, *Leisure Settings: Bourgeois Culture, Medicine and the Spa in Modern France* (Chicago and London: University of Chicago Press, 1998), 48–65

68. *Revue de Bretagne et de la Vendée*, prospectus 15 Dec. 1856; Guiomar, *Bretonisme*, 187–95

69. Frédéric Mistral, *Mes origines: Mémoires et récits* [1906] (Paris, Plon, 1937); Claude Morin, *Frédéric Mistral* (Paris, Fayard, 1993), 132–50

70. Cited by Roger Price, *The French Second Empire: An Anatomy of Political Power* (Cambridge, Cambridge University Press, 2001), 381

71. Jacques-Louis Hénon, *Discours sur l'administration municipale de Paris et de Lyon* (Paris, 1863)

72. Sudhir Hazareesingh, *From Subject to Citizen: The Second Empire and the Emergence of French Democracy* (Princeton, Princeton University Press, 1998), 287–305

73. Comité de Nancy, *Un Projet de décentralisation* (Nancy, 1865)

74. B. Basdevant-Gaudemet, *La Commission de décentralisation de 1870* (Paris, PUF, 1973)

CHAPTER 3: A DIVIDED SOCIETY

1. Balzac, *Les Paysans*, in *La Comédie humaine*, IX (Paris, Gallimard, 1978), 71, 91, 126, 347

2. Georges Lefebvre, 'Répartition de la propriété et de l'exploitation foncières à la fin de l'Ancien Régime', in Lefebvre, *Études sur la Révolution française* (Paris, PUF, 1954), 201–22

3. Georges Lefebvre, *Les Paysans du Nord pendant la Révolution française* (Paris and Lille, 1924), 11, 536–47

4. Anne Jollet, *Terre et société en révolution* (Paris, Comité des Travaux Historiques et Scientifiques, 2000), 496–9

5. Jean-Claude Farcy, *Les Paysans beaucerons aux XIXe siècle* (2 vols, Chartres, Société Archéologique d'Eure-et-Loire, 1989), I, 134–5

6. James R. Lehning, *The Peasants of Marlhes: Economic Development and Family Organization in Nineteenth-century France* (London, Macmillan, 1980), 115–17

7. Agricol Perdiguier, *Mémoires d'un compagnon* (Paris, Maspéro, 1977), 40–53

8. Natalie Petiteau, *L'Horlogerie des bourgeois conquérants* (Paris, Belles-Lettres, 1994), 37–49

9. Margaret H. Darrow, *Revolution in the House: Family, Class and Inheritance in Southern France, 1775–1825* (Princeton, Princeton University Press, 1989), 210–19

10. Alain Corbin, *The Life of an Unknown: The Rediscovered World of a Clog-maker in Nineteenth-century France* (New York, Columbia University Press, 2001), 51–9, 208–9

11. Gay Gullickson, *Spinners and Weavers of Auffay: Rural Industry and the Sexual Division of Labour in a French Village, 1750–1850* (Cambridge, Cambridge University Press, 1986), 78–111

12. Lehning, *The Peasants of Marlhes*, 39–41

13. Peter M. Jones, *Politics and Rural Society: The Southern Massif Central, c. 1750–1880* (Cambridge, Cambridge University Press, 1985), 58–9

14. John Merriman, *The Stones of Balazuc* (New York and London, Norton, 2002), 86–97

15. Donald Reid, *The Miners of Decazeville: A Generation of Deindustrialization* (Cambridge, Mass., Harvard University Press, 1985), 33

16. Paul Bairoch, *La Population active et sa structure* (Brussels, Éditions de l'Institut de Sociologie de l'Université Libre de Bruxelles, 1968), 97, 99

17. Jones, *Politics and Rural Society*, 62–6

18. Alain Corbin, *Archaïsme et modernité en Limousin au XIXe siècle, 1845–1880* (Paris, Marcel Rivière, 1975), I, 18–225; Annie Moulin, *Les Maçons de la Creuse: Les Origines du mouvement* (Clermont-Ferrand, Institut d'Études du Massif Central, 1986), 39–291

19. Martin Nadaud, *Léonard, maçon de la Creuse* (Paris, Maspéro, 1982), 37–46, 67–76, 135–47, 184–7. See also Gillian Tindall, *The Journey of Martin Nadaud: A Life and Turbulent Times* (London, Chatto & Windus, 1999), 19–141

20. Louise A. Tilly and Joan W. Scott, *Women, Work and Family* (New York and London, Methuen, 1987), 94; Claire Auzias and Annita Houel, *La Grève des ovalistes, Lyon, juin–juillet 1869* (Paris, Payot, 1982), 31

21. Lehning, *The Peasants of Marlhes*, 46

22. Jean-Baptiste Dumay, 'Memoirs of a Militant Worker from Le Creusot', in Mark Traugott, ed., *The French Worker* (Berkeley, University of California Press, 1993), 310–16

23. Perdiguier, *Mémoires d'un compagnon*, 130–39, 150–53, 192–3, 284, 298, 303

24. Nadaud, *Maçon de la Creuse*, 87, 129–30

25. Ibid., 60, 65–7, 121–2, 196–200

26. Norbert Truquin, *Mémoires et aventures d'un prolétaire (1833–1887)*, ed. Paule Lejeune (Paris, L'Harmattan, 2004). Large extracts are translated as Norbert Truquin, 'Memoirs and Adventures of a Proletarian in Times of Revolution', in Traugott, ed., *French Worker*, 251–308. See also Michelle Perrot, 'A Nineteenth-century Work Experience as Related in a Worker's Autobiography: Norbert Truquin', in Steven Kaplan and Cynthia Koepp, eds, *Work in France: Representations, Meaning, Organization and Practice* (Ithaca, Cornell University Press, 1986), 298–316

27. *L'Artisan: Journal de la Classe Ouvrière*, 17 Oct. 1830. See also William H. Sewell, *Work and Revolution in France: The Language of Labour from the Old Regime to 1848* (Cambridge, Cambridge University Press, 1980), 197–8

28. Émile Coornaert, *Le Compagnonnage en France du Moyen Age à nos jours* (Paris, Éditions Ouvrières, 1966), 62–8

29. Sewell, *Work and Revolution*, 201–18; Tony Judt, *Marxism and the French Left: Studies in Labour and Politics in France, 1830–1981* (Oxford, Clarendon Press, 1986), 59–63

30. Eugène Fournière, *La Règne de Louis-Philippe*, vol. VIII of Jean Jaurès, *Histoire socialiste de la Révolution francaise* (Paris, Rouff, 1901), 152–60; Robert Bezucha, *The Lyon Uprising of 1834* (Cambridge, Mass., Harvard University Press, 1974). See above, pp. 52–3

31. Georges Duveau, *1848: The Making of a Revolution* (London, Routledge & Kegan Paul, 1967), 100

32. Truquin, *Mémoires et aventures*, 17

33. David I. Kulstein, 'The Attitude of French Workers towards the Second Empire', *French Historical Studies* 2/3 (1962), 356–75; Bernard Ménager, 'Force et limites du Bonapartisme populaire en milieu ouvrier sous Le Second Empire', *Revue Historique* 538 (1981), 371–88

34. J. Albertini, 'Le Rapporteur de la loi sur les coalitions', in Anne Troisier de Diaz, ed., *Regards sur Émile Ollivier* (Paris, Publications de la Sorbonne, 1985), 97–121

35. Jean-Baptiste Dumay, *Mémoires d'un militant ouvrier du Creusot, 1841–1905* (Paris, Maspéro, 1976), 128. See also Fernand Huillier, *La Lutte ouvrière à la fin du Second Empire* (Paris, Association Marc Bloch, 1957), 53

36. Françoise Raison-Jourde, *La Colonie auvergnate de Paris au XIXe siècle* (Paris, Ville de Paris, 1978), 67, 86, 123–5, 141–2, 151–2

37. Nicolas Papayanis, *The Coachmen of Nineteenth-century Paris* (Baton Rouge, Louisiana University Press, 1993), 52–66

38. Jean Le Yaouancq, 'La Mobilité sociale dans le milieu boutiquier parisien au XIXe siècle', *Mouvement Social* 108 (July–Sept. 1979), 89–112

39. Michael B. Miller, *The Bon Marché: Bourgeois Culture and the Department Store, 1869–1920* (London, George Allen & Unwin, 1981), 25–45

40. Robert Gildea, *Education in Provincial France, 1800–1914: A Study of Three Departments* (Oxford, Clarendon Press, 1983), 147

41. Guizot letter of 4 July to *instituteurs* cited by Maurice Gontard, *Les Écoles primaires de la France bourgeoise, 1833–1875* (Toulouse, Institut Pédagogique National, 1964), 5

42. Gontard, *Les Écoles primaires de la France bourgeoise*, 30

43. Gildea, *Education in Provincial France*, 196–7

44. Alphonse Daudet, *Le Petit Chose* [1868] (Paris, 1947), 160

45. Alain Prost, *L'Enseignement en France, 1800–1967* (Paris, Colin, 1968), 32–4, 225, 231

46. Balzac, *Le Père Goriot* (Paris, Garnier-Flammarion, 1966), 108–9

47. Alexandre Dumas, *Mes mémoires*, II (Paris, Gallimard, 1957), 76–183

48. J. M. and Brian Chapman, *The Life and Times of Baron Haussmann* (London, Weidenfeld & Nicolson, 1957), 7–50

49. Pierre Jacomet, *Avocats républicains du Second Empire* (Paris, Éditions du Panthéon, 1933), 78–98; Philip Nord, *The Republican Moment: Struggles for Democracy in Nineteenth-century France* (Cambridge, Mass., Harvard University Press, 1995), 121–33

50. André-Jean Tudesq, *Les Grands Notables en France, 1840–1849* (Paris, PUF, 1964), 381. See also Vincent Wright, *Le Conseil d'État sous le Second Empire* (Paris, Colin, 1971), 191–200

51. Vincent Wright, 'Les Directeurs et secrétaires généraux des administrations centrales sous le Second Empire', in François de Baeque et al., eds, *Les Directeurs de ministère en France, XIXe–XXe siècles* (Geneva, Droz, 1976), 46

52. Christophe Charles, *Les Hauts Fonctionnaires en France au XIXe siècles* (Paris, Gallimard/Julliard, 1980), 24–6.

53. Général du Barail, *Mes souvenirs* (Paris, 1913), I, 1, 46; Rafe Blaufarb, *The French Army, 1750–1820: Careers, Talent, Merit* (Manchester and New York, Manchester University Press, 2002), 164–97; William Serman, *Les Origines des officiers français, 1848–1870* (Paris, Publications de la Sorbonne, 1979), 76–106, 200–235

54. Jean Walch, *Michel Chevalier: Économiste saint-simonien, 1806–1879* (Paris, Vrin, 1975); Pierre Leroux and George Sand, *Histoire d'une amitié*, ed. Jean-Pierre Lacassagne (Paris, Klincksieck, 1973)

55. Jules Simon, *Victor Cousin* (Paris, Hachette, 1887), 9–13; Simon, *Premières Années* (Paris, Flammarion, 1901), 115–287; Alan B. Spitzer, *The Generation of 1820* (Princeton, Princeton University Press, 1987), 72–91; Paul Gerbod, *La Condition universitaire en France au XIXe siècle* (Paris, PUF, 1965), 28–36

56. Balzac, *Eugénie Grandet* (Paris, Gallimard, Folio, 1972), 24–5, 33, 119, 222

57. Balzac, *Le Père Goriot*, 86, 94–7, 135–6; Balzac, *La Maison Nucingen*, in *La Comédie Humaine*, VI (Paris, Gallimard, 1977), 338–40

58. Balzac, *Eugénie Grandet*, 122

59. Claude Fohlen, *L'Industrie textile au temps du Second Empire* (Paris, Plon, 1956), 69–71; Tudesq, *Grands Notables*, 263–5

60. Jean-Pierre Chaline, *Les Bourgeois de Rouen: Une Élite urbaine au XIXe siècle* (Paris, FNSP, 1982), 114–17; Serge Chassagne, *Le Coton et ses patrons: France 1720–1840* (Paris, Éditions de l'École des Hautes Études en Sciences Sociales, 1991), 585

61. Dominique Schneider, ed., *Les Schneider, Le Creusot: Une Famille, une entreprise, une ville, 1836–1960* (Paris, Fayard, 1995), 149–52, 271–4; Agnès Diangio, *Schneider et Cie et les travaux publics (1895–1949)* (Paris, École des Chartes, 1995), 41–4

62. Pierre Barral, *Les Périer dans l'Isère au XXe siècle* (Paris, PUF, 1964), 24–117; Madeleine Bourset, *Casimir Périer: Un Prince financier au temps du Romantisme* (Paris, Publications de la Sorbonne, 1994), 44–85

63. Bertrand Gille, *Histoire de la Maison Rothschild* (2 vols, Geneva, Droz, 1965–7), I, 48–64, 164; François Caron, *Histoire des chemins de fer en France, 1740–1883*, I (Paris, Fayard, 1997), 172–3; Jean Autin, *Les Frères Péreire: Le Bonheur d'entreprendre* (Paris, Perrin, 1984)

64. Robert Forster, 'The Survival of the Nobility during the French Revolution', *Past & Present* 37 (1967), 71–86; Donald Greer, *The Incidence of the Terror during the French Revolution: A Statistical Interpretation* (Cambridge, Mass., Harvard University Press, 1935), and *The Incidence of Emigration during the French Revolution* (Cambridge, Mass., Harvard University Press, 1951)

65. Michel Figeac, 'La Noblesse bordelaise au lendemain de la Révolution', *Histoire, Économie et Société* 3 (1986), 381–405; Tudesq, *Grands Notables*, 293–5, 350; Reid, *Miners of Decazeville*, 15–18

66. General Pierre de Pelleport, *Souvenirs militaires et intimes* (Paris, 1857), I, 4, cited by Natalie Petiteau, *Élites et mobilités: La Noblesse d'Empire au XIXe siècle, 1808–1914* (Paris, La Boutique de l'Histoire, 1997), 155

67. François Lalliard, 'La Fortune du Maréchal Berthier, prince de Wagram et de Neuchâtel', *Revue d'Histoire Moderne et Contemporaine* 42/3 (1995), 454–80

68. Petiteau, *Élites et nobilités*, 210–13, 224–6

69. Gordon K. Anderson, 'Old Nobles and *Noblesse d'Empire*, 1814–1830: In Search of a Conservative Interest in Post-revolutionary France', *French History* 8 (1994), 163–4; Tudesq, *Grands Notables*, 123–4

70. Comte d'Haussonville, *Ma jeunesse, 1814–1830* (Paris, 1885), 24–87, 229–90

71. Alfred de Vigny, *Mémoires inédits* (Paris, Gallimard, 1958), 189

CHAPTER 4: RELIGION AND REVOLUTION

1. The most up-to-date work on the curé d'Ars is Philippe Boutry and Michel Cinquin, *Deux pèlerinages au XIXe siècle. Ars et Paray-le-Monial* (Paris, Beauchesne, 1986), and Boutry, *Prêtres et paroisses au pays du curé d'Ars* (Paris, Cerf, 1986), but see also Abbé Francis Trochu, *The Curé d'Ars: St Jean-Marie-Baptiste Vianney (1789–1859)* (London, Burns & Oares, 1927), Abbé Alfred Monnin, *Le Curé d'Ars* (4th edn,

Paris, Gervais, 1884), Mgr René Fourrey, *Jean-Marie Vianney, Curé d'Ars: Vie authentique* (Paris, Desclée, De Brouwer, 1981). See also Elisabeth Sainte-Marie Perrin, *Pauline Jaricot: Foundress of the Association for the Propagation of the Faith (1799–1862)* (London, 1928)

2. Pierre Pierrard, *Histoire des curés de campagne de 1789 à nos jours* (Paris, Plon, 1986), 86

3. Louis Pérouas, *Les Limousins, leurs saints, leurs prêtres du XVe au XXe siècles* (Paris, Cerf, 1988), 146

4. Michel Lagrée, *Histoire du diocèse de Rennes* (Paris, Beauchesne, 1979), 189; Lagrée, *Mentalités, religion et histoire en Haute-Bretagne au XIXe siècle: Le Diocèse de Rennes, 1815–1914* (Paris, Klincksieck, 1977), 179–90; Pérouas, *Les Limousins*, 146

5. Pierrard, *Histoire des curés de campagne*, 90–91, 102–3

6. Ibid., 127–37, 174–5

7. Gérard Cholvy, *Être chrétien au XIXe siècle, 1790–1914* (Paris, Seuil, 1997), 66–8

8. Alain Corbin, *Village Bells: Sound and Meaning in the Nineteenth-century French Countryside* (London, Papermac, 1999), 35–7, 42–3, 98–102, 119–20

9. J. Michel Phayer, 'Politics and Popular Religion: The Cult of the Cross in France, 1815–1840', *Journal of Social History* 11 (1978), 346–65

10. Cholvy, *Être chrétien*, 196; Yves-Marie Hilaire, *Une Chrétienté au XIXe siècle? La Vie religieuse des populations du diocèse d'Arras, 1840–1914* (Lille, Presses Universitaires de Lille, 1977), I, 70–82, 400–406; Hilaire, 'Notes sur la Religion Populaire au XIXe siècle', in *La Religion populaire: Paris 17–19 octobre 1977* (Colloques internationaux du CNRS, Paris, CNRS, 1979), 193–209

11. A. Corbon, *Le Secret du peuple de Paris* (Paris, Pagnerre, 1863), 302–3

12. Ibid., 303–9, 352–6

13. Gérard Cholvy and Yves-Marie Hilaire, *Histoire religieuse de la France contemporaine, 1800–1880* (Toulouse, Privat, 1985), 274

14. Christiane Marcilhacy, *Le Diocèse d'Orléans sous l'épiscopat de Mgr Dupanloup* (Paris, Plon, 1962), 49, 324–6

15. Timothy Tackett, *Religion, Revolution and Regional Culture in Eighteenth-century France: The Ecclesiastical Oath of 1791* (Princeton, Princeton University Press, 1986), appendix III, 364–6; Pérouas, *Les Limousins*, 14, 138–47

16. Hilaire, *Une Chrétienté au XIXe siècle?*, 629–49

17. J. Peter and Ch. Poulet, *Histoire religieuse du département du Nord pendant la Révolution, 1789–1802* (Lille, Facultés Catholiques,

1930–33), I, 130; Joseph Deschuytter, *L'Esprit public et son évolution dans le Nord de 1791 au lendemain de Thermidor An II* (Gap, L. Jean, 1959), I, 139–76

18. Maurice Rey, ed., *Les Diocèses de Besançon et de Saint-Claude* (Paris, Beauchesne, 1977), 142–56

19. Paul Huot-Pleuroux, *Le Recrutement sacerdotal dans le diocèse de Besançon de 1801 à 1960* (Paris, Neo-Type, 1966), 473–81

20. Armand Audiganne, *Les Populations ouvrières et les industries de la France* (Paris, 1860), I, 197–8

21. Cholvy and Hilaire, *Histoire religieuse*, 269

22. Claude Muller, *Dieu est Catholique et alsacien: La Vitalité du diocèse de Strasbourg au XIXe siècle, 1802–1914* (Hagueneau, Société d'Histoire de l'Église de l'Alsace, 1987), 631–6, 677–706, 851–61

23. Esther Benbassa, *The Jews of France: A History from Antiquity to the Present* (Princeton, Princeton University Press, 1999), 99

24. Paula E. Hyman, *The Emancipation of the Jews of Alsace: Acculturation and Tradition in the Nineteenth Century* (New Haven, Yale University Press, 1991), 12–23

25. Marquis de Noailles, *Le Comte Molé, 1781–1855* (Paris, Champion, 1922), I, 97

26. Benbassa, *Jews of France*, 88–95; Hyman, *Emancipation of the Jews*, 17–23

27. Muller, *Dieu est Catholique*, 740–47

28. Michael Burns, *Dreyfus: A Family Affair, 1789–1945* (London, Chatto & Windus, 1992), 3–69

29. James N. Hood, 'Protestant–Catholic Relations and the Roots of the First Popular Counter-revolutionary Movement in France', *Journal of Modern History* 43 (1971), 245–75; Gwynn Lewis, *The Second Vendée: The Continuity of Counter-Revolution in the Gard, 1789–1815* (Oxford, Clarendon Press, 1978), ch. 1

30. Lewis, *Second Vendée*, ch. 6

31. Report of school inspector, 15 July 1850, cited by Robert Gildea, *Education in Provincial France, 1800–1914: A Study of Three Departments* (Oxford, Clarendon Press, 1983), 79. See also Louis Secondy, 'Aux origines de la Maison de l'Assomption Nîmes, 1844–53', in René Rémond and E. Poulat, eds, *Emmanuel d'Alzon dans la Société et l'Église du XIXe siècle* (Paris, Le Centurion, 1982), 241–50

32. Audiganne, *Populations ouvrières*, II, 202–5

33. Cholvy and Hilaire, *Histoire religieuse*, 258

34. Michel Lagrée, 'Emergence d'une terre fidèle', in Jean Delumeau, ed.,

Le Diocèse de Rennes (Paris, Beauchesne, 1979), 169; Lagrée, *Mentalités*, 117

35. Lagrée, *Mentalités*, 119–23
36. On 'blue Christianity' see Bernard Plongeron, *Théologie et politique au Siècle des Lumières, 1770–1820* (Geneva, Droz, 1973), 149–82; Lagrée, *Mentalités*, 73–91
37. Claude Langlois, *Un Diocèse breton au début du XIXe siècle* (Paris, Klincksieck, 1974), 580–93
38. Abbé Jean-Marie Téphany, *Vie et oeuvres de Mgr Joseph-Marie Graveron, évêque de Quimper et de Léon* (Paris, Vivèds, 1870), I, 422
39. Michel Lagrée, *Religion et cultures en Bretagne, 1850–1950* (Paris, Fayard, 1992), 65–72
40. Ernest Renan, *Souvenirs d'enfance et de jeunesse* (Paris, Garnier, 1973), 82–3
41. Michel Lagrée, *Religion et modernité: France XIXe–XXe siècles* (Rennes, Presses Universitaires de Rennes, 2002), 119
42. Ruth Harris, *Lourdes: Body and Spirit in the Secular Age* (London, Allen Lane, 1999), 33–172
43. Chateaubriand, *Génie du christianisme* (Paris, Gallimard Pléiade, 1978), preface of 1st edn, 1282; *Mémoires d'outre-tombe* (Paris, Gallimard Pléiade, 1951), II, 399, 437, 461
44. Chateaubriand, *Génie du christianisme*, 555, 802, 1086, 1099
45. Ibid., preface of 1826, 460
46. Quoted by Edmond-Henri-Adolphe Scherer, *Études critiques de la littérature contemporaine*, IV (Paris, Calmann-Lévy, 1886), 61
47. Félicité de Lamennais, *Essai sur l'indifférance*, in *Oeuvres complètes* (4 vols, Paris, 1836–7), I, 30–34, II, 103–5, 176, 203. See also Jean-Marie Derré, *Lamennais, ses amis et le mouvement d'idées à l'époque romantique* (Paris, Klincksieck, 1962)
48. Geoffrey Cubitt, *The Jesuit Myth: Conspiracy Theory and Politics in Nineteenth-century France* (Oxford, Clarendon Press, 1993), 84–95
49. *L'Avenir*, prospectus, 20 Aug. 1830
50. Père Baron, *La Jeunesse de Lacordaire* (Paris, Cerf, 1961), 90, 183–4, 227–30
51. Montalembert to Lamennais, 26 Oct. 1830, in Georges Goyau and P. de Lallemand, eds, *Lettres de Montalembert à Lamennais* (Paris, Desclée, De Brouwer, 1932), 2–3; R. P. Lecanuet, *Montalembert, I: Sa jeunesse, 1810–1830* (Paris, C. Poussielgue, 1910), 5–17, 101
52. Montalembert to Lacordaire, 22 June 1831; Lacordaire to Montalembert, 29 July 1831, in P. de Lallemand, *Montalembert et ses amis dans le Romantisme* (Paris, 1927), 149, 191

53. Lamennais, *Paroles d'un croyant*, in *Oeuvres complètes*, XI, 32–5, 101–2, 130–31

54. Lacordaire to Montalembert, 6 Oct. 1834, in Montalembert, *Oeuvres polémiques* (Paris, 1868), III, 432

55. Montalembert to Lamennais, 30 Jan. 1835, in Goyau and Lallemand, eds, *Lettres de Montalembert à Lamennais*, 272

56. Mme Émile de Girardin, *Lettres parisiennes*, I (Paris, 1856), 63–5, letter of 8 Mar. 1837

57. F. Lamennais, *Le Livre du peuple* (Paris, 1838), 73, 91, 160, 181–9

58. Jules Bertaut, *Le Faubourg Saint-Germain* (Paris, 1935), 325–42

59. Guy Bedouelle, *Lacordaire, son pays, ses amis et la liberté des ordres religieux* (Paris, Cerf, 1991)

60. Pierre Pierrard, *Louis Veuillot* (Paris, Beauchesne, 1998), 18–45

61. Michelet and Quinet, *Les Jésuites* (Paris, 1843), 9–10, 88, 114–16, 241; Paul Viallaneix, *Michelet, les travaux et les jours, 1798–1874* (Paris, Gallimard, 1998), 132–6, 261–5; Cubitt, *Jesuit Myth*, 108–12, 137

62. Edgar Quinet, *L'Enseignement du peuple* (Paris, 1850), 25

63. Pierre N. Fortis, 'Lamennais and *Le Peuple Constituant*', in University of Paris X-Nanterre, *Actes du Colloque Lamennais* (Paris, Université de Paris X-Nanterre, 1975), 165

64. *L'Ère Nouvelle*, 19 Apr., 1 May 1848. See also Jean-Baptiste Duroselle, *Les Débuts du Catholicisme social en France, 1822–1870* (Paris, 1951), 295–303

65. Fortis, 'Lamennais and *Le Peuple Constituant*', 186–93

66. *L'Ère Nouvelle*, 1 Sept., 16 Oct. 1848; Ambrosio Romero Carranza, *Ozanam et ses contemporains* (Paris, Éditions Françaises d'Amsterdam, 1953), 314–20. See also Duroselle, *Débuts*, 306–10

67. Montalembert, article in *L'Ami de la religion*, 21 Oct. 1848, in *Oeuvres polémiques et diverses*, I (Paris, 1860), 500–503

68. Victor Hugo, speeches of 18 Oct. 1849 and 15 Jan. 1850, cited in René Rémond, *L'Anticléricalisme en France de 1815 à nos jours* (Paris, Fayard, 1976), 135–6, 140–41

69. See above, p. 78

70. Quinet, *L'Enseignement du peuple*, 25, 21, 105, 121

71. Cited by Eugène Tavernier, *Louis Veuillot* (Paris, 1913), 287

72. Montalembert, letters to Cavour, 22 Oct. 1860 and 20 Apr. 1861, in *Oeuvres polémiques et diverses*, II (Paris, 1860), 655–6, and III (1868), 57–8

73. Louis Veuillot, *Le Parfum de Rome* (2 vols, Paris, 1862), 291

74. H. W. Wardman, *Ernest Renan: A Critical Biography* (London, Athlone Press, 1964), 78

75. Ernest Renan, *Vie de Jésus: Édition populaire* (Paris, Calmann-Lévy, 1914), 2–3, 37, 69–70, 252–3

76. Ferdinand Buisson, *Souvenirs, 1866–1916: Conférence faite à l'Aula de l'Université de Neuchâtel, le 10 avril 1916* (Paris, Fischbacher, 1916), 10–11; Pierre Zind, *L'Enseignement religieux dans l'instruction primaire en France, 1850–1873* (Lyon, Centre d'histoire du Catholicisme, 1971), 281–2

77. Ligue de l'Enseignement, *Bulletin du Mouvement d'Enseignement par l'Initiative Privée* 5 (15 Feb. 1870), 72–3. See also A. Dessoye, *Jean Macé et la fondation de la Ligue de l'Enseignement* (Paris, 1883), 19–69, and Katherine Auspitz, *The Radical Bourgeoisie: The Ligue de l'Enseignement and the Origins of the Third Republic, 1866–1885* (Cambridge, Cambridge University Press, 1982), 51–122

CHAPTER 5: 'LE MALHEUR D'ÊTRE FEMME'

1. Madame de Staël, *Delphine* (Paris, Éditions des Femmes, 1981), I, 26–7, 32. See Angelica Goodden, *Madame de Staël: Delphine and Corinne* (London, Grant & Cutler, 2000); Madelyn Gutwirth, *Madame de Staël, Novelist* (Chicago and London, University of Illinois Press, 1978); J. Christopher Herold, *Mistress to an Age: A Life of Madame de Staël* (London, Readers Union, 1958); Maria Fairweather, *Madame de Staël* (London, Constable, 2005)

2. Maria Edgeworth to Henry Edgeworth, 16 Jan. 1803, in Christine Colvin, ed., *Maria Edgeworth in France and Switzerland: Selections from the Edgeworth Family Papers* (Oxford, Clarendon Press, 1979), 82–3, 56 note. See also Marilyn Butler and Christine Colvin, 'Maria Edgeworth and Delphine', *Cahiers Staëliens* 26–7 (1979), 80

3. Simon Balayé, 'Un Émissaire de Bonaparte: Fiévée, critique de Madame de Staël et de Delphine', in ibid., 107–8

4. André Burguière, 'La Révolution française et la famille', *Annales ESC* (1991), 151–68; Susanne Desan, *The Family on Trial in Revolutionary France* (Berkeley, Los Angeles and London, University of California Press, 2004), 93–118

5. Suzanne Desan, 'Reconstituting the Social after the Terror: Family, Property and the Law in Popular Politics', *Past & Present* 164 (1999), 81–121; Desan, *The Family on Trial*, 178–238

6. Desan, *The Family on Trial*, 283–310; Theresa McBride, 'Public

Authority and Private Lives: Divorce after the French Revolution',
French Historical Studies 17 (1992), 747–68

7. Balzac, *Physiologie du mariage* (Paris, Gallimard, 1971), 70, 84, 122,
   251; Patricia Mainardi, *Husbands, Wives and Lovers: Marriage and
   its Discontents in Nineteenth-century France* (New Haven and London,
   Yale University Press, 2003), 70–71, 87, 112

8. Whitney Walton, 'Republican Women and Republican Families in the
   Personal Narratives of George Sand, Marie d'Agoult and Hortense
   Allart', in Jo Burr Margadant, ed., *The New Biography: Performing
   Feminity in Nineteenth-century France* (Berkeley, Los Angeles and
   London, University of California Press, 2000), 103–23; Whitney
   Walton, *Eve's Proud Descendants: Four Women Writers and Repub-
   lican Politics in Nineteenth-century France* (Stanford, Stanford Univer-
   sity Press, 2000). See also Madeleine Lassère, *Delphine de Girardin*
   (Paris, Perrin, 2003), Phyllis Stock-Morton, *The Life of Marie d'Agoult,
   alias Daniel Stern* (Baltimore and London, Johns Hopkins University
   Press, 2000), Mona Ozouf, *Women's Words: Essay on French Singularity* (Chicago and London, University of Chicago Press, 1997),
   111–31 on Sand, and Belinda Jack, *George Sand* (London, Chatto &
   Windus, 1999)

9. Lassère, *Delphine de Girardin*, 39

10. Théophile Gautier, *Souvenirs romantiques* (Paris, Garnier Frères,
    1929), 206

11. Daniel Stern (Marie d'Agoult), *Mes souvenirs* (3rd edn, Paris, 1880),
    210, 221

12. Jack, *George Sand*, 1–112

13. Sand, *Story of My Life* (1991), 169, cited by Whitney Walton, 'Repub-
    lican Women and Republican Families', 109

14. Marie d'Agoult and George Sand, *Correspondance*, ed. Charles E.
    Dupéchez (Paris, Bartillat, 1995), letters of Marie d'Agoult, 24 Sept.
    1835 and George Sand, end Sept. 1835

15. George Sand and Gustave Flaubert, *Correspondance* (Paris, Calmann-
    Lévy, 1904), e.g. letters of Jan., Mar. and Oct. 1867

16. Sarah A. Curtis, *Educating the Faithful: Schooling and Society in
    Nineteenth-century France* (Delkalb, Northern Illinois University Press,
    2000), 25

17. J.-C. Chasteland and R. Pressat, 'La Nuptualité des générations
    françaises depuis un siècle', *Population* 17 (1962), 215–40

18. Claude Langlois, *Le Catholicisme au féminin: Les Congrégations
    françaises à supérieur-générale au XIXe siècle* (Paris, Cerf, 1984),
    205–8, 273, 522

19. Mgr Francis Trochu, *Jeanne Jugan, Sister Mary of the Cross: Foundress of the Institute of the Little Sisters of the Poor, 1792–1879* (London, Burns & Oates, 1950), 117

20. Curtis, *Educating the Faithful*, 25

21. Susan Bachrach, 'La Féminisation des PTT en France au tournant du siècle', *Mouvement Social* 140 (1987), 69–87

22. Colette Cosnier, *Marie Pape-Carpentier: Fondatrice de l'école maternelle* (Paris, Fayard, 2003); Jean-Noël Luc, *L'Invention du jeune enfant au XIXe siècle: De la salle d'asile à l'école maternelle* (Paris, Belin, 1997)

23. Ernest Renan, 'Ma soeur Henriette', in *Oeuvres complètes*, IX (Paris, Calmann-Lévy, 1960), 456

24. Ibid.

25. J.-V. Daubié, *La Femme pauvre au XIXe siècle* (Paris, Guillaumin, 1866), 151–64, 182–93, 319–23; Raymonde Bulger, 'Julie-Victor Daubié (1824–1874). Ses modes particuliers d'occupation de l'espace public', in Alain Corbin, Jacqueline Lalouette and Michèle Roit-Sarcey, eds, *Femmes dans la cité, 1815–1871* (Grâne, Créaphis, 1997), 287–92

26. Françoise Mayeur, *L'Éducation des filles en France au XIXe siècle* (Paris, Hachette, 1979), 113–38; Mgr Dupanloup, *La Femme studieuse* (7th edn, Paris, 1900), 132

27. Yvonne Kniebiehler and Catherine Fouquet, *La Femme et les médecins* (Paris, Hachette, 1983), 193–6

28. Bonnie G. Smith, *Ladies of the Leisure Class: The Bourgeoises of Northern France in the Nineteenth Century* (Princeton, Princeton University Press, 1981), 35–79, 129–44

29. Bernadette Angleraud, *Les Boulangers lyonnais au XIXe et XXe siècles* (Paris, Christian, 1998), 76–80

30. Martine Segalen, *Mari et femme dans la société paysanne* (Paris, Flammarion, 1980), 19–31, 94–110

31. Theresa McBride, *The Domestic Revolution: The Modernisation of Household Service in England and France, 1820–1920* (London, Croom Helm, 1976), 11–14, 35, 45; Pierre Guiral and Guy Thuillier, *La Vie quotidienne des domestiques en France au XIXe et XX siècles* (Paris, Hachette, 1978), 123, 65, 148–50

32. Anna Emilie Hamilton, 'Considérations sur les infirmières des Hôpitaux' (medical thesis, Montpellier, 1900), 122

33. Suzanne Voilquin, 'Recollections of a Daughter of the People', in Mark Traugott, ed., *The French Worker* (Berkeley, University of California Press, 1993), 93–113

34. Louise A. Tilly and Joan W. Scott, *Women, Work and Family* (New York and London, Methuen, 1987), 94–7; Mainardi, *Husbands, Wives and Lovers*, 26; Katherine A. Lynch, *Family, Class and Ideology in Early Industrial France: Social Policy and the Working-class Family, 1825–1848* (Madison, University of Wisconsin Press, 1988), 77–93

35. Louise Tilly, 'Structure d'emploi, travail des femmes et changements démographiques dans deux villes industrielles: Anzin et Roubaix, 1872–1906', *Mouvement Social* 105 (1978), 33–58

36. Claire Auzias and Annik Houel, *La Grève des ovalistes: Lyon, juin–juillet, 1869* (Paris, Payot, 1982), 25–125

37. Alain Corbin, *Women for Hire: Prostitution and Sexuality in France after 1850* (Cambridge, Mass., Harvard University Press, 1990), 38–49, 162–3

38. Myriam Harry, *La Vie de Jules Lemaître* (Paris, Flammarion, 1946), 121–46. See also Joanna Richardson, *The Courtesans: The Demi-monde in Nineteenth-century France* (London, Weidenfeld & Nicolson, 1967)

39. See for example Joan B. Landes, *Women and the Public Sphere in the Age of the French Revolution* (Ithaca and London, Cornell University Press, 1988)

40. Madame de Staël, *De la littérature considérée dans ses rapports avec les institutions sociales* (Paris, Garnier, 1998), 325–32

41. Cited by Geneviève Fraisse, *Reason's Muse: Sexual Difference and the Birth of Democracy* (Chicago and London, University of Chicago Press, 1994), 11–22

42. Jean-Pierre Chaline, 'Sociabilité féminine et "maternalisme": Les Sociétés de Charité Maternelle au XIXe siècle', in Corbin et al., *Femmes dans la cité*, 69–78

43. Karen Offen, *European Feminisms, 1700–1950: A Political History* (Stanford, Stanford University Press, 2000), 103; Janise Bergman-Carton, *The Women of Ideas in French Art* (New Haven, Yale University Press, 1995), 68–9, 84–5

44. Gautier, *Souvenirs romantiques*, 210

45. Mme Émile de Girardin / Le Vicomte de Launay, *Lettres parisiennes*, III (Paris, 1856), 25 Mar., 9 Nov. 1844

46. Daniel Stern [Marie d'Agoult], *Essai sur la liberté* (Paris, 1847), 94–103

47. Michèle Riot-Sarcey, *La Démocratie à l'épreuve des femmes: Trois figures critiques du pouvoir* (Paris, Albin Michel, 1994), 49–73

48. Offen, *European Feminisms*, 100

49. Doris and Paul Beik, eds, *Flora Tristan, Utopian Feminist: Her Travel*

Diaries and Personal Crusade (Bloomington, Indiana University Press, 1993), 112–22

50. Cited by Michelle Perrot, *Les Femmes ou les silences de l'histoire* (Paris, Flammarion, 1998), 310. See also Máire Cross and Tim Gray, *The Feminism of Flora Tristan* (Oxford and Providence, Berg, 1992)

51. Offen, *European Feminisms*, 110–11

52. Cited by Riot-Sarcey, *La Démocratie à l'épreuve des femmes*, 192

53. George Sand, *Correspondance*, XVIII: *1847–1848* (Paris, Garnier, 1971), letter to editors of *La Réforme* and *La Vraie République*, 8 Apr. 1848, 391–2, letter to Comité de la Gauche, Apr. 1848, 401–3, and to her son, Maurice Dudevant-Sand, 23 Apr. 1848, 359–60. See also Bernard Hamon, *George Sand et la politique* (Paris, L'Harmattan, 2001), 245–78, and Walton, *Eve's Proud Descendants*, 206–9, 214–16

54. Daniel Stern [Madame d'Agoult], *Histoire de la Révolution de 1848* (new edn, Paris, 1896), II, 158–60

55. Offen, *European Feminisms*, 127–8

56. P.-J. Proudhon, *Système de contraditions économiques ou philosophie de la misère II*, *Oeuvres complètes*, II (Paris, Marcel Rivière, 1923), 197

57. P.-J. Proudhon, *De la justice dans la Révolution et dans l'Église* (Paris, Garnier, 1858), III, 337, 372–3, 417

58. Juliette Adam, *Mes premières armes littéraires et politiques* (Paris, 1904), 68

59. Juliette La Messine, *Les Idées anti-Proudhoniennes sur l'amour, la femme et le mariage* (Paris, Alphonse Taride, 1858), 56–76, 84–8, 95–7

60. Jenny d'Héricourt, *La Femme affranchie* (Brussels and Paris, F. van Meenan, 1860), 43–5, 163, 180

61. P.-J. Prouhon, *La Pornocratie ou les femmes des temps modernes*, in *Oeuvres complètes*, XV (Paris, Rivière, 1939), 331, 346, 368

62. Émile Ollivier, *Journal, 1846–1869* (Paris, Julliard, 1961), I, 144–5, 300–314; Adam, *Mes premières armes littéraires et politiques*, 91, 101–3; Sylvie Aprile, 'La République au salon: Vie et mort d'une forme de sociabilité politique', *Revue d'Histoire Moderne et Contemporaine* 38 (1991), 477–80

63. Patrick Kay Bidelman, *Pariahs Stand Up! The Founding of the Liberal Feminist Movement in France, 1858–1889* (Westport, Conn., Greenwood Press, 1982), 75–8

64. G. Richelot, *La Femme-Médecin* (Paris, 1875), 27–8

CHAPTER 6: ARTISTIC GENIUS AND BOURGEOIS CULTURE

1. Chateaubriand, *Mémoires d'outre-tombe* (Paris, Gallimard Pléiade, 1951), I, 444–5

2. Lamartine to Comte de Virieu, 23 Mar. 1820, in *Correspondance*, II: *1813–1820* (Paris, 1873), 456

3. Théophile Gautier, *Souvenirs romantiques* (Paris, Garnier Frères, 1929), 190, 193

4. Gérard Unger, *Lamartine: Poète et homme d'état* (Paris, Flammarion, 1998), 31–156

5. Hubert Juin, *Victor Hugo*, I: *1802–1843* (Paris, Flammarion, 1980), 264; Graham Robb, *Victor Hugo* (London, Picador, 1997), 61–3

6. Alexandre Dumas, *Souvenirs romantiques et littéraires* (Paris, Tallandier, 1928), 70

7. Ibid., 115

8. C.-A. Sainte-Beuve, review in *Le Globe*, 2/9 Jan. 1827, in *Critique et portraits littéraires*, I (Paris, 1839), 537

9. Gautier, *Souvenirs romantiques*, 5–31, 75–89; Charles Pichois and Michel Brix, *Gérard de Nerval* (Paris, Fayard, 1995), 48–66

10. Sainte-Beuve to Hugo, Feb. 1830, in his *Correspondance générale* (Paris, Stock, 1935), I, 179

11. Michel Ross, *Alexandre Dumas* (Newton Abbot and London, David & Charles, 1981), 70–108

12. Dumas, *Souvenirs romantiques*, 190–91

13. Eugénie de Guérin, *Journal et fragments* (Paris, Didier, 1874), 121, entry of 5 May 1837

14. Sainte-Beuve to Hugo, 14 Apr. 1831, *Correspondance générale*, I, 228; Sainte-Beuve, *Critiques et portraits littéraires*, II (Paris, 1841), 146

15. Robb, *Hugo*, 185

16. Eugène de Mirecourt, *Fabrique de romans: Maison Alexandre Dumas et Compagnie* (Paris, 1845); F. W. J. Hemmings, *The King of Romance: A Portrait of Alexandre Dumas* (London, Hamish Hamilton, 1979), 121–38

17. Ross, *Dumas*, 227–31

18. Eugène Delacroix, *Journal* (Oxford, Phaidon, 1980), 62, entry for 5 Feb. 1847

19. Dr Louis-Désiré Véron, *Mémoires d'un bourgeois de Paris* (Paris, G. Le Prat, 1945), I, 177; Henri Martineau, *Stendhal et le salon de Madame Ancelot* (Paris, Le Divan, 1932)

20. Stendhal, *Souvenirs d'égotisme* (Paris, Le Divan, 1950), 55–6

21. Mérimée to Beyle, 15 Mar. 1831 in Prosper Mérimée, *Correspondance générale, I: 1822–1825* (Paris, Le Divan, 1941), 89; Stendhal to Mme Albertine de Rubempré, 6 Feb. 1831, in Stendhal, *Correspondance, II: 1821–1834* (Paris, Gallimard Pléiade, 1967), 225

22. Graham Robb, *Balzac* (London, Picador, 1994), 47–194

23. Sainte-Beuve to Victor Pavie, 18 Sept. 1831, in *Correspondance générale*, I, 263

24. Gautier, *Souvenirs romantiques*, 109

25. Ibid., 162–3; Pierre Pellissier, *Émile de Girardin, prince de la presse* (Paris, Denoël, 1985), 163–4

26. James Smith Allen, *In the Public Eye: A History of Reading in Modern France, 1800–1914* (Princeton, Princeton University Press, 1991), 27, 38, table A

27. Quoted by Henri Desmons, 'L'Office en librairie au XIXe siècle', in Jean-Yves Mollier, ed., *Le Commerce de la librairie au XIXe siècle, 1789–1914* (Paris, IMEC Éditions/Éditions de la Maison des Sciences de l'Homme, 1997), 195

28. Françoise Parent-Lardeur, *Lire à Paris du temps de Balzac: Les Cabinets de lecture à Paris, 1815–1830* (Paris, Éditions de l'EHESS, 1981, 1999), 117, 125

29. Jean-Jacques Darmon, *Le Colportage de librairie en France sous le Second Empire* (Paris, Plon, 1972), 38–203; Martyn Lyons, *Readers and Society in Nineteenth-century France* (Basingstoke, Palgrave, 2001), 134–42

30. Parent-Lardeur, *Lire à Paris*, 117–29

31. Gilles Feyel, 'La Diffusion nationale des quotidiens parisiens en 1832', *Revue d'Histoire Moderne et Contemporaine* 34 (1987), 60–64

32. David S. Kerr, *Caricature and French Political Culture, 1830–1848: Charles Philippon and the Illustrated Press* (Oxford, Clarendon Press, 2000), 7–137; Robert Justin Goldstein, *The Censorship of Political Caricature in Nineteenth-century France* (Kent, Phion, Kent State University Press, 1989), 119–68

33. Pellissier, *Émile de Girardin*, 22–99, 121

34. Sainte-Beuve, 'Balzac', Nov. 1834, in *Critiques et portraits littéraires*, III (Paris, 1841), 57–8; Sainte-Beuve, 'De la littérature industrielle', *Revue des Deux Mondes*, 1 Sept. 1839, in his *Portraits contemporains*, I (Paris, 1855), 489–96

35. Claude Bellanger, ed., *Histoire générale de la presse française*, II: *1815–1871* (Paris, PUF, 1969), 120, 122

36. Pellissier, *Émile de Girardin*, 102–14

37. Bellanger, ed., *Histoire générale*, 119–20; W. Scott Haine, *The World of the Paris Café: Sociability among the French Working Class, 1789–1914* (Baltimore, Johns Hopkins University Press, 1996), 213–14; Alexis de Tocqueville, *Souvenirs*, in *Oeuvres complètes*, XII (Paris, Gallimard, 1964), 120–21

38. Marvin Carlson, *The Theatre of the French Revolution* (Ithaca, Cornell University Press, 1966), 280–87

39. Herbert F. Collins, *Talma: A Biography of an Actor* (London, Faber & Faber, 1964); Anne Martin-Fugier, *Comédienne: De Mlle Mars à Sarah Bernhard* (Paris, Seuil, 2001)

40. Juste Olivier, *Paris en 1830: Journal* (Paris, Mercure de France, 1951), 58

41. F. W. J. Hemmings, *Theatre and State in France, 1760–1905*, II (Cambridge, Cambridge University Press, 1994), 106–28; Jules Janin, *Dubureau: Histoire du théâtre à quatre sous* (Paris, 1881), 34, 59–62; Maurice Albert, *Les Théâtres des boulevards, 1789–1848* (Paris, 1902), 268–93

42. Olivier, *Paris en 1830*, 58

43. Dumas, *Souvenirs romantiques*, 146–91; Anna Gaylor, *Marie Dorval: Grandeur et misère d'une actrice romantique* (Paris, Flammarion, 1989), 101–5

44. Stendhal, *Oeuvres complètes. Mélanges II: Journalisme* (Paris, Cercle du Bibliophile, 1972), 52–7, entry for 1 Sept. 1822; Jacques de Plunkett, *Fantômes et souvenirs de la Porte Saint-Martin* (Paris, Ariane, 1946), 70–147; Albert, *Les Théâtres des boulevards*, 367–8

45. Olivier, *Paris en 1830*, 292–3

46. Jules Janin, *Critique dramatique*, III: *Le Drame* (Paris, 1877), 309

47. Henry Monnier, *Sélections* (Paris, Mercure de France, 1939), 9–28. See also Edith Melchior, *The Life and Times of Henri Monnier, 1799–1877* (Cambridge, Mass., Harvard University Press, 1950)

48. Martin-Fugier, *Comédienne*, 42–50, 122–6, 130–34, 150–53, 181–6

49. Dr Véron, *Mémoires d'un bourgeois de Paris*, II, 217

50. Charles Hervey, *The Theatres of Paris* (Paris and London, 1846), 98

51. Jean-Claude Yon, *Eugène Scribe, la fortune et la liberté* (Saint-Genouph, Librairie A.-G. Nizet, 2000), 29–95

52. Sainte-Beuve, *Portraits contemporains*, II (Paris, 1855), 100

53. Marie-Véronique Gautier, *Chanson, sociabilité et grivoiserie au XIXe siècle* (Paris, Aubier, 1992), 45–7; Concetta Condemi, *Les Cafés-Concerts: Histoire d'une divertissement (1849–1914)* (Paris, Quai Voltaire, 1992), 23–34

54. Adam Carse, *The Life of Julien* (Cambridge, Heffer, 1951), 7–32

55. Nerval, *L'Artiste*, 31 Mar. 1844, cited by Raphaelle Legrand and Nicole Wild, *Regards sur l'Opéra-Comique: Trois siècles de vie théâtrale* (Paris, CNRS, 2002), 123

56. Karin Pendle, *Eugène Scribe and the French Grand Opera of the Nineteenth Century* (Ann Arbor, University of Michigan Press, 1979), 427–72; Jane Fulcher, *The Nations' Image: French Grand Opera as Politics and Politicized Art* (Cambridge, Cambridge University Press, 1987), 57–103

57. Gérard Monnier, *L'Art et ses institutions en France: De la Révolution à nos jours* (Paris, Gallimard, 1995), 124–41; Dominique Poulot, 'La Visite du muse: Un Loisir édifiant au XIXe siècle', *La Gazette des Beaux Arts* 101 (1983), 187–96; Balzac, *La Maison du Chat-qui-pelote*, in *La Comédie Humaine*, I (Paris, Gallimard, 1976), 54. I am very grateful to Camilla Murgia for help with the following paragraphs.

58. Anne Jourdan, *Napoléon: Héros, imperator, mécène* (Paris, Aubier, 1998), 199–202

59. M. E. J. Delécluze, *Louis David: Son école et son temps* (Paris, 1855), 265–96

60. M. A. Dupuy, ed., *Vivant Denon, Directeur des Musées sous le Consulat et l'Empire: Correspondance, 1812–1815*, II (Paris, Éditions de la Réunion des Musées Nationaux, 1999)

61. Marie-Claude Chaudonneret, *L'État et les artistes: De la Restauration à la Monarchie de Juillet* (Paris, Flammarion, 1999), 76; Albert Boime, *Art in an Age of Counterrevolution, 1815–1848* (Chicago and London, University of Chicago Press, 2004), 133–49; Lorentz Eitner, *Géricault's Raft of the Medusa* (New York, Phaidon, 1972)

62. Delécluze, *Louis David*, 382–4

63. Léon Rosenthal, *Du Romantisme au Réalisme: La Peinture en France de 1830 à 1848* (1st edition, 1914; Paris, Macula, 1987), 110–18; Chaudonneret, *L'État et les artistes*, 84; Boime, *Art in an Age of Counterrevolution*, 196–210, 225–31

64. Rosenthal, *Du Romantisme au Réalisme*, 15, 40

65. Monnier, *L'Art et ses institutions en France*, 140

66. Thomas W. Gaetgens, *Versailles: De la résidence royale au musée historique* (Paris, Albin Michel, 1989)

67. Cited by Albert Boime, *Thomas Couture and the Eclectic Vision* (New Haven and London, Yale University Press, 1980), 136

68. Alexandre Dumas fils, *La Dame aux camélias* (Paris, Calmann-Lévy, 1956), 87–9; F. W. J. Hemmings, *Culture and Society in France, 1848–1898* (London, Batsford, 1971), 47–9

69. Joanna Richardson, *Baudelaire* (London, John Murray, 1994), 1–149

70. Gautier, *Souvenirs romantiques*, 273

71. Charles Baudelaire, 'Salon de 1846', in *Oeuvres complètes*, II (Paris, Gallimard Pléiade, 1976), 431–2

72. Gautier, *Souvenirs romantiques*, 290

73. Richardson, *Baudelaire*, 236–50

74. Flaubert to Baudelaire, 13 July 1857, in Flaubert, *Correspondance*, II: *1851–1858* (Paris, Gallimard Pléiade, 1980), 744–5

75. Maxine du Camp, *Souvenirs littéraires* (Paris, Aubier, 1994), 200

76. Herbert Lottman, *Flaubert* (London, Methuen, 1989), 29–125

77. Flaubert to Louis Bouilhet, 14 Nov. 1850, in Flaubert, *Correspondance*, I (Paris, Gallimard, 1973), 708

78. Sainte-Beuve, review in *Le Moniteur Universel*, 4 May 1857, cited by René Descharmes and René Dumesnil, *Autour de Flaubert* (Paris, 1912), I, 59

79. Mlle Leroyer de Chantepie to Flaubert, 18 Dec. 1856, in Flaubert, *Correspondance*, II, 654–5

80. René Dumesnil, *La Publication de 'Madame Bovary'* (Amiens, E. Malfère, 1928), 74–88; Yves Leclerc, *Crimes écrits: La Littérature en procès au XIXe siècle* (Paris, Plon, 1991), 21–74, 139–88; Dominick LaCapra, *Madame Bovary on Trial* (Ithaca and London, Cornell University Press, 1982); Tony Tanner, *Adultery in the Novel: Contract and Transgression* (Baltimore and London, Johns Hopkins University Press, 1979)

81. Edmond and Jules Goncourt, *Journal*, I: *1851–1865* (Paris, Robert Laffont, 1989), I, 923; Robert Baldick, ed., *Pages from the Goncourt Journal* (London, Penguin, 1984), 80, entry for 21 Jan. 1863. See Jean de Cars, *La Princesse Mathilde: L'Amour, la gloire et les arts* (Paris, Perrin, 1988), 295–314

82. Goncourt, *Journal*, II: *1866–1886* (Paris, Robert Laffont 1989), 8; *Pages from the Goncourt Journal*, 116, entry for 12 Feb. 1866

83. Zola, *La Tribune*, 28 Nov. 1869, in *Oeuvres complètes*, X: *Oeuvres critiques I* (Paris, Cercle du Livre Précieux, 1968), 918

84. George Sand, *Questions d'art et de littérature* [1878] (Egham, Runnymede Books, 1993), 406

85. George Sand to Flaubert, 6 Sept. 1869; Flaubert to Sand, Mar. 1870, in Sand and Flaubert, *Correspondance* (Paris, Calmann-Lévy, 1904), 177, 206–7

86. Jean-Yves Mollier, *Michel et Calmann Lévy ou la naissance de l'édition moderne, 1836–1891* (Paris, Calmann-Lévy, 1984)

87. Jean-Yves Mollier, *Louis Hachette* (Paris, Fayard, 1999)

88. Bellanger, ed., *Histoire générale*, 298

89. Arthur Meyer, *Ce que mes yeux ont vu* (Paris, Plon, 1911), 185–6; Henri Thévenin, *Les Créateurs de la grande presse* (Paris, Spes, 1934), 151–8

90. Roger L. Williams, *Henri Rochefort: Prince of the Gutter Press* (New York, Scribner, 1966), 3–36

91. Morienval, *Les Créateurs de la grande presse*, 168–224; Michael B. Palmer, *Des petits journaux aus grandes agences: Naissance du journalisme moderne* (Paris, Aubier, 1983), 24–30

92. *Mémoires de Thérésia, écrites par elle-même* (8th edn, Paris, Dentu, 1865), 246. See also Gautier, *Chanson*, 58–9 and Condemi, *Les Cafés-Concerts*, 59–109

93. Bizet to his mother, 9 Dec. 1859, in Georges Bizet, *Lettres* (Paris, Calmann-Lévy, 1989), 118–19. See also Steven Huebner, *The Operas of Charles Gounod* (Oxford, Clarendon Press, 1992), 22–110, and J.-G. Proud'homme and A. Dandelot, *Gounod (1818–1893): Sa vie et ses oeuvres* (Paris, 1911), 218–24

94. Hervé Lacombe, *Les Voies de l'opéra français au XIXe siècle* (Paris, Fayard, 1997), 55, 78; Hector Berlioz, *A Life of Love and Music: Memoirs* (London, Folio Society, 1987), 419–24

95. Jean-Claude Yon, *Jacques Offenbach* (Paris, Gallimard, 2000), 131

96. Jean-Claude Yon, 'La Création du Théâtre des Bouffes-Parisiens (1855–62) ou la difficile naissance de l'opérette', *Revue d'Histoire Moderne et Contemporaine* 39 (1992), 575–600

97. *La Vie Parisienne*, 7 Jan. 1865, quoted in Yon, *Offenbach*, 307

98. Patrice Higonnet, *Paris, Capital of the World* (Cambridge, Mass., Harvard University Press, 2002), 186; Yon, *Offenbach*, 346–53

99. Champfleury, *Le Réalisme* (Paris, Hermann, 1973), 165–6, cited by Hemmings, *Culture and Society in France*, 97, 105

100. Hemmings, *Culture and Society in France*, 95, 98–9

101. Gerald M. Ackerman, *The Life and Work of Jean-Léon Gérôme* (Paris, ACR Éditions, 1986); Marius Vachon, *William Bouguereau* (Paris, Lahure, 1900); Louise d'Argencourt, ed., *William Bouguereau (1825–1905)* (Paris, Musée du Petit Palais, 1984)

102. Alan Krell, *Manet* (London, Thames & Hudson, 1996), 28, 47–56; Philip Nord, *Impressionists and Politics: Art and Democracy in the Nineteenth Century* (London and New York, Routledge, 2000), 15–19

103. Émile Zola, *Mes Haines: Causeries littéraires et artistiques* (Paris, Charpentier, 1879), 292, 307

CHAPTER 7: THE FRENCH IN A FOREIGN MIRROR

1. Stendhal, *La Chartreuse de Parme* (Paris, Gallimard, 1962), 15–16
2. Stendhal, *Rome, Naples et Florence en 1817*, in *Voyages en Italie* (Paris, Gallimard Pléiade, 1973), 83
3. Stendhal, *Promenades dans Rome* [1828], in *Voyages en Italie*, 663
4. Chateaubriand, *Voyage en Italie* [1827], in *Oeuvres romanesques et voyages*, II (Paris, Gallimard Pléiade, 1969), 1457–8
5. Germaine de Staël, *Corinne ou l'Italie* (Paris, Gallimard, 1985), 47, 65, 96, 115, 183
6. Stendhal, *Vie de Henri Brulard* (Paris, Gallimard, 1973), 430–35
7. Stendhal, *Rome, Naples et Florence en 1817*, 6–9, 72–6, 100, 113, 603, 655; *Promenades dans Rome*, 656
8. Edgar Quinet, *Italie* [1836], in *Allemagne et Italie* (Paris and Leipzig, 1839), 158–62
9. Gustave Flaubert, *Voyage en Italie*, in *Oeuvres complètes*, X (Paris, Club de l'Honnête Homme, 1973), 371–6
10. Edgar Quinet, 'Les Révolutions d'Italie', in *Oeuvres complètes*, IV (Paris, Pagnerre, 1857), 491–519
11. Hipployte Taine, *Voyage en Italie*, II: *Florence et Venise* (Paris, Hachette, 186), 53
12. Taine, *Voyage en Italie*, I: *Naples et Rome* (Paris, 1872), 98–111
13. Germaine de Staël, *De l'Allemagne* (Paris, Garnier-Flammarion, 1968), I, 115–16
14. Ibid., 57
15. Ibid., 55–67
16. Edgar Quinet, *L'Allemagne et la Révolution* [Oct. 1831], in *Allemagne et Italie*, *Oeuvres complètes*, VI (Paris, Pagnerre, 1857), 135–48
17. Quinet, *1815 et 1840* (Sept. 1840) and *Avertissement au pays* (1841), in *Oeuvres complètes*, X (Paris, Pagnerre, 1858), 31–52
18. Edmond About, *La Prusse en 1860* (Paris, 1860), 5–24; Émile Ollivier, *L'Empire libéral*, V (Paris, 1910), 157–9
19. Ernest Renan, *La Réforme intellectuelle et morale*, in *Oeuvres complètes*, I (Paris, Calmann-Lévy, 1947), 327–8
20. Joseph Fiévée, *Lettres sur l'Angleterre* (Paris, 1802), 118–32, 166–205. See also Jean Tulard, *Joseph Fiévée: Conseiller secret de Napoléon* (Paris, Fayard, 1995)
21. Jean-Baptiste Say, *De l'Angleterre et des Anglais* (Paris and London, 1815), 3–31

22. Stendhal, *Souvenirs d'égotisme*, in *Oeuvres intimes* (Paris, Gallimard Pléiade, 1955), 1477–83, 1505

23. Robert and Isabelle Tombs, *That Sweet Enemy: The French and British from the Sun King to the Present* (London, Heinemann, 2006), 331–2

24. L. Simond, *Voyage en Angleterre pendant les années 1810 et 1811* (Paris, 1817), II, 129, 286

25. Édouard de Montulé, *Voyage en Angleterre et en Russie pendant les années 1821, 1822 et 1823* (Paris, 1825), I, 126–32

26. Nassau Senior to Tocqueville, 17 Feb. 1835, Tocqueville to Senior, 21 Feb. 1835, in *Alexis de Tocqueville and Nassau William Senior, 1834–1859* (London, 1872), 4–8

27. Léon Faucher, *Études sur l'Angleterre* (Brussels, 1845), I, 27–31

28. Flora Tristan, *Promenades dans Londres* [1840] (Paris, Maspéro, 1978), 130–33

29. Stendhal, *Souvenirs d'égotisme*, 1481

30. Baron d'Haussez, *Great Britain in 1833* (London, 1833), I, 69, 70–71, 156–67

31. Faucher, *Études sur l'Angleterre*, II, 166–218

32. Tristan, *Promenades*, 208

33. De Montulé, *Voyage*, I, 267–8. See also Simond, *Voyage*, I, 171–2

34. Louis Blanc, *Lettres de l'Angleterre*, 1st series, I (Paris, 1865), 329–32; 2nd series, II (Paris, 1867), 13–14

35. Chateaubriand, *Atala* and *René*, in *Oeuvres romanesques et voyages*, I (Paris, Gallimard Pléiade, 1969)

36. Thomas Fleming, *The Louisiana Purchase* (Hoboken, NJ, John Wiley, 2003)

37. Lafayette to Jefferson, 8 Oct. 1804, in Gilbert Chinard, ed., *The Letters of Lafayette and Jefferson* (Baltimore, Johns Hopkins University Press, 1929), 230–34

38. Jefferson to Lafayette, 14 Feb. 1815, Lafayette to Jefferson, 1 June 1822, in ibid., 367, 408–9

39. Auguste Levasseur, *Lafayette en Amérique en 1824 et 1825* (Paris, Baudoin, 1829), I, 463–75, II, 163–73, 602

40. Cited by George Wilson Pierson, *Tocqueville and Beaumont in America* (Oxford, Oxford University Press, 1938), 36

41. Tocqueville, diary entry, 15 May 1831, cited by ibid., 70

42. Tocqueville, *De la démocratie en Amérique*, I [1835], 1st part, ch. III

43. Ibid., 2nd part, ch. IX

44. Beaumont to his sister Eugénie, 14 July 1831, in Pierson, *Tocqueville*, 192–4

45. Tocqueville, *De la démocratie en Amérique*, I, 2nd part, ch. X
46. Ibid., 462
47. Gustave de Beaumont, *Marie ou l'esclavage aux États-Unis* (Brussels, Hauman, 1835), I, iii, 118, 176–87, II, 62, 109–13
48. Count de Rochechouart, *Memoirs*, ed. Frances Jackson (London, John Murray, 1920), 161
49. Ibid., 254
50. Ernest Lavisse, *Souvenirs* (Paris, Calmann-Lévy, 1912), 110
51. De Montulé, *Voyage en Angleterre et en Russie*, II, 64, 105, 190, 218–33
52. Irena Grudzinska Gross, *The Scar of Revolution: Custine, Tocqueville and the Romantic Imagination* (Berkeley, Los Angeles and Oxford, University of California Press, 1991), 2–12
53. Marquis de Custine, *La Russie en 1839* (Paris, 1843), IV, 57–8
54. Ibid., II, 61–3
55. Ibid., I, 255
56. Ibid., 141–9, II, 213–14, III, 115, 208
57. Alexandre Dumas, *Mémoires d'un maître d'armes ou dix-huit mois à St-Pétersbourg* (Brussels, 1840)
58. Alexandre Dumas, *Impressions de voyage en Russie* (4 vols, Paris, 1865–6), II, 172–3, 193, 214–15, IV, 251–71
59. Théophile Gautier, *Voyage en Russie* (2 vols, Paris, 1866–7), I, 125, 233, 254–7, II, 43, 106, 118–21
60. See above p. 20
61. Chateaubriand, *Itinéraire de Paris à Jerusalem*, in *Oeuvres romanesques et voyages*, II (Paris, Gallimard Pléiade, 1969), 1052, 1100
62. Lamartine, *Voyage en Orient* (Paris, Honoré Champion, 2000), 43, 110
63. Ibid., 143
64. Ibid., 301, 575, 746
65. Juliette Adam, *Mes premières armes littéraires et politiques* (Paris, 1904), 231. She claimed to have heard this story from Émile de Girardin.
66. *Le National*, 3, 4, 7 Oct. 1840
67. Eugène Guichen, *La Crise d'Orient de 1839 à 1841 et l'Europe* (Paris, Émile-Paul Frères, 1921)
68. *Le National*, 15, 16, 22, 30 Apr. 1840
69. Thiers, speech of 14 May 1840, in *Discours parlementaires*, IV (Paris, Calmann-Lévy, 1879), 648
70. Tocqueville, 'Travail sur l'Algérie' (Oct. 1841), in *Oeuvres complètes*, III.1 (Paris, Gallimard, 1962), 214, 220, 239–68. See also Melvin

Richter, 'Tocqueville on Algeria', *Review of Politics* (1963), 362–98. I am grateful to Michael Stitt for this reference.

71. Gérard de Nerval, *Voyage en Orient*, in *Oeuvres complètes*, II (Paris, Gallimard Pléiade, 1984), 250, 262–78, 342, 450–57, 506–7

72. Gustave Flaubert, *Voyage en Orient* (Lausanne, Éditions Rencontre, 1964), 102–81; Flaubert to his mother, 8 Mar. 1850, in *Correspondance*, I (Paris, Gallimard Pléiade, 1973), 596

73. Flaubert, *Voyage en Orient*, 214–19, 255–61

74. Flaubert to Gautier, 13 Aug. 1850, in *Correspondance*, I, 663

75. Flaubert to Mlle Leroyer de Chantepie, 11 July 1858, in *Correspondance*, II (Paris, Gallimard, 1980), 822

76. Édouard Lockroy, *Au hasard de la vie: Notes et souvenirs* (Paris, Grasset, 1913), 47–9

77. Henriette Renan, *Souvenirs et impressions* (Paris, La Renaissance du Livre, 1930), 193–203

78. Renan to his mother, 27 Dec. 1864, in *Lettres de famille*, in *Oeuvres complètes*, IV (Paris, Calmann-Lévy, 1960), 1435–6

79. Ferdinand de Lesseps, *Souvenirs de quarante ans* (Paris, 1887), I, 233–47, II, 31–2, 134, 223–45, 759–67

80. Renan, speech of 23 Apr. 1884, cited by Lesseps, *Souvenirs*, II, 532–3

CHAPTER 8: WAR AND COMMUNE, 1870–1871

1. *Journal Officiel de l'Empire Français*, 16 July 1870, 1260–61

2. Informer report of 7 July 1870, cited by Stéphane Audoin-Rouzeau, *1870: La France dans la guerre* (Paris, Colin, 1989), 45

3. General Trochu, *L'Armée française en 1867* (Paris, Amypt, 1867), ch. 7

4. Alain Corbin, *The Village of Cannibals: Rage and Murder in France, 1870* (Cambridge, Polity Press, 1992), 112

5. Michael Howard, *The Franco-Prussian War* (London, Rupert Hart-Davis, 1961), 222

6. Louis Veuillot, article of 14 Aug. 1870, in *Paris pendant les deux sièges* (Paris, Victor Palmé, 1872), I, 13–16

7. J. P. T. Bury, *Gambetta and the National Defence: A Republican Dictatorship in France* (London, Longman, 1936), 125

8. Victor Hugo, 'Aux Français', 17 Sept. 1870, in *Actes et paroles, 1870-1871-1872* (Paris, Michel Lévy, 1872), 15

9. Juliette Adam, *Mes illusions et mes souffrances pendant le siège de Paris* (Paris, 1906), 64, entry of 13 Sept. 1870

10. *Télégrammes militaires de M. Léon Gambetta, 9 Oct. 1870–6 Feb. 1871* (Paris, 1871), 20

11. Howard, *Franco-Prussian War*, 252–4; John Horne and Alan Kramer, *German Atrocities, 1914: A History of Denial* (New Haven and London, Yale University Press, 2001), 141–2

12. *Télégrammes militaires*, 30 Oct. 1870, 36; Audoin-Rouzeau, *1870*, 227

13. *Affaire de la capitulation de Metz: Procès Bazaine* (Paris, Moniteur Universel, 1873), 195–6

14. *Journal Officiel de la République Française*, 15 June 1871, 1364, 1367

15. Gustave Flaubert and George Sand, *Correspondance* (Paris, Calmann-Lévy, 1904), 236

16. Jacques Rougerie, 'L'A.I.T. et le mouvement ouvrier à Paris pendant les événements de 1870–71', in his *Jalons pour une histoire de la Commune* (Paris, PUF, 1973), 16–17

17. Louise Michel, *Mémoires* (Paris, 1886), 169–71

18. Martin Philip Johnson, *The Paradise of Association: Political Culture and Popular Organization in the Paris Commune of 1871* (Ann Arbor, University of Michigan Press, 1996), 39, 46

19. *La Patrie en Danger*, 30 Oct. 1870, '1792–1870'

20. Cited by Charles Rihs, *La Commune de Paris* (Paris, Seuil, 1973), 56. See Johnson, *Paradise of Association*, 17–53

21. Caroline Schultze, *La Femme-médecin au XIXe siècle* (Paris, 1888), 19; Adam, *Mes illusions*, 225, entry of 18 Nov. 1870

22. Goncourt Journal, 1 Nov. 1870, cited by George J. Becker, *Paris under Siege, 1870–1871: From the Goncourt Journal* (Ithaca and London, Cornell University Press, 1969), 130–31

23. Francisque Sarcey, *Le Siège de Paris* (Paris, 1871), 163–4

24. Adam, *Mes illusions*, 272, entry for 15 Dec. 1870

25. Sarcey, *Le Siège*, 144–50

26. Adam, *Mes illusions*, 285, 294–5, entries for 23 Dec. 1870, 1 Jan. 1871; Goncourt Journal, 26 Dec. 1870, 14 Jan. 1871 in Becker, *Paris under Siege*, 178, 197

27. Adam, *Mes illusions*, 303, 306, entries for 6, 7–8 Jan. 1871

28. Comte de Falloux, *Mémoires d'un royaliste*, II (Paris, 1888), 443–4

29. *La Patrie en Danger*, 16 Nov. 1870

30. *Le Cri du Peuple*, 22 Feb. 1871

31. Gustave Lefrançais, *Souvenirs d'un révolutionnaire* (Brussels, 1902), 466–7

32. *Le Grand Colère du Père Duchesne*, 30 *ventôse* Year 79/20 March 1870
33. Goncourt Journal, 28 Mar. 1871, in Becker, *Paris under Siege*, 236
34. Goncourt Journal, 2 Apr. 1871, in Becker, *Paris under Siege*, 239
35. Marcel Dessal, *Un Révolutionnaire jacobin: Charles Delescluze, 1809–1871* (Paris, Rivière, 1952), 366–7
36. Marx, *The Civil War in France*, in *Marx and Engels: Selected Works in One Volume* (London, Lawrence & Wishart, 1968), 276
37. Robert Tombs, *The War against Paris* (Cambridge, Cambridge University Press, 1981), 92–120
38. Dessal, *Un Révolutionnaire jacobin*, 392–3
39. Carolyn Eichner, *Surmounting the Barricades: Women in the Paris Commune* (Bloomington and Indianapolis, Indiana University Press, 2004), 69–95; Johnson, *Paradise of Association*, 246–53, 267
40. Prosecution in trial of five *pétroleuses*, 3 Sept. 1871, cited by Edith Thomas, *The Women Incendiaries* (London, Secker & Warburg, 1967), 151. See also Gay Gulickson, *Unruly Women of Paris: Images of the Commune* (Ithaca, Cornell University Press, 1996), and David Barry, *Women and Political Insurgency: France in the Mid-nineteenth Century* (Basingstoke, Macmillan, 1996)
41. Veuillot, article of 29 May, in *Paris pendant les deux sièges*, 407
42. Goncourt Journal, 2 Apr. 1871, in Becker, *Paris under Siege*, 310–11
43. Flaubert to Sand, 10 June 1871, in *Correspondance*, 252

CHAPTER 9: CONSENSUS FOUND: FRENCH POLITICS, 1870–1914

1. Flaubert to Sand, Sept. or Oct. 1871, in George Sand and Gustave Flaubert, *Correspondance* (Paris, 1904), 282–3; Ernest Renan, *La Réforme intellectuelle et morale* [1871], in *Oeuvres complètes*, I (Paris, Calmann-Lévy, 1947), 373, 375
2. Léon Gambetta, speeches at Bordeaux, 26 June 1871, and Angers, 7 Apr. 1872, in *Discours et plaidoyers politiques*, II (Paris, Charpentier, 1881), 15–34, 226–47, and speech at Nantes, 16 May 1873, in *Discours et plaidoyers politiques*, III (Paris, Charpentier, 1881), 374–9. See also J. P. T Bury, *Gambetta and the Making of the Third Republic* (London, Longman, 1973)
3. Comte de Falloux, *Mémoires d'un royaliste*, II (Paris, 1888), 461; Pierre Guiral, *Adolphe Thiers* (Paris, Fayard, 1986), 460

4. *Le Pays*, 18, 19, 20, 23 Oct. 1871; Maurice Flory, 'L'Appel au Peuple napoléonien', *Revue Internationale d'Histoire Politique et Constitutionnelle*, new series, II (1952), 215–22. See also John Rothney, *Bonapartism after Sedan* (Ithaca, Cornell University Press, 1969), and Karen Offen, *Paul de Cassagnac and the Authoritarian Tradition in Nineteenth-century France* (New York and London, Garland, 1991), 64–6

5. Jean T. Joughin, *The Paris Commune in French Politics, 1871–1880* (Baltimore, Johns Hopkins University Press, 1955), 79–82

6. *Journal Officiel de la République Française*, 14 Nov. 1873, 6981–2. See text in Robert Gildea, *France, 1871–1914* (2nd edn, London and New York, Longman, 1996), 88–9

7. Duc de Broglie, *Mémoires*, II (Paris, Aux Armes de la France, 1941), 152. See Jean-Claude Wartelle, 'L'Élection Barodet, avril 1873', *Revue d'Histoire Moderne et Contemporaine* 27 (1980), 601–30

8. Falloux, *Mémoires d'un royaliste*, II, 549

9. Duc d'Audiffret-Pasquier, *La Maison de France et l'Assemblée Nationale: Souvenirs, 1871–1873* (Paris, 1938), 61–3; Falloux, *Mémoires d'un royaliste*, II, 575. See also Marvin Brown, *The Comte de Chambord* (Durham, NC, Duke University Press, 1967), 102–38, and Samuel Osgood, *French Royalism since 1870* (The Hague, Martinus Nijhoff, 1970), 19–29

10. *Le Pays*, 17 Mar. 1874; William H. C. Smith, *The Bonapartes* (London and New York, Hambledon & London, 2005), 206

11. *La République Française*, 21 July 1874

12. *La République Française*, 21 Nov. 1873, cited by Bury, *Gambetta and the Making of the Third Republic*, 186

13. De Broglie, *Mémoires*, II, 256, 278

14. Ibid., 345; Paul Smith, *A History of the French Senate*, I: *The Third Republic, 1870–1940* (Lewiston, Queenston, Lampeter, Edwin Mellen Press), 30–34

15. Henri Wallon, *La Terreur* (Paris, Hachette, 1873), I, ii

16. Smith, *History of the French Senate*, 136–52

17. Gambetta, speech at Auxerre, 1 June 1874, in *Discours et plaidoyers politiques*, IV, 144–5

18. Bury, *Gambetta and the Making of the Third Republic*, 276–80, 299

19. Joseph Reinach, *La Vie politique de Léon Gambetta* (Paris, 1918), iii

20. Quoted by Sylvie Aprile, 'La République au salon: Vie et mort d'une forme de sociabilité politique, 1865–1885', *Revue d'Histoire Moderne et Contemporaine* 38 (1991), 480. See also Manon Cormier, *Madame*

Juliette Adam ou l'aurore de la IIIe République (Bordeaux, Delman, 1934), 174–81

21. Charles de Freycinet, *Souvenirs, 1848–1878* (New York, Da Capo Press, 1973), 368

22. Louis Blanc, *Discours politiques, 1847–1881* (Paris, 1882), 290–91, 295–9

23. Jacques Ollé-Laprune, *La Stabilité des ministres sous la Troisième République, 1870–1940* (Paris, Librairie Générale du Droit, 1962), 128–30

24. See for example Paul Cambon to his wife, 7 Dec. 1881, in Cambon, *Correspondance*, I: *1870–1898* (Paris, Grasset, 1940), 144

25. Ferry, speech of 22 Feb. 1883, in *La République des citoyens*, ed. Odile Rudelle (Paris, Imprimerie Nationale, 1996), II, 149

26. Robert de Jouvenel, *La République des camarades* (Paris, Grasset, 1914), 22–45; Mattei Dogan, 'Les Filières de la carrière politique en France', *Revue Française de Sociologie* 8 (1967), 472, 482–3; Jean Estèbe, *Les Ministres de la République, 1871–1914* (Paris, FNSP, 1982), 86–95, 149–80; Pierre Guiral and Guy Thillier, *La Vie quotidienne des députés en France de 1871 à 1914* (Paris, Hachette, 1980), 31–6, 70–78, 194–220

27. Cited by Jean-Michel Gaillard, *Jules Ferry* (Paris, Fayard, 1989), 94–5; Jean-Baptiste Duroselle, *Clemenceau* (Paris, Fayard, 1988), 63–7

28. Jules Ferry, Bordeaux speech of 30 Aug. 1885, in *La République des citoyens*, II, 339–40

29. Jules Ferry, Le Havre speech of 14 Oct. 1883, in *La République des citoyens*, II, 181

30. Jean-Marie Mayeur, *La Vie politique sous la Troisième République, 1870–1940* (Paris, Seuil, 1984), 116–17

31. Institut Français d'Histoire Sociale 14 AJ 99 *bis*, tract of Commune révolutionnaire, June 1874

32. Madeleine Rebérioux, 'Le Mur des Fédérés', in Pierre Nora, *Les Lieux de mémoire* (Paris, Gallimard, 1984), I, 619–49

33. *L'Égalité*, 23–26 May, 14 July 1880. See Jacques Girault, 'Les Guesdistes, la Deuxième *Égalité* et la Commune', in Jacques Rougerie, ed., *Jalons pour une histoire de la Commune* (Assen, Van Corcum, 1973), 421–30

34. Maxime du Camp, *Les Convulsions de Paris* (4 vols, Paris, Hachette, 1878–80), I, iii–iv, IV, 450–51

35. Joughin, *The Paris Commune in French Politics, 1871–1880*; Rosamonde Sanson, *Les 14 Juillet: Fête et conscience nationale* (Paris, Flammarion, 1976), 34–51

36. Brousse, speech on 25 Sept. 1882, in Parti Ouvrier Socialiste Révolutionnaire Français, *Compte rendu du 6e Congrès national tenu à Saint-Étienne du 25 au 30 septembre 1882*, 87–9

37. Ferry, Épinal speech, 26 Aug. 1887, in *Discours et opinions*, ed. Paul Robiquet, VII (Paris, 1898), 627

38. Leslie Derfler, *Paul Lafargue and the Flowering of French Socialism* (Cambridge, Mass., Harvard University Press, 1998), 61–3

39. *Le Figaro*, 22 Feb. 1890, quoted by Zeev Sternhell, *Maurice Barrès et le nationalisme français* (Paris, Colin, 1972), 236–7; Sternhell, 'National Socialism and Anti-Semitism: The Case of Maurice Barrès', *Journal of Contemporary History* 8/4 (1973), 47–66

40. *L'Intransigeant*, 15 Oct. 1889; Édouard Drumont, *La Dernière Bataille* (Paris, Dentu, 1890), 182–91; Stephen Wilson, *Ideology and Experience: Antisemitism in France at the Time of the Dreyfus Affair* (Rutherford, Madison, Teaneck, Farleigh Dickinson University Press, 1982), 171–3

41. Jean Bouvier, *Les Deux Scandales de Panama* (Paris, Julliard, 1964)

42. Maurice Charnay, *Les Allemanistes* (Paris, Marcel Rivière, 1912); Michel Winock, 'La Scission de Châtellerault et la naissance du Parti "allemaniste", 1889–1891', *Mouvement Social* 75 (1971), 33–62; Michel Winock, 'Jean Allemane: Une Fidélité critique', in Rougerie, ed., *Jalons pour une Histoire de la Commune*, 373–80

43. Maurice Dommanget, *Histoire du premier mai* (Paris, Société Universitaire d'Éditions et de Librairie, 1953), 94–110

44. Derfler, *Paul Lafargue*, 87–100; Dommanget, *Premier mai*, 146–52

45. Rolande Trempé, *Les Mineurs de Carmaux, 1848–1914* (2 vols, Paris, Éditions Ouvrières, 1971); Harvey Goldberg, *Life of Jean Jaurès* (Madison, University of Wisconsin Press, 1962), 5–106

46. James Joll, *The Anarchists* (2nd edn, London, Methuen, 1979), 113–19; *L'Assassinat du Président Sadi Carnot et le procès de Santo Ironimo Casiero* (Lyon, Presses Universitaires de Lyon, 1995)

47. Jean Maitron, *Le Mouvement anarchiste en France*, I (Paris, Maspéro, 1975), 252–4; Jean Grave, *Le Mouvement libertaire sous la Troisième République* (Paris, Les Oeuvres Représentatives, 1930); Felipe Alaiz et al., *La Vie et l'oeuvre de Sébastien Faure* (Paris and Brussels, Éditions Pensée et Action, 1961)

48. *La Cocarde*, 19, 20, 22 Sept. 1894; Sternhell, *Maurice Barrès et le nationalisme français*, 199–213; Sternhell, *La Droite révolutionnaire* (Paris, Seuil, 1978), 62–3

49. Pelloutier, 'L'Anarchisme et les syndicats ouvriers', *Les Temps Nouveaux*, 2–8 Nov. 1895; Jacques Julliard, *Fernand Pelloutier et les*

origines du Syndicalisme d'action directe (Paris, Seuil, 1971); Georges Suarez, *Briand*, I: *1862–1904* (Paris, Plon, 1938)

50. J. E. H. Hayward, 'The Official Social Policy of the Third Republic: Léon Bourgeois and Solidarism', *International Review of Social History* 6 (1961), 19–48; Marcel Ruby, *Le Solidarisme* (Paris, Librairie Gedalge, 1971)

51. Eugene Owen Golob, *The Méline Tariff: French Agriculture and Nationalist Economic Policy* (New York, Columbia University Press, 1944); Pierre Barral, *Les Agrariens français de Méline à Pisani* (Paris, Colin, 1968), 86–7; Michael S. Smith, *Tariff Reform in France, 1860–1900: The Politics of Economic Interest* (Ithaca, Cornell University Press, 1980), 197–210; Hermann Lebovics, *The Alliance of Iron and Wheat in the French Third Republic, 1860–1914: Origins of the New Conservatism* (Baton Rouge and London, Louisiana State University Press, 1988), 107–8, 124–7

52. Sanford Elwitt, *The Third Republic Defended: Bourgeois Reform in France, 1880–1914* (Baton Rouge and London, Louisiana State University Press, 1986), 55–183; Janet Horne, 'L'Antichambre de la Chambre: Le Musée social et ses réseaux réformateurs, 1894–1914', in Christian Todalov, ed., *Laboratoires du nouveau siècle: La Nébuleuse Réformatrice et ses réseaux en France, 1880–1914* (Paris, EHESS, 1999), 122–6

53. J.-M. Mayeur, 'Droites et ralliés à la Chambre des Députés au début de 1894', *Revue d'Histoire Moderne et Contemporaine* 13 (1966), 117–35

54. Leslie Derfler, *President and Parliament: A Short History of the French Presidency* (Boca Raton, University Presses of Florida, 1983), 58–61

55. Robert J. Young, *Power and Pleasure: Louis Barthou and the French Third Republic* (Montreal and Kingston, McGill-Queen's University Press, 1991), 4–48

56. Cited by Georges Lachardelle, *Le Ministère Méline* (Paris, J. L. L. d'Artrey, 1928), 31–2

57. Pierre Sorlin, *Waldeck-Rousseau* (Paris, Colin, 1966), 347–86

58. Duroselle, *Clemenceau*, 430–31

59. Louis Leblois, *L'Affaire Dreyfus: L'Iniquité, la réparation* (Paris, Quillet, 1929), 1–37; Leblois, *Scheurer-Kestner* (Paris and Nancy, Berger-Levrault, 1898), 39–45; Joseph Reinach, *Histoire de l'Affaire Dreyfus*, II (Paris, 1903), 208, 505–25, 623–54, III (Paris, 1903), 137

60. Reinach, *Histoire de l'Affaire Dreyfus*, III, 145–6

61. Émile Zola, *La Vérité en marche* (Paris, Bibliothèque Charpentier, 1901), 73–93

62. Léon Blum, *Souvenirs sur l'Affaire* (Paris, Gallimard, 1935), 28–9, 97–101; Robert J. Smith, 'L'Atmosphère politique à l'École Normale Supérieure à la fin du XIXe siècle', *Revue d'Histoire Moderne et Contemporaine* 20 (1973), 248–68

63. Janine Ponty, 'La Presse quotidienne et l'Affaire Dreyfus en 1898–1899', *Revue d'Histoire Moderne et Contemporaine* 21 (1974), 193–220

64. Reinach, *Histoire de l'Affaire Dreyfus*, III, 341–2

65. *L'Intransigeant*, 22 Feb. 1898

66. Sternhell, *La Droite révolutionnaire*, 222–31

67. Mildred Headings, *French Freemasonry under the Third Republic* (Baltimore, Johns Hopkins University Press, 1949), 98–9

68. Reinach, *Histoire de l'Affaire Dreyfus*, III, 580

69. Wilson, *Ideology and Experience*, 179–96

70. Maurice Larkin, '"La République en danger?" The Pretenders, the Army and Déroulède, 1898–1899', *English Historical Review* 100 (1985), 85–105; Larkin, *Religion, Politics and Preferment in France since 1897: La Belle Époque and its Legacy* (Cambridge, Cambridge University Press, 1995), 19–24

71. Jean-Pierre Rioux, *Nationalisme et conservatisme: La Ligue de la Patrie Française, 1899–1904* (Paris, Éditions Beauchesne, 1977); Sternhell, *La Droite révolutionnaire*, 131–7; Pierre Birnbaum, 'Affaire Dreyfus, culture catholique et antisémitisme', in Michel Winock, ed., *Histoire de l'extrême droite en France* (Paris, Seuil, 1993), 103–8

72. Charles Maurras, *Au Signe de Flore: La Fondation de l'Action Française, 1898–1900* (Paris, Grasset, 1931); Victor Nguyen, *Aux origines de l'Action Française: Intelligence et politique à l'aube du XXe siècle* (Paris, Fayard, 1991); Yves Chiron, *La Vie de Maurras* (Paris, Perron, 1991), 152–87; Winock, ed., *Histoire de l'extrême droite en France*, 125–39; Eugen Weber, *Action Française: Royalism and Reaction in Twentieth-century France* (Stanford, Stanford University Press, 1962), 3–43

73. Berny Sèbe, 'From Thoissy to the Capital via Fashoda: Major Marchand, Partisan Icon of the Right in Paris', in Jessica Irons, ed., *Paris and the Right in the Twentieth Century* (Newcastle, Cambridge Scholars, 2007), 18–42

74. Joseph Caillaux, *Mes mémoires*, I: *1863–1909* (Paris, Plon, 1942), 27–120

75. Zola to Lucie Dreyfus, 29 Sept. 1899, in *La Vérité en marche*, 172

76. Smith *History of the French Senate*, I, 270–72

77. *La République Française*, 20 Nov. 1899

78. Speech of 2 June 1900, in Waldeck-Rousseau, *La Défense républicaine* (Paris, Charpentier, 1902), 193–4

79. Declaration by Camille Pelletan, cited in Jean-Thomas Nordmann, *La France radicale* (Paris, Gallimard Julliard, 1977), 44–6

80. In general on the Radicals see Judith Stone, 'The Radicals and the Interventionist State: Attitudes, Ambiguities and Transformations, 1880–1910', *French History* 2/2 (1988), 173–86; Serge Berstein, 'La Politique sociale des républicains', in S. Berstein and Odile Rudelle, eds, *Le Modèle républicain* (Paris, PUF, 1992), 189–208; Gérard Baal, *Histoire du Radicalisme* (Paris, La Découverte, 1994), 37–46; Berstein, *Histoire du Parti Radical*, I: *1919–1926* (Paris, FNSP, 1980), 40–86; Peter J. Larmour, *The French Radical Party in the 1930s* (Stanford, Stanford University Press, 1964), 60–77

81. Robert de Jouvenel, *La République des camarades* (Paris, Grasset, 1914; 1934), 14

82. Derfler, *President and Parliament*, 63–5

83. Weber, *Action Française*, 41–2

84. *La Petite République*, 9 June 1898

85. Jean Jaurès and Jules Guesde, *Les Deux Méthodes: Conférence, Lille, 1900* (2nd edn, Paris, 1925), 5–39

86. *4e Congrès international du Parti Socialiste Français, Tours, 2–4 mars 1902* (Paris, 1902, 1975), 116–20, 153–4

87. CGT, *XIVe Congrès national corporatif tenu à Bourges du 12 au 20 septembre 1904* (Bourges, 1904), 207–16; Frederick Ridley, *Revolutionary Syndicalism in France* (Cambridge, Cambridge University Press, 1970)

88. On anarcho-syndicalism see Ridley, *Revolutionary Syndicalism in France*; Peter Stearns, *Revolutionary Syndicalism and French Labour* (New Brunswick, Rutgers University Press, 1971), and Edward Shorter and Charles Tilly, *Strikes in France, 1830–1968* (Cambridge, Cambridge University Press, 1974)

89. Jean Jaurès, *Histoire socialiste de la Révolution française* [1901–4] (Paris, Éditions Sociales, 1968–72), I, 475–7, VI, 517–18

90. *4e Congrès international du Parti Socialiste Français, Tours, 2–4 mars 1902*, 137–43

91. Fernand Hauser, *Une Mystère historique: L'Affaire Syveton* (Paris, Librairie Universelle, 1905); Mermeix, *La Mort de Syveton* (Paris, Fayard, 1925)

92. Larkin, *Religion, Politics and Preferment in France since 1897*, 39–52; François Vindé, *L'Affaire des Fiches, 1900–1904: Chronique d'une scandale* (Paris, Editions Universitaires, 1989)

93. *Congrès Socialiste International, Amsterdam, 14–20 août 1904*, introduction by Georges Haupt (Geneva, Minkoff Reprint, 1978); Julius Braunthal, *History of the International, 1864–1914* (London, Thomas Nelson, 1966), 280–84

94. David Watson, *Georges Clemenceau* (London, Eyre Methuen, 1974), 198

95. Jeanne Simone Pocquet, *Le Salon de Madame Arman de Caillavet* (Paris, Hachette, 1926), 239

96. Georges Wormser, *La République de Clemenceau* (Paris, PUF, 1961), 210. In general, Jacques Juliard, *Clemenceau, briseur de grèves* (Paris, Julliard, 1965)

97. Suarez, *Briand*, II: *1904–14* (Paris, Plon, 1938), 243–6; Julian Wright, 'Social Reform, State Reform and Aristide Briand's Moment of Hope in France, 1909–1910', *French Historical Studies* 28/1 (2005), 31–67

98. Suarez, *Briand*, II, 280–95

99. Baal, *Histoire du Radicalisme*, 57–8

100. J. F. V. Keiger, *Raymond Poincaré* (Cambridge, Cambridge University Press, 1997), 94

101. Ibid., 125

102. Émile Roche, *Avec Joseph Caillaux: Mémoires, souvenirs et documents* (Paris, Université de Paris–I, 1980), 34; Caillaux, *Mes mémoires*, III: *1912–1930* (Paris, Plon, 1947), 55–6

103. Keiger, *Raymond Poincaré*, 117

104. Young, *Power and Pleasure*, 104–16

105. Caillaux, *Mes mémoires*, III, 78; Suarez, *Briand*, II, 441–54

106. Peter Shankland, *Death of an Editor: The Caillaux Drama* (London, Kimber, 1982); Edward Berenson, *The Trial of Madame Caillaux* (Berkeley, Los Angeles and London, University of California Press, 1992)

CHAPTER 10: RECONCILING PARIS AND THE PROVINCES

1. Charles Rihs, *La Commune de Paris 1871: Sa structure et ses doctrines* (Paris, Seuil, 1973), 165

2. Jean-Pierre Machelon, 'La Troisième République', in Louis Fougère, J.-P. Machelon and François Monnier, *Les Communes et le pouvoir de 1789 à nos jours* (Paris, PUF, 2002), 357

3. Robert Tombs, 'Paris and the Rural Hordes: An Exploration of Myth and Reality in the French Civil War of *1871*', *Historical Journal* 29/4 (1986), 795–808

4. Arthur de Gobineau, *Ce qui est arrivé à la France en 1870* (Paris, Klincksieck, 1970), 75, 94. This text was written in 1870–71.

5. Henri Wallon, *La Révolution du 31 mai et le Fédéralisme en 1793, ou la France vaincue par la Commune de Paris* (Paris, Hachette, 1886), I, i–iv, II, 432–6

6. Machelon, 'La Troisième République', 398–400

7. Mattei Dogan, 'Les Filières de la carrière politique en France', *Revue Française Sociologique* 8 (1967), 468–92

8. Alexandre Pilenco, *Les Moeurs du suffrage universel en France, 1848–1928* (Paris, Revue Mondiale, 1930), 221

9. Henri Lerner, *La Dépêche: Journal de la démocratie: Contribution à l'histoire du Radicalisme en France sous la Troisième République* (Toulouse, Université de Toulouse-Le Mirail, 1978), 134–43. The comment was made by *L'Assiette au beurre*, 29 Aug. 1905.

10. Mattei Dogan, 'La Stabilité du personnel parlementaire sous la Troisième République', *Revue Française de Science Politique* 3 (1953), 319–48

11. Joseph Barthélemy, *Le Gouvernement de la France* (Paris, Payot, 1924), 73

12. Paul Smith, *A History of the French Senate*, I: *The Third Republic, 1870–1940* (Lewiston, Queenston, Lampeter, Edwin Mellen Press, 2005), 83.

13. Jean Lenoble, *P.-E. Teisserenc de Bort: Gentilhomme limousin: Sénateur, ministre, ambassadeur, 1814–1892* (Limoges, SELM, 1977)

14. Émile Combes, *Mon ministère: Mémoires, 1902–1905* (Paris, Plon, 1956), 69

15. Edmond About, *Alsace 1871–1872* (Paris, Hachette, 1873), 251–62

16. Alfred Wahl, *L'Option et l'émigration des Alsaciens-Lorrains, 1871–1872* (Paris, Ophrys, 1974), 102–34, 190–91

17. Alphone Daudet, 'La Dernière Classe', in *L'Événement*, 13 May 1872, and in *Contes de lundi* [1873] (Paris, Flammarion, 1974)

18. L. Schoumaker, *Erckmann-Chatrian: Étude biographique et critique d'après des documents inédits* (Paris, Les Belles-lettres, 1933), 150–76

19. Erckmann-Chatrian, *Histoire du plébiscite* [1872], in *Contes et romans populaires*, XI (Paris, Pauvert, 1963), 269–75

20. Erckmann-Chatrian, *Le Brigadier Frédéric* [1874], in *Contes et romans populaires*, XII (Paris, Pauvert, 1963), 187–8, 262–77; *Le Banni*

[1881], in *Contes et romans populaires*, XIII (Paris, Pauvert, 1963), 212–330

21. G. Bruno (pen-name of Augustine Fouillée), *Le Tour de France par deux enfants* [1877] (New York, American Book Company, 1902), 184; Jacques et Mona Ozouf, *Le Tour de France par deux enfants*, in Pierre Nora, ed., *Les Lieux de mémoire*, I (Paris, Gallimard, 1984), 291–321

22. Michael Burns, *Dreyfus: A Family Affair, 1789–1945* (London, Chatto & Windus, 1992), 54–84

23. Dan P. Silverman, *Reluctant Union: Alsace-Lorraine and Imperial Germany, 1871–1918* (University Park and London, Pennsylvania State University Press, 1972); Jean-Marie Mayeur, 'Laïcité et question scolaire en Alsace et Moselle', in René Rémond, ed., *Forces religieuses et attitudes politiques dans la France contemporaine*, Colloque de Strasbourg 1963 (Paris, 1965), 239–49

24. Eugen Weber, *Peasants into Frenchmen: The Modernization of Rural France, 1870–1914* (London, Chatto & Windus, 1977), 67

25. Jean-François Chanet, *L'École républicaine et les petites patries* (Paris, Aubier, 1996), 206

26. Archives Départementales (AD) du Nord, 1N122, Conseil Général, report of Inspecteur d'Académie Brunel to Conseil Général, 31 July 1888, p. 663

27. Claude Mauron, *Frédéric Mistral* (Paris, Fayard, 1993), 242–4, 273–4

28. Frédéric Mistral, *Discours de Santo Estello* [15 Aug. 1888] (Avignon, J. Roumanille, 1888), 13

29. Jean-Marie Carbasse, *Louis-Xavier de Ricard: Félibrige rouge* (Montpellier, Éditions Mireille Lacave, 1977), 93, 144

30. Ibid., 151

31. Charles Maurras, *L'Étang de Berre* (Paris, Champion, 1915), 127–31

32. Charles Maurras, *L'Idée de la décentralisation* (Paris, 1898), 44

33. Maurice Barrès, *Assainissement et fédéralisme: Discours prononcé à Bordeaux le 29 juin 1895* (Paris, La Revue Socialiste, 1895), 7–8

34. Jean Charles-Brun, *L'Évolution félibréenne* (Lyon, Paquet, 1896), 26–7

35. Julian Wright, *The Regionalist Movement in France, 1890–1914: Jean Charles-Brun and French Political Thought* (Oxford, Clarendon Press, 2003), 117, 148 and passim; M. Nuyttens, *Camille Looten (1855–1941): Priester, Wetenschapsman en Frans-Vlaams Regionalist* (Louvain, Louvain University Press, 1981); Alain Deniel, *Le Mouvement breton* (Paris, Maspéro, 1976), 27

36. Jean-Paul Brunet, *Saint-Denis: La Ville rouge, 1890–1939* (Paris, Hachette, 1980), 61–92

37. Yves-Marie Hilaire, *Histoire de Roubaix* (Dunkerque, Westhoek-Éditions, 1984), 195; Joan Scott, 'French Socialist Municipalities in the 1890s', *Mouvement Social* 111 (1980), 145–53

38. Machelon, 'La Troisième République', 432–5

39. William B. Cohen, *Urban Government and the Rise of the French City: Five Municipalities in the Nineteenth Century* (Basingstoke, Macmillan, 1998), 252–3

40. Jean Lorcin, 'Une Utopie fin de siècle au pays noir: Le Socialisme municipal à Saint-Étienne en 1900', *Mouvement Social* 184 (1998), 53–73; Lorcin, 'Le Socialisme municipal en France: Le Cas de Saint-Étienne; modèle ou exception?', in Uwe Kühl, ed., *Der Munizipalsozialismus in Europe* (Munich, R. Oldenbourg, 2001), 66–77

41. Dominique Schneider, ed., *Les Schneider: Le Creusot: Une Famille, une entreprise, une ville* (Paris, Fayard, 1995), 166, 299–316

42. Hilaire, *Histoire de Roubaix*, 200–202

43. Edouard Baratier, *Histoire de Marseille* (Toulouse, Privat, 1973), 408–10

44. Françoise Bayard and Pierre Cayez, *Histoire de Lyon*, II (Le Coteau, Éditions Horvath, 1990), 355–63; Bruno Benoit, 'Le "Augagneurisme" ou l'expérience du socialisme municipal à Lyon (1900–1905)', in Kühl, ed., *Der Munizipalsozialismus in Europe*, 47–58

45. Édouard Herriot, *Jadis*, I (Paris, 1948), 123–60

46. AD Nord 2V76, subprefect of Hazebrouck to prefect of Nord, 16 Oct. 1882

47. AD Nord 1T123/5, notes of the archbishop of Cambrai, 11 Dec. 1901

48. Suzanne Berger, *Peasants against Politics* (Cambridge, Mass., Harvard University Press, 1972), 150

49. Caroline Ford, *Creating the Nation in Provincial France: Religion and Political Identity in Brittany* (Princeton, Princeton University Press, 1993), 161–5

50. Chanet, *L'École républicaine et les petites patries*, 284–9, 319–20, 344–6

51. Cited by Anne-Marie Thiesse, *Ils apprenaient la France* (Paris, Maison des Sciences de l'Homme, 1997), 18

52. Circular of education minister Maurice Faure to rectors of academies, 25 Feb. 1911, cited by Thiesse, *Ils apprenaient la France*, 9–10

53. Thiesse, *Ils apprenaient la France*, 11; Chanet, *L'École républicaine et les petites patries*, 347–9

54. Wright, *The Regionalist Movement in France*, 121–2, 126, 153–4; François Monnet, *Refaire la République: André Tardieu, un dérive réactionnaire (1876–1945)* (Paris, Fayard, 1993), 49–52

55. Joseph Paul-Boncour and Charles Maurras, *Un Débat nouveau sur la République et la décentralisation* (Toulouse, Société Provinciale d'Édition, 1905), 12–27

56. André Tardieu, *Le Temps*, 28 July 1903, cited in Paul-Boncour and Maurras, *Un Débat nouveau*, 103–4, and Thiébaut Flory, *Le Mouvement régionaliste français* (Paris, PUF, 1966), 14

57. Clemenceau, *L'Aurore*, 31 July 1903, and *La Dépêche*, 8 Apr. 1904, and Charles Maurras, *La Gazette de France*, 30–31 July 1903, cited by Paul-Boncour and Maurras, *Un Débat nouveau*, 85, 115, 121, and Flory, *Le Mouvement régionaliste français*, 14–17

58. Paul Joanne, *Itinéraire général de la France: Bretagne* (Paris, Hachette, 1892), xvii

59. Stephen Harp, *Marketing Michelin: Advertising and Cultural Identity in Twentieth-century France* (Baltimore and London, Johns Hopkins University Press, 2001), 50–79

60. Ibid., 85

61. Touring Club de France, *Sites et monuments: L'Armorique* (Paris, 1901), 14

CHAPTER 11: CLASS COHESION

1. Émile Zola, *La Terre* [1887], in *Les Rougon-Macquart*, IV (Paris, Gallimard, 1966), 391–2, 367, 747–50, 792–4, 811. On the *bande d'Orgères* see above, p. 22

2. Émile Guillaumin, *La Vie d'un simple* [1904] (Paris, Stock, 1943), 172–3, 284; R. Mathé, *Émile Guillaumin, l'homme de la terre et l'homme de lettres* (Paris, Nizet, 1966)

3. Pierre Barral, 'Le Monde agricole', in Fernand Braudel and Ernest Labrousse, eds, *Histoire Économique et Sociale de la France*, IV/1 (Paris, PUF, 1979), 352

4. Roger Thabault, *Mon village: Ses hommes, ses routes, son école* (Paris, FNSP, 1982), 103, 157, 160

5. Jean-Claude Farcy, *Les Paysans beaucerons au XIXe siècle* (Chartres, Société Archéologique d'Eure-et-Loir, 1989), II, 668–711

6. Laura Levine Frader, *Peasants and Protest: Agricultural Workers, Politics and Unions in the Aude, 1850–1914* (Berkeley and Los Angeles, University of California Press, 1991), 25

7. Annie Moulin, *Peasantry and Society in France since 1789* (Cambridge, Cambridge University Press, 1991), 63, 101; Paul Bairoch, *La Population active et sa structure* (Brussels, Éditions de Sociologie de l'Université Libre de Bruxelles, 1968), 96–7

8. Georges Le Bail, *L'Émigration rurale et les migrations temporaires dans le Finistère: Thèse pour le doctorat* (Paris, 1913), 35–59; Louis Chevalier, *La Formation de la population parisienne au XIXe siècle* (Paris, PUF, 1950), 207–11

9. Bairoch, *La Population active et sa structure*, 96, 104, 136, 146, 189

10. George Duby and Armand Wallon, *Histoire de la France rurale*, III (Paris, Seuil, 1976), 210–13, 451

11. Pierre Boisard, *Camembert: A National Myth* (Berkeley, Los Angeles and London, University of California Press, 1992), 85–7

12. Ronald H. Hubscher, *L'Agriculture et la société rurale dans le Pas-de-Calais du milieu du XIXe siècle à 1914* (Arras, Commission Départementale des Monuments Historiques du Pas-de-Calais, 1980), 481–506

13. Rémy Pech, *Entreprise viticole et capitalisme en Languedoc-Roussillon* (Toulouse, Université de Toulouse-Le Mirail, 1975), 70

14. Leo Loubere, *The White and the Red* (Albany, State University of New York Press, 1978), 299

15. Thabault, *Mon village*, 145–9, 154–5

16. Suzanne Berger, *Peasants against Politics: Rural Organization in Brittany, 1911–1967* (Cambridge, Mass., Harvard University Press, 1972), 64–5, 75–8

17. René Braque, 'Aux origines du syndicalisme dans les milieux ruraux du centre de la France', *Mouvement Social* 42 (1963), 79–116; Philippe Gratton, *Les Luttes de classes dans les campagnes* (Paris, Anthropos, 1971), 59–106

18. Émile Guillaumin, *Six ans de lutte syndicale* (Moulins, Éditions des Cahiers Bourbonnais, 1977); Gratton, *Les Luttes de classes*, 256–91

19. Gratton, *Les Luttes de classes*, 140–90; Félix Napo, *1907: La Révolte des vignerons* (Toulouse, Privat, 1971); J. Harvey Smith, 'Agricultural Workers and the French Winegrowers' Revolt of 1907', *Past & Present* 79 (1978), 101–25; Jean Sagnes, 'Le Mouvement de 1907 en Languedoc-Roussillon: De la révolte viticole à la révolte régionale', *Mouvement Social* 104 (1978), 3–30; Levine Frader, *Peasants and Protest*, 122–47

20. Émile Zola, *Germinal* (Paris, Fasquelle, 1971), 277; Elliott M. Grant,

Zola's 'Germinal': A Critical and Historical Study (Leicester, Leicester University Press, 1970), 7–11

21. Odette Hardy-Hémery, *De la croissance à la désindustrialisation: Un Siècle dans le Valenciennois* (Paris, FNSP, 1984), 32–4

22. Rolande Trempé, *Les Mineurs de Carmaux, 1848–1914* (Paris, Les Éditions Ouvrières, 1971), I, 149, 186; Gérard Noiriel, *Les Ouvriers dans la société française, XIXe–XXe siècles* (Paris, Seuil, 1986), 89, 110

23. Michelle Perrot, 'Les Classes populaires urbaines', in Braudel and Labrousse, eds, *Histoire Économique et Sociale de la France*, IV/1, 457

24. Bairoch, ed., *La Population active et sa structure*, 167

25. Yves Lequin, 'Labour in the French Economy since the Revolution', in *Cambridge Economic History*, VII (Cambridge, Cambridge University Press, 1978), 299–302; Perrot, 'Les Classes populaires urbaines', 458–60; Gérard Noiriel, *Le Creuset français: Histoire de l'immigration XIXe–XXe siècles* (Paris, Seuil, 1988), 137–42; Nancy Green, *Les Travailleurs immigrés juifs à la Belle Époque: Le 'Pletzel' de Paris* (Paris, Fayard, 1985), 97–153

26. Yves Lequin, *Les Ouvriers de la région lyonnaise, 1848–1914* (Lyon, Presses Universitaires de Lyon, 1977), I, 85–9, 119–20

27. Helen Harden Chenut, 'Troyes, capitale de la bonneterie: La Ville comme vitrine vers 1900', in Louis Bergeron, ed., *La Révolution des aiguilles: Habiller les Français et Américains, 19e–20e siècles* (Paris, EHESS, 1996), 65

28. Michael P. Hanagan, *The Logic of Solidarity: Artisans and Workers in Three French Towns, 1871–1914* (Urbana, University of Illinois Press, 1980), 61–2

29. *L'Éclaireur de Saint-Chamond*, 23 July 1899, cited by Hanagan, *Logic of Solidarity*, 187

30. Jeanne Bouvier, *Mes mémoires* (Paris, La Découverte/Maspéro, 1983), 108

31. Donald Reid, *The Miners of Decazeville: A Genealogy of Deindustrialisation* (Cambridge, Mass., and London, Harvard University Press, 1985), 91–106

32. Michelle Perrot, *Les Ouvriers en Grève: France, 1871–1890* (2 vols, Paris and The Hague, Mouton, 1974), I, 352

33. Ibid., 161–4

34. Jules Ferry, speech at Saint-Dié, 2 Oct. 1887, in *Discours et opinions*, ed. Paul Robiquet, VII (Paris, 1898), 92

35. Perrot, *Les Ouvriers en Grève*, II, 439

36. Georges Lefranc, *Le Mouvement syndical sous la Troisème République* (Paris, Payot, 1967), 106

37. Hanagan, *Logic of Solidarity*, 187, 155–9

38. Perrot, 'Les Classes populaires urbaines', 523

39. F. Caron, 'Les Mécaniciens et chauffeurs de locomotives du réseau du Nord de 1850 à 1910', *Mouvement Social* 50 (1965), 3–40

40. Lequin, *Les Ouvriers de la région lyonnaise*, II, 254

41. Joël Michel, 'Syndicalisme minier et politique dans le Nord-Pas-de-Calais: Le Cas de Basly', *Mouvement Social* 87 (1974), 9–33

42. Peter Schöttler, *Naissance des Bourses du Travail: Un Appareil idéologique d'état à la fin du XIXe siècle* (Paris, PUF, 1982); Hanagan, *Logic of Solidarity*, 87–125

43. E. Levasseur, *Questions ouvrières et industrielles sous la Troisième République* (Paris, Arthur Rousseau, 1907), 274

44. Steven M. Zdatny, *The Politics of Survival: Artisans in Twentieth-century France* (New York and Oxford, Oxford University Press, 1990), 5–10; Geoffrey Crossick and Heinz-Gerhard Haupt, *The Petite Bourgeoisie in Europe, 1780–1914: Enterprise, Family and Independence* (London and New York, Routledge, 1995), 44–6; Monique Peyrière, 'L'Industrie de la machine à coudre en France, 1830–1914', in Bergeron, ed., *La Révolution des aiguilles*, 99–109

45. Émile Zola, *Au bonheur des dames* [1883], in *Les Rougon-Macquart*, III (Paris, Gallimard, 1964)

46. Bernard Marrey, *Les Grands Magasins des origines à 1939* (Paris, Picard, 1979), 97–109, 261

47. Philip Nord, *Paris Shopkeepers and the Politics of Resentment* (Princeton, Princeton University Press, 1986), 21–59

48. Alain Faure, 'L'Épicerie parisienne au XIXe siècle, ou la corporation éclatée', *Mouvement Social* 108 (1979), 120

49. Françoise Raison-Jourde, *La Colonie auvergnate de Paris au XIXe siècle* (Paris, Ville de Paris, 1976), 331–52

50. Thabault, *Mon village*, 164

51. Theresa McBride, 'A Woman's World: Department Stores and the Evolution of Women's Employment, 1870–1914', *French Historical Studies* 10/4 (1978), 669–70; Michael B. Miller, *The Bon Marché: Bourgeois Culture and the Department Store, 1869–1920* (London, George Allen & Unwin, 1981), 78–9

52. Leonard R. Berlanstein, *The Working People of Paris, 1871–1914* (Baltimore and London, Johns Hopkins University Press, 1984), 7, 9

53. Roger Magraw, *Workers and the Bourgeois Republic: A History of the French Working Class*, II (Oxford, Blackwell, 1992), 14

54. Quoted by Crossick and Haupt, *Petite Bourgeoisie in Europe*, 84
55. Michel Crozier, 'White-collar Unions: The Case of France', in Adolf Sturmthal, ed., *White-Collar Trade Unionism* (Urbana, University of Illinois Press, 1966), 100–104; H. Stuart Jones, *The French State in Question: Public Law and Political Argument in the Third Republic* (Cambridge, Cambridge University Press, 1993), 75–7
56. Cited by Jacques and Mona Ozouf, *La République des instituteurs* (Paris, Seuil, 1992), 245
57. Robert Gildea, *Education in Provincial France: A Study of Three Departments, 1800–1914* (Oxford, Clarendon Press, 1983), 128
58. Ozouf, *La République des instituteurs*, 234
59. Maurice Barrès, *Les Déracinés* [1897] (Paris, Plon, 1972), 142–3
60. Henry Bérenger, *Les Prolétaires intellectuels en France* (Paris, Éditions de la Revue, 1901), 35–46
61. Georges Weisz, *The Emergence of Modern Universities in France, 1863–1914* (Princeton, Princeton University Press, 1983), 242
62. Barrès, *Les Déracinés*, 28
63. Antoine Prost, *Histoire de l'enseignement en France, 1800–1967* (Paris, Colin, 1968), 355
64. Gérard Vincent, *Les Professeurs du second degré* (Paris, Colin, 1967), II, 50, 52
65. Christophe Charle, *La République universitaire, 1870–1940* (Paris, Seuil, 1994), 103
66. Édouard Herriot, *Jadis*, I (Paris, 1948), 123–47
67. Robert J. Smith, *The École Normale Supérieure and the Third Republic* (Albany, State University of New York Press, 1982), 34–45
68. Jean Guéhenno, *Changer la vie: Mon enfance et ma jeunesse* (Paris, Grasset, 1961), 128–219
69. Weisz, *Emergence of Modern Universities*, 236, 238, 246
70. Jacques Léonard, *La Médicine entre les pouvoirs et les savoirs* (Paris, Aubier, 1981), 292–8
71. Bérenger, *Les Prolétaires intellectuels en France*
72. Jean-Baptiste Duroselle, *Clemenceau* (Paris, Fayard, 1988), 41–92
73. Léonard, *La Médicine*, 281; Paul Smith, *A History of the French Senate*, I: *The Third Republic, 1870–1940* (Lewiston, Queenston, Lampeter, Edwin Meller Press, 2005), 84
74. Émile Combes, *Mon ministère: Mes mémoires, 1902–1905* (Paris, Plon, 1956), 6–69
75. Weisz, *Emergence of Modern Universities*, 236, 238, 246
76. Jeanne Siwek-Poudesseau, *Le Corps préfectoral sous la Troisième et Quatrième Républiques* (Paris, Colin, 1969), 30–37

77. *Paul Cambon, ambassadeur de France, par un diplomate* (Paris, Plon, 1937); Geneviève Tabouis, *The Life of Jules Cambon* (London, Jonathan Cape, 1938)

78. Christophe Charle, 'Les Milieux d'affaires dans la structure de la classe dominante vers 1900', *Actes de la Recherche en Sciences Sociales* 20–21 (1978), 83–96; Charle, 'Le Recrutement des hauts fonctionnaires en 1901', *Annales* 35 (1980), 380–409; Charle, *Les Hauts Fonctionnaires au XIXe siècle* (Paris, Archives, 1986), 183–202, 211

79. Bernard Auffay, *Pierre de Margerie (1861–1942) et la vie diplomatique de son temps* (Paris, Klincksieck, 1976)

80. Charle, 'Le Recrutement des hauts fonctionnaires en 1901', 380–409

81. Christophe Charle, *Les Élites de la République, 1880–1900* (Paris, Fayard, 1987), 282, 312; Robert A. Young, *Power and Pleasure: Louis Barthou and the French Third Republic* (Montreal and Kingston, McGill-Queen's University Press, 1991), 76–7

82. Bérenger, *Les Prolétaires intellectuels en France*, 46

83. Édouard Charton, *Dictionnaire de professions* (3rd edn, 1880), entry, *ingénieur*; Terry Shinn, 'Des corps de l'état au secteur industriel: Genèse de la profession d'ingénieur, 1750–1920', *Revue Française de Sociologie* 19 (1978), 39–71

84. Maurice Lévy-Leboyer, 'Le Patronat français, 1912–73', in Lévy-Leboyer, ed., *Le Patronat de la seconde industrialisation* (Paris, Éditions Ouvrières, 1979), 154–6; Lévy-Leboyer, 'The Large Corporation in modern France', in A. D. Chandler and H. Daems, eds, *Managerial Hierarchies* (Cambridge, Mass., Harvard University Press), 132–3

85. Eric de Schodt, *Gustave Eiffel, un illustre inconnu* (Paris, Pygmalion, 2003)

86. James M. Laux, *In First Gear: The French Automobile Industry to 1914* (Liverpool, Liverpool University Press, 1976), 12–54

87. André Gueslin, ed., *Michelin, les hommes du pneu* (Paris, Éditions de l'Atelier, 1993), 17–88

88. Patrick Fridenson, *Histoire des Usines Renault*, I: *La Naissance de la grande entreprise, 1898–1939* (Paris, Seuil, 1972), 30–63; Anthony Rhodes, *Louis Renault: A Biography* (London, Cassell, 1969)

89. Dominique Schneider, ed., *Les Schneider: Le Creusot: Une Famille, une enterprise, une ville* (Paris, Fayard, 1995), 111–16, 216–78

90. Jean Bouvier, *Le Crédit Lyonnais de 1863 à 1882* (Paris, SEVPEN, 1961), II, 702–28, 747–69

91. Charle, *Élites de la République*, 168

92. Elisabeth de Gramont, *Pomp and Circumstance* (London and New York, Jonathan Cape, 1929)

93. George D. Painter, *Marcel Proust: A Biography* (London, Pimlico, 1996), 150–53

CHAPTER 12: SECULARIZATION AND RELIGIOUS REVIVAL

1. Joseph Powell, *Two Years in the Pontifical Zouaves* (London, 1871), 247–60; Robert Tombs, 'Paris and the Rural Hordes: An Exploration of Myth and Reality in the French Civil War of 1871', *Historical Journal* 29/4 (1986), 801

2. Louis Veuillot, *Paris pendant les deux sièges* (Paris, Victor Palmé, 1872), 14 Aug. 1870, I, 13–16

3. Ibid., 15 June, 8 July, 24 Aug. 1871, II, 407, 490, 516; Pierre Pierrard, *Louis Veuillot* (Paris, Beauchesne, 1998), 167–77; J. M. Roberts, *The Paris Commune from the Right* (London, Longman, 1973), 8

4. Thomas Kselman, *Miracles and Prophecies in Nineteenth-century France* (New Brunswick, Rutgers University Press, 1983), 113–19; Philippe Boutry and Michel Cinquin, *Deux pèlerinages au XIXe siècle: Ars et Paray-le-Monial* (Paris, Beauchesne, 1980), 175–223; Ruth Harris, *Lourdes: Body and Spirit in the Secular Age* (London, Allen Lane, 1999), 210–73; Joseph F. Byrnes, *Catholic and French Forever: Religious and National Identity in Modern France* (Pennsylvania, Pennsylvania State University Press, 2005), 95–109

5. Raymond A. Jonas, 'Monument as Ex-voto, Monument as Historiosophy: The Basilica of Sacré-Coeur', *French Historical Studies* 18/2 (1993), 482–502

6. Jacques de Biez, *E. Frémiet* (Paris, 1910), 134–42

7. Claude Langlois, *Le Catholicisme au féminin: Les Congrégations françaises à supérieure générale au XIXe siècle* (Paris, Cerf, 1984), 321; Pierre Pierrard, 'Les Origines de l'enseignement supérieure catholique à Lille', in *Ensemble d'Écoles Supérieures et de Facultés Catholiques* 35/1 (1975), 3–33

8. Gambetta, Saint-Quentin speech of 16 Nov. 1871, *Discours et plaidoyers politiques*, II (Paris, Charpentier, 1881), 175–8; J. P. T. Bury, *Gambetta and the Making of the Third Republic* (London, Longman, 1973), 66–70

9. Bury, *Gambetta and the Making of the Third Republic*, 394–8

10. Gambetta, Romans speech, 18 Sept. 1878, in *Discours et plaidoyers*

politiques, VII (Paris, Charpentier, 1884), VIII, 242; J. P. T. Bury, *Gambetta's Final Years* (London, Longman, 1982), 85

11. Jacqueline Lalouette, *La Libre Pensée en France, 1848–1940* (Paris, Albin Michel, 1997), 92–128, 261, 351–3

12. Robert Gildea, *Education in Provincial France: A Study of Three Departments, 1800–1914* (Oxford, Clarendon Press, 1983), 143–5, 163–4

13. Gerd Krumeich, *Jeanne d'Arc in der Geschichte* (Sigmaringen, Thorbecke, 1989), 175–81

14. *Centenaire de Voltaire: Fête oratoire présidée par Victor Hugo, 30 mai 1878* (Paris, Dentu, 1878), 68; Jean-Marie Goulemot and Éric Walter, 'Les Centenaires de Voltaire et de Rousseau', in Pierre Nora ed., *Les Lieux de mémoire*, I (Paris, Gallimard, 1984), 381–408; Olivier Ihl, *La Fête républicaine* (Paris, Gallimard, 1996), 102–6

15. Michel Richard, 'Les Ministres protestants du cabinet Waddington', in *Les Protestants dans les débuts de la Troisième République, Bulletin de la Société d'Histoire du Protestantisme Français* (1979), 199–226

16. Paul Bert, speech of 15 Aug. 1880 at Coulanges-sur-Yonne, in his *Leçons, discours et conférences* (Paris, Charpentier, 1881), 450

17. Françoise Mayeur, 'Les Protestants dans l'instruction publique au début de la Troisième République', in *Les Protestants dans les débuts de la Troisième République*, 37–48

18. Bert, speech of 21 Mar. 1880 at Le Havre, in *Leçons, discours et conférences*, 411

19. Mgr Freppel, speech in Chamber, 21 Dec. 1880, in *Oeuvres polémiques* (Paris, Société Générale de Librairie Catholique, 1881), 428, 469

20. Jean Faury, *Cléricalisme et anticléricalisme dans le Tarn, 1848–1900* (Toulouse, Université de Toulouse-Le Mirail, 1980), 123–61

21. Jules Ferry, speech in Chamber, 23 Dec. 1880, in *La République des citoyens*, ed. Odile Rudelle (Paris, Imprimerie Nationale, 1996), II, 28–41

22. Ferry to Pope, 26 June 1883, cited in Pierre Chevallier, *La Séparation de l'Église et de l'école: Jules Ferry et Léon XIII* (Paris, Fayard, 1981), 446. See also Jean-Marie Mayeur, *La Question laïque, XIXe–XXe siècles* (Paris, Fayard, 1997), 51–4

23. Jules Ferry, speech of 21 Dec. 1888, in *Discours et opinions*, VII (Paris, 1898), 129

24. Gildea, *Education in Provincial France*, 111, 130, 148, 167

25. A. Lanfrey, 'Église et monde ouvrier: Les congréganistes et leurs écoles à Montceau-les-Mines, 1875–1903', *Cahiers d'Histoire* 23 (1978), 51–71; see also Jean Bruhat, 'Anticléricalisme et mouvement ouvrier en France avant 1914', *Mouvement Social* 57 (1966), 61–100

26. Yves-Marie Hilaire, 'Les Ouvriers de la région du Nord devant l'Église catholique, XIXe–XXe siècles', *Mouvement Social* 57 (1966), 181–210; Gérard Cholvy and Yves-Marie Hilaire, *Histoire religieuse de la France contemporaine*, II: *1880–1930* (Toulouse, Privat, 1896), 180

27. See file on Flamidien Affair in AD Nord 1T123/12; Gildea, *Education in Provincial France*, 131–2; Danielle Delmaire, *Antisémitisme et Catholicisme dans le Nord pendant l'Affaire Dreyfus* (Lille, Presses Universitaires de Lille, 1991), 209–22

28. Cholvy and Hilaire, *Histoire religieuse*, II, 198

29. F. A. Isambert, *Christianisme et classe ouvrière* (Paris, Casterman, 1961), 74

30. Gérard Cholvy, *Christianisme et société en France au XIXe siècle* (Paris, Seuil, 2001), 120–21

31. Cholvy and Hilaire, *Histoire religieuse*, II, 197, 199

32. Louis Pérouas, *Les Limousins: Leurs saints, leurs prêtres du XVe au XXe siècle* (Paris, Cerf, 162–76; Lalouette, *La Libre Pensée en France*, 388

33. *Bulletin de la Société d'Histoire du Protestantisme Français*, 3rd series 6 (1887), 447

34. Eugène-Melchior de Vogüé, *Notes sur le Bas-Vivarais* [1893], cited by André Siegfried, *Géographie électorale de l'Ardèche sous la IIIe République* (Paris, Colin, 1949), 65

35. *La Rèpublique des Cévennes*, 17 Nov. 1902

36. Michael Burns, *Dreyfus: A Family Affair, 1789–1945* (London, Chatto & Windus, 1992), 76–90

37. Michael Marrus, *The Politics of Assimilation: A Study of the French Jewish Community at the Time of the Dreyfus Affair* (Oxford, Clarendon Press, 1971), 31; Esther Benbassa, *The Jews of France: A History from Antiquity to the Present* (Princeton, Princeton University Press, 1999), 108–36

38. Quoted by Nelly Wilson, *Bernard-Lazare: Anti-Semitism and the Problem of Jewish Identity in Late Nineteenth-century France* (Cambridge, Cambridge University Press, 1978), 76

39. Albert de Mun, *Ma vocation sociale* (Paris, 1908), 40

40. Albert de Mun, speech of 8 Sept. 1878, *Discours*, I: *Questions sociales* (Paris, Poussielgue, 1888), 299–300

41. In general see Benjamin F. Martin, *Count Albert de Mun, Paladin of the Third Republic* (Chapel Hill, University of North. Carolina Press, 1978), and Charles Molette, *Albert de Mun, 1872–1890* (Paris, Beauchesne, 1970)

42. Alexander Sedgwick, *The Ralliement in French Politics, 1890–1898*

(Cambridge, Mass., Harvard University Press, 1965); William Burridge, *Destiny Africa: Cardinal Lavigerie and the Making of the White Fathers* (London and Dublin, G. Chapman, 1966); J. Dean O'Donnell, *Lavigerie in Tunisia, 1825–1892* (Athens, University of Georgia Press, 1979)

43. *Le Figaro*, 8 Jan. 1890; Maxime Lecomte, *Les Ralliés: Histoire d'un parti, 1886–1898* (Paris, Flammarion, n.d.), 230

44. Rosemonde Sanson, 'La "Fête de Jeanne d'Arc" en 1894: Controverse et célébration', *Revue d'Histoire Moderne et Contemporaine* 20 (1973), 444–63

45. *La Revue Socialiste* 18 (June 1886), 505–14

46. *La Croix*, 22 Nov. 1894, cited by Pierre Sorlin, *'La Croix' et les Juifs* (Paris, Grasset, 1967), 109–10

47. *La Croix*, 3 Nov. 1894, cited by Sorlin, *'La Croix' et les Juifs*, 110–11; Delmaire, *Antisémitisme et Catholicisme*, 209–22; Ruth Harris, 'The Assumptionists and the Dreyfus Affair', *Past & Present* 194/1 (2007), 182–3. I am indebted to Ruth Harris for her conceptualization of the Dreyfus Affair as a religious war.

48. Letter of Lemire, 25 Feb. 1887, cited by Jean-Marie Mayeur, *Un Prêtre démocrate: L'Abbé Lemire, 1853–1928* (Paris, Casterman, 1968), 43

49. Suzanne Berger, *Peasants against Politics* (Cambridge, Mass., Harvard University Press, 1972), 46–7; Caroline Ford, *Creating the Nation in Provincial France: Religion and Political Identity in Brittany* (Princeton, Princeton University Press, 1933), 124–34

50. *La Justice Sociale*, 15 and 22 July 1893

51. Stephen Wilson, 'Catholic Populism in France at the Time of the Dreyfus Affair: The Union Nationale', *Journal of Contemporary History* (1975), 667–705

52. Maurice Barrès, *Scènes et doctrines du nationalisme* (Paris, 1902), 41

53. Ernest Renauld, *Le Péril protestant* (Paris, 1899); Pierre Froment, *La Trahison protestante* (Paris, 1899); Jean Baubérot, 'L'Antiprotestantisme politique à la fin du XIXe siècle', *Revue d'Histoire et de Philosophie Religieuses* 53 (1973), 177–221

54. *L'Action Française, première année*, 1 Oct. 1899, 235–60

55. Le Père Didon, *L'Esprit militaire dans une nation: Discours prononcé à la distribution des prix des Écoles Albert-le-Grand et Laplace, le 19 juillet 1898* (Paris, 1898), 19

56. Stephen Wilson, *Ideology and Experience: Antisemitism in France at the Time of the Dreyfus Affair* (Rutherford, Madison, Teaneck, Farleigh Dickinson University Press, 1982), 125–59

57. Barrès, *Scènes et doctrines du nationalisme*, 152–3

58. Léon Blum, *Souvenirs sur l'Affaire* (Paris, Gallimard, 1935), 101

59. *Le Figaro*, 1 Dec. 1897, and *L'Aurore*, 22 Feb. 1898, in Zola, *La Vérité en marche* (Paris, 1901), 17, 104

60. Anatole Leroy-Beaulieu, *Les Doctrines de la Haine* (Paris, 1902)

61. Raoul Allier, *Voltaire et Calas: Une Erreur judiciaire au XVIIIe siècle* (Paris, Stock, 1898)

62. Lalouette, *Libre Pensée en France*, 198–9

63. *La Dépêche de Toulouse*, 25 July 1898, cited by René Rémond, *L'Anticléricalisme en France de 1815 à nos jours* (Paris, Fayard, 1976), 201

64. F. Buisson, *Le Colonel Picquart en prison: Discours prononcé le 10 mai 1899* (Paris, Ollenorff, 1899), 11

65. René Waldeck-Rousseau, *La Défense républicaine* (Paris, Fasquelle, 1902), 82; Harris, 'The Assumptionists and the Dreyfus Affair', 201–7

66. Ford, *Creating the Nation in Provincial France*, 150–63. See also Judith F. Stone, 'Anticlericals and *Bonnes Soeurs*: The Rhetoric of the 1901 Law of Associations', *French Historical Studies* 23/1 (2000), 103–28

67. Émile Combes, *Mon ministère: Mémoires, 1902–1905* (Paris, Plon, 1956), 34, 78

68. Joseph Paul-Boncour, *Entre deux guerres: Souvenirs sur la IIIe République*, I (Paris, 1945), 143

69. Jean-Marie Mayeur, *La Séparation de l'Église et de l'État* (Paris, Julliard, 1966); Maurice Larkin, *Church and State after the Dreyfus Affair: The Separation Issue in France* (London, Macmillan, 1974)

70. Albert de Mun, *Les Responsabilités de M. Waldeck-Rousseau* (Paris, 1902); Benjamin Martin, 'The Creation of the Action Libérale Populaire', *French Historical Studies* 9 (1976), 660–89; Martin, *Count Albert de Mun*, 154–202

71. Yves Déloye, *École et Chrétienneté: L'Individualisme républicain de Jules Ferry à Vichy* (Paris, FNSP, 1994), 284; Gildea, *Education in Provincial France*, 115–17

72. Michel Lagrée, *Religion et cultures en Bretagne, 1850–1950* (Paris, Fayard, 1992), 171–2, 411–14; Yves Lambert, *Dieu change en Bretagne: La Religion à Limerzel de 1900 à nos jours* (Paris, Cerf, 1985), 116

73. Jacqueline Roux, *Sous l'étendard de Jeanne: Les Fédérations diocésaines de jeunes filles, 1904–1995* (Paris, Cerf, 1995), 37–45

74. Kselman, *Miracles and Prophecies*, 164–5

75. Lagrée, *Religion et cultures en Bretagne*, 69

76. Marc Sangnier, speech at opening of Sillon in 10th *arrondissement*, Paris, in *Discours*, I: *1891–1906* (Paris, Bloud, 1910), 139

77. Debate of 9 Mar. 1905, in *Discours*, I, 139

78. Charles Molette, *L'Association Catholique de la Jeunesse Française,
1886–1907* (Paris, Colin, 1968), 501–19; Lagrée, *Religion et cultures
en Bretagne*, 187–92

79. Charles Maurras, 'Le Dilemme de Marc Sangnier', in *L'Oeuvre*, II
(Paris, 1921), 28

80. Madeleine Barthélemy-Madaule, *Marc Sangnier, 1873–1950* (Paris,
Seuil, 1973), 15–16

81. Richard Griffiths, *The Reactionary Revolution: The Catholic Revival
in French Literature, 1870–1914* (London, Constable, 1966); Frédéric
Gugelot, *La Conversion des intellectuels au catholicisme en France,
1885–1935* (Paris, CNRS, 1998)

82. Raïssa Maritain, *Les Grandes Amitiés: Souvenirs* (New York, 1941),
provides an evocative account of this journey. See also Léon Bloy,
Journal, II (Paris, Mercure de France, 1958), 308–64; Joseph Bollery,
Léon Bloy: Essai de biographie, III (Paris, Albin Michel, 1954), 361–
5

83. Ernest Psichari, *Lettres du centurion: Oeuvres complètes*, III (Paris,
Louis Conard, 1948), 226, 239, 245–6, 274–5, 320; Agathon, *Les
Jeunes Gens d'aujourd'hui* (Paris, Plon, 1913). Agathon was the *nom
de plume* of Henri Massis and Gabriel Tarde.

84. Pie Duployé, *La Religion de Péguy* (Paris, Klincksieck, 1964), 13,
130

85. Charles Péguy, *Notre jeunesse*, in *Oeuvres en prose, 1909–1914* (Paris,
Gallimard, 1957), 646. See also Eric Cahm, *Péguy et le nationalisme
français de l'Affaire Dreyfus à la Grande Guerre* (Paris, Cahiers de
l'Amitié Charles Péguy, 25, 1972), 154–60; Géraldi Leroy, *Péguy entre
l'ordre et la Révolution* (Paris, FNSP, 1981), 213–39

86. Maritain to Péguy, 2 Feb. 1910, cited by Duployé, *La Religion de
Péguy*, 643–4; Raïssa Maritain, *Les Grandes Amitiés*, 269–74;

CHAPTER 13: FEMINISM AND
ITS FRUSTRATIONS

1. Gyp, *Autour du mariage* (Paris, Calmann-Lévy, 1883), 19–23

2. Ibid., 299–300

3. Gyp, *Autour du divorce* (43rd edn, Paris, Calmann-Lévy, 1893),
388

4. Jules Lemaître, review of 22 Aug. 1886, in *Impressions de théâtre.
Première série* (Paris, 1890), 302–5. See also Alison Finch, *Women's*

Writing in Nineteenth-century France (Cambridge, Cambridge University Press, 2000), 181–2

5. Willa Z. Silverman, *The Notorious Life of Gyp: Right-wing Anarchist in Fin-de-Siècle France* (New York and Paris, Oxford University Press, 1995), 56. See also Michel Missoff, *Gyp et ses amis* (Paris, Flammarion, 1932)

6. Anne-Marie Sohn, *Chrysalides: Femmes dans la vie privée (XIXe–XXe siècles)* (Paris, Publications de la Sorbonne, 1996), I, 511

7. Ibid., 75–84, II, 914

8. Paul Bourget, *L'Irréparable* [1883] (Paris, Plon, 1928)

9. Léon Blum, *Du Mariage* [1907], in *L'Oeuvre, 1905–1914* (Paris, Albin Michel, 1962)

10. Sohn, *Chrysalides*, II, 551, 574–5

11. Rachel G. Fuchs, *Poor and Pregnant in Paris: Strategies for Survival in the Nineteenth Century* (New Brunswick, Rutgers University Press, 1992), 106–22, 184–225

12. Zola, *Nana* [1880], in *Les Rougon-Macquart*, II (Paris, Gallimard Pléiade, 1961), 1213; Sohn, *Chrysalides*, II, 745, 760–71

13. J. Dartigues, *De l'amour expérimental ou les causes de l'adultère chez la femme au XIXe siècle* (Paris, 1887), 144. See also Michelle Perrot, ed., *A History of Private Life*, IV: *From the Fires of the Revolution to the Great War* (Cambridge, Mass., Harvard University Press, 1990), 590–602, and Laure Adler, *Secrets de l'alcôve: Histoire du couple* (Paris, Complexe, 1990), 140–47

14. André Armangaud, 'Mouvement ouvrier et néo-malthusianisme au début du XXe siècle', *Annales de Démographie Historique* (1966), 7–21; Arsène Dumont, *Dépopulation et civilisation: Étude démographique* (Paris, 1898)

15. Alexandre Dumas *fils*, *L'Homme-Femme* (Paris, 1872), 69–70, 175–6. See also Joëlle Guillais, *Crimes of Passion: Dramas of Private Life in Nineteenth-century France* (Cambridge, Polity Press, 1990), 136–76, and Annelise Maugue, *L'Identité masculine en crise au tournant du siècle, 1871–1914* (Paris, Rivages, 1987), 35–6; Ruth Harris, *Murder and Madness: Medicine, Law and Society in the* Fin de Siècle (Oxford, Clarendon Press, 1989), 289–90

16. Zola, *Nana* [1880], in *Les Rougon-Macquart*, II, 1464

17. Charles Virmaître, *Trottoirs et Lupanars* (Paris, 1895), 89–93; Alain Corbin, *Women for Hire: Prostitution and Sexuality in France after 1850* (Cambridge, Mass., Harvard University Press, 1990), 122–6, 174–6

18. Sohn, *Chrysalides*, II, 929

19. Paul Bourget, *Physiologie de l'amour moderne* (Paris, Plon, 1891)

20. Henry Bataille, *Maman Colibri*, in *Théâtre complet*, III (Paris, Flammarion, 1924), 239, 294–8, 314, 388–9. See also Maugue, *L'Identité masculine en crise*, 92–3

21. Roderick Phillips, *Putting Asunder: A History of Divorce in Western Society* (Cambridge, Cambridge University Press, 1988), 425–7; Antony Copley, *Sexual Moralities in France, 1780–1990: New Ideas on the Family, Divorce and Homosexuality* (London and New York, Routledge, 1989), 115–29; Adler, a *Secrets de l'alcôve*, 184–213

22. Frances L. Clark, *The Position of Women in Contemporary France* (London, P. S. King, 1937), 181

23. Alfred Valensi, 'L'Application de la loi du divorce en France' (law thesis, Montpellier, 1905), 91, 175, 184–5

24. See above, p. 335

25. Statements of Henriette Caillaux to the Assize Court of the Seine, *Gazette des Tribunaux*, 21/22 and 23 July 1914.

26. *Gazette des Tribunaux*, 30 July 1914. See Peter Shankland, *Death of an Editor: The Caillaux Drama* (London, Kimber, 1981) and Edward Berenson, *The Trial of Madame Caillaux* (Berkeley, University of California Press, 1983)

27. Paul Bairoch, ed., *La Population active et sa structure* (Brussels, Éditions de l'Institut de Sociologie de l'Université Libre de Bruxelles, 1968), 167–9

28. See, for example, Paul Leroy-Beaulieu, *Le Travail des femmes au XIXe siècle* (Paris, 1873); Fernand and Maurice Pelloutier, *La Vie ouvrière en France* (Paris, 1900), 92–124; E. Levasseur, *Questions ouvrières et industrielles en France sous la Troisième République* (Paris, Arthur Rousseau, 1907), 275–7, 537–40

29. Yvonne Kniebiehler and Catherine Fouquet, *La Femme et les médecins* (Paris, Hachette, 1983), 227–30

30. Madeleine Guilbert, *Les Femmes et l'organisation syndicale avant 1914* (Paris, CNRS, 1966), 13

31. Jean-Paul Burdy, Mathilde Dubesset and Michelle Zancarini-Fournel, 'Rôles, travaux et métiers de femmes dans une ville industrielle: Saint-Étienne, 1900–1950', *Mouvement Social* 140 (1987), 35

32. Sohn, *Chrysalides*, I, 144

33. Helen Harden Chenut, 'The Gendering of Skill as a Historical Process: The Case of French Knitters in Industrial Troyes, 1880–1939', in Laura L. Frader and Sonia O. Rose, *Gender and Class in Modern Europe* (Ithaca and London, Cornell University Press, 1996), 77–88

34. Jeanne Bouvier, *Mes mémoires: Une Syndicaliste féministe, 1876–1935* (Paris, La Découverte/Maspéro, 1983), 55–93

35. Marilyn J. Boxer, 'Women in Industrial Homework: The Flowermakers of Paris in the Belle-Époque', *French Historical Studies* 12/3 (1982), 407–13

36. Judith G. Coffin, *The Politics of Women's Work: The Paris Garment Trades, 1750–1915* (Princeton, Princeton University Press, 1996), 126–56

37. Tessie P. Liu, *The Weaver's Knot: The Contradictions of Class Struggle and Family Solidarity in Western France, 1750–1914* (Ithaca, Cornell University Press, 1994), 162–79

38. Guilbert, *Les Femmes et l'organisation syndicale*, 231

39. Bouvier, *Mes mémoires*, 103

40. Guilbert, *Les Femmes et l'organisation syndicale*, 29

41. Madeline Guilbert, *Les Fonctions des femmes dans l'industrie* (Paris and The Hague, Mouton, 1966), 47

42. Laura L. Frader, 'Engendering Work and Wages: The French Labour Movement and the Family Wage', in Frader and Rose, *Gender and Class in Modern Europe*, 150

43. Charles Sowerwine, 'Workers and Women in France before 1914: The Debate over the Couriau Affair', *Journal of Modern History* 55 (1983), 411–41

44. Raymond Grew and Patrick J. Harrigan, *School, State and Society: The Growth of Elementary Schooling in Nineteenth-century France* (Ann Arbor, University of Michigan Press, 1991), 265, 287, 298

45. Guilbert, *Les Femmes et l'organisation syndicale*, 14; Fernand Braudel and Ernest Labrousse, eds, *Histoire économique et sociale de la France*, IV/1 (Paris, PUF, 1979), 458

46. Susan Bacharach, 'La Féminisation des PTT en France au tournant du siècle', *Mouvement Social* 140 (1987), 69–87

47. Grew and Harrigan, *School, State and Society*, 291

48. Danielle Delhome, Nicole Gault and Josiane Gonthier, *Les Premières Institutrices laïques* (Paris, Mercure de France, 1980), 87, 107–11, 139

49. Françoise Rozenzweig, 'Pauline Kergomard née Reclus (1838–1925) ou comment devient-on républicaine?', in Alain Corbin, Jacqueline Lalouette and Michèle Roit-Sarcey, eds, *Femmes dans la cité, 1815–1871* (Grâne, Creaphis, 1997), 185–202; Anne T. Quartararo, *Women, Teachers and Popular Education in Nineteenth-century France* (Newark, University of Delaware Press, 1995), 116–49; Sharif Gemie, *Women and Schooling in France, 1815–1914: Gender, Authority and Identity in the Female Schooling Sector* (Keele, Keele University Press, 1995), 157–70

50. Karen Offen, 'The Second Sex and the *baccalauréat* in Republican France, 1880–1924', *French Historical Studies* 13 (1983), 252–86

51. Françoise Mayeur, *L'Enseignement secondaire des jeunes filles sous la Troisième République* (Paris, FNSP, 1977), 241–91; Jo Burr Margadant, *Madame le Professeur: Women Educators in the Third Republic* (Princeton, Princeton University Press, 1990), 47–143; Marguerite Aron, *Le Journal d'une Séverine* (Paris, Alcan, 1912), 232

52. George Weisz, *The Emergence of Modern Universities in France, 1863–1914* (Princeton, Princeton University Press, 1983), 246

53. Eve Curie, *Madame Curie: A Biography* (New York, Doubleday, 1939)

54. G. Richelot, *La Femme-Médecin* (Paris, 1875), 18, 65; Caroline Schultze, *La Femme-Médecin au XIXe siècle* (Paris, 1888), 16–28; Kniebiehler and Fouquet, *La Femme et les médecins*, 196–9; Harris, *Murders and Madness*, 16–77

55. Felicia Gordon, *Integral Feminist: Madeleine Pelletier, 1874–1939: Feminism, Socialism and Medicine* (Cambridge, Polity Press, 1990), 13–57

56. Colette Yver, *Les Cervelines* (Paris, 1908), 9–10; Colette Yver, *Princesses de science* [1907] (Paris, Calmann-Lévy, 1923), 255. See also Maugue, *L'Identité masculine en crise*, 43–53

57. Patrick Kay Bidelman, *Pariahs Stand Up! The Founding of the Liberal Feminists Movement in France, 1858–1889* (Westport, Conn., Greenwood Press, 1982), 80. See above, p. 368

58. Bidelman, *Pariahs Stand Up!*, 108–25; Steven C. Hause, *Hubertine Auclert: The French Suffragette* (New Haven, Yale University Press, 1987), 79–92; Mona Ozouf, *Women's Words: Essay on French Singularity* (Chicago and London, Chicago University Press, 1994), 132–58

59. Léon Richer, *Le Droit des Femmes*, 20 May 1888, cited by Bidelman, *Pariahs Stand Up!*, 92

60. Louise Michel, *Le Droit des Femmes*, 6 Sept. 1885, cited by Bidelman, *Pariahs Stand Up!*, 129; Hause, *Hubertine Auclert*, 64

61. Alexandre Dumas *fils*, *Les Femmes qui tuent et les femmes qui votent* (Paris, Calmann-Lévy, 1880), 214

62. Bidelman, *Pariahs Stand Up!*, 178–80; Corbin, *Women for Hire*, 216–30

63. Steven C. Hause and Anne R. Kenney, *Women's Suffrage and Social Politics in the French Third Republic* (Princeton, Princeton University Press, 1984), 34–53

64. Mary Louise Roberts, 'Acting Up: The Feminist Theatrics of Marguerite Durand', *French Historical Studies* 19 (1996), 1120. Republished in Jo Burr Margadant, ed., *The New Biography: Performing Feminity in Nineteenth-century France* (Berkeley, Los Angeles and London,

University of California Press, 2000), 171–217. See also Jean Rabaut, *Marguerite Durand (1864–1936): 'La Fronde' féministe ou 'Le Temps' en jupons* (Paris, L'Harmattan, 1996)

65. Bouvier, *Mes mémoires*, 101

66. Charles Sowerwine, *Sisters or Citizens? Women and Socialists in France since 1876* (Cambridge, Cambridge University Press, 1982), 77

67. Silverman, *The Notorious Life of Gyp*, 158; Roberts, 'Acting Up: The Feminist Theatrics of Marguerite Durand', 1126–7

68. Laurence Klejman and Florence Rochefort, *L'Égalité en marche: Le Féminisme sous la Troisième République* (Paris, FNSP/Des Femmes, 1989), 109

69. Sylvie Fayet-Scribe, *Associations féminines et Catholicisme* (Paris, Éditions Ouvrières, 1990), 57; Odile Sarti, *The Ligue Patriotique des Françaises, 1902–1933: A Feminine Response to the Secularization of French Society* (New York and London, Garland, 1992), 124–5

70. Hause, *Hubertine Auclert*, 186–200; Gordon, *Integral Feminist*, 85–101

71. Emmeline Pankhurst, *My Own Story* (London, Eveleigh Nash, 1914), 10–11; Christabel Pankhurst, *Unshackled: The Story of How We Won the Vote* (London, Hutchinson, 1959), 16–18, 200–218; E. Sylvia Pankhurst, *The Suffragette: The History of the Women's Militant Suffragette Movement, 1905–1910* (London, Gay & Hancock, 1911), 224–32, 365–7; Hause and Kenney, *Women's Suffrage*, 108–13. See also Sandra Stanley Holton, *Feminism and Democracy: Women's Suffrage and Reform Politics in Britain, 1900–1918* (Cambridge, Cambridge University Press, 1986), Laura E. Nym Mayhall, *The Militant Suffrage Movement: Citizenship and Resistance in Britain, 1860–1930* (Oxford, Oxford University Press, 2003), and June Purvis, *Emmeline Pankhurst: A Biography* (London, Routledge, 2002)

72. Julian Wright, 'Social Reform, State Reform and Aristide Briand's Moment of Hope in France, 1909–10', *French Historical Studies* 28/1 (2005), 31–67

73. Hause and Kenney, *Women's Suffrage*, 130–31

74. Gordon, *Integral Feminist*, 96, 109–13

75. Auclert, letter of 27 Apr. 1910, cited by Hause and Kenney, *Women's Suffrage*, 290, note 20; Pelletier, letter of 2 Nov. 1911, cited by Gordon, *Integral Feminist*, 18

76. Sowerwine, *Sisters or Citizens?*, 124–38

77. Hause and Kenney, *Women's Suffrage*, 99

CHAPTER 14: MODERNISM AND MASS CULTURE

1. Anne Martin-Fugier, *Les Salons de la IIIe République: Art, littérature, politique* (Paris, Perrin, 2003), 188–93; Joachim Kühn, *La Princesse Mathilde, 1820–1904* (Paris, Plon, 1935), 341–6

2. Alphonse Daudet, *Trente ans de Paris* (Paris, 1888), 336

3. Francis Steegmuller, *Maupassant* (London, Collins, 1950), 107

4. Robert Baldick, ed., *Pages from the Goncourt Journal* (London, Penguin, 1984), 330–31, entry for 18 Aug. 1887

5. J.-K. Huysmans, *L'Art moderne* [1883] (Paris, Plon, 1908), 128, 271

6. *Gauguin by Himself*, ed. Belinda Thomson (Boston, New York and London, Little, Brown, 2000), 23

7. See Malcolm Bradbury and James McFarlane, eds, *Modernism, 1890–1930* (London, Penguin, 1976); Bernard Smith, *Modernism's History: A Study in Twentieth-century Art and Ideas* (New Haven and London, Yale University Press, 1998); T. J. Clark, *Farewell to an Idea: Episodes from a History of Modernism* (New Haven and London, Yale University Press, 1999)

8. Ex-Madame Paul Verlaine [Mathilde Mauté], *Mémoires de ma vie* (Seyssel, Champ Vallon, 1992), 76. See also Jerrold Siegel, *Bohemian Paris: Culture, Politics and the Boundaries of Bourgeois Life* (London, Penguin, 1987), 246–64, and Joanna Richardson, *Paul Verlaine* (London, Weidenfeld & Nicolson, 1971)

9. Quoted by Martin-Fugier, *Les Salons*, 187–8

10. Édouard Dujardin, *Mallarmé par un des siens* (Paris, Messein, 1936), 25

11. Huysmans, *À rebours* (Paris, Gallimard, 1977), 327. See in general Jean Pierrot, *The Decadent Imagination, 1880–1900* (Chicago and London, Chicago University Press, 1981)

12. Maurice Barrès, *Le Secret merveilleux* [1892], in *Du Sang, de la volupté et de la mort* (Paris, 1921), 101–3

13. Wladyslawa Jaworska, *Gauguin and the Pont-Aven School* (London, Thames & Hudson, 1972), 75–82, 124; Claire Frèches-Thory, *Les Nabis* (Paris, Flammarion, 1990), 10–19

14. Maurice Denis, *Journal*, I: *1884–1904* (Paris, La Colombe, 1957), 62–4

15. Jaworska, *Gauguin and the Pont-Aven School*, 151

16. Aurélien Lugné-Poë, *La Parade* (3 vols, Paris, Gallimard, 1930–33),

I, 189–94, II, 53–5; John A. Henderson, *The First Avant-Garde, 1887–1894* (London, Harrap, 1971), 96–7, 144, 156

17. Léon Bloy, review in *Le Chat Noir*, cited by Robert Baldick, *The Life of J.-K. Huysmans* (Oxford, Clarendon Press, 1955), 90; Abbé Mugnier, *Journal (1879–1907)* (Paris, Mercure de France, 1985), 62, 72–8, 133, 149, 166–7

18. Denis, *Journal*, I, 63, 130–40, 172–82; Musée des Beaux-Arts, Lyon, *Maurice Denis* (Ghent, Snoeck-Ducaju & Zoon, 2000), 96–102

19. Camille Pissarro, *Letters to his Son Lucien* (London, Kegan Paul, 1943), 170–71, letter of 13 May 1891

20. Félix Fénéon, *Oeuvres plus que complètes* (Geneva, Droz, 1970), I, 54, 72–6, 174–83; John G. Hutton, *Neo-Impressionism and the Search for Solid Ground: Art, Science and Anarchism in* Fin de Siècle *France* (Baton Rouge and London, Louisiana State University Press, 1994), 49–59, 101–8, 173–5, 188–9

21. Julia Daudet, *Souvenirs autour d'un groupe littéraire* (Paris, Charpentier, 1910), 80

22. Jeanne Simone Poquet, *Le Salon de Madame Caillavet* (Paris, Hachette, 1926), 38–47, 125–34; see also Martin-Fugier, *Les Salons*, 165–72

23. Marie-Claire Bancquart, *Anatole France: Un Sceptique passionné* (Paris, Calmann-Lévy, 1984), 138–9

24. Léon Blum, 'En lisant', 1903–5, in Blum, *L'Oeuvre, 1891–1904* (Paris, Albin Michel, 1954), 85, cited by James Smith Allen, *In the Public Eye: A History of Reading in Modern Europe* (Princeton, Princeton University Press, 1991), 120

25. Myriam Harry, *La Vie de Jules Lemaître* (Paris, Flammarion, 1946), 119–87; Martin-Fugier, *Les Salons*, 166–73. On the Comtesse de Loynes see also above, pp. 57–8

26. Jules Lemaître, *Theatrical Impressions* (Port Washington, New York and London, Kennicat Press, 1970), 125–7, 136–8

27. Augustin Filon, *De Dumas à Rostand: Esquisse d'un movement dramatique contemporain* (Paris, Colin, 1898), 295

28. Michael de Cossart, *The Food of Love: Princesse Edmond de Polignac (1865–1943) and her Salon* (London, Hamish Hamilton, 1978), 26–103; Martin-Fugier, *Les Salons*, 140–41; Jessica Duchen, *Gabriel Fauré* (London, Phaidon, 2000), 44–113; Jonathon Brown, *Claude Debussy* (London, Pavilion, 1996), 43–62; Arnold L. Haskell, *Ballet Russe: The Age of Diaghilev* (London, Weidenfeld & Nicolson, 1968)

29. Gertrude Stein, *Picasso* (Paris, Librairie Floury, 1938), 26, 31, 62; Fernande Olivier, *Picasso and his Friends* (London, Heinemann, 1964), 82–8, 139–40

30. Elizabeth Cowling, *Picasso: Style and Meaning* (London, Phaidon, 2002), 160–62

31. Guillaume Apollinaire, *Chronique d'art (1902–1918)* (Paris, Gallimard, 1960), 73–4

32. Roger Shattuck, *The Banquet Years: The Arts in France, 1885–1918* (London, Faber, 1958), 208–19

33. George D. Painter, *Marcel Proust: A Biography* (London, Chatto & Windus, 1966), I, 95–8, 146–54, II, 293

34. Proust, *À la recherche du temps perdu* (Paris, Gallimard, 1968–9), I, 19

35. Painter, *Marcel Proust*, II, 163–204, 296–7

36. Alain Pagès, 'L'Expérience du livre: Zola et le commerce de la librairie en France au XIXe siècle', in Jean-Yves Mollier, ed., *Le Commerce de la librairie au XIXe siècle, 1789–1914* (Paris, IMFC, 1997), 428

37. James Smith Allen, *In the Public Eye: A History of Reading in Modern France, 1800–1945* (Princeton, Princeton University Press, 1991), 80

38. Jean-Paul Dekiss, *Jules Verne l'enchanteur* (Paris, Félin, 1999), 169; Henri-Jean Martin and Roger Chartier, eds, *Histoire de l'édition française*, III: *Du Romantisme à la Belle Époque* (Paris, Promodis, 1985), 202

39. Anne-Marie Thiesse, *Le Roman quotidien: Lecteurs et lectures populaires à la Belle Époque* (Paris, Le Chemin Vert, 1984), 17–21, 155; Smith Allen, *In the Public Eye*, 117–20

40. Thiesse, *Roman quotidien*, 28, 123–4; Dominique Kalifa, '"Zigomar", grand roman sériel (1909–13)', in his *Crime et Culture au XIXe siècle* (Paris, Perrin, 2005), 176–88

41. Sophie Grandjean, 'Les Éditions Fayard et l'édition populaire', in Mollier, ed., *Commerce de la librairie*, 229–32; Jean-Paul Colin, *La Belle Époque de roman policier français: Aux origines d'un genre romanesque* (Lausanne and Paris, 1999), 13–15

42. Claude Bellanger, *Histoire générale de la presse française*, III: *De 1871 à 1940* (Paris, PUF, 1972), 300–316, 399–404; Francine Amaury, *Histoire du plus grand quotidien de la IIIe République: Le Petit Parisien, 1876–1944* (Paris, PUF, 1972), I, 265–75, II, 864; Marjorie A. Beale, *The Modernist Enterprise: French Élites and the Threat of Modernity, 1900–1914* (Stanford, Stanford University Press, 1999), 53–5; Dominique Kalifa, 'Les Tâcherons de l'information: Petits reporters et faits divers à la Belle Époque', *Revue d'Histoire Moderne et Contemporaine* 40 (1993), 578–603

43. Jean-Yves Mollier, 'La Librairie du trottoir à la Belle Époque', in Mollier, ed., *Commerce de la librairie*, 234–40

44. Jean-Paul Sartre, *Words* [1964] (London, Penguin, 2000), 37, 47; Jean-Yves Mollier, 'Un Parfum de la Belle Époque', in J.-P. Rioux and J.-F. Sirinelli, eds, *La Culture de masse en France de la Belle Époque à aujourd'hui* (Paris, Fayard, 2002), 89–90

45. Baldick, ed., *Pages from the Goncourt Journal*, 374, entry for 13 Mar. 1892; W. Scott Haine, *The World of the Paris Café: Sociability among the French Working Class, 1789–1914* (Baltimore and London, Johns Hopkins University Press, 1996), 20–57, 227–8; Charles Rearick, *Pleasures of the Belle Époque: Entertainment and Festivity in Turn-of-the-Century France* (New Haven and London, Yale University Press, 1985), 58–83; Jerrold Siegel, *Bohemian Paris: Culture, Politics and the Boundaries of Bourgeois Life* (London, Penguin, 1987), 216–39

46. Yvette Guilbert, *La Chanson de ma vie: Mes mémoires* (Paris, Grasset, 1927); Bettina Knapp and Myra Chapman, *That was Yvette: The Biography of the Great Diseuse* (London, Frederick Muller, 1966); Charles Virmaître, *Trottoirs et Lupanars* (Paris, 1895), 149–51; Richard Harding Davis, *About Paris* (New York, Harper & Brothers, 1895), 81; Rearick, *Pleasures of the Belle Époque*, 83–91

47. Georges Sadoul, *Le Cinéma français, 1890–1962* (Paris, Flammarion, 1962), 13–17; Jacques Deslandes and Jacques Richard, *Histoire comparée du cinéma*, II: *1896–1906* (Paris, Casterman, 1968), 103–5, 304–17, 411–60; Emmanuelle Toulet, 'Le Cinéma à l'Exposition Universelle de 1900', *Revue d'Histoire Moderne et Contemporaine* 33 (1986), 179–209; Kalifa, '"Zigomar", grand roman sériel (1909–13)', 182

48. *Les Sports Athlétiques*, 12 Dec. 1891, cited by Eugen Weber, 'Gymnastics and Sport in *Fin de Siècle* France', *American Historical Review* 76/1 (1971), 85; Eugen Weber, 'Pierre de Coubertin and the Introduction of Organised Sports into France', *Journal of Contemporary History* 5 (1970), 3–16; Richard Holt, *Sport and Society in Modern France* (Basingstoke, Macmillan, 1981), 40–72; Philip Dine, *French Rugby Football: A Cultural History* (Oxford and New York, Berg, 2001), 23–46

49. Holt, *Sport and Society*, 91–100; Philippe Gaboriau, *Le Tour de France et le vélo: Histoire sociale d'une épopée contemporaine* (Paris, L'Harmattan, 1995), 35–51; Christopher Thompson, 'Controlling the Working-class Sports Hero in Order to Control the Masses? The Social Philosophy of Henry Desgranges', *Stadion* 27 (2001), 139–51

CHAPTER 15: REBUILDING THE NATION

1. Frederic H. Seager, 'The Alsace-Lorraine Question in France, 1871–1914', in Charles K. Warner, ed., *From the Ancien Régime to the Popular Front* (New York and London, Columbia University Press, 1969), 114

2. Paul-Marie de la Gorce, *La République et son armée* (Paris, Fayard, 1963), 14

3. Edgar Quinet, *La République: Conditions de la régenération de la France* (Paris, Dentu, 1872), 47, 63

4. Richard D. Challener, *The French Theory of the Nation in Arms, 1866–1939* (New York, Columbia University Press, 1955), 39–40

5. Alan Mitchell, '"A Situation of Inferiority": French Military Reorganisation after the Defeat of 1870', *American Historical Review* 86/1 (1981), 50–51; Annie Crepin, *La Conscription en débat, ou le triple apprentissage de la nation, de la citoyenneté, de la République (1798–1889)* (Arras, Artois Presses Université, 1998), 210–26

6. Gambetta, Saint-Quentin speech, 16 Nov. 1871, *Discours et plaidoyers politiques*, II (Paris, Charpentier, 1881), 172, cited by Seager, 'The Alsace-Lorraine Question in France', 112, and J. P. T. Bury, *Gambetta and the Making of the Third Republic* (London, Longman, 1973), 65–8

7. Alan Mitchell, *The German Influence in France after 1870* (Chapel Hill, University of North Carolina Press, 1979), 162–6

8. J. P. T. Bury, *Gambetta's Final Years, 1877–1882* (London and New York, Longman, 1892), 186, 268–9; Anne Hoguenhuis-Selverstoff, *Juliette Adam, 1836–1936* (Paris, L'Harmattan, 2001), 102–7; Bertrand Joly, 'La France et la revanche (1871–1914)', *Revue d'Histoire Moderne et Contemporaine* 46 (1999), 326–42

9. Jean-Jacques Becker and Stéphane Audouin-Rouzeau, *La France, la nation, la guerre, 1850–1920* (Paris, Sedes, 1995), 135–7

10. See above, pp. 294–5

11. Ernest Renan, *Qu'est-ce qu'une nation? Conférence faite en Sorbonne le 11 mars 1882*, in *Oeuvre complètes*, I (Paris, Calmann-Lévy, 1882), 12–28

12. Ernest Lavisse, *Souvenirs* (Paris, Calmann-Lévy, 1912), 110–12

13. Ernest Lavisse, 'L'Enseignement historique en Sorbonne et l'éducation nationale', *Revue des Deux Mondes*, 15 Feb. 1882, in Lavisse, *Questions d'enseignement national* (Paris, 1885), 42–3; Pierre Nora, 'L'Histoire de France de Lavisse', in *Les Lieux de mémoire*, II.1: *La Nation* (Paris, Gallimard, 1986), 317–75

14. Ernest Lavisse, *La Deuxième Année d'histoire de France* (Paris, 1884), 341–3

15. Félix Dupanloup, *Second Panégyrique de Jeanne d'Arc prononcé dans la cathédrale de Sainte-Croix, le 8 mai 1869* (Orléans, 1869), 35; Jacques de Biez, *Un Maître imagier: E. Frémiet* (Paris, 1896), 178; Gerd Krumeich, *Jeanne d'Arc in der Geschichte: Historiographie, Politik, Kultur* (Sigmaringen, Thorbecke, 1989), 160

16. Albert Réveille, 'Vercingétorix et la Gaule au temps de la conquête romaine', *Revue des Deux Mondes*, 3rd period, 22 (15 Aug. 1877), 867; Anne Pingeot, 'Les Gaulois sculptés, 1850–1914' and Antoinette Ehrard, 'Vercingétorix contre Gergovie', in Paul Viallaneix and Jean Ehrard, eds, *Nos ancêtres les Gaulois: Actes du Colloque International de Clermont-Ferrand* (Clermont-Ferrand, Association des Publications de la Faculté des Lettres et Sciences Humaines de Clermont-Ferrand, 1982), 255–61, 307–15; Eugen Weber, 'Gauls versus Franks: Conflict and Nationalism', in Robert Tombs, ed., *Nationhood and Nationalism in France from Boulanger to the Great War, 1889–1918* (London, HarperCollins Academic, 1991), 14–15; Krzystof Pomian, 'Francs et Gaulois', in Pierre Nora, ed., *Les Lieux de mémoire*, III: *Conflits et partages* (Paris, Gallimard, 1992), 81–91; Michael Dietler, '"Our Ancestors the Gauls": Archaeology, Ethnic Nationalism and the Manipulation of Celtic Identity in Modern Europe', *American Anthropologist* 96/3 (1994), 590–92, 41–105

17. Commandant Galliéni, *Voyage au Soudan français: Haut Niger et Pays de Ségou, 1879–1881* (Paris, Hachette, 1885); Marc Michel, *Galliéni* (Paris, Fayard, 1989), 14–110; André Le Révérend, *Un Lyautey inconnu: Correspondance et journal inédites, 1874–1934* (Paris, Perrin, 1980), 44–138

18. Vicomte E.-M. de Vogüé, diary entry of 13 July 1879, in *Journal: Paris–Saint-Pétersbourg, 1877–1883* (Paris, Grasset, 1932), 90

19. Jules Ferry, speeches of 5 and 9 Nov. 1881 in Odile Rudelle, ed., *La République des citoyens* (Paris, Imprimerie Nationale, 1996), II, 232–57; Henri Brunschwig, *Mythes et Réalités de l'impérialisme colonial français, 1871–1914* (Paris, Colin, 1960), 55

20. De Vogüé, diary entry of 28 June 1882, in *Journal: Paris–Saint-Pétersbourg*, 312

21. Winfried Baumgart, *Imperialism: The Idea and Reality of British and French Colonial Expansion, 1880–1914* (Oxford, Oxford University Press, 1982), 62

22. *La Justice*, 28 Sept. 1882, cited in E. Malcolm Carroll, *French Public Opinion and Foreign Affairs, 1870–1914* (New York, Century, 1931), 96–7

23. Paul Déroulède, *Le Livre de la Ligue des Patriotes* (Paris, 1887), 3, 123, 289

24. Charles de Freycinet, *Souvenirs, 1878–1893* (New York, Da Capo Press, 1973), 268–9

25. Ferry, *La République des Citoyens*, II, 284; Jean-Baptiste Duroselle, *Clemenceau* (Paris, Fayard, 1988), 226

26. Lucien Descaves, *Sous-offs: Roman militaire* (Paris, Tresse & Stock, 1889); Georges Darien, *Biribi* (Paris, Société Le Gadenet, 1966); George Courteline, *Le Train de 8h47*, in his *Théâtre, contes, romans et nouvelles, philosophie, écrits divers et fragments retrouvés* (Paris, Robert Laffont, 1990), 579–663; Jean Rabaut, *L'Antimilitarisme en France, 1870–1975* (Paris, Hachette, 1975), 34–58, has extracts from *Sous-offs* and *Biribi*

27. *Marcel Cachin vous parle* (Paris, Éditions Sociales, 1959), 15; on Fourmies see above, p. 267

28. George F. Kennan, *The Decline of Bismarck's European Order* (Princeton, Princeton University Press, 1979), 161

29. E.-M. de Vogüé, *Le Roman russe* (Paris, Plon, 1886)

30. Hoguenhuis-Selverstoff, *Juliette Adam*, 217–34

31. René Girault, *Emprunts russes et investissements français en Russie, 1887–1914* (Paris, Colin, 1973); Herbert Feis, *Europe, the World's Banker* (New Haven, Yale University Press, 1930), 23, 51, 74, 210–34; Rondo Cameron, *France and the Economic Development of Europe, 1800–1914* (Princeton, Princeton University Press, 1961), 486

32. Pierre Renouvin, 'Les Relations franco-russes à la fin du XIXe et au début du XXe siècle', *Cahiers du Monde Russe et Soviétique* I (1959), 128–47; Hoguenhuis-Selverstoff, *Juliette Adam*, 237–8

33. C. M. Andrew and A. S. Kanya-Forster, 'The French "Colonial Party": Its Composition and Influence, 1885–1914', *Historical Journal* 14 (1971), 99–128; Stuart Michael Persell, 'Joseph Chailley-Bert and the Importance of the Union Coloniale Française', *Historical Journal* 17 (1974), 176–84; C. M. Andrew, 'The French Colonial Movement during the Third Republic: The Unofficial Mind of Imperialism', *Transactions of the Royal Historical Society* 26 (1976), 143–66; Stuart Michael Persell, *The French Colonial Lobby, 1889–1938* (Stanford, Hoover Institution Press, 1983), 9–48; Christopher Andrew, *Théophile Delcassé and the Making of the Entente Cordiale* (London, Macmillan, 1968), 9–44; Roland Villot, *Eugène Étienne* (Oran, L. Fouque, 1951); John C. Wilkinson, *A Fatal Duel: 'Harry Allis' (1857–95), a Behind-the-Scenes Figure in the Early Third Republic* (Darlington, Serendipity, 2006)

34. *Le Drapeau*, 1 Oct. 1898
35. Roger Glenn Brown, *Fashoda Reconsidered: The Impact of Domestic Politics on French Policy in Africa, 1893–1898* (Baltimore, Johns Hopkins University Press, 1970), 95
36. E.-M. de Vogüé to Lyautey, 2 Oct. 1898, in Lyautey, *Lettres de Tonkin et de Madagascar, 1894–1899* (Paris, Colin, 1933), 619
37. Brown, *Fashoda Reconsidered*, 100
38. Ibid., 116; Darrell Bates, *The Fashoda Incident of 1898: Encounter on the Nile* (Oxford, Oxford University Press, 1984), 142–68
39. Christophe Charle, *Naissance des 'intellectuels': 1880–1900* (Paris, Éditions de Minuit, 1990), 200, 212, 222
40. General Galliéni, *Neuf ans à Madagascar* (Paris, Hachette, 1908), 161–2; Pascal Venier, 'The Campaign of Colonial Propaganda: Galliéni, Lyautey and the Defence of the Military Regime in Madagascar, 1899–1900', in Tony Chafer and Amanda Sakhur, eds, *Promoting the Colonial Idea: Propaganda and Visions of Empire in France* (Basingstoke, Palgrave, 2002), 29–39
41. Jean-Charles Jauffret, *Parlement, gouvernement, commandement: L'Armée de métier sous la 3e République, 1871–1914* (Vincennes, 1987), II, 910–17; Douglas Porch, *The March to the Marne: The French Army, 1871–1914* (Cambridge, Cambridge University Press, 1981), 67–72, 164
42. Maurice Larkin, *Religion, Politics and Preferment in France since 1890: The Belle Époque and its Legacy* (Cambridge, Cambridge University Press, 1995), 36–50. See above, p. 283
43. Judith F. Stone, *Sons of the Revolution: Radical Democrats in France, 1862–1914* (Baton Rouge and London, Louisiana State University Press, 1996), 273–98
44. Émile Combes, 'Discours de Clermont-Ferrand', in *Une Campagne laïque (1902–1903)* (Paris, 1904), 370–72
45. Michael Vann, 'All the World's a Stage, Especially in the Colonies: L'Exposition de Hanoi, 1902–3', in Martin Evans, ed., *Empire and Culture: The French Experience, 1830–1940* (Basingstoke, Palgrave Macmillan, 2004), 181–91
46. Andrew, *Théophile Delcassé*, 181–213
47. Kim Mulholland, 'Rival Approaches to Morocco: Delcassé, Lyautey and the Algerian–Moroccan Border, 1903–1905', *French Historical Studies* 5/3 (1968), 328–43; Persell, *The French Colonial Lobby*, 50–52; William A. Hoisington, *Lyautey and the French Conquest of Morocco* (Basingstoke, Macmillan, 1995), 25–6
48. Andrew, *Théophile Delcassé*, 274–301

49. Eric Cahm, *Péguy et le nationalisme français de l'Affaire Dreyfus à la Grande Guerre* (Paris, Cahiers de l'Amitié Charles Péguy, 25, 1972), 29–30

50. Jean Maitron, *Le Mouvement anarchiste en France* (Paris, Maspéro, 1975), I, 371 note

51. Paul Louis, *Le Colonialisme* (Paris, Bellais, 1905), 5–107

52. *L'Humanité*, 28 Dec. 1905

53. Jean Jaurès, speech to SFIO congress of Nancy, 13 Aug. 1907, in *Oeuvres*, V (Paris, Rieder, 1933), 106–10

54. Jean Jaurès, speech at Tivoli-Vauxhall, 7 Sept. 1907, and *L'Armée nouvelle* [1910], in *Oeuvres*, V, 128, 290–382

55. Charles Péguy, *Notre patrie*, in *Oeuvres en prose, 1898–1908* (Paris, Gallimard, 1959), 801–53; Cahm, *Péguy et le nationalisme français de l'Affaire Dreyfus à la Grande Guerre*, 27–38

56. Claude Digeon, *La Crise allemande de la pensée française, 1870–1914* (Paris, PUF, 1959), 495–518; Eugen Weber, *The Revival of National Sentiment in France* (Millwood, NY and Berkeley, Kraus Reprint/ University of California Press, 1980)

57. Archives de la Préfecture de Police BA 1340, speech of Déroulède, 22 May 1907; Bertrand Joly, *Déroulède: L'Inventeur du nationalisme français* (Paris, Perrin, 1998), 346–7

58. Paul Déroulède, *Hommage à Jeanne d'Arc: Discours prononcé à Orléans le 8 mai 1909 au banquet de la Ligue des Patriotes* (Paris, Bloud, 1909), 2

59. Maurice Barrès, *Scènes et doctrines du nationalisme* (Paris, Plon-Nourrit, 1925), II, 115–30

60. Ibid., I, 92; Yves Chiron, *La Vie de Barrès* (Paris, Godefroy de Bouillon, 2000), 21–2

61. Barrès, *Colette Baudoche* (Paris, 1909), 231–52

62. Ernest Psichari, *Terres de soleil et de sommeil*, in *Oeuvres complètes*, I (Paris, L. Conrad, 1948), 278–81; Frédérique Neau-Dufour, *Ernest Psichari: L'Ordre et l'errance* (Paris, Cerf, 2001), 16–120; Henri Massis, *Notre ami Psichari* (Paris, Flammarion, 1936), 51

63. Joseph Caillaux, *Mes mémoires*, II: *1909–1912* (Paris, Plon, 1943), 205. See above, p. 286

64. Marshal Joffre, *Memoirs*, I (London, 1932), 24–5

65. Porch, *March to the Marne*, 171–86

66. Sonia E. Howe, *Lyautey of Morocco: An Authorized Life* (London, Hodder & Stoughton, 1931), 218–20, 264; Porch, *March to the Marne*, 118–30; Marjorie Farrar, *Principled Pragmatist: The Political Career of Alexander Millerand* (New York and Oxford, Berg, 1991), 136–49

67. Jules Maurin, *Armée, guerre, société: Soldats languedociens, 1889–1919* (Paris, Publications de la Sorbonne, 1982), 268–72, 312–13; Guy Pedroncini, ed., *Histoire militaire de la France*, III: *1871–1940* (Paris, PUF, 1992), 85–115

68. Max Ferré, *Histoire du mouvement syndicaliste révolutionnaire parmi les instituteurs* (Paris, Société Universitaire d'Éditions et de Librairie, 1954), 164–70

69. Ernest Psichari, *L'Appel des Armes*, in *Oeuvres complètes*, II (Paris, L. Conran, 1948), 14–93, 117–75; Massis, *Notre ami Psichari*, 77–8

70. Agathon, *Les Jeunes gens d'aujourd'hui* (Paris, Plon-Nourrit, 1913)

71. Message of Poincaré, 20 Feb. 1913, cited in Jean-Jacques Becker and Stéphane Audoin-Rouzeau, *La France, la nation, la guerre, 1850–1920* (Paris, Sedes, 1995), 252–3

72. Charles Péguy, *L'Argent suite*, in *Oeuvres complètes*, XIV (Paris, NRF, 1932), 66, 128

73. Pascal Blanchard and Sandrine Lemaire, *Culture coloniale: La France conquise par son Empire, 1871–1931* (Paris, Autrement, 2003), 107

74. Cited by Becker and Audoin-Rouzeau, *La France, la nation, la guerre*, 269

75. Jacques Julliard, 'La CGT devant la guerre, 1900–1914', *Mouvement Social* 49 (1964) 47–62; Jolyon Howorth, 'French Workers and German Workers: The Impossibility of Internationalism, 1900–1914', *European History Quarterly* 15 (1985), 71–97

76. *La Guerre Sociale*, 4–10 Feb., 6–12 May 1914

77. Jean-Jacques Becker, *Comment les Français sont entrés dans la Guerre* (Paris, FNSP, 1977), 335–7

78. Jean-Jacques Fiechter, *Le Socialisme français de l'Affaire Dreyfus à la Grande Guerre* (Geneva, Droz, 1965), 209

CONCLUSION: 1914

1. Victor Boudon, *Avec Charles Péguy: De la Lorraine à la Marne* (Paris, Hachette, 1916), 147

2. Charles Horne, *The Great Events of the Great War* (New York, National Alumni, 1923), II, 281–2

3. Maurice Barrès, *L'Écho de Paris*, 17 Sept. 1914, in Éric Cahm, *Péguy et le nationalisme français de l'Affaire Dreyfus à la Grande Guerre* (Paris, Cahiers de l'Amitié Charles Péguy, 25, 1972), 2–35

4. Ibid.
5. Boudon, *Avec Charles Péguy*, xiii–xiv, 10–13, 173
6. Ibid., xiii–xv
7. Ibid., 100, 115–16, 171; Maurice Barrès, *Mes cahiers, 1896–1923* (Paris, Plon, 1994), 759

Index

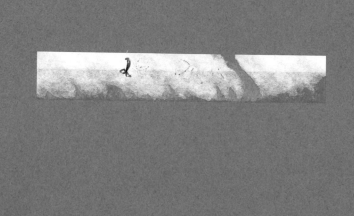